Praise for *Cuba since the*

"A courageous and formidable balance sheet of the Cuban Revolution, including a sobering analysis of a draconian 'reform' program that will only deepen the gulf between revolutionary slogans and the actual life of the people."
—Mike Davis, professor, University of California, Riverside; author, *Planet of Slums* and *In Praise of Barbarians*

"'My political roots are in the classical Marxist tradition that preceded Stalinism in the Soviet Union,' writes Samuel Farber at the beginning of his book. Based on that political and theoretical outlook, opposed as much to neoliberal thought as to the perversions of Stalinist and postmodern communist statism, Farber sets out to critically explore the course followed by the society, government, and power structures that emerged from the Cuban Revolution of 1959. His field of research covers the irreducible hostility of the US establishment, Cuba's historical inheritance, and the alternatives and decisions of its leaders in the last decades, up to and including the problems and challenges they face in these times. His study ends with a careful analysis of the premises and reform proposals currently being discussed in Cuba. A necessary and suggestive reading for all of those concerned with Cuba's future and with the threat posed by the imperial power over the entire Caribbean region."
—Adolfo Gilly, professor, history and political science, School of Social and Political Sciences, Universidad Nacional Autónoma de México; author, *The Mexican Revolution*

"This important, very well-written, and quite interesting book, evaluates the fifty-two years of the Cuban Revolution under a classical Marxist (pre-Stalinist) viewpoint. Samuel Farber doesn't pretend to be impartial: he advocates a transition toward a revolutionary, participatory, socialist democracy, based on majority rule, civil rights, and liberties. And yet his book is thoroughly, painstakingly documented, mostly with Cuban primary sources and a profound knowledge of the secondary literature. He evaluates, with surprising insights, Cuba's performance on national sovereignty, political democracy, economic growth, social welfare, race, gender, and the stand of domestic and external dissidents and critics. It is up-to-date, including an examination of the guidelines for the Sixth Party Congress, and ends with a good balance sheet and Marx and Engels' views. Expect a strong reaction both from the right and the left. Don't miss it!"
—Carmelo Mesa-Lago, Distinguished Service Professor Emeritus of Economics and Latin American Studies, University of Pittsburgh

"Samuel Farber's work on Cuba has long championed revolutionary democratic socialism from below. His latest book, a sophisticated and nuanced historical synthesis of the Cuban Revolution since 1959, provides an indispensable guide to the politics of a tiny island state that helped determine the history of Latin America and the dynamics of the Cold War in the latter half of the twentieth century. With a magisterial grasp of historical detail, and an incisive analytical eye, Farber offers an unparalleled cartography of the ideological debates and po-litical outcomes of Cuba's economic development, foreign policy, socio-cultural fluctuations in race and gender, and working-class and peasant realities under the rule of the Castro brothers. While acknowledging achievements of the rev-olutionary process in education and health, and defending Cuban sovereignty against imperial intervention, Farber shatters many of the idyllic myths propa-gated by left-wing apologists for the regime's authoritarianism. The geriatric transition from Fidel to Raúl seems to promise a strategic shift toward a Cuban version of Sino-Vietnamese, state-led capitalism. A revolutionary democratic al-ternative, Farber shows, will only be possible through socialist resistance from below."

—Jeffery R. Webber, Queen Mary, University of London; author, *From Rebellion to Reform in Bolivia: Class Struggle, Indigenous Liberation and the Politics of Evo Morales*

"Farber's comprehensive and well-written assessment of Cuba's experience since 1959 is rooted in history, informed by the comparative sociology of communist regimes, and rich in insightful and feisty analysis."

—Jorge I. Domínguez, professor of Mexican and Latin American politics and economics, Harvard University

Cuba since the Revolution of 1959

A Critical Assessment

Samuel Farber

Haymarket Books
Chicago, Illinois

Published in 2011 by Haymarket Books
PO Box 180165
Chicago, IL 60618
www.haymarketbooks.org
773–583–7884

ISBN: 978-1-60846-139-4

Trade distribution:
In the US, Consortium Book Sales and Distribution, www.cbsd.com
In Canada, Publishers Group Canada, www.pgcbooks.ca
In the UK, Turnaround Publisher Services, www.turnaround-uk.com
In Australia, Palgrave Macmillan, www.palgravemacmillan.com.au
All other countries, Publishers Group Worldwide, www.pgw.com

Cover design by Eric Ruder
Cover image of a portrait of Fidel Castro hanging from the balcony of an apartment in Havana by
Rodrigo Abd, Associated Press.

Published with the generous support of Lannan Foundation and the Wallace Global Fund.

Printed in the United States by union labor.

Library of Congress cataloging-in-publication data is available.

10 9 8 7 6 5 4 3 2 1

Contents

Selected Chronology

Major Events in Cuban History, 1933–2010

August 1933–January 1934: Revolutionary overthrow of dictatorship of Gerardo Machado. United States refuses to recognize nationalist government of Ramón Grau San Martín. Army strongman Fulgencio Batista rises to power with US support.

1934: Platt Amendment is officially overturned, but the United States retains a naval base in Guantánamo Bay. Reciprocal Trade Agreement between Cuba and the United States is signed, reinforcing Cuba's sugar monoculture and lack of industrial diversification.

1934–1940: Batista controls Cuba through puppet governments.

1940: New Cuban Constitution is established.

1940–1944: Batista rules Cuba as constitutional president.

1944–1948: Batista's candidate (supported by the Cuban Communists) loses the election to Ramón Grau San Martín, and elected president serves his full term.

1948–1952: Carlos Prío Socarrás, the candidate of Grau San Martín's party, is elected but is unable to finish four-year term.

March 10, 1952: Retired general Fulgencio Batista overthrows Prío's government through a military coup, and constitutional government comes to an end.

July 26, 1953: Attack on Moncada barracks fails and the Castro brothers and followers are captured.

May 15, 1955: Batista decrees political amnesty, and the Castro brothers, the rest of the Moncada attackers, and other political prisoners are released from prison.

December 2, 1956: The *Granma* lands in Oriente Province, bringing Fidel Castro and eighty-one of his fellow anti-Batista fighters from Mexico.

March 13, 1957: Assault on the Presidential Palace by Directorio Revolucionario fails.

April 9, 1958: General strike fails. After the defeat of the general strike, Fidel Castro turns to greater emphasis on guerrilla strategy.

January 1, 1959: Dictatorship of Fulgencio Batista is overthrown and rebels take over.

May 1959: Agrarian Reform Law is enacted. Major growth of US opposition to Cuban government

November 1959: Tenth National Labor Congress. Fidel Castro directly intervenes to press for "unity" slate with pro-Communist delegates.

February 4, 1960: Soviet leader Anastas Mikoyan arrives in Cuba and signs trade treaty with Cuban government.

March 1960: US government adopts systematic covert action plans to overthrow Cuban government. Plans had been in preparation since late 1959.

May 1960: Fidel Castro achieves complete control of Cuban press and mass media. The USSR and Cuba resume full diplomatic relations.

June–July 1960: US-owned oil companies refuse to process Soviet oil and are then expropriated by Cuban government. Eisenhower abrogates Cuban sugar quota.

August–October 1960: Large-scale expropriation of US-owned property in Cuba.

October 1960: Full-scale US economic blockade of Cuba begins. Large-scale expropriation of property owned by Cuban capitalists is undertaken.

January 1961: United States breaks off diplomatic relations with Cuba.

April 15, 1961: US government directs bombing of Cuban airfields.

April 16, 1961: Fidel Castro declares "socialist" character of Cuban Revolution.

April 17, 1961: US-sponsored invasion of Cuba begins. (It is defeated after several days of fighting in south-central Cuba.)

1961: Formation of the Organizaciones Revolucionarias Integradas (ORI), uniting the three principal organizations that fought against the Batista dictatorship as a first step toward the formation of the Cuban Communist Party (CCP).

October 1962: Cuban Missile Crisis.

October 1965: CCP is founded.

1965–1968: UMAP (Unidades Militares de Ayuda a la Producción, Military Units to Aid Production) camps are established to extract forced labor from Cuban gays and political, religious, and racial dissidents.

1968: Cuban government embarks on "revolutionary offensive" nationalizing remaining small businesses. Preparations begin for a ten-million-ton sugar crop in 1970.

1971: Congress on Education and Culture marks high point of cultural, gender, and political oppression. Law against "loafing," to discipline Cuban workers, is also approved.

1975: First Congress of the CCP meets.

1976: Promulgation of new constitution.

Spring 1980: Exodus of 125,000 Cubans from the port of Mariel is accompanied by large-scale street harassment of those leaving the country.

1989–1991: Collapse of Soviet bloc in Eastern Europe and of the USSR.

1990: The Cuban government introduces major austerity measures as it proclaims a new "Special Period in Time of Peace."

1991: Fourth Congress of the CCP meets. Congress resolves that religious practitioners will no longer be barred from joining the party.

1992: US Congress approves Torricelli bill, tightening economic sanctions against Cuba.

1993: The possession and use of the US dollar is legalized in Cuba. The government also allows limited self-employment.

1996: The Cuban Air Force shoots down two civilian aircraft operated by the exile organization Brothers to the Rescue. The Helms-Burton bill further hardening the economic blockade against Cuba is passed by Congress and signed by Bill Clinton.

2003: Seventy-five dissidents are sentenced to long prison terms.

2010: Negotiations between Spain, the Catholic Church hierarchy, and the Cuban government lead to the release of the dissidents still in jail from the 2003 arrests, the great majority of whom are subsequently deported. Other prisoners are also released. In September, the government announces the layoff of half a million state workers.

November 2010: Raúl Castro announces that the Sixth Communist Party Congress will convene in April 2011 to discuss major economic changes on the island. A party conference will be subsequently held to address organizational questions.

Introduction

The Cuban Revolution of 1959 was the third Latin American social revolution of the twentieth century, after the Mexican Revolution that started in 1910 and ended in 1940 and the Bolivian Revolution of 1952. However, the Cuban Revolution had far deeper consequences than those other revolutions because of the economic and political system that the revolutionary government established on the island and the activist foreign policy it pursued. The Cuban Revolution was thus one of the most important events in the history of twentieth-century Latin America.

The Cuban Revolution had a profound influence on Latin America, particularly on the Latin American left, for whom the choice remained between a social democracy increasingly doing Washington's bidding and the politicking of bureaucratic Communist parties in a constant search for a "progressive bourgeoisie" to ally with. Cuba also had a substantial impact on the international left, including the opposition movements that emerged in the developed capitalist countries of Europe and North America, as it influenced the New Left of the sixties in those parts of the world. An important part of the international left had been disillusioned but had not entirely rejected the model of the USSR as a result of the invasion of Hungary and Khrushchev's speech denouncing the abuses of Stalin in 1956. These people saw the Cuban leadership as a breath of fresh air—less bureaucratic, more revolutionary and anti-imperialist, and therefore more attractive than the sclerotic Soviet bureaucracy.

Cuba's foreign policy has played a much larger role on the world stage than warranted by the nation's size and degree of economic development. Since 1959, it has challenged the imperial power of the United States in the latter's own backyard and confronted an American-sponsored invasion, in April 1961, and hundreds of other violent attacks, including numerous acts of terror and attempted assassinations against the island's leadership, particularly Fidel Castro. Cuba has also suffered an oppressive US economic blockade that has lasted over fifty years. Cuba's alliance with the Soviet Union, one of the two contending empires of the Cold War, helped to bring the world to the brink of nuclear warfare in October 1962. Its military intervention in Africa contributed to the defeat of South

African apartheid and the consolidation of Angolan independence. However, its much less known intervention in the Horn of Africa supported a bloody but supposedly "progressive" dictatorship in Ethiopia and indirectly helped that country in its military efforts to suppress Eritrean independence. The Cuban presence in Africa was a major contributor to its impact on the third world as Cuba became one of the leading countries of the "non-aligned" bloc. Finally, the Cuban regime has for more than twenty years managed to survive the fall of the Soviet Union—its principal patron and senior ally—and the East European Soviet bloc. In the company of North Korea, it continued to exist during that period without a major turn toward capitalism, as has been the case with China and Vietnam.

Zhou Enlai's quip that it was still too early to assess the impact of the French Revolution may have been an exaggeration, but it was a useful warning against the dangers of premature analysis. However, the information amassed on the nature and evolution of the Cuban system in its more than half a century of existence and the importance of that revolution allow and call for an assessment of what it has and has not accomplished. Central to any assessment of the Cuban regime and its long existence is an understanding of the nature of the Cuban political and social system, a source of deep contention between its political admirers and its detractors. Unlike Nasser's Egypt, Ben Bella's Algeria, Nkrumah's Ghana, or Sukarno's Indonesia, the regime created in the first years after the revolution was not merely "radical nationalist," as some have claimed.[1] "Radical nationalist" regimes typically favored substantial state intervention in the economy. This included significant nationalization of some major capitalist firms, but these regimes never really attempted to abolish capitalism or to own and control the whole economic life of society, much less expropriate small capitalists and shopkeepers, as was the case in Cuba, particularly after 1968. While the political systems of those radical nationalist regimes were usually dictatorial, they never attempted to subject all of "civil society" to state control. Unlike these regimes, Cuba's society, polity, and economy were based on the Soviet model of nationalizing the whole economy and creating a one-party state controlling virtually all aspects of social, political, and economic life in the country. To be sure, the Cuban version of this system had its own national characteristics, as was also the case with China and Vietnam. This is analogous to the economic and political systems of countries such as Japan, the United States, Sweden, and France, which are hardly identical but all share the capitalist mode of economic and social organization.

I have previously published two books[2] focusing on the background of the Cuban Revolution, with particular emphasis on its exceptional character in the Latin American context. The present work is of a different character. It attempts to present a historical synthesis and evaluation of the Cuban Revolution since 1959. While it is based on a substantial amount of primary research, it also relies on research conducted by other scholars, Cuban and foreign.[3] While I cover a substantial range of topics, I don't claim to be fully comprehensive and have been necessarily selective. I have concentrated, in particular, on those questions that I believe have been subject to a great deal of mythmaking, fallacies, and misunderstandings coming from a wide variety of quarters.[4] Besides being a work of historical synthesis, this book is also an attempt to be a political reflection on history and a search for a usable past, which hopefully will support the new voices emerging in Cuba advocating a progressive transition toward a revolutionary and democratic form of socialism. These new voices stand in contrast to the bunker mentality of the regime as expressed, for example, by the absurd 2002 amendment to the Cuban Constitution proclaiming that the present Cuban system was "irrevocable." The amendment seemed to assume that constitutional declarations can prevent a change or overthrow of the system and that the present generations can dictate what future generations will do.

This book could therefore be considered to be a form of advocacy and normative in its orientation. However, that does not mean that it is not concerned with accuracy, truthfulness, and clarity. I believe, contrary to much recent postmodernist theory, that there are such things as facts and that is a worthy goal to present reality as truthfully as possible. But as Frances Fox Piven, among many other social scientists, has explained, no one can be simply be an empiricist, a compiler of nothing but the facts. Judgments have to be made about which evidence is to be gathered, where to search for it, how to assess its reliability, and how to order, present, and interpret it. This means that the researcher always approaches the subject matter with a philosophy or at least the rudiments of a theory.[5] Moreover, my efforts at objectivity should not be confused with impartiality, or the refusal to take sides. My explicit political aim is to present an alternative view to two influential perspectives: first, the view of those opponents of the Cuban system who would replace it with the rule of the capitalist marketplace, whether in its neoliberal or social democratic versions, and a direct or indirect reassertion of US hegemony over the island; second, the arguments of those who apologize for the Cuban system, although sometimes under the cover of academic or journalistic detachment.

My work also stresses the role of politics and ideas in the Cuban Revolution. Karl Marx famously postulated in *The Eighteenth Brumaire of Louis Bonaparte* that "men make their own history, but they do not make it just as they please; they do not make it under circumstances chosen by themselves, but under circumstances directly found, given and transmitted from the past."[6] This is a dialectically elegant formula on the respective roles of agency and the objective limitations on that agency, and consequently on the possibilities and limitations of revolutionary action. But there is a certain tradition in Marxism that grasps only one of the horns of this dilemma and looks at the revolutionary process as a sort of automatic, disembodied process in which the well-known "objective conditions" are responsible for everything that happens. In this perspective, the purposes and choices of, and decisions taken by, revolutionary leaders, even if constrained by objective reality, are given practically no weight. My approach differs from that line of analysis, which views the development of Cuban Communism as a virtually automatic, predetermined response to objective economic, social, and political conditions as understood and acted upon by men whose guerrilla experiences conditioned them to act as realistic revolutionaries to ensure that their revolution survived.[7] The point is that the politics and ideologies—the ideas—of the revolutionary leadership were decisive in the face of the objective obstacles and crises they inevitably confronted as a result of their successful revolutionary movement. The freedom of action of the leaders of the revolution was greatly enhanced by the decay of Cuban political parties and the political and organizational weakness of the major social classes in Cuban society, which in turn created a political vacuum that the revolutionary leaders were quickly able to fill.[8] The politics and ideology of the revolutionary leadership played a particularly critical role in shaping the perception of danger, whether coming from inside or outside the island, and the appropriate responses to it. These leaders acted under serious external and internal constraints but were nevertheless autonomous agents pursuing independent ideological visions. They made choices, including selecting the Communist road for the Cuban Revolution.

◆ ◆ ◆

My political roots are in the classical Marxist tradition that preceded Stalinism in the Soviet Union. Soviet Stalinism established the structural paradigm of a one-party state ruling over the whole economy, polity, and society, a paradigm that was later implemented in its various national variations by countries such as China, Vietnam, and Cuba. Central to my perspective is a view of socialist democracy in which institutions based on majority rule control the principal sources of economic, social, and political power at the local and national levels. To be a fully participatory democracy it must be based on the self-mobilization and organization of the people, and the rule of the majority has to be complemented by minority rights and civil liberties.

An author with such views writing about the Cuban Revolution (or any other social revolution) must confront several intellectual and political perspectives that are so firmly entrenched that they have practically become common-sense assumptions among various sectors of the intellectual and political spectrum. A number of events since the seventies, including major changes in Western capitalism, the victory of Thatcher and Reagan's policies, the conversion of social democracy to neoliberalism, and the collapse of the Soviet Union and the Soviet bloc, have strengthened the deeply entrenched notion that there is no alternative to capitalism. However, it is important to understand that the move toward neoliberalism and capitalism was not just a matter of what degree of persuasiveness these ideologies had acquired during the forty years since the Great Depression, when capitalist and laissez-faire ideology were clearly on the ideological defensive. The success of this new capitalist ideological hegemony was even more a political and ideological reflection of the massive defeat suffered by the labor movement and the left throughout the world since the 1970s.

But a democratic revolutionary perspective has to contend with more than just the neoliberal and conservative center and right. We also find that many liberal moderate reformers seem to assume that a radical social revolution by its very nature inevitably becomes totalitarian. There is no better articulator of this perspective than the philosopher Karl Popper, who maintained that democracy is only compatible with localized reforms of specific institutions and that any attempt to transform society as a whole is inevitably totalitarian.[9] Other influential thinkers have considerably broadened and extended this perspective. Thus, for example, the former Polish activist and present newspaper publisher Adam Michnik, who was imprisoned on many occasions for his courageous opposition to the Communist dictatorship in his country, considers the concept of totalitarianism to mean much more than a system consisting of specific sociopolitical institutions and practices. Michnik extended the concept of totalitarianism beyond the one-party state, the abolition of civil liberties, and a secret police not subject to the rule of law to radical political change itself. Michnik even attributed a "pre-totalitarian" tendency to the old nationalist–social democratic Polish Socialist Party because it did not limit itself to what Michnik called a "clear-cut program of reform." Instead, the Polish socialists, according to Michnik, put forward a vision of a "Socialism [that] promised total change, building this promise on the complete negation of a world based on the exploitation and oppression of nations and individuals."[10] It follows then that for Michnik only a partial negation of the exploitation and oppression of nations and individuals is acceptable and democratic.

Popper's views, as echoed by Michnik and legions of defenders of liberal capitalist democracy, managed to identify totalitarian Stalinism, which did completely transform Soviet society, with any and all revolutionary attempts to change society as a whole, and thus intended to discredit those other efforts as well. Popper and his followers ignored another revolutionary tradition that has been profoundly antithetical to the spirit of totalitarian Stalinism and has forcefully made its presence felt in a long list of revolutionary movements and outbreaks starting with the 1871 Paris Commune and the multiparty Russian Soviets of 1905 and 1917–18.[11] These movements and institutions repeatedly tried to change society as a whole through the vehicle of a higher and better form of democracy than that of liberal capitalism—not through a totalitarian one-party state. The profound democratic spirit of this tradition was inexorably anchored in its profound egalitarianism, which did not explicitly or implicitly counterpose economic equality to democracy, as has been the case with Ernesto "Che" Guevara and the many other social and economic egalitarians who have supported the dictatorial rule of the one-party state.[12] It is certainly true that all these revolutionary attempts failed at consolidating their power beyond a brief period of time or, in the case of the Russian Revolution, were eventually reversed by Stalinism. We cannot of course prove that the radical changes made or proposed by those movements would have been institutionally viable in the long run. Nevertheless, the fact remains that they were usually crushed by hostile forces, and their failure cannot be attributed to any conceivable structural lack of viability of their social and political projects.

This view of revolutionary democracy or socialism from below assumes that people have the capacity and potentially the will to govern themselves and need no saviors or caudillos to protect them from their own errors as they learn and find their way to govern. Perhaps more difficult, but no less indispensable for popular self-rule, is the achievement of an independent, critical spirit immunizing people against the manipulation, demagoguery, and appeal to their lowest rather than highest sentiments that have been as much mainstays of dictatorial and authoritarian rule as brute force. Closely related to this need is the rejection of the unanimity of the armed camp that forbids internal criticism and dissent because it is supposedly going to help the external enemy. In fact this unanimity disguised as "unity" does far more to prevent the revolutionary society from addressing the social cancers growing within its midst, let alone kill democratic prospects, than to allow it to successfully face the political threats coming from inside and outside.

There are also people who are willing to accept that there are flaws, problems, or "errors" with the Cuban "revolutionary process," but still support the regime on the basis that one cannot expect "perfection," particularly in the context of economic underdevelopment.[13] But "perfection" is hardly the issue at stake here. This writer would be the first to insist that any authentic revolutionary democratic movement in Cuba would have, if victorious, encountered great obstacles and difficulties, which would have likely resulted in a flawed and problematic society. The problem is not that the present Cuban system is "imperfect" but that its very bureaucratic nature worsens people's living conditions and creates oppressive barriers to what people can do collectively and individually. Moreover, the government does not even try to rectify let alone abandon its dictatorial institutions and practices. In fact, the regime usually moves in the opposite direction and institutes "reforms" designed to ensure the permanence of the existing system. Therefore, the real issue is whether people in Cuba have the right to freely organize themselves to address the problems affecting their society; the only way in which they can effectively and productively to do so is when they have actual control over their social, political, and economic destiny. Thus, a people's democratic control over its own fate is not just a good thing in itself but also the most practical way by which people are likely to *care* and attempt to solve the problems affecting them.

There is a widespread, and often less than fully conscious, attitude on the left ignoring or justifying the absence of democracy and the systematic violation of civil liberties in Cuba because of the revolution's achievements, whether real or imagined, and particularly because of the country's stance against US imperialism. This attitude, at least implicitly absolving the revolutionary leaders of any blame for their decisions, choices, and actions, has deep roots on the left and precedes the Cuban Revolution. It was precisely such an apologetic approach that led the Russian socialist historian Roy Medvedev to sharply criticize Isaac Deutscher, one of Stalin's best-known biographers. Medvedev objected to the way in which Deustcher, in telling the story of industrialization and collectivization, argued that Stalin could be considered one of the greatest reformers of all times because he had put the ideas of the October Revolution and socialism into practice. The price was very high, but that only proved, according to Deutscher, the difficulty of the task.[14] The Gulag, purges, and the creation of famine resulting in the death of millions of people become, in Deutscher's "objectivist" analysis standing outside history as it is actually lived by its actors, unfortunately just the high price the Soviet people had to pay. For Deutscher, Stalin is merely a reformer instead of a mass murderer. This political stance is particularly obnoxious when those holding it would be horrified by the idea of living in the societies paying the "high price." That experience is for others to endure. While Isaac Deutscher did not write about Cuba and the Cuban Revolution, his approach has had a pervasive influence in legitimizing this type of apologetic analysis among left-wing people who may have never heard of the Polish Marxist historian.

Organization of This Study

I have organized the chapters around those questions that are essential to an understanding of the nature of the Cuban regime and to an evaluation of its accomplishments and failures in more than five decades in power; while taking this topical approach, I seek to maintain some chronological order and clarity.

Chapter 1 focuses on the issue of democracy and the process of establishing the institutions of the one-party state, and it questions the notion that the establishment of Cuban Communism was merely a reaction to US hostility. It also makes the case that the political and cultural repression by the Cuban government can be explained not as a justified response to internal and external danger but as an instance of systemic surplus repression, that is, repression that is well beyond any justifiable response to violent subversion. Chapter 1 also refutes a number of arguments that have been made in defense of the Cuban political system and discusses the relative cultural and political liberalization that began to be carried out in the nineties.

Chapter 2 looks at Cuba's performance in terms of its economic development and standard of living. It contends that even though Cuba achieved important gains in the areas of education and health, its overall economic performance has been unimpressive if not a failure. I consider various explanations to understand why, such as the impact of the US economic blockade and the internal contradictions of the bureaucratic economic system, with its very negative consequences particularly for agriculture.

Chapter 3 presents an analysis of Cuban foreign policy. It looks at Cuba within the framework of the foreign policy of revolutionary governments, such as those of the French and Russian Revolutions. The chapter also attempts to dispel the myths surrounding the foreign policy of the Cuban revolutionary government, namely that it was always primarily based on the principle of supporting revolution abroad. This requires an understanding of its various stages. I argue that after the late sixties it was the defense of Cuban state interests as defined by its leaders and the alliance with the Soviet Union rather than the pursuit of revolution as such that motivated Cuban foreign policy. This in turn explains Cuba's African policy and its quite different implications for Angola and for the Horn of Africa, a critical distinction usually ignored by the Cuban government and its defenders.

Chapter 4 analyzes the role of the Cuban working class before and after the revolution and how it was systematically deprived of its independent organization and power through a process that began shortly after the revolutionary victory. It also describes how the seesaws of the Cuban government's economic policy throughout its many decades in power affected its labor policies and the Cuban working class, and how neither Soviet-inspired material incentives nor Guevara's moral incentives did anything to increase the power of Cuban workers. It also presents a brief analysis of the proposals for workers' control that have been put forward by some of the present left-wing critics of the Cuban government on the island.

Chapter 5 discusses Cuban Blacks and racist patterns in prerevolutionary Cuba, including some critical historical events, such as the brutal suppression of a black independent political party in 1912. The chapter also explains why and how some aspects of racism were eliminated after the revolution while others remained entrenched and became even more pronounced in the "Special Period" that began in the early nineties. In light of the existence of postrevolutionary racism, the chapter questions whether present-day Cuban racism is to be understood as a prerevolutionary leftover or whether institutional racism was reformed but never ceased to exist in the island.

Chapter 6 analyzes the gender politics of the Cuban Revolution. It starts by looking at the situation of women and gays[15] before the revolution. It then assesses the postrevolutionary period based on a detailed presentation of the situation of women in such matters as employment, education, and political power. It also analyzes the problems created by women's "double burden" at work and at home and how poor living conditions have considerably worsened the weight of the "double burden." I also find the organization of women "from the top," by the official Cuban Federation of Women (FMC), to be an obstacle that has led to attempts by women to organize independently for their rights. I analyze the situation of gays after the revolution in some detail, and the question is raised why gays suffered a much worse fate than Cuban women, with some explanations given. The chapter also considers the relative improvement of the situation of gays after the nineties in the context of the overall liberalization in the country.

Chapter 7 discusses the Cuban government's critics and opponents on and off the island. It describes the dissident political spectrum ranging from the hard right to Christian and Social Democrats. It discusses the issue of US financial aid to various dissidents in Cuba and presents a detailed analysis of the ideas and politics of Oswaldo Payá, the organizer of the Varela Proyect and the most prominent dissident in the island. I also assess the politics and ideas of critics and opponents on the left, a recent and growing phenomenon on the island, and their significance.

The conclusion briefly examines Marx's approach to the question of whether a particular political system or regime should be considered progressive, and the related but different question of whether it should be politically supported. The conclusion analyzes the record of the Cuban regime in light of these notions, particularly in terms of whether or not it has modernized Cuban society. Finally, the chapter discusses the implications of such an assessment for the political attitude that a left oriented toward self-emancipation and popular democracy should take vis-á-vis the Cuban regime.

A brief epilogue discusses the Sixth Congress of the CCP that took place in April 2011 and the program of significant social and economic changes that the government approved, as well as those changes that it has already carried out. The epilogue also attempts to interpret the meaning and significance of this new situation.

Chapter One

Toward "Monolithic Unity"—Building Cuban State Power from Above

The struggle against the Batista dictatorship of the fifties was a multiclass rebellion that focused on a demand for the restoration of constitutional rule and political democracy. It was only after the defeat of Batista on January 1, 1959, that the political revolution overthrowing the dictatorship became a social revolution radically transforming Cuba's class structure. This process included the revival of an anti-imperialism that had been moribund for two decades.

The eventual establishment of a Soviet-type regime in Cuba, the only one in the Western Hemisphere, cannot be explained in terms of generalizations about underdevelopment, dictatorship, and imperialism, which are common to the whole of Latin America. The single most important factor that explains the uniqueness of Cuba's development was the political leadership of Fidel Castro, which made a major difference in the triumph against Batista and in determining the course taken by the Cuban Revolution after it came to power. In turn, Castro's role was made possible by the particular socioeconomic and political context of Cuba in the late fifties.

Cuba, one of the more developed Latin American countries, had substantial capitalist, middle, and working classes. Yet these classes became politically weaker after the frustrated 1933 Revolution that overthrew the dictatorship of Gerardo Machado. This revolution produced no permanent resolution of any major social question but led first to counterrevolution and then to a variety of compromises and the unstable social and political modus vivendi of the next two decades of Cuban history.[1] While the Cuban capitalist class had developed significantly, particularly since World War II and its aftermath, it subordinated itself to politicians and military leaders such as Batista with whom the Cuban bourgeoisie had no close institutional or organic relationships. Nor did the Cuban bourgeoisie have an organic relationship to the armed forces as a whole, ever since a group of mutinous sergeants led by Batista in 1933 had replaced the traditional officer class rooted in the Cuban upper classes. The principal weakness of the Cuban capitalist class may have been its view of the US government as its political guarantor of last resort. This view was echoed by the geopolitical fatalism of most traditional Cuban politicians, as expressed by the notion that nothing important could be done in Cuba without US approval. This fatalistic view had tremendous resonance in Cuban political culture, particularly during the forties and fifties.

The substantial working class was highly organized in trade unions. But by the 1950s the unions had become extremely bureaucratic and corrupt, making it very difficult for this class to play the significant role in the struggle against Batista that it had played in the struggle against the Machado dictatorship in the early 1930s. Also, by the mid- to late fifties, the political parties, including the reform Ortodóxos, who had wielded substantial influence prior to Batista's seizure of power in 1952, had fallen apart, reflecting the political weaknesses of all of Cuba's social classes. The Movimiento de Resistencia Cívica (Movement of Civic Resistance), an organization formed by professional and other primarily middle-class elements, which played an important role in the struggle against Batista, dissolved itself into the 26th of July Movement in February 1959, a symptom of its political subordination to Fidel Castro. For its part, members of the nucleus of the revolutionary political leadership around Fidel Castro were not radical petty bourgeois, as the old Cuban Communists had claimed during the years before the triumph of the revolution. Instead, they were declassed in the sense that this group had no strong organizational or institutional ties to the petty bourgeoisie or to any of the country's major social classes. Most important of all, the total collapse of Batista's mercenary army provided this leadership with unprecedented opportunities without confronting the restraints and controls that a more politically articulated class system might have imposed.

However, the political monolith enshrining a single point of view and organization was not established immediately in Cuba. During the first year of the revolution, the tremendous enthusiasm and mobilization of the population took place in the context of a fairly open political life. Newspapers, magazines, and radio and television programs with political views ranging from the hard right to the hard left repeatedly clashed with each other. There were no legal or political restrictions to the free flow of ideas except that already at this early stage Fidel Castro was becoming an untouchable figure whom even right-wingers were afraid to criticize and only did so with a great deal of tact and diplomacy. The surging revolutionary tide created a highly charged political atmosphere. The clashes between the contending sides were usually sharp since the issues at stake, as in the case of the radical Agrarian Reform Law of May 1959 affected Cuba's class and property system in a fundamental way.

A wave of effervescent optimism had swept the country soon after Batista was overthrown. The great majorities of workers, peasants, students, and Cubans of many walks of life felt that they were politically free. The rotten social, political, and economic institutions of the failed republic would be transformed, although there was no clarity as to the manner, content, and form this would take. To use an expression that came into vogue many decades later, most Cubans felt that indeed "another world was possible." Yet at the same time the social conservatism of the forties and fifties that had been fostered by the chilling effect of the Cold War and by the relative prosperity brought about by the Second World War and the Korean War politically limited the radicalization that was unfolding in early 1959. The main subject of discussion was *reivindicaciones*, or material demands of a more or less immediate kind. The agrarian reform was seen mostly along the lines of social justice and the improvement of the living standards of agricultural wage workers and peasants, but certainly not in terms of any kind of anticapitalist revolution. This does not mean that there was no political radicalization taking place among the Cuban people; but it was a distinct kind of radicalization that at this time had little, if anything, to do with the state-collectivist ideology and practice eventually established in the country. Fidel Castro had, in February 1959, expressed his concern with this kind of "redistributive radicalism":

> One of the past epochs is still in the minds of the people . . . I have found it in rallies, in working-class rallies, for example. I have seen that in these rallies banners and demands are put forward in the same tone that was used when there was a nonrevolutionary Council of Ministers, a nonrevolutionary government . . . The masses don't realize that this is their government, that this is the government of the people, not at the service of vested interests, that for the first time in our history there is a government which is based on popular majorities. . . . One gets the sensation that they still have in mind the idea that government and people are two different things.[2]

A few days earlier, and in response to the same situation described by Castro, which had been aggravated by the politically amorphous character of the July 26th Movement, a radical nationalist editorialist for the movement's newspaper *Revolución* called for a membership-based revolutionary organization.[3] At this time, this would have excluded the old Communist Party. The call made by *Revolución* was ignored by Fidel Castro. Such an organizational effort would have required the elaboration of an explicit political platform tantamount to the creation of a political party at a "premature" moment from Castro's perspective. Instead, as we shall see below, Castro opted for another alternative during the first two years of the revolution, when the most critical changes determining the nature of the revolution were made. That was to take advantage of his overwhelming popular support and prestige to rally his supporters behind decisions he and his close associates had already made (even though on many occasions major features of these decisions were unexpected). For example, in the months preceding the Agrarian Reform Law just about every social and political sector of Cuban society was putting forward its own views on what the law should contain. Even the sugar mill owners and landlords were proposing their own agrarian reform that would of course have been no reform at all, while sweetening their proposals with the donation to the government of tractors and other agricultural implements. But Castro did not even hint at what kind of law he had in mind or how radical it would be until it was suddenly announced on May 17, 1959.

There were fairly frequent polemics within the revolutionary camp itself. For example, *Revolución* and *Hoy*, the daily organ of the PSP (Partido Socialista Popular), the old pro-Moscow Cuban Communists, were often in conflict over the controversial issues of the day. Although it was not fully spelled out, these two newspapers also fought over whether the Cuban Revolution should follow a left radical nationalist or a Communist course. These were the only two political options with significant support within the revolutionary camp after the liberals were pushed out or left the government of their own accord a few months after the victory of the revolution. The old Communists and their allies in the wing of the 26th of July Movement led by Ernesto "Che" Guevara and Raúl Castro fought the non-Communist radical nationalists of that movement. The PSP and their political allies won the battle when the polemics between radical nationalists and the old pro-Moscow Communists came to an end in September 1959,[4] although this was not clear at the time. As it turned out, however, they did not win the battle in their own terms because Fidel Castro, who had remained above the fray of these debates, soon proceeded to create his own kind of independent national Communism although in alliance with the Soviet Union.

Building the Apparatus of Control from Above

Thus, there was a new turn by late 1959 and early 1960 as the process of creating a political monolith and the apparatus of repression that went along with it got under way. Quite significantly, this process was directed not only against the traditional conservative and liberal opposition at home and US imperialism abroad but also against those within the revolutionary camp who opposed a Soviet-type course for the Cuban Revolution. Notwithstanding the conflict between radical nationalists and those supporting a pro-Communist course, Fidel Castro succeeded in homogenizing the revolutionary leadership and ranks without a full disclosure of his political agenda. Such a disclosure might have further encouraged criticism and, worse, the development of distinct revolutionary tendencies with clear programmatic alternatives, precisely what he wanted to avoid.

Instead, Fidel Castro preferred demagogic accusations of treason to justify the repression, including long-term imprisonment, of those who differed with him within the revolutionary camp. In October 1959, former schoolteacher and Rebel Army major Huber Matos resigned in protest over the growing Communist influence in the armed forces. Fidel Castro did not respond by owning up to socialism or Communism, although he had been attacking anti-Communism as divisive at least since he forced President Manuel Urrutia to resign in July 1959. At this time, besides preventing a greater ideological and political differentiation from emerging within the revolutionary camp, Castro was trying to delay a final and all-out confrontation with the bourgeoisie at home and US imperialism abroad, thereby maintaining the advantage of the element of surprise. So it was that, in a furious reaction, the revolutionary leader accused Matos of treason and had him sentenced to twenty years of prison in a show trial in which no conspiracy or incitement to violence on Matos's part was ever proved.[5]

The greatest exercise in grassroots democracy, described in much greater detail in chapter 4, took place in the union movement during the period of revolutionary pluralism from January until the first national revolutionary trade union congress of November 1959. At that congress, Fidel Castro personally intervened and imposed a union leadership slate with a much greater pro-Communist composition than was warranted by their numerical strength at the congress. Subsequently, after the congress concluded, the government launched a large-scale and ruthless purge of the union leaders who had resisted Communist influence. The unions were soon turned into a political monolith and policy tool in the hands of government, a state-controlled trade unionism organized along the lines of those in the Soviet bloc countries. At the trade union congress, as at Matos's trial, Fidel Castro did not openly acknowledge the eventual political goals he was pursuing through his critical interventions at those events.[6]

In January 1960, the print unions that had already come under government political control introduced *coletillas* (little tails) in Cuban newspapers. These were hostile comments placed at the end of each and every article critical of the government and its policies. This turned out to be a "transitional" measure that was no longer necessary after Fidel Castro seized all the critical and opposition presses in May 1960. No crisis, internal or external, or violent incidents presented a threat to the revolutionary government at this time. The seizure of the press was thus clearly a strategic choice based on long-term systemic political considerations rather than a defensive conjunctural action. In any case, the progovernment press already had more circulation than the newspapers opposing the government. This was due to the fact that the Castro regime had at its disposal all the newspapers, facilities, and equipment previously owned by Batista's supporters. For example, *Revolución* was published using the premises and equipment of the former pro-Batista newspaper *Alerta*. The Cuban government was certainly correct when it argued that the major media outlets the government had seized had been previously owned and controlled by rich people and companies that had the capital to buy them.[7] Certainly, it was hypocritical, and hardly democratic of the press owners, to control a good part of the media under the slogan "freedom of the press" when the overwhelming majority of Cubans did not have the material means to own and participate in the control of those media enterprises.[8] A few capitalists had hugely disproportionate access to the media and consequently to the shaping of public opinion. However, the press and media system that the Cuban government created was far *more* undemocratic than what it had replaced. Fidel Castro established media unanimity through the state monopoly of the mass media, whether major or minor, national or local.[9] Besides monopolizing the media, the Cuban government followed the model of the Soviet Union and soon took over even the smallest print shops and humblest mimeograph machines.

A Note on the Russian Revolution and Freedom of the Press

The Cuban revolutionary government never showed any concern with developing a democratic media that would preserve equal access to different points of view and diverse sectors of the population. This stance was fully consistent with the model of socialism that Stalin had established in the Soviet Union and that was followed, in a less extreme form, by his Soviet successors. By way of contrast, it is worth noting that before multiparty Soviet democracy disappeared during the civil war (1918–20) that followed the Bolshevik Revolution,[10] V. I. Lenin, following the assumptions of classical Marxism, made concrete proposals toward the establishment of a popular and democratic media system. In September 1917, shortly before coming to power, he specifically proposed that

> State power in the shape of the Soviets takes *all* the printing presses and *all* the newsprint and distributes them *equitably*: the state should come first—in the interests of the majority of the people, the majority of the poor, particularly the majority of the peasants, who for centuries have been tormented, crushed and stultified by the landowners and the capitalists.
>
> The big parties should come second—say, those that have polled one or two hundred thousand votes in both capitals. The smaller parties should come third, and then any group of citizens which has a certain number of members or has collected a certain number of signatures.[11]

In early November, shortly after the triumph of the revolution, Lenin suggested ten thousand as the number of citizens forming a group entitled to press facilities.[12] It is true that some of the other proposals that Lenin made in connection with the media were problematic, such as the extreme statification implied in his support for a state monopoly of advertising. This proposal would have prevented political organizations from supporting their own publishing activities by directly obtaining advertising funds from local unions, independent professionals, or even shopkeepers. If Lenin's concern was the equalization of advertising revenue to avoid the inequities of the bourgeois press system, then a progressive taxation of the more successful publications would have achieved a similar end without the dangers of extreme statification.

Lenin did not spell out whether present or former capitalists who had not violently opposed the revolutionary government should be entitled to have access to the press in strict proportion to their numbers in the population, or whether they should be disenfranchised regardless of their conduct. However, in July 1917, he announced that a revolutionary government would, at the appropriate moment, close down the bourgeois press.[13] Lenin made this pronouncement after *Pravda* had been shut down by the Provisional Government following the

"July days" of armed clashes between the Bolsheviks and the government, and the capitalist press was portraying Lenin as a German agent. His July 1917 pronouncement did not clarify whether this would be a temporary measure adopted as part of a state of emergency or if it was meant as a permanent policy regarding the press rights of former or remaining capitalists in a worker's state. Nevertheless, Lenin's proposals reveal a very different set of assumptions regarding the press under socialism from those that became the norm under his later dictatorial rule during and after the civil war, and even more so under the totalitarian media system established by Stalin in the late twenties.

The Creation and Consolidation of Cuba's One-Party State

In contrast to the Soviet Union and East European countries, the Cuban regime placed a great deal of emphasis on popular mobilization and participation. But that did not mean popular democratic control. The broad mass enthusiasm and participation did not translate into mechanisms and institutions of popular control from below. In the fall of 1959, the government created the peoples' militias. The new militias counted 100,000 members by April 1960, 200,000 by the end of that year, and as many as 300,000 people in 1961.[14] These were organized on a different basis from the politically pluralist and autonomous militias of the early stages of the Spanish Civil War, the armed defenders of the 1871 Paris Commune, or those of the Russian soviets of 1905 and 1917. The Cuban militias were born as the paramilitary wing of a highly centralized state where political unanimity was rapidly becoming the rule. The fact that the bulk of the Cuban militiamen may have been enthusiastic participants in the paramilitary force did not make the militias any more autonomous, democratic, or politically pluralist.

The second year of the revolution in 1960 also witnessed the establishment of the mass organizations that were to become the transmission belts for the implementation of governmental policy. These mass organizations were also to become the official alternatives to many of the existing independent associations that began to be shut down by the government. Among the organizational casualties of the early years of the revolution were the *sociedades de color*, which had been the organizational bedrock of black life in Cuba for many decades. An official organization "representing" black Cubans was never even established. There were a number of reasons for this, in particular the government's repeated claim that the revolution had eliminated racism on the island; therefore, the thinking went, an organization to defend blacks and oppose racism, even if it was government controlled, was not necessary. The revolutionary leadership adopted a different policy toward women. Influenced by the Soviet and Asian Communist models that incorporated women in the labor force and in other facets of social and political life, the government dissolved all existing women's organizations and established the official Cuban Federation of Women in August 1960. The organization, headed for many decades by Vilma Espín, Raúl Castro's wife, preempted the development of any independent women's organization, rejected feminism, and for the most part succeeded in isolating Cuban women from the worldwide explosion of the women's movement during the critical decades of the sixties and seventies.

Most important of all was the foundation of the Committees for the Defense of the Revolution (CDRs) in September 1960. The primary purpose of the CDRs was vigilance and repression. Fidel Castro clearly described the functions of the CDRs when he exhorted the Cuban people to "establish against the campaign of imperialism a system of collective revolutionary vigilance, in which everyone knows who everyone is, what each person who lives on the block does, what relations he had with the tyranny, to what he is dedicated, whom he meets, and what activities he follows."[15] While the CDRs helped to protect the Cuban revolutionary state from sabotage and other violent activities aimed at destabilizing it, they also functioned as a major mechanism to enforce political conformity and social control. The CDRs not only singled out to the authorities political malcontents and critics but frequently chastised people regarded as social deviants. This was specially the case during the witchhunt against gays and other "scum" (*escoria*) at the time of the Mariel exodus in the spring of 1980, discussed in greater detail below. All Cubans were required to participate in the CDRs, regardless of age or employment. Failure to do so was interpreted as unwillingness or resistance to being "integrated" into the revolutionary process, which carried serious educational and employment repercussions.

Mechanisms to enforce participation in the many activities sponsored by the regime were developed with a considerable degree of bureaucratic elaboration. A vast system of personal background information—primarily based on questionnaires popularly referred to as *cuéntame tu vida* (tell me your life story), concerning political attitudes, "voluntary labor," and membership and activities in "mass organizations"—became a taken-for-granted reality in Cuba. Each place of employment and every school kept an *expediente* (file) on every worker and student with that information along with routine data. However, with the passage of time and the consolidation of the regime, political vigilance became relatively less important. The CDRs spent a larger proportion of their efforts in other tasks such as the control of ever-increasing criminality and infectious diseases, urban agriculture, reforestation, and the collection of scrap and recyclable materials.[16] Participation has since become much more routinized, although even since the beginning there were people who joined the organization and just went through the motions of participating because they had no choice. As the economic crisis that began in the nineties forced people to spend inordinate amounts of time "resolving" the problems of getting food and other life essentials, they had less time to spend in the CDRs, which in some places virtually stopped functioning.

Regarding the organization of the ruling political party, the three major revolutionary organizations that had opposed the Batista dictatorship were brought together under the umbrella of the Organizaciones Revolucionarias Integradas

(ORI) in 1961, *after* the large-scale nationalization and other major changes establishing Cuban "socialism" had already been completed. In 1962, the ORI became the United Party of the Cuban Socialist Revolution (PURSC), which in turn became the CCP in 1965. In structural and institutional terms there was nothing original about the new Cuban model. Organized along the Soviet model of "democratic centralism," it was a single party that allowed no internal currents or factions. A constitution that enshrined the political monopoly of the CCP, thereby making any other competing parties illegal, was eventually adopted in 1976. The constitution also established the ruling party's monopoly over Cuba's mass organizations, such as the state's trade unions and women's organizations, which were to act as its transmission belts to the population at large. All organizations dedicated to the independent defense of the interests of workers, women, blacks, gays, and any other groups were left outside the bounds of the constitution and the law. Thus the question whether, abstractly speaking, a multiparty system was or was not a requisite for an authentic socialist democracy became moot.[17] Instead of leaving the conflicting interests of political, social, and economic life to freely resolve that question in practice, the government foreclosed any such pluralist possibilities through the use of state compulsion and force.

Stalinism Cuban-Style

By April 1961, when the Cuban government finally took the step of officially declaring itself to be "socialist," it had achieved an almost total control of the polity, economy, and society. Cuba, along the lines of the Soviet Union, China, and Eastern Europe, was well on the way to becoming a one-party state, increasingly controlling all social, political, and economic life on the island. It became a *totalitarian* country. This is an ambiguous term that has been often used for political purposes to discredit the opponents of the West in the Cold War. However, the term can be useful to designate something similar to what the Russian Communist leader Nikolai Bukharin called the "imperialist pirate state." This is a state whose social institutions "have a tendency to fuse with one another and to become transformed into one organization of the rulers . . . So there comes into being a single, all-embracing organization . . . with innumerable functions, with gigantic powers, with spiritual . . . as well as material methods."[18] A new class system based on the property form of state collectivism began to be established in Cuba. In this type of system, the state owns and controls the economy, and in turn the central political bureaucracy "owns" the state. Membership in the ruling class is determined by occupation of the centers of political power in a society in which political and economic power are fused. Power is monopolized at the top in a system that does not allow any *institutional* constraints by unions or any other popular organization independent of the one-party state.

Contrary to beliefs that have long been held by many liberals and leftists in the United States and elsewhere, the revolutionary leadership did not establish a Soviet-type system on the island merely as a reaction to the powerful hostile pressures of US imperialism, much less internal class forces in Cuba. Undoubtedly, the revolutionary leaders acted under serious internal and external constraints. The strong opposition of the US Empire to anything that would disturb the economic, political, and foreign policy status quo in its "backyard" weighed heavily on the political calculus of the revolutionary leaders. But at least as important was that these leaders indeed had a political and ideological view of reality that shaped their perceptions of danger, the appropriate responses to it, and especially what they regarded as the desirable form of social and political organization. As Ernesto "Che" Guevara told the French weekly *L'Express* on July 25, 1963, "Our commitment to the eastern bloc was half the fruit of constraint and half the result of choice."

An important feature of the Soviet-type one-party state is its built-in tendency to deal with political differences and dissidence through administrative and police methods rather than through political persuasion and argument. What could be called "surplus repression" is built into the very fabric of those societies precisely because they apply to peaceful political disagreements methods that from a democratic point of view can be considered legitimate only as a response to violent subversion.

These are the sorts of critical distinctions ignored by the Cuban government and its sympathizers abroad. They often argue that the Cuban government's wide-ranging repression and political control have been justified by the internal resistance offered by the Cuban upper classes and especially by the continual armed aggression sponsored by the United States of America. This aggression included the infamous US-sponsored Bay of Pigs invasion in April 1961 and a long string of failed assassination attempts and numerous other acts of sabotage and terrorism against Castro and other Cuban government officials, as well as the Cuban economy and civilians. These were organized by the US intelligence agencies and later by freelance right-wing Cuban terrorists originally trained by the CIA. The well-known cases of right-wing Cuban terrorists Orlando Bosch and Luis Posada Carriles are particularly illustrative. Although they were directly involved in the 1976 bombing of a Cuban passenger plane over Barbados that resulted in the deaths of seventy-three innocent civilians, the US government has abstained from directly prosecuting them for their terrorist crimes. However, in 2009, the federal authorities prosecuted Posada Carriles for having entered the United States illegally and also accused him of having lied about his involvement in terrorist activities. In January 2011 he went to trial for lying rather than for his terrorist activities and was shockingly declared not guilty by the jury.[19] Apparently, some terrorists are more equal than others.

Unquestionably, the revolutionary government has a right to defend itself from violent aggression by forces organized by and serving US imperial interests. For example, when right before the April 1961 US-sponsored invasion the

Cuban government detained tens of thousands of people suspected of potentially aiding the invaders, it could not have acted otherwise given the real threat it confronted from the United States. The problem, however, is that the government has used its legitimate self-defense needs as an ideological cover to justify a system that is intrinsically repressive regardless, as we have seen over more than five decades, of whether it is confronting violent opposition or peaceful dissent. No wonder then that the regime has often raised the specter of a US invasion to justify domestic repression. This was the case, for example, in March 2003, when for numerous reasons there was no possibility of Washington's carrying out that kind of aggression against Cuba. Nevertheless, it was necessary to evoke the possibility of a US invasion to justify the crackdown that resulted in the arrests of and long prison sentences given to seventy-five peaceful dissidents.

The Cuban government has certainly not engaged in the excesses of the height of Russian Stalinism during the period from the late 1920s to the early 1950s. Nothing the Cuban government has done is comparable to the massive purges and killings that terrorized the Russian people in the thirties, or to the establishment of a Gulag that sent millions of people into forced labor for economic and political purposes. While, as I suggested earlier, the economic power of the prerevolutionary Cuban upper classes was significant, their political weakness and fragmentation greatly facilitated their early and relatively easy defeat. A rural labor force composed primarily of rural workers rather than smallholding peasants significantly reduced the resistance to the government's nationalization and collectivization of the land. Moreover, Washington's decision to encourage the massive emigration of discontented Cubans had the unintended consequence of creating an escape valve that helped to diminish internal resistance and consolidate the Cuban regime.

Although large numbers of Soviet and East European functionaries, technicians, and security and armed forces personnel, and even some tourists, traveled to Cuba and lived there for considerable periods of time, their impact on the popular culture of the island was relatively small.[20] While the Cuban regime has been repressive and all-absorbing in its control of Cuban society, it has not deliberately set out to change the lightness, effervescence, and good humor typical of the Cuban character. That feature of Cuban society sharply contrasts with the dour and grim ambience that was found in Soviet and East European Communist societies. Through the years, many of those the prominent German writer Hans Magnus Enzensberger in *The Consciousness Industry* called "tourists of the revolution"[21] have chosen to concentrate on the character and personality of the Cuban people rather than on the social, economic, cultural, and political structures of Cuban Communism. These "tourists of the revolution" have praised the supposed uniqueness of "happy" Cuban socialism. The problem is that if one were to judge Cuba primarily on that basis, then Batista's Cuba would have also qualified as a brutal but "happy" capitalist dictatorship.

Political and Cultural Repression from the Sixties to the Eighties

The decades that followed the declaration of "socialism" in 1961 were characterized by the government's repression of nonviolent as well as violent opposition, and of dissident currents on the left as well as on the right. In the first half of the sixties, there were numerous rebel bands operating inside Cuba, particularly in the Escambray mountain range in the central part of the island.[22] While they were armed and often supplied by the CIA, after the defeat of the Bay of Pigs invasion in April 1961 these bands did not constitute a major threat to the regime, although they were undoubtedly a serious and costly nuisance. Many people were executed during the government military campaigns against the so-called bandits, and we may never know how many of these (including those executed without trial after capture) were actual armed rebels, collaborators, or innocent civilians. Nevertheless, there is at least one credible account of a forced relocation of thousands of people from the Escambray region in central Cuba. These people were compelled to move hundreds of kilometers to Pinar del Río at the western end of the island in the 1970s, years after the pacification of the Escambray mountain range had been concluded.[23]

From the mid- to late sixties, the Cuban government ran Unidades Militares para Ayuda a la Producción (UMAP) camps to isolate sexual, religious, and political dissenters. A still unknown number of gays, Catholics, Jehovah's Witnesses, Seventh-Day Adventists, and practitioners of certain Afro-Cuban traditions, such as the secret society of Abakuá, found themselves thrown together doing forced labor as a penalty for deviating from the ruling ideology and practices.[24] Between the end of 1967 and January 1968, the old Stalinist Aníbal Escalante was purged for a second time and after a political trial was sentenced to fifteen years in prison for having organized what in reality was no more than a discussion group. His "microfaction" had been meeting to analyze the shortcomings of the Cuban economy from an orthodox Soviet perspective and was friendly with a number of Soviet and Eastern European diplomats. These meetings were taking place at a time of tension between the Cuban government and the Soviet Union, including a serious reduction in economic aid by the Soviets, who were trying to force, and finally succeeded in obtaining, a modification of Cuba's foreign policy and domestic economic policies. It was clear that the Cuban government leaders were unwilling to openly debate the criticisms of the old Communists, which in fact predicted the economic debacle of the 1970 campaign for a ten-million-ton sugar crop.[25] Something similar had taken place a couple of years earlier, when conflicts with the Chinese government led Castro to ban literature that the Chinese had sent to Cuban army personnel. Rather than taking advantage of the occasion to openly debate the views of the Chinese, Castro simply suppressed their literature, treating it no differently from any right-wing or US imperialist propaganda.[26] Proponents of Black Power, who were seen by the government as divisive elements undermining national unity, were also persecuted, purged, and imprisoned. Prominent among these was the Black Cuban author Walterio Carbonell, a former Communist who had been Castro's ambassador to Tunisia and to the leadership of the Algerian FLN (Front de Libération Nationale), who resided in that country during their years in exile.[27]

Cultural Repression

In 1961, Fidel Castro announced his cultural policy with the slogan "Inside the revolution everything; outside the revolution, nothing." This was disingenuous and misleading on his part: he left out the key question of who decided what was and who qualified as being "inside the revolution." Or as José Manuel Martín Medem, the left-wing correspondent for Spanish television in Havana, put it many years later, "[Fidel Castro's] threat meant that bureaucrats and functionaries were going to decide who was writing *inside* and who was writing *against*.[28] The slogan was immediately followed by repressive measures directed not against right-wing counterrevolutionaries but against non-Communist leftists. *Lunes de Revolución,* the weekly mass-circulation literary and political supplement of the government newspaper *Revolución,* which published the writings of Sartre, Beauvoir, and a wide variety of non-Communist independent left-wing authors from all over the world, was closed. The documentary titled *PM,* depicting the apolitical pleasure-loving nightlife of poor people in Havana (directed by Saba Cabrera Infante, brother of Guillermo Cabrera Infante, the editor of *Lunes*), was also suppressed. Castro's 1961 slogan might have been interpreted as government censorship of "counterrevolutionary" content combined with a laissez-faire attitude toward cultural work with a politically neutral content regardless of the form in which it was expressed. However, things did not turn out that way. In a speech delivered on March 13, 1963, Castro thundered against what he called the lazy young children of the bourgeoisie. According to Castro, these youngsters walked around with very narrow pants and guitars and Elvis Presley–like attitudes and shamelessly took their licentiousness to the extreme of organizing effeminate shows in public places.[29] This speech served as the basis for a social policy that put in the same bag homosexuals, delinquents, lumpen elements, lazy people, imitators of Elvis Presley, and bourgeois and counterrevolutionary elements. The government's strategy to defend the revolution against US aggression reached the extreme of treating any song in the English language as a "weapon of the enemy" and rock and roll as a symptom of capitalist alienation.[30] Thus, for much of the sixties, censorship extended to such politically innocuous phenomena as the music of the Beatles.[31] In late 1968, a year during which much of the world had been shaken by political and cultural rebellion, the "hippie" style that had begun to attract some Cuban youth came under government attack. As the Cuban writer Julio César Guanche ironically pointed out, the once long-haired revolutionaries organized expeditions to the Coppelia ice cream parlor (a meeting place for Havana's urban youth) equipped with scissors to cut hippie hair and tight, clinging pants and suppress other "deviations from revolutionary morals."[32] That year also witnessed the "revolutionary offensive" under which the government nationalized even the tiniest hole-in-the-wall businesses and closed every bar and restaurant in Havana. Soon, certain holidays such as Christmas were no longer officially observed. All these measures were designed to encourage hard work and raise productivity and were a prelude to the campaign for a ten-million-ton sugar crop in 1970,[33] a campaign that seriously reduced production in other economic sectors and caused very grave damage to the Cuban economy. In October 1968, the poet and journalist Heberto Padilla's book *Fuera de juego* was awarded a prize by a jury convoked by the National Union of Cuban Writers and Artists (UNEAC). Padilla's book was attacked as "antirevolutionary" by the regime's hard-liners. The controversy provoked by this book ended three years later in 1971, when, after a month of ruthless interrogation, Padilla made a Stalinist-style confession, which provoked strong international protests by prominent left-wing figures such as Jean-Paul Sartre.[34] The prominent American cultural critic Susan Sontag was among those who protested Padilla's treatment in 1971. However, two years earlier she had claimed, with a blatant disregard for the facts, that "no Cuban writer has been or is in jail, or is failing to get his work published" and that the Cuban revolution was "astonishingly free of repression and bureaucratization."[35]

In 1970, a research project on Cuban families and communities that the American anthropologist Oscar Lewis and his team had been conducting with substantial assistance from the Cuban government was abruptly suspended by the authorities. Lewis was accused of a number of offenses, including being financed by the Ford Foundation, even though the government knew how the project was being financed during the time it lent it considerable support. Two years later, Raúl Castro even accused Lewis, a man broadly sympathetic to the Cuban government, of having established ties with counterrevolutionary elements before coming to Cuba and conducting espionage on the island under a progressive facade.[36]

Cultural Stalinism reached its high point in April 1971, when the National Congress of Education and Culture viciously attacked gay artists and intellectuals and approved banning gays representing Cuba abroad whether in artistic, political, or diplomatic missions. The Congress also attacked the Afro-Cuban Abakuá brotherhood, calling it a "focus of criminality" and "juvenile delinquency."[37] This began what the Cuban writer Ambrosio Fornet called the "Quinquenio Gris" (the Gray Five-Year Period), from 1971 to 1976. The architect Mario Coyula insisted it was more like a bitter fifteen-year period (Trinquenio Amargo) that had started in the second half of the sixties.[38] During this period, a series of "parameters" were imposed on professionals in the fields of education and culture to scrutinize their sexual preferences, religious practices, and relations with people abroad, along with other political and personal issues. At this time Cuban literature came closest to the model of Soviet socialist realism, at least in terms of its content. One striking example of this new line in the arts was the introduction of the detective novel under the sponsorship of the Ministry of Interior (MININT). The ministry established the National Prize for Police Literature to be awarded by juries formed by civilian writers supervised by a high-ranking intelligence officer. The first two prizes were awarded in 1973 to two works authored by two MININT lieutenants, but in subsequent years the prizes were awarded to civilian writers. In contrast to the police novel popular in capitalist countries, where the private detective plays the central role, the Cuban police novel inaugurated in the seventies had two central sets of actors. One involved the members of the intelligence agencies; the other were "the people," usually members of the CDRs, who collaborated and provided information to the intelligence agencies. This genre reached its peak in the first half of the seventies and declined considerably by the late eighties.[39] The official police novel was highly emblematic of the Cuban police state at its highest point of repression.

Margaret Randall, the American feminist writer then living as a left-wing exile in Cuba, describes the late seventies as an extremely painful period in her life. She was fired from her job, and while the government continued to pay her salary, she was never told the reasons for her firing. Years later, Randall described the prevailing atmosphere of oppression and reflected:

> For an activist there are probably few things worse than losing the confidence of your political comrades without reason. Because you have done nothing to lose it, there is nothing you can do to gain it back. Because you have given up so much to work for social justice and this work has become your identity, you feel as if your life itself may not be worth living. In the years about which I write, false accusations were often whispered about people—out of jealousy, vindictiveness, the rumor monger's desire to build himself or herself up, sometimes even out of the conviction a warning was necessary. Although I cannot remember a specific instance, I am ashamed to say that however unwittingly I too may have aided and abetted some half-truth or lies about others.[40]

From a different perspective and experience, the narrator of Leonardo Padura's *El hombre que amaba a los perros* (The man who loved dogs) remembers his youth in the late sixties and early seventies in Cuba and muses that in those years

> of the whole Western civilized and student world, we must have been the only members of our generation who, for example, never held a marijuana cigarette in our lips and who, in spite of the heat raging in our veins, were last to get rid of sexual atavisms, starting with the screwed-up taboo of virginity (there's nothing closer to communist morality than Catholic precepts). In the Spanish Caribbean we were the only ones who were totally unaware that salsa music was being born and that the Beatles (and the Rolling [Stone]s and Mamas [and Papas] too) were a symbol of rebellion and not of imperialist culture, as we were often told . . . We were, at the time, the last to know of the magnitude of the philosophical and physical wounds inflicted in Prague by tanks that proved to be more than a threat, of the massacre of

students in a Mexican plaza called Tlatelolco, of the human and historic devastation engendered by the Cultural Revolution of our beloved Comrade Mao, and of the birth, for people of our age, of a different kind of dream in the streets of Paris and in the rock concerts in California.[41]

The dark memory of the Trinquenio (or Quinquenio) unleashed a massive email protest in 2007 in reaction to a sudden reappearance of the three top bureaucrats who had managed the repressive cultural policies of that epoch: Luis Pavón Tamayo, Armando Quesada, and Jorge "Papito" Serguera. The presentation of these personalities on Cuban television as important contributors to Cuban culture caused consternation among many intellectuals and artists. They reacted with understandable fear, thinking that this might constitute the opening shot of a campaign to reintroduce a more repressive cultural policy under the aegis of Raúl Castro, who had just recently taken over from his ailing older brother Fidel. A veritable torrent of email articles circulated objecting to the reappearance of these former cultural functionaries and providing many fresh details of the horrors of that period. The protest succeeded in getting the government to admit that it had been an error to resurrect the three bureaucrats and that it would continue to pursue the more liberal policies that it had instituted since the nineties. The protest was politically limited in the sense that it generally neither challenged current censorship nor posed the question of who had given the orders to the three bureaucrats to carry out the repressive policies of the earlier period. However, the protest was, at least initially, truly spontaneous, a rarity in Castro's Cuba, and in that sense it empowered artists and intellectuals and opened up new vistas of protests on the island. The intellectuals' protest of 2007 also demonstrated the potential power of the new information technology as an avenue of protest. However, relatively few Cubans have access to computers on the island. Those who do usually use them at school or at work, with email being much more accessible than the Internet, which is restricted for both technical and political reasons.

The Mariel Exodus of 1980

The highly repressive spirit that animated cultural policies aimed at intellectuals and artists in the sixties and seventies affected more diverse and larger numbers of people when it was expressed in a far more brutal fashion during the Mariel exodus that took place in the spring of 1980. In January 1980, Fidel Castro conducted a massive shake-up of his government, which included the replacement of a large number of his cabinet ministers, in response to severe economic difficulties and popular discontent. Beginning in 1979 and early 1980 groups of people seeking asylum had forced their way into the Venezuelan and Peruvian embassies, the only way they could enter an embassy without the permission of the Cuban authorities. The asylum seekers were acting on the basis of an old Cuban and Latin American political tradition that had been abolished by Castro's government, even though hundreds of opponents of the Batista dictatorship had saved their lives by obtaining asylum in Latin American embassies. On April 1, 1980, five Cubans drove a bus through the Peruvian embassy's fence, but not before Cuban guards opened fire on the bus, which resulted in one of the guards being killed in the incident. The Peruvian government granted asylum to the five Cubans and refused to honor Castro's demand to hand them over for trial over the death of the guard.

Making what was probably the single biggest tactical mistake of his political life, Castro removed the guards from the Peruvian embassy, expecting perhaps that a couple of hundred people would enter it and in this manner disrupt the work of the Peruvian diplomatic corps. Instead, ten thousand Cubans took refuge on the embassy grounds in a very short period. This turned into a huge political setback for Castro, which he decided to turn around by opening the port of Mariel, situated in northwestern Cuba, to all Cubans wishing to leave the country, provided they were picked up from the island. A large flotilla of small boats arrived from Florida to pick up relatives and friends. But before they were allowed to depart from Mariel, the Cuban government forced them to take on board many other people, including several thousand inmates just released from prisons and mental institutions. After some 125,000 people—including a much higher proportion of black Cubans than had previously left the island—were allowed to land in Florida, president Jimmy Carter, succumbing to anti-immigrant and racist pressures, refused to take any more Cuban refugees. This was how Castro was able to change the political agenda and convert his political defeat into a political setback for Carter.

Meanwhile, inside Cuba, a veritable witchhunt was being orchestrated to humiliate and physically attack those departing the country. The Communist Party newspaper *Granma* set the tone by labeling the people who sought refuge in the Peruvian embassy as "in their great majority criminals, lumpen and anti-social elements, loafers and parasites . . . To judge by their dress, manners and language, seldom has such a 'select' group gathered anywhere . . . Even though in our country homosexuals are not persecuted or harassed, there are quite a few of them on the Peruvian embassy grounds, aside from all those involved in gambling and drugs who have no easy outlet for their vices here."[42]

CDRs and party groups organized mob action to yell obscenities, throw eggs and garbage, and paint demeaning slogans on the walls of the houses of those leaving the country. These actions were carried out with a special animus against those labeled as social deviants, especially gays.[43] Among those who left the port of Mariel was the gay writer Reinaldo Arenas, who had been earlier harassed and jailed.[44] This was probably the lowest point of Fidel Castro's regime, not in terms of actual repression—prison conditions endured by thousands of people were certainly worse—but in terms of the public humiliation and government-sanctioned disregard for human dignity. These repressive methods continued to be used, although on a much smaller scale and frequency, against dissidents, who were confronted by "rapid response brigades" attempting to break up their usually small demonstrations, and by organized mobs stoning and defacing their homes.

It would be a mistake to interpret the repression that reached its peak from the sixties to the eighties as an expression of irrationality and paranoia on the part of Fidel Castro and his close associates. There was an underlying political logic to the government's behavior. In the first place, the early adoption of the Soviet one-party state model established a substantial degree of path dependency (a social science term indicating that once a road is chosen certain consequences inevitably follow), which goes a long way in explaining the government's subsequent behavior. This feature of the Cuban system and the popular support and legitimacy enjoyed by the government encouraged a high degree of political voluntarism among the leadership. A popular and voluntaristic leadership with access to unlimited power resources tolerated no limits or restraints on the repression of what the government considered a cultural and political "softness" that the leaders perceived as an obstacle to the accomplishment of their political and economic goals.

The Rejection of "Formal Democracy"[45]

During the sixties and early seventies, the Cuban government rejected "formal democracy" and claimed that substantive and direct (nonrepresentative) democracy had been established on the island. This was supposedly accomplished through the armed militias and especially through the gigantic rallies that the Cuban government called in moments of political crisis and to mobilize in support of its new major policies. It was alleged that this proved that Fidel Castro always went to the people to get his policies approved and "voted" on (unanimously, to be sure). In reality, these rallies involved only the rubber-stamping of major decisions that Castro and his close inner circle had already made. Even half a million people at a public square were only a portion of Cuba's adult population in the early sixties. As the years passed, people increasingly became assigned, at the places where they worked or resided, to attend the big rallies called by the ruling party and its mass organizations. This does not necessarily mean that people were unwilling to attend, although with the passing of time increasing numbers of Cubans do try to stay home.[46] Many people enjoy progovernment rallies not necessarily because they are thrilled to support the government but because they offer good opportunities to stay out of work, socialize, and get some food, drink, and even free clothes,[47] which can otherwise be difficult to obtain. Most important of all, no discussion of views other than those of the Castro brothers ever took place at those giant rallies.

In any case, the political distinction between "formal" and "substantive" democracy is false and highly misleading, because there is no such thing as a "substantive" democracy that is not also "formal."[48] The Paris Commune and the Russian Soviets (before they lost their democratic character during the 1918–20 civil war) established democracy at work and throughout the rest of economic, social, and political life. These institutions, which are cited by others as classic examples of "informal, direct, nonrepresentative" democracy, established clear "formal" procedures for the election and recall of their delegates. In the case of the pre-1918 Russian Soviets, multiparty elections were held every three months, aside from the formal right of recall that could be exercised at any moment. Formal means also ensured the representational character of the higher decision-making bodies, a feature that counters the notion that these institutions were examples of "direct nonrepresentative" democracy. The delegates chosen by the local soviets went on to represent their electors in higher bodies.

These are the characteristics that endowed the Paris Commune and the soviets with a higher type of democracy than the one to be found in the "normal" electoral systems of political democracy in capitalist countries. It would thus be more useful to distinguish political democracy, which has substantial economic inequalities and authoritarian workplaces (even in the best of cases), from those historic attempts to democratize the *whole* of social life, including the economic and political systems. Sometimes, the democratic quality of countries pretending to be political democracies is so low that they can hardly be regarded as democratic in any sense of the term. This seems to be the case, for example, of Putin and Medvedev's Russian Federation, where administrative, police, and gangster measures such as assassination have been used to virtually stamp out opposition even though "free" elections, after which the votes have been duly counted, continue to be held. The problem with this Russian "democracy," however, is not that it is "formal."

The same approach can be applied to the problems of political democracy in the US context. The quality of political democracy in the United States has been considerably diminished by the electoral arrangements of its system of "checks and balances" inspired by the *Federalist Papers*, intended explicitly to check the popular will of majorities. The mechanisms to accomplish this goal included the Electoral College and the greater powers of the Senate compared to those of the House of Representatives though the Senate is actually elected on a far less democratic basis. In fact, until the twentieth century, senators were not popularly elected but instead appointed by state legislatures. Moreover, the "institution" of the filibuster makes the Senate, and by extension the political system, even less democratic. In addition, the legal obstacles to establishing third parties, the lack of proportional representation, and the drawing of electoral districts by the two principal political parties instead of an independent electoral authority have contributed to the impoverishment of political democracy. It goes without saying that the quality of American political democracy has been greatly reduced by the increasingly plutocratic course on which American politics has been embarked for a long time. The 2010 Supreme Court decision in *Citizens United v. Federal Election Commission* giving corporations the right to spend without limit in various forms of electoral activity confirmed and extended its plutocratic character.[49] This decision contributed to a substantial growth of corporate cash and anonymous contributions in the 2010 midterm elections,[50] with total electoral expenditures going up from $2.8 billion in the 2006 midterm elections to $4 billion in 2010.[51] Most important of all was the fact that the great majority of black people in the South did not have the right to vote until the mid-sixties. Today, there are constant attempts to reduce voting, particularly by African Americans and Latinos, by creating legal and bureaucratic obstacles to registration and through the disenfranchisement of people with a criminal record and lacking a driver's license or other identification documents.

In more general terms, there has been a serious deterioration of political democracy throughout the world. Political parties are increasingly empty of content and subject to the demands of the shallowest kinds of political marketing, a process that is aggravated by the huge costs of political media campaigns. Consequently, there is a lack of access to the big media for nascent movements and candidates who oppose the existing system. Parliamentary bodies have tended to decline, with many of their powers assumed by the executive branches, which unscrupulously use the doctrine of state secrets to protect their power. No wonder that political apathy, ignorance, and abstention have become prominent features of capitalist political democracy. While these are fatal to any notion of democracy built on the participation and control of an active and informed citizenry, they are certainly convenient and highly functional to a capitalist system that *structurally* privileges private and corporate economic power at the expense of public regulation and democratic control.

Institutionalization and the Adoption of "Formal Democracy"

The 1970s witnessed the "institutionalization" of the Cuban Revolution, which, as noted above, included the establishment of the first postrevolutionary constitution in 1976. With the institutionalization of the revolution, the government's definition of democracy in Cuba shifted considerably as it adopted the "formal democracy" model. It began to hold elections throughout the country that culminated in the establishment of the Asamblea Nacional del Poder Popular (National Assembly of Popular Power) as the forum for the discussion and enactment of laws. This is a very peculiar type of "democracy" with only one legal party and devoid of politics. Candidates from the lowest to the highest levels cannot present and campaign for their political programs and points of view; they can only publicize brief biographies describing their revolutionary merits and experience.[52] At the national level, the full assembly meets twice a year and for only two or three days on each occasion, although assembly commissions in charge of certain matters may meet for somewhat longer periods before submitting resolutions to the full plenary. In reality, the power lies with the Castro brothers and the Political Bureau of the CCP, which also controls this legislative body. In many instances, major policy changes have been announced without even a token gesture toward seeking approval from the assembly. This was the case, for example, with the decision to lease state land to private farmers, one of the most important reforms since Raúl Castro assumed full power in 2008. The new law was announced in the form of a decree shortly before the National Assembly of Popular Power was scheduled to meet.[53] Similarly, the very important decision to eliminate limits on state salaries was originally drafted by the Ministry of Labor in February 2008 and formally announced by Raúl Castro's government on April 12 of the same year[54] without the involvement of any Popular Power body. This was also the case for the layoff of half a million state workers decreed in September 2010. Earlier, on August 1, Raúl Castro announced to the National Assembly of Popular Power that self-employment would be expanded in light of the future reduction of state employment and that the self-employed would be also allowed to hire additional people.[55] The actual announcement of the massive layoff on September 13 was made by the CTC (Confederación de Trabajadores Cubanos, Confederation of Cuban Workers, the trade union central).[56] Again, the institutions of Popular Power were not involved in *deciding* anything related to these vital matters.

It is true that at the lowest municipal level, delegates are elected by secret ballot, among more than two, and up to eight, candidates nominated at open neighborhood meetings. Until 1992, popular election went no further than the municipal level, since members of the Provincial and National Assemblies were elected by the delegates to the Municipal Assemblies based on the candidates chosen by the party and the "mass organizations," also controlled by the party.[57] Since the constitution was amended in 1992, the principle of popular election has been extended from the municipal to the provincial and national levels. But there is a catch: candidates at the municipal level are nominated at the inclusive CDR meetings, but candidates at the provincial and national levels can be nominated only by the "commissions of candidacies" constituted by the mass organizations under the leadership of the CTC, all of which are controlled by the Cuban Communist Party.[58] Thus, the even stricter CP control at levels beyond the local results in ballots that have only one uncontested list of candidates. Voters can then vote for none, some, or all of those preselected candidates, who need to get more than 50 percent of the votes to be elected.[59] Popular Power institutions also operate at the local municipal level with significant administrative powers. However, they often do not have the material means to carry out such critical tasks as improving the housing situation, since the scarce resources are controlled by the central state, over which they have no say.[60] This is probably one of the reasons why there has been a noticeable decline of interest and participation in local Popular Power assemblies. Presiding officers feel pressure from those attending to go through the agenda quickly and finish the meeting as soon as possible.[61] In one particular local meeting called to nominate candidates, there was a general reluctance to nominate anybody. One person declined, and another person was nominated who had just moved into the neighborhood and was unknown to 98 percent of the people attending the meeting. In fact, the nominee was not even present when she was nominated; the person proposing her claimed that she had previously agreed to serve. Having completed the required procedures, and without any further discussion about the nominee, everybody voted in favor of nominating the proposed candidate, and the meeting was then quickly concluded.[62]

The Unity of the People

The refusal to allow substantive political debate among the various candidates at the lower levels of Popular Power elections, or anywhere else, is justified by the government on the grounds of maintaining national and revolutionary unity. As Raúl Castro declared in his speech of July 26, 2009, "Cuba will move forward with monolithic unity."[63] This is a very old slogan with roots that can be traced to the very beginning of the revolution—and this slogan of unity was counterposed to the development of authentic democratic institutions in the country. It is interesting to note that up to the earliest years after the victory of the revolution and *before* the adoption of the Soviet model, the revolutionary leaders implicitly acknowledged the existence of conflicting interests and views, although they insisted on their suppression for the sake of revolutionary unity. When Jean-Paul Sartre visited Cuba early in 1960 and asked Antonio Nuñez Jiménez, the head of the Agrarian Reform Institute, why a referendum was not held to validate the government and its policies and thus effectively respond to hostile criticisms, the Cuban leader symptomatically responded:

> For one single reason . . . We don't want to pay for the triumph of the revolution by wiping out the revolution. What is the meaning of our group? The unity of views, practical union. We are several in one. A single, same man everywhere at once . . . After it has chased out the *latifundistas*, an underdeveloped nation makes production the common denominator for all classes, their common interest. At present, what would an elected assembly be? The mirror of our discords.[64]

For Fidel Castro, the word *unity* has been a euphemism for monolithism and autocratic power. As early as 1954, almost five years before the victory of the revolution, he wrote to Luis Conte Aguero, then his close friend:

> Conditions which are indispensable for the integration of a truly civic moment: ideology, discipline, and chieftainship. The three are essential but chieftainship is basic . . . The apparatus of propaganda and organization must be such and so powerful that it will implacably destroy him who would create tendencies, cliques, or schisms, or would rise against the movement.[65]

Castro's long-standing views on these questions were the basis for an elective affinity with old Russian Stalinist arguments justifying the totalitarian one-party state in the Soviet Union. It is noteworthy that thirty-eight years after Castro wrote to Conte Aguero, he expressed similar views in regard to the Soviet Union in a long interview with Sandinista leader Tomás Borge. Castro criticized Stalin on a number of grounds, including the invasion of Finland and the Hitler-Stalin pact. But when Borge asked him, "What do you believe were Stalin's merits?" the first thing Castro mentioned was that Stalin "established unity in the Soviet Union. He consolidated what Lenin had begun: party unity."[66]

In comparison to Fidel Castro, Soviet Stalinism developed, as was its wont, a more "finished" and pseudo-Marxist argument to justify the one-party state. The Russian Stalinists maintained that since socialism had abolished the class struggle and unified the peasantry and the working class in the Soviet Union, and since conflicting parties have historically been established to represent the interests of conflicting classes, there was no need for more than one party. The current Cuban version, which began to be especially emphasized in the 1990s, takes for granted the Soviet notion of the homogeneity and harmony of popular interests and conflates it with its own interpretation of the political thought of José Martí, Cuba's founding father. In the late nineteenth century, Martí called for all groups and factions supporting Cuban independence from Spain to unite under the banner of the Partido Revolucionario Cubano (Cuban Revolutionary Party), which he founded and led in order to fight more effectively against Spain. The Cuban government claims that the Cuban people should stay monolithically united against the imperialist enemy, emulate Martí's model, and have only one party. Martí's call for unity for the sake of a cause was hardly unique in the annals of opposition and revolutionary movements. When Martí spoke about unity he was trying to overcome the petty jealousies and authoritarian tendencies of the insurgent caudillos in order to forge a united military but civilian-controlled campaign against Spanish rule on the island. In 1891, in a resolution that was considered a prologue to the foundation of the new party, Martí proclaimed that the new revolutionary party "will not work directly for the present or future dominance of any class of people, but for the organization, in accordance with democratic methods, of all the active forces in the Fatherland."[67] Martí attempted to accomplish his goals through political means: persuasion, education, and the creation of a united organization to achieve Cuban independence by force of arms against Spain. He did not advocate the forceful suppression, imprisonment, or execution of those Cubans who disagreed with him and resisted his efforts. Martí's views pertaining to "unity" in the struggle against Spain had absolutely nothing to do with the party system he or any other of the independence leaders thought should be established in a newly independent Cuban Republic, much less with the constitutional establishment of a one-party state outlawing other parties. Such an idea would have been most uncharacteristic of this man who was deeply steeped in the progressive and democratic political currents of the late nineteenth century.[68] Historically, the first attempt ever to create such a one-party political system controlling the whole life of a society occurred several decades after Martí's death in 1895.

Moreover, the Cuban people under the Castro brothers are not "united" in the sense of having transcended class and many other kinds of socially and politically rooted conflicts, nor were the Soviet people under Stalin and his successors. In reality, there is no such thing as a homogeneous social class with only one type of political consciousness and ideology. As Leon Trotsky succinctly put it in the 1930s:

> In reality classes are heterogeneous; they are torn by inner antagonisms, and arrive at the solution of common problems no otherwise than through an inner struggle of tendencies, groups, and parties. It is possible, with certain qualifications, to concede that "a party is a part of a class." But since a class has many "parts"—some look forward and some back—one and the same class may create several parties. For the same reason one party may rest upon parts of different classes. An example of only one party corresponding to one class is not to be found on the whole course of political history—provided, of course, you do not take the police appearance for the reality.[69]

There will always be a heterogeneity of views even within one stratum of a single class, due to unavoidable group and individual differences of opinion. The history of the Cuban Revolution is filled with such conflicts and differences even within the government camp itself. These differences may even involve serious strategic and tactical disagreements. This was the case with Fidel Castro's decision to embark on the eventually disastrous campaign for a ten-million-ton sugar crop in 1970, or with the earlier strategy adopted under pressure from the Soviet Union to reestablish sugar as the keystone of the Cuban economy.

Of course, the issue here is not advocacy of revolutionary "disunity" for its own sake. Every political leader, revolutionary or otherwise, will attempt to bring about "unity" in support of his or her programs and decisions. The question is whether such "unity" will be attempted through persuasion and other *political* means or through the use of administrative and police methods such as constitutionally outlawing other political associations and parties. Moreover, the airing of political differences in public strengthen popular political education and the potential for self-determination and management.

The Supposed Impossibility of Democracy in Cuba

The Cuban government has always claimed—both when it rejected and when it later adopted institutionalized "formal democracy"—that the Cuban Revolution embodies a superior type of democratic system. However, there is another current of thought, particularly influential among cultivated academic and intellectuals sympathetic to the Castro government, maintaining that the Cuban Revolution could not have been democratic. According to this argument, it was impossible for a socialist revolution that was also democratic to prevail in an economically underdeveloped country devoid of democratic traditions. Under the circumstances, the best that could have been expected was an "enlightened" dictatorship such as Castro's. But people making this argument stand outside the lived historical process. They make predictions with an assuredness and degree of certainty that is not warranted by a fluid situation that includes unforeseeable factors such as possible international (and not just national) repercussions of revolutionary outbreaks. Besides, democratic revolutionary socialism and a one-party Soviet-type dictatorship are not the only possible logical or historical outcomes of revolutionary processes whether in Cuba or elsewhere. At another level, such a fundamentally apologetic approach erases the boundaries between description and prescription. Even if we assumed that for a number of "objective" reasons, a socialist democracy was indeed not possible in Cuba and that the system established by Fidel Castro was "inevitable," that would not mean that such a system is worthy of support or apology. The "inevitability" of such a development is likely to be accompanied by eventual "inevitable" resistance to it. So the issue that arises in that context is, as always: which side are you on, the side of those who oppress or the side of those who suffer and resist that oppression?[70] Should intellectuals and academics identify with the problems that the elites confront and sympathize with their "dilemmas," or should they instead side with the oppressed and the resistance they engage in response to those in power?

There are "progressive" people abroad who support the Cuban government but admit that they could not tolerate living under its rule. The clear implication is that this regime is for Cubans to endure, but not for its academic, intellectual, and political sympathizers abroad. Gabriel García Márquez, a personal friend of Fidel Castro and defender of the Cuban system, once told the *New York Times* that he could not live in Cuba because he had not been through the process. García Márquez added: "I would miss too many things. I couldn't live with the lack of information. I am a voracious reader of newspapers and magazines from around the world."[71] Sometimes foreign sympathizers dislike certain aspects of Cuban government policy but take cover under a false cultural relativism to avoid criticizing the regime. Thus, in January 1972, a policy statement of the Venceremos Brigade, a North American organization sponsoring groups of volunteers regularly going to Cuba to assist in a variety of tasks, had to confront the Cuban government's hostile policies toward gays. Specifically addressing the antigay resolutions approved by the 1971 Congress on Education and Culture, the brigade insisted "this position was formulated by the Cuban people for the Cuban people.

It was not formulated for the U.S., or for any other country. Cuba is for Cubans, and while progressive and revolutionary people are always welcome in Cuba, the Cuban culture is not created for them in particular."[72]

This attitude can also be found commonly among academics specializing in Cuba, where it often takes the form of political relativism. For example, the British academic Antoni Kapcia sees the Cuban one-party system as "a vexed question since this system offends conventional western notions of a functioning democracy, defining Cuba as a dictatorship in most western countries' eyes."[73] In the first place, we may note Kapcia's rhetorical maneuver to avoid a straightforward statement of whether he thinks the Cuban government is or is not a dictatorship. But it is evident that this is a disingenuous tactic, since he is clearly trying to undermine the notion that Cuba is a dictatorship by relativizing that judgment as "Western" without actually saying or arguing that Cuba could be considered nondictatorial according to some "non-Western" criterion that is left unexplained. In these instances, as well as many others, cultural (and political) relativism evolves from a sound attempt to *understand* the meaning of social practices within their own cultural and political contexts into a thinly disguised form of tacit assent to oppression through equivocation or silence. If the assumptions of the Venceremos Brigade were correct, what consistent political basis is left to object to oppressive practices and solidarity with the victims wherever they may occur in the world? How can Kapcia's equivocations and evasions lead us to a clear understanding of what is or is not a dictatorship?

Repression and the Legal System

Since the early years of the revolution, the regime has shown little regard for legality, even for its own system of revolutionary laws and courts. In March 1959, amid the revolutionary trials of Batista henchmen that led to hundreds of executions and jail sentences, a revolutionary court in Santiago headed by Rebel Army major Félix Peña found forty-four Batista airmen innocent of war crimes. After a storm of protest ensued in Santiago, Castro ordered the pilots to be retried by a new tribunal formed by other high-ranking officers. Although no new evidence was produced at the second trial, all the airmen were convicted and sentenced to terms ranging from two to thirty years. Several witnesses who testified for the defense were imprisoned, the defense lawyers lost their jobs, and Major Peña apparently committed suicide.[74]

Throughout its history, the Cuban government has used the legal system in an arbitrary manner to stifle political dissent and opposition. Among the laws it has invoked to achieve this are those punishing enemy propaganda, contempt for authority (*desacato*), rebellion, acts against state security, clandestine printing, diffusion of false news, precriminal social dangerousness, illicit associations, meetings and demonstrations, resistance, defamation, and libel.[75] In a moment of highly unusual candor, former Cuban justice minister Roberto Díaz Sotolongo defended Cuba's law on "contempt for authority" by explaining that just as Spain had approved laws to protect the monarch from criticism, so was Cuba justified in protecting Fidel Castro, Cuba's "king," from criticism.[76]

The regime has also used repressive laws dating back to the prerevolutionary period, although with an entirely new purpose. The far greater enforcement capacity of Castro's government and the expansive spirit with which this older legislation has been redefined and applied have converted these old laws into something tantamount to new legislation. This is the case with the legal notion of "social dangerousness" originally established in the 1936 Social Defense Code. The 1979 Criminal Code, as modified in 1987, defines a person to be socially dangerous if that person engages in habitual drunkenness, drug addiction, or acts in a way that can be seen as falling under the vague and catchall category of "antisocial behavior." In such cases, the Criminal Code allows the state to impose "precriminal measures"—that is, punishment without trial—plus surveillance by the National Revolutionary Police and reeducation for periods of one to four years. Article 75(1) of the Criminal Code also allows for an individual to receive an "official warning" for having ties to people who are considered dangerous, a sort of "dangerousness" by proximity or association. As Amnesty International has pointed out, municipal tribunals have the authority to declare someone to be in a pre–dangerous criminal state. They can do so within such a short time—less than eleven days from charge to sentence—that they make it virtually impossible for the accused to mount an adequate legal defense. Since 2005, there appears to have been an increasing trend for the People's Municipal Courts to rely on these provisions to punish peaceful political activities and hinder freedom of expression. The law allows for "therapeutic measures," including detention in a psychiatric hospital until the subject is no longer dangerous. The open-ended nature of this measure gives the state tremendous power to abuse the rights of the mentally ill and of political opponents.[77] In the late eighties and early nineties, independent human rights organizations expressed concern about the use of psychiatric facilities for political purposes. In particular, the Cuban authorities were accused of having the dissidents Nicolás Guillén Landrian (a nephew of the famous Afro-Cuban poet Nicolás Guillén and a filmmaker, artist, and poet) and Jesús Leyva Guerra, a human rights activist, subjected to electric shock treatments.[78] In the late sixties, the left-wing lesbian writer Ana María Simó was jailed and afterward interned in a psychiatric institution, without any legal process.[79]

Faced with a large migration to the capital caused by the economic crisis of the nineties, the Cuban government had the legal, political, and military power to establish population control measures that most other less-developed countries facing similar crises have not. Because of the severe effects that the Special Period had in pushing people out of the Cuban hinterland, decree 217 of April 22, 1997, created strict internal migratory regulations for Havana,[80] although with dubious practical effect.

Yet the defenders of the Cuban system avoid the issue of the weight and oppressiveness of the Cuban state. Debra Evenson, a former law professor at DePaul University in Chicago and former president of the National Lawyers Guild, employed by the legal firm representing the Cuban government in New York, has articulated the notion that in Cuba "the collective good generally takes precedence over the individual."[81] Clearly, even the most egalitarian and democratic society will confront tensions and conflicts between the "collective good" and the "individual." However, it is disingenuous to hide under the benign term "collective good" to avoid describing and analyzing the overwhelmingly powerful Cuban state and how it relates to its individual citizens by denying them their political rights and civil liberties. More critical observers of the Cuban political scene seem to accept the Cuban government's definition of human rights in collective social terms while excluding the conception of human rights defined in terms of individual liberty, as if those two aspects of rights were necessarily exclusive of each other.[82] At the same time, democratic capitalist governments like to talk about human rights in terms of individual political liberties but play down if not ignore social and economic rights.

Fidel Castro's Cuba has had a long history of imposing imprisonment for political and economic crimes and for attempts to leave the country illegally. It has also resorted in the past to the extrajudicial practice of physically relocating to remote places dissident members of the CCP and government functionaries as a means to discipline them. Fidel Castro recently admitted that at one time there had been as many as 15,000 political prisoners in Cuba,[83] although on an earlier occasion he cited the figure of 20,000.[84] Starting in the late 1970s, when thousands of political prisoners were released, the number of political prisoners has been greatly reduced over the years, with an early July 2010 estimate of 167 of them in prison, thirty-four fewer than at the end of 2009. The great majority of these had been convicted for entirely peaceful political "crimes," such as publishing illegal material or organizing opposition meetings and peaceful demonstrations to demand the release of political prisoners. The above figures do not include short-term arrests (for a few hours or days at a time) of political dissidents who have criticized recent Cuban government policy. The government has increasingly relied on this tactic of short-term arrests to break up demonstrations, even though these are typically quite small, and to intimidate oppositionists. It is estimated that more than two thousand of those arrests occurred in 2010, compared with some 870 in 2009.[85] While the numbers of longer-term political prisoners were being reduced, prisoner Orlando Zapata Tamayo died in February 2010 as the result of a hunger strike in support of the demands of political prisoners for better conditions and release. Then activist Guillermo Fariñas began his own hunger strike along similar lines. This developing situation may have prompted the Cuban Catholic hierarchy and the Spanish and Cuban governments to engage in conversations concerning the fate of political prisoners during the spring and summer of 2010. On the basis of these talks, the Cuban government decided, in July 2010, to free 52 prisoners, 47 of whom had been among the 75 arrested and sentenced in the spring 2003 crackdown on dissidents. As it turned out, in the nine months preceding April 2011, 115 political prisoners were released, including the 52 who had remained in prison since the 2003 crackdown. Of the original prisoners, 103 emigrated to Spain with 647 relatives. Some 50 political prisoners remain on the island.[86]

Cuba currently has a very large number of common prisoners. The worldwide rate is 145 prisoners per 100,000 people, based on 2006 to 2008 figures; Cuba's rate of 531 prisoners per 100,000 people is the fifth highest of 218 independent countries and dependent territories. Cuba's record of imprisonment is only behind those of St. Kitts and Nevis (588), Rwanda (604), Russia (629), and the worst jailer of all, the United States of America (756 per 100,000 inhabitants).[87] As even defenders of the Cuban government have acknowledged, Blacks are overrepresented in the prison population, just as they are much more likely to be stopped by police for identity checks.[88] The Cuban government has also maintained the death penalty for numerous common and political crimes, although it appears that a de facto government moratorium on its application has been in effect for a number of years.[89]

Following the established practice in Soviet-type societies, the Cuban government has for many decades refused to acknowledge the political nature of many crimes regardless of whether these have been violent or nonviolent.[90] Accordingly, the government has always refused to grant political prisoners a different status from that of common prisoners, a distinction that is strongly rooted in Cuban and Latin American political culture and penal traditions. Historically, there has been a Latin American political practice of allowing political prisoners to dress in civilian clothes, create their own prison organizations, and organize their own, rather than submit to the jailers', political education. This held true, for example, for most of the time that Fidel Castro and his fellow Moncada attackers were in Batista's prison, from 1953 to 1955.[91] At least until the late seventies, the Cuban government carried out its most egregious abuses against the *plantados* (the planted ones), who for many years demanded to be treated as political instead of common prisoners. For this reason, they refused to attend the "political education" classes offered by the authorities as a condition of better treatment and eventual release. In the mid-eighties, much of the US press gave uncritical credence to an account of prison conditions in Cuba written by Armando Valladares, a right-wing former political prisoner of questionable credentials and credibility.[92] The Cuban official press, and its sympathizers abroad, had a field day discrediting Valladares in Cuba and throughout the world, with the implication that there was nothing problematic about prison conditions on the island. However, about the same time, Americas

Watch (the forerunner of Human Rights Watch) published a scrupulously objective yet devastating account by the former Cuban political prisoner and Christian socialist Jorge Valls. This account received little attention in the US press and was totally ignored by the Cuban press and government and its sympathizers abroad.[93] The true extent of the Cuban government's repression is yet to be unearthed. An authentic political opening in Cuba is likely to lead to a demand for access to the government archives, which might reveal, for example, the full story of the execution of General Arnaldo Ochoa and his associates in 1989.[94]

Popular Support and Manipulation

The Cuban government's repressive actions were considerably facilitated by the enormous popular support that the regime earned, particularly in the early years of the revolution. This was due to the government's radical reforms in land ownership, health, education, and social security affecting the great majority of the population, as well as its resistance to the US attempt to continue dominating Cuban affairs. But although it is crucial to be aware of the government's substantial fund of popular support, it is no less important to understand how it has been manipulated by the Fidelista leadership. For at least the first two years, Castro never presented, even to his most loyal followers, any specific program indicating where he intended to go politically. His method was to make sudden decisions and then present them, often at mammoth demonstrations, as accomplished facts. His personalistic modus operandi afforded him the advantage, from a narrowly tactical perspective, of surprising and defeating enemies, at home and abroad, at a minimal cost, particularly when it was accompanied by the very shrewd tactic of confronting one enemy at a time. This was a tactic that Castro used particularly during the early period of revolutionary consolidation. But such tactics, even when practically effective against internal and external enemies, also had the effect of preventing Castro's supporters from developing their own autonomous political consciousness so that they could cease being the objects, and become the subjects, of history.

Castro's manipulative strategy sometimes involved outright misrepresentation, as suggested by the agrarian reform legislated in May 1959 that barely mentioned cooperatives and the quite different one centered on state farms that was eventually implemented. As Joseph P. Morray, a contributor to the leftist magazine *Monthly Review,* commented about Castro's dissimulation in the early period of the revolution:

> The mark of a true revolutionary is that the content of his policy goes beyond his phrases. He must make it effective before it is understood by the guardians of the old order, lest it provoke an inconvenient prevention . . . Castro has demonstrated this quality . . . Castro's tone was moderate and conciliatory toward the United States. He had dropped the imperialism-baiting of his student days. He was not even identifying foreign private investment with imperialism. Many months would pass before Castro as Prime Minister

would join the Communists in hurling the unforgivable epithet "imperialist," which is also a manifesto, at the United States.[95]

One of the most striking examples of the manipulation of popular support by the revolutionary leadership was the forced resignation of President Manuel Urrutia. Early on the morning of July 17, 1959, newspaper headlines announced Fidel Castro's resignation as prime minister without explaining the reasons for such a dramatic and unexpected act. Many Cubans initially thought that Castro's announced resignation was his way of reaffirming his power in the face of the growing US hostility after the Agrarian Reform Law was approved in May 1959. Castro would receive a renewed affirmation of popular support, at which point he would return to his position as prime minister. Only the old Communists of the PSP immediately connected his resignation to their dislike for President Urrutia, who had recently made pronouncements criticizing Communism. He was a former provincial judge who had been rewarded by Castro with the presidency of the republic for having refused to condemn a group of 26th of July militants who had participated in an armed uprising against Batista.

In the morning students rallied at the University of Havana and then marched to the presidential palace in support of the Agrarian Reform Law and demanding that Castro withdraw his resignation. Upon arrival they were addressed by Armando Hart, the young minister of education. Throughout the rest of the day, the radio reported on the thousands of messages sent to Fidel Castro by unions and many other popular organizations demanding that he withdraw his resignation. The overwhelming majority of these messages were very similar to those that had been conveyed by the university students' demonstration earlier that day and by Hart's speech, and made no mention of President Urrutia.

That evening, Fidel Castro went on national television. To the surprise of the great majority of Cubans, he unleashed a savage political and personal attack on President Urrutia that was nothing less than a character assassination. He thundered against Urrutia for earning a big salary and building a fancy house for himself, and accused him of functioning in an obstructionist manner as president. But by far the main accusation was that Urrutia had gone out of his way to attack Communism on several occasions and particularly in a television interview that had aired some time before Castro's speech. Thus, the real motive for Castro's "resignation" was revealed after the Cuban people had been "warmed up" all day in support of the Maximum Leader.

Fidel Castro's "resignation" had been a very shrewd tactical move. Urrutia was a very weak opponent who could be easily eliminated, which would mark an important policy shift on the part of the government toward conferring a special status on Communist politics. In fact, in the next several months it became clear that Communists could attack anybody on the right and on the left, people within the revolutionary camp could not attack Communists without being called "divisive" and "counterrevolutionary" by Fidel Castro and his associates.

Fidel Castro's manipulation of popular support took on a much more ominous role in the Urrutia incident than in the special status conferred on Communist politics. Most Cubans saw Urrutia as superfluous and irrelevant and referred to him with the disrespectful moniker *cuchara* (spoon), meaning he was neither a fork (that pierces) nor a knife (that cuts). But he was not allowed to publicly defend himself against Castro's accusations. And as soon as Castro made his speech, the great majority of Cubans turned against Urrutia without the slightest question or doubt. With hindsight, it is clear that this was not the way for a revolutionary camp to settle the internal disputes that were inevitably bound to develop among its leaders. The dispute may have also reflected more than a difference of opinion and involved need to replace leaders who had been outflanked on the left by the radicalization of the revolution. However, the response should not have depended on the sole judgment of an individual, no matter how important, and certainly should not have entailed vicious personal slander and vilification (without the right of the accused to respond) as a political method. The method employed by Castro was consistent with the creation of uncritical mass support and adulation for a revolutionary caudillo, one with political plans and ideas. In the last analysis, however, the issue is not the reputation of Urrutia or any other leader who may have been disgraced by Fidel Castro, but the kind of revolution that was unfolding in Cuba.

The Relative Liberalization of the Nineties

The sharp economic crisis of the 1990s brought about a relative decrease of repression on the island. There was also a significant cultural relaxation. The sudden inability of the regime to maintain even the austere standard of living, meeting basic needs, to which the majority of the population had become accustomed created a climate of widespread discontent and unrest that could potentially have taken a political form. The economic crisis also negatively impacted the effectiveness of internal mechanisms of control, such as the CDRs. The government was forced to make concessions in a variety of areas, such as by an implicit toleration of the widespread petty corruption to which large numbers of Cubans had been forced to turn in order to survive. The previous thirty years had witnessed ebbs and flows of repression, such as when the liberation of a large number of political prisoners in the late seventies was succeeded by the government-sponsored brutality of the Mariel exodus in the spring of 1980. But no noticeable liberalization had previously taken place in connection with other political and economic changes, such as the political "institutionalization" of the seventies or the changes in economic organization under the influence of the Soviet Union in the same decade.

The Fourth Congress of the CCP, held in 1991, lifted the ban that had kept religious believers and practitioners from joining the ruling party and holding important positions in the government. This action revived religious practices among Cubans, whether Catholic, Protestant, Afro-Cuban, or even Jewish. This change in religious policy responded not only to the grave crisis developing at home but also to the Cuban government's increasing foreign policy need to relate to liberation theology circles in Latin America.[96] In the academic, cultural, and artistic worlds the relaxation of government controls encouraged the further development of small-circulation journals such as *Temas*, *La Gaceta de Cuba*, and *Criterios*. These liberal Communist organs began to dispense with the hackneyed language of the "party line" and engaged in serious social and political criticism, although within very clear limits.

A number of NGOs and research centers have since been allowed to function with a longer and looser leash. The popular counterpart of the liberalization that benefited the educated elites involved the toleration of a culture of complaint by individual citizens—certainly not of organized group activity outside of official channels. Beyond being allowed to be vented publicly, complaints have been sometimes *encouraged*, provided they are directed at specific individual office holders and never at the top political elite. Meanwhile, the mass media organs have maintained a strictly orthodox political orientation. They have also remained quite dull, although occasionally *Juventud Rebelde* has enlivened its coverage with investigative journalism pieces revealing the extent of corruption in the country. *Granma's* weekly section registering administrative complaints from the citizenry has been less revealing, but it orchestrated a "debate" on the privatization of small businesses such as cafeterias and restaurants to legitimate subsequent government actions to dump small enterprises plagued by waste, inefficiency, and theft.

Notwithstanding the relative cultural liberalization established since the nineties, the ruling party orthodoxy continues to be imposed in numerous ways, including a systematic censorship enforced through the Ideological Department of the Central Committee of the CCP, which sends its "orientations" about news content to all media organs.[97] International and national news is reported according to the political needs and convenience of the government. Sometimes, it takes several days until news of important events is disseminated because the government has to develop a "line" on the question, as had happened with the Soviet invasion of Afghanistan at the end of 1979. Since the Cuban government maintains friendly relations with the Chinese regime, which is one of its principal trade partners, negative news about that government is avoided, let alone any views or perspectives that might question its supposedly socialist character. Soviet publications had been widely distributed in Cuba since the sixties, but when publications such as *Sputnik* and *Moscow News* began to espouse the pluralistic perspectives of *glasnost*, they were banned, even if they rarely discussed Cuba, in

1989. Fidel Castro explained that these publications were banned because they were "full of poison against the U.S.S.R. itself and socialism. You can see that imperialism and reactionary forces and the counterrevolution are responsible for the tone."[98]

It goes without saying that any national news that might displease the government is suppressed, as was the case with the demonstration held by hundreds of students in Santiago de Cuba protesting poor living conditions and lack of safety for women students in the fall of 2007. The presence of riot police to quell a protest by Pakistani medical students objecting to the poor quality of their education at the Maximo Santiago Haza Medical School in Jaguey Grande, Matanzas, in the early part of 2010 was completely ignored by the Cuban media.[99] The important protest by intellectuals and artists in early 2007 was met with almost complete silence in the official media, so it was very difficult for the overwhelming majority of Cubans, who have no access to email, to find out what it was all about. The presence of censorship is also obvious even in matters of relatively little political import. In late 2010, the Cuban press gave no explanation of why Frederich Cepeda, Cuba's most valuable baseball player for seven years, was suddenly taken off the team for the Intercontinental Cup, failed to appear on the Sancti Spiritus roster for the Cuban league, and was then reinstated on that team.[100] Another example was the reporting on Javier Bardem's visit to the country in 2008. A very detailed biography of the Spanish actor appeared in the newspaper *Juventud Rebelde* but omitted any reference to his first Oscar nomination for playing the role of the Cuban dissident gay writer Reinaldo Arenas in Julian Schnabel's *Before Night Falls*.[101] Censorship is perhaps most striking in radio and television, which is under the aegis of the ICRT (Instituto Cubano de Radio y Televisión, Cuban Institute of Radio and Television), an institution despised by many artists and intellectuals for its censorious and arbitrary practices. Sometimes this censorship has been quite crude. One example is the deliberate failure to translate into Spanish Noam Chomsky's critique of the human rights situation in Cuba in an appearance on Cuban television during a visit to the island in 2003. Books, including those produced abroad, are not exempt from censorship. Even the relatively liberal annual book fair has ordered exhibitors to remove books written by critics and opponents of the regime, as happened with the Puerto Rico–based editorial house Plaza Mayor in 2004.[102]

Censorship reflects the government's fundamental elitism and lack of trust in what people may think and do when privy to unfiltered information. Censorship, and more generally the withholding of information from the mass of the population, demonstrates lack of respect for them, even contempt. This was clearly shown when in April 2009, Foreign Minister Felipe Pérez Roque and Vice President Carlos Lage were suddenly removed from office and the government found it unnecessary to provide a full explanation for the decision.[103] It is revealing in this context that since then a video detailing the government's version of that event has been produced but has been shown only to selected audiences of leaders and cadres of the CCP.

In October 2009, a column titled "Contra los demonios de la información secuestrada" (Against the demons of sequestered information) was published on the website of the official newspaper *Juventud Rebelde* but quickly removed by the Cuban authorities. In that column, José Alejandro Rodríguez, a journalist for that paper, pointed out that information is a double-edged sword that shines brightly but also reveals the dark holes of reality. Nevertheless, insisted Rodríguez, information is a public good, and we ought not to replace it with sanctioned and opportune information, virtual information, information-propaganda or convenient information, or information picked with tweezers. Information is information. Rodríguez concluded that the present-day handling of news in Cuba "obstructs the democratic potential [of socialism]" and that it is necessary to have a well-informed citizenry to achieve a "fuller and more democratic socialism."[104]

As I discuss in much greater detail in chapter 6, the official repression of gays, which once included the quarantining of AIDS victims, also began to be relaxed in the 1990s. At this time, a much more liberal and enlightened policy under the leadership of Mariela Castro Espín (a daughter of Raúl Castro) and CENESEX (Cuban National Center for Sex Education), which she directs, began to have some impact. CENESEX has advocated the legalization and facilitation of transgender surgery. None of this has meant, however, that Cuban gays have felt entirely free to come out of the closet or that discrimination has been eliminated. They, along with blacks, women, and workers, have not been allowed to organize independently to defend their interests, including the right to openly oppose and organize against the policies of the ruling party and state.

Restrictions on travel outside the country have also been liberalized. However, there is still no legal right to travel abroad and unauthorized entry or departure from the country has been illegal since the sixties. Permission to travel abroad is still a privilege granted by the state; it is very costly and requires much bureaucratic paperwork. Many political dissidents such as Yoani Sánchez, the editor of the *Generación Y* blog, have continued to be denied permission to travel abroad on numerous occasions, particularly because she was going to receive prizes for her dissident work from foreign institutions.[105] For the same reasons, Cuban dissident Guillermo Fariñas was also denied permission to travel abroad in late 2010.[106] Hilda Molina, a prominent neurosurgeon and former deputy of Cuba's National Assembly, was finally allowed to visit her son and family in Argentina in 2009 after fifteen years of waiting. Juan Juan Almeida García, a son of revolutionary hero Juan Almeida, and Bian Oscar Rodríguez Galá, a member of the critical rap group Los Aldeanos (The Villagers) have also been denied permission to leave the country.[107] Almeida was finally allowed to leave the island, after a long wait, in the summer of 2010, and Los Aldeanos were able to travel to southern Florida later that year. The absence of the right to travel has created, especially among young people, a powerful sense of isolation and frustration verging on claustrophobia. Indeed the absence of the legal right to travel and the great difficulty and expense required to obtain government permission to do so are undoubtedly among the most deeply felt sources of resentment of the government.

The government's liberalizing tendencies that began in the nineties has been anything but consistent. In April 2003, three young Black Cubans who attempted to leave the island illegally by hijacking a small ferry were, within a period of nine days, summarily tried and executed, even though they did not physically harm anyone during their failed attempt.[108] The previous month, seventy-five dissidents had been jailed and given long prison sentences.[109] As described by the left-wing reporter José Manuel Martín Medem, the whole affair showed clear evidence of entrapment, as several of the supposedly dissident initiatives to collaborate with the US government were actually proposed and carried out by state security agents pretending to be oppositionists.[110] The trial itself, as is usually the case with political cases in Cuba, was clearly arbitrary, and the sentences, the great majority of them ranging from fifteen to twenty-seven years in prison, were determined by the government in advance of the trial.[111] In the case of the seventy-five dissidents, the government invoked the Law for the Protection of Cuban National Independence and the Economy approved in 1999.[112] Among other things, this law made it a punishable crime to receive funds from hostile foreign forces, even if those funds are used to carry out entirely peaceful political activities or to write newspaper articles for hostile organs such as *El Nuevo Herald* in Miami. Some in the group did receive material aid from the US government in the form of publishing resources and stipends. But even if every one of the seventy-five had done so, the fact that their activities were of a peaceful nature should have made this issue not a police matter but rather a political question appropriate for public debate before the whole of Cuba. People could then have drawn their own conclusions as to the political trustworthiness and credibility of the government and its opponents. Moreover, this situation should not be judged in isolation from the overall context of the Cuban state's monopolizing the means of publication and broadcasting. In addition to lacking any legitimate avenue to express their ideas, dissidents are routinely denied educational opportunities and fired from their state jobs, which have historically constituted the overwhelming majority of the available jobs in Cuba. This situation has led some dissidents to the unfortunate, and in this case politically "Plattista" (after the Platt Amendment), conclusion that the enemy of their enemy is their friend, if not to becoming outright supporters of the United States, and thus they have become willing to receive aid from the US government. Unfortunately, this is a pattern with a long and sad history in opposition movements in Communist countries. If all Cubans, including peaceful oppositionists, were entitled to freedom of the press, speech, and assembly, and resources to exercise those rights were granted on some proportionate and equitable basis, then, and only then, could a case be made for criminalizing the receipt of material aid from the US government. The political approach I am suggesting here could become particularly relevant in a post-Castro Cuban transition, where massive American government resources might threaten to take over any electoral or political processes in the island. That would create a far more serious threat to Cuban national self-determination than whatever resources the US government currently distributes to a relatively small number of dissidents.

The 2003 crackdown, as harsh as it was, did not signal a general return, as some feared, to the earlier darkest practices of the regime's history. The relatively liberal policies of the government, particularly in the cultural and religious fields, have remained unchanged. This is mostly because the economic crisis and the decline of support for the regime that initially brought about the relative liberalization of the early nineties have not, on the whole, been reversed. As indicated earlier, estimates of the number of political prisoners have been substantially reduced from the three to four hundred of a few years ago. The policy that the Cuban regime maintained for many years of isolating the country from foreign cultural influences, of which the banning of long hair, certain types of clothing, and the music of the Beatles constituted the most absurd examples, has been reversed, particularly since the nineties. A statue of John Lennon was even erected in Havana, although it is worth noting that the Cuban government never publicly apologized or explicitly acknowledged the error of its former hostility to the British artist.

However, it is quite possible that the government may revert to the more repressive policies of earlier periods, particularly in a transitional situation after one or both Castro brothers have left the scene. In such a situation, a crisis of legitimacy may add fuel to the fire of popular discontent with the austerity and repressive measures that a regime dominated by the military may take, attempting to implement a Sino-Vietnamese model on the island.

Implications and Conclusions

Many of the matters explored in this chapter touch on problems that are not unique to the Cuban Revolution but relate to the crises of democracy, socialism, and their mutual relationship spanning the last century. Many decades ago, the authoritarian Indonesian leader Sukarno claimed to have established a new form of "guided democracy," as did many dictatorships throughout the world that claimed their own supposedly democratic "innovations." For its part, the Communist tradition originating in the Soviet Union has dismissed bourgeois capitalist democracy as being merely a matter of periodic elections where the people get to choose between competing set of agents acting on behalf of the capitalist class. This is a highly reductionist if not cartoonlike view of democracy under capitalism. To be sure, even in the best of cases, capitalist democracy, limited to the political sphere, is structurally designed to leave the realms of the economy and society to the "blind" dictates of private corporate property and the capitalist marketplace. The much-attacked welfare state and the usually diminished regulatory framework of capitalist economies do not fundamentally alter that reality. But a lot of what Communists and even some liberals consider to be capitalist democracy is not capitalist at all. If it had been left to the capitalists (and aristocrats), the British Parliament would have remained the highly undemocratic institution it was well into at least the 1860s, with a highly restricted property-based franchise and other serious limitations on democracy. Without working-class and popular struggle there would have been no male universal franchise starting in 1867, nor would there have been women's suffrage in the 1920s without the struggles led by the feminist movement in the United Kingdom as well as in the United States. The same applies to Cuba. Important democratic gains made by the Cuban people long before the 1959 Cuban Revolution were not gifts of the Cuban governments and upper classes. Women's suffrage, the eight-hour day, and welfare state reforms were the result of working-class and women's and other popular struggles in the wake of the 1933 Revolution. These and other social advances such as the establishment of extensive union rights for workers and social and economic rights for women were incorporated into the progressive and democratic 1940 constitution, in the name of which the revolution against Batista's dictatorship was conducted. I would therefore suggest that from a working-class and popular point of view, periodic elections are not the most important element of "capitalist" political democracy. The main value of that type of democracy, to the extent to which it has real substance, lies elsewhere. It is in the ability of the working class and other popular forces to organize freely and independently in pursuit of their interests and to create an alternative set of institutions, including their own media, to fight for their self-emancipation and against capitalist priorities and institutions.

While the Cuban experience is hardly unique when it comes to systematic violation of civil liberties and civil rights, it reinforces the need for the left to draw lessons from such historical events. The accumulated experiences of modern social revolutions strongly suggest that a socialist society based on democratic popular power must presuppose freedom of speech, press, and assembly, and of workplace and political organization. Along these lines, one international Marxist organization has proclaimed that a postrevolutionary socialist order must establish a number of fundamental rights. Among these are the necessity of written law, avoidance of retroactive delinquency, for the burden of proof to be on the accuser, the assumption of innocence until proven guilty, for accused individuals to determine the nature of their defense, full immunity of legal defenders from prosecution for lines of defense used in such trials, rejection of the notion of collective responsibility, a prohibition of torture, a suppression of the death penalty outside of civil war and war situations, a universal system of public trials by juries of peers, the democratic election of all judges, and the right of the mass of the working population to recall elected judges.[113]

The arguments against democracy in Cuba and other postrevolutionary societies usually share a number of unspoken and unexamined assumptions. One is the fundamentally pessimistic assumption that the forces supporting the successful revolution would, for some unexplained reason, be mute or at least politically inadequate and ineffective; they would therefore be unable to prevail against the opposition through persuasion and militant agitation without resort to force, even against peaceful opponents. At the same time, the defenders of the previous ruling class are deemed to be always able to confuse and win major sections of the population away from the revolutionary government. According to this view, that is why the new socialist government and its supporters are compelled, in order to preserve the successful revolution, to forcefully suppress the views of the opposition. It would be naive to assume that a counterrevolutionary opposition would be peaceful—the historical record shows exactly the opposite. However, there is no reason that a revolutionary government should "jump the gun" and act as if every act of opposition, by its very nature, would lead to violent subversion. This is something to be shown in practice rather than assumed beforehand.

Others on the left seem to share an unacknowledged assumption that the successful socialist revolution that brings about the final collapse of capitalism can happen only once, a sort of revolutionary socialist equivalent of Francis Fukuyama and his view of the end of history.[114] The historical record of the twentieth century makes this an unwarranted supposition. V. I. Lenin and the political tradition that followed in his footsteps made the valid claim that the political consciousness of the working class is uneven, that is, that some sectors of the working class are more politically active and revolutionary than others. This is also true for the political consciousness of the peasantry and other oppressed classes and groups. This unevenness is not likely to disappear immediately after capitalism has been overthrown by a successful socialist revolution. Therefore, when workers are confronting a postrevolutionary crisis, the gap between the less and more conscious among them may grow, isolating the more politically developed workers and their leaders from the mass of the population. The Russian Revolution is an example of how under any number of circumstances, including a devastating civil war, the revolutionary party can become isolated and deprived of political support, partly when a sizable proportion of its social base—the working class—physically disappears. This created a dilemma. Should the Bolshevik leadership have made an extraordinary effort to broaden the ruling party's political support by reaching out to prorevolutionary elements in other left parties with which the government may have been in conflict? Or should it have gone it alone and imposed, as it eventually did, a viciously repressive system such as Stalin's, to preserve the ruling party's monopoly of power?[115] The notion that what happened in Russia was exceptional because of the economic backwardness of the country and because of the civil war is unwarranted. The ruling classes of the most economically advanced countries with the strongest democratic traditions are not likely to peacefully agree to give up their economic and social power. They will sabotage and even destroy their productive property before handing it over. A socialist revolution is therefore more likely than not to inherit a society that has experienced a lot of destruction, making it very difficult for the new government to maintain, let alone improve, existing living standards at least for a number of years. If so, the possibility of a popularly supported capitalist restoration, even if temporary, may be rooted not only in counterrevolutionary conspiracies and actions but also in the material reality of postrevolutionary objective circumstances. It follows then that there may be the need to undergo a series of socialist revolutions before a new socialist political system and mode of production become stabilized and long lasting. In any case, there can be no advanced historical guarantees of socialist perpetuity except the perennial struggle of actual people to continue making socialism a historical reality.[116]

In conclusion, we do not know beforehand when a people and society are "ready" for democratic forms of economic, political, and social organization. We *can* look back and in retrospect realize that the rebel slave Spartacus and his comrades could not have succeeded in their emancipatory efforts and were bound to lose. In fact, it is most doubtful that the countries of Western Europe, let alone the rest of the world, were economically ready for socialist democracy at the time Marx and Engels published *The Communist Manifesto* in 1848. Looking back on the peasants' revolt in Germany of the sixteenth century and on rebel leader Thomas Munzer's historically grounded failure, Frederick Engels could remain sympathetic, identify with the peasant rebellions, and understand the reasons for Munzer's failure without apologizing for it. Thus, Engels reflected that

> the worst thing that can befall a leader of an extreme party is to be compelled to take over a government in an epoch when the movement is not yet ripe for the domination of the class which he represents, and for the realization of the measures which that domination implies . . . In a word, he is compelled to represent not his party or his class, but the class for whose domination the movement is then ripe. In the interests of the movement he is compelled to advance the interests of an alien class, and to feed his own class with phrases and promises, and with the asseveration that the interests of that alien class are its own interests.[117]

It is worth pointing out that Munzer never became the head of a stable national government, let alone of a new exploitative ruling class, so one can only imagine how much harsher Engels's critique would have been if he had been analyzing such a situation.

There is no school or university where workers and other exploited and oppressed people can go and learn to practice socialist democracy except the one wrought through their own efforts with the inevitable trials and errors. They are certainly not going to learn and develop "democratic traditions" from dictatorships that prevent them from carrying out that indispensable learning.

Chapter Two

Economic Development and the Standard of Living since the 1959 Revolution

The long-standing expectations of the Cuban people of economic development and a higher standard of living dramatically rose as the Cuban Revolution became a social revolution, transforming Cuba's class structure, after the political revolution had succeeded in overthrowing Batista's dictatorship in January 1959. For most Cubans, the time had finally arrived for agrarian reform, economic diversification, and industrialization to put an end to the country's historic dependence on sugar, chronic unemployment, and a low standard of living, particularly in the countryside.

In light of these aspirations, what balance sheet can be drawn of the economic successes and failures of the Cuban regime? More than fifty years after the victory of the revolution, the country has not become industrialized as the revolutionary leaders promised. Sugar production has dramatically diminished and is a shadow of its former self. However, this was not a result of successful agricultural diversification and industrialization. Instead, the decline of sugar was mainly due to the failure to adequately maintain and modernize the sugar mills, and to diversify into various sugar by-products. This governmental neglect long preceded the severe economic crisis of the 1990s. Agriculture never became diversified enough to satisfy domestic consumption and remains in dire straits. This has compelled the Cuban government to increasingly rely on food imports, especially from the United States. As far as industrialization is concerned, the biotechnology industry has advanced, but its promise has yet to be realized. While much exploration for oil in the Cuban waters of the Gulf of Mexico has taken place,[1] and is potentially very profitable, the actual extraction and sale of that oil are yet to begin. The most important recent economic activities on the island have been the extraction and export of nickel, in a joint venture with Canadian capital, and the export of medical and other services to other developing countries, particularly Venezuela, in exchange for oil. Tourism, in joint ventures with Spanish and other foreign capitalists, is also among the top earners and has come back with a vengeance. The prerevolutionary tourist industry, which preceded the era of jet travel and international mass tourism, with 200,000 to 250,000 annual visitors in the fifties, has been dwarfed by the massive tourist industry that has been growing since the nineties. Since 2004, the total number of tourists has surpassed two million a year.[2] Tourism has contributed to a growth of inequality and brought along with it the rise of prostitution, street hustling, and other social problems that the revolution was supposed to have eradicated. Quite significantly, Cuba has also come to rely heavily on remittances from abroad, particularly from Cuban Americans in southern Florida, which have become an essential means of survival for large numbers of Cubans.[3]

Contradictions of the Bureaucratic Economic System

The undoubtedly real effects of the US economic blockade have helped to hide from the Cuban people and the regime's sympathizers abroad the systemic inefficiency and waste inherent in the bureaucratic system of state collectivism that rules the island.[4] In this type of system, the economic surplus is not extracted in the form of profits from individual enterprise, nor is it realized through the market. Instead, it is obtained as a surplus product of the nation as a whole. The surplus is appropriated directly, through the state's control of the economy. This does not occur, however, primarily through the higher salaries of bureaucrats, which represent only a small part of the surplus product, as does the consumption of the ruling class in capitalist societies. The surplus product must also cover accumulation and investment, defense spending, and all other state expenditures.

This bureaucratic ruling class appropriates the economic surplus without any *institutional* constraints by unions or any other independent popular organizations. Omar Everleny Pérez Villanueva, a Cuban economist residing on the island, reported that during the period 1975–89, the rates of investment in the Cuban economy were on the average 25 percent of the gross national product. Pérez Villanueva further explained that "these levels of accumulation were possible because of the combined effect of existing restrictions on personal consumption and beneficial financing terms granted by socialist countries."[5] The prominent Cuban economist Carmelo Mesa-Lago calculated that during the earlier period of 1965 to 1970 the emphasis on capital accumulation at the price of reducing consumption rose to a high point, with the share going to the productive sphere increasing from 78.7 to 85.8 percent.[6]

Because of its closed bureaucratic and centralized nature, this system lacks transparency and open public discussions of its problems, except of course for those problems the regime chooses to publicize for its own purposes at the times it deems convenient. The episodic exposure of economic problems in the official media tends to be local in nature and obscures rather than clarifies their systemic nature. The regime often berates lower-level bureaucrats for their incompetence, publicly pressures workers to work harder, and, more generally, publicizes some deficiencies in order to promote ad hoc local "solutions" as a way of attempting to square the circle of the system's contradictions. Subordinates often tell their superiors what they would like to hear instead of the truth. In late 2010, Raúl Castro told Cuba's national parliament that "sometimes comrades, without a fraudulent purpose, transmit unverified false information provided by their subordinates. That is how they unconsciously end up telling lies. That false data can lead us to erroneous decisions with greater or lesser national repercussions."[7] In such ways information about the economy is systematically distorted, blocking transmission of the clear signals that are necessary for the proper functioning of an economic system. Authentic feedback, accurate information, and really independent initiatives from below, which imply a loss of control by the authorities, are discouraged by systemic features of the bureaucratic economic organization. Bureaucratic centralization also often entails a tremendous amount of waste. For example, a soft drink factory in western Cuba used to send its entire production to central warehouses in Havana, located over 200 kilometers away. From there the soft drinks to be consumed in western Cuba were sent back 200 kilometers to that part of the country. This arrangement, lasting a decade, was replaced in 2009 with one only somewhat less wasteful. Now the soft drinks are sent to the warehouse in the provincial capital some 70 kilometers away and then are sent back several dozen kilometers to the five municipalities located near the factory.[8] Similar problems have been reported in other parts of the country. A factory producing cookies and other sweets in the northern city of Caibarién in central Cuba used to send its production to Cienfuegos at the southern end of the province, and from there to the provincial capital located in the central part of the same region. It appears that in this case the bureaucrats eventually got it right and established direct delivery from the factory to the various provincial locations.[9]

Because of the existing authoritarian centralization, many government managers are unwilling to assume responsibility for their failure to meet economic targets. As a regional government economic executive recently told the official newspaper *Juventud Rebelde*, they are prone to "keep on the lookout waiting for the solution to come from the upper echelons when it is they who should have taken the initiative."[10] Other bureaucrats simply take actions that fall under their jurisdiction without regard to how they should be coordinated with actions taken elsewhere. The unilateral decision making and bad information, or the lack of information, have highly detrimental consequences since what has to be produced depends on other things that also need to be produced or imported. Carmelo Mesa-Lago reported that in the Cuba of the 1970s imported equipment often lay unused for years (sometimes rusting on the docks) because buildings to house it had not been constructed. Mesa-Lago also reported that during the seventies a large thermoelectric plant and several factories could not be put into operation because a vital part was missing, and light cranes were breaking down as a result of being used for excessively heavy loads. In agriculture, the construction of small dams was not being matched by the development of irrigation systems; therefore, much of the accumulated water was not used or was wasted.[11]

This kind of inefficiency continued to be a problem in 2009. Marino Murillo Jorge, the minister of economy and planning, complained that new electrical equipment acquired to save precious energy had been kept in storage instead of being installed promptly.[12] In the construction of tourist hotels, workers are often idle because "somebody" forgot to take the materials out of the warehouse or because the technicians who were supposed to supervise the work were not available at the work site.[13] The official press also reported that quality of work suffers as a result of lack of coordination among the different state enterprises responsible for the repair of water leaks. While one state enterprise is in charge of breaking up the street, a different one puts in the pipes, and if the job is badly done, the responsibility is spread among the different state enterprises, which means that in the end nobody takes responsibility.[14]

In the absence of an open and democratic public life, consumers lack the power to bring government economic planners to account. The lack of an open press and mass communications has facilitated cover-ups, corruption, and inefficiency. This allows bureaucratic production indexes to take on a life of their own, with little regard for quality and the variety of shapes, grades, and sizes that consumers need and want. In Soviet-type systems like Cuba's it often happens that if a factory has its output calculated in tons, then there will a systemic tendency to turn out fewer but heavier goods, rather than more varied and attractive ones.[15] Bureaucrats also develop relationships and become part of power networks that permit them to stockpile inputs and pay little regard to costs of production. Foreign reporters in Cuba have found that inefficient factories inflate their expenses to obtain more money from the government, and a generalized lack of attention to costs results in cases such as the plastics factory where $1.15 was invested for every dollar's worth of merchandise produced.[16] Sometimes a state firm does not pay the debts it owes to other state companies, and even if the guilty state manager is removed from the administrative post, this does not restore trust to the delinquent firm.[17] Such occurrences are part of the phenomenon of "soft budgets" in public enterprises, a central element of what the Hungarian economist Janos Kornai called "shortage economies" with their accompanying waste and inefficiency. The official Cuban press has acknowledged that the great difficulties of the Cuban economy include the waste of resources, the overuse of energy carriers, and the existence of idle plant in economic enterprises. However, the blame for these problems has been assigned to a lack of "economic culture"[18] rather than to the structure and organization of the economic system itself. These bureaucratic systems also create an unsolvable problem with incentives. The old maxim attributed to Soviet and East European workers that "they pretend to pay us and we pretend to work" fully applies to Cuba. This is evident in the visible lack of care that is noticeable regarding many different types of public sector property, from planes and hotels to parks and sidewalks. While economic hardship and the US blockade may explain the lack of building materials necessary for certain kinds of upkeep, they do not explain the absence of simple, labor-intensive activities that have no significant capital components, such as cleaning and sweeping.

The lack of workers' control and inadequate material incentives produce an indifference that is most evident in the service sector, where paradoxically substantial overstaffing can coexist with very poor service. At a small supermarket (barely 500 square meters in size) in Havana a young woman is in charge of keeping an eye on packages that cannot be brought into the store, and two guards search customers on their way out to prevent theft. This of course is not that different from many similar businesses located in poor areas in the United States and Latin America. But what is distinctive about Cuban bureaucratic practices at the retail level is the great deal of duplication and waste that contributes to very poor service. For example, the same small supermarket in Havana has a separate cashier for each type of merchandise. If a customer were to buy chicken, pasta, beer, toilet paper, and seasonings she would have to stand at five different lines in order to pay for her purchases at five different cashier stands.[19] This practice is not limited to the supermarket retail trade. A small establishment selling industrial products has five or six employees, each specializing in a certain number of products, but if one person is absent, none of the other employees, even if they are not busy, can be of any assistance. In addition, there are businesses that, although they are supposed to begin operations at 8:30 a.m., have not begun to do so even after 9:00 a.m. Meanwhile, the responsible employees are chatting away about matters not related to their work.[20] Workers in many of those establishments have no reason to care or "give a damn" when they neither are properly rewarded in material terms nor have any democratic political control of what happens in their workplace, much less the economy and society as a whole.

Besides these systemic flaws and contradictions common to all Soviet-type systems, Cuba has been affected by its own specific limitations generated by features of the imperialist division of labor and of economic underdevelopment such as the overwhelming concentration on the sugar industry. For all those reasons, the Cuban economy was not able to overcome most of its long-term problems in spite of the massive Soviet aid before the nineties, let alone after the economic crises provoked by the collapse of the Soviet bloc. Moreover, arbitrary interventions in economic affairs by Fidel Castro, the commander in chief, aggravated the problems that Cuba suffered as a Soviet-type economy for many decades. Although undoubtedly a very intelligent and talented man, Castro was not the expert he thought he was on everything under the sun, whether military strategy, baseball, agriculture, or cattle science, to name a just a few of his "areas of expertise." The overall balance of his personal interventions in economic affairs has been quite negative. Castro conducted an economically disastrous campaign for a ten-million-ton sugar crop in 1970, which failed to achieve its goals and greatly disrupted the rest of the economy. He was also responsible for the predictable failure of the F1 hybrid cows, a new breed of cattle, which he tried to develop on the island, against the advice of British experts he brought to Cuba in the sixties.[21] His penchant for economic "gigantism" led him to carry out such projects as the unnecessarily wide and wasteful eight-lane highway traversing a good part of Cuba. In the nineties, the Cuban leader was also responsible for a failed campaign to introduce the costly "micro-jet" method of irrigating banana trees. More recently, he was in charge of economic disruptions and improvisations that were part of his "Battle of Ideas." Fidel Castro's strong tendency to micromanage also silenced and paralyzed the initiatives of responsible and capable people who were simply afraid to contradict him. As René Dumont, the well-known left-wing agronomist, noted in the seventies, the person who opposes Fidel Castro is quickly rejected, and as a result when Castro sets forth a mistaken proposition nobody dares oppose him if they want to hold on to their job.[22] At the same time, when things went wrong, as they often did, rarely did Castro take responsibility and blame himself for the failures. For example, when it was revealed in the fall of 2004 that the use of high-sulfur Cuban oil had inflicted serious damage on thermoelectric plants, Castro blamed Marcos Portal, the minister of basic industry. In fact, Castro had promised Portal that the money saved from importing less oil would be invested in modernizing the equipment in the electrical plants. Instead, the Maximum Leader invested those savings in his pet projects related to the "Battle of Ideas."[23] All in all, Castro often created perfectly avoidable chaos and waste of resources.

Economic Underdevelopment Soviet-Style

In the last analysis, Cuba is an economically less developed country that lacks capital to invest in economic development. That creates many problems, which in turn interact with many of the negative features of Soviet-style economies to considerably deepen the crisis. Shortage of capital, and particularly hard currency for imports, in combination with the Soviet-style features of the Cuban economy, explains the poor quality and lack of variety of consumer goods on the island. However, shortage of capital is a relative concept: it has not stopped the government from maintaining a huge and economically unproductive internal security apparatus. This personnel and equipment are used, for example, to prevent the Cuban people from traveling outside the country as they see fit. The real external and internal threats to the regime that have existed for more than fifty years never justified such a massive, politically oppressive, and economically wasteful control machine since particular individuals under suspicion could always have been detained as they attempted to enter and leave the country. Something similar may be said about the expensive political and propaganda apparatus that the regime maintains on and off the island. Even after the retrenchment of Cuba's foreign policy that took place in the aftermath of the collapse of the Soviet bloc, its cost and dimensions are beyond the material means of a small and less economically developed country.

This combination of factors also helps to explain the problems with housing. Although practically free, Cuban dwellings have been in a state of ever increasing congestion and continual deterioration since well before the severe crisis of the early nineties. This goes back to the early years of the revolution, when the number of adequate housing units built from 1959 to 1963 dropped by one-third from 1964 to 1971. While the number of housing units built by the state rose in the seventies, it did not compensate for the loss of the existing housing stock during that period. Housing construction reached a historic high point in the eighties, but the goals for the construction of housing in the three five-year plans of 1981–90 fell short by 45 percent.[24] After this, the number of housing units built for every 1,000 people fell from 6 to 1.4 between 1989 and 2003–4, and increased to 4.6 in 2007. In 2008, 40,000 dwelling units were finished, but these were not able to compensate for those destroyed by the hurricanes that hit the island that year (hurricanes are much more destructive when houses have not been maintained and are in disrepair), so the housing deficit became 25 percent higher in that year than in 1989.[25] Undoubtedly, the lack of capital has been a critical factor contributing to the housing crisis. However, the great difficulties that individual dwellers face in maintaining buildings and making improvements tailored to their needs have considerably worsened the housing situation. This is the case for example with many of the low-income housing projects in East Havana, where bureaucratic administration and the poverty of the residents combine to produce very poor housing conditions.

The serious problems confronting transportation are yet another example of the effects of the lack of capital combined with the irrationalities of the Cuban economy. To be sure, there is lack of capital to acquire sufficient equipment and fuel. But the irregularities inherent to that sector—road conditions, traffic, and the need for careful maintenance and upkeep of vehicles, some of which are likely to have problems of different kinds and at different times from other vehicles—are not easily manageable by bureaucratic planning and administration. The government has begun to install GPS equipment in buses as a way to control some of those irregularities. Nevertheless, the official press has acknowledged that the installation of GPS equipment cannot address phenomena such as inadequate fare collection (including passengers handing over the fares to the drivers instead of depositing them in the collection boxes), lack of cleanliness, and drivers smoking inside the vehicles.[26] The lack of a sense of ownership, interest, and incentives, which is of course not limited to transport workers, has also led to high turnover among mechanics and other skilled workers and has contributed to poor vehicle maintenance.[27] Although serious problems with transport abounded long before the crisis of the nineties, they became considerably worse during the special period that began at that time. Transportation was then seriously curtailed with grave economic and social consequences, as people had great difficulty going to work and became isolated in their neighborhoods, unable to visit their relatives or participate in entertainment and cultural activities. Beginning in 2008 there was an improvement in urban transport, at least in Havana, with the importation of five hundred Chinese buses, which brought the total number of buses to 43 percent of what it had been in 1989.[28]

Soviet-type regimes tried to escape the rigidity of centralized bureaucratic planning by establishing special regimes in prioritized sectors of the economy. This is how, for example, the military-industrial sector was helped by the priority system in the Soviet Union although at the steep price of exacerbating imbalances among the various branches of the economy.[29] There are numerous examples of the use of the economic priority system in Cuba. These include Fidel Castro's disastrous attempt to achieve a ten-million-ton sugar crop in 1970 and the disruptions created by the ad hoc economic interventions of his "Battle of Ideas" at the beginning of the twenty-first century.[30] More successful was the special dispensation that Castro gave to Eusebio Leal, the official historian of Havana, to carry out extensive renovations in a section of Old Havana. Leal became the virtual owner of the tourist-oriented corporation Habaguanex with almost complete freedom of action while ignoring the various bureaucracies and reporting directly to the Maximum Leader. Worth noting, however, is the substantial degree to which the projects carried out by Habaguanex were financed out of its own profits.[31]

The Problem of Having "Strong Thumbs, No Fingers"

Yet Cuba, like the other Soviet-type systems, has been able to do some things better than others. It is worth noting how Cuba's achievements and failures resemble those of the Soviet Union, China, and Vietnam before these countries took the capitalist road, suggesting that systemic similarities are more significant than national idiosyncrasies and variations on the general Soviet-type model. Central to Cuba's achievements and failures is a feature of Soviet-type economies that the political scientist Charles E. Lindblom referred to as "Strong Thumbs, No Fingers."[32] Having "strong thumbs" allows the government to mobilize large numbers of people to carry out homogeneous, routinized, and repetitive tasks that require little if any variation, initiative, or improvisation to adapt to specific conditions and unexpected circumstances at the local level. Thus, for example, it is possible to organize a massive vaccination campaign and take other preventive medical actions that are fairly standardized. Following the same principles, you can organize an effective civil defense system that goes house to house evacuating people to centrally located shelters in advance of a hurricane (in contrast with the criminal neglect that accompanied Hurricane Katrina and its devastating impact on New Orleans in 2005). Or you can implement a national education curriculum that is comprehensively carried out in a uniform fashion throughout the country. Cuba also implemented an effective universal pension and retirement system with uniform rules and regulations and got rid of the patchwork of inadequate pension and retirement systems with much less than universal coverage that existed previous to the revolution. Thus, revolutionary Cuba did well in making major improvements in its health, social security,[33] and education systems. These are precisely the areas where other Soviet-type revolutions also did relatively well, although it should again be noted that in these matters Cuba generally started from a higher prerevolutionary base than such countries as Russia, China, and Vietnam.

The Case of Cuban Agriculture

The Cuban economy's bureaucratic centralized administration, lack of capital, and lack of nimble "fingers" prevent it from addressing issues of variety, size, design, and taste in consumer goods, and from acquiring the precision required for *timely* coordination of complicated production and distribution processes in all modern economic sectors. These major systemic flaws are most strikingly evident in agriculture, which given the vagaries of climate and local conditions, is far more "irregular" and requires more local initiative, intensive care, and individual motivation than the relatively homogeneous conditions prevailing in industrial production. That is why agriculture has been the most notable Achilles' heel of Soviet-type economies. This is also true in the case of Cuba, where the worst economic performance in recent years has been in agriculture. From 1989 to 2007 agricultural production fell from 10 to 4 percent of the GDP, which means that the country has had to import 84 percent of its basic foods, and even then it is incapable of satisfying existing needs.[34] This is the main reason why the food items provided by the ration card (and paid for in national currency) have in recent years covered less than two weeks of people's monthly needs and have been curtailed even further.

It is worth noting that consistent with the historical record of Soviet-type economies, the Cuban agricultural sector composed of private farms and relatively autonomous cooperatives—organized as the cooperatives of Producción Agropecuaria (CPA) and of Créditos y Servicios (CSS)—is more productive than the state sector.[35] In particular, although private farmers and the CSSes closely aligned with them accounted, in 2010, for 24 percent of the productive land, they produced 57 percent of agricultural goods in the country.[36] The state agricultural sector is plagued by a number of systemic structural problems. One of the most important problems is the low productivity resulting from a number of features of state agriculture, particularly bureaucratic overstaffing. According to Cuban government sources, the state agricultural sector suffers from an excess of nonproductive personnel accounting for no fewer than 89,000 workers, or 26 percent of the people working in that sector.[37] The overstaffing occurs at all levels of agricultural enterprises. For example, the drastic restructuring that took place under the government's Perfeccionamiento Empresarial (enterprise improvement)[38] policy in one agricultural enterprise near Guantánamo in eastern Cuba actually reduced the administrative personnel from 66 to 11 people while the number of security guards was reduced from 200 to only 16.[39] These reforms carried out from the top may temporarily increase productivity through the drastic reduction of personnel and the considerable squeezing and sweating of the few who are left at work. However, these types of reforms do little if anything to change what is in reality the principal factor underlying low productivity: the poor motivation of the state agricultural workers. An article in the official press analyzing the problems of the enterprises working under the system of Perfeccionamiento Empresarial pointed out that even in those supposedly "reformed" work centers "the workers see as normal going to work and failing to obtain the necessary productive results."[40] These workers neither control the productive process nor are offered adequate material rewards for their work, and even if they receive a wage increase according to the new policy of payment according to performance, there is not much to buy in the peso-denominated stores.

In the municipality of Guisa in eastern Cuba the production of coffee went down considerably in 2009 (Cuba spends almost $50 million a year buying coffee abroad) because the coffee plants were allowed to become too old. As the official daily *Granma* acknowledged, this happened in part because of lack of technical knowledge and in part because of a lack of care among cultivators.[41] Government administrators often lack the highly specific local knowledge required to achieve desired goals and in the process conserve resources. One such administrator told peasants to cut costs by using shorter wooden sticks to build the fences surrounding a farm. The peasants looked at each other and smiled without saying a word. They knew that the sticks had to be longer because otherwise cows would lean over the low fence and eat the buds, plus short sticks are more likely to rot.[42]

By the time agricultural goods reach their final destination, they are often unfit for human consumption because they have been damaged or spoiled in the long bureaucratic and tortuous road that they usually travel from farm to consumer—according to one reporter, that road includes eleven transfer points.[43] The transport of agricultural goods is further complicated by necessary unevenness of deliveries. From Sunday to Wednesday, there is relatively little supply of those products to the markets, but from Thursday to Saturday deliveries increase sharply and strain transport as well as the storage capacity of the warehouses.[44] The poor organization of transport in turn creates problems with packaging. Since the state transport organization is not accountable to the local agricultural enterprises, empty packages are often not returned to the point of origin, resulting in a considerable worsening of the shortage of containers.[45] It remains to be seen whether the new measures adopted in a place like Artemisa in western Cuba requiring a return of the empty boxes after the crops are delivered will actually take place and be sufficiently generalized to have the desired effect.[46] In 2009, an agricultural enterprise in eastern Cuba lost more than 6,000 pounds of mangoes because of the lack of packaging and difficulties with fuel and transport.[47] All these problems came to a head when a big scandal broke out in September of that year, as the official press revealed that tons of agricultural produce were rotting near Havana because of a lack of packaging, transportation, and coordination among the various official entities involved in the agricultural sector.[48]

In addition to the problems with transporting agricultural products from the farms to the consumers, there are transportation problems within the agricultural enterprises themselves. In the rice-rich region of Vertientes in eastern Cuba, a large state agricultural enterprise required a minimum of a hundred carts to handle the one million pounds of rice cultivated on a daily basis but had only forty at its disposal. Moreover, the administrators had failed to organize a gradual step-by-step transport of the rice to the mills to avoid the bottlenecks created when the crop reached its peak. However, in fairness to the administrators, this was in part due to problems in obtaining fuel. As a result, considerable amounts of cultivated rice were likely to remain unprocessed.[49] For all these reasons, official agricultural production figures are dubious indicators of food consumption, even if the figures have not been intentionally falsified.

Undoubtedly, the undercapitalization of Cuban agriculture plays an important role in the chronic problems of food production on the island that I have just described. But it is equally clear that whatever problems are caused by undercapitalization are greatly magnified by the rigid bureaucratic controls and centralization prevailing in the country. For example, the inflexible rule that forbids private farmers from delivering food directly to the urban markets and consumers often results in a waste of scarce transportation and energy resources. The numerous trucks that transport passengers to the capital are forbidden to transport agricultural products even if there is space available. Aside from the economic irrationality and inefficiency that these rigid rules create, they also become, as the official Communist Party organ *Granma* put it, "sources of lawbreaking and bribes."[50] Only trucks connected to the state enterprise charged with food procurement (Acopio) are allowed to bring agricultural produce to the cities. Farmers must often wait a long time for the Acopio trucks to arrive, at the risk of spoiling the harvest. Then, as I indicated earlier, these vehicles in turn do not move directly from farm to market but go through a complicated series of intermediate stages. The food situation in the capital was made much worse when in a further attempt at bureaucratic government control, most of the 1,300 places where food was sold to consumers in the Havana area were closed in 2008. A private farmer was quoted in the official press as saying that instead of the 600 sales points that remained in the capital, 2,000 were actually needed.[51]

Thus, Cuban agriculture lacks the "nimble fingers" required to successfully complete the cultivation and prompt delivery of farm products to the mostly urban consumers. In sum, as René Miyares, a farm co-op administrator, told *Juventud Rebelde*, to ensure the availability of fruits such as mango, guava, and papaya it is necessary to gather them with great care to avoid damage and to transport them fresh to their destinations on a daily basis. These are tasks that, according to Miyares, Acopio is not equipped to carry out.[52]

The Decline of Sugar

The production of sugar—the mainstay of the Cuban economy for two centuries—has declined to such a dramatic extent that the government has had to import sugar from Brazil and Colombia to fulfill its contractual obligations with China, which is the principal foreign consumer of Cuban sugar.[53] In 2006 and 2007 Cuba had to import sugar even to satisfy domestic demand.[54] Production has fallen from its historic averages ranging from 4.5 to 7.2 million tons in the 1950s[55] and 7 to 8 million tons in the second half of the 1980s[56] to 1 and 1.5 million tons in recent years. According to the official daily *Granma*, the 2009–10 crop was the worst since 1905 due to drought and poor organization. The Sugar Ministry found that eighteen of forty-four sugar mills suffered from lack of discipline in matters of technology and direction as well as deficiencies in work organization. By the end of the sugar season in late May, factors such as these were blamed for the loss of no less than 41.3 percent of the total number of days programmed for the grinding of sugar.[57]

In reality, the problems experienced in these last several sugar seasons are only the tip of the iceberg of a process of decay. For many years, the government paid inadequate attention to the need for the technical upkeep and improvements that would have made sugar production more efficient. Moreover, while foreign importers pay dollars for the sugar they import, the Cuban government pays state sugar enterprises in pesos at the absurd rate of one peso per dollar, a small fraction of the prevailing market rate. However, these enterprises have to buy some imported supplies in dollars, thus contributing to the decapitalization of the industry, a situation which was further worsened when between 1997 and 2002 it reduced peso investments in sugar by 54 percent while its peso investments in all sectors grew by 8 percent.[58]

The land reserved for the sugar plantations, like the rest of the island's agricultural areas, was poorly treated during several decades, including those preceding the crisis that began in the nineties, and was affected by erosion, overexploitation, salinity, high acidity, poor drainage, and compaction of the earth. As a result, according to information provided by experts in the Cuban Ministry of Agriculture in November 2009, 70 percent of the arable land in the country has poor fertility.[59] The price of sugar, which has remained low for most of the time that has elapsed since the seventies, was also a major contributor to the lack of economic viability of Cuban sugar. Faced with such a grim situation, the government, long before the crisis of the nineties, and perhaps because it was complacently relying on Soviet economic subsidies, made insufficient attempts at diversification.[60] This could have included the production of renewable energy based on bagasse and straw, alcohol, paper, cardboard, and animal feed, not to mention ethanol, which was the road followed by other sugar giants such as Brazil.[61] Instead, in 2002, the government was forced to dramatically downsize the industry, shutting down and dismantling 71 of 156 sugar mills, all of them built long before the revolution. More than half of the 400,000 sugar workers were moved to other occupations.[62] This meant that when the price of sugar later went up there was insufficient production to capitalize on the more favorable world market conditions, leading to a loss of 60 to 65 million dollars in 2010.[63] Current government plans indicate that the Sugar Ministry will be closed and replaced by a state-run corporation that will attempt to revitalize the industry by allowing foreign investment along lines similar to current arrangements in the nickel (Cubaniquel) and oil and gas (Cubapetroleo) industries.[64]

The Land Usufruct Program

The considerable amounts of idled sugar land have remained fallow instead of being converted to alternative productive uses. Thus, the total amount of cultivated land fell by 33 percent from 1998 to 2007. In 2008, Cuban official government sources indicated that 50 percent of agricultural land in Cuba was unutilized or underexploited.[65] More recently, the same government sources also expressed preoccupation with the fact that only 6 percent of the people working the land were young. Beyond the fact that only 24 percent of the population is rural, many young rural people have no motivation or incentive to work on the land and are studying trades or professions unrelated to agriculture.[66]

In response to the ongoing serious crisis in agriculture, legislation was approved in summer 2008 to provide small state-owned parcels of land in usufruct to private farmers for renewable periods of ten years. These parcels are typically 33.2 acres in size (equivalent to the old Spanish measurement of a *caballería*) although in certain instances they can be as large as 99 acres. The new private farmers are compelled to sell most of their production—as high as 70 percent in many instances—to the state (Acopio) at prices determined by the government, while they are allowed to sell the remainder on their own. However, the process of getting the distributed land to produce has been plagued with problems and bureaucratic delays. It may take as long as 128 days to process a land request, even though the land distribution program was established as a way to provide an immediate response to the critical and pressing food scarcities affecting the country.[67] By April 2011 the government had distributed 63 percent of idle land in the country. Of the land that was distributed, only 77 percent was actually being utilized. More than 70 percent of the recipients had no previous agricultural experience.[68] A long report published in 2009 in the official daily *Juventud Rebelde* revealed that up to that point 60 percent of the distributed land was full of weeds (*marabú*) and there were serious problems with the clearing process, usually carried out via the environmentally harmful practice of burning. There were also problems with fencing the land and especially with the lack of tools, machinery, protective equipment such as gloves, and an overall lack of technical advice and help. The report indicated that only 16.7 percent of those who received the land had actually been farmers who were extending their holdings. More than 80 percent of the beneficiaries had never had any land, and most of them probably lacked any previous agricultural experience.[69] Other reports have confirmed the general findings of the article in *Juventud Rebelde* and indicated that the new farmers have also had problems obtaining seeds and fertilizer as well with adverse climate conditions and lack of water.[70] The government has acknowledged that it had not paid private farmers on time and that some local officials lied to cover up the problem.[71] Delaying payments to private farmers adds insult to injury, considering that the state often pays less for the same product to the private and cooperative sector than to the state farms. For example, private and cooperative farmers get 130 pesos less for every one hundred pounds of rice than the state farms delivering the same product.[72] Moreover, when it comes to purchasing tools and supplies even the state enterprises under Perfeccionamiento Empresarial (enterprise improvement) often have to use, like the regular sugar state enterprises, dollar-equivalent hard currency (CUCs) while the government pays them for the produce in national currency (pesos).[73]

Nevertheless, there are indications that at least some people who benefited from the land distribution carried out by the government are responding with increased effort and production. A cooperative in Punta Brava near Havana reported a doubling of its crops within just a year. Private peasants seem to be saving in the use of equipment and inputs, ingeniously finding substitutes for hard-to-obtain fertilizers and cultivating every available inch of land to maximize agricultural output.[74] Still, the government reforms that might have conceivably provided some nimbler fingers for Cuban agriculture may prove to be inadequate for a number of reasons, including government ineptitude and the substantial bureaucratic state controls that remain in force. At the end of the first three quarters of 2010 overall (nonsugar) agricultural production had been reduced by 5.1 percent when compared with the analogous period in 2009, while cattle production had grown minimally with a 0.3 percent increase.[75] The terrible 2008 hurricane season was not likely to have been a major factor in the agricultural decline that took place between 2009 and 2010. However, it is difficult to estimate the extent to which the international Great Recession that began in 2008 and had a substantial impact on the Cuban economy may have affected the availability of agricultural inputs and resources. In any case, Raúl Castro announced in late 2010 that the government would consider expanding the land usufruct program with the distribution of additional acreage to successful farmers.[76]

The severe scarcities provoked by the major economic crisis of the nineties, and the sudden lack of access to gas-guzzling tractors, chemical fertilizers, and other expensive inputs, led the government to experiment with low-input organic agriculture in urban areas—with savings in energy and distribution costs. However, the government has provoked resistance and controversy with its introduction of transgenic crops into Cuban agriculture, as in the case of the variety of corn named FR-Bt1.[77] The regime has also recently began to develop pilot programs in suburban agriculture.[78] While urban agriculture has made significant contributions in, for example, the production of vegetables,[79] its overall contribution toward resolving the problems of Cuban agriculture and adequately feeding the population has been small. This reality runs contrary to the grandiose claims for urban agriculture made by apologists for the Cuban government abroad.[80] Not surprisingly, these apologists ignore the downside of certain forms of urban agriculture. Most important of all are the health dangers posed by the dreaded dengue fever, the serious illness transmitted by the *Aedes aegypti* mosquito, the campaign against which has been a long-standing concern of the Cuban people and authorities. The official daily *Granma* while describing the health situation in the José Martí district in Santiago de Cuba expressed concern about the serious sanitary violations it found there. These violations included the presence of pigs, poultry, house-grown crops, and makeshift water containers without the required precautions in buildings that constitute one of the principal residential communities of the country.[81] Beyond the critical health issues, it is also important to underline how forms of urban agriculture, often in combination with other forces affecting Cuban society, have had a very negative effect on the quality of urban life. The prominent Cuban architect Mario Coyula Cowley has written about the banana trees, hens, pigs, oil tanks used as water containers, wire fences, and carports covered with sheet metal—reflecting heat and returning to the street rainwater previously absorbed by green areas—that are now seen throughout urban Cuba. According to Coyula, this constitutes a process of primitivization that has created a "new rusted and rotting urban landscape." He adds that streetscapes have been losing transparency and fullness, and that the original facades, which at one time were maintained even on the most modest dwellings, are now hidden by junk architecture that now overwhelms street views.[82]

Nevertheless, in spite of the serious problems with Cuban agriculture, those with access to hard currency have been eating better, at least until a new economic crisis was unleashed by the terrible 2008 hurricane season and the severe world recession in early 2009. In part this has become possible because agricultural imports from the United States—allowed under the "humanitarian" exceptions to the blockade granted in 2001—greatly increased for several years. From the beginning of the "humanitarian" exports to Cuba in November 2001 until March 2007, 1.5 billion dollars' worth of goods had been sent to Cuba.[83] This made the United States Cuba's fifth-largest trading partner and principal supplier of food. Because of the serious impact that three terrible hurricanes had on Cuban agriculture in 2008, these exports increased to 710 million dollars in 2008 alone.[84]

US imports have the advantage of the proximity of American suppliers and ports to Cuba. However, the US government prevents Cuba from exporting goods or services to the United States to earn the dollars with which to pay for US imports, nor does it permit Cuba to acquire the agricultural and processed goods on even short-term credit. Cuba must pay cash even before the goods have actually been delivered. Because of these political obstacles imposed by the US government and the impact of the 2008 world recession on Cuba, US food sales to Cuba declined by 35 percent in the first five months of 2010 compared to the similar period in 2009. This steep decline followed a 24 percent drop in sales to the island in 2009 after the above-mentioned record sales in 2008.[85]

The Impact of the US Economic Blockade

For a long time, the Cuban government and its supporters have claimed that most of the Cuban economy's problems are due to the American economic blockade of the island. There is no doubt that economic activity in Cuba would increase substantially if the blockade were eliminated. American tourism would increase significantly—at least eight hundred thousand additional visitors a year, according to estimates—although that would of course require significant new investments in hotels and other tourist facilities. American oil corporations would most likely join the firms from many other countries that are already exploring for oil in the Cuban waters of the Gulf of Mexico. American pharmaceutical companies would quickly become involved in the Cuban biotechnology industry (some have already obtained permission from the US government to do so on a very limited basis). New American investments and the opening of the US market might stimulate certain segments of Cuban agriculture, which is presently in such dire straits, and even encourage the creation of maquiladora-type manufacturing on the island. Cuba could also obtain credits from American banks for its imports from the United States. But obtaining any long-term loans would probably require that Cuba settle its many debts, perhaps even including those with the Club of Paris, the payment of which Cuba suspended in 1986, several years before the collapse of the Soviet Union and the beginning of the "Special Period" on the island. Finally, shipping costs would be significantly reduced since foreign vessels could load and unload merchandise at Cuban and US ports during a single trip, something they cannot presently do under the US blockade.

However, in order to draw a historical balance sheet of the economic effects of the blockade,[86] it is necessary to consider a number of other factors. As much as it has tried, US imperialism was largely unsuccessful in drawing other capitalist powers into its economic blockade of Cuba. The United States was not able to prevent Cuba from trading with Latin America or with industrialized capitalist countries in Western Europe, Asia (Japan), and particularly Canada and Spain. The principal obstacle to Cuba's economic relations with the non-

US industrial capitalist world was Cuba's lack of goods to sell and hard currency to pay for imports, not Washington's political pressure on its allies. Of course, the absence of economic relations with the United States greatly reduced Cuba's access to dollars with which it could have increased its trade relations with the rest of the capitalist world. It is revealing that the rise of the world price of sugar to record levels in the first half of the 1970s (it increased fifteenfold from 1968 to 1974) led to a major growth of economic interaction between Cuba and the capitalist world. The non-Communist world's share of Cuban exports rose to an all-time high of 47.3 percent in 1972 and remained high at 43.3 percent in 1974. At the same time, the non-Communist world's share of Cuban imports reached 39.5 percent in 1974 and peaked at 51.4 percent in 1975.[87] In addition, Cuba received more than 6 billion dollars in credits and loans from many of these industrialized capitalist countries until the Cuban government suspended the service of these debts several years before the collapse of the Soviet bloc. However, in spite of this growth in its economic interaction with the non-US developed capitalist world, Cuba was not able to significantly diversify its economy beyond sugar, one of the traditional goals of the Cuban left well before the Cuban Revolution. Most important of all, because of the American blockade, Cuba received massive Soviet aid from the early sixties to the end of the eighties. Even though there is much debate on the exact value of the Soviet aid, even the most conservative estimates would place it well above Cuba's calculated losses from US economic aggression during that period.[88] Between 1960 and 1990, Cuba received about 65 billion dollars from the Soviet Union under very favorable terms (aside from other credits and aid from the CMEA [Council for Mutual Economic Assistance, also known as COMECON, or Communist economic bloc], Eastern European countries, and China). Two-thirds of that Soviet aid was in nonrepayable donations in the form of price subsidies, and one-third involved credit and loans of which Cuba repaid almost nothing.[89] Of course, this aid did not fully compensate the island for the major disruptions caused to its economy by the need to radically reorient its economic relations with the outside world. This included the retooling of its US-equipped physical plants to the machinery and spare parts imported from the Soviet Union and Eastern Europe. Nevertheless, in spite of this massive aid, Cuba managed only a modest annual rate of growth of slightly over 2 percent in its best years during the seventies and eighties.

The Cuban government, however, has obtained great political benefits from the undoubtedly criminal US blockade, which violates Cuba's right to national self-determination. As numerous observers have noted, the American blockade has been an invaluable source of internal cohesion and support for the regime. This became particularly important after the international events of the late eighties and early nineties placed into question, if not discredited, the viability of the Soviet model in the eyes of the Cuban people. The Cuban leadership had to shift its ideological proclamations in an increasingly nationalist direction and played down somewhat its proclaimed adherence to socialism and Marxism.

Economic Development and Human Welfare

Contrary to the claims of the Cuban government and its supporters abroad, Cuba's material achievements, taken as a whole, have been poor, particularly since the collapse of the Eastern bloc in the early nineties. However, it is difficult to find economic indexes that offer fully reliable measurements of Cuba's advances and setbacks as a Soviet-type, less economically developed society. The Gross Domestic Product (GDP) is a problematic index[90] that continues to be a subject of controversy even in the nontechnical mass media.[91] Nevertheless, the GDP can be a useful although admittedly crude indicator of economic dynamism and progress. In any case, the Cuban government itself regularly publishes GDP figures as a yardstick to measure its own economic performance, although it has made some controversial adjustments to the index.[92] According to GDP figures, Cuba has fared very poorly in comparison with its neighbors. In 1950, Cuba ranked tenth in per capita GDP among forty-seven countries in Latin America and the Caribbean. Close to sixty years later, in 2006, Cuba ranked seventh from last and was ahead of only Haiti, Honduras, Nicaragua, Bolivia, El Salvador, and Paraguay. Of course, Cuba's growth rate has been very uneven, reflecting major crises and changes throughout the revolutionary period. While its overall annual growth rate for the period 1959–2006 was only 0.92 percent, it varied widely. For the years 1959–70 it had a 0.62 percent annual decline, whereas for the years 1971–89 it had an annual increase of 2.04 percent. This latter period included the most productive years during the sugar boom of the seventies and the implementation of the more orthodox Soviet model of enterprise financing, which came to an end in the eighties. In the early nineties, Cuba's economy experienced a dramatic fall after the collapse of the Soviet Union, and it fell by more than one-third by 1993.[93] Since then, until 2008, the island went through a slow but steady recovery, although with setbacks, which probably brought it back to the GDP levels it had reached in 1989.[94] Undoubtedly, joint venture partnerships between the Cuban government and foreign capital have played an important role in this relative recovery. By 2002, joint ventures accounted for nearly 50 percent of exported goods and were especially important in mining, oil, natural gas, telecommunications, rum, and tourism.[95] Martha Lomas, minister for foreign investment and economic collaboration, reported to the National Assembly of People's Power in July 2007 that in 2006 Cuba had 981 million dollars of income due to foreign investments and that the direct sales of the joint ventures accounted for 8 percent of GDP.[96]

If we judge Cuba by the GDP index, the economic performance of the Castro regime has been at best mediocre. The annualized Cuban growth rate of per capita GDP in the prerevolutionary period of 1950–58 was 1.61 percent, almost double the 0.92 percent rate achieved from the 1959 revolutionary victory until 2006.[97] Cuba's low economic performance in comparison with the rest of Latin America and the Caribbean is particularly evident in such indexes as the number of personal computers and access to the Internet on the island. This is partly the result of poverty and the US economic blockade—which has not allowed Cuba access to the fiber-optic underwater network connecting other Caribbean islands—and partly the result of the government's desire to maintain as much control as possible over all politically troublesome technologies. The Ley de Seguridad de Información (Law of Security of Information) forbids open access to the Internet in private homes, although some people in good standing with the government do enjoy the privilege. The Cuban government recently allowed the post office to establish cyber-cafés on its premises, but so far only for email and "intranet" connections, which mostly provide access to Cuban websites. Access can also be obtained at the tourist hotels, but it is very expensive (from 7.50 to 12.50 dollars an hour according to the hotel's category).[98] Moreover, many critical blogs are not accessible within Cuba because the government has put filters in place to restrict access.[99] The government has also banned parabolic antennas and resorted to punishments ranging from heavy fines and confiscation of goods to three years' imprisonment in an only partly successful effort to limit the number of Cubans who smuggle the antennas used to watch Spanish-language telecasts from south Florida.[100] According to the International Telecommunications Union, 34.8 percent of the population of Latin America had access to the Internet in 2010 while only 14.0 percent of Cubans did.[101] However, a Cuban government survey also conducted in 2010 showed that only 2.9 percent of the people interviewed had direct access to the Internet during the previous year.[102] According to the report, 5.9 percent of these people used private connections, 59.9 percent went online at school, 7.4 percent, at work and 15.9 percent used the Internet account of another person. The same survey found that 5.8 percent of those surveyed had used email services. The Cuban government has made it clear that the submarine fiber-optic cable between Cuba and Venezuela that is supposed to be completed in 2011 will improve the quality of the existing transmissions but will not bring about a greater access to information technology.[103]

While the number of telephone mainlines in Cuba has also been low, there has been a significant expansion of telephone installations carried out by ETECSA, which until recently was a joint venture enterprise of the Cuban government with Italian capital. As a result, the number of telephone fixed lines more than doubled between 2000 and 2009 (4.4 to 10.42 per hundred people). However, this was still much less than the 17.8 average for Latin America and the Caribbean region in 2008. Nevertheless, the tripling of mobile phones between 2008 and 2010 has compensated for the relatively poor coverage of the fixed telephone network. Raúl Castro's government legalized the acquisition of mobile phones, although the need for hard currency to purchase them and pay for calls has limited their use. By 2009, the total rate of telephone ownership had risen to 15.5 percent, the lowest in the Latin American and Caribbean region, of which 5.0 percent were mobile.[104] However, the continued increase of mobile phones in use, which in 2010 surpassed the number of fixed lines (1,007,000 mobile as against 1,004,000 fixed lines),[105] suggests that the gap between Cuba and the rest of Latin America and the Caribbean will probably narrow to some degree in the coming years.

Human Development

How have the majority of the Cuban people fared in terms of their material well-being since the victory of the revolution in 1959? Are their lives better than before the revolution as well as in comparison to those of people living in other countries in Latin America and the Caribbean?

It is widely recognized that per capita income is not a satisfactory indicator of material well-being. The *Human Development Report* of the United Nations Development Program (UNDP) has, since 1990, attempted to provide a balanced view of economic performance by combining income, health, and education statistics in its annual Human Development Index (HDI). The HDI presents problems similar to those of the GDP,[106] but mostly of a different sort. Although this index does capture important elements of the quality of life in a country, it entirely ignores others. Most important of all, the index is not designed to capture and measure the hardships in countries where the economic problems of underdevelopment intersect and combine with those of Soviet-type societies. Thus, the HDI does not measure any of the elements that make for very difficult living conditions in Cuba. These include the low quantity and quality of food, housing, clothing and toiletries, the poor state of roads, urban and interurban bus and railway transport, and the inadequate delivery of basic necessities such as electricity and water. Least of all does the HDI measure the difficulties of daily life as measured by the amount of time people have to spend in obtaining such life essentials as food and basic services.[107] Moreover, indexes can be deceptive if they are viewed in isolation without regard to related matters such as maintenance and upkeep. Take, for example, the case of water. Viewed in one way, Cuba does extremely well by international standards, with 95 percent of the population having access to drinking water, with 74 percent obtaining it through indoor piping and the remaining 21 percent through access to multi-family wells and various types of public pipes. Yet serious water shortages are a normal condition of life in Cuba. This happens in part because of seasonal droughts in certain regions, particularly in the eastern part of the island. However, the most important cause of the shortage of water is the very deteriorated infrastructure (broken pipes and numerous leaks) going back to well before the Special Period of the nineties. Much of this equipment was installed before the revolution. Other contributing factors have been the misuse and waste of water in agriculture and the loss of water in homes due to people leaving their taps open because of the lack of a stable and permanent water supply. Moreover, the shortage and expense of acquiring the parts necessary to fix and maintain domestic water installations have significantly aggravated the problem. These various factors lead to a loss of 58 percent of the water pumped by the country's aqueducts and a 70 percent loss in the case of the Havana metropolitan area.[108]

Other illustrative examples of the kinds of hardships suffered under the particular conditions existing in Cuba can be found in the travails of obtaining food. The young Cuban left-wing critic Daisy Valera has written about how she spends Saturdays and Sundays procuring food rather than relaxing after a demanding workweek. She has to stand in line numerous times, even in front of lemon stands, where the exasperated buyers suffering the tropical heat are likely to end up screaming at each other and even fighting. When Valera goes to buy fruit, there are only two choices, and as a result she once consumed only guava juice for three months because she does not like papaya. Besides being tired at the end of her food-shopping journey, Valera is upset because she knows there are people who don't have to spend their weekends looking for food because they have access to hard-currency supermarkets where they can find what they want with less trouble.[109] Valera has also written about the hardships involved in traveling by bus from Havana to visit her relatives in central Cuba (approximately 200 miles) during summer vacation time. Since she had not made a reservation a full month in advance, it took her two hours waiting in line just to place her name on the list and then an additional fifteen hours until she was able to leave. Her trip was not cheap (travel to some provinces costs as much as 200 pesos, which is only slightly less than half of the median monthly wage of 429 pesos in 2009). Many of these problems might be explained by Cuba's poverty (few buses and expensive oil). But what can't be explained by the poverty of the country, especially if we consider the widespread overstaffing in state-run institutions such as bus terminals, is the lack of care and consideration for the customers. As Valera tells it, she found a terminal too small to prevent overcrowding and heat and without a restricted area for smokers. The floor of the terminal was filthy, and no one knew where to find water, unless one bought it from old men selling plastic bottles for five pesos each. The sole food stand that sells in pesos closes early so those who have to wait in the bus station for the rest of the night have to buy far more expensive food available only for hard currency. Valera points out that improvements could be easily made, such as opening larger waiting areas with more seats available and ensuring that adequate food is on offer to the public. But, as Valera concludes, no one can find those who are responsible for poor treatment and inefficiencies, and what is worse, no one has the courage to protest in hopes of change.[110]

Since Cuba has done well in health and education, two of the three elements of the HDI, it is not surprising that it has done much better by this indicator than by GDP figures alone. When the UN's *Human Development Report* was first published in 1990, before the collapse of the Soviet Union, Cuba ranked seventh among the nations of Latin America and the Caribbean, and it continued to rank seventh in the 2007/2008 HDI rankings, behind Barbados, Argentina, Chile, Uruguay, Costa Rica, and the Bahamas. However, these figures have been seriously questioned by the economists Carmelo Mesa-Lago and Jorge F. Pérez-López, who argue that the lack of basic statistics to estimate the economic component of the HDI makes it technically impossible to determine the HDI for Cuba. In fact, the 2001 edition of the *Human Development Report* excluded Cuba and eleven other countries from various tables because of a "lack of reliable data." This continued to be even more of a problem in the 2010 *UNDP Human Development Report*, where Cuba was omitted from the major UNDP HDIs due to lack of reliable information.[111] Mesa-Lago and Pérez-López are particularly puzzled by Cuba's sudden improvement in its ranking for the years 1997–2000. They claim that this was in part a result of deficiencies in the measurement of all the three basic indicators that underlie the index, and more important, a change in methodology used to estimate the economic index.[112] Cuba has also done relatively well in the UN's Human and Income Poverty index, ranking sixth in Latin America and the Caribbean, behind Barbados, Uruguay, Chile, Costa Rica, and Argentina. However, this index is also based on criteria closely related to health, education, and income. The only exception is the addition of an indicator regarding the proportion of the population using improved water sources. This is different from the regular and consistent delivery of water, a big problem that, as I suggested above, frequently reaches crisis proportions in Cuba and is not measured by this indicator.[113]

In the last analysis, there is a connection between the realities that the GDP and HDI attempt to measure. It must be recognized that for at least the two decades after the collapse of the Soviet Union the Cuban government maintained a commitment to the maintenance of the country's welfare state throughout the severe economic crises it confronted. Until recently, Cuba has been spending one-third of its GDP on social programs, the highest proportion in Latin America. But this has confronted Cuba with a serious problem, even in the short and medium term. The lack of economic growth inevitably impacts the state's ability to continue funding its social policies.[114]

Health

One of the most significant achievements of the revolutionary government was in health care. From 1959 to the end of the 1980s, right before the collapse of the Soviet bloc and the USSR, important improvements had been registered in all health indicators. Thus, for example, during that period the number of physicians rose from 9.2 to 33.1 per 10,000 inhabitants, hospital beds increased from 4.2 to 5.4 per 1,000 inhabitants, and the infant mortality rate fell from 33.4 to 11.1 per 1,000 live births.[115] In 1995, life expectancy had reached 74.83 years, an increase of 16 years since the last prerevolutionary census was taken in 1953.[116] These achievements are well known, and the Cuban government has received justified praise on that account. Far less known is the fact that when the revolutionary leaders took power they did not confront as dismal a health situation as those encountered by other successful third world revolutions such as the Chinese and Vietnamese, and were thus able to build on a relatively higher base. As Jorge Ibarra, a Cuban historian residing on the island, has pointed out, in the 1950s Cuba held third place in Latin America in the number of persons per medical doctor, behind Uruguay and Argentina.[117] The island also had the third lowest infant mortality rate in Latin America, behind Argentina and Uruguay,[118] and was among the leading countries in Latin America in terms of life expectancy.[119] Ironically, the origin of Cuba's relatively advantaged position in Latin America was the US military occupation of Cuba from 1898 to 1902. During the three-year period 1899 to 1901 the American occupation authorities carried out extensive sanitation campaigns and reforms that dramatically reduced infectious epidemic diseases and the ensuing high death rates.[120]

The biggest health problem of prerevolutionary Cuba was that the relatively high health averages for Cuba as a whole hid dramatic differences between the urban (57 percent of Cuba's population in 1953) and rural areas (43 percent). The contrast was even greater between the capital city, Havana (21 percent of Cuba's total population), and the rest of the country. Sixty percent of physicians, 62 percent of dentists, and 80 percent of hospital beds were concentrated in Havana. In 1956–57, four out of five rural workers could receive medical attention only if they paid for it, and since most of them could not afford it, this meant that the majority of this important group of poor Cubans had no access to medical care.[121]

Health Care since the Special Period of the Nineties

The Special Period brought about by the collapse of the Soviet bloc in the late eighties and the Soviet Union in the early nineties had a noticeable impact on Cuban health standards and significantly reduced the gains achieved in the previous thirty years. There was actual hunger on the island during the worst years of the crisis in the first half of the nineties. The serious nutritional deficiencies of this period provoked an epidemic outbreak of optical neuropathy, which affected more than fifty thousand people from 1991 until it was partially controlled in 1993.[122] The regime tried hard to maintain a health service network, which although considerably thinned was still comprehensive and national in scope. In this sense, the Cuban government did a much better job than many other Latin American countries faced with a similar set of objective circumstances probably would have. On the positive side, between 1990 and 2002 the number of physicians continued to increase relative to the size of the population. Infant mortality continued to decline with a rate of 4.7 (per thousand live births) in 2008 and 4.8 in 2009, which is, according to UNICEF, a rate superior to that of the United States.[123] But other health indicators fell sharply in 1993–95, and although they later recovered, they did not reach the levels attained in 1989. This held true for the number of hospital beds and the maternal mortality rate, which went up from 29 per 100,000 in 1989 to 49 per 100,000 in 2006.[124] Also, the percentage of the population immunized against contagious diseases in 2002 was between 25 and 90 percent lower than in 1989 for the five main vaccines, and Cuba came to rank eighth in the region in mortality from contagious diseases.[125] In 1999, health care expenditures per capita were still below their 1989 level.[126] This decline in health standards is especially worrisome in light of the decline in nutrition. In 2002, the caloric intake and consumption of protein among Cubans ages fourteen to sixty-four were respectively 57 percent and 68 percent below recommended standards.[127]

Among the causes of the decline in health care during the period after the fall of the Soviet Union were severe scarcities of spare parts for medical equipment, materials for laboratory tests, and anesthetic drugs, along with problems in the delivery of potable water and sewage services and shortages of medicine. Although two-thirds of medicines are manufactured in Cuba, these often involve imported raw materials, which are subject to the instability of markets, credits, and finances. These objective economic obstacles in combination with serious organizational impediments and inefficiencies create what the official daily *Granma* referred to as "controlados en descontrol" (controlled substances out of control).[128] First aid and over-the-counter remedies from aspirin to Imodium have also been difficult to get, and the official Cuban press has echoed complaints about the irregular distribution of sanitary pads for women.[129]

The buildings in which clinics and hospitals are located are often in such poor condition that they themselves constitute a health hazard. A letter published in *Granma*'s Friday section, dedicated to readers' complaints, strongly objected to the "great quantity" of cockroaches running around inside a provincial hospital in Santiago de Cuba.[130] Besides operations having to be delayed because of the lack of anesthetics, patients often have to bring food, bedding, and other essential supplies to the hospitals. The prominent Cuban writer Leonardo Padura has also called attention to the practice of doctors receiving gifts from their patients,[131] an important part of the informal practices in the health system that have developed as ways for people to deal with shortages and organizational inefficiencies.[132]

Since 2003, medical care has been seriously hurt by the government's export of about a third of Cuba's doctors to other countries.[133] By far the largest number of doctors are sent to Venezuela, which in exchange sends oil to Cuba. This oil for doctors exchange had a particularly negative impact on the otherwise highly regarded family doctor program established in 1984, because it has considerably increased Cuba's patient-doctor ratio. Many specialists have also been sent to Venezuela, thereby increasing waiting periods for many types of operations, and sometimes the performance of delicate medical tests such as colonoscopies is delegated to far less trained technicians, with consequent danger to patients. The armed forces and state security services have their own medical facilities, which are not as exposed to the severe problems of the medical care administered to the great majority of the population. The growing medical tourism industry to service foreigners and the medical system for the political elite are of a much higher quality than that available to the vast majority of the population.

A big scandal broke out in January 2010 when at least twenty-six patients died at Havana's Psychiatric Hospital as a result of an unusually cold Cuban winter, with a low of 3.6 degrees Celsius (38.5 F) in the area where the hospital is located. Although the Ministry of Public Health claimed to have ordered an investigation, it provided an immediate explanation for the deaths. According to the ministry the reasons included prolonged cold temperatures and risk factors associated with mental illness, physical deterioration due to old age, respiratory infections in a year when these ailments reached epidemic proportions, and complications from chronic diseases, mostly cardiovascular and cancer.[134] While the ministry's explanation underlined the factors that made those patients highly vulnerable, it did not even hint at the inadequate care that must have played an important role in so many *simultaneous* deaths.[135] Some time later, an inquisitive foreign reporter found out that relatives of the victims were visited by the authorities, who pressured them not to give him any more interviews because journalists had a "counterrevolutionary" interest in slandering Cuba.[136] Eventually, a trial was held a year later at which the prosecution claimed that the theft of clothing and food played an important role in the tragic events at the hospital. Thirteen hospital administrators, including high-ranking ones, were given prison sentences ranging from six to fifteen years; in addition, one hospital cook was sentenced to six years and one administrator was fined. No functionaries from the Ministry of Public Health responsible for the oversight of the hospital were charged or accused of negligence, let alone malfeasance.[137]

Thus, on one hand, the Cuban health system is justifiably proud of its achievements abroad in countries such as Haiti, Bolivia, Nicaragua, Ecuador, and Venezuela and the training of foreign doctors at the Latin American School of Medicine on the island. But on the other hand, it is increasingly failing to attend to what should be its first priority: the proper care of its Cuban patients. This actually undermines the sentiments of solidarity that Cubans may have toward people abroad. Tremendous waste and inefficiency are evident throughout the health system, as is the case for the Cuban economy as a whole. Very expensive equipment stored in ophthalmology warehouses is not utilized. The new burn unit of the well-known Calixto García Hospital located next to the University of Havana's main campus had not been used even for a single day more than two years after it had been inaugurated. The roof had fallen on several occasions, and the very expensive bathtubs for burned people could not be used because of a lack of water pressure. The new state-of-the-art operating room in the same hospital was also unusable, since it had a roof that leaked when it rained as well as dozens of leaks in the water pipes. Tiles continually came off the walls, perhaps because some of the cement was stolen at the time of its construction. Something similar happened during the construction of the Almejeiras Hospital, which ended up providing materials for the repair and expansion of many residential dwellings in central Havana.[138] Thus, the rampant law-breaking in the country has also had a serious effect on the health system.

Education

The Cuban revolutionary government was also successful in raising educational standards although, as in the case of health, it took off from a relatively high base in comparison with the rest of Latin America. According to the Cuban census of 1953—the last count before the 1959 Revolution—76.4 percent of the adult population could read and write, a level that trailed behind only Argentina (86.4 percent), Chile (79.5 percent), and Costa Rica (79.4 percent).[139] But just as in the case of health indicators, the national educational averages hid huge differences between the rural and urban populations. Whereas in 1953 the rate of illiteracy for the Cuban nation as a whole was 23.6 percent and the rate for Havana was only 7.5 percent, 43 percent of the rural population could not read or write. This was hardly surprising in light of a finding of a survey of rural workers, which showed that 44 percent of them had never gone to school, compared to only 26 percent of the urban population.[140] The large differences in health and educational levels and other standard-of-living issues between the urban and rural citizens of prerevolutionary Cuba were an expression of the imperial and uneven economic development[141] that afflicted the country. While the living conditions were dismally poor in the countryside, there was nevertheless a fairly advanced system of transportation and communications throughout the island. In fact, Ernesto "Che" Guevara recognized that Cuba's relative advancement in communications and other technical matters had allowed for the centralized control of some enterprises, thereby facilitating state economic planning.[142]

According to the 1970 Cuban census (the first after the revolutionary victory), the urban-rural illiteracy gap had been cut almost in half (from 12 and 42 percent, respectively, in 1953 to 7 and 22 percent in 1970). This was a result of the 1961 literacy campaign as well as other major efforts by the revolutionary government to raise educational standards.[143] Even more impressive was that elementary school education reached almost 100 percent of the school population by 1970–76, well above the 1953 levels. Again, the greatest difference in educational coverage had been in the rural areas. In 1958–59, while the countryside accounted for 43 percent of the population, it had only 30 percent of the elementary school teachers and student enrollment.[144] With respect to university education, enrollment actually declined from 1958 to 1961 and by 1970 was still below the prerevolutionary level. However, by 1972 that level had been recovered, and then it continued to increase until reaching 10.8 percent of the relevant age group in 1976.[145]

Education, like health, was seriously impacted by the Special Period that began in the nineties. In real terms, the educational budget contracted by 38 percent from 1989 through 1997. This resulted in deterioration and shortages ranging across the board, from lack of pencils and books and overall decay of buildings, equipment, and laboratories to cutbacks in school meals. The decline of enrollment in elementary schools was minimal, but the decline in enrollment in secondary education was significant, as it fell from 90.2 percent in 1989 to 74.5 percent in 1994, and then rose to 79.4 percent in 1998, still close to 11 percentage points below 1989.[146] Nevertheless, at end of the nineties more than 97 percent of children between the ages of six and fourteen were enrolled in school, and retention rates in elementary, secondary, and vocational and technical school were over 95 percent.[147]

However, a new crisis has affected the Cuban educational system in more recent years. Among the causes of the recent educational crisis has been an exodus of teachers from classrooms because of the low peso salaries prevailing in that sector. The teachers were replaced with televised classes and with inadequately trained high school graduates who sometimes knew less than their pupils. Not surprisingly, privately paid tutoring has flourished, and it is sometimes dispensed by the very same public school teachers that teach during the regular sessions. These practices have become so widespread that they were reported with concern by the official newspaper *Juventud Rebelde* on March 30, 2008.[148] Then, Raúl Castro's government decided to invite retired teachers to return to the classrooms, allowing them to continue to earn their full pension incomes in addition to collecting the full regular salaries. Subsequently, teacher salaries were also increased by the approximate equivalent of 7 dollars a month. By the beginning of the school year in September 2009, more than 4,000 retired teachers had accepted the government's offer, but according to Ena Velázquez, the minister of education, this still left a shortage of 8,000 teachers in the country as a whole. In the case of Havana, the teacher deficit accounted for fully one-third of the teaching positions in the capital.[149] A report in the official press claimed that the situation had further improved by summer 2010, with the number of retired teachers returning to the classroom having increased to 10,000. In addition 2,000 teachers who had been working in "political and mass organizations" and 1,741 other teachers who had left the profession had all decided to return to the classroom. Conversely, the same report noted that 7,487 people preparing to become teachers had abandoned their studies.[150] Notwithstanding the loss of so many future teachers, the government has continued to move away from Fidel Castro's favorite methods of addressing the crisis in education such as televised classes and improvised training of high school graduates. Thus, it has brought back to life older and more traditional training schools for teachers in elementary school and day care centers[151] and given new emphasis to the sixteen university-level schools of education.[152]

Fidel Castro's "Battle of Ideas" and the New Expansion of Higher Education

Hardest hit by the economic crisis of the nineties was enrollment in higher education. While it had reached a high point of 23 percent of the university-age population in 1987, it declined to 12 percent in 1998–99,[153] and by 2002–03 it was still 20 percent below the 1989–90 level. Nevertheless, in the early years of the twenty-first century, university enrollment began to grow in certain disciplines such as the humanities and the social sciences, almost tripling the number of students registered in those fields. Many of these were the future social workers that Fidel Castro began to use as his shock troops to attempt to solve numerous problems in the country, including corruption at gas stations. At the end of 2003, it was announced that an additional 107,000 students would be enrolled in higher education, signifying an increase of 56 percent in a single year. To accomplish this, the then existing seventeen universities were to be expanded with the creation of 732 higher education centers in municipalities and a corresponding 83 percent increase of professors, most of them adjunct. This was the "universalization of higher education" that had become part of Castro's "Battle of Ideas."[154] This sudden explosion in higher education raised obvious questions regarding the quality and training of the new professors and programs, and particularly about the employment opportunities the tens of thousands of new students would find upon graduation.[155] Perhaps Castro was trying to make the best of a bad situation that combined substantial youth unemployment with rising corruption and law-breaking in the country[156] by prolonging schooling, even if such a change would create some new problems later.

Closely related to Castro's expansion of higher education was his rediscovery of the "culture of poverty."[157] In what turned out to be the last major series of interviews that Castro granted to a foreign journalist before he became seriously ill in 2006, he stated that "at the beginning [of the revolution] we eliminated some marginal neighborhoods. But already a culture of marginality had been created [so] that even if you make new houses for them, the phenomena that took place in those areas persevere. That is a culture that replicates itself among a generation and then with their children."[158] Castro's adoption of this theory was full of ironies. At the time of its heyday in the sixties and seventies, Oscar Lewis's theory had been subject to withering criticism from leftist and Marxist social scientists for its focus on values at the expense of material factors such as inequality, lack of material resources, and issues of social and economic injustice.[159] Moreover, there was an even greater irony in that Lewis's major research project in Cuba that began in 1969 was designed to demonstrate that the "culture of poverty" did not exist in a socialist system such as Cuba's and was unique to capitalism.[160] In spite of this, as I showed in chapter 1, Lewis and his project had been expelled from the island.

In addition, Castro added a twist to his "culture of poverty" theory that had a special resonance in Soviet-type societies such as Cuba with their highly selective educational institutions, such as the famous Lenin School outside Havana. Castro indicated that his government had found there was an inverse relationship between knowledge, culture, and crime. As an example, he stated that only 2 percent of prison inmates in Cuba were children of professionals and intellectuals. The country's selective and meritocratic education system had created a situation where the children of workers and of Afro-Cubans tended to remain in the lower levels of society. He explained that this had happened

> because the parental level of schooling, even when there has been a revolution, continues to have a tremendous influence on the eventual fate of the children. And you see that the children whose parents come from the humblest sectors, or with less knowledge, don't get the necessary grades to enter the best schools. And that tends to perpetuate itself through the decades. And if you leave things as they are, you can predict the children of those people will never be directors of enterprises, managers, or occupy important positions because you cannot direct anything without a university education. What they can expect, in the first place, is to go to prison.[161]

According to Fidel Castro, the Cuban government began to tackle the problem of educational disadvantages in 2001 by substantially expanding access to higher education through a system of university extensions in a variety of locations such as municipalities, sugar mills, and even prisons. As Castro explained it, this expansion transformed people between seventeen and thirty who had not finished their secondary education into state-supported university students. Some, for a variety of reasons, were neither studying nor working when they were drafted into the program. It also turned into adjunct professors personnel who had been laid off from the administrative staff of enterprises such as the sugar industry.[162]

Raúl Castro's Change of Course in Higher Education

Fidel Castro's experiment with the "universalization" of higher education did not last long, and soon after his younger brother Raúl took over, the government made a substantial change of course in its approach to university admissions and the nature of higher education. The change of course was underlined by official exposés of the very poor preparation of students at all levels. Much has been made in the official Cuban press about atrocious spelling mistakes found among students, including those attending university. In response, elementary schools, following the "orientation" of the Ministry of Education, have established "spelling Fridays" as the time to concentrate on remedying such educational deficiencies.[163] A diagnostic test in grammar administered to 150,655 university students flunked 20,000 (13 percent), of whom 7,900 (5.2 percent) were in their last year of studies.[164]

Most important of all the new measures adopted by Raúl Castro's government was a new emphasis on entrance exams for the various universities in the country. The exams were introduced in the fall of 2009 in the municipal (evening) university campuses and for regular daytime students in the 2010–11 academic year. All those aspiring to enter the university will now have to take and pass exams with a higher minimum grade of 60 in Spanish, mathematics, and Cuban history,[165] although school averages will also be taken into consideration. Moreover, all future class assignments, exams, and degree theses will be subject to a *descuento ortográfico* (spelling penalty), which could even lead to an F grade. This penalty will be more flexible during the initial year but will become more rigorous in the subsequent stages of student careers.[166] The government has left no doubt that a different philosophy of higher education has been put in place, notwithstanding the ritual invocations of Fidel Castro's ideas on the matter. The official press has used phrases such as "opportunity for all, admission only for those who are well prepared"[167] and "people will have to study to enter the university," stating that "equality consists in that everybody can go to the university, but admission will have to be earned."[168] Top educational authorities in Cuba have warned that the state cannot continue to invest in higher education unless the universities adopt efficiency measures. They also argue that these institutions "should strive for quality instead of social promotion."[169]

The authorities have also stressed the need for a new political emphasis in the content of higher education. Minister of Higher Education Miguel Díaz-Canel Bermúdez, a member of the Political Bureau of the Communist Party, described this renewed political effort as "the shaking up of classrooms with systematic and profound ideological political work." The minister reiterated the old notion that the university was only for revolutionaries, although he clarified that this did not mean the government was contemplating a campaign or process of "purging."[170] The new philosophy for higher education also places great emphasis on remedying the lack of fit between university degrees and the country's economic needs. In particular, the university will have to readjust its priorities and pay much more attention to agricultural issues and problems.[171] It is estimated that Cuba has a deficit of three thousand agricultural engineers.[172]

The new emphasis on practical education is also to be extended beyond the university to all educational levels. A subject called "work education" (*educación laboral*) will be taught in all grades of basic secondary education. In addition, visits will be arranged to production and service centers in the community, conversations with "outstanding" workers and "heroes of labor" will be promoted, and students will be linked with productive tasks, mainly in the schools themselves.[173] It is clear that the long-standing practice of sending young city dwellers to "help" in agricultural tasks in the countryside is being eliminated. Raúl Castro announced at the end of 2009 that the provision of room and board to 126,000 preuniversity students was coming to an end and that 80,000 additional students would be transferred from the country to the cities, thereby saving 139 million pesos.[174] The official press has repeatedly lamented the lack of vocational education and called for giving new value to the skilled trades, which are very important to society, and getting away from parents' obsolete ideas about their children becoming university graduates. The education of young people must be linked to production so that they can be more easily trained as the skilled workers and midlevel technicians that the country requires.[175] One major problem with this new approach is the disastrous state of technical education in many Cuban schools presumably dedicated to that purpose. For example, a polytechnic school established in the sixties in what used to be a prestigious private Catholic school has deteriorated considerably. A technical student supposedly training to be a transport technician at that school complained that "here one learns very little, there are no tools, and I have not yet taken apart an engine." In another technical school designed to train carpenters, masons, mechanics, and machinists the equipment was missing, deteriorated, or obsolete. Moreover, the workshops lacked tools and did not have enough specialized teachers.[176]

Employment

One of the greatest problems of the prerevolutionary economy, with great impact on Cuban political consciousness and behavior, was a high degree of chronic unemployment, both in the countryside and the city. The sugar industry, by far the single most important source of employment, operated for an average of only ninety-five days per year in the postwar period,[177] leaving hundreds of thousands of rural workers to fend for themselves for the remainder of the year (*tiempo muerto* or dead season). The 1943 Cuban census, which was conducted during the dead season, registered a national unemployment rate of 21.1 percent, but when the next census was taken ten years later during the sugar harvest, the national unemployment rate was found to be only 8.4 percent. Weekly sample rates taken between 1956 and 1957 to check for seasonal fluctuations showed an unemployment rate of 20.7 percent in the dead season and 9 percent during the harvest for an average unemployment rate of 16.4 percent, with an additional underemployment rate of 13.8 percent. Additional samples taken in 1957 and 1958 showed average unemployment rates of 12.4 and 11.8 percent, respectively, with a corresponding underemployment rate of 7.6 and 7.2 percent for the two years.[178] It has been estimated that for the entire period of the prerevolutionary republic (1902–58) the number of jobs grew only 39 percent as much as the size of the employable population.[179] Approximately 50,000 young people entered the labor force every year in the years immediately preceding the revolution. Thus, while approximately 150,000 job seekers entered the Cuban economy between 1955 and 1958, only 8,000 new jobs were created in industry.[180]

After the overthrow of Batista at the end of 1958, the new revolutionary government made strong efforts to combat unemployment through a very extensive public works program, particularly during the dead season that began in early 1959. However, this was not sufficient to eliminate unemployment, since many capitalists refused to invest in and expand their businesses. This was particularly evident in the very important sector of private construction, which came to a virtual halt in response to the government's legislation substantially reducing urban rents. Tourism, one of the important sources of employment, was also drastically reduced, in great part because of the political hostility toward Cuba sponsored by Washington. Thus, there was still an average unemployment rate of 13.6 percent in 1959 and 11.8 percent in 1960, with a rate of underemployment of 12.1 percent in both years.[181] Castro's nationalization of the whole economy completed in 1968 with the "revolutionary offensive" that nationalized even the tiniest "hole in the wall" businesses, allowed the government, like its Soviet-type counterparts in Asia and Europe, to take measures that made it possible to claim that it had eliminated unemployment. Accordingly, the 1970 Cuban census revealed only 1.3 percent unemployment in the labor force, the lowest in Latin America.[182] After that low point, unemployment increased somewhat, in part because of the campaign for higher productivity, inspired by the orthodox Soviet economic model, that was undertaken in Cuba in the seventies. The rate of unemployment reached 3.9 percent in 1974 and as much as 5.4 percent by 1979. However, it appears that by 1980, with the help of the massive exodus through the port of Mariel, the male unemployment rate temporarily stabilized at 2.5 percent and the female rate at 7.8 percent of the labor force.[183] Then, the entry into the labor force of the baby boomers produced in the early years of the revolution may have helped to raise the visible unemployment rate to 5.5 percent in 1981.[184]

Notwithstanding its growth in the seventies, unemployment was still far below the rate of the prerevolutionary fifties and the early years of the revolution. The revolutionary government had undoubtedly succeeded in virtually eliminating one of the major and chronic problems of the Cuban economy. As the economist Carmelo Mesa-Lago has explained, this was accomplished through four means. First, substantial emigration opened about 200,000 jobs in Cuba in the sixties. Second, those below seventeen and above sixty-two years of age were removed from the labor force through the expansion of education and social security. Third, by the elimination of seasonal unemployment in the countryside. This was accomplished through rural to urban migration and "overstaffing" in state farms, guaranteeing jobs throughout the year. Fourth, employment was expanded in the social services, the armed forces, and the bureaucracy, coupled with "overstaffing" in industry and subsidies to redundant urban workers, all of which prevented open unemployment in the cities.[185]

The measures taken to eliminate unemployment were obviously a mixed bag: some very positive measures, particularly in the areas of education and social security, and an "overstaffing" that would necessarily lead to a substantial reduction in the productivity of the Cuban economy. But even this sort of reduction of productivity is a more complicated issue than what it is made to appear or what mainstream economists would have us believe. Barring any significant improvement in the economy's technology, in machinery, or in the organization or motivation to work, an easing of the capitalist speedup and super-exploitation at work is bound to result in some reduction of productivity. Moreover, a certain degree of loss of productivity is desirable for the sake of equity as employment is spread among a larger number of people in order to share more widely the benefits of a steady income and the other advantages of regular employment.

However, it is clear that the low productivity and inefficiencies of the Cuban economy, as is generally the case in Soviet-type economies, went far beyond what could possibly be justified on the grounds of a more humane workplace or considerations of equity. The built-in inefficiencies of the highly bureaucratic Communist economies systematically misused and wasted human effort and labor, a flaw as serious as the harmful effects of the systematic unemployment of capitalist economies. Fidel Castro himself called attention to the evils of bureaucratic overstaffing through comments he made in a number of speeches in 1964:

> Where there is one bureaucratic employee in excess in an unnecessary position, there is a man living at the expense of the worker . . . In small enterprises where the former capitalist owners maintained few employees, we now see three to four times that number . . . It is necessary that we avoid the inception of a parasite class living at the expense of productive work . . . We have accomplished nothing if we previously worked for the capitalist and now we work for another type of person who is not a capitalist, but who consumes much and produces nothing . . . The standards of living of the people cannot be raised while what one produces must be divided among three.[186]

The existence of a motivated labor force could have substantially compensated for the loss of productivity generated by bureaucratic overstaffing and the strong tendency toward organizational chaos in the Cuban and other Soviet-type economies. Of course, overstaffing and chaos themselves undermine worker motivation. In any case, since the victory of the revolution worker apathy has historically been one of the major weaknesses of the Cuban economy.

Employment since the Special Period of the Nineties
The 35 percent decline in economic output and 32 percent decline in productivity[187] brought about by the collapse of the Soviet bloc and the Soviet Union in the late eighties and early nineties produced a substantial increase in open and

hidden unemployment on the island. The virtual collapse of sugar production to 20–25 percent of its historic levels later added over 100,000 former sugar workers to the ranks of the unemployed, although most of these were soon relocated to other jobs or to training. Yet the official unemployment rate has for the most part remained remarkably low, with rates such as 7.9 percent for the period 1989–95, 4.5 percent for 2001, 3.3 percent for 2002, 2.3 percent for 2003,[188] and the even lower figure of 1.6 percent at the end of 2008.[189] This has led to the almost comical situation in which the government claims a very low official unemployment rate at the same time that the official Cuban press complains about large numbers of unemployed youth. In a *Juventud Rebelde* article published in March 2007, it was reported that 282,515 young people in Cuba, including 3,000 members of the Communist Youth, do not work or study.[190] Later the same year, *Juventud Rebelde* more specifically reported a total of 4,253 unemployed young people in Guantá-namo Province and 29,975 in the province of Santiago de Cuba.[191] Two years later, a more detailed report of employment in that city indicated that 27.4 percent of graduates from various educational programs had still not been provided em-ployment and revealed that the overall rate of unemployment in the region had reached 13.3 percent, and 22.08 percent among women, in 1997.[192] In March 2008, *Granma* found that 20 percent of the economically active population of Havana did not work even when there were thousands of unfilled job vacancies.[193] The large numbers of unemployed youth is due, at least in part, to a resistance to registering for employment with the municipal authorities for fear that the reg-istrant may be sent to work in undesirable jobs in agriculture, construction, and community services. Young people disappear from the official job market and end up idle, or engaged in the ubiquitous illegal economic activities.[194] The low peso pay rate prevailing in most government jobs is also a powerful factor dissuading people, particularly the young, from working.

However, another fundamental problem facing the Cuban economy has been a substantial underutilization of the workforce, or underemployment. The United Nations Economic Commission for Latin America (ECLA) called this "equivalent unemployment" and estimated that it had grown from 7.9 percent in 1989 to 34 percent in 1993, and then descended to 25.1 percent in 1998, after which date the ECLA inexplicably stopped publishing this type of data.[195] Carmelo Mesa-Lago calculates that if we add hidden to open unemployment, over 30 percent of the Cuban labor force could have been considered unemployed at the end of the nineties.[196]

Another problem faced by the Cuban authorities is that people who are sup-posed to be and are counted as working may still not do a full day's work. In May and June of 2008, specialists of the Ministry of Labor and Social Security found in a study of 2,042 enterprises and work centers that 60 percent of the workers were in various ways falling short of fulfilling their normal daily work obligations. The 26,622 violations of labor discipline that were detected included late arrivals at work (46 percent), taking longer than the periods assigned for breaks and meals (19 percent), lack of fulfillment of work hours (13 percent), leaving before the end of the workday (10 percent), carrying out nonauthorized activities while at work (5 percent), and leaving one's work post without authorization (4 percent).[197]

Inequality and Poverty

It is generally recognized that until the early nineties, Cuba had done best in Latin America and the Caribbean in achieving low levels of inequality of wealth and income, thus demonstrating that the island, like many other Soviet-type societies, was much better at distributing than at producing goods. This has been consistent with the visual impression that Cuba makes on many visitors: generalized poverty and scarcity but much less evidence of beggars and other instances of extreme destitution than in other Latin American countries. Cuba achieved the greatest degree of equality in the first several years after the victory of the revolution (1959–64). Inequality grew somewhat during the period of greatest economic growth, from 1971 to 1985. The subsequent 1986–90 period of "rectification of errors" that witnessed a resurgence of Guevaraist economic policies had a rather mixed impact on equality. On one hand, wage and income differences were reduced and rationing was expanded. But on the other hand, the black market expanded in response to the scarcity of consumer goods and excluded the poor, as did the privileged access of the elite to consumer goods through special stores, separate hospitals, recreational villas, and trips abroad.[198] This incidentally raises key issues that have usually been overlooked by Western sympathizers with Cuba and other Soviet-type societies. These people, residing in capitalist countries, are accustomed to money's powerful and exclusive role in obtaining consumer goods and the good things in life. Consequently, they have a great deal of difficulty understanding how *political access*, often to *free* goods, such as free travel abroad representing government-financed institutions, frequently becomes more important than money for obtaining valuable goods in Soviet-type countries. While the official salaries of the political elite are not necessarily much higher than those of most people, they nevertheless live considerably better lives. Thus, the demand that certain goods should be made available to those who have the money to buy them, instead of the government limiting access for political reasons, becomes in these societies a paradoxical yet elementary democratic demand. The right to travel abroad, the absence of which is widely resented in Cuba, is a good case in point, since the politically connected are allowed to travel, often at government expense, with far greater frequency than the rest of the population. In this sense, extra-economic political privilege in Soviet-type countries such as Cuba, which is not registered by the usual measurements of inequality utilized by economists, resembles the role played by extra-economic factors in precapitalist feudal and absolutist systems.

Since the two-tier economy of hard currency and pesos was legally established in 1993, inequality has been unleashed. It has been estimated that some 60 percent of Cubans have access to hard currency, although in varying quantities. Those who have relatives abroad are more likely to get hard currency remittances, as are those Cubans who live in the Havana metropolitan area and have jobs bringing them into contact with tourists. Both of these groups tend to be disproportionately white: black Cubans have been much less likely to emigrate, and there has been substantial racial discrimination in employment in the tourist industry in favor of Cubans regarded as having *buena presencia* (good presence or appearance), which is code for whiteness. Estimates made by several Cuban and foreign economists have shown a significant deterioration in the Gini coefficient that measures the degree of equality (with 0 signifying complete equality and 1 the highest inequality).[199] The economists Claes Brundenius and John Weeks have pointed out that prior to the victory of the revolution in 1959, the Gini coefficient for income was 0.55, which was "far from the highest in Latin America but well above the level for developed countries." From that relatively high point inequality descended significantly over the next twenty-five years and reached a Gini coefficient of 0.22 in the mid-eighties.[200] Then it changed for the worse in the nineties, with one estimate placing it at 0.40 in 1996 and 0.41 in 1999. Using data provided by a Cuban economist from a government research center, the Danish economist Rikke Fabienke estimated that the Gini coefficient had risen as high as 0.55 in December 1995. If correct, this estimate would have brought Cuba to prerevolutionary levels of inequality and would have surpassed the levels of inequality in fourteen other countries of Latin America.[201] Since then, a Cuban economist claimed to have estimated the Gini coefficient at 0.38 in 2002.[202] In any case, Raúl Castro made it clear in 2008 that "socialism means social justice and equality, but equality of rights, of opportunities, not of income. Equality is not egalitarianism." He added that egalitarianism is in the last instance "a form of exploitation: that of the good worker by the worker who is not, or even worse by the lazy worker."[203]

Besides creating significant inequality, the two-tier economy of hard currency and pesos has also generated serious distortions in the labor market. People working in the public sector—whether as street sweepers or medical doctors—are paid in pesos, while those working in the private sector are more frequently paid in hard currency, whether as tutors, maids, or private plumbers or carpenters. As we saw above, there has been a massive exodus of public school teachers to the tourism sector, where even though workers are paid in pesos by the state (including those people working in joint venture enterprises) they receive hard currency tips. The government has attempted to compensate for this disparity by giving hard currency bonuses and in-kind rewards. Many Cubans working for the government, particularly those in high-priority sectors such as oil and the tourism and nickel industries, may get part of their salary paid in hard currency plus a monthly *jaba* or shopping bag full of basic necessities such as food or clothing.[204] However, even with these bonuses and rewards the state often cannot compete with the private sector (legal and illegal) in terms of compensation. Taking all the relevant factors into account, the Cuban economists Omar Everleny Pérez Villanueva and Pavel Vidal Alejandro have estimated that while a gradual recovery in real wages had begun in the mid-1990s, they were still, at the close of 2008, only 24 percent of what they had been in 1989.[205] Moreover, from 1989 to 2007 the real value of the average pension had declined by 61 percent even though pensions accounted for 6.6 percent of the Gross Domestic Product.[206]

It is evident that poverty grew significantly during the "Special Period" that started in the early nineties. In the late nineties, thirty-six municipalities, all located in the eastern part of the country, were found to be in a highly "critical" or "severely depressed" state of development.[207] Urban poverty was estimated at 20 percent in 2002.[208] Interestingly, the Cuban economist Ángela Ferriol conducted a household survey in Havana in 2002 asking people whether they considered themselves poor, nearly poor, or not poor with respect to several indicators. The percentage of the population that defined themselves as poor or nearly poor was 41 to 54 percent. With regard to income, 31 percent considered themselves poor and 23 percent nearly poor; with regard to food, 21 percent poor and 24 percent nearly poor; with regard to housing, 22 percent poor and 19 percent nearly poor; and with regard to overall living conditions, 23 percent poor and 20 percent nearly poor.[209] Most disturbing is the growth of several shantytowns such as El Fanguito in the Havana metropolitan area and the practice of rummaging through garbage—referred to by such terms as *buceo* (diving) or *tanqueo* (tanking)—looking for things to retrieve and sell.[210]

Poverty has a very different meaning when people have the hope and reasonable expectation that life will get better, if not for themselves, at least for their children's generation. From this perspective, improvements in the standard of living and social mobility play a critical role in keeping hope alive. Contrary to widely shared misconceptions, aspirations for social mobility need not include Horatio Alger, rags-to-riches expectations, which are infrequent if not rare even in rich societies, but rather the desire to move into the immediately adjacent upper stratum, sometimes even within the same social class. For example, many workers can hope that education and the acquisition of skills may improve their life and those of their children while they remain in the working class. If the state of the economy makes this an unreachable goal, they may lose hope for what their country has to offer and aspire to emigrate or drop out of the working class and make a living through various "hustles" or even law-breaking activities. A little-noticed factor underlying the high degree of popular support for the Cuban government in the early decades of the revolution was the considerable social mobility that developed from 1959 to 1975. The Cuban social scientist Mayra Espina Prieto explains that this involved a movement from the working class, the peasantry, and other social sectors toward various forms of intellectual work, a clear case of traditional upward mobility. But, according to Espina Prieto, there were also massive movements from groups of private-sector employees, small owners, semi-proletarians, and the unemployed toward the working class connected to the state sector of the economy. While there has been some social mobility in recent years, it has not been of the same magnitude as in the first two revolutionary decades. Espina Prieto notes that the least mobile have been agricultural cooperative members, followed by state-sector technicians and workers.[211]

The Problem of Corruption

Among the worst consequences of the grave economic crisis that began in the nineties has been a qualitative growth of corruption, which in turn has very serious economic as well as moral and political consequences. Massive law-breaking is bound to occur when the ration book covers the food needs for only twelve days of every month while nonrationed goods are mostly available in hard currency and at least 40 percent of the population has access only to Cuban pesos. In other words, law-breaking has become a way of life in Cuba for the sake of survival. The top leadership has had little choice but to tolerate much of this behavior because the alternative would be to launch a massive campaign of police repression and terror without a guarantee of success.

Nevertheless, in an important speech delivered at the University of Havana in November 2005, Fidel Castro warned that corruption could bring about the destruction of the revolution from within, a goal that the internal counterrevolution and the United States had failed to achieve from without. The wave of corruption has been long lasting and has affected all levels of Cuban society. Examples of low-level corruption affecting average citizens are numerous, with some of these publicized by the official press. In October 2006, *Juventud Rebelde* ran an investigative report detailing how customers were systematically cheated in retail establishments such as cafeterias and shoe and watch repair services.[212] For at least three years, *Granma* has been reporting on the important social and economic damages caused by frequent theft of "angular" sections of high-tension electric towers, notwithstanding the risk to life and increased criminal penalties. According to the authorities, pieces of steel taken from the towers have been used for such diverse purposes as building carports and barnyards.[213] There are other examples of low-level but economically damaging corruption publicized by the government press. These include theft and vandalism of public telephones,[214] theft of water for agricultural purposes,[215] theft of screws from the metal rods bus passengers hold onto while the vehicle is in motion,[216] and theft of pipes, air tanks, valves, and other parts from railroad wagons (hoppers) used to spread stones on the railway lines—more than half of these wagons had to be taken out of service because of the thefts of parts.[217]

The official press has paid far less attention to growing corruption at the high levels of government, which is of course much more important than the disrupting but ultimately petty crimes that it likes to dwell on. In 2010, managers at Habanos, a cigar-maker, were questioned concerning claims that 60 million dollars were missing. Pedro Álvarez, the former head of Alimport, the agency in charge of food imports from the United States, was arrested at his home and taken to jail in handcuffs, but he later managed to evade the authorities and leave the country.[218] General Rogelio Acevedo, whose military career began as a teenage guerrilla soldier fighting the Batista dictatorship in the Sierra Maestra, was forced to resign as head of the Instituto de Aeronáutica Civil de Cuba (Civil Aeronautic Institute of Cuba). It seems that the managers of Cubana de Aviación, the state airline company, were using the planes as if they were their private property, leasing them and pocketing the proceeds. Emboldened by their success, Cubana's managers were even planning to buy small planes to "steal" customers from the airline whose interests they were supposed to protect. At the same time, Ofelia Liptak, General Acevedo's wife, was involved in a corruption scandal at Alimentos Rio Zaza, a food enterprise where she was an important executive. The head of this enterprise was Roberto Gabriel Baudrand Valdés, a Chilean who suddenly died as a result of what the authorities claimed were breathing problems caused by his having ingested prescription drugs and alcohol. Baudrand Valdés was in turn a close associate of the Chilean Max Marambio, the head of Salvador Allende's personal security team and a personal friend of Fidel Castro who became a successful businessman with important investments in Cuba. After the scandal broke out, the Cuban authorities tried Marambio in absentia and sentenced him to twenty years in prison.[219] These incidents indicate that corruption has reached a new level, as was also suggested by the fact that at about the same time, the Contraloría General (General Controllers' Office), a new agency created by Raúl Castro, announced that it would immediately audit 750 state enterprises.[220]

According to Esteban Morales Domínguez, a black professor who has written about racial problems on the island and has often appeared on Cuban television as an expert on the United States, the increasing corruption was much more dangerous for the revolution than the so-called internal dissidence. Morales Domínguez indicates that the land distribution program has been plagued with fraud, favoritism, bureaucratic slowness, and illegality, and that a lot of merchandise illegally finds its way from wholesale state enterprises to the street markets. Morales Domínguez adds that such phenomena constitute a true counterrevolutionary force that can do away with the revolution, a force which is located not below but above, at the very level of the government and state apparatus. More ominously, Morales Domínguez insists, there are people in the state and government who are strengthening themselves financially, so when the current regime falls they will have almost everything prepared to transfer state property into private hands, as happened in the Soviet Union.[221] Morales's article must have gravely offended the highest authorities, for after its publication he stopped appearing on the *Mesa Redonda* (Round Table), the most important political program in Cuban television, and some time later was expelled from the CCP.[222]

The Impact of the World Recession

Right after three hurricanes caused serious damage to Cuban agriculture and housing in 2008, the most serious world recession in many decades brought to an end the relative degree of economic recovery that had taken place in Cuba, particularly from 2004 through 2007. Since tourist installations were not seriously affected by the 2008 hurricanes, Cuba was able to establish a new record for tourist visits with an increase of 81,000 tourists, for a total of 2.4 million in 2009. However, even though more tourists came to the island, they were spending less, which resulted in an 11 percent decline in tourist income in comparison with 2008.[223] The situation improved in 2010 with the arrival of more than 2.5 million tourists and the growth of tourist income outpacing the number of tourist arrivals.[224] Most important of all, while there was only a slight decline in the production of nickel in 2009, the world recession caused a 72.3 percent fall in prices from peak to trough, sending them even below production costs, before they began to recover in 2009 and 2010.[225] In fact, Cuba lost 120 million dollars because a failure to meet nickel production targets prevented the country from taking advantage of the higher prices in 2010.[226] Nickel had recently become the principal sector of the Cuban economy, an even more important earner of hard currency than tourism and the export of medical and other services. Cuban ports also registered a considerable decline of foreign trade, with a significant reduction not only of exports but also of food imports from the United States. Commerce with China, Cuba's second largest trade partner after Venezuela, fell by a third.[227] There was also a reduction in the foreign sales of such products as tobacco, more difficulty in obtaining foreign credit (never easy since Cuba has acquired many debts going as far back as its suspension of debt payments to the Club of Paris in 1986), and worrisome predictions of a drop of tourism in the future.[228] Meanwhile, the import bill for oil and food in 2008 went up by 41 percent. This helped to reduce economic growth to 4.3 percent in 2008, the smallest growth for the Cuban economy in seven years. Cuba did even worse in 2009, with an annual growth rate of 1.4 percent. However, as Osvaldo Martínez, an important Cuban government economist, pointed out, the Latin American and Caribbean region as a while had done even worse, registering a decline of 1.8 percent during the same period.[229]

A national survey of enterprises conducted by *Juventud Rebelde* showed that curtailment of energy consumption and the lack of raw materials and other inputs had already had a serious impact on the national economy. Production had been reduced or entirely shut down in a whole range of enterprises, including dairies, suppliers of mineral water and soft drinks to the tourist industry, and factories producing wires, tiles, tires, and sanitary equipment.[230] Meanwhile, the number of joint ventures with foreign investors in Cuba slightly increased, after declining 22 percent from 2002 to 2008, even though those investors have complained about the difficulties they have faced in sending hard currency abroad from the accounts they maintain with government banks in Cuba.[231] The de facto freezing of their bank accounts, even if temporary, bodes ill for the possibility of new investments on the island in the future, which in any case have become more difficult to obtain due to the world economic crisis. A new twist to the Cuban government's involvement with foreign capitalists is the creation of more than a hundred joint venture enterprises *abroad* taking advantage of Cuba's scientific and technical know-how. These include such diverse ventures as medical industries in Asia, hydraulic projects in the Sahara, an ice-cream factory in Angola, and a five-star hotel in China.[232]

One aspect of this new crisis that has particularly worried the Cuban people is the possibility that blackouts, one of the worst features of the Special Period of the nineties that had recently been eliminated, might return.[233] Beginning on June 1, 2009, strict economizing measures were taken throughout Cuba, with particular emphasis on the use of electricity in the workplace. An enterprise that consumes over its top limit may lose electric services; in the case of residences, electricity may be cut off for seventy-two hours for a first-time violation of the new consumption norms. The official press has pointed out that the use of electricity had significantly increased since the beginning of 2009 and had reached "alarming" proportions in the spring of that year. Special emphasis was placed on the massive waste and inefficiencies in the state sector, where three thousand violations were discovered by government inspectors.[234] Inspectors also revealed, according to the official press, that 10 percent of the homes that were visited were stealing electricity.[235] Shops have been ordered to switch off their refrigerators for two hours a day, and bakeries are prohibited from baking in the evening, when power consumption peaks.[236]

Cuba's Economic Reforms—a Tentative Beginning

The decline in agriculture and manufacturing has led Cuba's economy, as indicated above, to become primarily centered on the nickel industry and on services, particularly tourism and the export of medical services abroad. However, the slow and gradual recovery of the middle of the first decade of the twenty-first century has been replaced, as we saw above, by a serious crisis. The 6 percent rate of growth that had been originally forecast by the government for 2010 was reduced to 1.4 percent,[237] although at the end of 2010, the Cuban government claimed a 2.1 percent growth of GDP for that year and projected a growth of 3.1 percent for

2011.[238] The rate of gross fixed capital formation, which in 1989 had reached 25.6 percent of GDP, has since then registered annual percentages below 10 percent in many years (compared with a regional average of 22.4 percent), which is insufficient for capital replacement. A new decline began to take place in 2009 and the first quarter of 2010 with a 15 percent fall in investments. Cuban economists calculate that a 25 percent rate of fixed capital formation is needed to maintain sustained economic growth.[239] In terms of foreign debt, Cuba's total external debt in hard foreign currency had increased considerably by 2008. It amounted to almost 46 billion dollars, the equivalent of 380 percent of annual exports, compared to the regional average of 83 percent.[240] Even more disturbing was the sharply upward trend of the debt, which had increased, according to ECLA's estimates, by a factor of 1.7 between 2004 and 2008.[241] If we look at the balance of trade, Cuba had reached a deficit of 7.9 billion euros in 2008, because exports stagnated while imports rose sharply by 43 percent. According to the Cuban Ministry of Foreign Trade, the deficit worsened in the first quarter of 2009, since 78 percent of foreign trade consisted of imports while only 22 percent was exports.[242] The situation improved in 2010 with a 21 percent rise of exports while imports rose by only 1 percent in the first three quarters.[243] But perhaps the most problematic feature of the Cuban economy is its historically low productivity. While the official rate of labor participation in the economy is 73.6 percent, 18 points above the median for Latin America and the Caribbean, its productivity has been poor and it actually declined by 1.1 percent in 2009.[244] This may have led Raúl Castro to proclaim on July 26, 2009, that economic problems would not be solved by people yelling "Fatherland or death" or "Down with imperialism," and that the Cuban people had to work harder to increase production, particularly on the land.[245]

After he took office initially in 2006 and then more permanently in 2008, Raúl Castro began to make some economic changes in an ad hoc and sometimes contradictory manner in response to specific problems and crises. For example, in order to solve the problem of teachers' mass desertion of the classroom, the government allowed Cubans to have multiple jobs, which of course contradicted its effort to get as many people gainfully employed as possible. The government also tried hard to resolve contradictions within the existing socioeconomic and political system. Thus, while the official press continued to complain about tens of thousands of idle young people, the government postponed the age of retirement, thereby effectively increasing the people in the labor force; the aging of the population also pointed to a looming crisis in the financing of social security.

Nevertheless, it was possible to detect the first tentative steps in the direction of a Cuban version of the Sino-Vietnamese model (that is, political dictatorship combined with a state-directed capitalism), even if the pace of change was slow and uncertain. As I noted above, substantial changes have been made in the educational system as the regime moves away from some of Fidel Castro's plans and ideas toward a more conventional model of education. The land-distribution program, with all its inadequacies, such as the oppressive and incompetent role played by the state requisition agency, is part of this trend. The Cuban government has also begun to allow foreign investors to lease government land for up to ninety-nine years to make possible the construction of golf courses surrounded by luxury housing, beachfront timeshares, and vacation homes for affluent tourists.[246] There has been more official recognition of the importance of individual initiative, motivation, and material incentives as spur to increased production and efficiency in agriculture. Increasingly, articles in the official press point a critical finger at the lack of stimulus to producers and the absence of care that typically goes along with it.[247] These media organs have also suggested that cash wages are more effective as work stimulus than store vouchers, since the store may not have what the worker needs to buy but what somebody decided to make available for purchase.[248] Thus, it is not surprising that the government eliminated the previously existing limits to state salaries at about the same time that a system of payment according to performance was put into place.[249]

The government media have also criticized the misuse of agricultural state assets, such as people using tractors as a means of transportation instead of agriculture. They have praised the initiative and inventiveness of individual farmers who look everywhere they can for abandoned bicycle parts, tubing, and springs that can be put together and converted into plowshares.[250] Moreover, the willingness of the official press to publicize *some* of the complaints voiced at a congress of small farmers that took place in May of 2010 is significant and is further evidence of the changes in official ideology that are slowly but surely taking place. These published complaints included concerns about matters such as the superfluous nature of the Ministry of Internal Commerce, the inadequacy of state procurement and transportation policies, the lack of water, and difficulty in obtaining agricultural inputs.[251] *Granma* conducted a long-lasting "debate" on the desirability of privatizing restaurants and cafeterias as a way of preparing the population for the privatization of a good part of retail trade while allowing hardliners to let off steam in the Friday editions of this Communist Party organ.

In 2010 the government took a major step suggesting a more definite and qualitative turn toward a state-directed capitalism. For some time, Raúl Castro had been talking about how an estimated one million people holding one-fifth of all jobs on the island would need to be relocated from their current employment. Taking what could perhaps be considered a "compromise position," the government finally announced in September 2010 that half a million workers, or almost 10 percent of the 5.1 million labor force, would be laid off during the following year. From then on, the state was only going to hire people to work in those areas of the economy where historically there had been labor shortages, such as agriculture, construction, teaching, the police forces, and industry. To help absorb the displaced workers the government was to grant 250,000 licenses for self-employment, and 200,000 additional state jobs were to be created by converting state businesses into employee-run cooperatives.[252] If we leave aside the urban and rural co-ops, some 450,000 private farmers plus 450,000 self-employed people in the cities would be officially allowed to hire additional people. This would involve at least 900,000 people—or 17.6 percent of the labor force.

It is possible that some of the newly self-employed people will get help from outside Cuban capital, particularly from southern Florida, a practice that has already been taking place to some extent. Until recently, the US government rules governing the provision of "humanitarian assistance" to relatives on the island that were liberalized shortly after Obama came into office did not specify whether the people sending remittances could take stakes in private businesses on the island. In any case, the United States had no way of tracking whether the money is being used to buy soap or the raw materials to make soap to sell.[253] New measures adopted by the Obama administration in January 2011 permit Americans to send money (up to $500 per quarter) to Cuban citizens who are not family members—except for senior members of the Castro government and the CCP—to support "private economic activity."[254] There has always been a section of the American political establishment that thinks it is important to provide money to private enterprises in Cuba to the extent that is possible. With the new opportunities for legal investments, there might be renewed pressure to modify the US economic blockade to permit larger remittances. While the Cuban government would probably favor such a development, the regime is likely to demand that the infusion of foreign money be channeled through state banks. This is already the case for the small amount of credits (490,000 euros or 680,000 dollars) granted by the Spanish Agency for International Cooperation for Development (Agencia Española de Cooperación Internacional para el Desarrollo) to finance some Cuban agricultural investments beginning in 2011.[255]

The consequences of the measures adopted by the Cuban government in 2010 are uncertain because there has not been a situation like this since the sixties. This is uncharted territory—especially if self-employed Cubans succeed in getting substantial investment money from Cuban friends and relatives in south Florida. While the success of the new entrepreneurs is doubtful in the short and medium run in light of the existing economic and political circumstances, a minority may succeed and come to constitute a legal petty bourgeoisie on the island. They will thus become very junior partners to the central political bureaucracy, which will share economic power with this new group. But there is also the question of political power, and the central bureaucracy is not going to share power with newly minted capitalists unless they totally assimilate into the ruling group.

The massive layoffs announced in 2010 were to be accompanied by a withdrawal of subsidies to the population, including far less generous unemployment compensation for those who have lost their state jobs. Moreover, the items covered by the ration card continue to be reduced. From 2009 to 2010 potatoes and peas had been taken off the rations list, and their prices soared. The ration for beans was cut by one-third, and for salt by nearly half. Rationed coffee went from 10 cents per four-ounce packet to five pesos of an equal weight of supposedly more concentrated beans. Gasoline prices went up by between 10 and 18 percent. The authorities also announced that the price of electricity would go up from 15 to 284 percent.[256] As of January 1, 2011, bathing soap, toothpaste, and detergents were removed from the rations list and had to be acquired at unsubsidized prices.[257] Overall, by the end of the third quarter of 2010 prices of agricultural and cattle products had increased 4.5 percent compared to the previous year.[258] We may thus be witnessing the beginning of the end of the implicit "pact," which had already considerably deteriorated since the early nineties, by which the government guaranteed to the population a minimal but secure standard of living in exchange for a tacit acceptance if not active support for the regime. This is bound to produce a great deal of popular discontent, although it is hard to predict how that discontent will express itself.

Chapter Three

Cuba's Foreign Policy—between Revolution and Reasons of State

Revolutions and Their Foreign Policies

The great revolutions of the modern era have usually had a substantial impact on other countries. Authentic social upheavals have reverberated in other lands as the idea spread that there are alternatives to oppressive systems and that "another world is possible." This is why successful revolutions often stimulated emulation, even imitation. Certain types of revolutionary governments have developed policies and organizational means through which to spread their influence and in many cases have helped to organize movements and uprisings in foreign countries similar to the ones that brought them to power. Successful revolutions have also had to deliberately structure their relations with other governments and have been compelled to design foreign policies to relate in some fashion to the frequently hostile world around them. Because they created new revolutionary paradigms with a vast worldwide influence, I will briefly examine the cases of the French and Russian Revolutions to illuminate some of the relevant issues in this context.

The French Revolution

The French Revolution that began in 1789 greatly influenced people throughout the European continent, Latin America, and even Asia. It had a major influence in the growth of secularism and nationalism, and it became a radical model for the separation of church and state, the abolition of feudal privileges, radical land reform, and the establishment of modern, secular republics throughout the world. The ideology of the French Revolution also contained important elements of universalism and internationalism that became expressed in matters such as the granting of equal citizenship to Jews and the abolition of slavery, which had a direct impact on the French colony of Saint-Domingue (renamed Haiti after independence). But the French Revolution had, above all, an internal perspective: the building of a French nation that was secular and republican. Because the revolution was short lived, its potential role as an organized revolutionary center did not materialize.

Although the French revolutionaries started out with a national internal perspective, they were forced to turn their eyes abroad when the king and important sections of the nobility and the church took residence in various West German cities, as they concluded that only foreign intervention could restore the old regime. The war with the counterrevolutionary foreign powers that started in April 1792 had become, by June 1793, both a civil and foreign war for the survival of a revolution in a country that was now helpless and bankrupt. Sixty out of the eighty departments of France were in revolt against Paris, while the armies of the German princes were invading France from the north and east and the British were attacking from the south and west.[1] The radicalizing logic of a revolutionary war that was going badly led to the overthrow of the moderate Girondins by the radical sansculottes, who were the main social base of what became the Jacobin Republic in the same month of June 1793.[2]

The sansculottes welcomed the mobilization of the whole population for the revolutionary war as the way to defeat foreign intervention and domestic counterrevolution and as the only road to achieve social justice. Indeed, it was the Jacobin government that abolished all remaining feudal rights without indemnity and abolished slavery in the French colonies, thus helping to create the conditions for the emergence of the black republic of Haiti.[3] In his classic *The Black Jacobins*, C. L. R. James movingly narrates the arrival of the multiracial delegation from Saint Domingue to the convention in Paris that granted them full credentials as deputies on February 3, 1794. The next day, Bellay, the Negro delegate from Saint Domingue who had purchased his freedom from slavery, gave a fiery oration pledging blacks to the cause of the revolution and asking the convention to declare slavery abolished. A motion to that effect was duly made and approved by acclamation followed by long and repeated bursts of applause.[4]

Although the revolutionaries succeeded in defeating the foreign and native forces trying to restore the old order, in July 1794, when the end of the war was at hand, Robespierre and his close associates were overthrown and executed by order of the convention. After a rightward-moving interregnum, Napoleon Bonaparte eventually took control and consolidated his power in 1799. As his foreign military campaigns developed, impulses toward imperial conquest, exploitation, and the interests of the French state as defined by the newly minted emperor took increasing precedence over the liberating impulses he had inherited from the French Revolution.[5] Nevertheless, Napoleon imposed a series of liberating and modernizing changes throughout Europe. Thus, for example, slavery was soon eliminated in the continent, and important modernizing reforms were adopted in education, law (Code Napoleon), and such matters as the metric system (to this day successfully resisted by the United States of America). It is important to note that Napoleon's reforms, which had been militarily imposed from above, had been preceded by a great deal of sympathy for the French Revolution in Europe, particularly in the Low Countries, the Rhineland, Switzerland, Ireland, Poland,

and parts of Italy. This included large numbers of the most talented and brilliant poets, philosophers, scientists, educators, engineers, and musicians who supported the revolution. Many of these—such as Kant, Hegel, Wordsworth, Blake, and Coleridge—would become classic figures of the Western intellectual and cultural canon. Beethoven dedicated his *Eroica Symphony* to Napoleon but revoked his dedication when Napoleon declared himself emperor.[6]

The Russian Revolution

Like the French Revolution, the 1917 October Revolution had a great international impact, stirred a great deal of political unrest throughout the world, and deepened immediate revolutionary prospects in several European countries. But unlike the French Revolution, the Russian revolutionary government quickly became an organizational center for spreading and helping to organize revolutions abroad. The Communist International (Comintern) was founded in 1919 for this purpose, as a disciplined organization to bring forth and lead the struggles for world revolution. The Comintern was also dedicated to extending Bolshevik politics and its model of political organization to the international Communist movements as clearly spelled out in its twenty-one conditions for admission.

The Russian Revolution of October 1917 took place in a qualitatively different world from that of its French predecessor. Vast changes had taken place, in particular the birth and development of industrial capitalism and the working-class movement that grew along with it. The growth of the working-class movement strengthened an internationalist perspective that had already begun to develop in Europe since the French Revolution. By the 1860s, Karl Marx, himself highly influenced by that great revolution, was helping to organize the Working Men's International Association. This was the first international association of unions and working-class groups of diverse political leanings, the main activity of which was to organize workers to prevent scabbing across European national boundaries.[7] Later, Marxism became the most influential ideological and political current in the workers and socialist movement of many countries. Many international socialist congresses, invoking Marxist theory and politics, went on the record reaffirming the internationalism of member parties and their opposition to inter-imperialist wars. Things turned out differently. After the outbreak of the First World War in August 1914, most of the socialist parties ended up supporting their respective "fatherlands"; only a minority, primarily but not exclusively composed of revolutionaries, remained opposed to the imperialist war on internationalist grounds. Among the people leading this internationalist minority were figures such as V. I. Lenin, Leon Trotsky, and Rosa Luxemburg. For this group of Marxist leaders, internationalism constituted not simply a body of political beliefs and practices but also an identity. They saw themselves primarily as internationalists and only secondarily as Russian, Polish, or German. Many Marxist revolutionaries of Jewish origin refused to join Jewish socialist political groups, such as the Bund, that were fighting against the anti-Semitism prevalent in the czarist empire. These Jewish Marxist revolutionaries, such as Trotsky and Luxemburg, were by no means indifferent to the plight of the Jews. Indeed, they genuinely saw their liberation emerging not out of their particular national struggles but as a result of the victory of the working-class movement and international socialism.[8]

The Internationalist Perspective of the Russian Revolution

Two things need to be stressed about the 1917 October Revolution in explaining its foreign policies. First, at the time—in 1917—every leader of the Bolshevik Party, including Stalin, held that in order to successfully institute socialism in Russia the revolution had to spread to the economically advanced countries in a relatively short period. Otherwise, the capitalist economy and its world imperialism, especially given the overall economic underdevelopment of Russia, would defeat the socialist direction of the revolution. For the Bolshevik leaders a successful revolution in a developed capitalist economy such as Germany—a revolution they thought was imminent—would assist in the economic development of revolutionary Russia. This would shortcut the process of primitive capitalist accumulation that would require the exploitation of Russian workers and peasants just as it did during the capitalist industrialization of countries such as Britain.

Second, for the Bolshevik leaders, the foreign policy of revolutionary Russia had to be conducted in an open, transparent, and altogether different manner from that of the imperialist capitalist powers. Accordingly, the Bolshevik government opened the archives of czarist diplomacy, published all secret treaties, and renounced the advantages that Russia was to gain from them. Thus, for example, a Bolshevik declaration addressed to the "Moslem Toilers of Russia and the East" proclaimed that Constantinople was going to remain in the hands of the Muslims themselves instead of those of foreign powers. The same declaration added that the agreements on the partition of Persia concluded between Great Britain and Russia in 1907 and on the partition of Turkey (the secret Anglo-Russian Pact of 1915) and the seizure of Armenia had been torn up and annulled.[9] When the revolutionary government's delegation went to Brest Litovsk in 1918 to negotiate with the German officers the conclusion of the First World War, the members of the Russian delegation headed by Trotsky proceeded to fraternize with and agitate against the war among the German troops stationed there. The revolutionary negotiators were also under strict instructions not to fraternize with their counterparts, who were to be regarded as their enemies and not as "fellow diplomats" on the other side of the bargaining table.

An Unanticipated Dilemma at Brest Litovsk

Only a few months after having taken power, the revolutionary government was confronted with a crisis that created serious tension between its revolutionary commitments and the defense and consolidation of the new revolutionary state. One of the principal demands of the Bolsheviks in the Russian Provisional Government had been its withdrawing from the First World War, to put an end to Russia's participation in an imperialist war and to the devastation it had brought on the Russian people. They promised that once in power they would, if necessary, unilaterally withdraw from the war. The Bolsheviks expected that once this happened, the German government would agree to cease hostilities against the revolutionary government in Russia or, better yet, would be overthrown or be forced by the German workers to sue for peace. This did not come to pass. Far from agreeing to an immediate peace, the German General Staff continued to press its military advantage and take over increasingly large chunks of Russian territory. From their position of strength, the Germans demanded increasingly onerous terms from the revolutionary government as conditions for peace. Lenin argued for acceptance of the German terms on grounds that given the existing relation of forces, the more Russia waited, the more Germany would advance and exact even more onerous concessions from the revolutionary government. The left Socialist Revolutionaries (SRs), who represented the radicalized peasantry and were the Bolshevik's coalition partners in the revolutionary government, and the left Communists, led by major leaders such as Nikolai Bukharin, rejected Lenin's position of compromise. These left tendencies argued for the continuation of hostilities based on a revolutionary guerrilla war, a sort of new front to undermine German power from within instead of the conventional military imperialist policies that Russia and the Entente had conducted against the Germans. Trotsky argued for a middle position of neither peace nor war, whereby Russia would demobilize its armed forces but refuse to sign the onerous peace treaty that Germany was demanding.[10] The contending Bolshevik factions carried over the debate about how to achieve peace in public and in a no-holds-barred fashion consistent with their politics of openness. This, incidentally, belies the notion that the Bolsheviks were a monolithic party from the very beginning and that there were no important differences between Lenin's rule and that of Stalin. The debate was settled in practice in favor of Lenin as the Germans continued to advance, making moot Trotsky's and the left Communist and left SR's positions. The revolutionary government ended up ceding territory to an imperialist capitalist power in exchange for its survival. Lenin's position underlined necessary compromises as an intrinsic part of revolutionary politics.

When the war with Germany was finally over, revolutionary Russia had to confront another source of tension between its internationalism and its interest in defending the revolutionary state when it had to define its relations with the existing capitalist states, particularly those on its borders. The question for the revolutionary government was, what implications would the establishment of normal diplomatic relations with a capitalist state have for the relations between Russia and the revolutionary movement in that capitalist country?

One possible solution was to declare that the official relations pursued by the Russian revolutionary government with a capitalist government would not be binding on the Russian Communist Party. This would have formally freed the Russian party to support the revolutionary movement against a government with which the Russian state maintained normal relations. Although the Russian government invoked this distinction between party and state for many decades, it was dismissed by the capitalist states as overly formalistic, as a distinction without a difference. And in fact, after Russia became a one-party state, this became not only a distinction without a difference but an absurdity. As it turns out, this could be considered an argument for the greater practicality of a pluralist, against a monolithic, revolutionary society and government. It would be far more difficult for a foreign capitalist state to demand unanimous respect and support from the citizens of a revolutionary state for the diplomatic agreements reached by its government if such unanimity did not exist on any matter, whether domestic or foreign.

Not too long after Brest Litovsk in the spring of 1918, Lenin's government was asked by Turkey's Mustafa Kemal in 1920 to provide military and diplomatic support. In spite of the great difficulties that Russia confronted at the time, it signed a treaty of friendship and aid with Kemal in March 1921 and provided him with money and weapons. From a revolutionary standpoint, such aid could be politically justified since the Turks were confronting an armed imperialist intervention conducted by the Entente through the agency of the Greek army. However, the Soviet leaders were also interested in developing an alliance with Turkey to guarantee their southern frontiers, the oil of the Caucasus, and navigation on the Black Sea. This meant that there were state interests mixed in with revolutionary considerations strictly speaking for their decision to enter into the agreement. But there was a big problem: while the Kemalists were asking for Soviet aid, they were viciously repressing the peasant movement fighting for agrarian reform and the Turkish Communist Party, which had just been formed. A month and a half before the signing of the Soviet-Turkish alliance in Moscow, the Kemalists had arrested, strangled, and thrown into the sea forty-two well-known Communist militants. Other Turkish Communists were put on trial for "high treason." The Russian Communist leadership kept quiet, fearing a breach with Kemal, and the issue of Turkey was kept entirely off the agenda of the 1921 Third Congress of the Comintern. It was only many months after the treaty of friendship and fraternity between the Soviet government and Turkey was signed on March 16, 1921, and after a deterioration in relations between the two countries had taken place, that the Soviet press condemned the atrocities in Turkey.[11]

In April 1922 Soviet Russia reached an agreement with Germany known as the Treaty of Rapallo (after the Italian town in which it was signed). Under this treaty, both sides renounced all territorial and financial claims against the other and agreed to normalize their diplomatic and trade relations. After the signing of the treaty, Germany became the capitalist state with which Russia maintained the most active economic relations. German industry and technicians contributed to the industrialization, and even to the armament, of Soviet Russia. Moreover, in the 1920s, the Soviet government secretly allowed German military engineers to develop in Soviet territory types of weapons that had been forbidden to Germany by the Treaty of Versailles. In fact, the German and Soviet armies established a collaborative relationship.[12] However, the Comintern appears to have followed a different policy with regard to Germany than it did with Turkey. The same 1921 Third Congress of the Comintern that kept silent about the killing of the Turkish Communists adopted a resolution protesting the repression of German Communists after the insurrectionary "March action" in 1921.[13] Much more important was Soviet Russia's readiness to support revolutionary action in Germany notwithstanding its amicable diplomatic, economic, and even military relations with that country. Thus, for example, at its June 1923 enlarged plenum, which took place after the Treaty of Rapallo was signed, the Executive Committee of the Communist International approved the policy of the German Communist Party (KPD) of preparing the conditions for a possible revolutionary outbreak. When a general strike broke out in Berlin in August 1923, Zinoviev, the president of the Comintern, decided that power was now within reach in Germany. In mid-September, the Comintern executive committee summoned the German Communist leaders to Moscow, where an agreement was reached to immediately prepare for an armed insurrection. The uprising was eventually arranged for the first week of October and then suspended, but the Hamburg Communists did not learn in time of the suspension. Several hundred Hamburg Communists fought for three days against the army and the police without receiving any support from the working class in the city. This episode turned into a big setback for the German Communists.[14]

It is clear that Moscow often misread the German situation and provided poor advice and direction to the German Communists.[15] But what is most relevant for my present purposes is that the good relations established between Germany and Russia under the spirit of the Treaty of Rapallo did not prevent the Russian Communist leadership from encouraging and helping to organize revolutionary outbreaks in Germany.[16] A major difference between the cases of Turkey and Germany was that Germany, unlike Turkey, was central to the revolutionary perspectives of the Comintern. In addition, Germany did not present the difficult and complicated question of how to relate to a bourgeois nationalist leader such as Mustafa Kemal who was resisting imperialism.

Stalin and the End of Marxist Internationalism

By the end of the twenties, following the transition period that began with Lenin's withdrawal from political activity some nine months before his death in January 1924 and the subsequent interregnum that lasted a few years, Joseph Stalin consolidated his rule. He established a totalitarian political system with a new bureaucratic class ruling over the working class and peasantry. The policy adopted under his rule was based on the worst traditions of Great Russian chauvinism, asserting the superiority of Russians over other nationalities, the beginnings of which Lenin noticed and fought during the last days of his political life.[17] This nationalism was also focused on achieving the industrialization of the country, which was implemented through the super-exploitation of Soviet workers and peasants. This was precisely the type of policy that the Bolsheviks had refused to consider at the time of the 1917 revolution, to avoid going through a process analogous to what Marx had described and called "primitive capitalist accumulation" in volume 1 of *Capital*. However, while it took about two centuries for British capitalism to carry out this bloody process, Stalin was determined to accomplish it during the first five-year plan he inaugurated in 1928. The cost of Stalin's policies in terms of the loss of human life, impoverishment of the peasantry and working class, growing inequality, and even a deliberate creation of famine in the Ukraine was truly staggering. Yet this approach to "building socialism" was the single most important feature of the new "Marxism" that Stalin succeeded in establishing. This was also the "Marxism" that became hegemonic throughout the world and would be emulated, albeit with modifications and adaptations, by successful Communist movements in countries such as China, Vietnam, and Cuba. Thus, instead of the "dictatorship of the proletariat"[18] that Engels had seen embodied in the highly democratic Paris Commune, the model that became prevalent throughout the world was the very undemocratic and oppressive one-party state that Stalin consolidated in the Soviet Union.

Stalin's "socialism in one country" meant first that Russia would be industrialized and turned into a great power without relying on any outside material aid. Second, the tension between Russian state interests and international revolution that Lenin's government and the early Comintern faced would be "resolved" by simply eliminating it in favor of Russian state interests. Communist parties abroad were to exist as a function of the interests and security of the Russian "socialist" fatherland as defined by Stalin. Accordingly, the principal duty of the foreign Communist parties became the protection of the interests of the Soviet Union and faithful compliance with the party line as it emerged from Moscow, even if this meant sacrificing political advantages, including revolutionary possibilities, at home. As a result, a qualitative change took place in the Comintern. Under Lenin, the Russian Communists had already acquired decisive power in an organization that was not based, as it was supposed to be, on an equal union among Communist parties. The organization did permit discussion among independent-minded people with diverging views and was genuinely, if often with mistaken policies, dedicated to the goal of international revolution. Under Stalin, however, the Comintern became a monolithic structure that imposed absolute unanimity on foreign Communist parties in pursuit of Russian state interests, pure and simple. Stalin followed the foreign policy of an empire, but a unique empire that could count on the unconditional support of an international movement, which in some countries such as France, Indonesia, and Italy eventually became truly massive in character.

Stalin's slogan of "socialism in one country" did not mean, as some have mistakenly thought, "socialism in *only* one country." Stalinist Russia was interested in the extension of what it called socialism to other lands provided that it did not endanger the interests and security of the Russian socialist fatherland. The Stalinist foreign policy methodology could be fruitfully compared to the investment policy of well-established capitalist corporations aimed at protecting earlier investments and making sure, as much as possible, that their new investments will be profitable. Stalin emerged from the Second World War in a relative position of strength that enabled him to engage in a massive expansion of his empire into Eastern Europe. This expansion was a fairly safe bet; Stalin pursued it at the least possible risk and expense. While he was willing to expand his power into Eastern Europe, Stalin's own estimate of his national and international position led him to oppose and sacrifice the revolutionary possibilities that existed in the China of the mid-twenties and the Spain of the late thirties. In doing so, he totally disregarded the interests of the revolutionaries and Communists of those countries, at whose expense he carried out his policies. When it comes to taking risks, revolutionaries have usually not behaved like business firms. Although sometimes tactically cautious, they have had to be strategic risk takers, not for the sake of adventure but because of a willingness to subordinate narrow short-range organizational interests to the larger political project of revolution.

The traditional terms *right* and *left* are not applicable to Stalin's foreign policy. Although after the mid-thirties he adopted a more conciliatory "right" Popular Front policy of alliance with other left parties and even the "progressive bourgeoisie," he had imposed a harsh and sectarian "left" Third Period policy in the late twenties and early thirties. Both policies had equally negative consequences for Communist movements abroad. Similarly, in 1926 he took a "right" position by opposing the Chinese Revolution, and the following year he took a "left" position by directly ordering his Comintern agents to organize the disastrous Canton rising.[19] Stalin ordered the Communist parties of Latin America to organize Popular Fronts throughout the continent. However, in Brazil, the tension and conflict between the government and the Communists led the Communist Party under Luiz Carlos Prestes to organize an armed uprising in November 1935 sanctioned by Moscow, notwithstanding its Popular Front line.[20] After the end of the "Patriotic War" with the defeat of Fascism in 1945, Stalin turned from his "right" policy of alliance with capitalist democracies to the "left." Through his spokesman, the French Communist Jacques Duclos, he denounced the American Communist leader Earl Browder for his "right" inclinations and policies, even though Browder had been implementing Stalin's policies of the previous period.[21] In keeping with Stalin's strategy to advance Soviet interests, the Cuban followers of his successors pressured the Cuban revolutionary leaders to adopt more radical policies during the first few months of the 1959 Cuban Revolution. But they later tried to restrain Castro and his associates when they went faster and farther than anything they or the Soviet Union had anticipated.[22]

The Foreign Policy of the Cuban Revolution

It is quite remarkable that an island the size of Pennsylvania with a current population of some eleven million people (approximately six million at the time of the 1959 Revolution) and limited industrial and economic resources was able to develop such a wide-ranging and influential foreign policy. Cuba's diplomacy as well as its military has played a significant and sometimes critical role not just in the Western Hemisphere but in Africa, the Middle East. and Asia, particularly Vietnam. In a long interview with Ignacio Ramonet shortly before the Cuban leader withdrew from public view due to a serious illness, Fidel Castro provided a brief but remarkable survey of Cuba's activities abroad. He underlined the well-known Cuban military presence in Angola in the seventies and eighties, which at one point reached fifty-five thousand soldiers and defeated the South African army in conventional warfare involving tanks, planes, and artillery. Castro also included lesser-known episodes of Cuban foreign policy such as his support of Algeria's independence struggle and the Cuban arms and soldiers that were sent to aid that country in its 1963 war against Morocco. He also revealed that an entire Cuban tank brigade was stationed in Syria (facing the Golan Heights) from 1973 to 1975 after the Israeli victory in the fall 1973 Yom Kippur War. He added that Cuban blood was shed in the (former Belgian) Congo, in the independence struggle of Guinea and Cape Verde led by Amílcar Cabral, and in Nicaragua and Grenada.[23] However, Castro did not mention to Ramonet anything regarding his major military intervention in the Horn of Africa, which was surpassed in size only by his intervention in Angola. Neither did he mention that in 1965 Cuba also sent troops to the Congo (Brazzaville) to train military forces that were fighting for the independence of Portugal's African colonies, and to Guinea to help Sekou Touré to maintain internal order and repel foreign aggression.[24]

Because of its activist foreign policy, the Cuban government has been regarded by many Latin American and other leftists as a consistently anti-imperialist force and a stronghold of progressive and national liberation movements. The reputation the Cuban leaders enjoy has been reinforced by the contrast between the island's historic opposition to US imperialism and the political surrender to the Washington neoliberal consensus of many well-known personalities, including many former leftists and revolutionaries. However, a careful examination of Cuban foreign policy reveals that while it is true that Cuba has followed a consistent policy of opposition to the imperialism sponsored by the United States and its Western allies, it has not followed that policy toward other imperialist aggressors. In fact, the Cuban government has taken the side of oppressor states on various occasions. How can

Cuba's contradictory policies regarding the right of nations to self-determination be explained?

From the very beginning, the principal focus of Cuban foreign policy has been its relationship with the United States, an imperial power that played a dominant role in Cuban affairs for at least sixty years before the revolutionary victory in 1959.[25] The revolutionary government's conflict with Washington, which has lasted well over five decades, has to a large extent framed Cuba's relations with the rest of the world. After Washington failed in its attempt, in 1958, to replace Cuban dictator Fulgencio Batista with a "safe" provisional government of its own choosing, it recognized the revolutionary government shortly after it came to power. In the early days of the Cuban Revolution, the US executive branch adopted a stance best described as worried vigilance, expressing neither sympathy nor hostility toward the Cuban government and exerting subtle but steady pressure while maintaining cautious diplomatic-style correctness. This changed after the radical Agrarian Reform Law adopted by Castro in May 1959. At that point, the US government became openly critical and demanded prompt compensation for the US lands to be seized under the new law. The US government concluded, although it did not publicly state, that the Cuban government would not cede to US pressure and had to be replaced. Thus, it initially encouraged internal opposition to the regime, but by the end of 1959, it began to implement a program to get rid of the Castro government by force. In a fundamental sense, the die was cast by February 1960, when the Eisenhower administration systematized its various initiatives to get rid of the Castro leadership.[26] In the years that followed, American efforts to overthrow the Cuban government included sponsorship of invasions, diplomatic boycotts, economic and naval blockades (in the context of the missile crisis of October 1962), economic sabotage, and numerous assassination attempts and terrorist attacks.

A commonly held view among American liberals is that the specific Cold War policies pursued by the Eisenhower and Kennedy administrations pushed Fidel Castro and his government into the arms of the Soviet Union and Communism. This reactive approach makes two critical assumptions: that the United States could have adopted significantly different policies and that the politics of the revolutionary leaders were merely a reaction to US policy regarding the Cuban Revolution. The fact is, however, that the United States acted toward Cuba the same way it had acted toward other Latin American countries long before the Cold War: leaving democratic political rhetoric aside, what really counted for Washington was the defense of US economic, political, and military imperial interests in its geopolitical "backyard." Regarding the politics of the Cuban revolutionary leaders, it should be noted that they were not political automatons that merely reacted to US policy. Although they acted under serious internal and external constraints, they were autonomous agents with a political history of their own and pursued independent political and ideological visions. These leaders made choices, including selecting the Communist road for the Cuban Revolution.[27]

Cuba's Foreign Policy in the First Year of the Revolution

Until the Cuban Revolution's social radicalism became evident after the victory of January 1, 1959, it was able to maintain amicable relations with a vast spectrum of Latin American political opinion and governments. At this early time, the horizon of the revolutionary government was almost limited to the Western Hemisphere. The only exception was Franco's Spain, with whom relations were difficult the first couple of years but then became quite amicable. However, as a result of Cuba's growing conflict with the United States, the break with the pro-US Latin American social democracy—Venezuela's Acción Democrática, Costa Rica's Partido de Liberación Nacional, Puerto Rico's Partido Popular Democrático—was not late in coming. In March 1959, the Costa Rican José Figueres in a visit to Cuba spoke in defense of the American side in the Cold War. David Salvador, the head of the Cuban trade unions and a radical nationalist who had Communist roots but was opposed to the local Communists,[28] publicly reproached the Costa Rican leader.

Among the little-known features of this early period were outbreaks of spontaneous popular expression of revolutionary solidarity with various Latin American countries. In April 1959, some eighty, mostly Cuban, insurgents acting on their own initiative, although with the apparent consent of the Cuban government, landed in Panama in an unsuccessful attempt to overthrow the government of that country.[29] In March and May of the same year, Cuban government forces stopped two expeditions headed for Haiti and Nicaragua to fight against the dictatorships of François Duvalier and Anastasio Somoza.[30] The Cubans headed for Nicaragua were strongly criticized by Major Camilo Cienfuegos, the head of the Cuban army, for having placed the revolution in a compromising situation. Besides, Cienfuegos insisted, "the oppressed peoples of America must make their own revolutions, because those revolutions would otherwise be discredited as having been made by foreigners, and would become an embarrassment for those peoples who would have demonstrated a lack of courage in freeing themselves from their own chains."[31] It was not uncommon during the early period of the revolution for Cuban activists to publicly raise funds in support of causes such as the liberation of the Dominican Republic from Trujillo's dictatorship. Fidel Castro was wary of these spontaneous initiatives, a "street internationalism," which he saw as a potential source of unanticipated international conflicts. Thus, when the Cuban government itself sponsored expeditions against the governments of Nicaragua, Haiti, and the Dominican Republic that same year[32]—while Trujillo, the Dominican dictator, organized expeditions against the Cuban government—it brought to an end freelance foreign policy. Earlier, in February 1959, Fidel Castro had clamped down on another kind of independent initiative involving peasant land occupations that had been encouraged by some of the old pro-Moscow Cuban Communists who in that period were attempting to pressure Castro from the "left."[33]

The Sources of Cuba's Foreign Policy

By the end of 1959, as a total break with the United States was becoming increasingly likely, Fidel Castro began to forge an alliance with the Soviet Union and the local Communists. With freelance foreign policy out of the way, the fundamental elements of Cuban foreign policy began to crystallize. This policy drew from three principal sources, the weight of which varied throughout the Cuban revolutionary trajectory. The first was the USSR's Stalinist politics, transmitted through increasingly direct contacts starting after Soviet emissary Aleksandr Alekseev's arrival in Cuba on October 1, 1959.[34] Allied with, and reinforcing the influence of, the Soviet Union were the Cuban Communists, whose power was rapidly growing in the island. Although these two forces were very close to each other, their interests were not always identical. Thus, for example, Cuban Communist leaders had been concerned for some time with the possibility that Fidel Castro could become a Latin American Nasser who would build a close relationship with the Soviet Union but ignore and even repress local Communists. The Cuban Communists were also concerned with the possible negative implications of the Soviet policy of "peaceful coexistence" with the United States, a policy that a major power like the Soviet Union could afford but that could have had very different consequences for a small, vulnerable country like Cuba.[35]

The second major source of Cuba's foreign policy was the independent Communist perspective of Ernesto "Che" Guevara, who according to his biographers was a self-described admirer of Stalin even after Khrushchev's revelations of the Russian leader's crimes in 1956.[36] Guevara was an ally of the old Cuban Communists from 1957 to 1960, a decisive period during which the key decisions about the kind of society that would be built in Cuba were made. But after 1960, Guevara's views and practices began to differ from those of the USSR and the old Cuban Communists on matters of domestic and foreign policy. The Soviet Union and the old Cuban Communists were supporting the "right-wing" Popular Front approaches, which as I earlier indicated, were initially developed in the mid-thirties by the Soviet Union and the Communist Parties involving alliances with forces to their right including the "progressive bourgeoisie." Guevara's approach was more similar, although not identical, to the far more intransigent and aggressive policies that Stalin adopted during other periods.

The third major source of Cuba's foreign policy was a non-Marxist but militant tradition of left-wing Latin American solidarity that had flourished on the island since the twenties and thirties. The Cubans and other Latin Americans involved in the freelance expeditions against the governments of Panama, Haiti, and Nicaragua in 1959 represented this ideological and political current. Historically, this tendency was associated with such figures as César Augusto Sandino in Nicaragua, Antonio Guiteras in Cuba, the Puerto Rican nationalist, Pedro Albizu Campos, and Lázaro Cardenas in Mexico. Another was the young Fidel Castro, who in 1947 enrolled in the ill-fated Cayo Confites expedition aimed at overthrowing Rafael Trujillo's dictatorship in the Dominican Republic. The expedition was organized by the Caribbean Legion, an eclectic group of idealistic democrats, nationalists, and criminal elements and was supported by influential populist and social democratic politicians in Cuba, Venezuela, and Costa Rica. The following year, while attending a student congress in Bogotá, Colombia, Fidel Castro became involved in the "Bogotazo," the riots that followed the assassination of the popular Colombian Liberal Party leader Eliecer Gaitán in April 1948.[37]

Although often characterized as "petty bourgeois" by the pro-Moscow Communist parties and by non-Communist Marxists, this current was "classless" in the sense that it had no firm, organic links to any class institutions or organizations whether petty bourgeois, working class, or labor. The "classlessness" of this current was ideologically and politically expressed in a disdain for theory, Marxist or otherwise, and an exaltation of the "man of action" in search of exciting and dangerous adventures and extraordinary and romantically stirring experiences. This orientation had an elective affinity with voluntarist versions of Marxism (Maoism, Guevaraism) that emphasized the power of the political will and minimized the importance of economic and other objective conditions. This current was also nationalist, secular, and "populist" in the precise sense that it rarely had a class analysis of society and it framed its perspectives in terms of the people against the powerful. It was a "left" populism in the sense that it supported radical action on behalf of the poor. Opposed to these were the views of the traditional Communist Parties, which espoused an economistic or objectivist view of Marxism and minimized the importance of revolutionary action.

The Two Stages of Cuban Foreign Policy

Immediately after having consolidated his control over the island's foreign policy by the end of 1959, Fidel Castro adhered to a policy that was predominantly a mixture of Guevara's brand of independent Communism and the Caribbean and Latin American tradition with which he had been associated since the late forties. This early period marked the high point of the Cuban Revolution's impact on Latin America, an impact that transformed the left, threatened various governments in the region, and forced the United States to respond with its Alliance for Progress, at best a mild reformist program.

During this period, Cuba's policy in Latin America involved open and aggressive support for guerrilla movements and harsh denunciation of the traditional Communist Parties on the continent that criticized and opposed such policies. This was a period of high revolutionary ardor and militancy on the island. The Cuban leaders were only beginning to consolidate themselves as a ruling group, to clearly define the interests of the state they were forging, and to differentiate it from their revolutionary leadership of the liberation movements on the continent and elsewhere. It was during this initial period that the Cuban leadership put forward guerrilla warfare as the strategy for the Latin American left. According to this strategy, articulated in its clearest and perhaps most one-sided form on behalf of the Cuban leaders by French thinker Régis Debray,[38] guerrilla struggles were to be conducted under the guidance of the *foco* theory. Following this approach, an armed minority would take control of one or more strongholds, from which the "liberation" of the rest of the country would be launched. This political strategy played down, if it did not explicitly rule out, the self-organization of the working class and peasantry. The agency and method of overthrowing the old ruling classes has a decisive impact on the nature of the new society that emerges from a successful revolution. Had the guerrilla movements been successful in Latin America based on the application of Debray's theory, the resulting new regimes would have been unambiguously elitist. Besides, any successful guerrilla movement in the Latin America of the sixties supported by the Cuban government would have more likely than not copied the elitist Cuban one-party state model. As it turned out, the guerrilla movements of the sixties failed in Argentina, Bolivia, Guatemala, Peru, and Venezuela.

These years were also characterized by a lot of friction with the Soviet Union, which under the pressure of the United States had been forced to reaffirm the notion that the Western Hemisphere was an indisputable part of the North American sphere of influence. Following this geopolitical logic, Moscow kept pressuring Havana to withdraw its open support of the Latin American guerrillas. It did not succeed in its efforts until the late sixties. Cuba-USSR relations reached a low point when the Soviet Union made an agreement with the United States to resolve the 1962 missile crisis without consulting with the Cuban government. Fidel Castro publicly, and with a great deal of bitterness, complained about the behavior of the Soviet leaders, who had apparently forgotten that Cuba was a sovereign state. The conflicts between Fidel Castro and the Soviet leaders, as well as between Castro and the leaders of several pro-Moscow Latin American Communist Parties, continued to grow throughout the second half of the sixties. In August 1967, Fidel Castro condemned the assistance provided by the Soviet bloc to Latin American capitalist countries such as Venezuela and Colombia. Shortly after, Cuba's top leaders boycotted the celebrations of the fiftieth anniversary of the Russian Revolution in Moscow and sent a lower-ranking official. Fidel Castro and his close associates criticized the Soviet leaders on many other matters, including what they considered Moscow's weak response to the US attack on North Vietnam. The USSR in turn took a dim view of the social and economic policies that the Cuban leaders were pursuing at home, which differed from the Soviet approach to economic management. The growing tension reached a critical point in early 1968 when Fidel Castro announced that the Soviets had significantly reduced their oil deliveries to Cuba. Shortly after, the Soviets also suspended the shipment of military supplies and technical assistance to the island.[39]

For many sympathizers with the Cuban regime, Cuba's unquestionably militant policy of the sixties followed the principles of revolutionary internationalism of classical Marxism. That, however, is a superficial and essentially misleading analogy. Notwithstanding the solidarity Fidel Castro and his close associates might have genuinely felt with Latin America, their political concerns were fundamentally nationalist. It would be more appropriate to speak of the Cuban leadership's "inter-nationalism" than of the internationalism of classical Marxism. In addition, the type of "socialism" that was being propagated by the Cuban leadership, a variant of the Soviet model, was qualitatively different from the fundamentally democratic character of classical Marxism, which made central to its politics the notion of the self-emancipation of the working class. By the sixties, Fidel Castro and his associates had become firmly wedded to the institutional structures of the one-party state along the general lines of the Soviet model established under Stalin. The fact that the Cuban leaders modified the model in certain respects, like placing a greater emphasis on popular mobilization—not to be confused with popular control—did not alter the fundamental structural kinship between the two models. The guerrilla theories of the Cuban leaders and of Régis Debray expressed a view of the world quite alien to classical Marxism. Furthermore, while implementing the guerrilla strategy for most of Latin America, Fidel Castro was already forging friendly, not merely diplomatically "correct," ties with such countries as the PRI's Mexico and Franco's Spain, two of the three countries (the third one being the United States) with the strongest historic ties to Cuba.

Finally, Cuba's foreign policy has had a particular kind of impact on domestic matters, which has seldom been discussed. Cubans on the island do not have access to essential facts regarding the political and socioeconomic organization and internal affairs of countries with which the Cuban government maintains friendly relations, and do not have the avenues to discuss their merits and flaws. This was as true throughout the sixties and seventies regarding Cuba's relations with Mexico and Spain (after the initial years of friction with Franco) as it is true today of relations with Russia and China. Even politically educated Cubans know little about what is going on in China, with which Cuba maintains very active diplomatic and economic relations, a country that is officially considered "socialist" by the Cuban regime and media. In a strange contribution to the Marxist approach to political consciousness, the Cuban people are supposed to develop internationalist sentiments and politics on the basis of systematically induced political ignorance, or misinformation, about countries friendly to the Cuban leaders.[40]

The early period of conflict between Cuba and the Soviet Union came to an end with Castro's speech supporting the Soviet and Warsaw Pact countries' invasion of Czechoslovakia in 1968. This speech showed Castro to be still very critical of the USSR and East European Communist countries and was more a defense of the Stalinist model of the one-party state than of the Soviet bloc as such. Beyond the political debt he had incurred to the Soviet Union because of its indispensable economic support, the Cuban leader clearly stated his opposition to Alexander Dubcek's reforms. In his indictment of the Czechoslovakian reformers, Fidel Castro claimed that "a real liberal fury was unleashed; a whole series of political slogans in favor of the formation of opposition parties began to develop, in favor of openly anti-Marxist and anti-Leninist thesis . . . in short, that the reins of power should cease to be in the hands of the Communist party . . . and in fact certain measures were taken such as the establishment of a bourgeois form of 'freedom' of the press. This means that the counterrevolution and the exploiters, the very enemies of socialism, were granted the right to speak and write freely against socialism."[41]

Cuba's Foreign Policy Adapts to Soviet Demands

At this time, after several years of pressure from the Soviet Union, Havana withdrew its open support of the Latin American guerrillas. Fidel Castro yielded to Soviet pressure, but not entirely: he continued to support insurgent movements in Latin America in a more discreet and limited manner, under the control of Major Manuel "Redbeard" Piñeiro. It was at this junction that Castro began to move toward a second foreign policy stage more closely associated with the traditional Soviet approach. However, even during this period of close partnership with the Soviet empire, there were certain objective features regarding Cuba's position in the Western Hemisphere and in the world that made its foreign policy more militant than the Soviet Union's. Cuba's geographical location within the geopolitical sphere of influence of the American empire, and its small size and relative economic underdevelopment, forced it to maintain a substantial degree of militancy to be able to survive as a society with an economic and social system inimical to Washington's.

During this stage of closer ties to the Soviet Union, Castro supported the suppression of the Eritrean national movement in the seventies and, with much discomfort and in a low-key manner, the Soviet invasion and occupation of Afghanistan that began in late 1979 and continued through the eighties.[42] Until then, Cuba managed to play an important leadership role in the movement of "third world" countries in a manner that was usually compatible and supportive of Soviet goals. Even when Castro's policies were closest to those of the Soviet Union, in terms of both his domestic and foreign policies, he avoided a total identification with the Soviet leaders in the eyes of the world. But his attitude toward Soviet actions in Afghanistan created a big problem in his relationship with the nonaligned countries because most of the nonaligned bloc was strongly opposed to that occupation. As it happened, Cuba had just been elected to head the nonaligned movement at a meeting in Havana a few months before the Soviets invaded Afghanistan.

As it shifted away from open support of guerrilla warfare in Latin America, Cuba became increasingly interested in Africa, a region on the fringes of the American geopolitical sphere of influence where Cuban initiatives were more compatible with Soviet foreign policy. Besides, there were fewer political risks to Cuba's intervention in Africa than in Latin America. In the case of Latin America, the Cuban government was challenging legal governments, while in Africa it opposed colonial powers and defended established regimes.[43] Cuba's political and military presence in Africa (and other parts of the world) also had a significant effect on the balance of its power relations with the Soviet Union. Its global presence along with its development into a significant military power gave Fidel Castro greater leverage and room for negotiation with the Soviet leaders, who for these reasons could not treat Cuba as if it were a mere East European satellite. The conflict between China and the Soviet Union and what was once called "Communist polycentrism" helped to give the Cuban government even greater room to maneuver with Moscow. At the same time, the substantial subsidies the island received from Moscow and its economic dependence on the USSR allowed it, until the late eighties, to maintain a standard of living that, although certainly austere, covered the most basic material needs of its population. The Soviet Union was able to compel Cuba to purchase its poor-quality consumer and industrial products at questionable prices, but it failed in its efforts to establish medium-range missiles (1962) and a nuclear submarine base (1970) on the island. Nevertheless, Moscow was able to use Cuban ports and airports to service its warships and aircraft and to establish a base (at Lourdes, near Havana) for electronic intelligence gathering and communications facilities.[44]

African Nationalism

During the second stage of its foreign policy in the seventies and eighties, Cuba's strategy was oriented toward building an alliance with African nationalism. Eventually, this alliance required the commitment of qualitatively far greater human and material resources than those Cuba ever invested in Latin America. In the course of implementing that strategy, Cuba took independent initiatives without consulting the Kremlin, although they were generally compatible with the overall strategy of Soviet policy in the region even if occasional tactical disagreements arose between Cuba and the USSR. The Cuban government was able to kill two birds with one stone. It was able to exercise its own military and political muscle on the African continent without the risk of causing the clash with the Soviet Union that Fidel Castro's earlier aggressive support of guerrilla warfare in Latin America had provoked.

In the case of Angola, Fidel Castro's strategy, combined with his alliance with the Soviet empire, allowed him to play a very important role in the defense of that country against Western imperialism and its right-wing UNITA (União Nacional para a Independência Total de Angola, National Union for the Total Independence of Angola) agents. During the initial months of the Angolan operation, Cuba handled the transportation of its troops by itself but used USSR-supplied weapons. Later on, the Soviets took over the transportation operation and supplied the Cubans with a variety of weapons to stop the domestic and foreign enemies of Angolan national self-determination.[45] The Cubans, in alliance with the MPLA (People's Movement for the Liberation of Angola–Labor Party, Movimento Popular de Libertação de Angola–Partido do Trabalho) and with the help of the Namibian independence fighters, eventually won this conflict and delivered a heavy military and political blow against the South African armed forces, the backbone of apartheid.[46] This victory also opened the way for the independence of Namibia in the late eighties.[47]

However, Cuban aid was not free of cost to the Angolan people. Cuban troops actively intervened in internal disputes within the Angolan MPLA, such as when they ensured the victory of the faction supporting Agostino Neto against the faction supporting Nito Alves.[48] Of course, the issue here is not whether Alves may have been better or worse than Neto, but that foreign forces were intervening and in fact deciding the outcome of an MPLA and Angolan internal matter. This Cuban intervention in the internal affairs of an African country was not unprecedented. Earlier, in 1966, Cuban troops actively intervened in the Republic of the Congo (Brazzaville) to protect the government of President Alphonse Massemba-Debat and put down a mutiny by military tribesmen loyal to Captain Marien Ngouabi.[49] Fidel Castro's government's interventions in the internal affairs of African countries sometimes grew out of the Cuban government's taking responsibility for the personal security of political leaders.[50]

Cuba's indiscriminate alliance with African nationalism also involved support for the bloody regimes of Idi Amin in Uganda and Nguema Macias in Equatorial Guinea.[51]

In the conflict between Eritrea and Ethiopia, Fidel Castro followed a different course than in Angola. Cuba had initially supported the Eritrean struggle for independence from the Ethiopian regime headed by Emperor Haile Selassie. But when Selassie was overthrown by the Dergue, a group that eventually came under the leadership of Mengistu Haile-Mariam and adopted a strong left-wing nationalist stance favorable to the Soviet Union, Castro radically changed his tune: he decided to ally himself with Ethiopian nationalists against the Eritrean nationalists. Castro now opposed the Eritrean struggle with the claim that it was secessionist and would destroy the territorial integrity of Ethiopia.[52] In fact, Eritrea had been a separate nation that had been colonized by Greater Ethiopia and afterwards annexed to it. Thus, the Cuban government moved from supporting Eritrean independence (up to July 1975) to an uncommitted neutral position (July 1975 to February 1977) to adopting the Ethiopian view that defined the Eritreans as "secessionists." In a speech delivered on April 26, 1978, Fidel Castro tried to justify his government's new position on Eritrea by comparing the Eritrean liberationists to the secessionists in the American South who provoked the American Civil War. As Nelson P. Valdés pointed out, this was a baseless comparison for a number of reasons, including the fact that the American South had been an integral part of the United States since its inception and did not constitute a separate nation. Besides, the Eritrean struggle was a truly popular movement unblemished by the racism of the Southern whites who wanted to secede.[53] Fidel Castro's support for the Dergue was not only rhetorical: he refrained from becoming directly involved in the Eritrean fighting, but the Cuban government trained and armed the Ethiopian forces and provided logistical support and supplies. It also directed the Cuban armed forces to relieve the Ethiopian troops on the Ogaden front, the site of the war between Ethiopia and Somalia, which made it possible for the Ethiopians to continue their war versus the Eritreans.[54]

Cuba's major military involvement on the side of Ethiopia in the Ogaden is a textbook example of a "war of choice" instead of a war of "duty"—solidarity with a liberation movement against imperialism—and certainly not a war of necessity for self-defense. The Cuban government intervened in the Ogaden to support not only the Ethiopian Dergue but also the USSR's side in the Cold War. Until the overthrow of the Ethiopian emperor Selassie, Cuba and the Soviet Union had aligned themselves with the self-proclaimed left-wing regime of Mohamed Siad Barre in Somalia. The left-wing evolution of the Ethiopian Dergue that overthrew Selassie led to a complex process whereby Ethiopia and Somalia ended up switching sides in their Cold War alliances. Meanwhile, in the Ogaden region of Ethiopia, irredentist groups organized by the Western Somali Liberation Front, aided by Somalia, took advantage of the Ethiopian government's precarious position to escalate a war of secession. The rebels almost won when 40,000 regular Somali troops invaded the Ogaden and in less than two weeks captured 112 towns and 85 percent of the region.[55] This was the point at which Cuban military intervention was decisive in helping the Ethiopian government to successfully reverse the situation. Somali actions clearly violated the sacrosanct rule adopted by postcolonial black Africa barring the redrawing of the admittedly arbitrary borders inherited from the colonial powers. According to this agreed-upon rule, borders could not be changed no matter how legitimate a case ethnic or even national groups had to secede from one country and join another. Yet it is very difficult to find a justification for Cuba's active involvement except in geopolitical Cold War terms. The Ogaden war was certainly very different from the conflict in Angola, where a newly independent African country was fighting for its self-determination against Western imperialism and apartheid South Africa. Although the United States had initially intended to support and arm the Somalis, it changed its mind when the Somali army invaded the Ogaden.[56] Apparently the US government hedged its bets. On the one hand, it informed Saudi Arabia, Iran, Egypt, and Pakistan, all armed with US weapons, that the American government would not object if they provided arms to the Somalians. On the other hand, Washington had just decided to "reciprocate the Ethiopians' desire to talk to us about their present predicament."[57] Nevertheless, the United States did warn Ethiopia that it would reassess its supposed policy of neutrality in this conflict if Ethiopia took the war into Somalia itself. Cuba, Ethiopia, and the Soviet Union promised that this would not happen, and they kept their word.[58]

Cuban military intervention in the Horn of Africa grew very rapidly from four hundred advisers to seventeen thousand regular troops in the first three months of 1978.[59] It was closely coordinated with the Soviet Union from the very beginning, and the Soviet Union played a more dominant role in the conflict than it had in Angola. For the USSR the Horn of Africa was strategically much more important than Angola: the port facilities at Massawa and Assab along the Eritrean coast, overlooking Saudi Arabia, would allow it to control the only dependable seaway from the western part of the Soviet Union to Vladivostok in the Far East.[60] The Ethiopian nationalist dictatorship's alignment with the Soviet Union in the Cold War turned it, for Cuba as well as for many in the international left, into a "progressive" force regardless of its bloody crimes at home. Nevertheless, although African progressive opinion welcomed Cuban support for Angola, it was much more ambivalent with respect to Cuban military intervention in the Horn of Africa.

Cuba's military intervention in Africa involved the rotation of hundreds of thousands of troops and, as I suggested above, dwarfed by comparison its involvement in Latin America and other parts of the world. Besides its cost to the Cuban people in terms of the loss of lives,[61] there were substantial economic losses as well. In addition to military personnel, a large number of Cuban technical personnel, construction workers, and even bus and truck drivers were sent to Africa.[62] It is estimated that between 1975 and 1991, more than 430,000 Cubans served in military and civilian capacities in Angola alone. By the mid-1980s, Angola had become the standard tour of duty for Cuban youth.[63] This exodus negatively affected Cuba's economic growth and the standard of living of the Cuban people, as expressed, for example, in the reduction in the housing units built on the island.[64] On the other hand, the Soviet Union might have limited the massive aid it sent to the island during that period had Cuba not so actively intervened in Africa.

Reasons of State

In spite of having been forced by the Soviets to curtail its support for Latin American guerrilla forces, Cuba continued to back the anti-imperialist movements in the continent. It played an important role, for example, in the overthrow of Anastasio Somoza in Nicaragua in the late seventies. But to fully comprehend Cuban policy in Latin America, it is essential to understand that its support of any anti-imperialist movement has always been subordinated to the interests of the Cuban state as defined by its leaders. Based, in part, on Jorge I. Domínguez's analysis on how the Cuban state has always adjusted its foreign policy to advance its own goals,[65] it is clear that in its state-to-state relations, the Cuban government has subordinated its support to opposition movements in any given country to the benefits it could obtain from its relations with the government of that country. Cuba has, as a general rule, even in its first foreign policy stage in the early sixties, refrained from supporting revolutionary movements against governments that had good relations with Havana and rejected US policy toward the island, independent of the ideological coloration of those governments. One possible exception may have been the normal diplomatic ties that Cuba maintained with the shah of Iran while reaching out to the Iranian People's Party (IPP), which was plotting against him. But after the shah was overthrown, the Cuban government returned to its usual policy when it broke with the IPP and cultivated friendly relations with Ayatollah Khomeini.[66]

Relations with Mexico

The most paradigmatic cases of the "reasons of state" direction of Cuban foreign policy are the very amicable relations that Cuba maintained with Mexico under the Institutional Revolutionary Party (PRI) and with Franco's Spain. The PRI-led regime was the only Latin American government that in the early sixties refused to comply with the US-controlled Organization of American States (OAS)'s instruction to its member states to break diplomatic relations with Castro's government. The PRI played a clever double game, expressing sympathy for Castro's government, in part to pursue its own "national interest" in Caribbean affairs and in part to co-opt its internal left discontent, while secretly collaborating with US government agencies in a number of hostile activities against Cuba. The no longer reform-oriented, but still nationalist and statist, PRI leaders—some of whom were only beginning to adopt neoliberalism as their banner—felt a certain degree of sympathy for the Cuban leaders based on their own nationalism and to a lesser extent because of their roots in the much decayed but still relatively recent Mexican Revolution. One of the Mexican groups most supportive of the Cuban government was the statist "dinosaur" but nationalist PRI faction led by Fernando Gutierrez Barrios, a sinister figure who headed the secret police from 1964 to 1970 (and who, quite ironically, had been personally involved in the arrest of Fidel Castro and his fellow revolutionaries in Mexico City in 1956) and was governor of the state of Veracruz from 1986 to 1988. The Cuban government responded to the sympathy of the then still dominant PRI statist "dinosaurs" by withholding public criticism of their crimes and corruption and by presenting to the Cuban people a benevolent image of the PRI's Mexico as a progressive political system. Consistent with this orientation toward Mexico, the Cuban press and government kept silent and failed to condemn the Plaza de Tlatelolco massacre of hundreds of students in October 1968, prior to that year's Olympic Games.[67] Moreover, the Cuban government did not support the guerrilla movements that erupted in Mexico in the late sixties and early seventies.

Relations with Spain

One of the most peculiar but little-known aspects of revolutionary Cuba's foreign relations is the lasting friendly relationship it established with Franco's regime in Spain. Few people off the island are aware of the enormous importance that the Spanish Civil War and its Francoist sequel had for Cuba, and particularly for the Cuban Communist and non-Communist left. On a proportional basis, Cuba sent more volunteers to fight in support of the Spanish republic than any other country in the Western Hemisphere, and opposition to the Franquista dictatorship was a major issue for the Cuban left throughout the forties and fifties. Relations between revolutionary Cuba and Spain were rocky during the first couple of years, and included an ugly incident on January 21, 1960, when the Spanish Francoist ambassador tried to burst in on a televised interview with Fidel Castro to protest the Cuban leader's attacks on the Spanish Embassy in Havana. Franco privately expressed his criticisms of the Spanish ambassador's undiplomatic behavior,[68] and by January 30 an agreement had been reached by the two countries to continue normal diplomatic relations with the acknowledgment by the Cuban leadership that no counterrevolutionary activity existed that could be attributed to the Spanish government.[69] A week later, the Spanish press officer in Havana informed Madrid that with one minor exception, the press, and particularly its progovernment sector, abstained from any attack on Spain following a government order that also forbade the publication of articles, editorials, or commentaries written by Spanish exiles, or anything about their activities.[70] Save for a couple of isolated incidents in the early sixties, relations between Cuba and Spain then settled into a quiet, friendly economic and diplomatic exchange that lasted for many years beyond Franco's death in the mid-seventies.[71] Curiously, the Falangist press sometimes sounded like the North American liberal media when it argued, as did *Arriba* in late 1963, against a US foreign policy that was pushing Fidel Castro into the arms of Moscow.[72] Franco thought that the Americans had been misinformed about the intentions of the Fidelistas and should have supported them to prevent the introduction of Russia and its Cuban agents into the revolutionary process.[73] The Spanish government resisted pressures from Washington to cut its trade relations with Cuba. For example, when during the Johnson administration Spain signed a three-year trade agreement with Cuba, Washington announced that it would cut its "aid" to Spain. In response, Franco's government reminded the United States that the assistance it provided Spain was not "aid" but a treaty obligation in exchange for the military bases that the United States was allowed to have in Spain. The US government was forced to "eat crow" and reverse its earlier decision.[74] In 1964, Spanish diplomats sponsored secret negotiations between Cuba and the United States that failed to achieve any results.[75]

Fidel Castro was less than candid when he claimed, in his interview with Ignacio Ramonet, that he maintained friendly relations with Franco at the same time that he remained closely connected with Spanish Communists such as La Pasionaria.[76] Castro did not mention that, in contrast to the Cuban press's pervading criticism of the Franco regime before the revolution, it maintained almost complete silence with respect to Spanish affairs throughout the sixties and seventies.[77] After Franco died in November 1975, the Cuban government observed all the official niceties required between two countries maintaining normal diplomatic relations. However, the Cuban media went beyond those diplomatic requirements and did not publish or transmit a critical word about the character of Franco's regime of almost four decades.[78] Castro's explanation of why Franco maintained such good relations with revolutionary Cuba reveals how right-wing nationalism can converge with Castro's nationalism. He said that Franco grew up in the Galician port of El Ferrol, the headquarters of the Spanish navy squadron that was annihilated by the US navy on the southeastern end of the island during the Spanish-Cuban-American War in 1898. According to Castro, the humiliation inflicted on the Spanish navy by the United States shaped Franco's critical attitude toward the American empire and its relations with Cuba. But Castro also suggested that there was a link between his worldview and Franco's: his admiration for the precapitalist values of chivalry and honor as he saw them in his father and his Spanish Jesuit high school teachers. This helps to explain why Castro officially honored the heroism of the Spanish sailors who suffered that 1898 defeat by the US navy in the bay of Santiago de Cuba.

Castro plays down the significant economic ties that Spain and Cuba maintained during the late Francoist period and suggests that by confronting and resisting the United States, the Cuban people "have reclaimed Spanish sentiment and honor. That historic almost sentimental factor must have influenced Franco's attitude. I don't believe in economic explanations, nor in explanations of any other type" (regarding Franco's attitude and behavior toward Cuba).[79] While it is true that the economic relations between Franco's Spain and Cuba were more important to the island republic than to the former "mother country," maintaining relations with Cuba was important to Franco not only to protect the substantial Spanish community on the island but to maintain a degree of autonomy from the United States. Moreover, there were powerful historic links between Spain and Cuba, as it and Puerto Rico were the last two Spanish colonies in the Western Hemisphere. Franco was interested in keeping Cuba within the Hispanic "family" of nations, where Spain tried to play a leading role, and preventing a repetition of the Mexican case—meaning Cuba breaking diplomatic relations with Franco's government and officially recognizing the Spanish Republican government in exile.[80]

After Franco's death, the relationship between Cuba and Spain continued to be very good under the Union of the Democratic Center (UCD) administrations from 1976 to 1982. Since then, the governments led by both the Socialist Party (PSOE) and the conservative Popular Party (PP) have maintained very active relations with the island, although there has generally been considerably more political and diplomatic conflict with the conservative governments particularly those under the leadership of José María Aznar. After the two "Brothers to the Rescue" planes piloted by Cuban Americans were downed by Cuban authorities in 1996, and the US Congress approved the Helms-Burton legislation tightening the economic blockade that was signed by President Bill Clinton, both the PP and the PSOE opposed the new law, as did the European Union as a whole.[81] This reaction was partly in protest against the extraterritorial features of the law, punishing European corporations investing in enterprises originally owned by Americans that had been nationalized by the Cuban government in the early sixties. While the US government tightened the economic blockade of the island, in December 1996 the European Union, with Spain playing a leading role in all matters related to Cuba, adopted the Common Position, the first article of which reads,

> The objective of the European Union in its relations with Cuba is to encourage a process of transition to pluralist democracy and respect for human rights and fundamental freedoms, as well as a sustainable recovery and improvement in the living standards of the Cuban people. A transition would most likely be peaceful if the present regime were itself to initiate or permit such a process. It is not European Union policy to try to bring about change by coercive measures with the effect of increasing the economic hardship of the Cuban people.[82]

The Cuban government objected to the Common Position as the interference of a group of foreign states in its internal affairs and pointed out that the European Union was using a double standard when dealing with other states accused of human rights violations such as Morocco, Israel, Guatemala, Turkey, and China.[83] The Cuban government also pointed to a number of related events that had preceded the adoption of the Common Position. Included among these was the May 1996 visit by US vice president Al Gore to Madrid, which led to an alliance with the Aznar government to develop a common policy on Cuba. At this time, Spain announced the termination of its humanitarian aid to the island, and the Hispano-Cuban Foundation (promoted by the right-wing Cuban American National Foundation) was established in Madrid.[84] Beyond the occasionally serious political and diplomatic frictions brought about by the Common Position, the merits of which continue to be debated in Spain and the rest of Europe to the present day, its principal economic effect has been to deny Cuba access to certain aid programs sponsored by the European Union. The key programs have been the Lomé Convention of the seventies and eighties addressing issues of commercial access, commodity export compensation, and financial aid and the subsequent Cotonou Agreement on development, economic, and trade cooperation adopted in 2000 (and revised in 2005 and 2010). It appears that Havana felt that the political price to be paid, including political commitments that Cuba would have to make in the area of human rights, was not worth the economic gains to be obtained by participating in cooperation aid programs.[85]

Relations with Latin America and the Caribbean

Cuba has removed its support of progressive and revolutionary movements in countries willing to suspend hostilities against it. Castro told a Brazilian publication in 1977 that "if a revolutionary movement emerges in a nation that has relations with Cuba and respects our sovereignty, in spite of our sympathy for that revolutionary movement, we will abstain from supporting it."[86] Perhaps the most extreme example of the application of this norm of Cuban foreign policy is the diplomatic and commercial relations it maintained with Argentina after the military coup of 1976 at the expense of the opposition movements in that country. Like the great majority of Latin American nationalists, right and left wing, Castro also supported Argentina against the United Kingdom in the Malvinas (Falklands) War of 1982.[87] In the case of El Salvador, in 1983 Castro declared he was ready to suspend his support for the FMLN (Frente Farabundo Martí de Liberación Nacional—Farabundo Martí Front for National Liberation) on the condition that the United States stop supporting the Salvadorean government. This proposal was consistent with Castro's view that it was necessary to stop the war in El Salvador to protect Cuba and Nicaragua from US attacks and with Castro's support for the ERP (Ejército Revolucionario del Pueblo), the FMLN faction led by Joaquín Villalobos, who advocated a war strategy leading to negotiations. Villalobos's strategy was opposed by the FPL (Fuerzas Populares de Liberación, Popular Forces for Liberation) led by Salvador Cayetano Carpio—Comandante Marcial—who argued for the perspective of a Maoist-type "prolonged popular war." Marcial was more independent from the Cuban government and refused to blindly follow the strategic and tactical orientations laid out by Fidel Castro. Villalobos, on the other hand, spent many hours face to face with Castro listening to his experiences, ideas, tactics, and views about the nature of revolutionary war. The fact that Villalobos shared responsibility for the murder of Salvadoran poet Roque Dalton did not diminish the Cuban leader's support for him, although Fidel Castro has since—and quite characteristically—claimed to have been unaware of his Salvadoran protégé's role in that murder. Soon afterward, Villalobos betrayed the rebels, signed a pact with ARENA (Alianza Republicana Nacionalista, Nationalist Republican Alliance), the Salvadoran right-wing party responsible for the death squads that murdered peasants and trade unionists. He later became an adviser to the Colombian government in its fight against the FARC (Fuerzas Armadas Revolucionarias de Colombia–Ejército del Pueblo, Revolutionary Armed Forces of Colombia–People's Army) guerrillas,[88] and more recently an adviser to the PAN (Partido Acción Nacional, National Action Party) conservative Mexican government.

The Cuban government has consistently opted for dividing and undermining movements not aligned with its policies and interests. This is why in 1966 Fidel Castro opposed the movement led by Yon Sosa in Guatemala and supported the movement led by Luis Turcios Lima.[89] This was also the reason why in the seventies, when Cuba resumed relations with the traditional Communist Parties that recognized the leadership of the Cuban government, Castro reestablished ties with the PCV (Partido Comunista Venezolano, Venezuelan Communist Party) and broke with the movement led by Douglas Bravo, which it had previously supported at the expense of the Venezuelan Communists.

In the seventies and eighties, Castro implemented an openly pragmatic policy of establishing ties with any Latin American or Caribbean country willing to have relations with Havana. This included a wide diversity of governments. Some may even have claimed to be revolutionary but in fact were either reformist or had not changed the status quo at all (Jamaica, Mexico, Panama, and Peru). Some were conventional regimes with no revolutionary pretensions (Barbados, Colombia, Guyana, Trinidad and Tobago, and Venezuela), and some were military regimes of a conservative and even repressive nature (Ecuador and Argentina).[90] Relations with countries such as Guyana presented a problem for the Cuban government when Forbes Burnham, who had been previously linked to Washington and the CIA, defeated the left-wing and longtime Cuban ally Chedi Jagan in the 1964 elections in that country. Eventually, Burnham began to make overtures to Cuba, to which Cuba responded with the establishment of very friendly—not just formal and diplomatically correct—relations. These relations were not regarded as totally acceptable by Caribbean progressive opinion because of the internal character of the Burnham regime.[91] Whatever damage to its prestige among Caribbean progressives the Cuban government suffered because of its relations with Burnham was more than compensated by the regard it garnered for its vigorous support for Maurice Bishop and the New Jewel movement in Grenada in the late seventies and early eighties. It is worth noting that the Cuban government refrained from any military actions that might have prevented the 1983 overthrow of Bishop, as it had done, as we saw above, on several occasions in Africa.[92] In overall terms, the Cuban government has tended, for long-standing cultural and political reasons, to pay relatively less attention to the non-Spanish-speaking Caribbean than to Latin America and Caribbean countries such as Puerto Rico and the Dominican Republic.[93] Cuba's support for Puerto Rican self-determination and independence has been long-standing and outspoken, and has been undoubtedly reinforced and perpetuated by the decades-old conflict between Havana and Washington. While it is true that as Rubén Berrios, the Puerto Rican social-democratic and proindependence leader, put it, support for Puerto Rican independence is "close to the heart" of the Cuban leadership,[94] it remains to be seen what will happen to that sentiment in the event of a future normalization of relations between Cuba and the United States.

The Cuban policy of broadening relations with Caribbean and Latin American governments became more viable after the OAS decided, in 1975, to lift its multilateral sanctions against Cuba and allow each of its member states to decide what relations they would have with the island. This was the beginning of a long process that culminated with the 2009 election of Mauricio Funes as the FMLN candidate in El Salvador. Shortly after, that country resumed diplomatic relations with Havana, as did Costa Rica in the same year. The United States was then left as the only government in the Western Hemisphere to not have reestablished diplomatic relations with Cuba. This can be seen in part as the success of the foreign policy that Cuba has followed during the last twenty years. After 1989, the collapse of the Soviet bloc and the Soviet Union, and the serious economic crisis that it provoked in Cuba reinforced the pragmatism of Cuba's foreign policy to such a degree that Fidel Castro closed the Department of the Americas led by Major "Redbeard" Piñeiro, who had directed Cuba's clandestine activities in the continent. Since then, the Cuban government has emphasized its opposition to American imperialism and neoliberalism more than to capitalism itself. In the case of Luiz Inácio Lula da Silva's neoliberalism in Brazil, and in spite of Fidel Castro's criticism of that country's ethanol policies, he and Raúl continued to support the Brazilian leader while ignoring the left-wing splits from Lula's party, the PT (Workers' Party). In his long interview with Ignacio Ramonet, Castro lavished all sorts of praise not only on Lula but also on conservative personalities such as Charles de Gaulle, King Juan Carlos of Spain, and Pope John Paul II.

The Cuban government's foreign policy, including its support or lack of support for causes abroad, has been a function of its perception and definition of what it needs for its own survival and what is in the best interests of the Cuban state. The Cuban leaders were also constrained by their unequal alliance with the Soviet Union, and while they certainly have a political ideology, they have worn it as a loose garment that allows plenty of room for maneuver needed in their foreign policy decisions. In that sense, Cuban foreign policy, to the considerable extent that it is based on considerations of realpolitik, bears a strong kinship with the foreign policy of Joseph Stalin and his successors. This has been particularly the case with the Cuban government's attitude toward friendly capitalist governments, and toward factions of revolutionary movements and Communist Parties favored by the Cuban leadership in their struggle with other factions. However, Cuba never attempted to reproduce the tightly disciplined international movement that the Comintern (later the Cominform, established in 1947) managed from Moscow.

Foreign Policy and National Independence

Cuba began to considerably reduce its "globalism" even before the collapse of the Soviet Union in 1991. Negotiations leading to the eventual withdrawal of Cuban troops from Angola had already begun to take place under Gorbachev in the late eighties. The collapse of the Soviet Union forced an even more drastic limitation of Cuban "globalist" politics. The severe economic crisis that the Soviet collapse brought about on the island made it impossible for Fidel Castro to continue playing the international role he had played in the past. Cuba's regular armed forces were reduced by more than 80 percent, from a total of some 297,000 as late as 1991 to some 55,000 in 2005.[95] Notwithstanding the Cuban government's implementation of the alternative strategy of "Guerra de Todo el Pueblo" (War of All the People) to defend the country against a potential foreign invasion, there is no doubt that Cuba's military capability has seriously deteriorated. This becomes even more evident when taking into account problems such as lack of preparedness and training due to shortages of fuel and spare parts for military equipment.

The severe reduction of Cuba's military capability is an example of what economists and other social scientists call a "natural experiment." It retrospectively demonstrates that this reduction has made virtually no difference in terms of US imperial aggression. This does not mean that the Cuban government could have reduced its armed forces to zero without any consequences for its survival from US hostility. However, it underlines the fact that Cuba's powerful armed forces had many purposes beyond the defense of the country against US aggression. It is true, however, that the principal but not exclusive goal of Cuban foreign policy was to ensure the country's independence and the regime's survival in the face of the long-standing and unremitting hostility of the American empire.

In light of this, what has the Cuban government accomplished in terms of national independence some two decades after the collapse of the Soviet empire? Is the Cuba of 2010 under less foreign control than it was before the victory of the revolution in 1959?

Although the Platt Amendment that legally subordinated Cuba to the United States in a quasi-colonial manner was formally abolished in 1934, this did not eliminate Cuba's political, economic, and military subordination to the United States. The new relationship, which lasted until 1959, was similar to the type of dependency that many ostensibly independent countries in Africa and Asia retained with their former colonial masters, a dependency that was deplored by third world nationalists as neocolonialism. However, for over three decades Cuba was as dependent on the Soviet Union in economic and political terms as it had previously been on the United States. Therefore, it could be argued that Fidel Castro had merely replaced one imperial master with another. But the nature of Cuba's relationship with the USSR differed from the relationship that the East European satellite states maintained with the Soviet colossus. With the exception of Yugoslavia and arguably Czechoslovakia, East European Communist Parties had come to power under the sponsorship of the Soviet Red Army. They remained in power as long as the Soviet Union was able and willing to protect them from their own populations and from the Western powers. That was not the case with Cuban Communism: it has survived for over two decades the collapse of the USSR and the Soviet bloc. Yet the Cuban leaders were not as independent from the USSR as they might have liked, and even less than they would have liked others to think. Because of its heavy subsidy, the Soviet Union was able to pressure Fidel Castro to change not only his foreign policy but also his internal economic policy. That was why from the early seventies until the mid-eighties Castro abandoned Guevaraist economic centralization and "moral" incentives for the Soviet model of "material" incentives and a greater degree of autonomy for enterprise administrations. However, he returned to some of the Guevaraist policies during his "rectification" campaign in the mid-eighties. The Soviet Union, fearful of the consequences of too open a challenge to American hegemony in the Western Hemisphere, was able to make Fidel Castro abandon his 1960s policy of open support for guerrilla warfare in Latin America. Cuba may not have been a USSR satellite in the manner of countries such as East Germany and Poland, but it was subordinate to the Soviet Union in some key respects. Nevertheless, Cuba's vigorous political and military activities abroad substantially helped to compensate for its dependence and subordination, particularly economic, to Moscow. Therefore, the claim that the Cuban leadership merely replaced Washington with Moscow as its imperial patron, beyond its mechanical character, is also inaccurate.[96]

In any case, the Cuban leaders had more independence from Moscow than the prerevolutionary governments had from Washington. The relationship that Cuba maintained with the Soviet Union for roughly three decades could be more accurately described as that of a junior partner than that of a satellite, and, as suggested by Piero Gleijeses, was analogous to the relationship that has existed between Israel and the United States.[97] But what allowed Cuba, a small and, unlike Israel, relatively poor and underdeveloped country, maintain its junior status vis-à-vis the Soviet Union instead of becoming a mere satellite? What leverage did Cuba have in this highly unequal relationship? First, as we indicated above, the Cuban leaders owed their power on the island to their own political efforts; they did not owe it to the Soviet Union. Also, their very existence and survival ninety miles from Florida as a thorn in the side of the United States was important to the USSR in the context of the Cold War. However, Castro's most important bargaining tool was his intervention abroad, which, in the jargon of international relations, has been labeled as truly "globalist."

It is evident that the collapse of the USSR and the Soviet bloc has significantly increased Cuba's exposure to and dependence on foreign capitalist investment and the capitalist world market. Cuba has increasingly been forced to rely on economic activities such as tourism and nickel extraction financed primarily by Spanish and Canadian capital and on a substantial trade with China. These, along with the export of professional services to Venezuela in exchange for oil, have become the basis of Cuba's economic survival, particularly in light of the severe reduction of sugar production and the crisis in food production and agriculture on the island. Besides the considerable growth of inequality that this new economic situation has generated, Cuba's heavy dependence on the world market and foreign investment seriously qualifies and limits its political independence.

National Independence and the Future Transition

The Cuban government's willingness to challenge the US empire in its own backyard brought down the wrath of Washington, which attempted by every means, including numerous assassination attempts and acts of terrorism, to overthrow the revolutionary government. The high points of these efforts included the failed April 1961 invasion, which was followed by a campaign of sabotage and assassinations, the so-called Operation Mongoose, which lasted until January 1963. By the mid-sixties, the CIA had begun to reduce the scope of hostilities against Cuba with the closure of Radio Americas on Swan Island (from which its broadcasts to Cuba were launched) and the shutting down of its Miami station, a process that was not completed until the early seventies.[98]

However, sabotage actions launched from the United States continued to take place sporadically in the seventies and eighties. For example, in February 1976 a Soviet freighter was attacked near Cuba, and two fishing boats were attacked in April. These incidents were followed by various other fatal attacks, most notably those aimed at the overseas facilities of Cuban airlines, culminating with a major disaster in Barbados. A Cuban plane carrying athletes and other civilian travelers, both Cuban and foreign, had just departed from that island when it was destroyed by a bomb, killing all seventy-three people aboard. It appears that while this was not explicitly a CIA operation, the agency was aware of its likelihood and did nothing to prevent it.[99] The Cuban right-wing campaign of violence launched from the United States continued in the eighties. Shortly before Reagan's electoral victory in 1980, the Miami-based group Omega 7 assassinated a member of the Cuban mission to the United Nations in New York. President Carter communicated his condemnation to the Cuban government and promised to prosecute the murderers.[100] Carter's pronouncements did not stop Alpha 66, another right-wing terrorist group, from publicly daring the US government to invoke the US Neutrality Act against them.[101] These acts of terrorism and sabotage continued even until the late nineties. In 1997, several bombings in Havana hotels resulted in the death of an Italian tourist, but by then it was clear that for some time the main focus of attention of the US government and the Cuban American right wing had moved to the political arena. The Cuban American National Foundation obtained far greater success in making life difficult for the Cuban government and people through the strengthening of the economic blockade than any act of sabotage and terrorism had ever achieved.

The passing from the scene of one or both Castro brothers is likely to renew the process of restoring economic and diplomatic relations between the United States and Cuba. Powerful agribusiness and shipping interests in the West, Midwest, and South of the United States, which have engaged in hundreds of millions of dollars of trade every year with Cuba under the 2001 "humanitarian" exceptions to the blockade, have long been pushing in that direction. Congressional Republicans and Democrats were close to approving legislation that would have weakened, if not eliminated, the blockade had it not been for George W. Bush's threats to veto such laws. Even though President Barack Obama won Florida in 2008 over the opposition of the Cuban hard right, he has acted cautiously in terms of eliminating the existing political and economic measures against Cuba. Meanwhile, what used to be the Cuban American right-wing monolith in south Florida has become somewhat divided. This fragmentation is likely to grow if a transitional regime after the Castro brothers were to welcome investments from Cuban American capitalists while still barring them from political power.

American liberals and some members of the US political establishment have often advocated negotiations with Cuba. They have argued that negotiations would lead to a modification or end of the American economic blockade on the pragmatic grounds that the Cuban leadership would have to reciprocate with concessions and adopt a less antagonistic stance toward the United States. An American initiative of this kind may or may not have such an outcome, depending on the other considerations that may affect Cuban and US foreign policy. For example, in November 1974, when the Cuban right wing in south Florida was still only a negligible political factor, Henry Kissinger, on behalf of the Ford administration, began secret negotiations with the Cuban government. As a result of these negotiations, Cuba extradited the hijacker of a US plane and returned the ransom it had seized in another hijacking. In August 1975, Washington softened the economic blockade by withdrawing the threat of withholding aid to countries whose ships carried goods to and from Cuba and by allowing the docking in the United States of ships of third countries trading with Cuba. It has been argued that Cuba's involvement in the war in Angola ended the secret talks, the process of détente, and the possibility of normalizing relations between the two countries in November 1975. There is some truth to that claim, as Fidel Castro later acknowledged that normalization of relations with the United States was not then a priority of Cuban foreign policy. As Julia E. Sweig has pointed out, Cuba's leaders had learned to live without the United States, were subsided by the Soviet Union, and had more to gain by involvement in Africa than by returning to a more docile relationship with the United States.[102] However, as we shall see below, there were important political forces and developments in US domestic and foreign policy that blocked such an important change as normalizing relations with Cuba.

Negotiations were resumed by the Carter administration in 1977. There were mutual concessions between the two countries that included the establishment of diplomatic "interest sections" in Washington and Havana and the lifting of the ban on tourist travel to the island. (The travel ban, lifted in 1977, was reinstated by the Reagan administration in 1982.) But Cuba's decision to send troops to Ethiopia and Washington's objections to the presence in Cuba of certain kinds of Soviet military equipment and personnel helped to bring this new détente to an end. Carter and Castro still managed to reach various agreements afterward. These covered smaller matters such as increased cooperation between the US Coast Guard and its Cuban equivalent, the Border Guard Troops, and the repatriation of US citizens living in Cuba. In late 1978, Fidel Castro released most political prisoners, and about one thousand of them left for the United States. In 1979, Cuban Americans were for the first time allowed to visit their relatives on the island, and large numbers of them did so.[103] Thus, the changes that took place in the mid- and late seventies in US-Cuban relations, while registering some improvements, were not dramatic and did not lead to a full normalization of diplomatic and economic relations between the two countries.

Meanwhile, political pressures in the United States began to grow against the normalization of relations with Cuba. Although several members of the Carter administration were in favor, Zbigniew Brzezinski, Carter's powerful national security adviser, opposed it.[104] The American right wing was becoming very agitated over the negotiations concerning the transfer of sovereignty over the Panama Canal. This had been an important issue in the 1976 elections, and the negotiations concluded in August 1977, leading to eventual Panamanian control of the canal. In September 1977 US negotiations with Cuba were suspended until after the Panama Canal treaties were ratified by the Senate. This suspension turned out to be indefinite.[105] Faced with an attack from the right on the issue of the Panama Canal treaties, the Carter administration decided to shore up its right flank by adopting a tougher posture on Cuba.[106]

By 1979, the international situation confronting Washington had changed in a way that strengthened the hand of the hard-liners who opposed a normalization of relations with Havana. The Carter administration had been weakened by the Iranian hostage crisis and the Soviet invasion of Afghanistan, while Fidel Castro had assumed the leadership of the nonaligned movement, more Cuban troops were moving into Africa, and the Sandinistas had ousted the Somoza regime in Nicaragua. This made it easier for Brzezinski and Robert Pastor, his deputy for Latin America, to lobby against any more "concessions" to Cuba. The resignation of "moderate" Secretary of States Cyrus Vance, who was supportive of a rapprochement with Cuba, helped to seal the fate of such initiatives.[107] In the eighties and nineties relations between Cuba and the United States worsened under both Republican and Democratic administrations. The collapse of the USSR and the Soviet bloc encouraged the notion in both Washington and Miami that the Cuban regime was in its last throes and that its death could be accelerated by a tightening of the economic blockade of the island. The combined impact of the Torricelli (1992) and Helms-Burton (1996) Acts greatly strengthened the economic blockade but failed to bring about the overthrow of the regime.

The fact that the negotiations approach did not work in the seventies does not mean it might not work under the vastly different circumstances of the early twenty-first century, since Cuba has become a far less important issue on the American foreign policy agenda after the collapse of the Soviet Union. However, apart from whatever pragmatic advantages negotiations may have, there is a principled democratic case to be made for ending the American blockade of Cuba. Simply put, the blockade should be unilaterally ended by the United States based on the old established political grounds that each nation has a right to determine its own destiny and that the United States has no right to impose any socioeconomic or political system on other countries. This principle does not depend on whether the Cuban regime is or is not worthy of support. That is something that the Cuban people should determine unencumbered by foreign pressures or demands. Ironically, the implementation of this principle would have an important practical consequence. It would undermine the principal anti-imperialist rationale for Cuba's undemocratic one-party state: the regime's argument that monolithic unity is necessary as a defense against foreign aggression. Yet Democrats and Republicans are highly unlikely to adopt such an approach for many reasons, including the corruption of American political culture under the impact of the United States' long imperial experience.

Beyond Cuba's increasing dependence on the world market, what is likely to remain of its past progress in limiting foreign control once both Castro brothers have left the scene and the country's new leaders possibly embark on the pursuit of a Sino-Vietnamese type route toward capitalism? The Soviet subsidies that allowed the Cuban government to maintain an austere standard of living covering the most basic needs of the population had the curious effect of allowing Fidel Castro and his close associates to pay less attention to economic development. Economic development has been a central feature of Communist ideology, particularly in its third world versions, in some countries constituting the raison d'être of its leaders and providing an ideological justification for their political power. Will there be a resurgence of Communist concern with economic development in Cuba once Fidel Castro has departed from the scene along with his spartan combination of militarism and constant preaching against the sins of the "consumer society"? This process has already begun to occur under the rule of Raúl Castro and is likely to accelerate even further after his death.

The ample history of Communist transitions to capitalism shows that it is highly unlikely that it will take even a relatively benign form in Cuba. Those transitions have been characterized by "shock therapies," including sharp reductions of "welfare state" protections and spending enforced by dictatorial rule. In Cuba this may take place in the openly despotic Chinese form or in the cosmetically disguised Russian style. (These two countries share with Cuba the important fact that their Communism originated in homegrown revolutionary upheavals.) In the case of Cuba, which does not have the economic resources and potential of China or even Vietnam, such a neoliberal course is likely to be accompanied by growing US control over the economic affairs of the island, with International Monetary Fund–style structural adjustment, privatization, and austerity policies. However, this does not necessarily mean that the United States will reassert itself politically in pre-1959 neocolonial fashion. In fact, it is likely that under this scenario the US government might provide some political concessions to the future Cuban dictators such as returning the Guantánamo Naval Base to Cuba, particularly if an army-led Cuban government reassures the United States that it can deliver law and order on the island.[108] This base lost its military strategic value a long time ago, and President Obama promised that its use as a prison camp for the so-called war on terrorism detainees would come to an end, although it is not clear if and when that will come to pass. Such types of political concessions might provide a convenient cover for making Cuba safe for capitalism through radical changes regarding property, social welfare, labor, and overall macroeconomic policies. At the same time, superfluous political provocations that could ignite a nationalist response would be minimized, if not avoided. Whether this is a likely scenario or not, the degree to which Cuba's reduction of foreign control is permanent will be known only after a post-Castro transition has taken place.

Chapter Four

Cuban Workers after the 1959 Revolution— Ruling Class or Exploited Class?

Cuban Workers before the Revolution

At the time of the victory of the revolution, the Cuban working class, whether urban or rural, was not socialist in any meaningful sense of the term, nor did it lend its own distinctive character to the Cuban Revolution led by Fidel Castro. Although it is true that at least beginning in 1956 most workers had become hostile to the Batista dictatorship and sympathized with the Castro-led revolution, their opposition was not expressed in active, organized class terms. As Castro himself pointed out in his unusually frank speech of July 26, 1970, "In 1959 the majority of our people weren't even anti-imperialists. There was no class consciousness. Only class instinct, which isn't the same."[1] The following year Castro elaborated on this theme before the leaders of the Chilean labor movement: "At the triumph of the revolution, from the point of view of leadership and cadres, we couldn't count on a tried, awakened workers' movement. We didn't have one ... We counted on the support of the workers and farmers—a very broad base— but we didn't have what could be described as a tried, organized, and awakened workers' movement. That's the way things were."[2]

The origin of the Cuban working class goes back to the nineteenth century and particularly to the first two decades of the twentieth century. Sugar monoculture originated in the 1790s, but the entry of US capital at the end of the nineteenth century and especially after the Cuban Republic was officially established in 1902 marked a qualitative new stage in the island's economy and polity. The Platt Amendment to the 1901 Cuban Constitution guaranteeing US control over Cuban affairs greatly facilitated the huge economic expansion of the period 1900–25. Besides introducing an uneven development into the Cuban economy, with sharp differences between urban and rural Cuba, the economic boom of the early twentieth century signified the integration of the Cuban economy into the US economy. From a Cuban perspective, this was not just capitalism but also imperialism.

By the early 1950s Cuba had been substantially urbanized. The census of 1953 counted 5.8 million people on the island, with 57 percent urban and 43 percent rural. The US Department of Commerce, basing itself on the figures provided by the same census, classified 22.7 percent of the Cuban labor force under the category of craftsmen, foremen, operatives, and kindred workers, 7.2 percent as clerical and kindred workers, and 6.2 percent as sales workers. Service workers, except private household, constituted 4.2 percent and private household workers 4.0 percent of the labor force. These categories could be considered a rough approximation of the urban working class, for a total of 44.3 percent of the labor force. Farm laborers (including unpaid family workers) constituted 28.8 percent of the labor force, which could be seen as a rough approximation of the rural working class. This class grouping was more than twice the size of the 11.3 percent of the labor force that was classified as farmers and ranchers. Of course, a large proportion of the farmers and ranchers were quite poor, and there was a great deal of movement between the two rural class groupings,[3] as well as significant migration from the rural to the urban areas.

The "class instinct" that Fidel Castro referred to in his 1971 speech developed as a result of a history of nonsocialist but militant struggles of a trade-union character. The pattern of struggle of the prerevolutionary Cuban working class could be described as "trench class warfare": constant efforts to push back whatever advances the enemy would make, with some success in making inroads into enemy territory. However, it had no strategy, even on a theoretical level, for taking state power and reshaping society. Its ideology was one of neither social revolution nor business unionism. It rather followed the path of militant reformism, particularly in the forties and early fifties, and was shaped by a long line of historical events and ideological influences. In the nineteenth century, Cuban workers, particularly in the tobacco industry, had created labor unions and other working-class organizations under the influence of the Spanish anarchist movement. By the late twenties, the Cuban Communist Party (founded in 1925), a part of the Communist International that was increasingly coming under the control of Stalin, grew in influence and replaced anarchism as the principal radical ideology in the labor movement. Cuban Communist influence in the labor movement ascended during the Depression years, notwithstanding its ultra-left and sectarian Third Period, which lasted from 1928 to 1934. The peak of Communist influence in the Cuban labor movement began in 1938. At that time its opportunistic Popular Front policy made it possible for the party to make a deal with Batista (during his first period in power that ended in 1944), exchanging political support for the general for control of the labor movement. Once the Cold War began, however, the liberal populist but corrupt Cuban governments that succeeded Batista acceded to US pressures and purged most Communist leaders from the unions.

Thus, after 1947, the mostly corrupt American-type business unionism, which also had long-standing roots in the Cuban working class, acquired renewed but not entirely unchallenged influence over Cuban unions. As a result, the Communist Party's strength in the Cuban labor movement declined sharply after 1947. A 1956 survey conducted by the Popular Socialist Party (PSP), the name adopted by the Communists at the time of the Soviet alliance with the United States during the Second World War, indicated that only 15 percent of the country's two thousand local unions were led by Communists or by union leaders who supported collaboration with the PSP.[4] However, even at the height of its influence, the Communist Party was in close competition with various "populist" parties. "Pro-Communist" workers would often support Communist trade-union leaders but ended up voting for one of the various "populist" parties. The "pro-Communist" inclination of many workers was a result not of Communist political education but of the respect they felt for Communist leaders, who were seen as personally honest and dedicated, an important trait in what was a very corrupt political system. However, this personal respect was often tinged with nationalist political suspicion of Communist loyalty to a foreign power.

There was a substantial difference between the kind of influence the Communists had in the early revolutionary 1930s, when politics and trade unionism were closely tied together, and after 1938, when the party veered toward open reformism. Moreover, during the Soviet alliance with the United States during the Second World War, Communist policy clearly became class collaborationist. Communists' control of the labor movement gave them power and influence in the working class. However, only a small number of workers who were active Communist Party members, and not simply members of Communist-led unions or registered Communist in the official electoral lists, were actually educated or indoctrinated in hard Communist politics.

The initial reaction of the working class to the military coup that brought Batista back to power in 1952 was no different from that of the rest of Cuban society. Mostly everyone reacted with surprise first and then apathy. Only the student movement and a few political activists reacted in a militant manner. As time went by, however, anger and indignation against the government increased among the majority of the Cuban people, although "middle-class" elements and organizations played a more vocal and leading role than workers in expressing it. Cuban workers were under a double dictatorship: that of Batista in the country as a whole, and that of Eusebio Mujal—the top union leader acting as Batista's agent—in the trade unions. As a result, workers had no readily available organizations through which they could articulate their discontent. As oppressed individuals, increasingly hostile to Batista, they were unable to consistently respond as a class, that is, through a trade union or any other form of class organization. To have done so, they would have had to develop a clandestine union or shop-floor structure in opposition to both the dictatorship and its trade-union collaborators, a task in which they only attained a limited degree of success during the last two years of the Batista dictatorship.

Instead of addressing the concrete organizational and political factors that helped to demobilize workers, Fidelista leftists like Régis Debray attributed the inability of the working-class movement to play a central role in the struggle against Batista to a supposed bourgeoisification of the workers by the city.[5] Perhaps a Gallic penchant for excessive abstraction permitted Debray to propose such an interpretation without the slightest effort to address the concrete working and living conditions of the Cuban urban working class during that period. Nevertheless, a remarkably similar analysis was put forward by the liberal American historian Theodore Draper. Without paying much greater attention than Debray to the actual conditions of the urban working class, Draper attributed the lackluster role played by Cuban workers to their having become a relatively privileged class in the prerevolutionary period.[6]

It is true that on coming to power in 1952, Batista immediately made a deal with the corrupt top union bureaucracy to not pursue an aggressive policy against the unions, the membership of which included then about one-half of the approximately two-million-strong Cuban working class. Instead, Batista opted for a strategy of gradually but steadily eroding working-class gains. Strikes, including two failed political general strikes in 1957 and 1958, and other forms of independent working-class activity were repressed, so the workers lost substantial ground during the seven-year-long dictatorship. Their losses along with their political disgust with the regime's brutality and corruption produced a great deal of animosity against the regime among workers, just as it did with the rest of the population.

Cuban Workers after the Victory of the Revolution

The general strike that took place immediately after Batista fled the country in the early hours of January 1, 1959, was not a class but a national action called by Fidel Castro and the 26th of July Movement. Practically the whole population supported the strike, including the Cuban bourgeoisie and the middle classes, which were still enjoying their "honeymoon" with the revolutionary leaders. The January 1959 strike was the rebels' insurance policy against any possible coup aimed at preventing them from achieving a total victory. The strike became a national holiday when for a whole week tens of thousands of people lined up to greet Castro and the rebel army in their slow procession from the east of the island toward Havana.

Soon after, a huge wave of labor conflicts and strikes erupted throughout the country, expressing the pent-up economic and political frustrations of the Cuban working class during the Batista years, as well as the great expectations aroused by the revolution. Among many labor conflicts, there were work stoppages in twenty-one sugar mills due to wage demands. Unemployed railway workers and workers who had lost their jobs at a closed paper mill near Havana went on a hunger strike. Employees of the Compañía Cubana de Electricidad, the US-owned national electrical utility, declared a slowdown to demand a 20 percent increase in wages, and six hundred workers who had been dismissed by the company in the previous two years demonstrated at the Presidential Palace to demand their reinstatement.[7] Fidel Castro and the revolutionary government tried to solve the myriad labor problems that confronted them during this early period with a clear and strong tilt in favor of the workers. Measures such as substantial reduction in urban rents decreed in March 1959 contributed to the development of the distributive radicalism that characterized the early period of the revolution. Castro, like any other intelligent observer, must have been aware that such radicalism was the keystone for growing mass support for the revolutionary government. On various occasions, as I indicated in chapter 1, he expressed his concern with the type of consciousness prevailing among the working class. Perhaps anticipating rougher times ahead, Castro tried to "educate" the masses to trust and rely on the regime rather than simply supporting a government that was delivering the goods.

Castro's government, very much afraid of losing control of the working class, let alone afraid of economic instability, tried to discourage strikes. The government convinced the new revolutionary union movement led by David Salvador, a former Communist who had become a 26th of July Movement leader in the clandestine struggle against Batista, to go along with its efforts in this direction. For their part, the Communists still had an arms-length relationship with the government and tried to push it in a more radical direction. While the PSP voluntarily avoided calling for or encouraging strikes even in the earliest days of the revolution, the party took the position that "strikes, when they are necessary and just, help rather than harm the Revolution."[8] The friction between Fidel Castro and the PSP increased when several Communists reportedly encouraged a few instances of "spontaneous" land seizures. In response, Castro made clear in a televised interview on February 19, 1959, that any persons involved in seizing land without waiting for the Agrarian Reform Law would be engaging in criminal conduct and lose their right to any benefits from the law.[9] Three days later the Communists retreated and agreed "that it was necessary to put a stop to the anarchic seizures of land."[10]

Shortly after Batista fled the country, union halls throughout the island were occupied by revolutionary trade unionists of various stripes, with those associated with the 26th of July Movement most numerous and influential. These new leaders quickly proceeded to purge all the supporters of Eusebio Mujal—the "Mujalista" labor bureaucrats who had collaborated with the Batista dictatorship. A vigorous organizing campaign was quickly launched that greatly enlarged the already sizable, although bureaucratic and corrupt, union movement. In the spring, every single local union in the country held elections, and these were followed by elections at the regional and national level. This turned out to be the most important exercise in autonomous grassroots democracy during the revolutionary period. The

candidates associated with the 26th of July Movement emerged as the overwhelming winners, and the Communists managed to obtain only some 10 percent of the
union posts (some of the elected 26th of July Movement candidates did have
Communist sympathies). In any case, the outcomes of the spring union elections
were remarkably consistent with the results of the union survey the PSP had conducted in 1956.

The election results prodded the Communists into putting a great deal of
effort to increasing their influence in the organized working class, which, as one
might expect, provoked a great deal of conflict with their political opponents inside the unions. Nevertheless, the elections of delegates in early November for
the Tenth Congress of the CTC (Confederación de Trabajadores de Cuba, Confederation of Cuban Workers) that was to take place later that month produced
results very similar to those of the spring elections. Once the congress began, it
was clear that the Communist delegation would take a drubbing and would be
excluded from the leadership bodies of the labor confederation. At this point,
Fidel Castro intervened and a different leadership slate was approved. While
well-known Communist unionists were kept off the slate, the so-called unitarian
elements of the 26th of July Movement, who were friendly to the Communists
and were led by Jesús Soto were given a predominant and controlling role.

After the congress concluded, the Labor Ministry, under Fidel Castro's
control, assisted by the Communist union leaders and the "unitarian" elements
friendly to them, began to purge a large number of trade union leaders who
had resisted Communist influence, accusing them of being "Mujalistas."[11] The
purge took place by means of purge commissions and carefully staged and controlled union meetings instead of new elections. About 50 percent of the labor
leaders, most of whom belonged to the 26th of July Movement and had been
freely elected in the spring 1959 local and national union elections, were removed; many were persecuted and jailed as well. Veteran PSP cadres and their
"unitarian" collaborators took over those leadership positions. Castro and his
revolutionary government enjoyed such great support in 1959 and 1960 that
any labor leader they chose could have easily been removed from office had
there been new elections; any slate of candidates supported by Castro and his
government would undoubtedly have won.[12] However, from the Cuban leader's
long-term perspective, new elections would have allowed the unions to retain
their autonomy. The purges allowed the unions to be turned into his policy
tools at a point when he had begun to move politically toward the Soviet Union
and the Cuban Communists.

In August 1961, less than two years after the fateful Tenth Congress of the
CTC, the government approved new legislation that brought the nature and function of Cuban trade unions into alignment with those of the Soviet bloc. According to the new law, the main objectives of the unions were to help in the
attainment of the national production and development plans; to promote effi-

ciency and expansion of social and public services; to improve the administration of all sectors of the economy; and to carry out political education.[13] A few years later, a CTC Declaration of Principles and Union Statutes further elaborated on the role and duties of the Cuban unions as the government's agents to impose production discipline. The unions had to organize socialist emulation and unpaid labor; strictly apply labor legislation, work quotas, wage scales, and labor discipline; promote an increase of output; improve the quality of production; reduce costs and maintain equipment; develop political consciousness; and expand recreational, sports, and cultural facilities.[14] Eventually, the unions were reorganized into fewer national unions such that all workers in a given industry, regardless of their job description, belonged to the same industrial unions. Membership in the unions was supposedly "voluntary," a convenient fiction accepted by some foreign observers who somehow failed to notice and acknowledge the enormous coercive pressures to join the "mass organizations" of a one-party state.[15]

The Eleventh CTC Congress, which took place in November 1961, could not have been more different from the congress two years earlier. Unanimity had now replaced controversy. With no contest allowed for the leading positions at stake, all leaders were elected by acclamation. Not surprisingly, old Stalinist leader Lázaro Peña regained the position of secretary general that he had last held in the forties under Batista. Of the seventeen national union leaders in 1959, only five remained in the twelve-member leadership group "elected" at the conclusion of the congress. In order to save production costs, the Eleventh Congress also agreed to give up gains that many unions had won before the revolution. It approved the eight-hour day, thereby adding work time to those union members who had already gained the seven-hour day. The nine days of sick pay, previously paid automatically, would be paid only to those who could prove that they were actually sick. The extra month's pay as an end-of-the-year bonus was abolished. Although an abstract case could be made for the desirability of at least some of these changes in a new socialist order, here they were imposed from above with little or no discussion. There was no open confrontation with the opposing views actually held by a large number of Cuban workers, who could not openly express them, nor organize in support of what they thought. Undoubtedly, the benefits that the workers had otherwise obtained from the revolution along with the then-prevailing revolutionary fervor in the country greatly facilitated the government's ability to establish its vision of the role of workers and unions under its version of socialism.

Even the dramatic change of leadership carried out at the 1961 congress did not put an end to the process of erasing all remaining traces of independent unionism. By the end of the Twelfth CTC Congress in 1966, only one of the members of the 1961 national committee remained. Of the twenty-five other heads of labor federations in 1961, only one remained in office by 1966. After 1961, several top leaders of the CTC had been removed and others appointed by the party's political bureau, not by the CTC itself,[16] without even the slightest regard for formality and appearances. In any case, the radical change in leadership personnel within such a short period of time was a faithful reflection of the no less drastic change that had taken place in the nature and function of the Cuban unions. In fact, the revolutionary leaders were politically quite upfront about the changes that they had established in the unions. Vice Premier Raúl Castro declared that "yesterday it was necessary [for unions] to struggle continuously in order to gain certain advantages, to obtain a little more from the profits being made by the magnates. Today the great task confronting the CTC and the unions is to increase production, recruit voluntary workers, tighten labor discipline, push for higher productivity, and improve the quality of what is produced."[17] In what amounted to a veritable "educational" campaign, similar pronouncements were continually being made throughout the early sixties by "new" Communist leaders such as Fidel Castro as well as by the members of the Communist "old guard" such as Blas Roca.[18]

As one might expect, the character of collective bargaining itself also changed. The Ministry of Labor published a model collective-bargaining agreement in 1962 with instructions on how to implement it throughout the various sectors of the economy. This model agreement followed closely the Soviet regulations on collective bargaining published in 1947.[19] Regarding the right to strike, during the first five years after the victory of the revolution in 1959, various laws were enacted to regulate labor conflicts. The Ley de Justicia Laboral (Law of Labor Justice), enacted in 1964 and put into effect at the beginning of 1965,[20] did not mention strikes, following the Stalinist theory that since the workers were the owners of the means of production they could not strike against themselves. In fact, the right to strike had been explicitly mentioned only in the regulations that were in force until 1960. In June 1961, Ernesto "Che" Guevara had put forward the notion that "the Cuban workers have to get used to living in a collectivist regime and therefore cannot strike."[21] Therefore, it was hardly surprising that the 1964 law did not mention strikes and neither did the "socialist" 1976 constitution, even though the progressive prerevolutionary constitution of 1940 had explicitly declared the constitutional standing of the right to strike in its article 71.

Indeed, the main overall purpose of the 1964 law was to strengthen labor discipline and increase productivity. The law singled out for punishment not only those workers who committed economic crimes like fraud but also those who displayed signs of laziness, vagrancy, absenteeism, tardiness, foot-dragging, or lack of respect for superiors, and who damaged equipment. The law paired violations with three grades of punishment: light, moderate, and serious penalties. Light penalties ranged from a simple warning to a small wage cut. Moderate punishment included a major wage cut or transfer to a different job in the same work location. Serious penalties ranged from transfer to a different location, which could be far from family members, to loss of employment.[22] In mid-1969, a little over ten years after the victory of the revolution, the minister of labor announced that the government was preparing regulations for the "labor file" or identity card carried by every Cuban worker. The official unions did not discuss the original draft; they were eventually given some input into how the regulations were to be administered after they became law in September 1969. The labor file, or the "workers' biography," as the minister of labor called it, would include the workers' merits, such as, for example, overfulfillment of work quotas or overtime work without pay, as well as demerits such as absenteeism, negligence in handling equipment, and nonfulfillment of work quotas. The "labor file" would also record any sanction or punishment applied to the worker by any of the relevant disciplinary bodies and courts.[23]

Notwithstanding all the mechanisms of control that were introduced in the sixties to make Cuban workers more productive, the government did not feel they were effective enough. For one thing, absenteeism grew throughout the late sixties and reached some 20 percent of the labor force by late 1970. On October 15, 1970, Minister of Labor Jorge Risquet, who had been politically formed in the ranks of the old Communist Party, proposed resolution number 425, which in effect was a vagrancy or antiloafing law that called for the placement of nonproductive workers in labor camps. From the government's point of view, this was preferable to imprisonment since the labor camps would achieve the double purpose of contributing to production and simultaneously segregating "lazy" people and preventing them from influencing other workers. Before becoming law, the proposal was presented for public discussion, supposedly to obtain the workers' opinions but in reality to engage in a one-sided government media campaign in support of the objectives and procedures of the proposed law. The campaign succeeded in incorporating some 100,000 men into production, which was after all one of the central objectives of the proposed legislation. Finally, on March 15, 1971, the government enacted the Law against Laziness. According to this law, all men between the ages of seventeen and sixty had to put in a full workday. Anyone who missed or left work for fifteen days or more without justification or who had been reprimanded by his work council at least twice would be classified as being in a "precriminal state of loafing," while recurrent absentees would be charged with the "crime of loafing." Sanctions ranged from house arrest to internment in a rehabilitation center doing forced labor for a period ranging from one to two years. The law also lengthened the incarceration period and even authorized the use of capital punishment for serious crimes such as "economic sabotage." In all cases, the courts were to consider such factors as age, the record of labor and social activities of the accused, and the personal and family factors that may have affected the behavior of the guilty party.[24] We do not know the extent to which the law was implemented in practice.

At the time, it was noted that the law against absenteeism and "loafers" had actually been in the works for a considerable amount of time before it was proposed in late 1970 and enacted into law in the spring of 1971. The preamble to the law had actually been written as early as 1968, but the law had not been decreed then because government leaders thought that certain prerequisites had to be fulfilled before it could be effectively implemented. According to the Cuban minister of labor, these prerequisites included (1) the total eradication of the private sector, excepting small farms, making it impossible to hide the person's employment status, (2) creation of personnel records for every worker, which were inaugurated in 1969, and (3) a census of the population in order to have exact information on manpower by region, zone, and street block.[25]

Seesaws in Economic and Labor Policy

The Cuban regime, like those that have ruled over other Soviet-type systems in Eastern Europe and Asia, has been trapped within the contradictions peculiar to its own mode of production and class rule that I discussed in earlier chapters. Since no particular set of policies has been able to resolve those basic contradictions, a regime has shifted among alternative approaches in its economic policies. These included shifts from economic centralization to decentralization, and from a partial utilization of market mechanisms—well short of a full market economy—to a repudiation of such mechanisms. The government has similarly shifted in its labor policies. From 1963 to 1965, the revolutionary leaders put into effect a Soviet-influenced system of wage scales, work quotas, labor norms, and output standards.[26] Then, in the second half of the sixties, the government allowed the unions to decline and tried to improve production through the creation and encouragement of "vanguard workers." In addition, as we shall see later in this chapter, the regime would at various times change its emphasis from so-called moral to material incentives and back again to the former.

Alternating between the "Soft" Line and the "Hard" Line

The regime's effort to tighten the screws on the working class through such measures as the creation of the labor file in 1969 and the Law against Vagrancy in 1971 was not the only posture that the government adopted toward the Cuban people in connection with their work duties. While preparing for the campaign against vagrancy and loafing, the regime became aware of the danger of completely alienating the working class, something that would have sapped its legitimacy and undermined the degree of consent necessary for the hegemony of any relatively stable modern ruling class. On August 1, 1970, Minister of Labor Risquet starkly presented one horn of the dilemma confronting the regime:

> Theoretically, the administrator represents the interest of the worker and peasant state, the interest of all the people. Theory is one thing and practice another . . . The worker may have a right established by the Revolution [that

is not respected or a complaint against the administration] and there is no one to defend him. He does not know where to turn. He turns to the party and it does not know [about the worker's right] or it is busy mobilizing people for production . . . the party is so involved with the management that in many instances it has ceased to play its proper role, has become somewhat insensitive to the problems of the masses . . . If the party and the administration are one, there is nowhere the worker can take his problem . . . The trade union either does not exist or it has become the vanguard workers' bureau.[27]

In the subsequent months, however, Risquet apparently feared that workers might take too seriously the government's new move to revitalize the trade unions and provide them with too effective a means to defend themselves from bureaucratic abuse. Faced with this new potential problem, the minister of labor presented the other horn of the dilemma confronting a regime that would not compromise its power in the face of a possibly growing workers' autonomy:

> The fact that Fidel and I have suggested that the workers should be consulted does not mean that we are going to negate the vanguard role that the Party must play . . . [There should not be] expectations or hope for magic solutions.[28]
>
> The decision and responsibility [in the enterprise] fall to the management, whose job is to take the daily necessary measures required by the process of production . . . One thing that is perfectly clear is that the management should have—and does have—all the authority to act. It is charged with a responsibility and it has the authority to make decisions.[29]

The "Democratization" of the Unions

In 1970, one year after having introduced the "labor file" and while preparations were being made to implement the law against vagrancy and loafing, the regime, following its characteristic seesaw between "harder" and "softer" lines, called for a democratization of the unions. However, this was not going to be the kind of union democracy that existed in 1959, when political and ideological currents confronted each other and strongly competed for union office from the lowest local level to the highest positions in the CTC. This time, "democratization" was limited to the opening of the lower levels of union officialdom to relatively free and competitive elections.[30] However, as was later the case with the so-called Popular Power elections, the union electoral procedures prohibited candidates from campaigning or advertising their candidacy, which precluded any 1959-style political and ideological debate. An electoral commission was authorized only to publicize the candidates' past "merits" on bulletin boards and murals. Notwithstanding its apparent willingness to allow for a substantial turnover of the lower union officialdom, the government continued to use both pressure and manipulation throughout the electoral process. When some union members complained about the continued use of the methods of the sixties, the minister of labor responded that the critics were "counterrevolutionaries" and "demagogues."[31] Even so, the elections, conducted by secret ballot instead of acclamation, resulted in a wholesale rejection of the officeholders; only 27 percent were reelected. This electoral practice continued for several years, and in 1978, for example, 54 percent of local trade union leaders were newly elected.[32]

It was clear that the government intended to use this new form of union elections as a mechanism for the workers to "let off steam" by allowing them to kick out low-level union leaders. Still, the union would have to support the policies of the national union and political leadership of the country. Fidel Castro dispelled any doubt about this being the purpose of the elections when he declared that "the [elected official] will have the moral authority of this election, and when the Revolution establishes a line, he will go out to defend and fight for that line."[33] It was also quite evident that the party was continuing to direct the unions. In 1973, Raúl Castro justified why this had to be so: "It is necessary to keep in mind that the working class considered as a whole . . . cannot exercise its own dictatorship . . . Originating in bourgeois society, the working class is marked by flaws and vices from the past. The working class is heterogeneous in its consciousness and social behavior . . . Only through a political party that brings together its conscious minority can the working class . . . construct a socialist society."[34]

The "democratization" of the seventies did not even imply that the unions had the power to interfere with the government's control of the economy, including such matters as establishing the nature of the economic plan, the wage fund, and personnel policies.[35] Workers and union leaders alike were very clear about the function that the unions had acquired. In a study conducted in 1975, most rank-and-file workers and union leaders defined production as the most important task of the unions. Only two of the fifty-seven who were interviewed mentioned the defense of worker interests as the primary function of the unions; eight mentioned both increasing production and defending workers.[36]

Nonunion Labor Bodies: Technical Advisory Councils, Grievance Commissions, and Labor Councils

The same shift between more "democratic," softer policies and harsher policies took place in nonunion labor bodies that were nevertheless attempting to address various labor problems confronting the regime. Such were the cases of first the Technical Advisory Councils and the Grievance Commissions and later the Labor Councils. Early on, in 1960, the Castro government established technical advisory councils in nationalized enterprises, allegedly to encourage worker participation in management. However, these councils pursued, at best, only educational goals, since they never had any collective decision-making power. In fact, Ernesto "Che" Guevara stressed their educational character when he proclaimed his hope that the councils would make it possible for the workers to understand that they had to "sacrifice an easy demand today to achieve a greater and more solid progress in the future."[37] Decision making was a power that the revolutionary leaders had made the exclusive prerogative of the management appointed by the central government. Thus, Guevara also described the structure of power and authority as "collective discussions, one-man decision-making and responsibility."[38] When the councils were abolished in 1962, Guevara further explained that the councils had constituted a first effort to "establish meaningful links between workers and plant management. At that time, we manifested great prejudices about the ability of the working class to elect their membership adequately . . . Mass participation in the elections was poor. The elections were bureaucratic."[39]

Shortly after the Technical Advisory Councils were created, the tremendous power that the state had acquired over the whole economy confronted it with the far-from-simple need to design mechanisms to address the inevitable workers' complaints in every workplace. Initially, these complaints were handled at the lowest workplace level by Grievance Commissions (Comisiones de Reclamaciones), which existed from 1961 to 1964. These commissions were elected jointly by the workers, local management, and the Ministry of Labor, although the ministry exclusively maintained the right to issue a final decision on any labor dispute.[40] Nevertheless, it seems that some Grievance Commissions turned out to be too lenient from the government's point of view, as they often took the side of the workers against management. This led the Minister of Industries Guevara to complain that "the grievance commissions are a barrier creating contradictions . . . [they] will be able to accomplish a very useful task only provided that they change their attitude. Production is the fundamental task."[41]

The "soft" Grievance Commissions were abolished by the earlier mentioned Law of Labor Justice (Ley de Justicia Laboral), which went into effect on January 1, 1965, and, as we already saw, tried to implement a "harder" line toward the workers. The new legislation replaced the Grievance Commissions with Labor Councils (Consejos de Trabajo) established in all work centers and consisting of five members elected by the workers, provided that those elected were "disciplined" people, had a "socialist attitude toward work," and had no record of absenteeism. Above the local councils, the law established two higher bodies that heard cases on appeal. The members of these bodies were not directly elected by the workers but appointed by the Ministry of Labor, state managers, and the unions; the representatives of the first two bodies constituted the majority in the appeal boards. The law permitted managers in the workplaces to impose punishments directly. These included wage deductions, postponement of vacations, transfers, and temporary discharge. In exceptional cases, a workplace manager could terminally fire a worker without any rights of appeal. The law also empowered the Ministry of Labor to dismiss and change members, annul a council decision, or recall a case heard by a council and to make a final decision without any further right to appeal.[42]

The councils declined during the late sixties and early seventies, but they underwent a rebirth toward the end of the seventies, with the number of cases adjudicated nearly doubling in comparison with the early seventies. The introduction of Soviet methods of enterprise self-financing, reinforcement of material incentives, and revitalization of the unions in the seventies brought about a substantial increase in worker grievances. Although the government placed the councils under CTC jurisdiction in the late seventies, lack of discipline and low productivity continued to plague the Cuban economy.[43] In the face of the systemic crises and insoluble contradictions that continued to affect the Cuban economy, the "harder" line established in 1965 came to be considered "soft," and the government once again called for a new "hard" line. In 1979, one of the worst economic years before the collapse of the Soviet Union in the early nineties, Fidel Castro told the National Assembly: "Today our labor laws are actually protecting delinquency . . . the lazy, absentee worker . . . not the good worker."[44]

In 1980, not too long after Castro's speech, the government took away from the Labor Councils the power to adjudicate cases of labor discipline, arguing that they were not efficient in resolving disputes and that they had failed to improve discipline and productivity. The government introduced decree number 32 giving management full power to enforce labor discipline, including the authority to fire workers. Workers could appeal managerial decisions in the municipal courts. At the same time, the government issued decree number 36 to regulate management, although managers were subject to discipline by their ministries and not by the workers. In light of the power that management had acquired, which it used in excess, the unions were given ability to implement some corrective measures. The management excesses that resulted from the implementation of decree number 32 were thus curbed somewhat, and the unions were able to obtain compensation out of enterprise funds for workers who had been unjustly punished. The suggestion by several worker assemblies that compensation for workers in such situations be taken out of manager salaries was, unsurprisingly, rejected. Cuban workers continued to be dissatisfied with the government's relatively lenient attitude toward managers, a sentiment that was even noted by the CTC congress of 1984.[45]

The ups and downs of both the Grievance Commissions and the Labor Councils demonstrated the futility of the Cuban government's perennial attempts, like those of Soviet-type governments in Eastern Europe and Asia, to "square the circle" of its own contradictions. As one might expect, the periodically shifting institutional arrangements and policies could not but fail to address the fundamental contradictions of the system. The removal of the fear of unemployment (fired workers were usually offered jobs in another workplace), the dearth of consumer goods, the low hopes of economic improvement whether through individual or collective means, and the lack of economic or political control over their lives left Cuban workers with little motivation to work steadily, hard, or well.

Workers' Motivation—Material and Nonmaterial (Moral) Incentives

In 1951, less than a decade before the victory of the Cuban Revolution, the International Bank for Reconstruction and Development (IBRD, later part of the World Bank) published a massive report on the Cuban economy. Written from a modernizing but conservative laissez-faire point of view, the report found plenty to criticize in the Cuban economy. It took particular exception to what it saw as the economic "distortions" produced by strong state intervention in the economy, particularly in the area of collective bargaining (for example, compulsory government arbitration of labor disputes) and in the laws protecting job tenure, which made it difficult to fire workers. However critical of the legal and political environment affecting labor relations in Cuba, the report glowingly appreciated the Cuban workers themselves. According to the report, the quality of Cuban labor was good and compared favorably with that of countries with large native American populations such as Mexico and the Central American republics. The average Cuban worker was willing to work and able to learn—qualities that the report said were necessary for high levels of production. Rural Cubans of all social levels and ethnicities, even in comparatively remote areas, were accustomed to the idea of producing for a market or working for wages. Repair and maintenance of equipment, work at the ubiquitous sugar mills, and the increasing use of automobiles and tractors had established some degree of familiarity with machinery throughout the island and led to a fairly widespread development of mechanical skills.[46] Five years later (only three years before the victory of the Cuban Revolution), a US government guide for American businessmen repeated much of the assessment of labor relations put forward by the IBRD's *Report on Cuba.* However, the US government guide was more insightful than the *Report* about the high aspirations of Cuban workers and was, if anything, even more positive about the qualities of labor on the island:

> The worker in Cuba is self-respecting, intelligent, abstemious, and alert. He learns routines with ease and shows aptitude in acquiring mechanical skills. Ambitious enough to respond to incentive, he has wider horizons than most Latin American workers and expects more out of life in material amenities than many European workers. His health is good and, although his education may be deficient, his native intelligence permits him to overcome this obstacle in most instances. His goal is to reach a standard of living comparable with that of the American worker.[47]

A few years later, after the victory of the revolution on January 1, 1959, almost the entire Cuban economy was nationalized starting with most industry, commerce, and land in the early sixties and ending with the tiniest street-corner businesses in 1968. A quite different picture started to emerge of the motivation and quality of Cuban labor, at least in the pronouncements and complaints voiced by government leaders. Workers' motivation, or the lack of it, became a big problem for decades to come, as did, among other issues, the quality of work, absenteeism, and people showing up to work but working fewer hours than required by the established schedules.

What happened? How did this new state of affairs come about? Given the short period that had elapsed since the IBRD's and US government's reports, it was obvious that the answer had to be found in the changes in social organization and circumstances of work and society at large and not in the physical or psychological makeup of the Cuban workers themselves. In trying to interpret this conundrum, defenders of the Cuban government leaders have, with a degree of plausibility, blamed people's lack of motivation to work on a number of factors, including a substantial reduction of the scourge of massive unemployment, the increase in the social wage as a result of social legislation, and the reduction of consumer goods due to the US economic blockade. However, these explanations ignore the systemic causes of economic crisis inherent in the island's bureaucratic system itself, which I discussed in chapter 2. The defenders of the Cuban government do not adequately explain why, for example, total agricultural output declined by 23 percent from 1961 (when state economic planning began) to 1969, or why per capita food production was 28 percent lower in 1969 than it had been in 1959.[48] There is little doubt that in addition to the US economic attacks on the island's economy, the bureaucratic nationalization of Cuban agriculture with the resulting major organizational inefficiencies, poor incentives and motivation of rural workers, and other related bureaucratic problems was a key factor explaining the decline in food production.

With little to buy and with the option of collective actions such as strikes precluded by the repressive nature of the political system, workers voted with their feet or, as the social scientist Albert Hirschman noted, "exited" the state economy through a variety of means. By the early sixties, workers recognized that they could earn enough money to buy the scarce rationed items by working only fifteen or twenty days a month.[49] Thus, absenteeism continued to be a problem. According to Castro, in August and September 1970, 20 percent of the workforce was absent on any given day. In January 1971, in the midst of the sugar harvest, absenteeism among agricultural workers in Oriente Province was still 23 percent.[50] Fifteen years later, at the Third Party Congress that took place in 1986, Fidel Castro complained about people cutting short their workday and argued that socialism could not be constructed if only 80 percent, 75 percent, or 70 percent of work hours were fulfilled.[51] The same complaints extended not only to absenteeism and the number of hours worked but also to the quality of products and services. In September 1989, the government seriously penalized railroad workers for negligence, poor discipline, and unacceptable work habits.[52]

In response to these serious labor problems the government alternated between the use of material and nonmaterial (moral) incentives, just as it had with the other policies I discussed earlier, in order to elicit a greater commitment and dedication to work among the Cuban people. In Cuba, as well as in other Communist countries, the use of material or nonmaterial incentives have affected and were affected in turn by other important economic policies and strategies. Included among these were planning methods, the allocation of resources, the organization of the enterprise, and such social and political matters as income equalization and mass mobilization for economic purposes.[53] For example, when in the 1970s Cuba adopted the policy of material incentives, it did so along with taking up the Soviet model of self-financing enterprise and the creation of a somewhat higher degree of unemployment and income inequality. Contrary to a widespread perception, the policy of material incentives has not necessarily been more economically or politically liberal from a working-class perspective. It can, as in the extreme case of Stalin's Russia, sharply increase industrial speed, unpaid overtime, deteriorating working conditions, and rivalry among workers.

On the other hand, the Cuban government's adoption of Guevaraist "moral" incentives in the years 1966 to 1970 and during the period of "rectification of errors" from 1986 to 1990 was accompanied by a greater degree of income equality and a stronger antimarket orientation. This approach also tended to rely heavily on labor mobilization through the mechanism of "voluntary labor," whose voluntary nature is questionable given that the state with all its coercive mechanisms was the agency soliciting "volunteers." Voluntary labor was also economically quite wasteful when it involved bringing "volunteers" to the countryside. Urban transplants had to be transported, housed, and fed. The expenditures involved in bringing urban "volunteers" to the countryside could have been put to much better use by improving the living conditions of agricultural workers both for its own sake and to discourage rural to urban migration. City dwellers' lack of experience and familiarity with the nature and conditions of agricultural work throws into question the degree to which they made a significant difference in solving agricultural labor shortages. The alleged educational and political benefits of manual labor could have been achieved far more cheaply by urban volunteers helping in local factories or through community work in such tasks as repairing and cleaning streets, social centers, libraries, schools, and hospitals.

When "moral" incentives failed to achieve their goals, as they frequently did, the Cuban government often resorted to coercion and the militarization of labor. This was particularly evident in agriculture, with the introduction of military discipline and officers at the head of state farms, and the use of militarized labor brigades in construction.[54] In Communist systems, forced labor has tended to play a greater role than in the democratic capitalist countries. In nationalized economies, the much lower incidence of unemployment has diminished the role and meaning of the economic coercion (the great majority of people must work so they don't starve) that plays such a central role in capitalism. The lower level of unemployment is arguably a major reason that physical coercion has played a greater role in Communist than in capitalist societies.[55]

Certain economic and social conditions have encouraged the use of material and nonmaterial or "moral" incentives. Scholars have discerned a pattern of economic conditions that have encouraged the abandonment of material incentives and the adoption of nonmaterial ones in Communist societies such as Cuba. John M. Montias points out that these are situations in which "top level decision makers know too little about the availability of factors [of production] and their productivity in any forthcoming period" to design plans that can serve as guidelines for local decisions. It is difficult to administer material incentives when "supply conditions at the factory level are too chaotic," and when it is not possible for managers "to distinguish the adverse effects on outcomes of lack of effort or discipline" by their subordinates from the negative effect on output of poor conditions and other causes.[56] In the case of China under Mao, the stress on "moral" incentives was historically associated with a process of sharply increasing investment that left fewer resources for consumption. As high investment and "moral" incentives further developed and deepened, dislocation and discontent began to grow among workers and peasants because of the ever-diminishing material rewards for increasing work. Eventually, the regime was forced to grant certain concessions that often took the form of more material incentives. This is what happened with the Great Leap Forward during the years 1958 to 1961. The regime was forced to abandon that campaign, given dangerously low food consumption and poor morale, even in army units. The peasants were then encouraged to reapply themselves to agriculture by returning to private plots, rural markets, piece rates, and bonuses paid by sharply reduced capital accumulation.[57]

In Cuba, Fidel Castro tried for the first time to implement a Guevarist economic policy based on "moral" incentives from 1966 to 1970. Emphasis on capital accumulation at the expense of consumption reached a high point. A large increase in national savings was to be achieved by reducing consumption through the expansion of rationing, the export of products previously consumed at home, and the reduction of imports considered superfluous. The investment share going into production increased from 78.7 to 85.8 percent between 1965 and 1970, the highest proportion ever achieved during the revolutionary period.[58] However, with the exception of a few agricultural and industrial products, there was a general decline in output in the Cuban economy, in great part because the absence of both a central plan and coordination among special plans led to shortages in inputs, bottlenecks, shutdowns, and proliferation of incomplete projects. Improvements in certain sectors of the economy were offset by declines in other sectors.[59] Soon, strong pressures from the Soviet Union led to the abandonment of this strategy and the adoption of more orthodox Soviet methods in the seventies. Cuba, with neither the size nor the resources of China, was far more economically dependent on the Soviet Union.

Economic policies originally inspired by Guevara were again put into effect during the "Rectification of Errors" period from 1986 to 1990, which was designed to combat a number of ills such as a considerable slackening of work effort, a virtual disappearance of volunteer labor, and nepotism.[60] Output quotas were generally increased, and wages, bonuses, prizes, and overtime funds were usually reduced. Unpaid voluntary work and labor mobilization were revived, and new construction contingents were created. The use of "moral" incentives increased, although material incentives were maintained in some areas of the economy such as tourism. While lip service was given to increased worker participation in economic functions, managerial control of the workforce was actually reinforced.[61] At the beginning of the Rectification Period, the Central Committee of the Communist Party criticized the unions for their "indolence and tolerance" of lack of discipline and excessive salaries. The task of the unions was to make sure that their members put in a full day at work. Two years later, in 1988, Fidel Castro noted that Japanese workers had only six paid vacation days a year while Cuban workers had thirty, although shortly after this he explained that he was not advocating an elimination of vacation days, only saying that workers had to "work hard" to improve productivity.[62]

This was a period of poor economic performance starting in 1986, the year Cuba stopped paying the debt it had contracted with the countries of the Club of Paris. Figures published by the Cuban National Bank in 1995 showed that the GDP during this period declined annually by 1.3 percent in absolute terms and by 2.3 percent in per capita terms. Undoubtedly, exogenous factors such as drought, a decline in the world price of sugar, and deterioration in the terms of trade with the Soviet Union played a role. But the policies of the Rectification Period itself, such as elimination of the private farmers' market, and the lack of a coherent economic model had very negative effects.[63] The collapse of the Soviet bloc and the USSR in the late eighties and early nineties brought this period to an end, as these major events delivered a huge blow to the Cuban polity and economy. In any case, as the Cuban government oscillated between "material" and "moral" incentives, there is one method the Cuban government never tried because of its ideological proclivities and organizational class interests. I would call this method "political" incentives: democratic control of the economy, polity, and society, including control of the workplace by the workers. According to this approach, only by participating and controlling their own productive lives do people become interested in and responsible for what they do for a living day in and day out; that is, only thus do they get to care and give a damn. In this sense, workers' democracy can be seen both as a good in itself—people taking control of their lives—and as a truly productive economic force.

After the fall of the Soviet Union and the loss of its economic support, a Special Period began and with it a decline of "moral" incentives, a rise in substantial inequality, and the creation of a dollar economy alongside the peso economy. Many enterprises were shut down for a variety of reasons, including lack of inputs and frequent blackouts. The number of excess workers rose very quickly while labor productivity fell precipitously, although most workers continued to receive their salaries. In this new situation, unpaid voluntary labor and military mobilization for productive purposes became irrelevant. The government adopted a number of measures such as allowing mothers to stay at home for longer periods, relocating workers with the help of unemployment compensation, and creating new jobs in economic sectors such as joint ventures with foreign capital, agriculture, and self-employment. However, governmental restrictions and harassment greatly limited the development of small businesses and artisan occupations.[64] Beginning in the mid-nineties, hundreds of thousands of workers were "rationalized" out of their jobs, particularly in the declining sugar industry. Some were shifted to new state jobs, some stayed home while receiving a state subsidy, and others became self-employed.[65] Later on, Fidel Castro took advantage of this economic situation to carry out a short-lived expansion of higher education.

Workers and the Economy under Raúl Castro's Rule

As we saw in chapter 2, since Raúl Castro took over when his brother Fidel became seriously ill in 2006, he has taken a number of measures that he claims will improve the economy, while the key institutions of the one-party state that control the country's economy remain fundamentally unaltered. Raúl Castro eliminated the upper limits on government salaries and began to introduce the practice of payment according to performance. Thus, for example, in the region of Sancti Spíritus in central Cuba, 68 percent of the workers were paid according to productive results at the end of 2009, a proportion that was to be expanded to include 76 percent of workers during the first trimester of 2010. Salvador Valdés Mesa, secretary-general of the CTC, warned that the state could not continue to subsidize workers who have been laid off but must reorient them to more needed productive labor.[66] But two months later Raúl Castro declared that the state could not be responsible for the relocation of laid-off workers and that the "citizens" themselves should be the most interested in finding a socially useful job. The Cuban leader warned that if the economy did not correct its problems, the island's political system would be at risk.[67]

In September 2010 the government announced that 500,000 state workers would be laid off during the coming year, with a large portion of them becoming self-employed. As a measure significantly increasing (for the first time since the sixties) a private sector in the Cuban economy to cover close to 17 percent of the labor force, the announcement attracted the attention of the world media. Understandably, far less attention was paid to the ways and manner in which the layoffs will be carried out. According to the government, the process of determining who will be kept and who will be let go from their state jobs was to be guided by the principle of "proven fitness" (*idoneidad demostrada*). Everybody will be treated equally regardless of whether they are old or young, man or woman, so clearly neither seniority nor any form of "affirmative action" for blacks or any other disadvantaged groups will be taken into account. And who will determine specifically who is suitable and who is not? This will be the job of a Committee of Experts (Comité de Expertos) that will be elected in a general assembly of workers, who will be presented with a slate prepared by the management and the official union. Voting will take place by a show of hands. It is not difficult to predict that given the prevailing political conditions in Cuba, this voting exercise will be purely cosmetic. However, it is significant that the government has excluded from the jurisdiction of the Committee of Experts the determination of the employment fate of cadres and leaders. Decisions about which cadres and leaders will stay and which ones will go will be taken by the bodies and authorities authorized to appoint or elect them. The same will apply to managers.[68]

Workers who were relocated to other jobs in the state sector will receive salaries corresponding to their new positions. The laid-off workers will receive one extra month's pay, at which point the worker's employment relationship with the state will be terminated. If after one month the laid-off worker has not been able to find other employment, she will be further compensated with 60 percent of her basic salary for a period based on her length of service. Compensation will be paid for one month for those who have worked from ten to nineteen years, two months for twenty to twenty-five years, three months for twenty-six to thirty years, and five months for those with more than thirty years of service. However, those workers who "unjustifiably" turn down their reassignment to a new job in the state sector will be entitled to 60 percent of their basic salary for only one month.[69]

As we have seen, while the government was complaining about an excess of workers in the state sector, it was allowing workers to have more than one job and students to work part time.[70] While this seems illogical in light of the large labor surplus in the country, it appears to have been the government's response to the severe problem of highly inadequate peso salaries, thus underlining the contradictory forces at work in the Cuban economy. In any case, many people had already been working illegally outside their state jobs—in which they invested as little time and effort as they could get away with. Six months after multiple employment was initially allowed in mid-2009, fifty thousand people (out of a labor force of five million) were *officially* working at more than one job. It is revealing that 97 percent of these people were linked to the educational sector, given that low salaries had previously provoked an exodus of teachers and other personnel with grave consequences for Cuban elementary and secondary schools.[71]

The government's attempt to save resources has had widespread consequences, not least for the official ideology. The leadership's decision to wind down mobilizations of urban youth to work in agriculture was accompanied by unprecedented pronouncements by top leaders such as José Ramón Machado Ventura, Raúl Castro's number-two man and appointed successor. He declared that the "romanticism" of the big mobilizations should be left behind, since they ended up producing more losses than positive results. According to Machado Ventura, this reevaluation was particularly necessary now that the country was compelled to quantify even the most minimal expenditures.[72] To save on the substantial expenditures (including a great deal of theft) of the 24,700 canteens serving lunch to some 3.5 million people at their workplaces, the government also began to experiment with closing canteens at several ministries in Havana. To replace the canteens, workers were given 15 pesos ($0.75) to buy food on their own for every day they came to work.[73] This means that if a worker came to work every day, she would receive 360 pesos a month to buy lunch. This was the equivalent of 87.0 percent of the average monthly salary of 415 pesos at the end of 2008, thus creating the paradox of many workers getting an additional lunch income that was higher than their salaries.[74] What an implicit governmental admission of the harmful consequences of very inadequate salaries and economic irrationality! The official government media announced the following year that since the results of the experiment had been positive, the new policy of closing the workers' canteens would be extended to almost 20 percent of the national labor force.[75]

But what about the unions in Cuba today? What are they doing to protect the interests of the workers in this new era of wrenching and potentially transformational changes? Besides supporting and acting as government spokespeople on economic policy, although sometimes with a pinch of sweetener as in the case of the earlier cited pronouncement of official trade union leader Salvador Valdés Mesa, they seem to be increasingly integrated with management, even at the local level. Take, for example, the case of Juan Ramón Gamboa, a security guard in Las Tunas in eastern Cuba. A family emergency prevented him from attending a local union meeting, for which the *management* fined him with a 10 percent discount on his bonus, in both national and convertible currency. As it turned out, the meeting was canceled for lack of a quorum, and those who failed to attend were fined by the deputy director of the work center, the same person who was supposed to conduct the meeting. Not only had the administration supplanted the union outright, but to add insult to injury, it no longer called it a local union meeting but referred to it as a meeting of the union with the administration.[76] This was admittedly an extreme case, one that even got the attention of the official government press. However, it merely constituted, in fact, an excessive application of the general direction of a long-standing government policy. This was dramatically demonstrated by the fact that the official announcement of the half-million layoffs from the state sector in August 2010 was made by none other than the CTC[77] instead of by government employers—Raúl Castro or other high-level government leaders.

The Cuban Working Class and the Cuban Government

At no point have Cuban workers and peasants had any say in the government adoption of labor policies. Che Guevara's call for the workers and peasants to develop *conciencia* (consciousness) and adopt a revolutionary morality was tantamount to calling on them to take political and social responsibility without political and social power. Guevara's call for consciousness and morality also assumed a harmony of interests between the rulers and the ruled—between the givers and receivers of incentives. Even if there had been total economic equality in Cuba, there was still a division of labor where a few made decisions whose consequences were borne by those who had not made those decisions. That is why, in the last analysis, Guevara's call for "moral incentives" was a preachy sermon delivered by the subjects of history to the workers, who were reduced to being the objects of history. In light of the circumstances, the Cuban workers' and peasants' "exit" through absenteeism and other means of "withdrawing efficiency" (Thorsten Veblen) was a totally rational, although not necessarily fully conscious, response.

Nevertheless, ever since significant union turmoil and protests came to an end some time after Fidel Castro's intervention at the Tenth Congress of the CTC in November 1959, unofficial (illegal) union activity in Cuba almost disappeared. A short-lived dissidence did take place in the early nineties among union activists in the port of Havana. In July 1991, the national CTC leaders fired from their jobs and removed from their leadership positions in the Merchant Marine, Ports, and Fishing Union two men: Rafael Gutiérrez, an electrician in the port of Havana who was also arrested, and Alfredo González Poey, a member of the secretariat of the same union. Moreover, González was physically attacked by a group suspected of cooperating with the state security police. Manuel Manrique and Lázaro Cuesta Collazo, also merchant marine union members, were fired as well. The four victimized workers were associated with the small (and legally unrecognized) social democratic Harmony group.[78] Interestingly, it has been reported that the same port was shut down by a one-day strike organized in 1970 by the secret black Abakuá brotherhood, which for a long time had been influential among black longshoremen.[79] In general, however, beyond the relatively passive "exiting" and "withdrawal of efficiency," Cuban workers have collectively done little to significantly change their situation, much less to wrest political power from the structures of the one-party state.

The controlling and repressive capacity of the regime is an important factor but is insufficient to explain the behavior and attitudes of Cuban workers. The government was able to obtain and solidify massive working-class support in the early years of the revolution, when redistributive policies and social legislation improved working-class living standards. These gains, and the resurgent anti-imperialist national sentiment, obviously worked to the benefit of the regime. In subsequent decades, and until the devastating economic crisis of the early nineties, the government was also able to ensure a standard of living that, while modest and austere, eliminated economic uncertainty and anxiety as well as extreme hardship. As a result, the regime was able to maintain working-class political support, though it may not have been as enthusiastic as it was in the sixties. Even among those workers who were skeptical and no longer supported the regime, an implicit truce with the regime was maintained as long as minimal living standards were kept in place. Significant social mobility through the expanding system of higher education made many feel that life could be better for their children if not for themselves. And there was the possibility of emigration, which, while always difficult and costly, offered a possible route of escape from the dreariness and lack of consumer goods. The crisis of the nineties delivered a powerful blow to this fragile equilibrium. Support for the government substantially declined, and at the same time Cuban workers and peasants became consumed by the overwhelming daily tasks of "resolving" the day-to-day problems of getting food, clothing, medicine, and other essential goods. Increasing numbers of people have turned to the *bombo* (lottery) run by the US Interests Section in Havana. The winners obtain the highly prized visa to emigrate to the United States, although they also have to complete onerous and expensive procedures to obtain the Cuban government's permission to leave the country.

Current Proposals for Workers' Control

In recent years, a group of Marxist critics of the Cuban system led by retired diplomat Pedro Campos Santos have presented a reform program focused on the workplace. Coming from a Marxist perspective, Campos Santos's group places workers' control of production at the center of its advocacy for a socialism that is democratic and participatory. This is a rather distinctive standpoint, since other leftist critics have in the recent past concentrated on other types of economic changes such as the "market-socialist" type reforms that were proposed by the thinkers around the Center for the Study of America in the nineties. Many dissidents have advocated union independence from the state, but their implicit or explicit procapitalist perspective has obviously ruled out any consideration of workers' control over production.

Campos Santos's group has essentially been proposing a set of political incentives that have been excluded from consideration by the Cuban government's focus on material and "moral" incentives. As Campos Santos and his associates see it, the transition from what they have alternatively called "state socialism" and "state capitalism" to a democratic socialization requires a number of changes in the workplace. The most important involves putting small and medium-sized enterprises entirely under workers' management through freely elected workers' councils. For bigger enterprises of a strategic or national importance that are technologically advanced and demand large resources and a highly specialized personnel that can be provided only by the state budget or foreign capital, they propose joint management by the workers and the state. The reform program argues for a shift from payment of salaries to a partial distribution of the enterprise's surplus (after covering social security expenses and the necessary reinvestment in the enterprise and the economy as a whole). It also advocates voluntary cooperatives for small farmers, and for small industrial or service enterprises in sectors such as construction, restaurant, and repair workshops that tend to be staffed by artisan labor. Campos Santos and his associates maintain that Cuba is a society in transition to socialism whose forces of production are at a low level of development. Therefore, there is a sector of the economy in which production and services should be allowed to be conducted by individuals or families working for themselves, since "there is no capitalism in the absence of exploited salaried labor." Along the same lines, the reform program proposes that citizens be allowed the freedom to buy and sell their individual personal property such as vehicles and homes. The group also proposes democratic planning for the overall economy without specifying the institutional mechanisms to achieve it.[80]

For Campos Santos, a classical Marxist, the proletarian revolution consists of the working class seizing state power and using it to transform into public property the social means of production it seized from the bourgeoisie. That is how socialized production becomes possible based on a democratically designed plan. This perspective is worlds apart from the politics of nationalizing everything, including the tiniest one-person "businesses," that animated the so-called revolutionary offensive in Cuba in 1968. This "offensive" was partly rooted in the confusion between private property in general and capitalist private property in particular, a confusion that is typical of official Cuban state "socialism" and other similar "socialisms." The tenor and content of the proposals put forward by the group around Campos Santos incorporate the distinction that Friedrich Engels made in his *Socialism: Utopian and Scientific* between modern capitalism, in which production has become a social act but the social product is appropriated by individual capitalists, and socialism, in which both production and its appropriation have become socialized.[81] Following this distinction, it is the productive property requiring collective work that is the proper object of socialization, not individual or family production, much less personal property. This perspective differs not only from the past all-out nationalization policy of the Cuban government but also from the approach espoused by figures critical of that government such as Orlando Márquez, the official spokesman for the Catholic archdiocese of Havana:

> Is it possible to prove that it is a bad thing that one person shows entrepreneurial initiative [*iniciativa empresarial*] while another chooses to be a salaried employee? And if it is not possible to prove this, who would be interested in putting a brake on the growth of self-employment that allows the state and the family economy to breathe easier? How can a house or car be considered

"private property" when it cannot be [legally] sold or given away by its legitimate owner?[82]

In the first place, Márquez seems to conceive of people becoming workers or entrepreneurs purely as a result of individual choice in a fictional classless world. In addition, Márquez mixes up, just as the Cuban government had done for decades, personal and business property, self-employment, and employing others as if they were equivalent, ignoring that they involve different issues and criteria of social and economic organization. A later article by Márquez discussing the likely and *desirable* growth of the number of rich people on the island shows how his purely individualistic approach leads him to ignore not only the distinction between social and individual production but also the exploitation of other people's labor. Moreover, Márquez seems to think that creating a wealthier *country* is the same as or logically implies an increase in rich individuals. He also suggests, echoing the conservative Catholic resignation in the face of inequality and poverty, that "evil does not reside in wealth or poverty as such, but in the manner of living those realities, and in the honesty and goodness that we give to our lives, whether as wealthy or poor people."[83]

It is perhaps due to tactical reasons, as I have indicated elsewhere in this volume, that the reform program put forward by the Campos Santos group has not addressed questions pertaining to the one-party state, although it did advocate allowing the formation of tendencies within the ranks of the CCP. Democratic economic planning depends on whether the various political groups or parties can peacefully present their alternative visions or strategies for the economy and polity as a whole. In the last analysis, it is only through workers' actual control of their daily productive tasks and their real involvement in decision making for the whole of their society that the Cuban working class, along with its class allies, can truly become a ruling instead of an exploited class.

The reform program was supposed to be presented to the Sixth Congress of the CCP that was due to occur in 2002, was repeatedly postponed, and finally took place in 2011. Based on its nature and historical trajectory, there is no reason why the party leadership would pay any attention to this or any other reform program put forward by any group other than themselves. To consider such independent ideas and proposals, even if put forward by party members, would run contrary to the usually carefully choreographed agendas and unanimity on important matters typical of CCP gatherings. Of course, the party leadership modified its program to assimilate and deflect party and popular discontent in a manner that would not challenge its monopoly of power. Only a real independent social movement can put political weight behind truly democratic proposals and prevent their being ignored by the established powers. Similarly, only a workers' movement can make real (and institutionally viable) the call for workers' power made by critical intellectuals such as Campos Santos.

The Cuban Working Class and Its Future

A Cuban transition toward capitalism, whether in the Sino-Vietnamese or another form, may witness attempts to reestablish a free, independent, and politically conscious trade union movement, which will be based on a working class that became fairly educated during the Castro regime. This new trade unionism could attempt to make its biggest inroads in the "winning" sectors of the economy, which will likely have a fairly concentrated labor force that should not be too difficult to organize barring substantial state and capitalist repression. The new independent trade union movement (and, one would hope, the new democratic revolutionary left that will grow alongside of it) will have to address the gap between the "winning" and "losing" sectors of the post-Castro Cuban economy. It will also have to address the problem of the large and growing number of unemployed workers and organize against the repression that a post-Communist order is likely to carry out to "discipline" the Cuban working class. The present Cuban government's systematic prohibition and repression of any kind of popular independent movement will make these future tasks all the more difficult, just as it has made it very difficult to resist and combat current acts of exploitation and oppression.

Chapter Five

Racism against Black Cubans—an Oppression That Dared Not Speak Its Name

Blacks,[1] notwithstanding official Cuban census figures, probably became a majority of the people living in Cuba sometime during the latter part of the twentieth century. Three hundred fifty years of slavery and the widespread institutional racism that followed its abolition in 1886 turned blacks into the most important of the oppressed groups in Cuba, before and after the revolutionary victory of 1959. Nevertheless, due to the peculiarities of Cuban history, the oppression of black Cubans, before and after the revolution, has been, until very recently an oppression "that dares not speak its name."

Racial oppression in Cuba has been different from and less vicious than in the United States. However, contrary to the self-indulgent notion widespread among Cuban whites in south Florida and on the island that postcolonial Cuba has been free of racism, Cuban racism exists and has been cruel and oppressive. Yet there are important differences between the racial orders in the two countries, starting with their respective slave regimes. The late seventeenth-century legislation regulating slavery in the Spanish empire defined slaves as human beings instead of chattel and granted them some minimal legal rights. Thus, the Spanish legal system regarded the murder of a slave as a crime,[2] and allowed slaves to own property and to purchase their freedom outright or in small installments over time.[3] There were also laws affording some protection to families of slaves. However, the extent to which these laws were enforced is not known.[4] In the past, some important historians, such as Frank Tannenbaum, paid little or no attention to this problem and took Spanish law at face value as if it mirrored reality.[5]

In fact, life for African slaves in Cuba was so harsh that they often ended up escaping into maroon communities, or rebelling with more frequency than in the United States.[6] This greater militancy may have been due to circumstances that allowed them to retain a greater degree of cultural autonomy—including the preservation and observance of their traditional African religious practices—than was the case in North America. Perhaps even more important was their success in establishing African-based ethnic organizations (*cabildos de nación*) and secret societies such as Abakuá, which were widespread in Cuba but generally absent in the United States.[7] These differences were in part results of the Cuban slave system's continuous renewal through fresh imports from Africa for a substantially longer period than was the case in the United States.[8] The manumission rate in Cuba (and other Latin American countries)[9] was also significantly higher and led to a larger proportion of free blacks than in North America.[10] For example, in 1862, the 43.2 percent of the Cuban population that was black was composed of 26.5 percent slaves and 16.6 percent *libertos* (former slaves who had purchased their freedom or had been emancipated by their masters).[11] In sharp contrast, the 1860 US census showed black slaves as constituting 13 percent of the population while free blacks and mulattos accounted for only 1.5 percent of total inhabitants.[12]

Since the Spanish colonial migration to Cuba was predominantly composed of single men instead of families, as was the case in North America, there was a much greater degree of miscegenation on the island. This did not necessarily involve official marriages between whites and blacks (these were actually forbidden from the mid-1860s until the early 1880s)[13] and certainly nothing approximating an equality of conditions between Spanish men and their black sexual partners. Miscegenation led to the emergence of mulattos (*mulatos*) as an intermediate racial category that became part of a system of classification shared by whites and blacks alike. However, although acknowledged as an intermediate group, mulattos have been regarded as much closer to blacks than to whites.

Membership in the subordinate racial groups was never defined in Cuba as based on so-called hypo-descent[14]—better known as the "one drop of black blood rule"—that defined blackness in the United States. In Cuba, physical appearance continues to be the key factor determining racial affiliation. Unclear or ambiguous cases of racial identification have usually been "resolved" based on markers of social standing, with higher class membership identified with a higher level of whiteness. Thus, a well-off light-skinned mulatto can easily pass for white. Racist ideas concerning the "improvement" of the race through increased "whitening of offspring" and through the acquisition of "better" hair and other physical features are widely shared among the great majority of whites, and substantial numbers of blacks and mulattos as well.

Their relative prosperity and the fear of a repetition of the Haitian Revolution, which took place at the end of the eighteenth century (*otro Santo Domingo*, "another Santo Domingo"), made white native *criollos* (creoles) delay the armed struggle against Spain well into the second half of the nineteenth century.[15] Fear of being numerically overcome by blacks also made the colonial authorities resort to every means at their disposal to keep the island as white as possible. In 1815, they established a Junta de Población Blanca (Council for White Population) charged with increasing white immigration.[16] As a result, the Royal Decree of

1817, specifically directed toward attracting whites to the island, was approved, giving foreigners the same rights to purchase urban and rural property as Spaniards. White foreigners were also granted tax exemptions.[17] This decree was an early instance of a pattern of discriminatory immigration legislation that would continue unchanged through the first decades of the twentieth-century Cuban Republic. And so it was that Cuba managed to reestablish a white majority after the first half of the nineteenth century.[18] After the colonial census of 1861, registered whites constituted 56.8 percent of the population, and the 1877 census counted whites as 64.9 percent of people living on the island; no subsequent colonial or republican census registered a lower proportion of whites.

Now that white Cuban fears of "another Haiti" had receded, large numbers of white and black Cubans joined in the armed struggle against Spain in 1868. The principal white Cuban leader of the first war effort, Carlos Manuel de Céspedes, freed his slaves and exhorted them to join in the independence struggle.[19] The late arrival of Cuba to the Latin American struggle for independence from the Iberian powers meant that it would be conducted under the influence of more advanced social and political ideologies. The principal political leader of the third and final war of independence, which began in 1895, was José Martí (1853–95), a progressive thinker and writer. However, Martí, whose vast influence on Cuban politics—including race—is felt to this day, held to a firm "color-blind" perspective on the racial question. He strongly opposed racial discrimination and articulated an integrationist political program in which there were no black or white Cubans, just Cubans. This "color-blindness" led him to put on the same plane what he regarded as white and black racism. As he put it in the article "My Race" published in the exile newspaper *Patria* on April 16, 1893, white racist supremacists have no more right to complain about blacks who extol the character of their race than black "racists" have a right to complain about white racists. In the last analysis, Martí was an early advocate of the racial silence that would so strongly characterize subsequent Cuban history. A year earlier, in 1892, he had urged Cubans to stop talking about race: "This constant allusion to a man's color should cease."[20]

The third and last Cuban war for independence ended in 1898 with the US military intervention against Spain. As the price for withdrawing from the island and allowing the establishment of a nominally independent Cuban republic, the United States imposed the Platt Amendment, which gave Washington ample rights to intervene in the internal affairs of the newly established republic. On various occasions during the subsequent three decades the United States militarily occupied parts or the whole of the island, until the Platt Amendment was formally abolished in 1934. Even then, the United States retained its naval base in Guantánamo as part of the price for having abolished the amendment. The contributions of black Cubans, who were about two-thirds of those fighting in the third war of independence, were ignored by the American occupation authorities as well as by the Cuban republic that followed it. Racial discrimination by white

Americans and white Cubans continued unabated and provoked the formation of a black independent political party, the Partido Independiente de Color—PIC—in 1908. The party's program espoused general progressive demands such as the eight-hour day, free immigration for people of all races, legalization of common-law marriages, and land distribution to veterans of the wars of independence. The PIC also demanded black representation in the diplomatic service, the army, and the various branches of the government, but it did not argue for racial separation, and it endorsed the ideal of a racially integrated Cuban nation. However, PIC's emphasis on the independent character of the party meant that its membership was open to blacks and mulattos, not whites.[21]

In response to the creation of the PIC, the Cuban Congress approved in 1910 the "Morúa law" banning political parties organized along racial criteria.[22] The law was named after Martín Morúa Delgado, a black senator who argued that a black political organization would encourage the formation of exclusively white organizations and thus create a conflict with devastating consequences for the nation.[23] As an integrationist, Morúa was also concerned that separate black organization would further marginalize his people and deprive them of access to social, economic, and political opportunities. The PIC took up arms as a protest against the "Morúa law," and the "race war" of 1912 followed. This was not really a "race war" but a massacre of black Cubans. Some three thousand mostly unarmed black Cubans were killed over a period of two months, compared with sixteen government soldiers, some of whom died from friendly fire.[24] The "race war" had a truly traumatic effect on the social and political life of the country, and the norm of silence about race became truly entrenched. That does not mean that racial tensions and outbreaks were totally absent from Cuban politics. For example, part of the political opposition to the Machado dictatorship that was overthrown in 1933 had clear racist inclinations, which even led to racially motivated killings.[25] But race as a topic of discussion became increasingly delegitimized, as evidenced in the generally progressive constitution of 1940, in which the "Morúa law" became enshrined as constitutional principle.

After the 1930s, the populist-nationalist wing of the left, strongly influenced by the political ideas of José Martí, partook in the silence about race. However, things were different with the CCP—which faithfully followed the line laid out in Moscow by Stalin and his successors—founded in 1925. In contrast to the populist-nationalists, the Communists explicitly addressed blacks and the issues that specifically concerned them, and made a special attempt to recruit them. However, the Communist policy toward Cuban blacks changed in accordance with the Moscow party line. The Cuban Communists in the late twenties and early thirties advocated the recognition of a "black belt" nation in Oriente Province, just like Communists in the United States, who for some time advocated the creation of a separate "black belt" nation in the American South.[26] After the Communists were legalized in the late thirties, their approach to many issues was also affected by the domestic politicking the party conducted with its political partners of the day.

At the Constitutional Convention of 1940 the Cuban Communists advocated a policy similar to affirmative action in the United States. Such a policy would have guaranteed the participation of black workers in all sectors of the economy in a proportion similar to their presence in the total population of the province in which they lived. Later on, during the convention proceedings, the Communists modified their position to advocate for "fair" representation in all newly created jobs, a step back from their call for black representation in all jobs for fear that it might lead to the firing of white workers. In this fashion, the Communists addressed the objection that their original proposal would have created racial divisions among workers. Both Communist proposals were rejected, however, and the convention ended up approving the position put forward by the more conservative delegates, making racial discrimination in hiring and promotion practices unconstitutional.[27] Like several other progressive constitutional provisions, this was never really implemented by subsequent legislation, either because the legislation had no teeth or because it was never enacted.

Of a total of seventy-six delegates to the convention, only five were black or mulatto, and three of these were Communists. The Communists were the fifth largest party with 9 percent of the vote and 8 percent of the delegates. Half of them were black or mulatto, and a large percentage of the Communist candidates for convention delegates had also been black or mulatto.[28] By the forties and fifties, a significant proportion of the top Communist leadership was black (including Blas Roca, Lázaro Peña, and Salvador García Aguero) as was a significant part of the party's membership. However, even though blacks became an important group within the party, Communists never became as important within the Cuban black population as a whole. There, the hundreds of local branches of the black self-help social clubs (*sociedades de color*) constituted by far the principal form of black self-organization.[29]

Racist Patterns in Prerevolutionary Cuba

The massive immigration of Spaniards (principally from Galicia, Asturias, and the Canary Islands) that began in the late nineteenth century[30] and increased in the first two decades of the twentieth century was critical in maintaining an ample white majority in Cuba. This Spanish immigration was approximately twice as large as the number of black Caribbean workers, mostly from Jamaica and Haiti, who came to work in the sugar mills in the first two decades of the twentieth century. The number of black Caribbean immigrants was later significantly reduced by the expulsions decreed by the nationalist government that emerged from the 1933 revolution. As a result of these politically influenced demographic processes, the last prerevolutionary census of 1953 registered 72.8

percent of the population as white, with 12.4 percent Negroes, 14.5 percent mulattos, and 0.3 percent Asians. According to the same census, an increasing urbanization of black and mulatto Cubans had left only 19 percent of them working in Cuban agriculture.[31]

In the 1950s, right before the victory of the revolution, racial segregation existed in Cuba but, unlike the system of "Jim Crow" in the southern United States or South African apartheid, was not sanctioned by law. Public parks in several provincial cities (but not in the Havana metropolitan area) had separate areas for whites and nonwhites. White landlords often refused to rent houses and apartments to blacks, and many hotels did not allow blacks to register as guests.[32] Blacks were also unwelcome at the most popular nightclubs. A big public scandal erupted when the American/French star Josephine Baker was barred from the famous Hotel Nacional in the early fifties and suffered a similar fate at the equally famous Tropicana nightclub. Racially exclusive private social clubs monopolized access to most desirable beaches in the capital. The racist practices of private social clubs had other important consequences. For example, tens of thousands of Cubans obtained private health care provided by the Spanish regional associations, which for a relatively modest membership fee admitted whites of any national background but not blacks and mulattos. In the case of baseball, the most popular sport in Cuba, although professional teams were racially integrated, important amateur teams organized by the social clubs did not admit blacks and mulattos. Thus, while many white professional players were recruited from the amateur teams fielded by the discriminatory social clubs, black professional players, including such famous stars as Orestes "Minnie" Miñoso, were recruited from racially integrated teams sponsored by sugar mills and other industrial and commercial enterprises.[33] Public schools, from the elementary to the university level, were racially integrated, but the very important private schools, whether secular or religious, were overwhelmingly if not exclusively white. Some poor neighborhoods, such as the well-known barrio of Pogolotti located in the city of Marianao near Havana, were overwhelmingly black, but both white and black residents lived in many other poor neighborhoods.

Cuban whites monopolized private-sector white-collar employment and other forms of "nonmanual" labor, including sales positions in the most expensive Havana department stores such as El Encanto. Exclusion from this sector led to a protest campaign during the presidency of Carlos Prío Socarrás (1948–52) who issued a presidential decree outlawing racial discrimination in the filling of vacancies or newly created positions in industry and commerce. Prío and his minister of labor also asked the managers of some of the most noted department stores in Havana to include black women on their staffs. The response to the president's decree and requests to the big-store managers was poor. A few highly educated light-skinned mulatto women were hired in Havana's luxury stores for the 1951 Christmas season, but they were dismissed shortly after.[34]

Black Cubans were highly concentrated in various kinds of "manual" labor such as personal services and construction, although unlike the case of the United States in the twentieth century, this included ample representation in the skilled construction trades. Many of the children of the better-paid black and mulatto carpenters, masons, electricians, and plumbers were economically able to postpone entry into the labor force, enter the nonsegregated public university, and become professionals. A small but significant number of black Cubans were thus able to take advantage of those educational opportunities. This was reflected in the 1943 census, according to which blacks accounted for 5.8 percent of the engineers, 9.5 percent of the medical doctors, and 11.9 percent of lawyers and judges. Yet these were modest gains within a context in which blacks still constituted 36.3 percent of unskilled workers and 55.7 percent of domestic servants.[35]

Besides baseball, blacks were well represented in other professional sports such as boxing. In 1943 there was also a substantial black presence in the army (21.6 percent of the armed forces) and police force (14.7 percent),[36] including a few high-ranking officers, and the unions.[37] According to the 1943 census, black and white unemployment rates were about equal in agriculture, livestock, and fishing, manufacturing and mechanized industries, and some professions such as law and engineering. However, in other areas of the economy the rate of black unemployment was at least twice that of whites. That was the case of the relatively unimportant leather-processing industry as well as among the critically important government employees at the municipal, provincial, and national levels.[38]

The prerevolutionary Cuba of the 1950s had many of the characteristics of an ethnic and racial mosaic, with whites, blacks, mulattos, and a large number of immigrants, particularly Spanish, Chinese, Jamaicans, and Haitians, with much smaller numbers of Arabs (mostly Lebanese Christians) and Polish and Turkish Jews. Nevertheless, Cuba was not multicultural in the sense in which the term has been used in the United States during the last several decades. The predominant white Hispanic culture was sometimes implicitly identified with Cubanness. While there was an alternative model of Cubanness based on the mixed cultural nature of the society, the fact is that the powerful African component of Cuban nationality was not really appreciated except for its contribution to Cuban music. Whites looked down on traditional African religion, considering it with amused derision at best or as uncivilized savagery at worst. Nevertheless, twentieth-century Cuba was not a white settler society (in other words, white settlers of foreign origin ruling over natives with whom they refuse to integrate politically or culturally), as some observers have proposed.[39] The children of Spanish, Chinese, Arab, and Jewish immigrants considered themselves as politically and culturally Cuban as the mulatto and black population. Whites did not consider blacks and mulattos any less Cuban than they were, even though they looked down upon and discriminated against them. Similarly, black and mulatto Cubans looked at the whites born on the island as being no less politically and culturally Cuban than they were, even though they may have resented and hated the racial discrimination to which they were being subjected. This commonly shared national identity differed from the settler mentality that prevailed in such places as preindependence Algeria and apartheid South Africa. In addition, Cuban whites were, unlike the French Algerians and white South Africans, the clear majority of the population in prerevolutionary Cuba. In Cuba, the concept of race was not confused with the quite different concept of nation or national minority.

The 26th of July Movement and the Racial Question

Fidel Castro owes his political formation to the populist/nationalist wing of the Cuban left.[40] He was a congressional candidate of the Partido Ortodoxo in the June 1952 elections, which never took place because of Batista's military coup of March 1952. A large number of the participants in the attack on the Moncada barracks that Castro led on July 26, 1953, also came out of the youth wing of the Partido Ortodoxo. The Ortodoxos, like the Partido Auténtico from which they had split in the second half of the 1940s, were fully within the tradition of Martí and Morúa regarding the race question. This does not mean that the Auténticos and Ortodoxos were indifferent to racial discrimination or to black Cubans. In fact, like other parties, the Ortodoxos ran black candidates for office and expressed their sympathy for black Cubans through symbolic actions such as publicly associating with black boxing champions Kid Chocolate and Kid Gavilán.[41] However, in contrast with the Communists, neither Auténticos nor Ortodoxos would even consider advocating "affirmative action" policies or trying to recruit Cuban blacks as blacks.

Yet it would be a mistake to conceive of the Auténticos' and Ortodoxos' racial politics as purely a question of white populist political ideology. What most mattered in this context was the social milieu that constituted their main base of support, particularly during the late forties and early fifties. For the most part, white urban middle- and lower-income people who held jobs in the professions, artisan occupations, and the working class constituted this milieu. Although the term "petty bourgeois" has been used to describe this group, it is inaccurate. It does not apply, for example, to the very large group of somewhat educated and poorly paid white-collar employees in the unstable public sector (there was no civil service) who constituted an important part of this social base. This predominantly white milieu would have, at least initially, been indifferent if not hostile to "affirmative action" and other demands specifically addressed to black Cubans.

It is therefore not surprising that most of the important pronouncements of Fidel Castro and the 26th of July Movement omitted any reference to race or racial discrimination in Cuba. That was the case with "History Will Absolve Me," the radical speech delivered by Castro when he and his associates were tried for the 1953 Moncada assault, even though it touched on a large number of other problems that plagued Cuban society. Neither was race or racism mentioned in the *Manifesto of the Sierra Maestra* that Fidel Castro coauthored with Raúl Chibás, the brother of the deceased founder of the Partido Ortodoxo, and Felipe Pazos, a noted Cuban economist and president of the Cuban National Bank during the last Auténtico administration.[42] This was by far the most widely read pronouncement of Castro's movement against Batista because it was published by the mass-circulation magazine *Bohemia* in between two periods of censorship in July 1957. The "Program-Manifesto of the Movement" published in Mexico the same year made no reference to racism and maintained that the movement's ideal was the "organic unity of the nation" and that "no group, class, race, or religion should sacrifice the common good to benefit its particular interest." It added that the revolution's social order would "incorporate all, without privilege or exception."[43]

One exception to the generally silent treatment given to racism by Castro's movement was the "Manifesto No. 1 to the People of Cuba," dated August 1955. The manifesto called for the "establishment of adequate measures in education and legislation to put an end to every vestige of discrimination for reasons of race." However, this document had a limited circulation.[44] This silence over race was again more a by-product of the social and political milieu to which these documents were addressed than of Castro's personal political inclination. After all, he had been a member of the executive board of the University Committee to End Racial Discrimination when he was a law student at the University of Havana from 1945 to 1950.[45]

The participation of blacks and mulattos in Castro's 26th of July Movement is more difficult to assess. It seems that between one-fifth and one-fourth of the people who attacked the Moncada barracks were blacks and mulattos.[46] A smaller proportion of blacks and mulattos were part of the eighty-two-person group that brought Fidel Castro and his fellow fighters to Cuba in late 1956: it constituted 16 percent of the total expeditionary force, although 21 percent of the nineteen-person "Estado Mayor," or General Staff, were blacks and mulattos.[47] According to the 1953 Cuban census 26.9 percent of the Cuban population were black and mulatto. This means that the proportion of black and mulattos among the 1953 Moncada attackers was only slightly lower than their percentage in the country as a whole; however, the proportion of blacks and mulattos among the 1956 *Granma* expeditionaries was substantially lower. Nevertheless, the fact is that there were more blacks and mulattos among these two groups than among those who attended the numerous anti-Batista demonstrations by university and high-school students. This was not the result of any special black recruitment effort; that was not Fidel Castro's politics. More than anything else, it was an indirect effect of the more diverse class and occupational composition of Castro's fellow fighters. The list of the occupations of the participants in the 1953 attack on the Moncada barracks compiled by the historian Hugh Thomas includes accountants, agricultural workers, bus workers, businessmen, shop assistants, plumbers, and students.

In other words, they were mostly workers and thus more likely to include blacks and mulattos in their ranks. Nineteen of these men were with Castro on the *Granma*, and the social composition of this later group was also diverse, although more of them had higher education than those at Moncada.[48] It was probably more difficult for less-educated, poorer, and darker Cubans to go into exile abroad.

Although the majority of these two groups of fighters seem to have been workers by origin or current occupation, very few of them had been active in trade-union or working-class politics. It can therefore safely be concluded that these individuals were not representative of any one class or group in Cuban society, because they lacked organic institutional ties with any social class or stratum. That is why *classlessness* (in the sense of lack of roots or association with any class organizations or institutions) may be a closer approximation to an accurate description of these people than the much abused left-wing category "petty bourgeois."

Batista and Black Cubans

During the Batista dictatorship in the fifties there was an undercurrent of opinion, seldom articulated in public because it would have violated the rule of silence concerning racial matters, suggesting that Cuban blacks sympathized with the dictator. Batista came from a poor family in Oriente Province and had managed to become a sergeant stenographer in the Cuban army before coming to power for the first time in the military coup of September 1933. He was also the product of what was for Cuba an unusual racial mixture of white, black, and Cuban Amerindians (a virtually extinguished racial group on the island). In the fifties, his supporters referred to him as "the Indian" and wore small badges featuring reproductions of multicolored feathers. No matter how hard he tried, Batista (whose second wife, Marta Fernández, was as white as a Cuban woman could be) was never fully accepted in Cuban high society. He was reputedly turned down for membership by some of the most exclusive white social clubs. Back in the thirties, shortly after he rose to power, members of the white upper classes publicly showed their racial contempt for him on at least one occasion. They walked out en masse from the well-known Sans Souci nightclub, located on the outskirts of Havana, when Batista, his first wife Elisa Godínez, and associates showed up for a New Year's celebration.[49]

There is no hard evidence to support the notion of black support for Batista. However, the alternative proposition that blacks were underrepresented in the ranks and particularly in the leadership of the opposition to Batista has a more solid foundation,[50] although that changed after the Rebel Army recruited—in 1957 and 1958—a couple of thousand peasants from eastern Oriente Province, the geographical area with the highest proportion of blacks and mulattos in the country. Batista may have enjoyed some sympathy among blacks for a short period after the 1952 coup, particularly among members of the older generation, based on racial identification and Batista's support for the welfare state in the late thirties and early forties. But it is doubtful that much of that sympathy survived after 1956, when virtually the whole country turned against the dictatorship's brutality and corruption. As members of the working class, where they were overrepresented, blacks also suffered from the erosion of the gains that the unions had managed to obtain before 1952.

Black Cubans, however, had no organizational vehicles through which they could express their growing discontent. The unions, with their large black membership, had been captured by the government, and their bureaucratic leadership faithfully supported the regime. The other possible avenue for black political expression was the black and mulatto mutual-help societies, but they, unlike most of their white civil society counterparts, had been also captured by Batista's government. That is why not a single black or mulatto society was listed among the forty-two civic and professional associations that demanded Batista's resignation in March 1958.[51]

Notwithstanding the general rule of racial silence, well-known spokespersons for the Batista regime tried to exploit the supposed "special" feelings that blacks had for Batista. Among these were Senator Rolando Masferrer, the head of a private army of thugs called The Tigers, and the well-known mulatto journalist Ramón Vasconcelos, Batista's minister of communications. They claimed that Cuban blacks could not expect anything from the anti-black revolutionaries, who were being supported by the white professional middle classes.[52] Some anti-Batista groups implicitly accepted those claims and identified the regime with black Cubans. For example, an infamous cartoon of the Organización Auténtica—the armed group that supported former president Prío after he was overthrown by Batista—depicted Batista and his army as a gang of savages with clearly black African facial features.[53]

Black Cubans after the Revolutionary Victory

Like everyone else, blacks celebrated the revolutionary victory and lined up to meet the procession of rebel soldiers led by Fidel Castro that for a whole week traversed the island from east to west. The silence over racial matters began to be gradually breached during the first two months after the revolutionary victory of January 1. Early in January, the Communists, pressuring the government from the left, proclaimed the need for an official policy against discrimination and for concrete measures to make sure that blacks had access to all jobs—including those in the armed forces and all government institutions, including the diplomatic service.[54] Castro himself made brief critical references to racial discrimination on several occasions.[55] Nevertheless, there were reasons to fear that the rule of silence over racial matters might reassert itself. Writing in *Bohemia*, Cuba's most important magazine, in February, the black Cuban lawyer Juan René Betancourt, an opponent of Batista who took over, on behalf of the revolutionary government, as provisional supervisor of the National Federation of Black Societies (Federación Nacional de Sociedades de Color), warned against this danger. Betancourt argued that "it is impossible that anyone should believe, seriously and in good faith, that by ceasing to refer to 'blacks' and 'whites' the people will forget their existence, and racial discrimination will thus be liquidated by this miraculous method." He also warned against a repetition of what happened in 1902—the exclusion of blacks, including insurgent leaders, from the affairs of the new republic. While expressing his admiration and trust in Castro, Betancourt added that the racial problem could not be resolved with flattering proclamations nor with a handful of prestigious but token posts. He called instead for an organized, biracial drive against racism.[56]

Then Fidel Castro delivered a major speech on race on March 22, 1959. In that speech, Castro strongly criticized racism and identified two forms of discrimination: one that denied Afro-Cubans access to cultural centers and another, which was even worse, that denied them access to jobs. Therefore, he reasoned, the struggle to end racial discrimination at work was one of the main battles that the revolution had to fight. However, he contended that a law against discrimination was unnecessary, and instead he proposed a campaign condemning public manifestations of racism. He also promised to build better, racially integrated public schools, in which children of all racial groups would study and play together and recreation centers would be open to all citizens. Cubans would thus join in building a new fatherland free of discrimination.[57] Further, Castro announced that access to all beaches would be desegregated, including the very desirable resort areas such as Varadero. However, the official announcement made clear that people would have access to the sand and sea only. Private buildings, restaurants, and other facilities by the sea would remain available only to members. It was only after April 1960, when the government nationalized the private clubs, that these facilities became available to white and black people alike.[58] Meanwhile, Fidel Castro assured the members of private clubs that their "privacy" would be respected. The same gradual approach was followed regarding segregated public parks in various provincial cities. Instead of facing racist practices head on, the authorities rebuilt those parks and eliminated the layouts that had served racial segregation in the past.[59]

Although the content of Castro's March 22 speech was far from extreme, it was a major policy statement forthrightly opposing racism and as such a fundamental departure from the norm of racial silence. As a result, there was an immediate white backlash that was described by René Depestre, a black Haitian writer residing in Cuba and a frequent contributor to the island's publications:

> The entire white bourgeoisie and most white petit bourgeois, even those who would then have given their lives for the revolution, were panic-stricken as if the Cuban Prime Minister had announced an atomic attack against the island on the following morning . . . The whole sinister mythology constructed in

the days of slavery resurfaced in men's consciousness along with its imaginary procession of evil instincts, lubricity, physical filth, pillage and rape . . . The volcano of Negrophobia was in eruption.[60]

As Depestre pointed out, the negative reaction among whites was not limited to the conservative and counterrevolutionary opposition, and Castro, with a good ear for the popular mood, was well aware of that. Moreover, the white reaction exploded at an early point in the revolutionary process. At that time, the media, while personally respectful and deferential to Castro, had not yet been taken over by the government and was, from the hard right to the hard left, strongly debating the momentous issues that were confronting the country.

And so three days later, on March 25, Castro held a televised press conference during which he beat a retreat. He continued to insist that racial discrimination was socially and morally wrong, particularly in the area of employment, and strongly criticized those who called themselves Christian, educated, or revolutionary while being racist. At the same time, he tried to reassure white Cubans that private and personal spaces would be respected and that change in these areas would be gradual, accomplished through the color-blind education of new generations of Cubans. By upholding the traditional public-private divide in the context of racial integration, Castro explicitly disclaimed the possibility that whites would be forced to socialize with blacks. He continued to oppose the adoption of laws against racial discrimination and asked blacks to be more "respectful" than ever before and not to "give excuses" to those opposed to the revolution's battles for racial integration. The most important thing, Castro insisted, was to maintain unity in the face of those opposing the revolution from within and without the country.[61] There was thus the implication, which became increasingly explicit in the following years, that it was "divisive," if not "counterrevolutionary," for specific groups to raise grievances or demands not approved by the revolutionary leaders that "might play into the hands" of the regime's powerful opponents.

While Fidel Castro and other revolutionary leaders continued to make critical references to racial discrimination in some of their speeches, Castro's "clarifications" of March 25 helped to establish a tone that was defensive toward whites and benevolently paternalistic toward Cuban blacks. A large government advertisement published in the 26th of July Movement's newspaper *Revolución* in April and May 1959 carried the photograph of a black child pleading:

> I don't ask for much. I want to eat, get to know the taste of a pastry. The right to a glass of milk and a little bit of meat every day, to be healthy so, when I grow up, tuberculosis does not consume me. I want to play, to have a tricycle . . . to have a new toy. I want to study, to access books and a good school. In order for me to reach all that, it is necessary that my parents have a place to work. They don't want to send me to an institution. They want to earn what is fair in order to give me food, toys, education, so when I grow up, I can be something besides a shoeshine boy or a valet. If I become a good man, per-

haps my intelligence will generate some respect, and we all can get along and the races will understand each other. Perhaps when I become a man, people will have a clearer idea about life so when one of my children goes by, instead of saying "there goes a 'negrito' [little black boy]," they will come to say, "there goes a child." Isn't it true that I don't ask for much?[62]

Paternalism was expressed in a different but striking way in Castro's interactions with the few Cuban blacks who were among the Cuban exiles made prisoners after the failed US-sponsored Bay of Pigs invasion in April 1961. Fidel Castro gathered the prisoners in Havana's sports arena for a five-hour political show. He publicly interrogated many of them but seemed particularly offended when he came across black prisoner Tomás Cruz, of the invaders' paratroop battalion. Castro first said to Cruz, "What are you doing here?" and later told him that "he had the audacity to team up here to fight the Revolution along with that other [white] gentleman, with whom you were not allowed to bathe [at private clubs]."[63] Castro treated Cruz more as an ungrateful Negro than as a political enemy, which is what he was.[64] The attitude that Castro displayed toward the black Cuban counterrevolutionary was entirely consistent with the way the revolutionary leadership frequently addressed all Cubans. The leaders often stressed (and still do) what "the revolution" had done *for* this or that group or for all Cubans, as if "the revolution" were a disembodied entity that was something other than and apart from those Cubans who presumably benefited from it.

This is how things more or less stood until 1962, when, after the Castro government had nationalized most of the economy and radically transformed the country's class structure, it proclaimed that the problems of racial discrimination and racism had been resolved. From then on, issues pertaining to race and racism were essentially sidelined and ignored, and the rule of racial silence was restored.[65] To the degree that such a victory was accomplished, it was through the implementation of radical class-based measures, which substantially benefited blacks and mulattos because of their disproportionate presence among the laboring classes and the poor. By 1962, a literacy campaign, urban housing reforms, the establishment of "racially blind" centralized hiring for all job openings through the Ministry of Labor, and the nationalization of private education with the subsequent opening of those schools to Cubans of all backgrounds had already been carried out. The last reform, nationalization of private education, was particularly important in facilitating the significant social mobility that Afro-Cubans experienced after the sixties. To the extent that they were successful, these class-based reforms were by far the main basis of the progress that blacks achieved during the revolutionary period. Conversely, the major failures of the revolutionary government in improving the housing of most Cubans, particularly the working class and the poor, have resulted in Afro-Cubans continuing to have the worst and most de facto segregated housing on the island.

Initially, the old pro-Moscow Cuban Communists continued to press for racially based affirmative action in employment and other areas while they were not part of the revolutionary government and were pressuring it from the left. Thus, at the height of the racial discussion triggered by Castro's speeches at the end of March 1959, black Communist union leader Lázaro Peña proposed an affirmative action program to be carried out by the unions.[66] By the early sixties, however, once the old Communists were incorporated into the revolutionary leadership, they stopped raising issues that the regime wanted to avoid. The lack of black representation, particularly at the top leadership levels, was and continues to be a thorny problem with a great deal of potential for embarrassment. For example, Fidel Castro's decision to move himself and the Cuban delegation to the UN to Harlem's Theresa Hotel in the fall of 1960 was a brilliant political move and has been widely celebrated as such. But it is much less known that once Castro had decided on that shrewd move, he quickly flew black Cuban major Juan Almeida from Havana to New York to try to compensate for the fact that the seventy-seven-person Cuban delegation was lily-white.[67] On a few occasions in the past, however, Fidel Castro and the top leadership publicly raised the need to increase the number of Afro-Cubans at the higher levels of the party and government. Such was the case during the Third Congress of the CCP in 1986, where Castro also mentioned the need to promote women and young people, and again at the Fifth Congress of the party in 1997. But these occasional proposals did not translate into a public, permanent, and systematic program of affirmative action on the island.

In light of the Cuban government's tendency to sidestep the issue of racism, black independent organizations could have potentially fulfilled the indispensable role of pressing the grievances and demands that the government might oppose or find politically inconvenient to pursue. But the government's transformation of Cuban society in the early sixties left no room for the independent and voluntary organization of any group of Cubans, including black Cubans.[68] Instead, starting in 1960, the regime opted for the establishment of mass organizations, such as the trade unions and the CDRs, to act as transmission belts for the implementation of party and governmental policy. While the regime, following the pattern of Soviet-type countries, established a national women's organization— the FMC or Federation of Cuban Women (Federación de Mujeres Cubanas)— it saw no need to maintain an official organization to represent Cuban blacks. In any case, as we saw above, the racial problem had been declared solved by the early sixties.

Among the organizational casualties of the early years of the revolution were the sociedades de color, which had been the bedrock of black life in Cuba for many decades. For the most part, these were mutual aid societies that ranged from the exclusive Club Atenas in Havana patronized by the black elite to very humble associations in small provincial towns and sugar mill bateyes or villages.

In one of those modest, working-class social clubs, revealingly called Lovers of Progress (Amantes del Progreso), black men regularly met to drink and discuss politics, while children came to get help with their school homework and learn about the history of Cuban blacks, a subject matter virtually ignored by the public school system.[69] Sometime in 1959, government leaders decided to do away with this source of independent power. Juan René Betancourt, the provisional supervisor of the National Federation of Black Societies, after informing the government that the seventh national convention of the organization had been scheduled for the end of November 1959, unexpectedly found out through a radio broadcast that he had resigned "because of the pressure of other duties." The government was obviously opposed to any measure that could strengthen and consolidate an independent national black organization. This was the beginning of a process that by the mid-sixties eliminated the sociedades de color as a vital force in black Cuban society.[70]

After the Early Sixties—Racism Reformed but Not Eliminated

Had the sociedades de color remained alive, they would have had much to act on and oppose in the decades that followed the revolutionary changes of the early sixties. Black Cuban culture became a subject relegated to museums and to professional folkloric dance groups that often traveled abroad. The government, along with most of white Cuba, continued to look down on the religions of blacks as "backward."[71] If not openly repressed, as in the case of the Abakuá society (many of whose members were confined to the UMAP camps of the mid-sixties), black traditions and religions were put under heavy state control. This changed significantly during the economically dire Special Period of the nineties, once the Fourth Communist Party Congress in 1991 decreed the liberalization of religious practice in the country: the government began to encourage various expressions of black culture, traditions, and religion, particularly as important sources of tourist income.[72]

As in much of the rest of "nonrevolutionary" Latin America, the Cuban media tended to present the country as if it were only populated by whites. Even visitors to Cuba who were sympathetic to the revolutionary leadership took notice of this, as did for example Elizabeth Sutherland (also known as Elizabeth "Betita" Martínez), a Mexican American writer and editor who had been active in the black liberation movement in the United States. She spent the summer of 1967 in Cuba and remarked that not only were blacks still overrepresented in menial jobs such as street cleaners and ditch diggers, but whites were overwhelmingly predominant in posters, magazines, television program, movies, and the theater.[73] Things did not change much in the Cuban media for the next forty years. The hip-hop group Hermanos de Causa has renamed the ICRT (Cuban

Institute of Radio and Television), the state agency controlling all radio and television programming, the Cuban Institute for Racism in Television.[74] According to reports, the black staff of the ICRT has protested the absence of black faces in the Cuban media in recent years,[75] and the absence of black women in Cuban television was thoroughly documented in a study published in a Cuban blog in 2006.[76] Even the high-quality and frequently critical Cuban cinema has suffered from the same problem. Black actors have been given leading roles mainly in movies dealing with slavery or with issues of marginality, black religion, or breakdowns of social discipline and lawbreaking. Matters pertaining to discrimination and prejudice have been addressed only on infrequent occasions.[77]

Limitations on the participation of Cuban blacks and mulattos have been noted in fields such as ballet and competitive swimming, with pseudo-scientific explanations sometimes being put forward to rationalize and justify such practices.[78] For many years blacks and mulattos have been disproportionately represented in the prison population, which, as of 2008, was the fifth highest in the world on a per capita basis. A UN delegation that visited two Cuban prisons in 1988 confirmed that fact, which was also acknowledged by the high-ranking Cuban functionary who accompanied the delegation.[79] Blacks have been particularly victimized by the article in the penal code criminalizing "social dangerousness" (*peligrosidad social*). According to the 1979 Penal Code, individuals who demonstrate "a special proclivity" toward committing crimes can be punished with jail terms without even having committed criminal acts and without a formal trial. The concept of "social dangerousness" has most commonly been invoked in cases of chronic drunkenness, vagrancy, drug addiction, and other "antisocial" acts such as openly gay behavior. There is little available information on the racial impact that this law has had on the island. However, according to a study commissioned by Cuba's attorney general in 1987, out of a total of 643 cases of "social dangerousness" registered in the city of Havana between May and December 1986, blacks and mulattos represented 78 percent of those individuals deemed "socially dangerous." Revealingly, 84 percent of the "socially dangerous" individuals were between the ages of sixteen and thirty.[80]

Blacks have been also underrepresented in the top positions of political leadership. At the First CCP Congress, held in 1965, at the very most only 9 percent of the one hundred members of the party's Central Committee (CC) were black. This was virtually identical to the racial composition of the prerevolutionary Cuban Congress in 1945, when only 9.4 percent of the House of Representatives and 9.3 percent of the Senate were black.[81] More recently, in a thorough study published in 2004, Henley C. Adams showed that the black share of the main party and state organs was 32.3 percent—197 of a total of 610 people in those bodies. This is very close to the 35 percent of the population officially counted as black and mulatto in the 2002 census. However, Adams found that the proportion of black Cubans declined markedly in the exclusive institutions with decision-making power. Thus, in the Political Bureau, Council of State, and Council of Ministers, just 10 to 20 percent of members were black. The Council of State was the most racially diverse, and the Council of Ministers the least representative with only one black among its thirty-nine members, despite 12.1 pecent of the Central State Administration—the most senior state cadres—being black and mulatto.[82] A similar situation prevailed in the much less powerful ANPP (Asamblea Nacional del Poder Popular, or National Assembly of Popular Power). After the elections of 2003, 32.5 percent of the new ANPP members were black, 4.5 percent more than in the previous assembly. Among the newly elected members of the assembly, blacks constituted 38.5 percent, higher than their official proportion in the population of Cuba as a whole. Nevertheless, of the six new provincial assembly presidents, only one was black, the only Afro-Cuban among a total of fifteen. The low proportion of blacks in the more important provincial executive bodies reflects the pattern in the more powerful national bodies mentioned above.[83] With respect to the CC of the Communist Party, Adams showed that after the fifth, most recent, congress of the party in 1997, only 13.3 percent of the 150 members of the CC were black and mulatto, a decline of 25.6 percent from the previous committee. This represented a 77.4 percent decline from the high point of racial inclusion achieved at the third congress held in February 1986. With the exception of the two congresses held in the 1980s, the proportion of blacks has declined on other occasions as well.[84] In terms of military representation on the CC of the Communist Party, they overwhelmingly belonged to the senior ranks, composing 85.1 percent of those elected, with blacks constituting only 10.5 percent of this group. But among the fifteen lower-ranking officers elected to the CC, 40 percent were black.[85] This is consistent with the observations of Hal Klepak, a Canadian expert on the Cuban military, although Klepak notes that in comparison with their counterparts in other Latin American armies, blacks and mulattos have a significant presence in the upper ranks in the Cuban military.[86] However, we cannot generally speak of an uninterrupted linear progression of ever-rising racial inclusion at the top political leadership levels in Cuba. In fact, Adams's study points out that one of the major factors contributing to the underrepresentation of blacks in the high circles of power is their low holdover and high replacement rates during the periodic reshuffling of the political elites.[87]

Nevertheless, even the percentages cited by Adams greatly overestimate the proportion of Afro-Cubans in leadership bodies in comparison to the Cuban population as a whole. Adams compared the black presence among Cuban leaders to official census figures, on the supposition that these accurately represent the relative proportions of whites and nonwhites in Cuban society as a whole. However, these census figures undercount blacks and mulattos by a substantial number. Thus, if we take the prerevolutionary census of 1953 as a baseline, it is clear that at the time 12.4 percent of the population was counted as black, 14.5

percent as mestizos (a census category identical to mulattos), and 72.8 percent as white. The first postrevolutionary census of 1970 asked questions about race, but the results of such inquiries were never published. The two subsequent censuses of 1981 and 2002 showed that the black population of Cuba had decreased from 12.4 percent in 1953 to 12.0 percent in 1981 and to 10.1 percent in 2002, while the mestizo (mulatto) population had increased from 14.5 percent in 1953 to 22 percent in 1981 and 24.9 percent in 2002.[88] While the proportion of mestizos or mulattos has probably increased in Cuba in the last sixty years, very few people, including scholars writing about Cuba, believe that only 35 percent of contemporary Cuba is composed of blacks and mulattos. How can the discrepancy between those perceptions and the figures provided by the last two official censuses be explained? In a society dominated by racist values where most signs of black self-assertion have been suppressed, there will be a systematic tendency for people being counted to "upgrade" their racial status. Esteban Morales Domínguez, a black professor at the University of Havana, has pointed out that many people who are not white resist adopting a black or mulatto identity, an attitude that generates deception and hypocrisy and "distorts census figures."[89] Thus, the number of blacks and mulattos in Cuba must be much higher than the one registered by the official censuses.[90] If that is the case, then the proportion of blacks and mulattos holding high public positions is much smaller in comparison to the population as a whole than is suggested by the official figures.[91]

The Problems of the Special Period

The severe economic crisis brought about by the collapse of the Soviet Union and the Soviet bloc in the early nineties considerably worsened the position of blacks and mulattos in absolute and relative terms. As the country's GDP fell by more than one-third within a very short period, about 60 percent of the population began to increasingly depend on remittances from relatives abroad and a few hard-currency sources at home. Cuban blacks got a disproportionately small share of those remittances, if for no other reason than that, according to the 1990 US census, whites accounted for 83.5 percent of the Cuban immigrants living in the United States. A study published by the Cuban journal *Temas* estimated that whites were 2.5 times more likely to receive remittances than blacks and 2.2 times more likely to receive them than mulattos.[92] As the Cuban crisis deepened in the nineties, the tourist industry became the most dynamic of the emergent sectors of the economy and an important source of hard currency for those working in that sector. This led to the transformation of racial patterns of employment in the industry. In the early eighties, Afro-Cubans constituted a substantial proportion of those working in hotels, restaurants, and related services—38 percent according to the 1981 census.[93] The "Special Period" brought about such a major change that the study published by *Temas* concluded that although Afro-Cubans continued to be strongly represented in that sector, they worked mainly in the backroom jobs. The notion of *buena presencia* or "good appearance," closely linked to the racist notion that whites are more attractive—and also more acceptable to white tourists—than blacks, is a crucial factor determining who gets hired and promoted. According to the study, no more than 5 percent of the managers, professionals, and technicians in the tourist industry are black and mulatto.[94] The jobs that blacks have do not typically bring these workers into contact with the tourists, while whites predominate in jobs that do. It is therefore not surprising that whites received 1.6 times more tips than blacks and 1.4 times more than mestizos (mulattos.)[95]

Their substantially disadvantaged economic situation forces blacks and mulattos to work at other jobs in addition to their regular employment. Whites moonlight 2.7 times less than blacks and 1.4 times less than mulattos. In the emerging economic sectors such as tourism, moonlighting is 4.2 times less common than in the traditional economic sectors.[96] Besides moonlighting, people with little or no access to remittances resell products subsidized by the rationing system. Although the ration book typically covers less than half a month's needs, it included until very recently products such as cigarettes that many people choose to resell rather than consume.[97] Accordingly, whites resell rationed products 3.7 times less than blacks, and the latter 2.1 times more than mulattos. Workers in the emerging economic sectors are 2.1 times less likely to resell rationed products than people who work in the traditional economic sectors.[98]

Throughout the revolutionary period, Afro-Cubans suffered far more than whites from poor housing conditions. This situation became more acute during the Special Period. The inaccessibility of construction materials, sometimes even to those people with hard currency to buy them, considerably worsened during this time. The high degree of humidity, let alone the devastating effect of hurricanes (three in 2008 alone), made the situation even more intolerable. The study published in *Temas* pointed out that Afro-Cubans predominate in the most populous and depressed areas or neighborhoods, while whites are predominant in nicer residential neighborhoods, even though there are no rigid forms of racial segregation in the style of US ghettoes. While this situation improved somewhat in the eighties, that was no longer the case in the nineties due to the worsening economic situation.[99]

The economic crisis that began in the nineties also had a disproportionately negative impact on black youth, who were far more likely to be unemployed and relegated to marginal roles in the society than their white cohorts. Blacks and mulattos are also disproportionately represented among the hustlers and prostitutes who, among other marginal activities, cater to the tourist trade. Black youth are far more likely, as in the United States, to be subjected to police harassment and arrest. The hip-hop movement that has taken hold among a significant subset of black Cuban youth has become an important means of expressing their feelings of indignation and protest against police abuse.[100] Debra Evenson, a former law professor and former president of the left-wing National Lawyers Guild who became a legal representative of the Cuban government in New York, aptly summarized the situation:

> Criminal activity, such as theft, increased dramatically in the 1990s parallel to the economic crisis. Although many Cubans have resorted to illegal activity to "resolve" their individual economic needs, blacks have been and continue to be over represented in the prison population. There is a general perception among the population that street crime is primarily committed by blacks. The stereotype of the "*jinetera*" or prostitute in Cuba today is black or mulatta. The unfortunate result of these phenomena is the perpetuation of negative stereotyping of black youths, who are much more likely to be stopped by police in the street for routine identity checks.[101]

Historical Leftovers or Persisting Institutional Racism?

When confronted with the many expressions of racism in postrevolutionary Cuba, spokespersons and apologists for the regime have historically claimed that these are leftovers or remnants of the capitalist past that will fade with the passage of time. This type of explanation tends to emphasize the role of individual prejudice and minimize the role of ongoing institutional discrimination on the island. A frequent implication of this "remnant" or "leftover" argument is that expressions of racism will eventually disappear even in the absence of social and political action. When regime leaders have occasionally recognized that some action was needed, the urgency of the problem became diffused because racist ideologies and practices were seen as having limited social consequences due to the notion that they affected only private and family relations, over which the government had little control.[102]

Is there an alternative approach to that based on the Cuban government's explanations and apologies that would better explain prerevolutionary and postrevolutionary racism in Cuba? Such an explanation should start by dealing with racism as a system of power and social-structural relations. One racially defined group—Cuban blacks—has been historically deprived of power and access to resources as the result of being the object of discriminatory conduct by primarily the white upper and upper-middle classes. Discrimination suffered at the hands of the white lower-middle and working classes, while less weighty and consequential from a societywide perspective, has nevertheless been real as well.[103] From this perspective, the historical role of prejudice—expressed primarily as an individual attitude—has been to ideologically justify and help to maintain the power disparities essential to the continuation of racial discrimination, which constitutes the heart of racism. In Cuba, just as in the United States, discrimination has been primarily carried out through institutional arrangements. These include justice and correctional systems, housing and occupational patterns, and ruling party hierarchies, which, by virtue of being institutionally and systematically entrenched, do not depend on the prejudiced attitudes of individual power holders for their continuation and survival.[104]

From this perspective, it is clear that prerevolutionary Cuba was a racist society even though the overwhelming majority of whites, and a significant proportion of blacks, may not have seen it as such. Although Cuban racist patterns were different from those of the United States, both racist systems originated in slavery and continued to be reproduced by postslavery social and economic institutional arrangements. The Cuban Revolution succeeded in abolishing the system of private capitalism, establishing in its stead a new state bureaucratic system with a new type of ruling class. When it came to race, it carried out some important reforms in race relations, such as the desegregation of beaches and provincial parks, and class-based reforms, such as in the areas of education and health, that disproportionately benefited black Cubans. But only a long-lasting vigorous campaign of affirmative action and authentic multiculturalism could have brought about a clear break with the past—a revolution, and not just a reform, of race relations. This the revolutionary government did not do; the revolutionary leadership itself was a product of the racial silence and color-blind ideology prevailing in prerevolutionary Cuba. Blacks, just like workers, did not as a group have significant input into the revolutionary process, whether before or after the overthrow of Batista on January 1, 1959. Their concerns and grievances were thus not central to the revolutionary program as it evolved through time. The autonomous, independent organizations of blacks (as well as of workers) were abolished, and they were left with no agency of their own through which they could struggle for and force democratic and liberating changes.

Thus, institutional racism, although reformed, continued to exist in postrevolutionary Cuba and significantly worsened during the Special Period that began in the nineties. Racial prejudice continued to exist after the revolutionary victory, but not because it was, as the revolutionary leaders maintained, a remnant or leftover from the capitalist past. Instead, prejudices fed on the continuing reality of black powerlessness, disadvantage, and subordination in many areas of life. As the living conditions of black Cubans deteriorated during the Special Period of the nineties even more than those of whites, so did white prejudice significantly increase. In fact, the reforms carried out by the revolutionary government, which, although real, fell short of an overturn of the prerevolutionary racial order, had the perverse effect of creating new forms of racial prejudice. Thus, a forty-year-old Cuban white male physician could claim in the mid-eighties: "I have a theory that could be considered fascist, but to me blacks are inferior to whites in regard to their intelligence coefficient. In support of this theory I contend that in Cuba, where for thirty-five years blacks have had the same opportunities to study, there is no evidence that they can equal whites. How can one not think that genetic heredity affects them neurologically and makes them different, that is, inferior."[105]

Black Resistance and Consciousness in Cuba

In the sixties and seventies there were a number of small but significant racially oriented instances of opposition on the island, all of which were suppressed by the regime. The African American political scientist Mark Q. Sawyer has summarized the most important of these incidents. Sawyer tells us that in 1967, shortly before the World Cultural Congress held in Havana, to which important black Cuban figures were not invited, a group of them approached the revolutionary authorities to raise issues of concern to Cuban blacks. Cuban minister José Llanusa Gobels responded by calling these black leaders "seditious" and stated that the revolution would not allow activities that would divide the people along racial lines. Llanusa's defense of "national unity," like that of the rest of the revolutionary leaders starting with Fidel Castro, privileged whiteness: in the name of "unity," blacks and mulattos were asked to put aside their grievances. This meant that racial inequalities would be perpetuated.[106] Moreover, Llanusa indicated that only the government and party were authorized to theorize on matters of "culture" and that only hidden enemies would bring up a matter that had already been resolved at the beginning of the revolution. Several of those who met with Llanusa, such as Walterio Carbonell, were later arrested (Carbonell suffered many abuses that most likely contributed to his serious physical and mental health problems). The only black Cuban who was invited to attend the congress was the well-known old Cuban Communist poet Nicolás Guillén. Shortly afterward, in 1968 and 1969, a movement called Movimiento de Liberación Nacional (MLN) was organized by blacks who did not belong to the intellectual elite and who were apparently willing to resort to violent action. It was later broken up with a number of arrests and long prison sentences. Reportedly, MLN's connections with the secret religious society Abakuá, particularly influential among the stevedores in the port of Havana, allowed it to organize a one-day strike action at that port.[107] In 1971, the Black Power Movement, which drew inspiration and sustenance from the work and activities of Frantz Fanon and the Black Power movement in the United States, also became active. The government handled this group with a mixture of co-optation—rewarding some with government positions—and repression, jailing some and exiling others. Lastly, in the mid-seventies the Afro-Cuban Study Group, interested in African American culture, was formed. The group, heavily oriented toward black culture abroad, was very disappointed by the government's refusal to publish the Afrocentric work of Cheikh Anta Diop. This group was also repressed by the government.[108]

With the benefit of hindsight, it is easy to understand why the chances of any of these groups' getting significant support among Cuban blacks, were small.

At the time, the government had substantial support among whites and blacks and its powers of repression were both extensive and effective. This constellation of factors began to significantly change in the nineties. On one hand, the deteriorating economic situation affected black Cubans even more than whites. Although the rioters who shook the Havana seashore in the summer of 1994 did not specifically raise racial demands, they were disproportionately black and mulatto. On the other hand, the relative intellectual and political liberalization of the nineties allowed for a slow and gradual reopening of the subject of race. This is evident in certain small-circulation journals oriented to academics and intellectuals and in discussions that have occurred at the National Library and at the National Union of Cuban Writers and Artists (UNEAC).[109] Artistic exhibitions, such as the 1997 *Queloides I* exposition, and books and documentaries have also contributed to the creation of a more open climate concerning the discussion of racial questions.[110] For his part, Fidel Castro, in a major interview granted shortly before he fell seriously ill in 2006, acknowledged that Cubans of African origin live in worse housing, work at harder and lower-paid jobs, and receive from five to six times less in dollar remittances than their white compatriots.[111] But the heavy hand of censorship has by no means disappeared. For example, the participants in a panel discussion on the Partido Independiente de Color that took place in 2008, on the hundredth anniversary of its foundation, received instructions "from above" to stick to the historical topic and not to say anything about racism in present-day Cuba.[112]

Several black professionals and intellectuals also announced, in September 2009, that they would attempt to revive the Cofradía de la Negritud (loosely translated as Brotherhood of Negritude, CONEG), originally founded in 1998. CONEG's founding document makes clear it is not a political organization, that it does not intend to violate the law, and that it aspires to have a legally recognized existence. However, it pulls no punches when outlining how the Special Period disproportionately affected blacks, who were heavily concentrated in unskilled construction jobs and as "auxiliary workers" in the service sector. The document also explicitly criticizes Cuban blacks for not having taken advantage of the historic opportunities offered by the revolutionary victory in 1959 to organize themselves to achieve fundamental advances in the elimination of racial inequality. At the same time, it also notes that unlike in the case of Cuban women, blacks were not called upon by the government to organize as a distinctive group. While CONEG recognized that the Cuban Revolution had done much to eliminate racial discrimination on the island, there was still much to be done "because the fundamental bases of the problem have not essentially changed." CONEG calls for a number of concrete changes: it explicitly mentions the need for a program to reverse the historic, cumulative disadvantages of the black population in Cuba and calls for diverse measures directed against the prejudices held by a considerable number of white Cubans. CONEG further advocates efforts to raise the level of self-esteem of the black Cuban population and for greater community attention to the "very numerous black Cuban penal population."[113] In a 2007 letter to the executive director of the Superior Council of the Social Sciences, Norberto Mesa Carbonell, the principal leader of CONEG, spelled out a long list of actions that were required to eliminate racial discrimination in Cuba. These included affirmative action in Cuban universities, a proportional presence of black people in television, movies, and the ballet, and the sale of personal grooming products designed for the needs of blacks and mulattos. The letter also insisted on the right to legal recognition of social and community organizations contributing to the elimination of racism, discrimination, and racial inequalities.[114] More recently, CONEG wrote to the National Secretariat of the CTC expressing concern that racial discrimination may have been the determining factor for many black workers in the layoffs of half a million people announced in September 2010. The letter to the CTC based its concern on earlier cases of personnel restructuring, such as that of the Habana Libre Hotel in 1994, which resulted in what the letter described as "ethnic cleansing."[115]

The greater national and international attention to racial discrimination in Cuba has recently put additional pressure on the government to acknowledge that racism is a real problem in Cuba. In December 2009, Raúl Castro, in a speech to the National Assembly of Popular Power, expressed his sense of shame over the insufficient representation of women and blacks in positions of leadership in the country and promised to use all his influence to change the situation.[116] A few weeks later, *Mesa Redonda* (Round Table), the daily television program that has in recent years become the most important vehicle through which the country's authorities broadcast their positions on the political questions of the day, addressed the issue of racism on the island.[117] The timing of Raúl Castro's pronouncement and the *Mesa Redonda* program on race suggests that they may have been at least in part responses to an important event that took place outside Cuba. This was the declaration signed on November 30, 2009, by many prominent African Americans in support of the position taken by Professor Abdias Nascimento, a historic leader of the Black Movement of Brazil, demanding the release of black dissident Dr. Darsi Ferrer and criticizing racism on the island. The African Americans signing the declaration included such prominent black left personalities as Ruby Dee Davis, Cornel West, the Reverend Jeremiah A. Wright Jr., and Kathleen Neal Cleaver.[118] Needless to say, the document was strongly rejected by the Cuban press and the regime's spokespeople,[119] but it nevertheless stung them and may have had some beneficial effect.

A critical aspect of any possible future development on the racial front in Cuba is black consciousness and the direction in which it may be evolving. Historically, the significantly lower degree of physical racial segregation and the greater commonality of conditions between white and black Cuban workers, peasants, and the poor helped to produce a different type of racial consciousness from that in the United States. According to Carlos Moore, the Cuban intervention in Angola had a tremendous psychological impact on black Cubans, even those who were opposed to the regime. In particular, Fidel Castro's proclamation at the height of the intervention that Cuba was a "Latin African" country had a substantial impact on black Cubans, who, according to Moore, began to see foreign policy "as the most conducive arena for fulfillment of their ethnic aspirations."[120] There is reason to believe that the Cuban military interventions in Africa may indeed have resulted in military promotions as well as an increased representation in other official positions for black Cubans.[121]

More recently, interviews conducted by Sawyer on the island showed a wide spectrum of attitudes toward race among black Cubans, ranging from the view that race no longer matters at one end to the perception that the country is fundamentally racist at the other end. Few of the blacks and mulattos interviewed agreed with the old official line that race no longer matters and that those who bring up the issue of race are themselves racist. A young black nurse reflected that "there is a lot of racism in Cuba, and all of us blacks know it. We are discriminated against and need to stick together." A black Cuban lawyer in eastern Cuba, whose views were somewhere in the middle, declared: "I think of myself as both Cuban and black. It is confusing how many in the United States seem to think of themselves as black or white first and American second. I am Cuban. We are all Cuban, but at the same time there are differences."[122]

There is evidence suggesting that the cutbacks in social assistance, deterioration of social programs, and increasing levels of inequality have led a significant number of young black people to conclude that it is necessary to create an all-black organization.[123] Measures being announced in 2010 and 2011 by Raúl Castro's government, such as the shrinking and possible elimination of rationing and the laying off and relocation of as many as a million workers, may impact black attitudes toward the regime and, more generally, black consciousness. A Sino-Vietnamese market-type transition after the Castro brothers are gone from the scene is likely to exacerbate racial inequalities by neglecting if not abandoning the nonemergent sectors of the economy where blacks are disproportionately concentrated. An urban policy that, as in the case of the Havana metropolitan area, would continue to improve the whiter districts located near the Gulf of Mexico shore for the purposes of tourism and possible real estate speculation and neglect the much more heavily black "Havana Inland"[124] would exacerbate such inequalities. Cuban blacks would need to develop their own political perspectives and organizations to respond to such a worsening of conditions and growth of racial inequality.

Chapter Six

Gender Politics and the Cuban Revolution

The gender policies of the Cuban government have elicited much controversy during its more than five decades in power, particularly in regard to the treatment of gays. The government and its defenders have singled out prerevolutionary sexism or traditional "machismo" as the major culprit for the persistence of sexism after the revolution. Undoubtedly, there is still a traditional "machista" cultural inheritance on the island, but the current socioeconomic and political system brought about new systemic problems that especially affected women and helped to perpetuate sexism. Indeed, women have been prevented from acting and organizing independently to struggle against sexist oppression and to defend their interests. This has of course also been true for gays, who for decades were subjected to an oppression and abuse without precedent in the country's history.

Cuban culture is historically rooted for the most part in that of Spain, the colonial "mother country," which ruled the island for four hundred years. Under the colonial arrangement that Spain established in Cuba, men had unchallenged economic power, sole custody of their families, and complete sexual dominion over women.[1] The various cultural traditions that the African slaves brought to the island sometimes reinforced the sexist patterns established by the Spanish overlords, as various Afro-Cuban religious traditions and secret societies engaged in sexist practices to varying degrees.[2] On the other hand, these very African influences counterbalanced the rigidity of the Spanish version of Catholic culture since they did not share its quasi-medieval notions and obsessions with such matters as original sin and sexual purity, and generally brought to the island a more joyful attitude toward life. Moreover, the Catholic Church, in contrast with its strenuous efforts to proselytize Native Americans on the Latin American mainland, neglected missionary work among slaves and free blacks. In siding with Spain against the Cubans fighting for independence, the church further weakened its standing among black as well as white Cubans. Catholicism on the island was also buffeted by the influence of Enlightenment ideologies among the *mambises* (Cuban rebel troops), often transmitted by the Masonic lodges, to which the great majority of black and white independence leaders belonged.

The Legacy of the Struggle for Independence, Cuban Feminism, and the 1933 Revolution

After Spanish rule was abolished and the much less than sovereign Cuban Republic was established in 1902, a number of social forces came into play that to some degree modernized the country and modified the legacy of traditional Hispanic sexism. Most important were the reforms carried out in the early years of the Cuban Republic and in the aftermath of the 1933 Revolution, in which the women's movement that took shape in the twenties and thirties helped shape the reform agenda of that major, although largely frustrated, revolution.

Divorce

The roots of legal divorce on the island go back to the nineteenth century. A divorce law had been suggested by independence leaders as early as 1868 and was part of a larger struggle for the separation of church and state and to establish secular law and create social equality. A law establishing divorce was part of the Revolutionary Codes approved by Cuban rebels in 1896, while Spain was still in control of the island. Eventually, the Cuban Republic approved a no-fault divorce law in 1918.[3] The same law allowed women the right to have custody over children and to receive alimony and child support payments, and prescribed the terms of property settlements.[4] An earlier law approved in 1917 had given married women the right to administer and dispose of their property and to negotiate and enter into private and public property contracts.[5] By the 1950s, Cuba had one of the highest rates of divorce in Latin America.[6]

The Right to Vote and Social Legislation

In the 1920s, a number of women's associations and parties developed in Cuba, giving rise to the equivalent of what has been called "first wave" feminism in the United States. This first wave feminism was politically heterogeneous, ranging from conservatives to leftists, although the leadership was socially fairly homogeneous and was composed of white, educated middle- and upper-class women. The Cuban feminists of the period did not on the whole confront male power as a major cause of women's oppression. Particularly during the early years of the movement, they were interested in legal reforms that did not necessitate deep changes in the social structures—responsible for a great deal of social inequality—in the country. Although these early feminists were concerned with women's education and conditions of employment, their main focus was with women's right to vote, which they finally won in 1934, as an outcome of the 1933 Revolution.[7] In Latin America, only Uruguay, Brazil, and Ecuador had achieved women's suffrage before Cuba.[8]

Nevertheless, very few women were elected to national office in the years between 1934 and the 1959 Revolution. Only twenty-six women—twenty-three representatives and three senators—were elected to Congress during this period.[9] But the greater incorporation of women into the political process as voters further encouraged women's participation in student and union movements. An increasing number of women also became active in political parties, although typically in the subordinate "female sections" of those organizations. Women's demands helped to bring about a substantial body of social legislation enacted from the thirties to the fifties. These laws included the right to a twelve-week maternity leave, a requirement that factories and institutions that employed more than fifty women have nurseries for children under the age of two, and a prohibition of firing women workers when they got married. Female sales clerks at department stores also struggled for and won the right to sit down whenever their work allowed it. However, this type of legislation usually did not cover domestic or agricultural workers. Further, employers were repeatedly found to violate these laws or find ways to circumvent them. For example, the large Ariguanabo textile mill simply stopped hiring women, and the Woolworth chain of department stores, one of the biggest, began to hire only single women as "temporary" workers.[10]

During the 1930s the grounds for divorce expanded to include abandonment by either partner after only six months and separation after more than five years. Both partners were declared equally responsible for the material subsistence of the family, but an emphasis on parental income as the determining factor for custody made this modification harmful to women.[11] In 1940, a new and broadly progressive constitution codified the previous social legislation benefiting women and additionally prohibited the classification of children as legitimate or illegitimate. At the same time, however, the constitution eliminated many of the progressive implications of this measure by retaining the invidious distinction for purposes of inheritance.[12]

Feminist pressure undoubtedly helped to shape the progressive content of the constitution of 1940. The Third National Women's Congress was held in February 1939 and registered the increased political maturity and advances that had taken place since the first such congress in 1923. In the meantime the programs of the women's movement had expanded from a narrow set of women's issues to a view of women's oppression, which led to advocacy of more left-wing political solutions.[13] Unfortunately, although the 1940 Constitution confirmed the legal gains won in the thirties and earlier, it had the perverse effect of taking most of the wind out of the sails of the women's movement by demobilizing women politically. Many women's organizations continued to exist until they were disbanded by the revolutionary government in 1960. But their focus had shifted from legal and political issues such as suffrage and social legislation to welfare, education, and health projects, including community activities oriented toward resolving problems of poverty and disease among women and children.[14]

Abortion remained illegal. However, by the forties and fifties it was widely practiced throughout the island. In the cities, illegal abortions were fairly accessible and usually carried out by qualified professionals at prices within the reach of working-class women. In the rural areas, abortions were also frequent but more likely to be carried out by midwives and rural folk healers with the aid of rites, rituals, and home remedies.[15] In the period immediately preceding the revolution, Cuba was one of the Latin American countries with the highest incidence of abortion.[16]

The Education and Employment of Women

In addition to the impact of the legal and political changes implemented during the first fifty years of the Cuban Republic, traditional Spanish gender relations were affected by the significant, although limited, economic development brought about by the North American imperial masters who replaced the Spanish colonial overlords in 1898. The effect of this type of economic development was highly distorted, as reflected, for example, in the huge gap in living standards it perpetuated between city and countryside.[17] However, it brought about important material transformations on the island and had the unanticipated effect of introducing a degree of "Americanization" into Cuban culture,[18] which further blunted the edge of the prevailing Spanish patriarchal relations.

The main areas affected by this transformation were education and employment. By the 1950s, the proportion of females between five and fifteen years of age attending school was almost equal to that of males. The proportion of males who were illiterate (26 percent) exceeded that of females (21 percent), and only Argentina had a higher female literacy rate in Latin America (85 percent).[19] According to the 1953 census, women constituted 37 percent of university graduates.[20] By 1956–57, 45 percent of university students and 22 percent of professors were women. They were concentrated in certain professions: in the late 1950s, 622 women were studying in pharmacy, 430 in law, and 388 in philosophy and letters; only 7 women studied agricultural engineering, 4 civil engineering, and 3 electrical engineering.[21] Clearly, it was not exclusion but the gender division of labor that led women, particularly in the middle class, to be socialized and channeled into particular careers and professions. In any case, only a small proportion of young Cubans attended university at this time.

The gender division of labor was also evident in the labor market. Before the 1959 Revolution, the great majority of women were homemakers. According to the 1953 census only 13.7 percent of adult women were employed outside the home, and more than one-quarter of these were domestic workers[22] who were not protected by any labor or social legislation. Women were well represented (46 percent) in the professions and semiprofessions and were overrepresented in teaching, philosophy, and nursing. They constituted 82 percent of the teachers, 81 percent of social workers, and 68 percent of pharmacists. But women were only 13 percent of medical doctors, 17 percent of lawyers, and 5 percent of administrators and managers. They were also underrepresented (between 15 and 20 percent) among white-collar workers, and greatly underrepresented (between 2 percent and 10 percent) among blue-collar workers.[23] Significantly, women tended to occupy the extremes of the Cuban occupational structure. On one hand, as I indicated earlier, more than one-fourth of women working outside the home were domestic servants, while on the other hand, women accounted for more than 55 percent of professional and technical workers (38,616 out of 70,018).[24]

North American and European observers have tended to confuse the visibility and even flamboyance of prostitution in Havana with the quite different matter of its relative weight and importance within the Cuban economy and society as a whole. Thus, for example, Lourdes Arguelles and B. Ruby Rich argue that the only occupational sectors showing substantial growth in the fifties were tourism, drug distribution, gambling, and prostitution.[25] However, they provide no data supporting this contention and largely ignore the general economic context of the island in that period. In 1956, a high year for tourism, that economic sector earned thirty million dollars, which was barely 10 percent of what was earned by the sugar industry.[26] Nor do Arguelles and Rich say a word about the very large construction industry. This industry was attracting huge amounts of very conservative Cuban capital into the residential sector. Foreign capital was flowing into the facilities being built by the Moa Bay Mining Company for the mining and concentration of nickel and cobalt in eastern Cuba in the fifties,[27] and of course, into hotels for tourists as well. To get some perspective on the issues of tourism and prostitution in the fifties we should consider that somewhere between 200,000 and 250,000 tourists visited Cuba every year in the fifties, compared with well over two million for most of the first decade of the twenty-first century.[28] Meanwhile, the population of Havana only doubled during those fifty years.[29] It is estimated that by the end of the decade of the fifties there were 270 brothels and 11,500 women earning their living as prostitutes in Havana (there were far fewer prostitutes working outside of the capital). As shocking as the latter figure is, it pales in comparison with other data provided by the 1953 census for Cuban women overall. According to that census 87,522 women were working as domestic servants, 21,000 women were totally without employment and looking for work, and another 77,500 women were working for a relative without pay. Moreover, an estimated 83 percent of all employed women worked less than ten weeks a year, and only 14 percent worked year-round.[30] These were the far more shocking realities of the uneven development induced by the US empire and Cuban capital on the island, although they may not be as risqué and exciting to North American and European observers, whether left or right, interested in Cuban exoticism and difference.[31]

The Situation of Cuban Gays before the 1959 Revolution

Since the earliest days of Spanish colonialism on the island, gays were victims of deep discrimination and prejudice, but rarely as a result of open and official government policy.[32] The considerable oppression of gays in prerevolutionary Cuba was for the most part carried out by civil society in ways that only rarely were expressed in the media (except in depictions of gays as targets of comedic ridicule) or became objects of serious academic and professional research. Gay bashing and oppression was far more likely to be talked about than written about. Moreover, gays were much more socially ostracized in the countryside than in Havana.[33] These features of Cuban life were in great part due to the very deep closet in which gay people had been forced to live on the island. A lack of gay organizations cemented that reality. While the silence on racism masked at least an abstract recognition, on the part of most white Cubans, that racism was evil, particularly after the defeat of Nazism in the Second World War, that was not the case with homophobia, which was not even acknowledged as a social problem.

There were several pseudo-scientific "studies" on gays published, particularly in the late nineteenth and early twentieth century, which tended to portray them in a negative light. In 1906, the famed Cuban anthropologist Fernando Ortiz blamed Asians for being at least one of the "races" responsible for bringing such a *vicio execrable* (abominable vice) to Cuba.[34] References, frequently negative, to female homosexuality appeared in Cuban literature, as in the case of José Martí and his novel *Amistad Funesta* (Fatal friendship).[35] A far more positive tone could be noted in novels written in the twenties and thirties by authors such as Ofelia Rodríguez Acosta, Alfonso Hernández Cata, and Carlos Montenegro. Nevertheless, in 1928, prominent feminist leader Mariblanca Sabas Alomá targeted lesbianism for being a crime against nature and a behavior reflecting both deviance and excessive passion.[36]

The powerful biases against gay men—discrimination and prejudices against gay women were always less pronounced—had a great impact on the behavior of heterosexually oriented men. In general, machismo has always been as openly punitive toward deviations from traditional male appearance and manners as toward homosexual behavior as such. Men who appear to behave in an effeminate manner or with less than stereotypical masculinity are assumed to be homosexual regardless of whether they are gay.[37] In Cuban culture this led to an obsessive exactitude with which Cuban male youngsters were instructed by their older male peers on how precisely to shake hands, speak, stand up, and walk. Any "normal" male who deviated from this code ran the risk of being considered a "faggot" (*maricón*) and treated with repugnance and ridicule by Cuban men and women. Homosexuals who presented themselves in a more conventionally masculine manner were more likely to be tolerated, although still looked down upon, by most Cubans. These men were referred to as *entendidos*, as in *entendido pero no dicho* (understood but not stated).[38]

Although there were public homophobic acts, these were consistent with the prerevolutionary norm that antigay discrimination was primarily the domain of individuals and the institutions of civil society. Even when the police raided and arrested gay people in the establishments and public places where they tended to congregate, as happened, for example, in 1958, Batista's last year in power, the government did not use those incidents as occasions to score political or ideological points. It would have been seen as very strange if Batista's government had chosen to make a big political issue out of those raids. This stood in stark contrast with the occasional actions undertaken by the state against prostitution. For example, in January 1951, under the constitutional government of Auténtico president Carlos Prio Socarrás, the minister of the interior, Lomberto Díaz, launched a campaign to "clean" the barrio Colón, by far the neighborhood most associated with prostitution in the capital.[39] The campaign was widely discussed in the media and created a bit of a sensation among the people at large. The differential public treatment of prostitution and homosexuality might have been implicitly based on the individualistic and moralistic notion that prostitution involved an explicit moral choice while homosexuality was a moral, and perhaps a physical, weakness, affliction, or sickness. Besides, female heterosexual prostitution, while morally reprehensible to contemporaries, did not challenge heterosexual norms, while homosexuality did. It was also more acceptable to publicly talk about prostitution since it predominantly involved women and was supposed to be "the oldest profession," while gayness, mostly associated with men, was a far more uncomfortable topic for the politicians and media to handle.

Cuban Women after the Revolution

Women did not play central leadership roles in the struggle against the Batista dictatorship (1952–58), although their rank-and-file participation, particularly in the urban underground, has been underestimated.[40] It is true that because the women's movement, which had played a significant role in the revolutionary process of the thirties, had exhausted itself by the forties, there were only weak links of continuity between that movement and the women political activists of the fifties. A study conducted in Cuba in the late nineties found that the majority of these women activists were young, single, white, middle class, and educated and that their principal underground political activities were propaganda and fund raising. Only 23 percent of the women studied were members of or even aware of women's organizations.[41]

Consistent with social patterns in Latin America and elsewhere, many women leaders of the struggle against Batista were related to top male revolutionary leaders, as in the cases of Vilma Espín and Haydée Santamaría.[42] Celia Sánchez, Fidel Castro's close associate, was the first woman to participate in armed combat. However, it should be pointed out that Espín, Santamaría, and Sánchez were already local or secondary leaders of the movement before they met their future husbands.[43] In the summer of 1958, women were allowed to form their own Mariana Grajales platoon.[44] It is estimated that by the end of

1958 some three hundred women had participated as guerrilla fighters in the struggle against Batista.[45] This would have amounted to 10 percent of the total number of combatants if Fidel Castro's own estimate of three thousand rebel fighters when victory was achieved on January 1, 1959, is correct.[46] Besides propaganda and fund raising, women were active in the urban underground movement in such roles as nursing, providing shelter, and—taking advantage of the traditional role expectations of the Batista police when searching people—transporting hidden fighters and weapons in vehicles. Women lawyers represented imprisoned revolutionaries, and in proportionately much smaller numbers than men, they participated in street demonstrations and even planted bombs and hurled Molotov cocktails. Women also allowed their homes to be used for illegal political meetings and were involved in manufacturing weapons and uniforms.[47]

Once the revolutionary government consolidated itself and began to create a Soviet-type society on the island, women were mobilized on behalf of the type of modernization process typical of those social systems. In the case of Cuba, that strategy built on the significant degree of modernization that had been achieved in the prerevolutionary years and was characterized by a highly paternalistic style of government functioning. Central to this approach was the incorporation of women into the labor force as part of a strategy of economic development. The major incorporation of women in the paid labor force of the island did not lead to much political or theoretical discussion about its implications and consequences (although this changed somewhat with the relative liberalization of the nineties). Cuba did not directly experience the women's movement and sexual revolution of the sixties. Whatever progress was made in terms of women's rights in Cuba was not connected to the international women's liberation movement, but instead to the mobilization of women into the paid workforce outside the home. As the Cuban writer Reynaldo González put it: "We didn't live through the sexual revolution with all its problems, its positive aspects and also its excesses, its exaggerations too. Here we didn't go through it . . . In Cuba feminism is a sort of education of the female masses for work, but we have not had the theorizing that comes with this kind of work . . . The woman's revolution in Cuba didn't have any theorizing; it lacked that."[48]

While women's liberation was not the main goal of this economic strategy, it undoubtedly had an indirect liberating effect. The historian William H. Chafe makes a distinction between two kinds of social change that is illuminating in this context. One type of social change is brought about through structural, impersonal forces (such as the industrial revolution) that can dramatically alter the lives of people. The other type of social change is brought about by protest movements (such as the women's movement) that are consciously and deliberately struggling for specific liberating goals.[49] In the case of Cuba and other Soviet-type societies, Chafe's useful distinction gets somewhat more complicated, because the modernization brought about through economic development has been an explicit political goal of the state leadership and not the impersonal process typical of capitalist market societies. Of course, the leaders of Soviet-type societies including Cuba also support their own version of the liberation of women, although this type of "liberation" is clearly subordinate to the leaders' view of other government priorities and is subject to their control from above.

Organizing Cuban Women—from the Top

True to the Soviet-type socioeconomic and political patterns that the government established in the early sixties, the state swallowed up civil society almost in its entirety.[50] An intense process of politicization conducted totally from above was fundamental to the creation of the Cuban leviathan. As applied to Cuban women, this involved the creation in 1960 of the FMC as one of several state-sponsored "mass organizations." However, the FMC was not primarily concerned with women's liberation—or feminism—and it largely succeeded in keeping Cuban women isolated from the international women's movement at its most important moments. More than 920 preexisting women's organizations were disbanded and subsumed into the FMC. Since the women's movement on the island had faded into oblivion some twenty years earlier, this organizational transition was achieved smoothly and with little resistance, unlike the wrenching confrontations and purges that took place in 1959 and 1960 in the Cuban labor movement. None of the women's organizations had ever played the central role that the sociedades de color had played among Cuban blacks as recreational, cultural, and social welfare centers. As Fidel Castro's assistant and close confidant, Celia Sánchez functioned for many years as a sort of Cuban equivalent to Eva Perón, receiving letters from all over the country asking for help in resolving problems and correcting injustices.[51]

As a "mass organization" the FMC was supposed to recruit as many women as possible and thus act, like the trade unions and other "mass organizations," as a transmission belt for the far more exclusive Communist Party. In this the FMC succeeded: by 1975, it had expanded its membership to include some 80 percent of the adult women in the country.[52] It functioned first and foremost as an instrument for the mobilization of Cuban women. It turned hundreds of thousands of them into participants in a social and political process over which they neither had political control nor were being prepared to exercise it at any point in the future. To the considerable extent that it got women out of their homes, it liberated them from traditional and patriarchal authority relations even as it brought them into the still patriarchal but less intimate and far more impersonal authority of the one-party state and its institutions of control. The significant degree of personal and social liberation from traditional authority that women experienced was accompanied by an equally significant loss of their political freedom and ability to organize independently from the state.

Nevertheless, the FMC played an important role in several worthy campaigns. One was the literacy campaign of 1961, which eventually enrolled more than fifty thousand women, including many adolescent girls, who were often sent far from home and the oversight of their parents.[53] In addition, thousands of rural women were trained to use sewing machines, and they, in turn, were enrolled as instructors to even larger numbers of peasant women. Another FMC program engaged in the education and retraining of thousands of domestic servants, an occupation that was almost eliminated with the revolution after having included, according to the 1953 census, about 25 percent of employed women.[54] The FMC also developed programs to curb prostitution and retrain prostitutes, and to establish day care centers.[55] The FMC played a major role in recruiting female "volunteer" labor, an important feature of the Cuban economy. In 1970, for example, women contributed 20.1 million hours of volunteer labor to the sugar harvest. Women's volunteer labor accounted for 95.6 million hours in 1973 and "only" 49.3 million hours in 1975.[56]

The leadership of the FMC has functioned as a kind of discreet lobby within the ruling circles of the state and Communist Party, particularly in terms of legislation and administrative rules relevant to women. This was the case, for example, with the family code enacted in 1975 and with the reduction of the number of jobs and occupations from which Cuban women had been legally banned. The FMC was often an inside player in the battles over bureaucratic turf characteristic of Soviet-type systems. For example, the FMC lost an important bureaucratic battle when it was compelled, along with the CDRs, to eliminate its factory and occupational branches in the late 1960s. The official trade unions then assumed control of all organizational life in every work center and in the process established their own women's offices in each union local.[57]

While the FMC has been able to lobby the central political leadership behind the scenes, it cannot oppose that leadership, whether openly or otherwise, on any issue pertaining to women or anything else. FMC congresses offer an opportunity for a kind of "debate" designed to let off steam and deal almost exclusively with practical issues. No delegate to an FMC congress has been able to raise a question that challenged the government line on, for example, economic or foreign policy. Resolutions have been voted on by delegates raising their hands, and have been usually approved unanimously. Every congress unanimously approves a resolution in support of the revolutionary leadership and its policies.[58]

From its very inception, it was clear that the FMC was not an independent women's organization and that it had nothing to do with the women's liberation movement or feminism, which it rejected with hackneyed "Marxist" language, such as the use of "bourgeois" and "petty bourgeois" as terms of abuse. Vilma Espín, the head of the FMC, informed a reporter for *Ms.* magazine at the 1974 FMC congress that the Cuban women's revolutionary movement was "feminine, not feminist."[59] Although the term "feminine" in Cuban Spanish has a more ambiguous meaning (it can refer both to femininity and to womanhood) than in English, Espín's opposition to feminism, and by implication much of women's liberation, was crystal clear. Throughout its history, the FMC has been an extremely hierarchical institution that has never questioned patriarchal structures or practices and has for the most part shied away from engaging in gender analysis.[60] Its magazine *Mujeres*, which focused on women's contributions to the economy, education, and culture, has been infused with a traditional, paternalistic portrayal of women. In addition to statements by Fidel Castro praising exemplary women, much of its content has involved how to make toys, knit and sew, care for sick children, and use kitchen utensils, and other domestic matters.[61] Throughout the 1960s, every edition of *Mujeres* featured full-page fashion spreads, copied from North American publications such as *Glamour* and *Vogue*. During the mobilizations for volunteer labor in the countryside, the FMC and the CDRs sponsored beauty contests to select the "Stars of the Harvest." Each winner in 1968 represented a different crop, for whose cultivation she had to campaign.[62]

In contrast to other Latin American countries, Cuban society remained isolated from the international women's movement, particularly during the sixties, seventies, and eighties. The primary international contacts of the FMC during those years were limited to the women's organizations in the Soviet bloc and the Moscow-dominated International Democratic Federation of Women. Starting in 1987, however, FMC representatives began to develop contacts with Latin American feminists, particularly in Nicaragua and El Salvador. As support for feminism grew among the Latin American left and as feminism acquired a popular following, the FMC's replaced its antifeminism with a policy of cooptation signaled by the limited inclusion of a few feminist issues in the Cuban policy process.[63]

This parallels the growing relationship between the Cuban government and the proponents of liberation theology in Latin America in the eighties, which led to a considerable softening of the Cuban government line on religion both outside and within the island. However, the FMC's "flexibility" should not be overstated: its concessions to women's liberation fell far short of the equivalent concessions that the Cuban government granted to organized religions after the Fourth Party Congress in 1991. The FMC continued to be detached from the problems facing Cuban women under the "Special Period." In addition, most of its leaders refused to incorporate gender analysis and feminism in their work, and most importantly, they continued to suppress every effort by women to organize independently of the official state organization.[64]

Until 1999, the only Cubans who participated in Latin American women's *encuentros* (encounters) were FMC functionaries, and they typically did not actively report on these regional discussions after they returned home. This began to change in recent years when Cuban women who were not FMC bureaucrats were allowed to participate in the encounters with their Latin American counterparts.[65] In the early nineties, because the First Ibero-American Women and

Communication Congress was held in Havana, several Cuban women working in the field of communications were exposed to the gender concept. Influenced by these notions, these women established the Association of Women Communicators, or "Magín." Magín's main objective was to change women's image in the media. The group's founders included journalists, historians, and artists who were originally affiliated with the FMC and maintained cordial relations with its officials. Magín began to grow and soon had about four hundred members, mostly in Havana.[66]

Magín received help from American grassroots human rights and women's organizations that visited Cuba and brought them medicines, food, and resources for their workshops. UN agencies such as UNICEF and OXFAM helped Magín with financial resources and in giving them an international profile. However, as Sujatha Fernandes has argued, this transnational assistance introduced into Magín an advocacy logic that diverted its leadership from developing broader activist work. Magín's original decision to work within the media had come from its own leaders' direct experience in working in that profession, but the effort to make themselves attractive to international donors led them to narrow their focus. Instead of trying to build a broader movement reaching out to teachers, doctors, and all those involved with education and communication, they opted to turn Magín into a professional association for workers in the mass media. The influence of transnational organizations also led Magín to turn inward to questions of self-cultivation and self-esteem instead of organizing in pursuit of broader emancipatory goals.[67]

Magín's close ties with a number of state institutions, especially with the FMC, began to wear down, particularly over the question of *jineterismo* (the Cuban term for prostitution) and sex work. For the FMC, jineterismo was immoral and had to be "cleaned up." On the eve of the seventh congress of the FMC in 1995, Vilma Espín declared that prostitution occurred among "weak people, unethical families, young women who are a great shame to the country and do not pay attention to their moral degradation . . . The majority come from homes with little morality or are simply very depraved people who accept that their daughters live that way because they benefit from it."[68] For the women of Magín views such as this represented a self-righteous, moralistic, and conservative perspective. Magín held that Cuban women had the right to engage in jineterismo provided that they retained their dignity and self-respect. At the root of the differences between Magín and the FMC on this question were disagreements regarding morality and sexuality. Magín began to be perceived by the authorities as a threat to the state at a particularly bad time that coincided with the government's crackdown against critical institutions such as the Center for the Study of America (CEA). On March 23, 1996, Raúl Castro gave a speech denouncing Cuban NGOs, particularly those with ties to foreign NGOs. The attack against CEA was launched after this speech, and in September the Central

Committee of the CCP called a meeting of its executive committee with Magín's leadership to dissolve Magín. At the meeting, the Communist leaders argued that most independent organizations ended up subverting the revolution one way or another, because foreign money was always given in exchange for political loyalties. Magín was also denounced for duplicating the work of various official organizations, including the FMC, an illegal and prosecutable act in Cuba. Party leaders contended that an autonomous organization of women presented a risk to national unity and that therefore Magín would have to be disbanded. According to Sujatha Fernandes, Magín's women "accepted the decisions because they knew there were no other options if they did not want to be considered dissidents and have their professional lives in Cuba curtailed."[69] Shortly after Magín was disbanded, the government created with the support of the FMC a substitute organization, the Journalism Gender Circle, under its tight control.[70]

The case of Magín illustrates the Cuban one-party state's inability to allow any independent organization of women, or of any other group, even when it is not opposed to the government, as Magín certainly was not—it simply differed in some of its policies from the official mass organizations. The organization of the Cuban one-party state also points to the limits of the FMC itself. Through its many activities and its behind-the-scenes lobbying, the FMC could have at best protected some of what Maxine Molyneux has called women's "practical interests," which unavoidably result from the gender division of labor, such as the benefits they often obtain from welfare state legislation and institutions. But the FMC would not have been able to fight, except occasionally and on the margins, for what Molyneux calls women's "strategic interests," namely, those aimed at opposing patriarchy, such as abolishing the sexual division of labor, alleviating the burdens of domestic labor and child rearing, removing institutionalized forms of discrimination and male control and violence, establishing freedom of choice over childbearing, and constructing political equality.[71]

Women and Political Power in Cuba

In light of sexism on the island and Cuban women's secondary role in the struggle against the Batista dictatorship, it is not surprising that during at least the first postrevolutionary decade women had virtually no presence in the various leadership bodies of the revolutionary government. Through the late sixties and even early seventies, they were visibly absent from the cabinet, the trade union leadership, and the Political Bureau, the Secretariat, auxiliary commissions, and provincial branches of the CCP. By the late sixties, out of one hundred members of the Central Committee, only five were women. Of the twenty-seven members of the National Committee of Communist Youth, only one was female and only one was a black male.[72] Even though women constituted the great majority among members of the CDRs, a man always led this watchdog organization during those years.[73] It took fifteen years after the revolutionary victory for the first woman to be appointed to the Political Bureau of the CCP.[74]

The representation of women in the leadership of governmental institutions began to improve in the seventies and eighties,[75] although at a very slow rate. The one exception has been the national parliament, or National Assembly of Peoples' Power, one of the least powerful political institutions, which serves as a sounding board for the ruling party and as a cosmetic embellishment for the "democratic" pretensions of Cuban Communism. During its seventh legislative session (2006–07), 43.39 percent of the deputies were women. However, it is worth noting that even within the institutional structures of People's Power, the representation of women was substantially less at the local level (27.03 percent),[76] although this proportion increased to 33.4 percent in the elections held in 2010.[77] This has been usually attributed to two factors. First, many women, particularly after the crisis of the nineties, bore the burden of greater domestic demands (caring for children and obtaining scarce food and other material resources). Second, men tend to be unwilling to vote for women since there are more candidates than offices at the local level; this is not the case at the national level, where there is only one candidate for each office to be filled. This explanation is probably valid for what happens at the local level. But it fails to explicitly acknowledge that women appointed by the government at the national level are also far more likely to be important full-time functionaries with far more material resources and domestic help to take care of their household duties.[78]

Aside from the relatively powerless national parliament, women remain woefully underrepresented in the institutions with real power in Cuba. In general, there is an inverse relationship between the actual power of an institution and the presence of women in it.[79] In 2003, six women (19 percent) were members of the important thirty-one-person Council of State, and only two more were added five years later for a total of eight (25.81 percent).[80] Regarding cabinet positions held by women, Cuba ranked thirty-fifth in the world, with six women (16.2 percent) among the thirty-seven government ministers in 2005.[81] Women's membership in the CCP has significantly increased since the very low 10 percent level in 1967 but still constituted only 30 percent of the membership at the time of the Fifth Party Congress in 1997.[82] Of the 150 members of the Central Committee elected at that congress, only twenty members (13 percent) were women, and the Political Bureau elected after that congress had an even smaller proportion of women (8.3 percent).[83] Part of the reason for the underrepresentation of women in the higher echelons of the party and government is related to the heavy influence of army brass in those presumably political institutions. Women are almost invisible in the higher ranks of the army—only one woman is a general—and this obviously has had an impact on women's political representation at the highest levels.[84] The absence of women in the leadership structures of the CCP becomes striking when compared with the composition of the leaderships of the Sandinista Front for National Liberation in Nicaragua and the Farabundo Martí National Liberation Front in El Salvador. In 2001 both of these parties had, compared to Cuba, almost five times the number of women in their highest decision-making bodies. Both the Nicaraguans and the Salvadorans had put in place quotas to raise the level of women's participation in leadership.[85]

The inclusion of women as equal partners in the structures of power is important as a matter of principle—the right of oppressed groups to participate in any and all of the important positions in society, be they strictly political or otherwise. This is particularly the case for women, who usually account for half the population of any country. It is also important because of its consequences, not least being the improvement in self-esteem that is more likely to lead to even very young girls having far greater aspirations.

However, it is highly questionable whether such benefits include the notion that women occupying positions of power will necessarily bring a distinctive and more humane "women's sensibility" to the corridors of power[86] and that they will necessarily defend women's or, more broadly, progressive and popular interests. The examples of Margaret Thatcher, Indira Gandhi, and many other contemporary women leaders support the deep skepticism merited by such assumptions. Moreover, let us not forget that the promotion of women to positions of leadership in Nicaragua has not prevented the enforcement of one of the most repressive anti-abortion laws in Latin America.

Nevertheless, such notions are widespread among students of women in Cuba, including such critical and fine scholars as Lois Smith and Alfred Padula. These authors seem to view the policies and practices of the Cuban government solely in terms of their being based on interests "defined by a male elite."[87] Maleness, however, doesn't explain anything about the specific dynamics of any particular socioeconomic system, including Cuban Communism. Moreover, Cuban ruling-class men for the most part live with and form families with Cuban ruling-class women,[88] who, even if in a subordinate position in relation to their male partners, benefit from and have a common interest in defending their ruling-class interests. Besides, there is nothing in principle that forecloses the possibility that the Cuban regime could significantly expand the number of women in positions of leadership (even including a perfectly equal 50–50 division of top positions). That would be a good thing in terms of fully implementing inclusion principles. But it might not necessarily do anything at all to strengthen the interests and freedom of most Cuban women if these interests came in collision with the ruling social and economic system. This would be especially the case if Cuban women continued to be denied the right to form their own independent organizations to defend their interests even against state policies and actions.

The Education and Employment of Cuban Women

The literacy campaign and related educational campaigns conducted by the Cuban leaders resulted in a notable increase in school attendance at the lower educational level for both boys and girls in the early years of the revolution. However, this was not the case with respect to university education. As already indicated in the chapter on the economy, enrollment in higher education actually declined from 1958 to 1961 and by 1970 was still below the prerevolutionary level. By 1972 that level had been regained, and it continued to increase until reaching 10.8 percent of the relevant age group in 1976 and a high point of 23 percent of the population of university age in 1987. As a result of the economic crisis of the nineties, however, this proportion declined to 12 percent of the university-age group in 1998–99; by 2002–03 it was still below the 1989–90 level.[89] The number of women university students grew much more than the number of men. After 1980 women represented more than 50 percent of university graduates, and after the year 2000, more than 60 percent. In the academic year 2006–07, 65 percent of the graduates were women.[90]

In terms of employment, the early years of the revolution saw the incorporation of few women into the labor force: with the onset of rationing and the lack of consumer goods there was little incentive for women to go to work outside the home. Higher working-class incomes and several generous social policies, combined with the government's inability to provide sufficient day care centers, school and workers' cafeterias, laundromats, and other similar services, encouraged working-class women to stay at home.[91] Then, when the economy improved in the seventies due to a dramatic increase in the price of sugar, there was a boom in women's employment. The proportion of women of working age in the labor force rose from 24.9 percent in 1970 to 44.5 percent in 1979, which represented close to 30 percent of all Cuban workers.[92] However, this was not that different from other countries in Latin America: in 1980, 27.8 percent of Mexico's labor force, 27.4 percent of Argentina's, and 21.2 percent of Venezuela's work force were women. A few years later, in 1984, 40.8 percent of Colombia's labor force were also women.[93] We may conclude from these changes in the labor force throughout Latin America that a variety of socioeconomic factors, other than deliberate state policy as in the case of Cuba, were at work pushing women into the labor force. As the eighties progressed, more Cuban women went out to work outside their homes, so that by 1990 Cuban women constituted 39.6 percent of the labor force.[94] By the end of 2007, the proportion had increased to 40.04 percent. If we exclude the armed forces and look at only the state civilian sector, the figure rises to 46.2 percent of the workforce. The rate of economic participation among women was then 59.1 percent,[95] which obviously constitutes a huge difference from the 13.7 percent of Cuban women in the labor force registered by the 1953 census. Obviously, the Cuban government had succeeded in its goal of incorporating Cuban women into the labor force.

Cuban women have become a large majority of the professional and technical workers (65.6 percent) on the island and are mainly concentrated in the health and education sectors (56.0 percent of doctors as of 2007).[96] They have a presence in other fields, but they tend to hold low and intermediate positions. Technology continues to be controlled by men, and even though the majority of doctors are women, they constitute only 12.3 percent of surgeons and 10.7 percent of specialists in trauma and orthopedics.[97] Consistent with this tendency, women doctors tend to dominate in pediatrics, while men predominate in cutting-edge fields such as transplants.[98] Women's membership in the prestigious Academy of Science is comparatively low (26.3 percent), and even though for many years the majority of university graduates have been women, they account for only 31 percent of doctorates in science and 30 percent of academics who have been conferred special honors.[99] While 52.5 percent of university professors are women,[100] a 2004 study by the Cuban researcher Dayma Echevarría concluded that men were twice as likely to advance to positions of greater decision-making power than women in the Cuban economy and society as a whole.[101] Even Vilma Espín, for many years head of the official Cuban women's organization, complained that the "promotion logic" used to determine advancement in some places emphasized different qualities for men and women. According to her, male administrators tended to take into account physical appearance and marital status when hiring or promoting women. Women's sexual comportment has also made them targets of discrimination, as they are sometimes fired for "improper" behavior such as out-of-wedlock pregnancies or supposed extramarital affairs.[102] It is also known that at least as of the mid-eighties, 62.6 percent of men earned above-average salaries, while only 38.6 percent of the women did so,[103] and that under the impact of the economic crisis of the nineties women were typically overrepresented among the poor.[104]

The Cuban government has shown a greater predisposition to use quotas and affirmative action methods in relation to women than to black Cubans. This is consistent with the role of women in the very public process of mobilization and modernization and with the general silence and refusal to acknowledge racial discrimination at least until very recently—a Cuban social and political taboo rooted in causes going back decades before the 1959 Revolution. Thus, for example, in the seventies the government established gender quotas for enrollment in mid-level polytechnic education, which resulted in a considerable increase in women's enrollment during the 1975 to 1980 period.[105] However, the government has also used bans and quotas in a reverse direction to eliminate or limit the number of women in certain occupations. In 1976, the Labor Ministry barred women from almost three hundred job categories, claiming that these occupations presented special health hazards for women. In fact, this ban was due to the ministry's concern with placing laid-off, unemployed male workers, who had priority, in the government's view, over unemployed working women. By the mid-1980s, as a result of the changing demographic and economic situation and due to the objections raised by the FMC, the official women's organization, the list of jobs closed to women was reduced to about twenty-five.[106]

A similar situation arose in the eighties concerning medical school enrollment. After 1984, enrollment in medical training was limited to a 52:48 ratio of women to men; otherwise, women medical students would have outstripped men by a proportion of 3:2. Fidel Castro argued that since civilian medical aid was a critical component of Cuban foreign policy, and because women found it harder to go abroad for lengthy periods due to their greater family and personal responsibilities, the number of women doctors had to be reduced. In addition, many of the recipient countries had problems accepting and dealing with women doctors. Given the major party and foreign policy considerations involved in this case, the FMC refrained from intervening, and the reverse, although admittedly mild, medical quotas were adopted.[107]

Cuban Women's "Double Burden" and the Family Code

The much wider incorporation of Cuban women into the labor force might have had a liberating effect, in the sense of having allowed women to fulfill more of their work capacities and potential, stretching the boundaries of their aspirations, and diminishing the financial and other forms of control by husbands. However, it appears that many Cuban women had a different conception of liberation, at least in the late sixties. According to the anthropologist Ruth Lewis, the poor Cuban women she studied in the slums then thought of liberation in terms of release from outside work, taking care of their own homes, and having time to spend with their children.[108] Lewis's fieldwork findings were confirmed by surveys conducted by the FMC during the same period among much broader groups of women.[109] Moreover, much of whatever benefit Cuban women may have obtained from joining the labor force has been annulled by Cuban working women's continuing to be responsible, as has been the case in the rest of the Communist world, for most of the domestic duties that they were already carrying out before they went to work outside the home. Thus, the majority of Cuban women have ended up with a "double burden": working many hours outside as well as inside their homes.

On International Women's Day in 1975, the Cuban government enacted the Family Code, aimed at alleviating if not eliminating these "double burdens" demands on women. Accordingly, chapter 2, part 1, of the code affirmed the equality of the sexes in marriage. Article 27 strongly affirmed that the working spouse is legally expected to help with household chores as well as with the care of children, even if the other spouse does not work outside the home.[110] The Cuban public had been primed for the reception of the Family Code through extensive coverage in the official press. It was clearly liberating in its content, but it was a measure adopted from above without a corresponding movement from below that could have pushed for its full implementation in practice. Given the almost impossible task of legally enforcing the new law, only an independent grassroots women's movement might have brought it closer to implementation. Its abstract and somewhat rhetorical provisions presented other difficulties, particularly a differential class impact. Women workers noted that even if they divorced their husbands because they refused to help around the house, they would ultimately be left with complete responsibility for the domestic tasks without the additional resources available to many middle-class women. They also found the law's notion of women's right to "financial independence" from their husbands potentially troublesome, as it opened up the possibility of their having to end up supporting the family by themselves.[111] Fidel Castro's acknowledgment, years later, that there were no appropriate mechanisms to enforce legally mandated child support payments confirmed that such fears had been well founded.[112]

An official time study conducted in 2002, under the conditions of the Special Period, showed the continuing burdens of women's double burden. The study pointed out that in the poor working-class district of Old Havana women spent an average of 3.55 hours a day on domestic labor while men spent only 1.17 hours a day. In the town of Bayamo in eastern Cuba, women spent 4.39 hours while men spent only 1.28 hours on domestic tasks. In the rural areas, probably because of less access to even inadequate labor-saving devices, both sexes spent more time in domestic tasks, but women still carried most of the domestic burden. Thus, in the province of Granma in eastern Cuba, women spent 5.59 hours a day on domestic labor while men spent on average 2.25 hours a day. The study also estimated all paid and unpaid labor, inside or outside the home, in urban as well as rural areas. According to that estimate, in the country as a whole women spent 29 percent of their time on paid and 71 percent on unpaid labor, while men spent 67 percent of their time on paid labor and 33 percent on unpaid labor. In the urban areas unpaid labor accounted for 69 percent of the hours worked by women and 28 percent of the hours worked by men; in the rural areas these relative proportions were 80 percent for women and 40 percent for men.[113]

The Cuban government has argued that it has tried to address the situation by enacting the Family Code and through the many practical efforts of the FMC, the official organization of women, and that it is confronting a deepseated historically rooted machista inheritance. However, as in the case of racism, the governmental tendency to blame hangovers of prerevolutionary cultural norms for the present sexism is a handy way of abjuring political responsibility in the matter. Moreover, an account by Moníka Krause-Fuchs, Cuba's pioneering and well-known sex educator during the seventies and eighties, shows how the *current* attitudes and policies of the government functionaries of the period actively contributed to the reproduction and perpetuation of sexist attitudes and practices. She notes that at a Latin American Congress of Legal

Medicine meeting, the Cuban specialists told their Latin American colleagues that they did not understand or accept the legal concept of "marital rape." They indicated that "such a crime does not exist. When women get married, they know that they owe 'carnal access' to their husbands, it is an obligation. Period."[114] This attitude is not really surprising in light of the general official silence regarding the issue of domestic violence.[115]

Based on numerous visits to Cuban schools, Krause-Fuchs reported to the Ministry of Education (MINED) that the principles of coeducation were being applied in classrooms and on the job in the countryside. But when it came to cleaning and other domestic chores, the boys left those tasks to the girls. This included not only the cleaning of school facilities but also washing the boys' clothes while the boys rested, talked, or enjoyed themselves. The boys did not even carry the buckets of water required for washing their clothes. The girls accepted such tasks as an inevitable part of their gender and destiny. Moreover, they told Krause-Fuchs that they saw the boys as having sexual needs that if not satisfied might make them sick, and that girls had to provide them with proof of their love by having sex with them. In fact, a girl wishing to initiate a relationship with a boy was supposed to ask him if he wanted her to wash his clothes. Those girls who refused to abide by the rules of the game were labeled as bad, useless, and in the worst of cases, *tortilleras* (lesbians). In a memoir of her years in Cuba, the American writer Margaret Randall describes an identical situation at the elite Lenin School in the seventies. However, in that instance several girls rebelled, and before long the majority of the Lenin School's women students were refusing to wash the young men's clothes.[116]

Cuban schoolboys refused to attend Krause-Fuchs's conferences on contraceptive methods and family planning, because this was an issue of exclusive interest for the girls since they were the ones who would get pregnant. Asked about their promiscuity and their using women to satisfy themselves, the young men responded that men had to practice their manhood, "to know what to do at the moment of truth." As they told Krause-Fuchs, "practice is the criterion of truth, it is a principle of Marxism-Leninism, isn't it true?"[117]

In light of these attitudes and practices, Krause-Fuchs expected the educational authorities to become concerned and attempt to address them. However, she reported that while her conferences were packed with students, the local teachers in charge of sex education left the room as soon as they could out of embarrassment for their ineptitude and inability to deal with those issues, given the prevailing rules and their numerous prohibitions. But the reaction of the high-ranking functionaries of the Ministry of Education was worse. She relates that they seemed amused and laughed at some of the passages in her report. They did not understand her concern regarding the submissive attitudes of the girl students and their willingness to serve the boys. Although this was an attitude and practice tolerated and even encouraged by many of the teachers in the schools she visited, the high-ranking education functionaries thought Krause-Fuchs's reactions were exaggerated and told her, "But Monika, girls like to spoil boys, they like to wash their clothes, let them do it, they are doing nothing wrong."[118]

The Cuban government sometimes tended to encourage women to revert to traditional gender roles in response to the severe economic crisis of the nineties. In 1994, during the food shortages that characterized the worst years of the Special Period, Raúl Castro called for a new stress on food security as a key ingredient of the revolutionary struggle. In response to this call, the Asociación Cubana de Técnicos Agrícolas y Forestales (ACTAF, the Cuban Association of Agriculture and Forestry Technicians) developed a series of cooking classes for women. The ACTAF's intent was to raise nutrition levels in the country, but in the process it reinforced traditional gender roles.[119]

Living Conditions and Their Effect on Cuban Women

Housing

The problems of the Cuban system have had a special and disproportionate effect on women and their living conditions on the island. An example of the gender-specific way in which the system works against women is the housing situation, an endemic problem in the country. For many decades, there has been an increasing congestion and deterioration of apartments and houses. For a long time housing has been virtually free to the great majority of Cubans. Yet Cubans have paid a heavy price for housing, because of the high scarcity of living quarters and overall deterioration of the housing stock. A Cuban social scientist estimated that in the period from 1959 to 1985, that is, several years before the Special Period of the nineties, housing construction had been limited to 6.5 dwellings per 1,000 people, thereby creating a deficit of 888,000 housing units.[120] A revealing index of the growing congestion resulting from such conditions is that the proportion of grandchildren living in the same household as their grandparents practically doubled between 1953 and 1995. This was accompanied by a considerable increase in the number of sons-in-law and daughters-in-law living on the same premises as older heads of household.[121]

To be sure, the presence of extended family members in the household can be helpful for taking care of children and carrying out domestic chores. However, this is far outweighed by the numerous problems produced by multigenerational families living in small and inadequate quarters. We can find among these a lack of necessary privacy for intimate relations among couples and interference of in-laws in spouses' decision making. Moreover, these tensions are exacerbated by numerous other problems confronted by Cuban households, such as food shortages and the poor quality and unreliability of electrical appliances and labor-saving devices that are difficult to repair. This is a particular problem for women, who, as we saw above, are primarily responsible for household tasks. One of the little-noticed effects of poor and congested housing conditions is their contribution to the high rates of divorce (further discussed below) and to domestic violence.[122] Many average Cubans, including victims, prefer to keep silent about domestic violence because it is regarded as a private matter.[123] The shortage of housing frequently forces divorced people to continue living under the same roof and contributes to the rising level of domestic violence against women in Cuba. For example, in slightly more than the first four months of 2010, seventeen women had been murdered in the eastern province of Guantánamo, most at the hands of a husband, former husband, or boyfriend. This is a problem that has worsened in recent years and, as I suggested above, has been virtually ignored by the Cuban official media.[124]

The terrible hurricane season of 2008 destroyed many dwellings, particularly in small towns and rural areas, precisely because they were in poor condition and were thus very vulnerable to bad weather conditions. The national housing situation was not significantly improved when, according to a report submitted to the Cuban parliament, the government managed to build only 20,000 homes in 2009, meeting a little over 60 percent of its modest annual construction goal. In September 2005, Fidel Castro had pledged the construction of 100,000 homes per year, a target that was repeatedly reduced to become a goal of 32,000 for 2009. The government was unable to meet even this reduced goal.[125]

The housing conditions of Havana, with its approximately two million people, have been particularly bad. The Special Period that began in the nineties exacerbated the previously existing housing crisis. It was estimated in 2006 that 60 districts and 114 settlements in the capital were unhealthy.[126] By 2009, fifty years after the revolution, there were 12,000 people living in shelters and 120,000 waiting to be relocated to other dwellings because their homes were considered uninhabitable. A number of shantytowns such as El Fanguito (the little mud) have developed in Havana and the surrounding areas. It is worth noting that 80 percent of the housing stock in Havana was built before 1959, which suggests that much of this crisis is rooted in the lack of construction that preceded the Special Period.[127] This is particularly ironic in light of the prerevolutionary housing boom in the nation's capital. According to the census of 1953, more than one-third of the then-existing housing units in Havana had been built in the period from 1946 to 1953.[128] To be sure, this housing boom had been heavily skewed toward the middle and upper classes, and it was also an expression of the conservatism of Cuban capital. (US and other foreign capitalists did not generally involve themselves in residential construction.) Cuban investors preferred the perceived security of real estate to other forms of riskier commercial and especially industrial investments.

Child Care

The situation with child care has been better than with housing, if for no other reason than that the regime has historically made it a higher priority in the context of incorporating Cuban women into the labor force. The first government day care centers were opened in Havana in 1961.[129] In the sixties and seventies they developed in a way that led the political scientist Jorge I. Domínguez to describe them as "a mixture of impressive performance and frustration," particularly because the number of existing day care centers was below what was needed to meet the number of children registering. Only the erratic attendance of the children prevented this from becoming a serious overcrowding crisis.[130] Between 1970 and 1986 enrollment in day care centers more than doubled, from more than 47,000 to nearly 110,000 children; demand still outstripped capacity.[131] By 1990, right before social services of every kind were substantially affected and reduced under the Special Period, the day care capacity of the island had risen to 140,000 children. Since there were then 1.4 million women workers, this meant that there was only one opening for every ten women workers.[132] Of course, Cuban women attempted to fill this gap with informal agreements with relatives and neighbors involving every imaginable sort of arrangement, including barter and cash.

In her memoir, Monika Krause-Fuchs tells of how she had to resort to a number of *palancas* (pull or connections) to get one of her sons into one of the day care centers. Although successful in her efforts, she remained troubled and frustrated because of a chronic lack of qualified personnel at the time. (Although the memoir does not provide specific dates, the context suggests it was the early seventies.) Krause-Fuchs was particularly bothered by the irregular attendance, passivity, and irresponsibility of the caregivers or "educators" and the resulting lack of hygiene and disorder among the children. When confronted by Krause-Fuchs, one of the "educators" characteristically responded that there was nothing she could do since she was alone with the children in the absence of her fellow "educators" who were out sick, or because they had to resolve some problem, or because their bus had broken down.[133] More likely than not, these were not false excuses since day care workers—usually women—faced the same kind of difficulties navigating daily life in Cuba as the parents whose children they were supposed to care for.

The anthropologist Amelia Rosenberg Weinreb has noted how in recent years an increasing number of parents have been taking their children to *círculos particulares,* or private child care centers. Many state *círculo* instructors who were making 148 pesos a month (approximately $6) had quit their state jobs to work from their own homes, charging six to fifteen dollars a month per child enrolled, bringing them on the average one hundred dollars a month. According to Rosenberg Weinreb, their clients are parents who prefer to pack their own lunches for their children and bring their own toys and clothing, and they want their children to get individualized attention in a small group. Parents can also pick up and drop off their children at their own convenience, rather than at set hours.[134]

Efforts to bring in labor-saving devices, such as refrigerators and washing machines, in the seventies and eighties had only limited success.[135] As I previously indicated, when machines broke down, as they often did, it was difficult to get a state repairperson to fix them. Rigid bureaucratic rules continue to make the daily lives of women difficult. Parents, and particularly working mothers, needed more flexibility in handling their daily chores—including shopping, a lengthy and complicated task given the only sporadic, temporary access to various food items. The government would not find a way to keep the corner store open until 8:00 p.m.[136] *Granma* has acknowledged through its weekly complaints section that sale and distribution of sanitary pads is considerably hampered by the rigid and inflexible schedule that Cuban women must follow to obtain them from their local pharmacies.[137] These rigid bureaucratic rules were perhaps products of a shortage that had been ongoing for years. The production of sanitary pads was insufficient to meet more than 50 percent of demand because, as the government agency in charge of manufacturing and distributing the product claimed in 2003, there was a lack of money to buy the necessary raw materials, which were imported from China.[138]

Abortion and Contraception

For the first few years after the revolutionary victory in 1959, the Cuban government strictly enforced the existing anti-abortion legislation, which had been widely ignored in the prerevolutionary period. According to the Penal Code established in the late thirties, abortion was allowable only to save the life of the mother, if there were genetic or hereditary defects in the fetus, or if the pregnancy was caused by rape.[139] The new government policy, combined with the disappearance of contraceptive devices historically imported from the United States and a surge of revolutionary optimism, contributed to a baby boom that reached its peak in 1962.[140]

In 1965, for unknown reasons, the Ministry of Public Health reversed the government's anti-abortion policy, using the existing law that permitted abortions to save the life of the mother as the legal springboard to authorize abortion in all cases on demand. However, at the time women still required permission from their husbands to have an abortion. The new criminal code adopted in 1979 decriminalized abortions provided they followed the established health regulations. This made abortions for profit illegal. Abortions were to be freely provided by government physicians authorized to perform that procedure until the tenth week of pregnancy. Second- and third-trimester abortions had to be authorized by hospital directors.[141] The abortion rate, which before the adoption of the new criminal code had already been high, continued to rise for the next decades, reaching its highest point of 97 abortions per 100 births in 1986.[142] Then it declined to 52.5 in 2004, although this is still a high figure by international standards. It appears that some of the recent decline is due to the increasing use of "menstrual regulation," a method to prevent to-term pregnancies that can be used if a woman goes to see a gynecologist right after she detects a delay in her menstrual cycle.[143] Health authorities also recently introduced Levonorgestrel, the "morning after" pill, hoping to further reduce Cuba's high abortion rate.[144] Be that as it may, the high abortion rates on the island have been an important factor in the substantial decrease of fertility and the consequent aging of the population. Starting with an already low fertility rate of 1.8 in 1985, the Special Period depressed the rate even further to 1.6 in 1991 and to 1.3 in the especially critical years of 1993 and 1994.[145] The fertility rate rose to 1.7 in 2009, the highest of the preceding decade, but it is very unlikely to remain at that level.[146] Cuba's fertility rate has been low since 1978 (1.43),[147] and in any case below the replacement level, which requires an average of slightly more than two children per woman of childbearing age.[148]

Abortion in Cuba has been used as an important method of birth control, not as a supplement to contraception. Even when contraceptives were widely available, they were not always used.[149] Inadequate sex education programs and resistance to sex education have played a big role in this context. A survey of a thousand health workers conducted in 1986 revealed that even this group, which included gynecologists, had a poor grasp of the best methods of birth control, particularly for teenagers.[150] The prevailing opinion among young Cuban males that contraception was the exclusive concern of girls because they are the ones who get pregnant[151] is consistent with the high incidence of teenage pregnancies and abortions and with the data showing that first pregnancies are the most likely to be terminated.[152]

Irregular availability of contraceptives has also contributed to the high abortion rates on the island. Krause-Fuchs reports young women telling her: "Me take the pill? Where do I find them? It has been a long time since they were available in my province," and a mother asking her: "Doctor, could you get pills for my daughter? She cannot use an IUD, it hurts her, the doctor recommended taking the pill, but we cannot find them anywhere."[153] Krause-Fuchs relates that due to lengthy delays in the UN-supported construction of a factory to produce contraceptives, the Ministry of Public Health decided to import the pills to the island. However, due to budget reductions a few months later, the import of contraceptives was suspended because there were other things that the government considered to be more important to obtain from abroad.[154] The findings of Spanish social scientist Isabel Holgado Fernández, based on her observations during the decade of the nineties, concur with Krause-Fuchs's earlier observations. Holgado Fernández found a chronic deficit of contraceptives on the island due to the US economic blockade and administrative inefficiencies. She also found that domestically produced intrauterine devices have caused gynecological problems such as pelvic inflammation and infertility.[155]

Divorce

The growing incorporation of women in the labor force, combined with serious hardship in daily life and a favorable legal climate,[156] pushed the rate of divorce in Cuba to one of the highest in the world. In 1958, the year before the revolutionary victory, there was a divorce rate in Cuba of 9.09 per 100 marriages.[157] The rate then began to rise, and by 1970 there were 22 divorces for every 100 marriages, by 1981 there were 39, 61 in 1998, and almost 70 in 2004.[158] The ease and rapidity with which divorce can be obtained is related to the relative scarcity of property over which to haggle. In addition, as we saw earlier, the severe housing shortage that forces people to live with in-laws and other relatives contributes to marital tensions and unhappiness. Many of the social phenomena encouraging divorce on the island are hardly unique to the country. However, there is one distinctive feature of life in Cuba that may have had some, even if small, effect on the marriage and divorce rate. For many decades, the government provided a positive incentive for marriage by granting newly married people certain material advantages, such as making it easier for them to obtain honeymoon hotel accommodations, food and liquor for the wedding, and even some household effects.[159]

Cuban Gays after the Revolution

In spite of not having been allowed to organize independently to articulate and defend their interests, Cuban women benefited in some ways from the revolutionary process. Some traditional forms of patriarchal sexism have become weakened, such as the power of husbands at home. Women's incorporation into the labor force and the occasional implementation of affirmative action policies have led to a much greater occupational differentiation and to a larger number of women playing prominent roles in the economy and society. However, the opposite has been the case for Cuban gays, who have suffered greatly, particularly during the first thirty years of the revolutionary period. For reasons that will be elucidated later on, the Cuban government forced gays out of the closet and politicized their situation to significantly increase their oppression. As part of this process, the revolutionary leadership created a climate of opinion that not only dismissed gay oppression as a legitimate issue but also portrayed gay life as a symptom of social decay. For example, when in 1967 the British House of Lords accepted the Wolfenden Report and abolished the UK's laws against sodomy, the Cuban press portrayed the event as a further example of the decline of the British empire. *Bohemia*, Cuba's most influential magazine, marked the beginning of the gay liberation movement in the United States with a cartoon portraying, in a derogatory manner, two men getting married in a church ceremony.[160]

A long series of events are "high" points of the decades-long trajectory of the persecution of gay Cubans by the revolutionary government. As early as 1962, the government conducted a massive raid known as the "night of the three Ps," that is, *prostitutas* (female prostitutes), *proxénetas* (pimps), and *pájaros* (birds, one of the many derogatory Cuban terms for gay men). The raid netted thousands of people who were arrested and taken to police stations and city jails. The "operation" involved indiscriminate raids in certain neighborhoods—such as Colón, near Old Havana—known for their high concentration of prostitutes. This was accompanied by selective raids on people reported as sexual deviants on lists prepared by the CDRs. That is how the well-known gay playwright Virgilio Piñera ended up being arrested in his house, located some distance from Havana.[161]

In his March 13, 1963, speech at the University of Havana attacking lazy children of the bourgeoisie who imitated Elvis Presley and organized "freelance effeminate" shows, Fidel Castro explained that it was not so easy to straighten out an adult homosexual, or as he put it, "a tree that had grown twisted." Therefore, no drastic measures would be adopted against them, but young people aspiring to be homosexuals were a different matter. Castro added that he had observed that the Cuban countryside did not produce the "subproduct" of homosexuality.[162] Then, in 1965 the government erected the UMAP camps, where for some three years gays, along with Jehovah's Witnesses, many practitioners of Catholicism, members of Afro-Cuban secret societies such as Abakúa, and other "deviants" were forced to provide cheap, regimented labor for the Cuban state.[163] At about the same time, the Cuban state also established the Center for Special Education for boys considered to be "effeminate" and those raised by single mothers who were considered "at risk" of becoming homosexuals. The separation of these children from the regular public schools was obligatory since it was believed that they could "infect" their classmates.[164]

Coinciding with the international revolutionary year of 1968, the Cuban state undertook a "revolutionary offensive" at home. However, this was not an offensive against powerful and oppressive private and state structures as in Mexico City, Chicago, Paris, and Prague, but against the poorest and most marginal sectors of what remained of the Cuban petty bourgeoisie. To ensure that no nook or cranny of the Cuban economy remained outside the ownership and control of the state, all tiny businesses, including large numbers of small bodegas and bars, were either taken over by the government or closed. This was accompanied by a renewed persecution of homosexuals and prostitutes. In his speech of September 28, 1968, celebrating the eighth anniversary of the establishment of the CDRs, Fidel Castro denounced young Cubans whom he described as living in an "extravagant manner." These included those with long hair and fancy clothes, which were signs of moral degeneracy that would ultimately lead to political and economic sabotage. According to Castro, those youngsters were trying to introduce in Cuba a revived version of the Prague Spring, with street-walking prostitutes, the sale of women, parasitism, and ideological softening. He advocated forced labor in agriculture as punitive reeducation. The pronouncements of Castro and other revolutionary spokespeople were followed by mass shavings of long-haired men and the sending of miniskirted girls accused of sexual looseness to do forced labor in the countryside.[165] Castro also purged and imprisoned the "micro faction" of old Communists in February and supported the Soviet invasion of Czechoslovakia in August of that year.

This was followed by the "Quinquenio Gris" (Five Gray Years), which began in 1971 with the National Congress of Education and Culture resolving that because of the influence they could have on Cuban youth, "notorious homosexuals" were not to be tolerated in spite of their "artistic merits." Homosexuals who had direct influence on youth via artistic and cultural activities were to be transferred to other organizations. The congress also resolved that people whose morals undermined the prestige of the revolution would be barred from any group of performers representing Cuba abroad.[166] Some gay artists and intellectuals were protected from the drastic effects of the 1971 resolutions because of their links to institutions that enjoyed a certain degree of clout with Fidel Castro, in part because they were led by internationally prestigious and influential figures. Such were the cases of Alicia Alonso's Cuban National Ballet, Alfredo Guevara's ICAIC (film institute), and Haydée Santamaría's Casa de las Américas, the internationally known cultural center in Havana.

The official marginalization of gays had been anticipated by the University of Havana when it inaugurated in the mid-sixties a three-year-long campaign through the distribution of homophobic literature encouraging the repudiation of *enfermitos* (little sick ones) by fellow students and the public trials of hundreds of students. The purges required all students enrolled in a given department to attend a mass assembly to question the political attitudes and behavior of their classmates. The "jury" of the official student organization and the Communist Youth called witnesses to testify from the floor, but witnesses were afraid to defend accused students for fear of being accused themselves. These purges were aimed at both "counterrevolutionaries" and homosexuals, with the usual unanimous verdict of "guilty" resulting in expulsion from the university and inclusion of the assembly's findings in the *expedientes* (workplace and career records kept by the state) that were beginning to be used by this time. By the fall of 1965, purges had become so frequent that the leader of the Communist Youth promised to refrain from holding them during class time.[167]

The decade of the eighties began in spring 1980 with the Mariel exodus, which was used by the government as another opportunity not only to ridicule and attack gays but also to force their departure from the country. Some straight Cubans pretended to be gay in order to obtain the necessary government clearances and permissions to leave the island. In the United States, the National Gay Task Force (NGTF) estimated that out of a total of some 125,000 who left Cuba at that time, between 2,000 and 10,000 of the refugees were gay men and lesbians.[168]

Shortly after the Mariel exodus, the AIDS crisis broke out in the United States and elsewhere, eventually reaching Cuba. The Cuban government responded with some of the most extreme measures anywhere in the world. Mandatory screening for HIV infection began in 1986. The first tests focused on the highest-risk groups: those who had traveled abroad since 1975, particularly soldiers who had served in Africa. By April 1991, 9,771,691 people, almost the entire population, had been tested. HIV-positive people (902 cases in early 1993) were quarantined in sanatoriums and once they developed full-blown AIDS were transferred to hospitals. Although medical attention and living conditions in the sanatoriums were admittedly good and the policy was effective in reducing contagion, the government's policy was internationally criticized for its unnecessary harshness and ruthless display of state power over individuals. Basically healthy people were forced to live isolated, nonproductive lives while waiting to develop full-blown AIDS, a process that sometimes took many years, to then be moved to a hospital.[169] As Marvin Leiner has pointed out, the quarantine policy was used as a substitute for the absence of a serious educational program on AIDS. As with the Victorians' response to syphillis and gonorrhea, the Cuban government was trying to deal with AIDS while avoiding public discussion or education about sex and how to practice safe sex to limit the transmission of the virus.[170] The quarantine policy was discontinued in the nineties, but the earlier choices that the Cuban government made in dealing with AIDS revealed a lot about its historic attitudes to sex and sexual education, as well as about the vast capacities of the Cuban leviathan.

From a legal point of view, homosexuality was explicitly recognized in Cuba for the first time in the Penal Code adopted in 1979, even though laws against "socially dangerous" conduct that did not explicitly mention homosexuality had been used against gays for some time before then. Article 359 of the 1979 code explicitly defined homosexual conduct as constituting a "public scandal." Article 367 linked homosexuality to the corruption of minors. The article on "public scandal" established a sentence of three to nine months in prison, a fine, or both in cases where (1) a person made a public display of his homosexuality or solicited someone else to engage in homosexual conduct; and (2) a person engaged in homosexual acts in a public place or in a private place exposed to the involuntary view of others. The article on the corruption of minors established a sentence of one to eight years in prison for anybody who induced a minor less than sixteen years old, of either sex, to engage in homosexuality.[171]

The Liberalization of the Nineties and Its Effect on Cuban Gays

The cultural, religious, and intellectual liberalization that accompanied the sharp economic crisis of the nineties has included a more tolerant attitude toward Cuban gays, although there is still official resistance to the equal treatment of homosexuals.

In 1992, as part of the relative cultural liberalization that had begun to take place in the country, the Cuban playwright's Senel Paz's *El lobo, el bosque y el hom-*

bre nuevo (The wolf, the forest, and the new man) sold out to mixed straight and gay audiences in Havana. The play portrayed the friendship between a gay man and a straight Communist activist and was later made into *Fresa y Chocolate*, the successful 1994 film by noted Cuban director Tomás Gutiérrez Alea.[172] However, for many years the film was restricted to relatively small audiences, and it was not broadcast on Cuban television, by far the principal vehicle for viewing movies in Cuba, until 2007. It was only since 1999 that Cuban television had begun to present foreign films addressing gay issues. Along similar lines of relative cultural liberalization, the Asociación Hermanos Saíz, the official organization of young writers, has since 1998 been organizing a well-attended exhibition of homoerotic arts, but the official press has refused to publish even a press note announcing the event.[173] Since the nineties, a social and cultural center called the Mejunje located in Santa Clara in central Cuba transforms, with the support of the local authorities, into a nationally and internationally known gay club on weekends. When *Juventud Rebelde* published an article on the physical renovation of Mejunje's premises, it described in detail the cultural and theatrical activities that took place at the center but did not include a single word about the gay activities that so prominently took place there as well.[174] It is clear that official limits have been placed on the cultural liberalization that has taken place on the island.[175]

Most important of all, since 1993 the Cuban government has been treating HIV-positive Cubans on an outpatient basis, although it continues to retain admission into the sanatoriums as an option. In addition, CENESEX, led for many years by Mariela Castro Espín, Raúl Castro's daughter, has been advocating for the legalization and facilitation of transgender operations and gay marriage. Castro Espín publicly congratulated Mexico City for legalizing gay marriage and stated that this had not yet happened in Cuba due to "prejudices," without specifying whose prejudices she was referring to.[176] In May 2009 and 2010, Cuba officially celebrated the World Day against Homophobia. During the 2010 festivities, Mariela Castro Espín even hinted at the possibility that an officially sanctioned gay organization might be created in the future if "convincing proposals" were put forward. However, some participants in the festivities complained that police harassment of LGBT people continues at the places where they usually gather.[177] It is also worth noting that Castro Espín and CENESEX have encouraged the transformation of political complaints of Cuban gays (for example, the continuing police abuse notwithstanding changes in government policies) into cultural expression, which, even when expressing itself in a flamboyant manner, is fundamentally harmless. Resistance to Castro Espín's proposed reforms has not been limited to the "usual suspects" in the Communist Party hierarchy. The Catholic Church, which for decades has rather cautiously criticized the Cuban government on many different matters has vigorously expressed its conservative objections to the center's activities as well as the broadcast on television of *Brokeback Mountain*. The Catholic Diocese of Havana issued a scathing denunciation of what it saw as the government's campaign to promote homosexuality, transsexualism, and "sexual diversity."[178]

On the legal front, some of the harshest penalties against gays in the 1979 Penal Code were softened and even eliminated by changes that took effect in 1987. Provisions penalizing public displays of homosexuality and engaging in homosexual acts in public view were eliminated. However, the provisions concerning homosexual behavior that creates a "public scandal" because it offends public decency or because it importunes or bothers another person with solicitations to engage in homosexual acts are still on the books. Violations of these provisions can still be punished by prison sentences of three to twelve months, or a fine of between one hundred and three hundred *cuotas* (a *cuota* is equivalent to one day's minimum wage). Also, the maximum sentence was increased by three months in the revised code. The provision concerning minors below sixteen years of age remained unchanged. In addition, article 317 permanently bans from teaching or any other jobs involving children anybody who has been convicted of a sexual offense, even if this involves an insistent homosexual proposition to another *adult*.[179] More importantly, the 1987 code retains the catchall precriminal category of "social dangerousness," which does not explicitly mention homosexuality, but bans "the exploitation or practice of socially reprehensible vice" and "antisocial conduct" (article 73), which has been widely used for police repression of drunkards and drug addicts as well as gays.[180] Notwithstanding the liberalization that has taken place in the cultural, medical, and legal fields, the government's harassment of gays continues. This includes harassment of male transvestites who are arrested when they are found dressed in women's clothes[181] and the government's attempt in 2009 to disrupt the Mr. Gay Havana competition, a gay beauty pageant.[182]

These incidents point to the need for independent organizations to defend gays against government repression, a task that cannot be accomplished by CENESEX or any other official organization responsible to the government that finances them and controls them. That the Cuban government cannot be trusted on these matters was strikingly demonstrated in November 2010 when the Cuban delegation at the Third Commission of the UN General Assembly voted in support of an amendment that eliminated any explicit reference to sexual orientation in its periodic resolution condemning extrajudicial, arbitrary, or summary executions. Cuba was the only Latin American country that supported the amendment, promoted by Morocco and Mali. Among those opposing the exclusion were the center left governments of Venezuela, Ecuador, Brazil, Paraguay, and Uruguay, while Bolivia and Nicaragua were not present at the time of the vote.[183] In a formal statement, CENESEX and SOCUMES (Multidisciplinary Cuban Society for the Study of Sexuality) commented on the Cuban vote but limited themselves, with only a hint of displeasure, to noting its practical diplomatic and political effect. At the same time, they hastened to add that there were no laws in Cuba allowing the punishment of homosexuality as a crime. The fact remains that this declaration did not protest, or even register a clear objection to, the Cuban vote at the UN. After the shock that the vote produced among various groups in Cuba (as usual, the Cuban mass media completely ignored the controversy), the minister of foreign relations, Bruno Rodríguez Parrilla, and some of his aides met with the interested parties. The functionaries, besides detailing "the political manipulations of the powerful states against the underdeveloped countries" in the annual sessions of the UN General Assembly, listened to the arguments, concerns, and suggestions of the visitors and reiterated that there was no change of policy with regard to Cuba's opposition to discrimination on the basis of sexual orientation or gender identity. They further claimed that the vote in question was the result of "an unforeseen and conjunctural circumstance."[184] Sometime later, when the vote of the Third Commission came up for ratification at a subsequent meeting of the UN's General Assembly, the Cuban delegation absented itself and did not participate. This may have been a concession to the protests provoked by the earlier Cuban vote inside as well as outside the island.[185]

Several attempts by Cuban gays to organize independently—one example is the Gay and Lesbian Association (GLAC), which formed in July 1994—have been unsuccessful. Several GLAC members tried to form the GALEES—Grupo de Acción por la Libertad de Expresión de la Elección Sexual (Action Group in Support of Liberty of Expression of Sexual Choice)—but they were unable to receive any form of official recognition. On the island, the official act of denying or ignoring a request for recognition is equivalent to making a group illegal,[186] although the government may nevertheless choose to tolerate its existence.

The Roots of Homophobia during the Revolutionary Period

The widespread sexism that has existed in revolutionary Cuba, particularly against gays, has long been an uncomfortable issue for supporters of the Cuban regime, particularly in countries such as the United States where vital and influential women's and gay liberation movements developed in the wake of the 1960s. Susan Sontag, the prominent cultural critic (among others), tried during her Fidelista political phase to minimize the problem with a false cultural relativism full of condescension. As Sontag put it in 1969: "Suspicious as we are of the traditional puritanism of left revolutions, American radicals ought to be able to maintain some perspective when a country known mainly for dance, music, prostitutes, cigars, abortions, resort life, and pornographic movies gets a little uptight about sexual morals and, in one bad moment two years ago, rounds up several thousand homosexuals in Havana and sends them to a farm to rehabilitate themselves. (They have long been sent home.)"[187]

Many left-wing activist gays have had much more difficulty reconciling the sympathy they harbor for Castro's government with their own interests as gays and loyalty to oppressed gays in other countries, let alone the widespread hostility to Castro's government among gay communities all over the world. Left gay writers have tried to reconcile these conflicting sentiments with various interpretations of the Cuban regime's homophobia. Allen Young, a left-wing American gay writer and activist, put forward in 1981 a kind of "third world" explanation blaming Cuban homophobia on an ideology that according to him did not arise from Cuban political experience or Cuban culture. Instead, argued Young, the official Cuban ideology came "from the external tradition of European Marxism" as transmitted to the island by the PSP—the old Cuban Communist Party.[188] Years later, in 1996, Ian Lumsden, a gay Canadian left-wing academic and activist, developed an explanation similar to Young's, attributing Cuba's antigay persecutions not to Fidel Castro's views but to the influence of Soviet thinking, which considered homosexuality "a decadent bourgeois phenomenon." However, unlike Young, Lumsden pointed out that the Soviet position was a creation of Russian Stalinism and had been adopted after the decriminalization of homosexuality by Lenin's Bolshevik government.[189]

The 1917 Russian Revolution in fact removed all legal restrictions on sexual activity as such. In the particular case of gay sex, all voluntary homosexual relations for persons age fourteen and over were legalized. Beyond legalization, Soviet representatives maintained relations with the Institute for Sexual Science in Germany, which campaigned for the repeal of sodomy statutes and against homophobia in all its expressions. Moreover, as Soviet commissar of public welfare, Alexandra Kollontai campaigned for women's liberation against the enslavement of continuous childbearing and the burdens of domestic labor and child care. Communal restaurants, laundries, and child care facilities for working women were set up at her urging. In addition, laws against abortion were repealed, and contraception was made available to all. Divorce was greatly simplified, and equal pay for equal work was made a principle of the new state. The early Soviet courts even approved marriages between homosexuals, and, amazingly, there are recorded instances of sex change operations in the Soviet republic in the 1920s. It is true that many of these legal and political gains meant little in practice, given the lack of material resources to implement them and the sheer poverty of the country. However, it wasn't until the Stalinist thirties that homosexuality was recriminalized, abortion was outlawed, and a general offensive against many social advances of the twenties was carried out.

Contrary to the clichés tying "Marxism" with homophobia, the Bolsheviks were not the first socialists in the Marxist tradition to have defended gay rights. Far from being hostile to gays or to women's liberation, this tradition has a long history of struggle on these issues. For example, the German Social Democratic Party (SPD) had, before the Bolshevik Revolution, played a leading role in the campaign against the German antisodomy law and popularized gay issues in the pages of *Vorwarts*, the party newspaper.[190]

As convenient as it might have been for North American left-wing gay writers influenced by New Left ideology to blame the old Cuban Communists for the antigay venom on the island, Cuban reality points in an altogether different direction. Although the old Cuban Communists provided much of the ideological language to defend and justify such practices, the thrust and dynamism of those policies came primarily from Fidel Castro and the new Cuban Communist leadership. The new Cuban Communists were influenced, particularly in matters pertaining to gender politics, by ideologies and practices that had nothing to do with classical Marxism. In 1965, two years after his attack against gays in his speech of March 13, 1963, Castro clearly spelled out his position on various matters critical to the treatment of gay Cubans. First, homosexuals were to be banned from positions with a direct influence on young people, particularly in educational centers. Castro acknowledged that a homosexual could profess revolutionary ideology and exhibit a correct political position, in which case he should not be considered politically negative. However, he held that "we would never come to believe that a homosexual could embody the conditions and requirements of conduct that would enable us to consider him a true Revolutionary, a true Communist militant. A deviation of that nature clashes with the concept we have of what a militant Communist should be." Castro insisted on banning homosexuals from any position that could influence young people and strongly argued for the need, under the existing conditions in Cuba, to inculcate Cuban youth with a spartan spirit of discipline, struggle, and work. To encourage that spirit, Castro recommended the promotion of "activities related in some way with the defense of the country, such as sports."[191] It is worth noting in this context that the Jehovah's Witnesses, who refused to serve in the military, were persecuted by the Cuban state and were even driven underground for some twenty years after they were forced into illegality in the mid-seventies.

Implicit in this perspective were notions predominant in the traditional Hispanic culture on the island that gays were weak, ultra-sensitive, and even cowardly.[192] A similar set of attitudes led Che Guevara to contemptuously refer to the prominent gay Cuban playwright Virgilio Piñera as a "*maricón*" (faggot) when he saw one of his books at the Cuban embassy in Algiers in 1963.[193] Significantly, this was the same Virgilio Piñera who publicly admitted to his fear at the famous 1961 meeting when Fidel Castro proclaimed that everything would be permitted to intellectuals inside the revolution, but nothing outside of it. Fear was certainly not going to be an emotion easily accepted among the new tough and virile youth to be created in Cuba. Gays were seen as incapable of the tough, combative, and monolithic military culture averse to critical thinking (disguised as "revolutionary unity") that the revolutionary leadership wanted to promote in the country. Moreover, "studies" conducted in 1965 by the Ministry of Public Health had concluded that the homosexuals' alleged ideological weakness and vulnerability to imperial propaganda were socially contagious.[194]

As the historian Lillian Guerra has pointed out, the Cuban government had, starting in the 1960s, also associated gay life to the dreaded disease of "intellectualism," since as groups suffering from nonproductive, self-absorbed conditions they both subverted the high value that the leadership placed on manual labor. Thus, during the university purges in the sixties not only were homosexuals attacked but also male intellectuals who thought, read, talked, or debated too much. The greatest defects of the "intellectualized" students were their obsession with debating Marxism, disdain for agricultural labor, taste for abstract art, proclivity toward reading, inclination to share their opinion with others, and strong interest in other countries. In early 1966, Jaime Crombet, secretary general of the UJC (Unión de Jóvenes Comunistas—Union of Communist Youth), identified a range of anti-social tendencies related to homosexuality. These included intellectualism, "discussionism," egoism, autonomism, Trotskyism, and reunionism (the habit of holding many meetings to decide a question rather than taking action). It was clear all along that the remedy for all these kinds of defects was, as Fidel Castro had advocated for the "extravagant" manner of living of some young people, hard manual labor in agriculture as punitive "reeducation."[195]

In the last analysis, the problems of youthful "extravagance," homosexuality, and "intellectualism" had a common root in the decay and degeneracy of urban life. The regime's ideologues contrasted to this the mythical and archetypical "virile" virtues of the rural world. This was a theme hardly typical of the Stalinist "Marxism" of the old Cuban Communists, and far more in tune with the homegrown machismo of the new Fidelista Communists, which in some ways resembled the ideological style of Spanish Francoist traditionalism. A 1965 editorial in the daily newspaper *El Mundo* (seized by the government a few years earlier) is worth quoting at length:

> On a certain occasion, Fidel let us know that the countryside does not produce homosexuals, that this abominable vice does not grow there. True. The conditions of virility found among the Cuban peasantry do not permit it. But in some of our cities it proliferates . . . Against it, we are struggling and we will struggle until we eradicate it from a virile country, wrapped up in a life-and-death struggle against Yankee imperialism. And in this super-virile [*virilísimo*] country, with its army of men, homosexuality should not be and cannot be expressed by homosexual or pseudo-homosexual writers and "artists." Because no homosexual represents the Revolution, that is a matter for males [*asuntos de varones*], of fists and not of feathers, of fury and not of trembling, of sincerity and not of intrigues, of creative valor and not of meringue-coated surprises [*sorpresas merengosas*] . . . Unfortunately, this has become an alarming political and social matter . . . We are not talking about persecuting homosexuals but of destroying their position in society, their methods, their influence. Revolutionary social hygiene is what this is called.[196]

Starting in the early sixties, then, the most representative figures of the Cuban state proceeded to tap into traditional hostility and discriminatory cultural attitudes toward gays and to exaggerate and politicize their supposedly worst features. Thus gay oppression, which in prerevolutionary days had been an almost exclusive product of the "silent" working of civil society, became political, explicit, and often strident. Although this was not necessarily a fully conscious or cynical strategy, it was totally compatible with the political aims of the revolutionary leadership to use machismo as a tactic to further the "unity" of the country in support of their aims. In any case, the overall record of the Cuban government, particularly during the first thirty years after the 1959 victory of the revolution, clearly gives the lie to the notion that Cuban homophobia is simply or primarily a "cultural leftover" of the prerevolutionary period. Mariela Castro Espín herself has claimed that the "homophobic and machista culture, fundamentally inherited from Spanish colonial domination, has conditioned human relations and political decisions" and that the creation of the UMAPs "was a reflection of the social handling of those prejudices."[197] Needless to add, Castro Espín's explanation ignores the major role in the active encouragement of homophobia played by the revolutionary leadership, including Fidel Castro. It is not plausible to attribute the regime's homophobic record to the problems of "an imperfect revolution in an imperfect world."[198] Such an attribution might have perhaps been more appropriate had the regime consistently fought homophobia but for some reason failed in its efforts.

The gender and family policies of the Cuban government were made possible by and in turn further strengthened the control capacities of the Cuban state, which are qualitatively greater than those of any other country in Latin America. As Lois Smith and Alfred Padula put it when writing about the early decades of the revolution, "the state was becoming a member of the family" as the newly created mass organizations invaded the family's private sphere. The CDRs, the FMC, and the militias encroached on the time and attention of family members, and the surveillance functions of the CDRs had serious implications for family life and more broadly for privacy in general. Access to employment, housing, and education was heavily affected by people's participation in those organizations.[199] The periodic sending of children to the countryside for the purposes of education and voluntary labor also increased the power of the state in relation to children and their families. Of course, there were limits to the state's reach even from the sixties to the eighties, the period of the greatest political controls on the island. The fears fostered and exploited by the American Catholic Church and the US government during the heyday of the Peter Pan operation, which brought tens of thousands of children out of Cuba in the early sixties, were unfounded. The Cuban government never contemplated taking the custody of children away from their parents, much less sending them to be "reeducated" in the Soviet Union. Moreover, some of the Cuban state's efforts to penetrate family life undoubtedly had positive, liberating effects. Women joining the labor force acquired greater power within the family, could be more independent and assertive toward their husbands, were more likely to marry for love, and were more willing to risk divorce. The greater provision of state welfare services also diminished the power of authoritarian families over women.[200]

It is worth asking why the worst excesses of the Cuban government's gender discrimination were focused on gays and not on women. In traditional Hispanic culture, women are seen as complementary—although subordinate—to men and are not perceived as challenging (or mocking) men's roles in the same ways as gay men. (Lesbians are not taken very seriously and barely register in this context.) Women's nurturing and homemaking roles support men's struggling roles in the outside world: in their capacity as the "weaker sex" they make evident the indispensability of men's "tough" natures. In revolutionary Cuba women were supposed to play these roles, although in a substantially modified fashion, as they were also called on to help modernize the country by joining the labor force and becoming workers and professionals. Women contributed to what turned out to be a selective and uneven modernization that Cuban Communism, like similar systems in Asia and Eastern Europe, carried out, and that in the case of Cuba had substantial roots in prerevolutionary society. The liberating effects of this strategy, however, were subordinate to the government's modernization policy. When this course of action brought about serious frictions and role conflicts within the family, the Cuban government pretended to solve this with the mostly symbolic dispositions of the Family Code enacted in 1975. The government's policies toward women blunted but did not challenge traditional male power and certainly did not help to unleash the independent energies of women on behalf of their self-liberation.

As we saw above, the Cuban government was forced by the sharp economic crisis that began in the late eighties and was greatly exacerbated in the nineties to allow a number of changes in the country's policies. These included withdrawal from military activities abroad, a dramatic reduction of Cuba's armed forces, and liberalization of many government policies pertaining to religious and cultural matters. This significant change in the country's social and cultural ambience also led to a significant liberalization of the Cuban government's gender policies, ranging from the treatment of AIDS patients to the liberal educational activities of CENESEX. Even Fidel Castro himself adopted a tone different from that of the pronouncements he had made three decades earlier. In a long interview with Nicaraguan leader Tomás Borge in 1992, he insisted that he did not see homosexuality as a type of degeneracy and that he was absolutely opposed to all forms of repression, contempt, scorn, or discrimination toward homosexuals. In this interview, the Cuban leader also brazenly lied when he pretended that he had "never been in favor of, nor promoted, nor supported any policy against homosexuals." After listening to Castro's claims and disclaimers concerning Cuban gays, Borge asked Castro the critical question of whether a homosexual could become a member of the Communist Party. Castro dodged a direct yes or no answer but commented that while there had been many prejudices in Cuba with respect to this issue, there were other types of prejudices against which Castro and the leadership had chosen to focus their struggle.[201] In other words, gays could wait for the right to be admitted to the CCP. More recently, Fidel Castro is supposed to have taken personal responsibility for the persecution of gays in Cuba in a 2010 interview he granted to Carmen Lira Saade, the editor of the Mexican left-wing daily *La Jornada*. But on closer inspection it turns out that he is still disclaiming responsibility. According to this new version of events, Castro held himself responsible only for not having paid attention to the problem of the antigay campaigns since he was very busy with the October 1962 crisis, sabotage, armed attacks, and other life-and-death problems. Thus the Cuban leader is copping a plea: he was simply negligent rather than an active agent in fueling the flames of the antigay campaign.[202] Castro's excuse was echoed by his niece Mariela Castro Espín, who claimed that her uncle "had not been keeping in touch with what was happening in the UMAPs" because "his life was dedicated to the survival of the revolution . . . and . . . the laws favoring the rights of the people within the complex and tense international relations."[203]

While there was substance to the shift in Cuban gender policies since the nineties, it still fell far short of eliminating discrimination against homosexuals in many areas of Cuban life. Gays still cannot independently organize in defense of their interests to oppose government policy and actions whenever that may be necessary—and of course tens of thousands of gay Cubans are still compelled to live "in the closet." It goes without saying that Cuban women's need to fight for the "strategic interests" leading to their liberation cannot rely on the FMC, which in fact constitutes an obstacle to their liberation. They, no less than gays, need their own independent organizations to pursue that struggle.

Chapter Seven

Dissidents and Critics—from Right to Left

There were few political obstacles to building an opposition to the Batista dictatorship (1952–58), since it had a very narrow political and social base of support. Even the upper classes withdrew their tolerance for the dictatorship when its rapacious conduct and brutality also hurt them. Batista's repressive apparatus was politically isolated, and whatever motivation the armed forces had to support the regime was based on corporate privileges and corruption rather than on political ideology. Consistent with the nature of the regime, people informing the police about the activities of political opponents were usually morally depraved individuals who helped the authorities for mercenary reasons. One could also argue that the brutality of Batista's regime was in part due to its lack of social roots and political support in the country.[1] In turn, the shallow social implantation of the regime was key to its relative ineffectiveness in holding on to power.

In contrast to a regime like Batista's, the systematically repressive nature of Soviet-type regimes made it politically difficult to build enduring oppositions within those societies. On one hand, these regimes tended to leave no alternative but the adoption of an open and outright oppositionist stance to those who refused to surrender their political independence to the one-party state. Such a stance was likely to lead to imprisonment, exile, or in the best of cases political isolation and permanent unemployment. On the other hand, critics and even oppositionists were sometimes able to survive in the nooks and crannies of the system, attempting to channel and offer direction to the inevitable discontent that those systems produced. This was particularly true in decaying Soviet-type systems that had not been products of autochthonous revolutions and had been imposed on native populations by the Soviet Red Army. In any case, the task of opposition under these types of regimes was full of difficulties, practical and political.

Compared to Batista's regime, there was certainly no lack of physical brutality in the system run by the Castro brothers, particularly during the first twenty years of their rule. There were thousands of executions,[2] and there was large-scale imprisonment, throughout the revolutionary period, of tens of thousands of people under typically very poor living conditions and physical mistreatment.

This dwarfed in *numerical terms* the repression carried out by the Batista dictatorship, although, of course, that dictatorship did not face the violent external opposition of the United States, the most powerful empire of the twentieth century, as Castro's government did. In addition, the revolutionary leadership had to deal with the strong and often violent resistance of the Cuban bourgeoisie and other political opponents to the large-scale transformation of Cuba's social and economic structure. For those reasons, comparing the repression of the two regimes is to a considerable extent like comparing apples and oranges. Over the long haul, however, the Castro regime has primarily relied on forms of social and economic control rather than physical repression to consolidate its power. It has not matched the number of noncombatant opponents killed by several Latin American dictatorships such as those of Argentina and Guatemala. Nevertheless, it has been unequaled in Latin America in terms of its effective social, political, and economic control of the population under its rule, particularly until the early nineties. Among the mechanisms of control of the Cuban regime we find the restricted access to higher education and desirable employment, vigilance of the block committees, and other methods that I have described elsewhere in this volume. Compared to the situation under Batista, far larger numbers of people have "informed" the authorities about political, social, and economic deviance. But this function has been typically performed by average citizens, sometimes motivated by politics and ideology, sometimes by petty personal jealousies and desire for bureaucratic advantage, but usually not for monetary rewards. Since the early eighties and especially since the early nineties, "softer" socioeconomic methods of control have become more important as the use of physical brutality has declined, although the government has resorted to that whenever it found it convenient. Although significant liberalization has taken place in many areas of social and cultural life since the early nineties, the Cuban government still has vast social, economic, and political resources of control at its disposal. These are far more effective in achieving political control than the primitive repressive methods used by previous dictatorships such as those of Machado in the late twenties and early thirties and Batista's in the thirties and fifties.

The regime's reliance on socioeconomic methods of control assumes the existence of a substantial amount of popular legitimacy and support, the material basis of which was originally a significant improvement of the standard of living for the most materially deprived sectors of the population, social mobility, and nationalist anti-imperialism. However, the economic crisis of the nineties provoked by the collapse of the Soviet Union had a devastating effect on the Cuban economy and on the standard of living of the great majority of the population. Thus it is hardly surprising that popular support for the regime declined substantially; likely a majority of the population is now disaffected, even though they may see no realistic and desirable political alternatives on the horizon. Nor is it surprising that the regime has come to rely even more on nationalist anti-imperialism and opposition to the

United States' criminal economic blockade rather than on "socialism" as a way of maintaining whatever legitimacy and popular support it still retains.

Who Are the Cuban Dissidents and What Do They Stand For?

The origins of open and organized nonviolent political dissidence, as distinct from clandestine opposition groups attempting to overthrow the government by force, date back to 1976, when a group of former supporters of Castro's government came together to form the Cuban Committee for Human Rights (Comité Cubano Pro-Derechos Humanos). Among the founding members of this group were Gustavo Arcos Bergnes, who had participated in the attack on the Moncada barracks led by Fidel Castro on July 26, 1953, and was Cuban ambassador to Belgium in the early days of the revolution; Elizardo Sánchez Santa Cruz, a former professor of philosophy at the University of Havana who had been a member of the Juventud Socialista, the youth wing of the old PSP, and Ricardo Bofill, who spent time in prison as one of the members of Aníbal Escalante's old Communist "micro faction" in the late sixties. Inspired by, and trying to emulate, the dissident movements in Poland and Czechoslovakia, with which they tried to establish contact, the Cuban dissidents emphasized the peaceful nature of their efforts for both principled and practical political reasons. Although implicitly social democratic in outlook, the committee focused on investigating and denouncing the violations of human rights, that is, civil liberties, by the Cuban government. In the years that followed, the founding members of this committee would quarrel with each other and establish new groups such as the Cuban Commission for Human Rights and National Reconciliation (CDHRN—Comisión Cubana de Derechos Humanos y Reconciliación Nacional), established by Sánchez and others in 1987. With the passage of time, other dissident groups of varying political persuasions were organized, although again in clear contrast to the underground opposition groups of the sixties, they generally advocated a peaceful alternative to what they saw as the regime's systematic embrace of violence. For more than three decades, the regime has alternated between repression of these groups—including, as in the case of the trial of seventy-five dissidents in spring 2003, imposing of heavy prison sentences—and bare toleration of their activities. Even then, tolerated dissidents pay a price for being who they are. However, in light of the government's total control of the mass media, their activities are unknown to the great majority of Cubans except for when the government occasionally chooses to denounce them.

There have never been more than a relatively small number of dissidents, who are organized in many small groups. At the same time, there probably are many more silent dissidents, including people who occupy important positions in the country's economic, cultural, and even political spheres. This is an expression of the prevailing *doble moral* (double morality)—a substantial gap between what people say in private and in public. The open dissidents do not seem to have a social base in the sense of having relations with groups of peasants, workers, students, or any other significant social force. When such a relationship began to develop, as in the case in the early nineties of several union activists in the port of Havana, government repression made sure to put an end to that connection. The situation is somewhat different with Catholic dissidents who have a relationship with the church. However, the potential impact of this connection is greatly attenuated by the relative political weakness of Cuban Catholicism and by the great caution exercised by the Catholic hierarchy, which has sometimes provoked strong criticisms from Catholic and other dissidents.

As suggested earlier, there is a high price paid for dissidence in Cuba, including loss of employment in the public sector, which at least until very recently comprised the overwhelming majority of jobs in the country. In addition, dissidents are likely to lose access to higher education and may become subject to many forms of harassment and imprisonment. For obvious reasons, an increasing number of dissidents have grown up in and are a product of the revolution, although some, especially those who are Catholic, are the descendants of, and have family connections with, people who opposed the revolutionary government from the very beginning. Some dissidents worked for a long time in midlevel positions in the Cuban government, as in the case of the economist Oscar Espinosa Chepe. Others are related to major leaders of the old Communist Party, such as Vladimiro Roca, son of Blas Roca Calderío, one of the principal leaders of the PSP for many decades. It is worth noting that a significant number of well-known dissidents are black. Such are the cases of Vladimiro Roca, Manuel Cuesta Morúa, Oscar Elías Biscet, Jorge Luis García Pérez (Antúnez,) Darsi Ferrer, Guillermo Fariñas, Félix Bonné Carcassés, and Dimas Castellanos, as well as Orlando Zapata Tamayo, who died after a long hunger strike in 2010.

The political spectrum of dissident opinion in Cuba ranges from the hard right to moderate Christian democrats and moderate social democrats on the left. The political positions separating the various dissident groups and individuals generally do not include the use of violence against the regime, since peaceful opposition has become a virtual consensus position for politically active dissidents inside the island. The situation is quite different with respect to the US economic blockade, which is supported by many Cuban dissidents and opposed by some others. Dissidents who oppose the US economic blockade typically do so because they see it as a counterproductive, inopportune, and failed policy rather than on the grounds of national self-determination and anti-imperialism (in other words, that the United States has no right to use its economic power to impose its preferred economic and political system on Cuba). Similar differences of opinion exist with respect to whether Cuban dissidents should receive aid from US government agencies. Most controversial of all in dissident circles have been the issues of whether to advocate dialogue with the government and whether the opposition should attempt to operate within the political rules of the existing system to try to bring about democratic changes on the island.

While dissidents strongly criticize the Cuban political and economic system, they tend to say little, with some important exceptions noted below, about concrete alternatives, whether in terms of general economic organization or more specific matters such as education and health policy. Here one cannot help but recall Fidel Castro's manipulative political tactic from 1956 until as late as 1960 of saying as little as possible about his eventual political and economic goals for the country. While this tactic may have "fooled" Castro's opponents at home and abroad, it also "fooled" his loyal supporters.[3]

Nevertheless, practically all Cuban dissident currents accept the principles of the "market economy" (the term "capitalism" is usually avoided), which is practically taken for granted as a matter of common sense and the only possible alternative to the failures of the Communist economies. Dissidents supported the legalization of self-employment, as did most leftist critics of the regime and a good part of the government apparatus itself. But many dissidents, perhaps deliberately, blur the critical distinction between self-employment (or small family firms) and the far more expansive and general notion of reintroducing private enterprise, which they also support. However, dissidents do tend to avoid the issue of privatization of *existing* enterprises, including those that were built by the revolutionary government and were never privately owned. They also tend to keep silent on whether *large* enterprises solely owned by *Cuban* individuals or private corporations should be allowed on the island. Some of these dissident currents could have conceivably advocated a "mixed economy"—combining private enterprise in small firms with the state controlling large-scale industry—but, as far as I am aware, no dissident group has explicitly proposed such an alternative. It is not unusual for dissident programmatic pronouncements to omit any reference to matters of economic organization. This was the case for example of the unity statement in support of human rights, freedom, justice, and national reconciliation adopted by the most prominent dissident leaders ranging from the most right-wing to Christian and social democrats in April 2007. Such omissions are probably intended in part to avoid publicizing differences of opinion among dissidents and in part to downplay their common commitment to the fundamental principles of the "market economy."[4]

The "Moderate Dissident" Milieu

"Moderate dissidence" in Cuba is fundamentally defined by two political criteria. First, beyond support for a peaceful rather than violent strategy to achieve changes in the existing political system on the island, which is common to all dissident opinion inside the island, moderates tend to advocate some form of dialogue with the government to achieve their goals. Second, moderate dissidents share a critical attitude toward the economic blockade and other aspects of US policy toward Cuba. Thus defined, being a moderate dissident leaves a great deal of room for a wide range of political differences on other important matters, including the role that the state should play in the economy. Moreover, Christian democrats are likely to differ from other "moderate dissidents" on such matters as the separation of church and state. While the moderate opposition is highly critical of the Cuban one-party state as undemocratic and for ignoring the rule of law, it places a strong emphasis on criticizing what it perceives as the government's proclivity toward stridency, intolerance, and periodic resort to violent repression of opponents.

The moderates' emphasis on dialogue and national reconciliation may also be an implicit recognition of political weakness and a response to the fact that the government still enjoys legitimacy and popular support, even if it may no longer be that of the majority of the population. For many years, these groups as well as human rights supporters have also made repeated calls for "tolerance." Unfortunately, tolerance constitutes a poor and precarious attitudinal substitute for an institutional culture of rights that should be part of democracy as an everyday socioeconomic and political reality. Rights are about empowering people independently of the attitudes of those ruling over the country at any given point.[5] It was in this spirit that Thomas Paine more than two hundred years ago praised the new French Constitution because it "hath abolished or renounced toleration, and intolerance also, and hath established *Universal Right of Conscience.*" Paine added, "Toleration is not the opposite of intoleration, but is the counterfeit of it. Both are despotisms. The one assumes to itself the right of withholding liberty of conscience, and the other of granting it."[6]

The moderate dissident emphasis on tolerance points to the development of a new Cuban liberalism that has expressed itself with a great deal of sophistication in such venues as the high-quality and influential journal *Encuentro de la Cultura Cubana* and website *cubaencuentro*, both edited in Madrid. The journal, which stopped publication in 2009, was produced with excellent paper and multicolor graphic design, which allowed it to frequently reproduce works of art. *Encuentro* had the financial support, according to its publishers, of a wide variety of sources. This included agencies of the Spanish Foreign Ministry and the Spanish Socialist Party (PSOE), the federal government's National Endowment for Democracy, the Open Society Institute, and the Ford Foundation in the United States, the Swedish Olof Palme International Center and Social Democratic Party, the European Commission, and the Mexican journal *Letras Libres* among many other organizations and institutions.[7] In contrast to much of the archaic political discourse among Cuban Americans in south Florida, *Encuentro* was also very modern. *Encuentro* generally occupied, for most of its existence since its foundation in 1995, the center to center-right of the political spectrum, although not all contributors fit this characterization. In this sense, *Encuentro* was similar to the Mexican *Letras Libres*, and its predecessor *Vuelta*, in that prominent liberal center-right writers such as the Mexicans Enrique Krauze and Gabriel Zaid left their mark. The authentic achievements that were obtained in prerevolutionary Cuba hardly warranted the apologetic "Homenaje a la República" (Homage to the Cuban Republic) to which *Encuentro* dedicated one of its issues. This was undoubtedly an inappropriate way to refer to what by any reasonable account was a failed and corrupt social, economic, and political system.[8] Moreover, many articles in *Encuentro* criticized what they described as the intransigence and moral absolutism of revolutionary and reformist thought in Cuba sometimes going back as far as the late nineteenth century, accusing it of having engendered a political climate of intolerance and illiberalism hostile to democracy. Consistent with this intellectual and political orientation, *Encuentro* published in its pages the work of like-minded thinkers who became particularly influential in Eastern Europe in the late eighties and early nineties such as Poland's Adam Michnik and the Czech Republic's Vaclav Havel.[9] However, the international financial crisis that broke out in 2008 had a serious impact on the journal, which shortly after laid off almost all its personnel and ceased publication.[10] At the same time, a split among the editors led to the creation of the website *Diario de Cuba*, which is politically further to the right and competes with the older website *cubaencuentro*, which has become more open to social democratic and even some left perspectives.

Many moderate dissidents seem to understand, at least intuitively, that an open and explicit advocacy of a *capitalist* market economy is not going to have a great deal of appeal in a country where Communism was homegrown and not imposed by foreign troops. In Cuba, as in such countries as China and Vietnam, Communism has historically had much greater popular legitimacy and support than did the Communist systems that existed in places like Poland and Hungary. By the same token, the term "capitalism" became strongly associated with inequality and exploitation. Nevertheless, the moderates occasionally talk about granting equal legal standing to different forms of property, whether state, cooperative, or private, without specifying their respective dimensions, and also support the maintenance of a welfare state. However, one can only conclude on the basis of the moderate opposition's explicit programmatic statements and numerous evasions that they would favor a less generous welfare state than that promised, if not consistently delivered, by the social legislation of Cuban Communism.

One might have expected from Cuba's social-democratic dissidents at least some rhetorical attention to issues of class power and privilege. But the political positions adopted by some of the more prominent dissidents who claim to be social democrats seem to be in fact much closer to US-style liberal democracy. These dissidents perhaps adopted the term "social-democratic" in pursuit of international recognition and support from Latin American and European social-democratic parties, which have in most cases adopted neoliberal economics in practice if not in theory. Such is the case of the Arco Progresista (Progressive Arc), a coalition of small social-democratic groups led by, among others, Manuel Cuesta Morúa. He is a descendant of Martín Morúa Delgado, an important black Cuban politician of the early twentieth century. The political platform that the Progressive Arc presented in the summer of 2008 is written in vague liberal-democratic language. The platform argues that the challenges Cuba faces are not "simply ideological— right, center, or left—but national: what country, nation, and state we are going to give ourselves, and what is our position . . . about whether it is the right, center, or left that constitutes the best option for Cuba." The platform does vaguely advocate strengthening its political work in workplaces, which they acknowledge has been a deficit of the Partido Arco Progresista. But its most concrete proposal is the organization of a campaign to collect a million signatures for an agrarian reform that would distribute the land in order to augment agricultural production. The document did not even say a word in support of independent agricultural cooperatives or any other form of voluntary collective working of the land. This is a hardly surprising omission when the platform places the campaign for land distribution in the context of demanding a liberalization of labor and agricultural markets.[11] However, Cuesta Morúa has been an outspoken critic of racial discrimination and helped to found the Citizens' Committee for Racial Integration (CIR), which planned to hold regular discussion workshops and initiate a campaign against racist behavior by the police.[12] The Arco Progresista of which he is a leading member also strongly objected, from a working-class perspective, to the massive layoff of half a million workers announced by the revolutionary government in the fall of 2010.[13] In relation to the United States, Cuesta Morúa saw the younger Bush's very aggressive policies toward Cuba as deepening the error of treating the Cuban government as if it were a rebel that had to be disciplined by the United States.[14] Morúa's refusal, during the younger Bush's administration, to toe the US line, followed by an important sector of Cuban dissidents, earned him the ill will of the US Interests Section under James Cason, who spread the word that Morúa's people were Castro's puppets. Consistent with this line of thought, Dimas Castellanos, a supporter of Morúa, was denied a visa to enter the United States in 2004, when he was invited to attend the thirty-fifth anniversary of the Center for Cuban Studies in Miami.[15] More recently, Cuesta Morúa and the Arco Progresista launched a new political initiative called "Nuevo País" (New Country), claiming that Cuba was falling apart and needed a new foundation. The Nuevo País document strongly emphasized the need for an acceptance of pluralism—in terms of race, politics, sexual orientation, and religion, among others. However, the document objected to the mediating interference of institutions, political parties, interest groups, vanguards, and messianic movements, so one is left to wonder how the pluralism that was so fervently advocated is going to be expressed in organizational and institutional terms. In the end, the Arco Progresista's initiative advocates a reduction of the armed forces under strict civil and citizen control. It also advocates a welfare society where a sustainable, ecological, and durable development will be based on a combination of diverse forms of property in the framework of a market economy, distributive equity, and networks of social protection.[16]

One of the founders of Cuban dissidence in the seventies, Elizardo Sánchez Santa Cruz, who has achieved international prominence, is a moderate dissident who deserves special attention. A major part of Sánchez's reputation was due to his introduction of a modern form of human rights reporting: objective, cool, and as meticulous as the difficulties of human rights reporting on the island allowed. Increasingly, however, Sánchez also adopted a political posture along generally moderate social-democratic lines. He continued to oppose the blockade from a policy, rather than national self-determination, perspective. Thus, in connection with the US ban on travel to Cuba, he told the *New York Times* on April 22, 1997, that "American policy impedes the transformation we seek . . . how can one sincerely argue that the cause of a more open Cuba would not be advanced by having as many Americans as possible in the streets of Havana?"[17] In the face of the younger Bush's tough measures toward Cuba, Sánchez argued that restricting Cuban American travel to the island violated the fundamental right of freedom of movement and that providing direct financial aid to dissidents would be counterproductive.[18] However, as we shall see below, Sánchez changed his mind and later favored US financial assistance to Cuban dissidents. A 2006 cable from the US Interests Section (USINT) in Havana distributed by Wikileaks shows that Elizardo Sánchez and Vladimiro Roca had a meeting with Michael Parmly, the head of the Interests Section, to protest and ask for a reconsideration of the two-year-old ban of ten people from the USINT's two Internet centers. Sánchez and Roca claimed that these people had been unfairly blacklisted, perhaps at the request of rival dissidents. For his part, Parmly insisted that the ten were among a small number of Cubans whose Internet privileges "were revoked for repeatedly disturbing other users, mistreating USINT staffers, or committing other offenses."[19] Be that as it may, while this particular cable does not clarify the degree to which there might have been a working relationship between Roca, Sánchez, and the US diplomatic mission, it does show that both sides conceived of each other as an ally, even if they may have been mutually disappointed by each other's actions.

Most surprising was the Cuban government's accusation in 2003 that Sánchez was a double agent and had been an informant and collaborator of Cuban state security agencies. A video was televised showing Sánchez in the company of government agents and purportedly being decorated for the services he had rendered to the regime. Sánchez acknowledged the authenticity of the video but strongly denied that he had provided information or was an agent of the government. Instead he metaphorically claimed that he had sat down with Satan in hell itself, which was a very dangerous place. Sánchez insisted that he was there to convey a very generous proposal from a number of statesmen he had recently met suggesting a type of transition in which Fidel Castro himself would make the necessary reforms but would still govern Cuba until the end of his days. The major lesson Sánchez drew from this experience was that he had been a fool for talking to the government.[20]

What explains the campaign to discredit Elizardo Sánchez, particularly when the government showed that he was, after all, collaborating with it? Enrique Patterson, a prominent black Cuban intellectual in south Florida and former associate of Sánchez, argued that because of his political background, the Cuban dissident had contacts and relationships in the middle and not-so-middle regime spheres, which, politically ambitions as he is, he had cultivated with great patience. According to Patterson, the honor conferred on Sánchez may have been the work of a group in the regime conspiring with him in trying to undermine Castro. When the Cuban leader found out what was going on, he cracked down on the operation, singling out Sánchez as a political target. Patterson also saw Sánchez as looking forward to the moment when Castro passed from the scene and the regime reformists might propose a transition toward democracy. Sánchez would then be ready to join them, not as the opposition counterpart at the negotiation table but as a full member of the regime's reformist group. Whether Patterson's interpretation is correct or not, one cannot but agree with his conclusion that a "political dialogue should not be conducted with policemen."[21]

The moderate dissidents look favorably toward the liberalization of the economic blockade, including measures such as those adopted by the Obama administration in 2009 and 2011. In fact, in the summer of 2010, seventy-four moderate dissidents, including hunger striker Guillermo Fariñas, blogger Yoani Sánchez, Elizardo Sánchez, and economist Oscar Espinosa Chepe, signed a letter supporting proposed congressional legislation that would lift the US travel ban to the country for all Americans.[22] However, the Cuban moderates usually envision liberalizing changes in US policy in the context of an exchange: the Cuban government should respond to a softening of the blockade with domestic liberalizing and democratizing measures of its own. This exchange of supposed equivalents constitutes the commonsense perspective of most moderates on the island but also of liberals abroad, particularly in the United States. For example, in a 2009 report on Cuba, Human Rights Watch proposed such an exchange approach. However, the report additionally demanded that "before changing its policy, the US should work to secure commitments from the EU, Canada and Latin American allies that they will join together to pressure Cuba to meet a single, concrete demand: the immediate and unconditional release of all political prisoners."[23] Ten years earlier, while the human rights situation in Cuba was if anything worse than in 2009, Human Rights Watch published another report that also proposed the exchange approach. But unlike 2009, it placed far greater emphasis on the damage done by the US economic embargo on Cuba and did not recommend that the United States obtain commitments from other countries before making changes in its embargo policies.[24]

The "exchange" approach was also endorsed by Pope John Paul II during his visit to Cuba in 1998, when he proclaimed that the world should open itself to Cuba and that Cuba should open itself to the world. At first sight, the pope's exhortation appears to be very reasonable. But if we think about it a little more carefully, we can see that there a number of traps right below the surface plausibility of the slogan. The first trap is the notion, widely accepted by the US mainstream media, Washington's political establishment,[25] and moderate Cuban dissidents, that a US modification, let alone abolition, of the blockade should ultimately *depend* on the Cuban government's domestic liberalizing and democratizing responses. Not surprisingly, supporters of the Cuban government abroad, although not so much the Cuban government itself, make the opposite claim; namely, that the elimination of internal political repression in Cuba *depends* on abolition of the economic blockade. Implicit and sometimes explicit in these political rationales is the pretense, on the one hand, that the US blockade was established because Cuba is undemocratic, a laughable claim when one considers the long history of the US economic, military, and political support for the bloodiest procapitalist dictatorships. On the other hand, there is the mirror image pretense that the Cuban one-party Soviet-type state exists *because* of the US blockade. This assumes that the Cuban revolutionary leaders had been political blank slates, merely responding to US policies, and had no preferences and ideologies of their own, including no conceptions of desirable political or economic systems.

The political logic of this mutual concessions approach is that it implicitly rules out a demand for independent and unilateral actions—although in quite different spheres—on both sides of the Gulf of Mexico. It also establishes a false symmetry between the two countries and obscures the roots of the blockade, which was imposed by the US empire because the Cuban government challenged US power and control over the island, not because the Cuban government was undemocratic, which it certainly has been. That alone justifies the democratic demand for a unilateral and unconditional lifting of the blockade. Similarly, Cubans on the island, with the help of voluntary organizations abroad that are independent of foreign governments, such as Amnesty International, are entitled to press for civil liberties and internal democratic change quite independent of whether the US government modifies or abolishes the blockade.

There are also practical issues to be considered here. The fact is that the over fifty-year-old economic blockade has been an absolute failure in achieving its supposed objectives and has instead helped to impoverish the Cuban people. Many people on both sides of the Gulf of Mexico would agree with this assessment but claim that the exchange and negotiations approach is "practical" while the advocacy of unilateral actions is not. They argue that a process of give-and-take of mutual concessions would lead, on the one hand, to the eventual dismantling of the blockade and, on the other hand, to the complete liberalization and democratization of Cuban society. But the "unilateral action" approach is no less "practical." The unilateral abolition of the US blockade would completely undermine the Cuban government's remaining justification of repression in the eyes of the substantial number of Cubans who still support the government for nationalist and anti-imperialist reasons. Similarly, a unilateral abolition of the repressive machinery of the one-party state in Cuba would radically destabilize the false American political justification for it and would make the blockade of Cuba politically untenable.

The Posture of the Catholic Church

Cuba is not Poland, and it would be foolhardy to expect that the Cuban Catholic Church could play the same critical role as its Polish counterpart in helping to bring about the overthrow of Communism on the island. However, that does not mean that, as we shall see below, the Cuban Church may not be an important political actor in the country. Even before the revolution, Cuban Catholicism was politically weak for reasons deeply rooted in Cuban history. The church never showed the same degree of interest in proselytizing among black slaves and their descendants as it did among the Native American populations in countries such as Mexico and Peru, a population that was virtually wiped out in Cuba. The church also supported Spanish colonialism during the Cuban struggles for independence. Many of the Cuban independence leaders were Masons,[26] and even those who were not strongly anticlerical favored the strict separation of church and state, the policy adopted by the new nominally independent Cuban Republic in 1902. At the time of the 1959 Revolution, the church was also disadvantaged by the fact that a majority of the priests were Spanish.[27] Parishioners were mostly white, urban, and middle and upper class, and most peasants and rural workers had little contact with Catholic churches and priests. In sum, although the great majority of the population was nominally Catholic, only a relatively small minority actively practiced the Catholic religion.[28]

While the revolutionary government and the Catholic Church maintained friendly relations during the first year of the revolution, sharp clashes began to occur between them in 1960. In August, a "Pastoral Letter from the Cuban Episcopate" attacked Communism. The letter contained a mixture of themes: it condemned the dictatorial and terrorist character of Communism that enslaved people to the state, encouraged the abolition of the right of property, and pressured women to work outside the home. Consistent with the Catholic Church's traditional hostility to such notions as the class struggle, it also condemned Communism for being materialistic and atheistic.[29] A few days later, Fidel Castro made a strong counterattack that was followed by a systematic campaign against the church in the government press. There were street clashes, verbal attacks in the churches, the closure of various Catholic radio and television programs, and some arrests. Then, after the failed Bay of Pigs invasion of April 1961, in which two Catholic priests participated as chaplains, the revolutionary government dealt several fatal blows to the church. In June, the government nationalized private education, taking over the two Catholic universities and all of the 324 primary and secondary church schools. In September, 132 mostly Spanish priests were expelled, dozens of Catholic leaders were imprisoned, and religious processions were forbidden.[30] Two years later, in 1963, the church even lost control of the monumental Colón Cemetery, which was nationalized.[31] The end of Catholic education and the dramatic reduction in the number of priests and nuns (two-thirds of priests and nine-tenths of nuns had left the country) constituted a serious defeat for the church from which it never fully recovered. However, once the church had been thoroughly defeated, it did not take long before a normalization of relations came about between the government and the Catholic hierarchy. Much of this was due to the intervention of the Vatican through its emissary Monsignor Cesare Zacchi, who was its chargé d'affaires in Cuba from 1962 until 1975.[32] By the early seventies, a new entirely Cuban hierarchy was running the church.[33] After then, the church was able to survive with a substantially diminished number of parishioners by taking what was fundamentally a low political profile. While the church often adopted very moderately critical stances toward the government, it also took a position against the American economic blockade that diminished somewhat its political distance from the revolutionary leadership.[34]

Nevertheless, from the sixties until the Fourth Congress of the CCP in 1991, active practitioners of Catholicism, like those of other religions, were barred from membership in the ruling party and from the most important educational and employment opportunities. These repressive measures further weakened Cuban Catholicism, although since the religious liberalization of the early nineties, the church has significantly increased the number of its parishioners. According to the *National Catholic Reporter*, less than half of the population identified itself as Catholic in 2006.[35] The hierarchy, under the leadership of Cardinal Jaime Ortega Alamino (born in 1936), continues to be very moderate and cautious in its criticisms of the government. However, some Catholic clergy such as José Conrado Rodríguez, a parish priest in Santiago de Cuba, and laymen such as Dagoberto Valdés, former editor of the Catholic journal *Vitral* in western Cuba, have been far more outspoken in criticizing the regime. Others such as the highly cultured Monsignor Carlos Manuel de Céspedes, vicar general of Havana and a direct descendant of one of Cuba's most important founding fathers, also named Carlos Manuel de Céspedes, have managed to get along better with the government while retaining their political independence. On the eve of the celebration of what would have been Che Guevara's eightieth birthday on June 14, 2008, the official CCP daily newspaper *Granma* even published a long article by Céspedes praising the Argentinian-born leader. Nevertheless, Céspedes has argued that while the defense of national sovereignty does not allow for "flirtations" (*coqueteos*), everything should be open for discussion when it comes to sociopolitical and economic matters. Céspedes claims that while the 1976 constitution commands "a type of socialism that no longer exists," the majority of Cubans believe that there should be a socialism that is "more democratic and participatory, closer to what was the original project of social democracy."[36] The website *Espacio Laical Digital* (http://espaciolaical.org) sponsored by the Consejo Arquidiocesano de Láicos de la Habana (Lay Council of the Archdiocese of Havana) has provided a forum for liberal and social-democratic Catholics such as Roberto Veiga González and for left-wing critics of the regime (for example, Armando Chaguaceda) as well as for the work of Cuban economists abroad (such as Carmelo Mesa-Lago).

The Cuban government has allowed the Catholic Church to publish dozens of small parish and group publications and forty-six bulletins and magazines, and to establish twelve websites and seven electronic bulletins that reach about a quarter of a million people directly or indirectly.[37] Although of limited circulation (well below 5 percent of the adult population), these publications constitute the one significant exception to the Cuban government's monopoly on the printed word on the island. Among the most important websites sponsored by the church are the above-mentioned *Espacio Laical* (for lay Catholics) and *Palabra Nueva* (organ of the Archdiocese of Havana) that can be read by the small number of Cubans who have access to the Internet. The Catholic hierarchy has for many years also made requests to the Cuban government that fall within the broad scope of a democratization of the Cuban polity and society. This is the case, for example, of the hierarchy's demand for a "systematic space" in the government-controlled mass media[38] as well as access to the Internet and institutions such as prisons in order to minister to their faithful, a request that the government granted to all religious denominations in 2009.[39] Cardinal Ortega was even allowed to conduct a Christmas Mass in 2010 at the Combinado del Este, one of the principal prisons on the island.[40] The Catholic hierarchy's desire to train and import more priests also falls within the scope of a democratization of Cuban society. More problematic from a democratic point of view, as I will discuss below, are the demands made by the hierarchy and other Catholic circles for the establishment of religious schools on the island.[41]

The Cuban Catholic Church has for a long time been very concerned about what it sees as a decline of moral values and conduct on the island. A good part of this concern is fully justified and stems from the widespread youth anomie and generalized law-breaking and corruption in the country. This corruption is so vast that it led Fidel Castro himself to warn in a speech at the University of Havana in November 2005 that it could destroy the revolution from within and thus accomplish what US imperialism had failed to bring about for many decades. But much of the Cuban church's great concern about values and moral crisis is not based on specifically Cuban phenomena but reflects its traditional views on such matters as family life (for example, the rising divorce rate) and rejection of sexual freedom and other aspects of modernity. Like Catholic churches elsewhere in the world, the Cuban church opposes abortion and birth control and supports only traditional family forms. In recent years, the church has found itself in the position of pressuring a government institution to take a more conservative stance on the issue of gays. According to Mariela Castro Espín, the director of CENESEX, the Catholic Church communicated to the center its negative views about homosexual marriages. Castro Espín responded that neither homosexual marriage nor the adoption of children by homosexual couples was being considered, although in the future a reform bill would allow the legal recognition of same-sex unions with the same rights as civil unions among heterosexual couples. Castro Espín added that the June 2008 decision to carry out sex operations for transsexual persons, which had also been a matter of concern to the Catholic Church and other religious denominations, was still in force.[42] The church's conservative stance toward some of the reforms proposed by CENESEX is consistent with a socially conservative view of the world that has sometimes led it to make claims without any factual basis. For example, in the pastoral letter issued on February 25, 2003, Cardinal Ortega Alamino claimed that "experience demonstrates that sex, alcohol, and drugs are dangerously intertwined."[43] Several years later, Ortega lamented the decadence of Cuban society in more general terms. But he singled out for criticism "the unbridled sexual life, the lack of social engagement, the deafening music disregarding neighbors, the abuse of alcoholic beverages, or the murder of a priest in order to steal from him," an allusion to the killing of a Spanish priest in July 2009.[44]

Somewhat unexpectedly, Cardinal Ortega, the head of the Cuban Catholic hierarchy, found himself a negotiating partner with the Cuban and Spanish governments in 2010. This turned out to be a successful negotiation to obtain the release and deportation (almost entirely to Spain) of most of the fifty-two Cubans who still remained in prison as a result of the crackdown on dissidents that took place in the spring of 2003. Shortly after, the Catholic hierarchy also successfully intervened to allow Juan Juan Almeida, dissident son of revolutionary hero Juan Almeida, to travel abroad to receive medical treatment after years of the government's denying him permission to leave the country. The cardinal had earlier succeeded in temporarily stopping the harassment, at least in Havana, of small demonstrations that the Ladies in White were conducting to protest the imprisonment of their relatives. Beyond the obvious significance of these measures as marking liberalizing steps on the part of the Cuban political leadership, they also indicated the government's recognition of the Catholic hierarchy as an interlocutor and negotiating partner, with important implications for the future.

But why would the Cuban government grant such recognition to the Cuban church hierarchy? It is very unlikely that the Cuban government did so because it was responding and accommodating to a perceived growing popular support for the church inside the country. Instead, the government may have chosen the church as a negotiating partner because it is an important *Cuban* institution that is simultaneously part of a powerful *international* organization. Thus, on one hand, the government tried to avoid the impression of simply giving concessions to foreign countries (for example Spain, acting, as it has for many years, on its own behalf as well as that of the European Union). On the other hand, as part of an influential international organization, the Cuban church could serve some useful purposes as a lobbying and diplomatic force abroad. It is very revealing that Cardinal Ortega traveled to Washington in June and August 2010 and met with important figures in the Obama administration such as General James L. Jones, national security adviser, and Arturo Valenzuela, assistant secretary of state for Latin America.[45] Ortega told the *Washington Post* that Raúl Castro "has a desire for an opening with the U.S. government . . . he repeated to me on several occasions that he is ready to talk to the United States government directly, about every issue."[46] While it is doubtful that Ortega was functioning as an official diplomatic conduit between Havana and Washington, it was clear that he was playing an important role sounding out Washington on behalf of Havana.

Ortega's negotiating activities on behalf of political prisoners, which excluded the participation of dissidents, were criticized by moderate dissidents such as Yoani Sánchez.[47] Cardinal Ortega was also subject to a withering attack in a letter addressed to the pope signed by 165 dissidents, including such well-known right-wing dissident figures as Vladimiro Roca and Marta Beatriz Roque,[48] to which the church and Catholic publications responded vigorously.[49] Missing from all these criticisms and attacks was an admission that the church is not a democratic institution[50] and that it has its own corporate interests that are likely to benefit from its acting as an intermediary for the Cuban government. For example, the Cuban government materially contributed to the construction of a new building with modern facilities located 17 kilometers southeast of Havana to house the San Carlos and San Ambrosio Seminary, which had been originally located in Old Havana. Cardinal Ortega publicly expressed his gratitude to the Cuban government for its contribution when Raúl Castro and other high-ranking dignitaries attended the inauguration of the new seminary.[51]

The Moderate Catholic Dissident Milieu

There are political opposition currents in Cuba that although Catholic in inspiration, do not speak for the church, although they probably count on the sympathy of some of the hierarchy and many priests and rank-and-file practicing Catholics. Without a doubt, the most important of these has been the Christian Liberation Movement (CLM) founded in 1988 by Oswaldo Payá (who was born in 1952 and was thus seven years old at the time of the revolutionary victory). Cardinal Ortega has praised and congratulated Payá for the firmness with which he has upheld his ideals. But he has distanced himself from Payá's political activities on the grounds that the church does not support political projects.[52] In turn, Payá has not been shy in criticizing the Cuban Catholic Church for its timidity and caution in criticizing and opposing the Cuban government.[53] For instance, Payá criticized "some [Catholic] pastors" and the Spanish government for going along with the Cuban government in excluding dissidents from the 2010 negotiations to release political prisoners.[54]

Payá is probably the best known of the Cuban dissident leaders today, at least abroad. He opposes the US blockade (as bad policy rather than on the principled grounds of national self-determination) and has refused to accept US aid for him and for his small organization. Virtually unique among dissidents, his strategy has been to try to work within the Cuban legal and political system, a strategy that has been much attacked and vilified by the hard Cuban American right in south Florida. Following this strategy, he collected enough signatures to run as a candidate in the Popular Power elections in Cuba in 1992. Not surprisingly, the electoral application was ignored by the authorities. In 1998, Payá founded the Varela Project (named after Félix Varela, the early nineteenth-century Cuban pro-independence priest). The purpose of the project was to collect the ten thousand signatures required to initiate a referendum process to modify the 1976 constitution. Payá succeeded in collecting the signatures and presented them to the relevant government authorities on March 10, 2002. Soon after, the government proceeded to organize a referendum for a constitutional amendment proclaiming the "irrevocable" status of the existing "socialist" system, as if constitutional bravado could prevent the overthrow of the Cuban or any other system. Eventually, in January 2003, a spokesman for National Assembly president Ricardo Alarcón announced that the Constitution and Legal Affairs Committee had shelved Payá's amendment because it went against the very foundations of the constitution, among other reasons.[55] The text of Payá's proposed amendment emphasized a number of democratic demands on behalf of electoral reform, free speech, press, and association, and amnesty for nonviolent political offenders. It also advocated the legalization of private enterprise, whether individual or cooperative, without specifying its size. Payá's petition did proclaim that no person should be allowed to obtain income from exploitation of the labor of others. However, the overall context clearly indicated that his concept of exploitation accords with the term's commonsense usage meaning ill treatment of and excessive demands on workers.[56]

The Varela Project has become well known abroad, and a sector of the Spanish press has even frequently referred to Payá as the "Cuban Suárez," referring to Adolfo Suárez, Spain's prime minister after Franco's death.[57] Payá became known inside Cuba as well when former president Jimmy Carter visited the island in 2002 and explicitly referred to the Varela Project in his televised address to the Cuban people. Subsequently, Payá initiated the Heredia Proyect in 2007 and publicized it again in 2010.[58] The purpose of this new project is to gather signatures in support of a bill abolishing restrictions on the freedom of movement inside and outside the country and on the citizenship rights and property of past and future Cuban emigrants.[59] With his new focus on the right to travel and the right of emigrants to retain their citizenship rights and (mostly personal) property, Payá has touched on the policies that have probably created the greatest amount of resentment of the government among the Cuban population at large. Of course, very few Cubans are likely to hear about this new initiative.

Much less known than the Varela and Heredia projects is Payá's extensive work spelling out the views of his Christian Liberation Movement on basic principles for a new Cuban constitution and socioeconomic order. This is contained in his long "Documento de trabajo para el programa de transición" (Working document for the transition program), published on December 12, 2003.[60] Payá conceives of this document as his contribution to a "national Cuban dialogue" that he proposes to carry out on the island to establish the basis for a Cuban transitional program and government that would be subject to a popular referendum. During this transition the Cuban constitution of 1976 and its various amendments would be abolished, and preparations would be made for a new constitutional convention.

Payá's Working Document (henceforth referred to as WD) is without a doubt the most detailed political platform that any Cuban dissident leader has ever proposed. In light of Payá's prominence as the most important dissident leader, it deserves serious consideration, not least because it allows us to visualize the kind of socioeconomic and political order that he would attempt to establish in Cuba were he to emerge as a dominant leader in a post-Castro order. While the WD claims that its program is not focused on either capitalism or socialism,[61] this is a rhetorical evasion, since the program is quite obviously capitalist in its orientation. Thus, Payá recognizes and would guarantee the right not only to personal property but to entrepreneurial activity and businesses, and the right to private property over means of production, transport, and other sectors of the economy. Most critically, the program sets no limits on the size of such private enterprises, while vaguely promising that the law will regulate the exercise of the right of private property in accordance with the common welfare.[62] Along the same lines, when proposing that land be available for individual and other forms of ownership, it sets no limits to the size of private landholdings. The WD does prohibit land ownership by foreigners, who would, however, be allowed to lease land from Cuban owners.[63] For many decades this was a common way of circumventing Mexican agrarian reform legislation: making peasants the nominal "owners" of land that had been "leased" to their foreign or Mexican corporate employers. Regarding the mass media, the WD proposes that existing public enterprises be allowed to contract the services of private individuals or private enterprises, offer their spaces and lease their facilities for commercial ends, or even be partially privatized. They would be allowed to do these things while supposedly preserving the capacity of the state and society to offer all citizens a vehicle for free opinion and expression. Any enterprise, society, institution, or individual, whether Cuban or foreign, could establish new mass media institutions in conformity with future legislation to be approved.[64]

The WD claims to support democratic rights and freedoms. It endorses freedom of speech and association, the right to travel and the right to strike, habeas corpus, and abolition of the death penalty. It also advocates a total amnesty for those who may have committed abuses, crimes, and denunciations against other Cubans during the revolutionary period.[65] It justly promises to remove and eliminate all the powers, prerogatives, and privileges that the CCP gave to itself during its many decades in power. However, the WD contradicts its own professed democratic ideals when beyond promising those essential measures that would abolish Communist Party privileges and restore equality among all political parties, it pledges to altogether ban the CCP.[66] In addition to being undemocratic, this would be an ill-advised and foolish policy. It would mean nothing less than the political disenfranchisement and ostracism of tens of thousands of honest and sincere rank-and-file Cuban Communists who are not guilty of any crimes—hardly a good omen for a democratic and peaceful post-Communist transition. Moreover, the WD proposes violations of democratic rights and a fatal undermining of a politically informed and active citizenry when it advocates the banning of all political movement and party activity from all work centers, schools, universities, government installations, and police and military units.[67] Indeed, members of the military and police forces would not be able to belong to any political party, "because they have the sacred mission of defending the people and the rights of citizens above any party or political criteria."[68] Lastly, the WD advocates banning any institutions or organizations whose principles and activities go against people's fundamental rights, national independence, democracy, freedom, and national reconciliation and equality among Cubans,[69] without explaining who would determine whether an institution or organization has violated such a ban, and how. Payá's letter supporting the military coup against Hugo Chávez in 2002, which he subsequently tried to hide, also places much doubt over how consistently he supports democracy.[70]

One of the most troublesome aspects of Payá and the Christian Liberation Movement's approach is its clear failure to uphold the separation of church and state, a critically important feature of Cuban political life and culture ever since became a nominally independent republic in 1902. Thus, for example, article 35 of the widely respected constitution of 1940 unambiguously declared that "the Church shall be separate from the State, which cannot subsidize any cult." Curiously, the WD does take the trouble to declare that religious institutions will be separated from the state,[71] but it does not bother to address the critical issue of whether the state will be insulated from religious practices and institutions. Since, as we shall see below, Payá and the CLM support public financing of religious education, the omission is highly significant. Moreover, for unexplained reasons, the national council of the transitional government would include people recommended by lay Catholic organizations, as well as by the Baptist Church and the Masons.[72] The influence of Catholicism on the WD becomes crystal clear when it advocates the banning of abortion and possibly various kinds of investigations such as cell stem research when it forbids "any practice or investigation that manipulates or suppresses human life."[73] The WD also advocates the discouragement and elimination of pornography,[74] which would of course entail widespread artistic and cultural censorship.

According to the WD, private medical care would be allowed as a complement to free public health care and as a stimulus for the constant improvement of the latter. While the WD insists that under no circumstances would private health care be allowed to undermine free public health care, it does not say how it would prevent the sharp inequalities that have historically characterized two-tier medical systems (such as that of the United States).[75] Along similar lines, there would continue to be free public education at all levels, an education that would be secular and nonideological. But in a major substantial break with Cuban educational traditions, both prerevolutionary and postrevolutionary, the WD advocates that the state should finance religious schools that would be free of charge to students.[76] Remarkably, no political or philosophical argument is put forward to justify the use of public money to finance religious education. The document also puts forward the notion that parents have the right to choose the type of education for their children that conforms to their own values and religious beliefs.[77] This exclusively individualistic perspective allows for no consideration of the critical role of public education as a major democratic force in shaping the new generations and society as a whole. Neither does the document consider the role of public education in terms of social integration and class and racial equality. I would contend that making the case for democratic (not that of the present one-party state), universal, free, and compulsory public education need not violate religious liberty. Parents would still have every right to send their children to the religious schools of their choice on weekends (such as the well-established Sunday school tradition in many countries) or after the daily public school sessions are over.

A Note on the *Generación Y* Blog

A new phenomenon in the Cuban political scene is the proliferation of bloggers with a wide variety of political views, including some written by supporters of the regime.[78] Because of government harassment and restrictions, most critical and dissident bloggers use foreign servers and obtain expensive access to the Internet in tourist hotels. Unfortunately, few people in Cuba have the technical means and equipment to read these blogs. Those who do, usually at school or work, run the risk that administrators will accuse them of using public equipment and facilities for purposes unrelated to their studies or work.

The best-known blogger is Yoani Sánchez, writing on *Generación Y.*[79] Yoani's is a fresh and well-written column that appears approximately every other day. She comments mostly on the problems of everyday life that Cubans face and particularly focuses on material scarcities, bureaucratic obstacles and irrationalities imposed on the citizenry, and violations of civil liberties. Topics covered by her columns include the people who have been displaced, sometimes for years, by the collapse of buildings (August 21, 2010), the poor preparation of teachers and corruption in the schools (June 26, 2010), and prostitutes catering to Cuban men rather than to tourists (April 26, 2010). On more strictly speaking political topics, Sánchez has written about censorship, including the seizure of her own books that had been sent from abroad (April 8, 2010) and even the blocking by Cuban television of a fight that broke out among the players at a baseball game (March 24, 2010). She has also written about the numerous difficulties and obstacles that the government places in the path of citizens who want to travel outside the country (April 1, 2010). If effectiveness can be measured by the numerous attacks leveled against her by the apologists for the Cuban regime abroad (she is seldom mentioned by the official Cuban press), then she must be extremely effective.

Sánchez does not, unlike the great majority of dissidents, offer an explicit political alternative to the government, although one can infer an overall moderate liberal political posture from her many columns. She does not present herself as a politician, but she is of course no less political than the other dissidents. Hostile interviewers have quoted her as favoring the placing of certain economic sectors in private hands and the creation of a "sui generis capitalism" in a "sui generis island."[80] Even if these citations were inaccurate, other pronouncements do show her as at least implicitly favoring capitalism. She told a Venezuelan newspaper that she was much more optimistic about that country than about Cuba, because there were still structures of civil society that had not been eliminated and because "free enterprise survives, with many difficulties, but there it is and the basic structures of a democratic society have not been abolished" in Venezuela.[81] When discussing the problems of Cuban television, including the piracy of foreign productions and the state's political monopoly over the media, Sánchez argues that "a dynamic, attractive, and legal programming cannot be carried out while there is a total state ownership of the media," but fails to spell out any specific alternative to total state control.[82] Any reasonable reader may conclude that she is for capitalist investment in the media, which, given the nature of the business, would have to be quite substantial. If we compare Sánchez's writings with those that appear, for example, in the left-wing *HavanaTimes.org*, it is clear that she is far more concerned with issues of liberty and economic efficiency than with equality. Her particular focus was revealed by her column of November 1, 2010, in which she accused the government of forcing equality on the Cuban people. This is, to say the least, a peculiar attitude in light of the growing inequality on the island since the early nineties. Instead of talking about the concrete economic conditions in the country and the growing economic inequality, Sánchez claims that it was fortunate that collectivization had not erased the human desire for having a little piece of one's own and that forced egalitarianism had only encouraged people's wish to differentiate themselves from each other.[83]

Sánchez has criticized US policy toward Cuba (as bad policy rather than on the grounds of national self-determination) on many occasions and signed the dissident letter supporting legislation ending the US government's restrictions on travel to the island in 2010. In 2006, even before *Generación Y* existed, Sánchez and her husband, Reinaldo Escobar, expressed dislike of the hard-line Cuba policies adopted by the younger Bush's administration. They strongly criticized what they described as the "hegemonic arrogance of the United States" and how "United States policy towards Cuba, in its effort to democratize Cuba based on its own interests, is mistaken."[84] As revealed by Wikileaks, she told US diplomat Bisa Williams when the latter visited Havana in September 2009 that "restrictions only hurt us." Sánchez added, "Do you know how much more we could do if we could use PayPal or purchase things online with a credit card?"[85]

It is worth noting that Sánchez has used hostile language when discussing leftist critics of the Cuban government on at least two occasions. In October 2008, she described Eliecer Dávila, the information science student who famously confronted government leader Ricardo Alarcón at the UCI (Universidad de las Ciencias Informáticas, University of Information Science) in an incident discussed below, as "a victim and executioner of the lack of space for plurality and debate."[86] This was a veiled attempt to discredit Dávila by focusing on his past political monitoring activities at the UCI rather than on the political direction in which he was then moving. Sánchez's other attack, on leftist protesters in 2009, was of a similar nature. In an overall negative assessment of the letter rejecting the governmental bans and obstructions of cultural and social initiatives (which I also discuss below), she took the signers to task for their past ideas and remaining political illusions rather than stressing their new political direction. As Haroldo Dilla Alfonso has pointed out, she criticized them because at some moment they believed in the myth of Raúl Castro's reforms or because they supported the notion that the revolutionary process could reinvent itself. For Yoani Sánchez, concludes Dilla Alfonso, the authors of the letter "are nothing but a mask for conformism. There is no space for them on the Olympus."[87] A truly popular movement for democracy in Cuba would unavoidably involve hundreds of thousands of people who previously supported the government. Thus, Sánchez's resistance to political "contamination" could be seen as a mechanism for sectarian exclusion or, more likely, as an attempt to discourage the opposition movement from taking a left anticapitalist course.

The Hard Right

Generally, right-wing dissidents in Cuba are characterized by their support for the US economic blockade of the island. They usually have close ties to the diplomatic US interests sections in Havana, reflected in willingness to receive material aid from the US government, generally consisting of access to the Internet, computer and office equipment, living stipends, and even salaries.[88] However, some moderate social-democratic dissidents who have historically not supported the blockade are willing to receive US material aid as well. This may demonstrate the precariousness of a critique of US policy that is not based on the principled grounds of national self-determination. Rightists support the reintroduction of the market economy (most times a euphemism for capitalism, although the two terms are not identical) in Cuba. But that does not distinguish them since, as I have already indicated, Cuban moderate dissidents also support such a systemic economic change, although perhaps with more of a welfare state twist.

It is hard to estimate the number of right-wing dissidents and their support. It is not easy, to say the least, to openly proclaim those ideas inside Cuba, although some prominent dissidents have done so. In any case, it is difficult to interpret the meaning of silence under the political conditions prevailing on the island. Furthermore, one cannot accept at face value the Cuban government's attribution of right-wing ideas to its opponents, for these characterizations may be inaccurate or altogether false.

In contrast, it has been very easy to see the predominance of right-wing politics among exiled Cubans, particularly those in Miami and other parts of south Florida. This includes, of course, an important group, particularly among the older exiles of the sixties and seventies, that does not share the predominant nonviolent views of dissidents on the island. Miami became the operational center for US military and terrorist activity against the Cuban government as early as May 1959, when the CIA established its first front organization (the Double Check Corporation) in the city.[89] However, it was only in the fall of that year that a military strategy began to play a central role in US policy toward Cuba. In the period previous to the Bay of Pigs invasion of April 1961, thousands of Miami Cubans went on the CIA payroll. This was also the time when a political culture began to be established in the area that not only was right wing and antidemocratic but also manifested a highly distorted perception of political reality. In this political culture, the hand of Communism was seen everywhere. For example, moderately liberal critics of the US blockade of Cuba such as the editorial board of the *New York Times* have been considered by the Cuban American right wing to be either Communists or Communist dupes.

US government policy played a major role in creating a material base for what soon became a Cuban enclave in Miami. In 1966, the US Congress approved the Cuban Adjustment Act, granting Cubans arriving to the United States automatic asylum, a right that has not been available to Haitians or other refugees in Florida or elsewhere in the United States. The Cuban Refugee Program granted substantial financial assistance to Cuban refugees, who also became eligible for a variety of social services and low-interest college loans. Nevertheless, the great majority of Cuban refugees became workers in such industries as construction, garment, and trucking,[90] and for many decades their relative economic success was in part due to the very high participation of Cuban women in the labor force.

During the sixties and seventies, the politics of Cuban Miami served as auxiliaries of Washington's imperial designs on the island. Nevertheless, this did not prevent Cuban right-wing spokespeople from denouncing what they saw as "betrayals" such as John F. Kennedy's refusal to provide air support to the Bay of Pigs invaders in 1961. A qualitative change took place after 1980 during the Reagan administration. A group of Cuban American businesspeople under the leadership of Jorge Mas Canosa[91] founded the Cuban American National Foundation (CANF). CANF explicitly followed the model of AIPAC (American Israel Public Affairs Committee) in becoming a very effective lobbying and political machine on behalf of a hard right-wing line toward Cuba. Although quite right wing, CANF was modern, knew the ways and language of American politics, and has been successful in obtaining funding from the National Endowment for Democracy and the Florida state government.[92] As Guillermo J. Grenier and Lisandro Pérez have pointed out, the CANF knew how to function like legitimate interest groups, organizing campaign contributions, political fundraisers, lobbying, dissemination of information, and media relations. The CANF played a critical role in the passage of the 1992 Torricelli Act and the 1996 Helms-Burton Act, both of which tightened the US economic blockade of Cuba.[93] Clearly, none of the numerous right-wing groups and individuals who flourished in Miami but had remained within the bounds of traditional Cuban political culture could have possibly played such a role. While the foundation successfully imitated AIPAC in its lobbying and other legal political activities, it also financed and collaborated with the right-wing terrorist attacks against the Cuban government, which often involved the injury and death of innocent noncombatant civilians. Thus, in 1998, the acknowledged terrorist Luis Posada Carriles claimed that CANF had financed his activities. Then, in 2006, José Llama, a former board member of CANF, was arrested in Puerto Rico in 1997 for conspiring to kill Fidel Castro. Llama then publicly demanded that CANF repay the $1.4 million it had borrowed from him in the mid-1990s to help finance the acquisition of a fast boat and other supplies to attack Cuban targets.[94]

Throughout the eighties, the efforts of CANF and other Cuban American business groups, added to the sheer size of the Cuban community in greater Miami and their high election turnout rates, brought about Cuban American political control of the city. The city of Miami got a Cuban-born mayor, and Cubans also became city and county managers. Cubans controlled the city commission and constituted more than one-third of the Dade County delegation to the state legislature. In 1989, Cuban-born Ileana Ros-Lehtinen was elected to the US House of Representatives,[95] where she was joined in subsequent years first by Lincoln Díaz Balart and then by his brother Mario.

The new right-wing Cuban political ascendancy lost no time in establishing its hegemony by every means available, including the denial of fundamental civil and political liberties to those who deviated from its political line. Its political rule in Dade County gave the lie to the promise that the Cuban right would reestablish "freedom and democracy" on the island once Fidel Castro was removed from power. As soon as it came under Cuban American right-wing control, the Miami City Commission established a record for curtailing freedom of expression by denying permits for demonstrations and rallies not to its political liking.[96] Throughout the late eighties and early nineties, there was a drawn-out campaign of harassment against the Cuban Museum of Arts and Culture because it had shown the work of artists still in Cuba and those who had not denounced the Cuban regime. This included a city commission attempt to evict it from its premises and the Florida House of Representatives' cancellation of a $150,000 state grant. Most alarmingly, a bomb was left under the wheel of a museum board member's parked car, which destroyed the museum's glass front door when it detonated.[97]

The bombing of the Cuban Museum brings into focus the close political ties that the Cuban American hard right has had with Cuban right-wing terrorist[98] groups and individuals. In 1982, the Miami City Commission approved a $10,000 grant to the notorious terrorist group Alpha 66. In 1983, when Eduardo Arocena, leader of the terrorist group Omega 7, was arrested for plotting to kill the Cuban ambassador to the UN, Xavier Suárez, the Cuban American mayor of Miami, declared that he thought of Arocena as a freedom fighter, not a terrorist. In 1983, the Miami City Commission proclaimed a "Dr. Orlando Bosch Day" after he was arrested by Venezuelan authorities for planning the 1976 bombing of a Cubana plane, which killed all of its seventy-three civilian passengers.[99] Such terrorist activities had also previously resulted in the deaths of Cuban Americans in Miami who were seen as departing from the hard-right party line concerning Cuba. Luciano Nieves was shot to death in February 1975. In 1976, a bomb went off in the car of Emilio Milián, blowing his legs off. In the late seventies, Eulalio Negrín and Carlos Muñíz Varela, two advocates of the dialogue that was then taking place between the Cuban government and a group of Cuban exiles, were killed in Union City, New Jersey, and Puerto Rico, respectively.[100] Fortunately, numerous other violent acts of harassment, including bombings, did not result in fatalities. Among these were attacks on notable Cuban American dissenters from the hegemonic right-wing ideology such as María Cristina Herrera, founder of the Institute of Cuban Studies, Francisco Aruca of Marazul Travels and Radio Progreso, and Giselda Hidalgo, a trade unionist and human rights advocate.[101]

Aside from these acts of violence, other forms of political action have contributed to give a deservedly negative reputation to Cuban American–controlled Miami. Latin American and other artists who have performed in Cuba have been subject to cancellations and other reprisals if scheduled to appear in Miami.[102] Other right-wing Cuban American political actions have endangered race relations in south Florida, as when Nelson Mandela was treated shabbily when he visited the city in 1990. The mayors of Miami and Miami Beach, as well as the Miami-Dade Commission, under the pressure of Cuban American and to a lesser extent Jewish leaders, refused to meet or honor Mandela because the South African leader had refused to disavow Fidel Castro and Yasser Arafat. The African American community was of course offended and organized a fairly successful boycott against the city of Miami, which was only ended three years later with some concessions to the black community.[103] Last but not least, in late 1999 and the early part of 2000 there was the saga of the child Elián González. Elián's mother had died in an attempt to flee Cuba for Florida, but his father remained on the island and, with strong backing from the Cuban government, asked for his return. The numerous antics of the Cuban right wing, which sponsored and strongly encouraged the efforts of Elián's Miami relatives to keep him in the United States, seriously discredited Cuban American–ruled Miami in the eyes of the great majority of Americans. This included many conservatives who sympathized with the idea that since his mother had died, Elián should rejoin his father.[104]

It is not only Cuban American politicians who play important roles in this political right-wing world. Numerous Spanish-language radio stations have proliferated in Miami and transmit content that is typically vitriolic against the Castro government and anybody who even raises a mild objection to the economic blockade and other aspects of the US government policy toward Cuba. These stations have to one degree or another supported terrorist activities against the Cuban government, or against those people in the United States whom they perceive as sympathetic to or "soft on" the Castro regime. The same politics have historically characterized dozens of small newspapers, with many of them at various times supporting themselves by extorting contributions from Cuban American businesspeople.[105] In the early part of 1992, the Cuban hard right led by the CANF even conducted a boycott against the *Miami Herald*, the principal Miami newspaper.[106] This was part of a long-term and successful campaign to force the traditionally liberal organ to cave in and cater to the politics of the Cuban right wing, particularly in *El Nuevo Herald*, its Spanish daily edition.

The number and importance of right-wing terrorist incidents have substantially declined at least since the nineties. A certain degree of political relaxation has come to prevail in Miami, although protection of civil liberties is far from completely assured. In 2001, the threat of demonstrations by Cuban right-wing exiles over the presence of artists from Cuba compelled organizers of the Grammy Awards to move the show from Miami to Los Angeles. The hard-right establishment has increasingly concentrated on such matters as the above-mentioned unsuccessful campaign to try to keep Elián Gonzalez from being returned to his father in Cuba in late 1999 and early 2000. The Cuban American hard right has continued to campaign vigorously in support of the US economic blockade of the island, against the growing worldwide opposition to it. Last but not least, it has invested considerable energy in defending and trying to keep out of jail well-known terrorists such as Luis Posada Carriles.[107] (Orlando Bosch, another well-known bomber, deceased in late April 2010, had been living quietly in Miami, unmolested by a federal government presumably committed to the punishment of terrorists.) Elements of the hard right have also tried to obtain a presidential pardon for Eduardo Arocena, a Cuban American serving a long prison sentence for terrorist activities conducted in the United States against targets associated in some way with the Cuban government.[108]

During the eight-year rule of the younger Bush, the Cuban hard-right wing, led by the three south Florida Cuban American congresspeople, had a great deal of influence over Cuba policy. It played a major role in shaping a nearly five-hundred-page report by a presidential commission published in May 2004. This report recommended, among other things, a reduction of visits and money remittances by Cuban Americans to the island and an increase in monetary aid to Cuban critics of the government of Fidel Castro.[109] These measures were put into effect the following month. Earlier that year, the Cuban American members of Congress and their hard-right allies had put forward a plan for a post-Castro Cuba. It called for the privatization of joint ventures between the Cuban government and foreign investors. The plan also urged that government-owned land be redistributed to small- and medium-sized private farmers in order to foster a middle class. The new government would also make loans and credit lines available to the private sector to finance the reconstruction of infrastructure and to facilitate transfer of government property to private Cuban ownership. In an attempt to reassure people in Cuba, the plan advocated that urban dwellers should have the right to remain in their homes. However, in a flight of dangerous economic fantasy, the plan promised that the old owners would be compensated according to the replacement value of assets at the time they were confiscated.

Congressperson Ros-Lehtinen announced that the plan had the support of prominent dissidents in Cuba, including Oscar Elías Biscet and Marta Beatriz Roque, a position that Roque and two of her associates confirmed before a House subcommittee via telephone from the US Interests Section in Havana.[110] Biscet, who was born in 1961 and therefore grew up under Castro, is a black doctor and well-known Christian antiabortion activist who generally holds a right-wing worldview. At the same time, he claims to admire and to have been shaped by the influence of the nonviolent views of Thoreau, Gandhi, and Martin Luther King Jr. He has been jailed on several occasions by the Cuban authorities. His most recent imprisonment took place when he was one of the seventy-five dissidents arrested for peaceful dissent activity in the spring of 2003 and was given a twenty-five-year sentence. George W. Bush selected Biscet from among many imprisoned dissidents and conferred upon him (in absentia) the Presidential Medal of Freedom in 2007.

Marta Beatriz Roque, who was born in 1945 and was thus only thirteen years old when the revolution triumphed on January 1, 1959, was trained as an economist and taught at the University of Havana until she was dismissed for political reasons in 1990. Her endorsement of the 2004 plan announced by the Miami Republican House members is consistent with the declared purposes of the organization she founded in 2002. This was the Assembly to Promote Civil Society (Asamblea para Promover la Sociedad Civil), which opposed Proyecto Varela and converged with the exile groups in Miami that supported the US economic blockade of Cuba.[111] In addition, she has openly advocated US economic aid to Cuban dissidents and maintained close ties with James Cason, whom she called "a very, very great man."[112] Cason was the head of the US Interests Section in Havana during the younger Bush's presidency and was by far the most strident and provocative of US envoys to Cuba since 1959. Vladimiro Roca, son of one of the principal leaders of the old CCP, former Cuban Air Force pilot and government economist and an associate of Roque, also endorsed President Bush's tightening of the economic blockade. Roca called it "a gesture of solidarity with the Cuban people and with the opposition."[113]

Nevertheless, while Roque has generally been outspoken in favoring US sanctions against Cuba, she has occasionally moderated her positions and displeased the Cuban hard right in Miami. This happened in November 2006, after the Government Accountability Office (GAO) criticized USAID (US Agency for International Development) for its poor management of funds that had been appropriated for Cuban dissidents: one exile group had even used the money to buy Nintendo games and leather jackets. Roque issued a statement that was also signed by Vladimiro Roca, Elizardo Sánchez, and Gisela Delgado, which advocated the elimination of existing restrictions on remittances and travel to Cuba as a way of achieving greater efficiency in the distribution of USAID funds. Delgado, whose husband is a political prisoner, told a *Miami Herald* reporter that she wanted the bans on both US tourism and family reunification visits to be lifted. At the same time, Elizardo Sánchez, an opponent of the economic blockade for many decades, was now clearly arguing in favor of the distribution of US government money to dissidents and their families.[114] It is hard to tell how many of the dissidents agree with Sánchez's new position, but there is no doubt that they constitute a substantial group among Cuban dissidents.

In April 2008, Roque joined other dissidents to call for a Cuban transition within "an atmosphere of national reconciliation" and then asked President Bush to make it easier for Cuban Americans to visit family members on the island and send money to their relatives.[115] More than a decade earlier, she had been part of a group of four dissidents (with Vladimiro Roca, Félix Antonio Bonné Carcassés, and René Gómez Manzano) who wrote a document titled "The Homeland Belongs to All" critiquing the Cuban Communist "Project Document" for its Fifth Congress held in 1997. The dissidents' nine-page document thoroughly criticized the lack of political freedoms in the country and especially the poor performance of the economic system administered by the CCP. The dissidents' document was less detailed in its recommendations than in its criticisms but nevertheless called for political democratization as well as economic liberalization. Besides demanding that Cubans, just like foreigners, be allowed to invest in their country, the four dissidents suggested that "the Cuban community overseas . . . could undoubtedly contribute to a sustained economic recovery."[116] At the time, Roque and her three colleagues were sentenced to prison terms ranging from three and a half to five years under the charge of sedition for publishing this document. Roque and two others were released in May 2000, but Roca was forced to serve all but seventy days of his five-year sentence, perhaps because of his family background.[117] Roque was also part of the group of seventy-five dissidents who were arrested and sentenced in the spring of 2003, although she was released the following year because of poor health.

The "Neo-moderate" Opposition Abroad—a Tactical Turn?

For several years, a more "moderate" opposition stance has been winning ground among some former hard-right opponents of the Cuban government abroad, particularly in south Florida. There are many possible causes for this shift, but I would single out the Cuban government's success in surviving the collapse of the Soviet Union in the early nineties as the principal one. At the time, there had been a great deal of expectation in south Florida that the Cuban regime would soon collapse, an expectation that was well expressed in the title of the *Miami Herald*'s reporter Andrés Oppenheimer's book *Castro's Final Hour*, published in 1992.[118] Other causes of this shift were the declining importance of Cuba to US foreign policy after the end of the Cold War and the discrediting of the Cuban American right wing as a result of the Elián González affair in late 1999 and early 2000. Moreover, as the old hard-line generation has been dying out, their descendants have become Americanized and less concerned about Cuban affairs, while new Cuban immigrants coming from the island are motivated principally by economic concerns.

After CANF founder Jorge Mas Canosa died in 1997, his son Jorge Mas Santos took over the foundation and eventually moved it in a relatively "moderate" direction. However, the CANF remains a solidly right-wing organization in terms of its socioeconomic and political positions and overall support for the economic blockade of Cuba; only its posture and image have become "softer."

Still, the new "moderate" turn provoked an ultra-right split from the CANF in 2001. The splitters formed the Cuban Liberty Council under the leadership of Ninoska Pérez Castellón, a Cuban American woman whose father was a Batista police official accused of acts of torture and murder. She is married to Roberto Martín Pérez, a former Batista policeman whose father, Lutgardo Martín Pérez, was a high-ranking police official and a prominent member of Batista's repressive police machinery.[119] The Liberty Council in turn is close to the three Republican Cuban American congresspeople in south Florida (Ileana Ros-Lehtinen, David Rivera, and Mario Díaz Balart).[120]

With this split, the CANF's "moderate" image was solidified. The CANF's "moderation" earned the foundation a visit and speech by Barack Obama during the 2008 presidential campaign. The CANF and other "neo-moderate" elements put up serious Democratic candidates against the three incumbent Cuban American Republicans in what became the hardest-fought campaigns that these congresspeople had ever faced. These congressional contests pitted the "neo-moderate" Cuban American right against the Cuban American ultra-right. Confronting the opposition of the hardest Cuban right, the "neo-moderates" and the Obama campaign advocated relaxation of the economic blockade in order to permit Cuban Americans to visit the island more frequently and send more frequent and greater remittances to their Cuban relatives. However, the three Republican candidates still managed to win reelection by decisive margins, though that of Mario Díaz Balart against Joe Garcia, a Democratic Party operative and former executive director of CANF, was only 6.2 percentage points (53.1 percent for Díaz Balart versus 46.9 percent for García). Since then, Lincoln Díaz Balart has retired from Congress, and his brother Mario has moved over to run in Lincoln's district. Republican David Rivera then ran for Mario's seat in the 2010 elections and won 52.1 percent of the vote against 42.6 percent for Joe Garcia in a four way race,[121] which was part of a big swing to the right in Florida and many other states. One major reason why the hard-right Republican candidates have managed to retain their seats notwithstanding the changing political climate among Cuban Americans in south Florida is that the older exiles are far more likely to be US citizens and registered voters. The degree to which Cuban American attitudes toward relations with the island are reflected in their votes for Congress and other offices is still not clear. Nevertheless, it is significant that while Obama lost the overall Cuban American vote (while still managing to win the state of Florida), he did much better among younger Cuban Americans. It is estimated that in Miami-Dade County, 55 percent of Cuban Americans under the age of twenty-nine voted for Obama, while 84 percent of Cuban Americans over sixty-five years old voted for McCain. Overall, Obama obtained 35 percent of the total Cuban American vote, a 10 percent increase over the proportion that John Kerry obtained in 2004.[122] After Obama took office, the harsh restrictions on Cuban American travel and remittances to the island imposed by George W. Bush were repealed in 2009. Further liberalizing measures on sending money to the island and on travel by US citizens (short of removing the ban on tourism) were adopted by the Obama administration in January 2011.[123] Aside from those and other smaller policy changes and the adoption of a less strident rhetoric, particularly by the American diplomats in the Interests Section in Havana, the main features of the US economic blockade of the island have remained unchanged.

The shift in the Cuban American political mood has helped to bring about a wide-ranging political alliance under the "neo-moderate" umbrella. This alliance includes the Miami-based Instituto de Estudios Cubanos (Institute of Cuban Studies) a group of academics and professionals founded in the early seventies that criticized US policy toward Cuba and brought together traditional Cuban moderates, liberals, and people sympathetic to the Cuban regime. For many years, the institute was viciously attacked by the Cuban right wing in Miami as being "soft" on Castro and as *dialogueros* (supporters of a dialogue with the Cuban government), and, as I indicated earlier, its founder, María Cristina Herrera, escaped a terrorist attack in 1988. Although the institute has shed the leftist elements of its past in recent years, it is still politically very different from other political currents that have joined it under the "neo-moderate" umbrella. Among such forces we find the Unión Liberal Cubana led by the right-wing journalist Carlos Alberto Montaner, a onetime advocate of annexing Cuba to the United States; Hermanos al Rescate (Brothers to the Rescue) led by José Basulto, a man previously linked to right-wing terrorist violence who claims to have abandoned the armed struggle against the Cuban government; and Jorge Mas Santos's CANF. Other groups that have joined the coalition are closer to the older and more traditional Cuban moderates. These include the Cuba Study Group, an important group of moderate Cuban American capitalists led by Carlos Saladrigas, who has recently advocated freedom for all American citizens to travel to Cuba, and the Christian Democratic Party, a peculiar political entity that combines criticisms of US policy toward Cuba and a promarket liberal democratic political platform with strong ties with foreign right-wing figures such as former Spanish prime minister José María Aznar, a strongly conservative and authoritarian politician.[124] Last but not least, we find that the south Florida representatives of the moderate human rights and political groups on the island have also joined this "neo-moderate" political coalition.

From a programmatic point of view, the "neo-moderate" coalition outlined its positions when it came together several years ago and formed an organization called Consenso Cubano (Cuban Consensus), with a program called "Pilares para un Consenso Cubano" (Pillars for a Cuban Consensus). This program explicitly advocates a process of conciliation and a nonviolent transition in Cuba toward democracy, clearly defined in liberal democratic terms, based on a pact with the Cuban government. If the Cuban government proves to lack political will to achieve such a negotiated transition, then Consenso Cubano will support "other non-violent actions to which the Cuban people might resort." In the same spirit, Consenso proposes a general amnesty for all political crimes and the creation of something along the lines of the "truth commissions" that have been established in other postdictatorial, systems such as South Africa. The document endorses Cuban national independence "without imposition or intrusion by any other nation," thus trying to disassociate Consenso from the suggestion that the "neo-moderate" coalition is a tool of US imperialism.

While the document presents a clear view of the political system it envisions for Cuba, including the means to achieve it, it is often evasive and opaque when it broaches matters pertaining to the economic transformation of the country. The document endorses a "free-market economy," although it promises to pay "special attention to the fundamental principles of social justice" without specifying the manner in which it would accomplish such a goal. The matter of residential properties and small farms is discussed with the forthright recommendation of granting "clear and unhindered title to those persons who currently occupy those properties . . . without current restrictions [in other words, of the present Cuban government] and without fear of eviction, claims or levies by former owners." The document also advocates the right of the former owners to claim compensation from the state, but it doesn't say anything about how an impoverished Cuban republic could find the resources to compensate them. Neither does the document explain how many other social priorities would have to be sacrificed for a future Cuban government to be able to afford such compensation. The rights of Cubans to self-employment, to own property, and to form their own enterprises are recognized, and the document does not attempt to limit the possible size of those enterprises, nor does it suggest how the state might limit or regulate the private sector of the economy. The document is also silent about the thousands of enterprises currently owned by the Cuban state, particularly those that have been created since the revolution and were never privately owned. The "moderates" promise that the "free-market" system will "extend special consideration to society's most vulnerable sectors" and "uphold the principle of universal access to health care and education as national priorities." However, it does not say a word about whether such "access" will be free of charge or "tiered" along the historic lines of the US system of Medicaid for the poor and insurance and fee for service for those who are not eligible for the means-tested health care system.[125]

The incipient moderate ambience in south Florida's Cuban American community has been strengthened by a number of cultural events that have taken place since the fall of 2009. The Colombian singer Juanes organized a politically ambiguous giant peace concert at Revolution Square in Havana. Unusually for that venue, there were virtually no pronouncements of a political nature at an event that lasted several hours. The concert included many Latin American singers and musicians and some Cuban American artists, but not the better-known Gloria Estefan and Willy Chirino, who are openly hostile to the Cuban regime. The concert created an open split in south Florida, with Cuban moderates and liberals supporting it while the right wing opposed it. However, it is clear that the Cuban hard right clearly lost this round. It is estimated that an enormous 73 percent of Cuban Americans tuned in to the September 20 concert. An opinion poll conducted afterward found that Cuban American support for the concert had gone up from an initial 27 to 53 percent. The biggest change came among the older exiles, whose approval rose from 17 to 48 percent.[126] Since then this developing peaceful and even conciliatory atmosphere has been reinforced by the visit of several musical groups from the island, including the well-known band Los Van Van. While a relatively small group picketed the events, the concerts were uneventful from a political point of view. However, the fact that the visitors were interviewed in the most widely watched Cuban American and Latino news programs and talk shows in Miami suggests that the political atmosphere is softening in south Florida.

This is consistent with the findings of polls aiming to gauge the political attitudes of Cubans in Florida and New Jersey. For example, an April 2009 poll conducted by Bendixen and Associates found that 67 percent of Cuban Americans favored the elimination of restrictions on travel to Cuba for all Americans—and not just Cuban Americans. The same survey found that on the issue of economic embargo against Cuba, 42 percent believed that it should be continued, while 43 percent thought that it should be terminated.[127] Another poll conducted by the same firm in August 2009 continued to show the same even division among Cuban Americans on the question of the economic embargo—41 percent were against maintaining it while 40 percent were in favor of keeping it. Revealingly, 62 percent of Cuban Americans who arrived in the United States in the sixties or before wanted to retain the embargo, while most of those who arrived after the 1980s were in favor of ending it.[128] A year later, in July 2010, a study conducted by the University of Miami's Institute for Cuban and Cuban-American Studies found that 64 percent of Cuban Americans wanted to eliminate all travel restrictions to Cuba. This included 62 percent of those sixty-six years or older. Overall, the proportion of people supporting elimination of the travel ban had gone up 5 percent during the previous year.[129] However, such survey results must be viewed with caution, since they can be ambiguous. As late as March 2007, a poll conducted by researchers at FIU (Florida International University) showed that while 55.2 percent of Cuban American respondents strongly favored unrestricted travel to the island, 49.1 percent strongly favored food sales to Cuba, and 50.3 percent strongly favored a dialogue among Cuban exiles, dissidents, and the Cuban government, 57.5 percent strongly favored the tightening of the embargo, and 43.7 percent strongly favored US military action to overthrow the Cuban government. This may reflect an underlying attitude, at least among some Cuban Americans, favoring anything and everything that "might work"—not surprising in light of the survey's finding that only 23 percent of respondents felt that the embargo had worked well or very well.[130]

Critics and Opponents on the Left

By the fifties, no significant socialist or Marxist political tradition had survived on the island besides that of the old pro-Moscow Cuban Communists. The "Marxism" of the revolutionary period was overwhelmingly based on Soviet manuals translated into Spanish. It was only briefly in the late sixties and early seventies and again since the nineties that the liberalization in academic and intellectual circles has opened a space for the rediscovery of the best of the classical Marxist tradition. Union-based traditional social democracy was never important in the country, and the substantial anarchist influence in the trade unions came to an end by the 1920s. A left-wing nationalist tradition did survive in the forties and fifties, but its political influence was much weakened by the drift of many leaders and activists either toward the increasing moderation of populist governments and parties or toward political gangsterism. Unfortunately, these were the principal inheritors of that political tradition during those two decades.[131]

Throughout the revolutionary period, there have been critical voices on the left that did not challenge the fundamentals of the one-party state system. One current was the orthodox pro-Soviet faction led by Aníbal Escalante that was quickly suppressed in the late sixties. Far more interesting was a group of young philosophy professors at the University of Havana led by thinkers such as Fernando Martínez Heredia, which published a journal called *Pensamiento Crítico* from 1967 to 1971. The journal tried to support the revolution at home and abroad in an open, broad, nondogmatic manner, and was clearly influenced by international third world and New Left currents.[132] These sorts of efforts did not last very long. The journal was suppressed, and the Department of Philosophy was disbanded and eventually replaced by a group of academics toeing the government line. The eighties witnessed the development of several small left currents deviating from the official government line, but these were primarily of a cultural and artistic rather than political character as had been previously the case with *Pensamiento Crítico*. Groupings such as Castillo de la Fuerza and Proyecto Paideia proposed a dialogue with the Cuban state, searching for autonomous spaces to develop their own cultural programs. The state institutions rejected this approach. The Ministry of Culture as well as the ideological apparatus of the CCP refused to accept a new type of relationship proposed from the outside and shut down any possibility of an autonomous space functioning within their own structures. The government attempted to co-opt the nonconforming artists and in several cases facilitated their going abroad. Thus by the end of 1990 fifty-eight plastic artists were living outside the country, mostly in Mexico and Europe, not as dissidents or emigrants, but with permits to reside abroad.[133]

The government began to relent somewhat with the onset of the sharp economic crisis provoked by the collapse of the Soviet Union and the Soviet bloc in the late eighties and early nineties. Paradoxically, it was the economic crisis that brought about a degree of liberalization—not to be confused with democratization—that has survived until now. Of course, this relative liberalization did not mean an end to the political harassment of dissidents or an unconditional release of all nonviolent political dissidents. Indeed, the relative liberalization has been marred by several major incidents of repression. One was a crackdown on the CEA (Centro de Estudios sobre America, Center for the Study of America), a Communist Party think tank devoted to analysis of Cuban reality with a critical spirit and high intellectual and academic standards. Among its leading figures were the sociologists Juan Valdés Paz and Haroldo Dilla Alfonso (who later rejected the one-party state and is currently exiled in the Dominican Republic) and the economists Julio Carranza Valdés, Luis Gutierrez Urdaneta, and Pedro Monreal.[134] It seems that the CEA on several occasions came close to violating the rule that one can criticize even the bureaucracy, understood as the low- and middle-level functionaries, but never the political elite, who are supposed to be infallible.[135] The other major incident of repression was the March 2003 political crackdown on dissidence, which resulted in the imposition of long-term sentences on seventy-five people. At about the same time, three people who had unsuccessfully hijacked boats in order to leave the country were promptly executed even though no blood had been spilled in their attempt. However, neither of these acts of repression affected Cuban critical leftists, as had been the case with the CEA crackdown.

The period of relative liberalization that began in the nineties had a broad impact on the intellectual, academic, and artistic worlds. Since then, more critical voices, although well short of outright political opposition, which would automatically be a one-way ticket to dissident status, have begun to emerge in a number of sophisticated left-wing journals. These typically have a small circulation among educated and artistic elites. Among them are *Temas, La Gaceta de Cuba* (organ of the UNEAC, the writers and artists' union), and *Criterios*. These journals have on several occasions included contributions from exiled writers and academics, and they read very differently, in style and content, from the turgid, boring, and dogmatic *Granma*. Plastic artists and musicians, as we saw above, have been given more leeway, including much greater ease to travel abroad, and many writers and academics have also obtained this concession. *Temas*, which is the most important social science and intellectual journal in Cuba, often publishes factually rich and critical articles that nevertheless carefully avoid even an indirect questioning of the one-party system, much less its principal leaders. One good example of such a contribution provided highly revealing data on racial inequality in the country. However, the article did not address the political implications of its analysis, whether in terms of the adequacy of current government policy, the need for a systematic policy of affirmative action, or the need for an independent black organization, among other possible issues.[136] Although *Temas* is undoubtedly a forum for liberal Communist politics, it often "takes cover" by including representatives of quite conservative hard-line views and institutions among its panelists and roundtables. The notoriously repressive Jorge "Papito" Serguera was invited to participate in a panel discussion regarding the significance of the events of July 26, 1953 (the day Fidel Castro and his associates unsuccessfully attacked the Moncada barracks in Santiago de Cuba), for Cuban political culture.[137] More recently, a symposium on the current state and future of university education in Cuba included Georgina Fuentes Vicente, a professor in the Higher Institute of Police Science Eliseo Reyes of the Ministry of the Interior, the principal institution carrying out political repression in Cuba.[138]

La Gaceta de Cuba, the organ of the UNEAC, does not evidence a comparable effort to include party-line voices and appears to be more unambiguously liberal. There are many possible reasons for this, including the fact that on the whole *Temas* deals with politically far more sensitive matters than does *La Gaceta*. In any case, participants in the congress of the UNEAC in early April 2008 voiced strong criticisms of government censorship, particularly in the mass media. For example, the popular singer Amaury Pérez Vidal blasted the ICRT (Cuban Institute of Radio and Television) for its arbitrary and repressive censorship policies. (As expected, the mass media generally abstained from reporting on the many critical pronouncements made at the congress.) The website of the UNEAC has featured very critical articles, such as one by Arturo Arango in which he counterposed democratic socialism to the bureaucratic and centralized state and sympathetically discussed the activities of critical left groups on the island (see below).[139] The widely quoted and reproduced article by Esteban Morales Domínguez denouncing corruption and the likely privatization of public property by the people in power, which provoked his disappearance from the mass media and his expulsion from the CCP, also appeared on the UNEAC website.[140] After his expulsion from the party and removal from the mass media, Morales Domínguez published another critical article on political economy on the UNEAC website that was removed a few days after its publication.[141] Of course, this does not mean that UNEAC, which is after all an official institution, has ceased to support the regime; indeed, the opposite is evident in the reports and articles that appear on its website. Neither has the UNEAC stopped acting, whenever necessary, as a repressive arm of the Cuban one-party state. This was clear in the expulsion from the organization of the writer Manuel García Verdecia and the firing from his job of the novelist Rafael Vilches Proenza for "undue use of their Internet accounts," which the UNEAC considered "improper behavior for intellectuals committed to the revolutionary process."[142]

Several Cuban artists have been quite outspokenly critical while traveling abroad. Internationally known Cuban singer Silvio Rodríguez has publicly opined that the Cuban political system needs to be decentralized and modernized and has echoed the growing demand, particularly among young people, that the Cuban government permit people the right to travel abroad.[143] He later declared that "there are many things that need to be revised in Cuba" and expressed disappointment that these matters have thus far been dealt with only unofficially and have not been aired in the Cuban press.[144] Rodríhuez, however, has been careful not to break his ties with the Cuban establishment. The well-known black Cuban singer Pablo Milanés, who was a cofounder of the Nueva Trova, or new Cuban song, with Rodríguez, has been much harsher in his criticisms of the Cuban system. Milanés has stated that "Cuban socialism has stagnated": "we are paralyzed in every sense, with plans for a future that never arrives." In the same interview, he noted that with the election of a black president, the United States had "obtained the same as or more than we have achieved in Cuba, where black people don't yet have real power or real opportunities." As if that were not enough, Milanés added that he did not trust any Cuban leader over seventy-five years old (this obviously includes Raúl Castro and José Ramón Machado Ventura) and that since they had already had their moment of glory, it was time for them to retire.[145] These declarations were made while Milanés was touring in Spain. More than a year later, he argued that another revolution was needed since "the great sun born in 1959 has been filling with spots to the degree that it has aged." He added that he would prefer "change," since "elections are a democratic game in quotes that are also a farce."[146] The well-known Cuban singer Carlos Varela, in Miami in May 2010, condemned "repudiation acts" against the dissident Damas de Blanco (Ladies in White) and made several other very critical comments about the political situation in Cuba.[147]

Again, it is worth contrasting the openly critical stance often taken by several of the most important Cuban performers with the much more cautious stance typically adopted by liberal Communist academics, with important exceptions such as the above-noted case of Esteban Morales Domínguez. This may be partially explained by the greater ability of writers and performers to obtain independent financing abroad. Sometimes, however, a sophisticated liberal Communist stance simply becomes a cover for what is fundamentally an apology for the Cuban system. For example, in an article published in *La Jornada*, the Mexican left-wing daily newspaper, Rafael Hernández, the director of *Temas*, concocted a number of sophistries to justify the one-party state, the imprisonment of political dissidents, and the supposedly democratic character of the institutions of Popular Power.[148]

It is also worth noting that a number of younger Cuban scholars have taken on issues and political traditions that the older liberal Communist academics have tended to ignore. Among these are Julio César Guanche, who (in the company of some older academics who belonged to the CEA in the nineties, such as Juan Valdés Paz) works at the Centro para el Desarrollo de la Cultura Cubana "Juan Marinello." This center has become increasingly hospitable to critical thought.[149] Guanche has engaged in a dialogue with independent Catholic intellectual Roberto Veiga González in *Espacio Laical Digital*.[150] There are also young revolutionary socialist scholars such as Hiram Hernández Castro and Ariel Dacal Díaz. Hernández Castro has written positively about Rosa Luxemburg and her libertarian views about socialism. Dacal, in addition to having written much about the Soviet Union and Leon Trotsky,[151] helped to organize a meeting on the occasion of the ninetieth anniversary of the October Revolution in 2007, attended by some five hundred students, where the discussion focused on why that revolution became bureaucratized under Stalin. These discussions have taken place in the context of the post-1990 Cuban government's claim that Cuban Communism differs substantially from the system that prevailed in the Soviet Union and Eastern European countries and that it will therefore not suffer the same fate. With this claim the Cuban government opened the door to critical analysis of why those social and political systems collapsed. An obviously unintended consequence of permitting such writings and discussions is that they have become indirect and oblique means of discussing the defects and faults of the Cuban version of the same system.

The Development of a Left Critical Milieu

An important development of recent years has been the growth of a left-wing critical milieu, which expresses itself in a number of venues, but particularly in the website *HavanaTimes.org*. A number of young people contribute to the website and articulate a broad left-wing socialist and democratic critique of Cuban society and politics. Among these are Erasmo Calzadilla, Dmitri Prieto-Samsonov, and Daisy Valera. Like Yoani Sánchez in *Generación Y*, the contributors to *HavanaTimes.org* write about the problems of everyday life in Cuba as well as about more strictly speaking political topics, often producing sharp critiques of the nature of Cuba's political and social system.

Besides the young people who regularly contribute to *HavanaTimes.org*, there are also some older left-wing critics of the regime who come from a more orthodox Marxist background. Most important among these is the retired diplomat Pedro Campos Santos, whose views on workers' control I already discussed in chapter 4. He and his associates have written many articles, often published on the Catalonian website *kaosenlared.net*, and have elaborated their ideas in much greater detail than the contributors to *HavanaTimes.org*. They have argued for a participatory and democratic socialism and have emphasized the need for a transition from what they call statification to socialization. (They have often used the term "state capitalism" when describing the Cuban system.)[152] This requires, according to them, workers' control and self-management of the Cuban economy through the creation of workers' councils in all factories and offices in the country. These critics also favor the creation of genuine cooperatives and the legalization of small private enterprises. They propose that Cubans be allowed to buy and sell their personal property, including vehicles and houses. They demand that Cubans be afforded the right to travel abroad and within the island. Consequently, they advocate the elimination of decree 217 of 1997, which restricted the movement of people into the capital city of Havana.

Campos Santos has not yet, to my knowledge, challenged the primacy of the one-party state, although he has advocated an opening of the CCP to allow "diverse opinions and tendencies" within its ranks. His reform proposals were originally intended to be presented as submissions to the Sixth Congress of the CCP, which was supposed to have taken place as early as 2002 but, after a very long delay, was held in April 2011.[153] Those proposals said nothing about censorship and the need for openness and diversity in the mass media and very little about civil liberties and democratic political rights. They did advocate putting an end to the harassment of youth, blacks, and people from the interior of the country. Although Campos Santos clearly expressed hostility toward the dissident camp, he did advocate review of the harsh sentences that had been imposed on people arrested for "matters linked to political questions." However, his proposals hastened to add that the "help" that foreign governments have provided for the purpose "of subverting the order established by the constitution, should be declared illegal." The Sixth Congress, which concentrated on economic questions, ignored these proposals. It is not difficult to predict that the same will happen at the subsequent party conference to address organizational questions. These types of events never deviate from their carefully choreographed agendas.

Since he expressed these views Campos Santos has become much more explicit in spelling out his ideas about political freedom and democracy. He has argued for "the need to eliminate the criminalization of differences, including political ones, and to open spaces that allow the free expression of all forms of thought, even if we don't share them; a review of the judicial cases related to political matters and to adjust our legislation to the universal principles of the Universal Declaration of Human Rights and especially to the International Pacts on Civil and Political Rights, signed but not ratified by the government."[154] Campos Santos made a critical distinction between people found to have worked for enemy intelligence or practiced terrorism and people who have engaged in peaceful dissent and demanded reforms. The first group should be put on trial and sentenced, while the others should not be treated as if they were engaging in imperialist subversion.[155] In May 2009, Cuban government functionaries, under the pretext of administrative rules concerning the use of office computers, fired one of Campos Santos's collaborators from his state job for illegally emailing articles that he and Campos Santos had written for *kaosenlared.net*. Campos Santos vigorously protested this action,[156] as have others who have since written about the incident for *kaosenlared.net* and elsewhere.

Perhaps the single most important group within this critical left milieu is the Cátedra de Pensamiento Crítico y Culturas Emergentes "Haydée Santamaría." This group was founded in 2004–05 by an informal group of young social science professors and researchers under the auspices of the Asociación Hermanos Saíz, the official organization for young Cuban writers and intellectuals.[157] The Cátedra more recently gave birth to the Red Protagónica Observatorio Crítico (http://observatoriocriticodesdecuba.wordpress.com). The Red Protagónica has been involved in a number of ecological, historical, artistic, and editorial activities, covered in the *Havana Times* and other publications welcoming critical perspectives.[158] It has come to function as an umbrella group that includes other groupings such as Campos Santos's group and the critical black intellectuals organized in the Cofradía de la Negritud.[159] Members of the Red Protagónica and a number of other young Cubans of a leftist bent have developed an interest in recent years in revolutionary ideas ranging from anarchism to various currents of revolutionary socialism, from the antiparty tradition of Council Communism to Trotskyism. These groups are informal in nature and, for obvious reasons, tend to meet in homes rather than in more formal institutional settings. Yet, the various groupings that form this emerging left critical milieu have begun to engage in public activities such as carrying banners with ecological and socialist self-management slogans at May Day demonstrations since 2008 and organizing a small "march-performance" against (government) violence on November 6, 2009. At the 2010 May Day parade, the critical left groups marched together with banners proclaiming "Down with Bureaucracy/Long Live the Workers/More Socialism" and "Socialism Is Democracy/Dump the Bureaucracy."[160] The activists belonging to the Red Protagónica have joined with others in trying to make a connection with Afro-Cuban traditions through participation, symbolically proclaiming the need for an opening to "all roads," in the syncretic religious procession honoring St. Lazarus–Babalú Ayé on December 17. In conjunction with the Cofradía de la Negritud, the Red Protagónica has also honored the memory of the anonymous Afro-Cubans who as members of the fraternal society Abakuá organized an armed protest against the Spanish colonial authorities' execution of eight white medical students on November 27, 1871.[161]

Not surprisingly, the work of these overlapping groups has been obstructed as they have intermittently suffered bans, pressure, exclusions, firings, and arrests at the hands of the government authorities.[162] In light of these reprisals, a declaration of protest was published at the end of December 2009. The declaration objected in no uncertain terms to the various abuses that the government had carried out against the activists. It argued that the lack of respect for diversity undermined revolutionary unity and did not weaken the real counterrevolution, which in fact becomes stronger in the absence of a space for socialist criticism. But it also unambiguously proclaimed that "if capitalism is the power of capital against ordinary people, then we are against capitalism, but if 'socialism' is the power of a bureaucracy against the rest of society, then we are also against this 'socialism.'" The declaration was signed by a diverse group of people. This included older figures with a long record of participation in the Cuban government such as the veteran writer Félix Guerra and Pedro Campos Santos, who had also participated in some of the protest activities, and younger figures such as Armando Chaguaceda, a university professor, and Jorge Luis Acanda González, the son and namesake of a well-known Cuban academic and expert on Gramsci.[163] Since then, the Cuban Supreme Court upheld the firing of a philosophy instructor in a technical college in Havana, Erasmo Calzadilla, one of the principal writers for *HavanaTimes.org*. The Supreme Court disregarded some of the wildest accusations against Calzadilla, but it held that Calzadilla's classes "did not correspond to the approved academic program" and that he met "with students from and outside the school to discuss topics that [did] not correspond to the study plan" and thus constituted "a serious violation of job discipline."[164]

The people who belong to the new left-wing critical current do not see themselves as "dissidents," or even as "left-wing or revolutionary dissidents." Part of the reason for this is their understandable fear of being associated with political currents tied to Miami and Washington. Even if they have already experienced reprisals and punishment for their ideas, they still place themselves within the camp of "the revolution," although it is difficult to tell whether this is due to tactical self-protective reasons, political conviction, or a mixture of the two. For example, Campos Santos has often invoked the Castro brothers as a source of ideological legitimacy.[165] But it is Armando Chaguaceda, a young university professor and occasional collaborator on *HavanaTimes.org*, who has presented the most elaborate explanations of his posture toward the ruling group and the revolution. Chaguaceda, in an article he coauthored with Dmitri Prieto, a regular columnist for the *Havana Times*, invoked Adam Michnik to argue for the notion of a "self-limiting radicalism," which seeks to create islands of autonomy inside a regime that prefers an authoritarian monologue. According to Chaguaceda and Prieto, this radicalism is at the same time subversive and self-limiting. It is subversive because the government rejects any experience that disputes its own representation as "the only possible and institutional left." But it is also limited, because Prieto and Chaguaceda advocate a self-management, culturalist, and communitarian perspective that addresses certain aspects of reality but not the "hard nuclei of power."[166] Elsewhere, Chaguaceda has differentiated between the "revolution" and the "regime," which he defines as "the complex of institutions and norms tied to demands of *realpolitik* and the dictates of the dominant group at the hub of society." For Chaguaceda, the regime coexists with, overlaps with, and confronts the revolution, which he describes as a "wide repertoire of practices, values, speech, and customs, coming from vast social sectors (popular ones and the media) that at least call for the remembering of history, popular participation, equality, and social justice, as well as the rejection of all forms of domination and hierarchy."[167] Chaguaceda's description of the constitutive elements of "regime" and "revolution" are less than clear, particularly when he refers to the "complex of institutions and norms" that characterize the "regime," since we don't know its precise meaning. He does not explain whether his rather vague notion of "revolution" includes the institutions and practices of democracy in a socialist context. It is also unclear why Chaguaceda thinks that the "emancipatory character of radical social changes and the demolition of old hierarchies lasted—as sociological inertia—until the end of the '80s." It is certainly true that inequality has grown significantly since the nineties, but the degree of religious, academic, cultural, and, to a very limited degree, political liberty has also significantly increased since that time, so it is difficult to see how that would fit into Chaguaceda's analysis. Of course, it is possible to distinguish between "revolution" and "regime" at a much higher level of abstraction than that suggested by Chaguaceda. That would make it possible, as he argues, to "construct a critique from the left" in order to "delineate a new socialist project." This is certainly a praiseworthy and indeed indispensable goal, even if the distinction he makes between "revolution" and "regime" may have, as we shall see below, less than solid historical foundations.[168]

An important peculiarity of the Cuban Revolution is that it very rapidly passed from the moderate to the most radical stages under the same top leadership with very few important changes. This was also true of the Chinese Revolution, but even as Mao was making all sorts of concessions to moderate and conservative allies with such notions as the "block of four classes," there was never any doubt that the Chinese Communist Party was leading the revolution. In contrast, Fidel Castro did not begin political life as a Communist, much less as the head of Cuba's Communist Party, which was, in fact, suspicious of if not entirely hostile to him. So how did Castro end up leading a Communist-type revolution? Writers such as Theodore Draper have argued that the Cuban Revolution was a "middle-class" revolution that was betrayed by Fidel Castro.[169] However, using the concept of "betrayal" to analyze the common historical transition from political to social revolution is problematic, particularly in the case of the Cuban Revolution.

Leon Trotsky, for example, could legitimately raise the issue of betrayal of the Russian Revolution after the 1920s, since he was a leading member of a well-organized political party with an explicit set of principles and programs and an equally explicit and irrevocable class commitment. In that case it made sense to talk about the defense of principles of the October Revolution against Stalinist betrayal. In Cuba, however, the leadership of a revolutionary group was accepted by its supporters without even a pretense of programmatic or institutional controls over the leadership by the ranks. After the revolution moved from its multiclass democratic political origin to a new radical social stage in 1959, there were not, aside from the relatively small orthodox Stalinist party, significant leftist groups with political principles counterposed to the particular revolution that Fidel Castro and his close associates chose to lead. Once the revolutionary leadership adopted a clear Soviet-type course in the early sixties, some of the early non-Communist left-wing nationalist independents dropped their reservations, at least in public, and became functionaries of some importance. This was the case of such figures as Faustino Pérez and Marcelo Fernández Font, who remained in the government ranks as important functionaries but not as top political leaders. Other independent leftists sooner or later criticized and even attacked Fidel Castro. Aside from being persecuted, this left them politically isolated and without recourse to a non-Communist socialist group or heritage, which could have legitimated their political stance. Such were the cases of, for example, David Salvador, the main revolutionary trade union leader, and Carlos Franqui, the principal editor of *Revolución*. Therefore, it is difficult to make a *historical* case for the distinction between a "regime" led throughout more than fifty years by the same people and a "revolution," which never stood for a clearly defined program distinct from what the leaders said it was at any given point in time.

From Individual Complaint to Collective Resistance

The views and activities of the leftist critics of the government have to be understood as part of the molecular political changes that have become visible on the island in the early part of the new century. The year 2007 may have witnessed the beginning of a transition from the politics of individual complaint—which had gained particular currency with the crisis provoked by the collapse of the Soviet bloc in the early 1990s—to the politics of collective resistance. The year began with a protest by many Cuban intellectuals and artists against the public reappearance of three individuals associated with the highly repressive cultural policies that had purged numerous prominent intellectuals and artists in the darkest period of the 1970s: Luis Pavón Tamayo, Armando Quesada, and Jorge "Papito" Serguera. The protest was politically limited, since it never challenged current censorship nor generally raised questions about who had given orders to these repressive cultural functionaries back in the 1970s. But the protest was quite unusual for Cuba, as it started independently from any kind of government control through email, leading artists and intellectuals to flex their political muscles outside the control of the one-party state. Although the Cuban mass media almost ignored the protest and the government managed to contain it, the protesters succeeded in obtaining an official reaffirmation of the current relatively tolerant cultural policies.[170] In January 2008, a strong protest also occurred at a meeting at which government officials informed employees of joint ventures between the Cuban government and foreign companies that the under-the-table hard-currency salary supplements they received from their foreign employers would henceforth be taxed. The workers were particularly indignant because the Cuban government was already collecting their hard-currency salaries from these companies and paying them in far less valuable Cuban pesos.

However, the most serious potential threat to the Cuban government lies in the widespread and sometimes strong alienation of the young people on the island, which has been well described and analyzed by the historian Michelle Chase.[171] This alienation has expressed itself in a wide variety of ways. There is the hip-hop movement among young black Cubans, particularly those living in poor neighborhoods in East Havana who are sick and tired of police harassment and lack of access to hard currency, indispensable for buying clothes and other life essentials.[172] In September 2007, several hundred students openly demonstrated at the University of Oriente in Santiago de Cuba to protest poor living and educational conditions as well as lack of security for women students. The student protest, ignored by the government-controlled press, must have been quite serious, since the government found it necessary to hold a large official counterdemonstration in Santiago de Cuba in early October, reaffirming support for the regime. There are unconfirmed reports that many protesters were expelled from the university, but the government-controlled media have maintained total silence on the matter. And as I mentioned earlier, on November 6, 2007, about five hundred students at the University of Havana showed up to discuss what went wrong with the Russian Revolution—an indirect way of discussing Cuba's problems—at an event organized by the historian Ariel Dacal and others.

In early February 2008, on a video widely distributed over the Internet, students at the elite Universidad de las Ciencias Informáticas, located in what used to be the Soviet listening post at Lourdes, were shown confronting Ricardo Alarcón, the president of Cuba's National Assembly. They were protesting travel restrictions abroad, their inability to visit tourists facilities in Cuba,[173] the inequitable effects of the dual currency system, a lack of information about the candidates for the official parliamentary elections and their positions, and censorship preventing access to search engines such as Yahoo! The students were raising libertarian democratic demands from an explicitly revolutionary and socialist standpoint.[174] In his disingenuous response, Alarcón argued that most people in the world lacked means to travel and if everyone could travel there would not be enough resources to accommodate all this demand. He deliberately confused the issue of the legal and political right to travel with whether people could afford to do so. He also omitted the fact that in Cuba, for exclusively political reasons, some people had more "right" to travel than others.

The Road Ahead

It is unlikely that the dissident groups discussed earlier in this chapter, whether they are right wing or moderate or whether they accept US aid or not, will play an important role in a Cuban transition after the Castro brothers have departed from the scene. Not only are all these groups very small in size but they have not until now been able to link up with any important social force in Cuba. As revealed by a document released by Wikileaks, Jonathan Farrar, former head of the US Interests Section in Havana, sees the traditional dissidents as older people who "have little contact with young Cubans, and to the extent they have a message that is getting out, it does not appeal to that segment of society." Farrar describes these dissidents as "individuals with strong egos who do not work well together and are therefore easy targets for manipulation by the Cuban security services." Seeing no evidence that they have support among the people at large, he concluded that "it is unlikely that they will play any role in whatever government succeeds the Castro brothers" and suggested that "the most likely immediate successors to the Castro regime will probably come from within the middle ranks of the government itself." Farrar thinks that his government should look toward certain elements within the government and to the younger generation of "nontraditional dissidents" such as Yoani Sánchez.[175] In truth, dissidents and oppositionists have generally not played an important role in numerous post-Communist transitions, with the notable exceptions of Poland and, to a much lesser extent, Czechoslovakia.

In any case, an outright right-wing Cuban or Cuban American takeover of Cuba could happen only on the basis on an unlikely US military occupation of the island, which would probably require several hundred thousand troops, an option that was seriously considered only once, during the October 1962 missile crisis.[176] A Sino-Vietnamese–type transition led by the army, which has for a long time been heavily involved in the Cuban economy and particularly in the joint-venture enterprises with foreign capital, may lead the Cuban right, whether in Cuba or in south Florida, to play a different role. The heads of the Cuban Army might then welcome investments of the Cuban American capitalists with a clear understanding that the army would politically run the show. This would be similar to the role that overseas Chinese capitalists have been playing in China for a very long time, or the role that Russian business oligarchs have been playing under Putin and Medvedev. Such an alliance between Havana and a section of Cuban south Florida would certainly lead to a deepening of the split that has already begun to occur among Cuban American right-wing forces.

The development of a body of left critical opinion of a democratic bent inside Cuba is very recent; it is too early to tell whether it will grow into a significant force. There are many factors that may affect such a development, but I would point to the fate of the CCP as one of the important ones. It is almost certain that the party already contains a number of political currents that have not been allowed to openly express themselves. One current is certain to favor an opening to the capitalist market in its Sino-Vietnamese version. Another current, which has been called "Talibanes" in the past, was strongly represented in the no longer existing Grupo de Apoyo (Fidel Castro's staff) and had resisted economic and political reforms for some time. Some party functionaries and cadres of that ideological bent are likely to continue to do so in the future, but like the Gang of Four in China, from a statist neo-Stalinist perspective very hostile to any kind of democratic change. We cannot know whether major tendencies favoring socialist democracy are likely to come out of the party's ranks or, what is far more important, from popular protests that may erupt in the future.

Conclusion

Cuba Might Not Be
a Socialist Democracy, But . . .

Has Cuba Been Modernized?

We have seen how Cuba, well over fifty years after the triumph of the revolution, has fared under a number of criteria ranging from national sovereignty, economic growth, and standard of living to political democracy and freedom. We saw that Cuba's record under most of these specific criteria has been at best mixed, and most of all, that if socialism assumes an authentic democratic rule of the great popular majorities, then Cuba does not in any way qualify as a socialist society.

However, more than fifty years after the revolutionary victory, many would argue that even if Cuba is not socialist according to a popular democratic definition, the regime is worthy of support for other reasons. Some might claim that even though the Cuban regime is neither democratic nor socialist, it has modernized the country. The concern with modernization is by no means limited to social scientists and historians of a wide variety of persuasions but has in fact motivated, even if not fully articulated, a good part of the political support and sympathy for reformist and revolutionary regimes in the third world. The notion of modernity is complex and has encompassed a wide range of meanings, but my own understanding of it is closest to the one formulated by Ian Kershaw and Moshe Lewin:

> "Modernisation" need not have connotations of "improving" society, let alone democratising it. In sociological, political, and historical writing, it has implied the process of long-term change that transforms a society resting on agriculture and its related political and social structures and cultures into an industrial society based on technological advancement, secularised culture, bureaucratic administration, and extensive (however shallow) forms of political participation. These changes were compatible with the emergence of quite different political systems—with varying forms of authoritarianism as well as with democracy.[1]

Uneven modernity was a striking feature of the prerevolutionary Cuban republic that was primarily expressed by sharp contrasts between the rural and urban areas, which respectively accounted for 43 and 57 percent of the population.[2] This particular aspect of unevenness continues to hold true today except that three-quarters of the population is now urban, while the country has become a very low-productivity service economy with very uneven technological development (advanced biotechnology but backward telecommunications) rather than becoming industrialized. The general economic crisis that began in the nineties encouraged strong migratory movements to Havana from the interior and particularly from the easternmost part of the island. If nothing else, the recipients of hard-currency remittances from abroad are far more likely to be residents of urban than rural areas, which has a considerable impact on living standards. This makes the bigger cities *relatively* less depressed than the countryside, although this could change if the land usufruct program were to be more successful than the legalization of self-employment in the cities. In particular, a sharp reduction in sugar production to some 20 percent of its historic norms and a serious crisis in Cuban agriculture have reinforced the migratory trend. This led the Cuban government, as discussed elsewhere in this volume, to approve legislation strictly controlling migration to Havana, although it has had unclear practical results.

There is no doubt that the inclusiveness of secondary and especially elementary education, and to a lesser extent of higher education, has contributed to the modernization of the country. However, if we assume that the encouragement of a critical spirit should be part of a properly modern education, then the content of Cuban education has in many areas been far from modern, at least in terms of the social sciences taught at public schools and universities.[3] Censorship of historical facts and critical ideas, and a crudely tendentious manner of presenting approaches that differ from the official ideology of nationalist "Marxism-Leninism," which is sprinkled throughout the curriculum and also taught in regular prescribed courses, are hardly compatible with the encouragement of critical thinking. Nevertheless, that does not mean that students passively accept this and that there is not considerable skepticism and even occasional resistance to the official line.

It is perhaps ironic that the modernization of Cuba's system of higher education has made it much more similar to the system of research-oriented universities prevailing in the United States—which in turn was originally copied from Germany—than it was before the revolution. Notwithstanding the historic Cuban government's resistance to foreign and particularly English-language words, the Anglicism "master" (derived from the Latin *magister*) is now widely used in Cuba to describe a person who has obtained a master's degree. A doctorate is now conferred, as is usually the case in industrially developed and other modernized countries, on people who have completed postgraduate training and a thesis based on an independent research project. Obtaining a doctorate in today's Cuba requires a more demanding and lengthier course of study, research, and writing than it did before the revolution.

Similarly, the revolution confirmed and considerably extended the strong secular tendencies that were already prevalent in prerevolutionary Cuba. Even though the Catholic Church was able to regain some of its lost strength after the official discrimination against religious practitioners was lifted in 1991, it has never regained the influence it had before the victory of the revolution. Even then, the church's influence in Cuba was, by Latin American standards, rather limited. As we saw in the chapter on gender politics, the prerevolutionary secularization of the country had manifested itself in the rights that Cuban women had won to make contracts, own and administer property, vote, and divorce, although relatively few women worked outside the home. After the revolution, women were almost fully incorporated into the labor force with all the serious problems this entailed, given women's new "double burden" at work and at home made worse by difficult living conditions in the country.

In some ways, postrevolutionary Cuba has become more cosmopolitan, and in that sense more modern. Large numbers of Cuban students were trained at universities in the Soviet Union and Eastern Europe. Even larger numbers participated in wars abroad, particularly in Angola and the Horn of Africa, although often with racist ideological effects. Many white and even some black Cubans, appalled at witnessing the extreme poverty and unfamiliar cultural practices in those countries, explained them in terms of the old stereotypes affirming the supposed inferiority of the people there. For a long time, many young foreigners have come to study in Cuba, and even larger numbers of Soviet and East European technicians and military personnel spent time working on the island. Thousands of political tourists also visited the country and for several decades constituted the only significant type of tourism in Cuba, before the avalanche of mass commercial tourism that began in the nineties. However, this exposure to foreign peoples and experiences has been accompanied, perhaps paradoxically, by a claustrophobic climate encouraged, particularly among young people, by the absence of a legal right to travel even to nearby Caribbean islands.

As we have seen, there are several ways in which Cuba has, over more than five decades, become a more modern country in the sense delineated by Kershaw and Lewin above. Political participation without popular control has been virtually obligatory, although less so in recent years. However, compulsory political participation has been a very blunt instrument that has not prevented widespread cynicism and apathy, particularly among the young. But there is another, deeper sense in which Cuba has retrogressed and become *less* modern. While bureaucratization has risen to unprecedented heights, its character is often more reminiscent of premodern absolute despotism than of modern bureaucratic rule. To the degree that bourgeois revolutions advanced the impersonal rule of law and citizen rights against the arbitrariness and capriciousness of precapitalist states, they were more modern and progressive. It is true that Marx and Engels foresaw a future communist society where the state and consequently the very notion of individual rights and protection from that state would disappear. But this notion has been seriously misunderstood and distorted in a far from disinterested effort to legitimate the many different Soviet-type systems that were established after Stalin consolidated his power in the USSR. Marx and Engels saw the establishment of socialism as the result of a forceful revolutionary outbreak of relatively short duration arising as a revolutionary response of the working class and its allies to the profound crisis of capitalism. They foresaw a very different timetable for the transition from socialism to the higher stage of communism. As socialist society achieved increasing material abundance, civility, and cultural enlightenment, it would become increasingly noncoercive, which is not necessarily the same as conflict free. Rights and the state against which those rights are claimed would disappear for lack of use; in other words, they would gradually become superfluous and unnecessary. For example, free speech would be taken so much for granted that it would no longer have to be claimed as a right against the state or against other individuals and groups. Similarly, the material abundance of the higher phase of communist society would allow the progressive replacement of economically coercive labor (one has to work to make a living) by free, creative work.[4]

Many undoubtedly regard this as an unrealizable utopia. But there is no question that it is dramatically different from the supposedly socialist state immediately and forcibly eliminating group and individual rights and in the process becoming even more of an undemocratic leviathan than the prerevolutionary state. As we saw in chapter 1, the Cuban government has a long record of violating civil liberties, even orchestrating mob actions as in the case of the Mariel exodus in the spring of 1980 and subsequently using so-called rapid response brigades to crack down on dissent. In terms of its political life, the Cuban government does not respect the rule of law, and the courts, at least in political cases, do not have even relative autonomy and function as mere tools of the government. Worship of an omniscient Commander in Chief who claims expertise in widely different areas of human knowledge has considerably worsened this problem.

Is Cuba Progressive?

Some might claim that even if the Cuban regime has not fully achieved a modernization of the country, the Cuban revolutionary government is still progressive and deserves the political support of forward-looking people throughout the world. I am specifically referring to support for the revolutionary *government*, since to talk in vague terms of "supporting the revolution" often constitutes an evasion. One might perhaps "support the revolution" by hailing its overthrow of the prior socioeconomic and political system, but it is not logically or historically possible to avoid discussing the merits and demerits of the new system the revolutionary leaders put into place and considering whether it deserves support. Along parallel lines, the revolution certainly deserves support in terms of its efforts to determine its own destiny against the impositions of the US empire. But that should not be confused with the separate and distinct issue of whether one supports the existing Cuban political and socioeconomic system and the government's policies.

In this context, I am not very concerned with one particular left approach, heavily influenced by the Communist tradition founded by Stalin, that sees Cuba not only in a very positive light but also as a highly progressive socialist system. Sometimes, spokespersons for this tradition may rhetorically grant that Cuba is not "perfect." James Petras, for instance, when apologizing for the crackdown on dissidents in 2003, quickly dismissed the lack of democracy and freedoms on the island as the concern of "impotent intellectuals" in the United States who are "unable to threaten power" and are "therefore tolerated to meet, discuss and criticize."[5] At bottom, one of the points of departure of this school of thought is the fundamental assumption that only one system can possibly follow capitalism: socialism. This vulgar version of Marxism ignores the classical Marxist notion that the decay and crises of social systems in the past, as well as of modern capitalism, can produce other outcomes such as the mutual ruin of the contending classes,[6] leading to barbarism as a possible postcapitalist alternative. The perspective exemplified by Petras tends to be part of a broader, and naive, evolutionary view of history. In a sort of dime-store Hegelianism, it is assumed not only that history has an intrinsic goal and meaning but that it can only move forward or backward, toward or away from the desired socialist and communist goal. No allowance is made for the possibility that history may move "sideways," or in a contradictory fashion that moves at the same time both forward and backward.

I am very concerned, however, with a far more common and influential approach on the broad left that argues that while it is unfortunate that the Cuban regime is undemocratic and "sometimes" repressive, it is nevertheless a progressive regime that deserves political support and sympathy. For the very broad left the label "progressive" suggests government concern with the welfare of the majority of the population whether through economic regulation or direct action on behalf of working people and the poor. Because the Cuban government is seen as having promoted great advances in education and health and as showing concern for the fate of the poor, it qualifies as progressive. Thus, the "good things" that the Cuban government has been perceived as doing qualify it for the label "progressive" and the political support that goes along with it.

This does not mean that the soft defenders of the regime who think this way are not aware that the Cuban government also does "bad things." But through a very opaque and implicit, if not unconscious, method of evaluation, soft defenders reach the conclusion that the "good things" somehow have more weight and tilt the balance in the Cuban government's favor. It should be pointed out that this approach is by no means limited to the political left. Indeed, many right-wingers have claimed that while Chilean general Augusto Pinochet may have done some political "bad things," he also did many "good things" in the economic realm. Similar sentiments have been expressed in the past about right-wing authoritarian modernizers such as Lee Kuan Yew of Singapore.[7]

However, justifying political support on the basis of the balance of "good" and "bad" things a regime does is fraught with peril. In the first place, even the most atrocious political regimes can be found to have done "good" things. After all, did not Mussolini, as George Bernard Shaw liked to point out, make the trains run on time? Didn't Stalin industrialize the Soviet Union and militarily defeat Fascism? However, these regimes were so monstrous that it is very easy to quickly conclude that they had a highly negative balance sheet. Of course, the record of Cuban Communism is not as extreme. Nevertheless, if we follow the same approach of drawing up a balance sheet listing the "good" and "bad" things in the Cuban case, some questions inevitably arise. Are the "bad" things the Cuban government does (repression and suppression of democracy) a necessary cost of the advances that it has made in such fields as education and health? It would of course be impossible to make such a case. However, it could be more persuasively argued that while repression and the lack of democracy cannot be directly justified as a cost of the gains made by the revolutionary government, they can be justified as defending the government that made those gains possible against internal and particularly external enemies. As I have already shown in chapter 1, the undemocratic and repressive character of the Cuban government is general and systemic and not merely a situational justified response to specific threats to security. But there are other problems as well. Whatever the very long-lasting Cuban political regime may have accomplished at one point may have little relevance to subsequent generations of Cubans. This is evident in the disengagement and apathy if not complete alienation that Cubans of the younger generation are displaying. Moreover, the regime's efforts to show that other peoples are doing worse than Cubans will not necessarily be persuasive for large sectors of the population who quite justifiably feel that other peoples' miseries do not alleviate their own. These sorts of comparisons can even be ludicrous, as people in many of those countries mentioned above might have also been worse off *before* the 1959 revolution took place in Cuba.

Marx and Engels's Approach to Progress and Political Independence

In my view, Marx and Engels's political treatment of the question of progress is much preferable to the "balance between 'good and bad things'" approach and, as we shall see, highlights the need to maintain political independence from regimes and governments that may in some sense claim to be "progressive." These classic socialist thinkers discussed this question primarily in the context of the overthrow of feudalism, a decayed socioeconomic and political system that was systematically blocking and restraining political and economic change. Marx and Engels analyzed the overthrow of feudalism and the birth and development of capitalism primarily through their study of actual social processes that they saw as bringing about capitalist development and the working class that would necessarily grow alongside it. According to them, the working class was the first exploited class in history that because of its social and economic characteristics could emancipate itself and avoid the restoration of class rule that had typified all previous historic attempts at liberation, including the most recent bourgeois revolution.[8]

For Marx and Engels, the bourgeoisie, or any other social or political force, was progressive to the extent that it struggled to abolish the many reactionary features of feudalism. But for them, the fact that an act was progressive did not necessarily mean that it should be politically supported. Thus, Marx thought that rent of land is conservative while profit is progressive, but he had no intention of implying political support for the profit system. Even the awful era of the capitalist industrial revolution was progressive in relation to the old society it eliminated, but of course that did not mean that Marx and Engels were politically apologetic for or sympathetic to the atrocities associated with that process. While capitalist industrialism was progressive against the society it replaced, it was not progressive against the class struggle of the workers it exploited, which was politically supported by Marx and Engels.[9]

Thus, for Marx and Engels, the progressive actions taken by political leaders and social classes against feudalism were worthy of support only when they facilitated the growth of the working class and its ability to defend itself and increase its independent political and social power. In *The Prussian Military Question and the German Workers Party*, an 1865 popular pamphlet written by Engels and closely checked and amended by Marx,[10] the author declared that it was in the interests of the workers to support the bourgeoisie in its struggle against all reactionary elements so long as the bourgeoisie remained true to itself. What did Engels, and Marx, mean by conditioning the support of the workers on the bourgeoisie's remaining true to itself? For the classic socialist thinkers, the bourgeoisie remained true to itself only when it consistently demanded "direct universal suffrage, freedom of the press, organization and assembly, and abolition of all discriminatory laws against particular classes of the population." If the bourgeoisie were to consistently fight in this way, Engels and Marx concluded that it would not be able to "fight for its political rule, nor express this political rule in a constitution and laws, without at the same time putting weapons in the hands of the proletariat."[11] Clearly then, the classic socialist thinkers conditioned their political support for the bourgeoisie on the bourgeoisie's willingness to conduct the democratic struggle to the end without concessions to the feudal powers and interests. But what if the bourgeoisie, notwithstanding its hostility to feudal reaction, allies with it because of its even greater fear of the workers, as became the norm after the failed revolutions of 1848? As Engels and Marx explained in the same pamphlet, the workers' party will continue to forge ahead with the agitation that has been betrayed by the bourgeoisie "for civil liberties, freedom of the press, assembly and organization, in spite of the bourgeoisie. Without these freedoms the workers' party itself cannot act freely; in this struggle it is struggling for its own life-element, for the air which it needs to breathe."[12] This clearly indicated, as Marxist scholar Hal Draper has pointed out, that for Marx and Engels, the workers' fight for democratic rights and freedoms was carried out, in the last analysis, not on behalf of the democracy shaped and limited by capitalist interests. Instead, workers were fighting for the development of the fullest democracy: workers' democracy and workers' power.[13]

Marx and Engels's approach to progress and the maintenance of class political independence can be even more clearly seen in how they consistently approached the role of the various "progressive despots" of the nineteenth century. These were political and military leaders who struck blows for a number of progressive goals such as national unification against feudal fragmentation and privileges, but at the same time opposed and resisted democratic goals and struggles. While Marx and Engels freely acknowledged the "progressive" aspects of Napoleon Bonaparte's abolition of feudal institutions in his military campaigns throughout Europe, they became increasingly hostile to his despotism as their politics matured. A more important and telling test of Marx and Engels's approach to progress came up in the case of Germany's Bismarck. Engels acknowledged Bismarck's accomplishment in bringing about the successful unification of Germany, but he indicated that while a progressive aim was being carried out, it was not done in a way that he, Marx, or the workers should support. Engels, with Marx's agreement, welcomed the advances toward the national organization and unification of the German proletariat that Bismarck had brought about and that had established a new starting point for that class. Bismarck was facilitating a revolution, but that revolution could be furthered only by intransigent opposition to Bismark himself. It is very revealing in this context that when the Lassallean faction of German socialism flirted with Bismarck, Marx and Engels denounced and broke with them publicly.[14] Along similar lines, Marx was critical of Simón Bolívar. While supporting and affirming the progressiveness of the national liberation movement in South America, Marx criticized Bolívar for what he saw as his penchant for military dictatorship, authoritarianism, and arrogating arbitrary power for himself.[15] Thus, Marx and Engels's political attitude to progressive despots was consistent with their view of progress in other contexts. As Draper concludes with respect to Marx and Engels's attitude toward progressive political actors who were nevertheless adversaries of the workers' movement, "the objective progressiveness of a despot or exploiter meant merely that the enemy was compelled by history to help your cause despite himself: it could not for a moment induce you to change your mind about which side you were on. On the contrary, it was only the continued class struggle from below that could even squeeze the greatest historical advantage out of the 'progressive' social forces which were propelling your enemy on his path."[16]

Marx and Engels's analysis reflected not only the bourgeoisie's growing disinclination to support revolutionary action against the remnants of feudal Europe, but also the growing separation of national unification, equality, individual freedom, democracy, and other political goals of the struggle against feudalism from capitalist economic development. By the second half of the nineteenth century it was evident that there was no necessary connection between political freedom and capitalist economic growth, as was made very clear by the Bismarck regime in Germany and the Meiji Restoration in late nineteenth-century Japan. Modernizing authoritarian regimes in the twentieth century would make that separation even clearer.

It follows from the previous analysis that arithmetic addition and subtraction of gains and losses is the wrong approach to the question whether a social system or political regime is progressive and should be politically supported. Broadening the analysis of Marx and Engels, we can argue that there is one particular loss that cannot be compensated by any gain when it comes to the question of deciding whether a regime should be politically supported. This is the loss of class, group (whether defined by race, gender, or sexual orientation), and individual political autonomy and independence—and specifically, the loss of freedom to organize independently to defend class, group, and other democratic interests and associated civil and political freedoms to make such organizational independence possible and viable.

Epilogue

After the Sixth Party Congress

The period between September 2010, when the Cuban government announced massive layoffs, and April 2011, when the Sixth Congress of the Cuban Communist Party (CCP) took place, marks a distinctive turn in the history of Cuban Communism. This period witnessed tactical delays such as a postponement of the layoffs and government promises of popular reforms, such as allowing Cubans to travel outside the island[1] and legalizing the free purchase and selling of homes[2] and automobiles.[3] Nevertheless, the package of changes that the party congress approved and that Raúl Castro promised to carry out during the next five years[4] signifies a major retreat and shrinking of the Cuban welfare state and substantial insecurity for the half-million workers who will be initially laid off. Viewed as a whole, the changes that have been programmed also constitute an important turn toward a Cuban variant of the Sino-Vietnamese model combining capitalism with a substantial state economic presence and political authoritarianism. In my view, this will be more a result of the growing autonomy of enterprise managers from the central state authorities than through the expansion of self-employment and small enterprises. Meanwhile, the face of rural and urban Cuba has begun to change with the rapid spread of private employment, which has become particularly visible in the preparation and sale of food and in transport of passengers.[5] At the same time, items provided through the subsidized ration book are progressively being eliminated. Thus, for example, beginning on January 1, 2011, soap and other articles of personal hygiene were removed from the rationing system and began to be sold in stores at market prices.[6]

The Sixth Party Congress

The Sixth Congress of the CCP was nine years overdue (it was supposed to have taken place in 2002, five years after the 1997 Fifth Party Congress) when it finally took place in April 2011. This party gathering was convened to discuss only economic matters and to elect the new CCP leadership. Other political and organizational questions are to be addressed at a national party conference, which was originally scheduled for later in the year but was postponed to early 2012.

Why did Raúl Castro finally convene the congress after such a long delay? In the first place, it was to take the last steps in the consolidation of his political power. Raúl Castro strengthened his power considerably since he initially took over from his older brother Fidel in 2006 and his takeover became fully official in 2008. As of the time of this writing, spring 2011, the great majority of the government ministers are Raúl Castro's appointees, and under his influence the high military officialdom has continued to increase its power over the economy and political system. Although Fidel Castro has resumed political activity and has even given public speeches before large crowds, he has refrained from expressing his views on domestic policy. The "Reflexiones" columns that he regularly publishes in *Granma* and *Juventud Rebelde* are exclusively concerned with foreign policy and such matters as the environment. His presence at the final session of the congress suggests that he assented to the economic changes that his brother Raúl has begun to implement and to the new party economic program.

Second, Raúl's political consolidation enabled him to turn from more than a decade of near paralysis in economic policy, from the mid-nineties to 2006, and four years of hesitant, modest, and sometimes incoherent steps, from 2006 to 2010, to a qualitatively different set of economic changes, some of which he has already implemented. One involves the legalization of self-employment in 178 specific occupations and liberalization of the rules governing small private enterprises such as the *paladares* (small restaurants), by allowing them to increase the maximum number of patrons from twelve to twenty, and then to fifty in the spring of 2011.[7] In a more important turn in light of the regime's history, the authorities have officially allowed the hiring of employees who are not family members, thereby legalizing a practice that was already in existence and opening the door for its further expansion.

The government's concerns underlying these measures arise from the gravity of the economic situation. The government's program originally submitted in preparation for the Sixth Congress (*Draft Guidelines for Economic and Social Policy of the Cuban Communist Party*) explicitly acknowledges that the Cuban economy suffers from serious structural problems. However, it specifically mentions only deterioration of the country's trade balance, low productivity, capital loss affecting the productive base and infrastructure, and stagnation in the growth, and consequent aging, of the Cuban population,[8] and omits major problems such as the country's foreign debt.[9] As I indicated in chapter 2, Cuba's debt had increased, according to the UN's Economic Commission for Latin America (ECLA), by a factor of 1.7 between 2004 and 2008. As of that year, it amounted to almost forty-six billion dollars, the equivalent of 380 percent of annual exports, compared to the regional average of 83 percent.[10] The Cuban debt has caused serious concern among foreign creditors, including China.[11] The call for the Sixth Congress was made in November 2010,[12] two months after the announcement in September of the proposed massive layoff of half a million state workers. Raúl Castro and his associates obviously felt that they had arrived at a critical juncture and needed the endorsement of the highest party institution to strengthen their hand. The Cuban leader underscored the seriousness of the situation when he told the National Assembly of Peoples' Power on December 18, 2010, "Either we rectify or the time to continue teetering on the edge of the precipice is over and we will fall."[13]

The guidelines finally approved by the Sixth Party Congress cover 313 proposals under twelve headings. Whenever implemented, these measures will represent strong and bitter medicine for the bulk of the Cuban population. Although they could be considered a wish list that will not be fully implemented in the near future, they manifest an unmistakable political tone and coloration that indicates, in general terms, the direction in which the government would like to go. This includes a far greater reliance on market mechanisms, the self-financing and profitability of each individual enterprise, elimination of subsidies and social benefits, and liberalization of the rules governing small business and foreign investment. However, there are tensions and contradictions in these new guidelines. For example, the guidelines encourage foreign investment[14] and define "socialism" as equality of rights and opportunities, which it explicitly contrasts to egalitarianism.[15] At the same time, the primacy of planning over the market, and of state "socialist" enterprises over self-employment, cooperatives, and foreign investment, is reiterated. In addition, the document includes a vow to prevent the concentration of property in the hands of private individuals or legal entities. Nevertheless, the guidelines propose considering the use of market mechanisms and attempt to influence them.[16]

There are several major themes and proposals that, even if implemented only partially, will hurt the poorest and most vulnerable segments of the population. Among these are the abolition of subsidies, although the government claims they will remain available to the needy. The subsidies to be reduced or altogether abolished, including those benefiting the recipients of Cuban aid abroad, are these:

- Subsidies for worker education: workers will now have to study in their free time and only on the basis of their "personal effort," except in cases of special interest to the state.[17] That means that, in general, there will be no more paid study during work hours, scholarships, or any of the other means that have supported worker education in the past.
- Although workers' dining rooms will continue to function in those places considered by the government to be "indispensable," the food served will be provided at prices that are not subsidized.[18]
- The ration book, which is a form of regulated and egalitarian

distribution at subsidized prices, will be brought to a "gradual" and "orderly" end.[19]

• Cuba will seek, as far as possible, to be compensated for at least the costs of the collaborative solidarity it offers other countries.[20]

Government economists make a provocative point when they argue, to justify the elimination of subsidies, "that if the production of all items is subsidized, you will never know the cost of anything."[21] A more fundamental criticism would be that if "everything" were subsidized, the economy would in short order become severely inflationary and undercapitalized. The Cuban government has acknowledged that its economy is currently undercapitalized and suffered serious inflation in the nineties. Although the inflation was controlled, there was a substantial drop in real wages from which the Cuban people have yet to recover. But the alternative to "subsidizing everything" is not the elimination of all subsidies, or as government spokespeople put it, only subsidizing people and not goods and services. A rational economic policy can include a calculated and measured use of subsidies of goods and services for specific and thought-out purposes. Subsidies could be justified in terms of encouraging class equality, public welfare and the creation of a more educated citizenry and productive economy (e.g., worker education), and efficient use of energy and transport (e.g., mass public transit). Moreover, restricting public subsidies to those "in need" runs the huge risk of undermining political support for subsidies in general, as ample experience has demonstrated in the case of means-tested social programs in numerous countries. An alternative that may avoid or at least diminish these political costs might be to provide certain subsidized goods and services to all with benefits allocated on a sliding scale according to individual and family income.

Toward the aim of rationalizing the Cuban economy, the guidelines promise to advance toward monetary unity, taking into account labor productivity and other factors. This vague promise addresses the widely disliked and unjust system of double currency.[22] The principle of payment according to work performance instead of straight hourly wages and salaries is reiterated,[23] a notion fundamentally opposed to elementary trade-union principles. The program also vows to eliminate overstaffing in the state sector and to develop processes to dispose of state workers who do not meet the standards of individual competence or "proven fitness."[24] This suggests further layoffs beyond those decreed in September 2010 (and then delayed), not surprising in light of Raúl Castro's earlier talk about laying off a million people, or 20 percent of the labor force. The guidelines also propose the establishment of a relationship between the growth of labor productivity and workers' median income to maintain monetary equilibrium and the efficiency of the national economy.[25] According to the government, in 2010 labor productivity increased by 4.2 percent and median salaries by 4.4 percent.[26]

Most important of all are the guidelines' proposals, which have so far received relatively little attention, to establish greater enterprise autonomy. These proposals have a material basis of support: a major sector of the Cuban economy, including civilian and military joint ventures with foreign capital and economic enterprises administered by the armed forces, which has become the foundation for a new managerial and technocratic stratum in Cuban society. Needless to say, these people would derive much benefit from greater managerial autonomy, which would potentially place them on a path toward becoming a central part of a reconstituted ruling class. Raúl Castro, in his inaugural speech to the Sixth Party Congress, placed a new emphasis on decentralizing the administration of contracts and on giving enterprise (and ministry) functionaries greater power in appointing, substituting, and disciplining people without undue party interference.[27] An earlier article in *Granma* explicitly linked the lack of enterprise autonomy with the loss of capacity to move, react, and be competitive, which in many cases led these enterprises to perform poorly, ceasing to depend on their own income and instead relying on the state budget.[28]

Though these proposals in the "enterprise sphere" are sometimes contradictory in light of the central government's desire to retain control, even their partial implementation may have major consequences for the Cuban economy, polity, and society as a whole. The guidelines explicitly propose the following:

- The internal finances of an enterprise cannot be interfered with by people who are not part of it except as determined by legally established procedures.[29] This would presumably have barred Fidel Castro from personally intervening in the management of enterprises, as he was often inclined to do.
- Although enterprises make their own decisions and administer their working capital and investments without any outside interference, they must proceed within the limits established by the plan.[30] This potentially contradictory guideline does not specify what the specific limits are and is bound to produce friction and even law-breaking.
- Control of the enterprise is to be based primarily on economic and financial, without excluding administrative, mechanisms, thereby reducing the existing burdensome control of enterprises by the central government and increasing the rationality of information systems.[31]
- State enterprises that consistently show losses in their financial balances, have insufficient working capital, are not able to honor their debts with their own funds, or are negatively evaluated in their financial audits are to be liquidated or can be transformed into nonstate property.[32] This last provision opens the door to the

creation of cooperatives or to privatization. If implemented even partially, this proposal will increase the number of displaced workers and beyond that have obvious major consequences for the Cuban economic system.

- The losses of state enterprises will no longer be subsidized. State enterprises will not as a rule receive financing from the state budget to fulfill the production of goods and services.[33]

- The incomes of workers and managers will be "linked" to the "results" obtained by the state or nonstate enterprise for which they work.[34] The term "linked" (*vinculado*) is somewhat vague, in any case, this proposal conflicts with the earlier proposal that workers be paid according to their performance at work. Thus, if workers work hard and efficiently in an enterprise that is nevertheless unprofitable for other reasons (including the incompetence and malfeasance of state managers), their efforts will not be equitably compensated. The fact that managers' income would also be affected does not diminish the potentially unjust impact on workers.

- State enterprises will have the independent power to approve their own job positions and classifications within the norms of the plan, which will help to avoid unnecessary hiring.[35]

- The determination of prices of products and services that for economic and social reasons the state has an interest in regulating will be centralized, while other prices will be decentralized.[36] It remains to be seen how this guideline will be carried out in practice. To the extent that prices are decentralized, the door will be open to competition among state firms and with nonstate economic actors. If so, the role of "market principles" in the Cuban economy will increase.

- Provincial and municipal authorities will not be able to intervene in enterprise management.[37]

- Conditions will be created to decentralize the Investment Plan, and state enterprises, in addition to other pertinent government institutions, will have the power to approve investments.[38]

The "New Old" Party Leadership

Beside adopting the 313-point package of economic changes, the Sixth Party Congress also elected the leaders who will direct the affairs of the CCP until the Seventh Party Congress, which is supposed to take place in five years. On this occasion, it was announced that Fidel Castro would no longer hold any official party office. This was not surprising in light of his advanced age (eighty-five) and delicate health, even though he is undoubtedly doing better than in 2006, when he withdrew from the spotlight due to a life-threatening condition. Raúl Castro also announced the introduction of term limits for officeholders (two five-year terms), although this will have very little impact on him and on José Ramón Machado Ventura, the now officially appointed second in command in the hierarchy. Both will be in their late eighties, if they are still alive, when they reach the end of their two terms.

The Central Committee (CC) elected at the April 2011 party congress was reduced from 125 to 115 members. According to Raúl Castro, 31.3 percent of members of the new CC are blacks and mulattos, which is close to their proportion in the Cuban population as a whole if the 2002 official census figures (35 percent) are an accurate representation of Cuba's racial composition, and 41.7 percent are women.[39] Among those elected to the CC, twenty-five people (21.7 percent) have come out of the armed forces and are currently active, retired, or in charge of civil operations.[40] One of these twenty-five is Luis Alberto Rodríguez López-Calleja, a son-in-law of Raúl Castro, who is the head of the armed forces' business enterprises (GAESA–Grupo de Administración Empresarial S.A.). He is a rising figure who, given the current trajectory of the Cuban economy and polity, is likely to play a major role in any transition after the two Castro brothers are gone from the scene.

Things appear rather different when we look at the Political Bureau (PB)—the most powerful political body in the country—that was elected at the Sixth Congress. The PB was reduced from twenty-four to fifteen members and now includes only one woman and only three blacks or mulattos, well below the official proportions of those groups in the Cuban population as a whole. This "new" BP is actually an "old and more of the same" group with a median age of seventy-three. The predominance of the military is striking. Eight of the fifteen members either are currently active in the military or have a military background. The new membership of the PB also shows evidence of a great concentration of power. As Haroldo Dilla Alfonso points out, there are six members of the PB who are simultaneously president or vice president in the other two most powerful institutions, the Council of State and the Council of Ministers, and four of these six are in or came out of the military. Another six have a seat in at least one of these other two institutions, and three of these came out of the military. In sum, if to be a member of more than one of these institutions is an indicator of clout within the power structure, twelve of the fifteen PB members are in such a situation, and seven of these have a military background. This is a degree of concentration of power higher than those of all previous Political Bureaus.[41] The military's predominance over the party bureaucracy proper is clearly evident here. This is a particularly important phenomenon in light of the major role played by the armed forces in the Cuban economy, including the army's economic enterprises, its participation in joint ventures with foreign capital, and the program of *perfeccionamiento empresarial* (enterprise improvement). Finally, it is noteworthy that Abel Prieto, the minister of culture and one of the most liberal members of the Communist Party hierarchy, was dropped from both the PB and CC, as usual without any explanation for such a major demotion.

Discussion of the Communist Party Proposals

Raúl Castro called for an open discussion of the party's proposals among the Cuban people during a three-month period, from December 1, 2010, to February 28, 2011, with the promise that nobody would be prevented from expressing their ideas. This is not the first time that such an "open discussion" has taken place. It happened, for example, during preparations for the Fourth Party Congress in 1991 and again after Raúl Castro, in his speech of July 26, 2007, a year after he had taken over from his older brother Fidel, called for countrywide deliberations. These "discussions" have pretended to be democratic but take place within an organizational framework that denies and subverts the very essence of democracy. In the first place, the official party media have exclusive control of what and how to report on what transpires at discussion meetings in offices and factories. This control was wielded extensively in this as well as in the previous "open discussions" called by the higher party authorities. People participating in those discussions had no organization of their own, nor were they allowed to communicate and organize on behalf of their grievances with people participating in discussions in other workplaces. As a result, those participating in a discussion in any given setting faced the organization of the rulers, that is, the CCP, as isolated groups. From November 15 to November 30, the period immediately preceding the "open discussion" of the party's proposals in 2010, seminars were held in all the municipalities to prepare the cadres that were going to participate in the meetings with the party nuclei, workers, and communities.[42] This means, of course, that trained party cadres were going to be present at each discussion to "guide it" and transmit the party "orientations" that came from above. Still, these discussions did communicate to the party leadership much of the discontent and the complaints at the grass roots. These in turn resulted in mostly minor adjustments to the program that was eventually adopted at the congress, and the inclusion of several guidelines conveying some important promises to the Cuban people.

If we take as examples the final guidelines discussed above, we can see how several of them were modified and even softened somewhat:

- The original guideline on ending subsidies for worker education was modified to specify "except in cases of special interest to the state."[43]
- The notion of "gradualness" was added to the original guideline announcing the elimination of the ration book in an "orderly" manner.[44]
- The original guideline to link the income of workers to the results obtained by the enterprise was expanded to include managers.[45]

- The original guideline proposing that management control of an enterprise was to be based primarily on economic and financial instead of administrative mechanisms was modified to state that administrative mechanisms would not be excluded.[46]
- Notably, the option to transform enterprises that consistently showed losses into nonstate property had not been included in the original guidelines.[47]

However, by far the most important concessions to popular discontent were party and government promises to allow the legal buying and selling of homes and automobiles and especially the promise to allow Cubans to visit foreign countries without the very onerous present restrictions.

According to the party authorities, more than 395,000 opinions were accepted and included in the reformulation of the guidelines. Some 210,000 had to do with matters of implementation; more than 65,000 were doubts or preoccupations that the party intends to respond to through publicity and education programs. Another 62,000 opinions dealt with issues that were already addressed in various guidelines, and approximately 50,000 opinions were not accepted or will be studied at a later time.[48] According to Raúl Castro, almost all the changes to the original guidelines were made *prior* to the Sixth Party Congress. This occurred on March 19–March 20, 2011, at meetings of the PB of the party and the executive committee of the Council of Ministers. The secretariat of the CC, the central cadre of the CTC (central union), other mass organizations, and the Communist Youth organization also participated in these two-day gatherings. Raúl Castro did not explain why and how proposals were accepted, modified, or rejected except that forty-five opinions and proposals that would have permitted concentration of property and were thus in open contradiction to socialism were rejected.[49]

Thus, this discussion process, rather than having been a democratic debate, let alone democratic decisionmaking, was far more akin to a nationwide oral suggestion-and-complaint box. The CCP leaders responded to the thousands of opinions that the Cuban people submitted to them much like the owners and managers of a capitalist enterprise who implement those suggestions that they find most helpful to run their business and pacify the labor force. The discussion process that was carried out in Cuba was not even comparable to collective bargaining, let alone political and economic democracy. It is very revealing that final guideline 04 states that the structural and other changes proposed in the party program will be realized in "a programmatic fashion, with order and discipline, on the basis of the approved policy, *informing the workers and listening to their opinions.*"[50] I suppose that Cuban workers should be thankful for small favors. After all, the final guidelines did not pledge to refuse to provide information and ignore the workers' opinions!

Critiques and Evaluations of the Guidelines and the Government's New Economic Policies

The proposals made in the guidelines have been praised and criticized from a wide range of quarters. Most critics, from right to left, tend to agree that the government's extension of legal self-employment is a positive step. However, from the standpoint of those who favor the establishment of a capitalist "market economy" in Cuba, including those with a social-democratic orientation, the new economic changes leave much to be desired even if they have positive features. For one thing, the changes are seen as not having gone far enough. From this perspective, rather than allowing only a limited number of self-employed occupations, it would have made more sense to allow self-employment throughout the economy as a whole with perhaps a short list of *excluded* occupations, whether for economic or political reasons. Instead, the government published a list allowing self-employment in only 178 occupations (21 more than the 157 originally allowed by the 1993 reforms, which were reduced to 117 years later).[51] While this particular criticism has been raised by so-called free market economists, is it not necessarily exclusive to their perspective, and is in fact compatible with the Marxist notion that socialization and nationalization are pertinent only to social and collective, rather than individual or family, production. Of course, Marxists do not support let alone share the enthusiasm of the "free-marketeers" for an unlimited hiring of workers, but instead have been arguing for the development of self-managed cooperatives.

Another important matter raised by the party guidelines is taxation. The tax legislation that accompanied the reforms of the first half of the nineties established only one tax: an income tax for the self-employed, who were not obliged, unlike the rest of the population working for the state, to make social security contributions. The new regulations establish five taxes, including a 25 to 50 percent income tax and a 10 percent sales tax, which in combination constitute a very heavy tax load. The self-employed are now obliged to contribute to the social security fund at the rate of 25 percent, almost three times the average for Latin America. The government projects that as a result of the new taxes imposed on the self-employed (and those hiring others), fiscal income will increase 300 percent from 2009 to 2011, assuming a base of 250,000 newly self-employed people.

The Cuban government later promised to carry out annual reviews of the monthly minimal tax quotas in several self-employed activities in order to correct them if necessary, and it provided some tax concessions, particularly to people renting out apartments and houses and to those engaged in transporting Cubans.[52] Nevertheless, the heavy tax burden will probably lead to major tax evasion, illegal self-employment, and small-scale hiring, which as previous experience in many parts of the world has shown, is very difficult to detect and prevent.[53] At the macroeconomic level, economists analyzing Cuba from the fundamentally capitalist "free market" perspective have also argued that the centralized determination of prices is in contradiction to the decentralized decision-making allowed to enterprises in a variety of areas such as investment.[54] The government, in a perhaps desperate effort to maintain overall economic and political control of the new situation, is trying to have its cake and eat it too, thereby contradicting the inner logic of the market. It is likely that the "laws of the market" will end up prevailing but in an illegal, corrupt, if not gangster-type reborn capitalism, although with a heavy state presence in the economy.

Other criticisms, not necessarily linked to a "free market" or a socialist perspective for that matter, point to serious defects in the government's plans conducting the layoffs and incorporating former state workers into the self-employed sector. Although the government has postponed the layoffs, it has not canceled the plan to lay off half a million workers (and probably many more to be laid off at a later time). The government would not have even dared to propose this if it had to confront the power of a real trade union movement. As it turned out, it was the official union leadership that announced, without even a murmur of protest, the mass layoffs. State workers, many with only office experience, can make the transition to production or service work only after substantial retraining, an issue that has so far been entirely ignored by the government. This lack of retraining becomes even more of a problem when we consider that the government has excluded seniority, let alone any affirmative action criteria protecting women and black Cubans, as a consideration to determine the *idoneidad* (fitness) of those who will stay and those who will be let go. Thus, for example, a forty-five-year-old state worker with twenty years of office experience may be laid off and expected to make a living working for herself in the petty production and service private and cooperative economy. This problem will be aggravated by the recent substantial reductions in unemployment compensation that I discussed in chapter 4.

Critics also point out the problem of credits and inputs. Even though the government authorized the banks to grant credit necessary to start their ventures to small farmers and the urban self-employed,[55] there does not seem to be a major concern or priority placed on solving this critical problem. This becomes especially urgent in the case of the 200,000 people who will be laid off and expected to form cooperatives without even a mention of the need to develop cooperative banks.[56] As far as inputs are concerned, the government has significantly expanded the sale of construction materials and pledged to increase the variety and volume of some products, like food items such as eggs and rice, to satisfy the demand of self-employed workers. However, according to the government, these inputs will, at least for the time being, be available at stores selling at retail rather than wholesale prices.[57] With little or no access to retraining, credit, or wholesale inputs, the newly laid off people will likely add a new element to the problem of theft from state property and widespread law breaking on the island. Already millions of Cubans with no access to hard currency are forced to steal from the state because the ever-shrinking peso-denominated ration book does not even cover half of what they need to feed themselves.

A substantial sector of the international left, particularly in Latin America, has reacted positively to the Cuban government's recent economic turn. These leftists refuse to look at the facts and the direction in which Cuba is going. Or else they argue that "objective economic circumstances"—either the continuing US blockade or the collapse of the Soviet Union—have made such economic changes necessary. They choose to ignore how the state bureaucratic system, as I showed in detail in chapter 2, is a major source of economic waste and inefficiency in Cuba. The pro-Castro left also argues that the "reforms" were the result of a democratic process of discussion and consultation, an argument that totally ignores the realities of the monopoly of political organization and the media, as well as the many other undemocratic features of the Cuban one-party state. Finally, the regime defenders ignore the massive cuts in unemployment compensation, subsidies, and the ration book that have already begun to be implemented, and insist that Cuba's "social gains" in social welfare and economic equality will be maintained.[58]

A minority of critical leftists have strongly criticized the fashion in which the government proceeded, characterizing it, to take one example, as "brutal, bureaucratic, undemocratic, brusque and terribly late, forced by the crisis and involuntary, overbearing and without the slightest self-criticism."[59] I would argue, along with these critics, that the problem is not, as it is for the advocates of the capitalist "market economy," that the Cuban government's economic proposals do not go far enough, but rather that the proposed changes are going in the wrong direction. As an alternative, this political perspective advocated worker self-management, equality, and a democratization of the Cuban political system and society as a whole.[60] Other critical democratic leftists have pointed out that the government guidelines make no reference to the social costs of the adjustment proposed, nor do they mention those who will, on balance, lose. These are the most vulnerable groups—the elderly, women, less educated people, inhabitants of the less dynamic areas of the country, and so on—who until recently were covered by a paternalist/clientelist accord now in an open process of decomposition.[61]

The Road Ahead

It is difficult to predict the consequences of the new economic and social turn taken by the government. It appears that as the system clearly declines, the country's leadership is more explicitly turning to China and Vietnam as the models for Cuba's development. In April 2005, on the occasion of a visit by Raúl Castro to China, he told his hosts that "it was truly encouraging everything that you have done here . . . there are some people around who are preoccupied by China's development; however, we feel happy and reassured, because you have confirmed something that we say over there [in the West] and that is that a better world is possible."[62] This might have been a politically revealing but isolated throwaway comment. But more recently pro-Chinese pronouncements came from high Cuban officials *after* the Sixth Party Congress was called and the initial guidelines for it were published. Ricardo Alarcón, president of the National Assembly of Popular Power, met with his Chinese counterpart in late November 2010 and declared that "Cuba is prepared to take advantage of the development experience of China's reform and opening." [63] Even Fidel Castro was reported as praising China's "rectifications" and telling university students that "China is worth studying."[64]

One problem in forecasting future developments is that it is difficult to know which of the Communist Party's "shopping list" of 313 guidelines will end up being implemented. That might depend on the relation of forces among different sectors of the bureaucracy pushing for their own interests. If the managerial elements, particularly those linked to the armed forces, end up having the clout and coherence necessary to prevail, this might open the road to something similar to the "*nomenklatura* privatization" and economic looting that took place in the USSR in the nineties. This is precisely what, as we saw in chapter 2, Professor Esteban Morales warned about, which led to his getting barred from the official mass media and expelled from the CCP.[65]

Another issue is the possible fallout of the eventual massive layoffs without sufficient credit, inputs, and training necessary to start the new mini-enterprises and cooperatives that are supposed to absorb the laid-off employees. As we saw above, this might become a particularly acute problem in light of the sharp reductions in unemployment compensation that the government recently implemented. Whenever the government decides to carry out the massive layoffs, it will have to deal with a serious crisis. This might coincide with a crisis of legitimacy following the passing from the scene of one or both of the Castro brothers in the not too distant future (Raúl Castro turned eighty years old and Fidel Castro eighty-five in 2011). In any case, the Cuban version of Communism seems to be in decline. It has failed to achieve economic development on any terms, whether "socialist" or capitalist. As the Cuban people have come to realize this, a growing sense of hopelessness has developed among the population, particularly the youth, both white and black.[66] Increasingly, people see no future for themselves and their children. Cuba, in their eyes, has become a place to leave, to flee from.[67]

The transitions that took place in the former Communist countries and the forces and tendencies in Cuba analyzed in this book suggest that in the longer run there will likely be a full transition to a state-controlled form of capitalism in Cuba, particularly after the Castro brothers have died. The transition is likely to be led by the army and joint venture managers and technocrats, possibly in alliance with a small but growing petty bourgeoisie in Cuba and a wing of the Cuban capitalists in south Florida.[68] It is difficult to imagine a Cuban transition that would not involve the Cuban army playing a major role. First, the army is the best-organized institution on the island. Second, the army, following the Soviet model, has not been involved in internal repression except in situations of armed rebellion and combat. The last of these took place fifty years ago with the armed rebellions in the Escambray mountain chain in central Cuba. Under the Soviet model operating in Cuba, it is the state security organs, organizationally distinct from the armed forces, that are in charge of carrying out the tasks of internal repression. Third, due to compulsory military service, the Cuban army has been a more inclusive institution than the CCP. Fourth, the Cuban army has for a long time been a major player in Cuban economic life. The army's economic role comprises its own businesses, such as the huge business conglomerate GAESA which includes the tourist enterprise Gaviota,[69] and high-ranking army officers occupy leading positions in other key areas of the Cuban economy. In the process, the Cuban army has educated and developed an important group of technocrats who, together with a group of civilian technicians and managers, have for some time played a major role in the Cuban economy and society.

Those implementing the transition will likely disregard any social or human consideration standing in the way of the new state-controlled capitalist system. This may take the form of a military dictatorship sponsoring large-scale privatization and the consequent unemployment, reduction of social services, and other features of the usual neoliberal program. State policies will likely promote the "winners": tourism and the construction and consumer industries supplying it; extractive industries such as oil and nickel; biotechnology; and possibly a newly developed maquiladora industry. The "losers" will be neglected: a good part of "noncompetitive" manufacturing and, with some exceptions such as citrus, agriculture in general. If substantial amounts of oil are found in Cuban waters of the Gulf of Mexico, this will of course alter the country's economic prospects and ease the way for any state capitalist transition.

The direction in which Cuba seems to be going suggests that resistance is the most urgent priority for those who would endure negative consequences of the government's actions. Some might argue that since socialism of a democratic and revolutionary orientation is not likely to be on the immediate agenda, it is irrelevant and there is no point putting forward a socialist and democratic perspective and program to organize such resistance. However, a political vision advocating the democratic self-management of the Cuban economy, polity, and society as a whole would be most effective for shaping a compelling resistance. In invoking solidarity with the needs of the worst off and thus class, racial, and gender equality, a resistance movement would build unity against old and new oppressors. For example, a trade union movement that strongly defended workers in the "losing" sectors of the economy against the employer and government offensive would cement the solidarity of those workers with workers in the "winning" sectors, thereby building their united political power and potential for social transformation.

Such a vision would suggest that resistance is not futile, since there is an alternative to both capitalism and the failed "Communism" of Cuban history.

Though a struggle for this alternative society may not be on the immediate political agenda, a change in the relation of forces both nationally and internationally—such as a reversal of the defeats suffered by the labor movement and the left throughout the world since the seventies—in the not too distant future may make it a realizable political goal. In any case, the establishment of democracy in the Cuban economy, polity, and society at large will not be handed down as a gift by the people in power but will have to be obtained by struggles from below.

Acknowledgments

I want to thank Anthony Arnove, editor at Haymarket Books, who suggested this project and provided editorial guidance throughout. I am also very grateful to Dao X. Tran, who helped me resolve numerous editorial problems. Thanks also to Ruth Goring, who proofread the book, and to the production team at Haymarket Books: Rachel Cohen, Julie Fain, John McDonald, and Eric Ruder. I owe special gratitude to a number of people who have criticized and commented on various chapters: Mel Bienenfeld, Sebastian Budgen, Michelle Chase, Haroldo Dilla, Joel Geier, Adolfo Gilly, Thomas Harrison, Nancy Holmstrom, Dan Labotz, Charles Post, Corey Robin, Justino Rodriguez, Lance Selfa, Ahmed Shawki, Marina Sitrin, Stephen Steinberg, Frank Thompson, and Kit Wainer. I am also indebted to numerous friends in Cuba and the United States who generously responded to my various inquiries. I am solely responsible for the views expressed in this book. Finally, I want to acknowledge the invaluable help provided by several faculty and staff members at the Brooklyn College Library.

This work would not have been possible without the unstinting editorial collaboration and limitless intellectual and moral support of my wife, Selma Marks. To her, my gratitude and love.

Notes

In order to avoid printing the full addresses of some very long URLs, which the reader would be challenged to type into a browser, I have shortened some of them to just the top level of the domain name and trust that the reader will be able to search for the article using other location information such as author name, title, publication name, and date. And in order to facilitate readers finding sources in Spanish, I have included those citations in Spanish.

Introduction

1. Marifeli Pérez-Stable, *The Cuban Revolution: Origins, Course and Legacy*, 2nd ed. (New York: Oxford University Press, 1999), 61.
2. Samuel Farber, *Revolution and Reaction in Cuba, 1933–1960* (Middletown, CT: Wesleyan University Press, 1976), and Samuel Farber, *The Origins of the Cuban Revolution Reconsidered* (Chapel Hill: University of North Carolina Press, 2006).
3. Unless explicitly noted otherwise, I am responsible for all translations from Spanish.
4. While the great bulk of this work is new, small segments of the book overlap with two of my previous publications. I want to thank the publishers for their permission to use materials from those publications in this volume—*Revolution and Reaction in Cuba* and *Before Stalinism: The Rise and Fall of Soviet Democracy* (Cambridge: Polity Press, 1990). The latter book was also published by Verso in the United States.
5. Frances Fox Piven, "The Spirit of Rebellion: The Working Class in the Great Depression," introduction to the 2010 Haymarket Books edition of Irving Bernstein's *The Lean Years* as reprinted in the *International Socialist Review*, no. 72 (July–August 2010): 56.
6. Karl Marx, *The Eighteenth Brumaire of Louis Bonaparte* (Moscow: Foreign Languages Publishing House, n.d.).
7. James O'Connor, *The Origins of Socialism in Cuba* (Ithaca, NY: Cornell University Press, 1970), 11.
8. For a more detailed discussion of this matter see chapter 1, "Towards a Theory of the Cuban Revolution," in my *Revolution and Reaction in Cuba*, 3–27.
9. Karl Popper, *The Open Society and Its Enemies* (Princeton, NJ: Princeton University Press, 1971), and Karl Popper, *The Poverty of Historicism* (New York: Harper and Row, 1964).
10. Adam Michnik, *Letters from Prison and Other Essays*, trans. Maya Latynski (Berkeley: University of California Press, 1985): 89–90, 294.
11. Karl Marx, *The Civil War in France: With Other Writings by Marx and Engels on the Paris Commune* (Chicago: Charles H. Kerr, 1998); Leon Trotsky, *1905* (New York: Vintage Books, 1972); Farber, *Before Stalinism: The Rise and Fall of Soviet Democracy*. Other revolutionary outbreaks and movements were influenced by this tradition: the German revolution

of 1918, the tens of thousands of revolutionaries depicted by George Orwell in *Homage to Catalonia*, the Hungarian Workers' Councils in 1956, and important tendencies in the struggles in Chile from 1970 to 1973, Portugal from 1974 to 1975, Iran in 1979, and Poland in 1980–81. See, among other sources, Pierre Broué, *The German Revolution 1917–1923* (Chicago: Haymarket Books, 2006); Pierre Broué, *The Revolution and the Civil War in Spain* (Chicago: Haymarket Books, 2008); and Peter Fryer, *Hungarian Tragedy* (London: D. Dobson, 1956). For similar events and political tendencies in France 1968, Chile 1970–73, Portugal 1974–75, Iran 1979, and Poland 1980–81, see Colin Barker, *Revolutionary Rehearsals* (London: Bookmarks, 1987).

12. Advocacy of social and economic equality combined with political dictatorship has historic roots that can be traced all the way back to Babeuf, who argued for communist equality but also for the notion of an "educational dictatorship" over the people. Whether such an inherently contradictory combination can be realized in practice is of course an entirely different matter. See Hal Draper, "The Two Souls of Socialism," in Draper, *Socialism from Below*, ed. E. Haberkern (Atlantic Highlands, NJ: Humanities Press, 1992), 6–7.

13. See, for example, "An Imperfect Revolution in an Imperfect World," chapter 9 of Ian Lumsden's *Machos, Maricones and Gays: Cuba and Homosexuality* (Philadelphia: Temple University Press, 1996), 178.

14. Roy Medvedev, *Let History Judge: The Origins and Consequences of Stalinism*, ed. and trans. George Shriver, revised and expanded ed. (New York: Columbia University Press, 1989), 869.

15. I use the term *gay* rather than *LGBT* (lesbian, gay, bisexual, transgender) to be faithful to the naming conventions of the historical period during which these issues manifested themselves in Cuba.

Chapter One: Toward "Monolithic Unity"

1. For a full discussion of the 1933 Revolution and its consequences, see my *Revolution and Reaction in Cuba*.

2. Fidel Castro in an "Ante la Prensa" interview of February 19, 1959, in Fidel Castro, *Discursos para la historia* (La Habana: Imprenta Emilio Gall, 1959), 1: 11, 15–16.

3. *Revolución*, 16 febrero and also 15 abril 1959.

4. Euclides Vázquez Candela, "Saldo de una polémica," *Revolución*, 14 septiembre 1959.

5. Matos served his full term in prison and was released and left for Miami in 1979. Like so many others who endured these sorts of experiences, he made a sharp turn to the political right.

6. This does not mean that the eventual Communist outcome of the Cuban Revolution resulted from a conscious plan developed by Fidel Castro and his close associates in collaboration with the leadership of the old Communist Party *prior* to Batista's overthrow on January 1, 1959, as claimed by Tad Szulc and the south Florida Cuban American right wing. For a more detailed discussion of this issue see pages 59–63 of my book *The Origins of the Cuban Revolution Reconsidered*.

7. The well-known *New Yorker* columnist A. J. Liebling expressed a similar sentiment when he wrote that freedom of the press is limited to those who own one.

8. Fidel Castro recently elaborated at some length his views on freedom of the press under capitalism. See his "Otra vez la podrida OEA" (Once again the rotten OAS) in "Reflexiones del compañero Fidel," *Granma*, 10 mayo 2009, 1.

9. This did not preclude small journals oriented to elite intellectual, academic, and artistic audiences from occasionally deviating from official party orthodoxy as in the case of *Pensamiento Crítico* in the late sixties.

10. For a discussion of this process see Farber, *Before Stalinism: The Rise and Fall of Soviet Democracy*, particularly chapters 1 and 3.

11. V. I. Lenin, "How to Guarantee the Success of the Constituent Assembly," in *Collected Works*, vol. 25, *June–September 1917* (Moscow: Progress Publishers, 1964), 382. Lenin's emphasis.

12. V. I. Lenin, "Draft Resolution on Freedom of the Press," written November 4, 1917, in *Collected Works*, vol. 26, September 1917–February 1918 (Moscow: Progress Publishers, 1964), 283.

13. Albert Resis, "Lenin on Freedom of the Press," *Russian Review* 36, no. 3 (July 1977): 275.

14. Jorge I. Domínguez, *Cuba: Order and Revolution* (Cambridge, MA: Belknap Press of Harvard University Press, 1978), 208.

15. Cited in César Escalante, "Los Comités de Defensa de la Revolución," *Cuba Socialista*, 1 (septiembre 1961): 70.

16. Katia Siberia Garcia, "Comités de Defensa de la Revolución: Motivos para continuar," *Diario Granma* 13, no. 269 (25 septiembre 2009), www.granma.co.cu/2009/09/25/nacional/artic05.html.

17. Thus, for example, Ian Lumsden maintains that "democratization [in Cuba] does not necessarily require a multiparty system." Lumsden, *Machos, Maricones and Gays*, 200.

18. Cited by Stephen Cohen, *Bukharin and the Bolshevik Revolution: A Political Biography, 1888–1938* (Oxford: Oxford University Press, 1980), 397.

19. Peter Kornbluh, "A Former CIA Asset Goes on Trial," *Nation*, January 24, 2011, 24–26; "Jury Clears Cuban Exile of Charges That He Lied," *New York Times*, April 9, 2011.

20. Perhaps the biggest Russian cultural influences in Cuba were the consumption of certain kinds of food imported from the Soviet Union and especially the impact of televised Russian cartoons on Cuban children. See, for example, Gorki Aguila, "La nostalgia no es carne de puerco," *Encuentro de la Cultura Cubana* (Madrid), nos. 51–52 (invierno/primavera 2009): 187–89; and Jacqueline Loss, "Despojo de lo soviético en Cuba: La estética del adios," *Otro Lunes: Revista Hispanoamericana de Cultura*, no. 8 (2009), www.otrolunes.com/html/este-lunes-n08-a11-p03–2009.html. Loss's article includes some useful bibliographical references. See also various articles in the issue of the UNEAC's *La Gaceta de Cuba* mainly dedicated to discussing Soviet cultural influence in Cuba, no. 1 (enero/febrero 2010).

21. Hans Magnus Enzesberger, "Tourists of the Revolution," in *The Consciousness Industry: On Literature, Politics and the Media* (New York: Seabury Press, 1974), 129–57.

22. Domínguez, *Cuba: Order and Revolution*, 345–46.

23. For the large-scale forced relocation of thousands of people from central to western Cuba in the seventies, see "Pueblos cautivos: Entrevista con el doctor José Luis Piñeiro," *Encuentro de la Cultura Cubana* (Madrid), primavera 2001, 20, 228–31.

24. For additional details about the UMAP camps, see Lumsden, *Machos, Maricones and Gays*, 65–69.

25. Maurice Halperin, *The Taming of Fidel Castro* (Berkeley: University of California Press, 1981), 271–76.

26. Ibid., 202–04.

27. US black leaders Eldridge Cleaver and Robert Williams also had to leave Cuba because their views differed from those of the Cuban leadership. For a detailed account of Carbonell's and Robert Williams's relationship to Fidel Castro and the Cuban government, see Carlos Moore, *Pichón: A Memoir; Race and Revolution in Castro's Cuba* (Chicago: Lawrence Hill Books, 2008), 176, 220–21, 287, 339.

28. José Manuel Martín Medem, *¿Por qué no me enseñaste cómo se vive sin ti?* (Mataró, Spain: El Viejo Topo, 2005), 307. Author's emphasis.

29. Departamento de Versiones Taquigráficas del Gobierno Revolucionario, "Discurso pronunciado por el Comandante Fidel Castro Ruz, Primer Ministro del Gobierno Revolucionario de Cuba, en la clausura del Acto para Commemorar el VI Aniversario del Asalto

al Palacio Presidencial, celebrado en la Escalinata de la Universidad de la Habana, el 13 de marzo de 1963," www.cuba.cu/gobierno/discursos/1963/esp/fl30363e.html.

30. "El 'diversionismo' de la diferencia," *Cuba Revista Mensual* 11 (noviembre 2008). Reproduced in *Cuba a la Mano*, 17 diciembre 2008, http://cubaalamano.net/sitio/client/article.php?id=10637.

31. For more details on the suppression of the music of the Beatles in the sixties and their rediscovery in the nineties, see Juan José Castellanos, *El Sgto. Pimienta vino a Cuba en un submarino amarillo* (Havana: Editorial Letras Cubanas, 2000), 5–7, 144–48.

32. Julio César Guanche, "The Crisis of the Scissors," *Revista: The Harvard Review of Latin America* 8, no. 12 (Winter 2009), www.drclas.harvard.edu/revistaweb/1960s/cuba/guanche.

33. Julie Marie Bunck, *Fidel Castro and the Quest for a Revolutionary Culture in Cuba* (University Park: Pennsylvania State University Press, 1994), 144.

34. Guanche, "The Crisis of the Scissors," 25; Celestine Bohlen, "Heberto Padilla, 68, Cuban Poet, Is Dead," *New York Times*, September 28, 2000, www.nytimes.com/2009/09/28/arts/heberto-padilla-68-cuban-poet-is-dead.html.

35. Susan Sontag, "Some Thoughts on the Right Way (for Us) to Love the Cuban Revolution," *Ramparts*, April 1969, 18, 14. For the names of some of the writers arrested and repressed in the sixties (before the publication of Sontag's article), see Seymour Menton, *Prose Fiction of the Cuban Revolution* (Austin: University of Texas Press, 1975), 141.

36. Ruth M. Lewis, foreword to *Four Men: Living the Revolution; An Oral History of Contemporary Cuba*, ed. Oscar Lewis, Ruth M. Lewis, and Susan M. Rigdon (Urbana: University of Illinois Press, 1977), vii–xxx.

37. Carlos Moore, *Castro, the Blacks and Africa* (Los Angeles: Center for Afro-American Studies, UCLA, 1988), 304.

38. Ambrosio Fornet, "El quinquenio gris: Revisitando el término," 30 enero 2007, and Mario Coyula, "El Trinquenio Amargo y la ciudad distópica: Autopsia de una utopía," 19 mayo 2007, *Centro Teórico-Cultural Criterios*, www.criterios.es/cicloquinqueniogris.htm.

39. Claudia González Marrero, "La novela policial en Cuba durante la década del 70: Una literatura comprometida," *kaosenlared.net*, 25 octubre 2008. See also Daylet Domínguez, "Antiintelectualismo y género policial en Cuba," *Encuentro de la Cultura Cubana* 53/54 (verano/otoño 2009): 205–12.

40. Margaret Randall, *To Change the World: My Years in Cuba* (New Brunswick, NJ: Rutgers University Press, 2009), 212–16. Eventually, Randall received something close to an apology from Cuban State Security and shortly after left for Nicaragua, where the Sandinistas had just come to power.

41. Leonardo Padura Fuentes, *El hombre que amaba a los perros* (Mexico City: Tusquets Editores México, 2009), 78.

42. "Cuba's Position," editorial, *Granma Weekly Review*, April 13, 1980, 1.

43. Monika Krause-Fuchs, Cuba's well-known sex educator, described in some detail the awful incidents associated with the Mariel exodus and how they contradicted humanist and socialist values. Monika Krause-Fuchs, *Monika y la Revolución: Una mirada singular sobre la historia reciente de Cuba* (Tenerife, Canary Islands: Centro de la Cultura Popular Canaria, 2002), 245.

44. The experiences of Reinaldo Arenas were powerfully represented in Julian Schnabel's film *Before Night Falls*.

45. The term "formal democracy" is somewhat ambiguous but most commonly refers to political systems that have some features of democracy, particularly elections, but little real democracy, whether political or economic. Putin and Medvedev's Russian Federation would fit this description. The term was also applied to the various regimes that supported the United States in the Cold War and pretended to be democratic but were in fact dictatorships, such as Nicaragua under Somoza or the Philippines under Marcos. However, more relevant to my

present purposes is the use of the term "formal democracy" by supporters of the Soviet-type countries. These people often argue that civil liberties, elections, limits on the length of terms and reelections, and other features of "bourgeois" democracy are mere formalities that can be dispensed of in favor of the authentic democratic substance of those societies.

46. For some of the details of how Cubans go about avoiding attendance at marches, see the work by the anthropologist Amelia Rosenberg Weinreb, *Cuba in the Shadow of Change: Daily Life in the Twilight of the Revolution* (Gainesville: University Press of Florida, 2009), 153.

47. In January 2000, while on a visit to Cuba, I witnessed a demonstration in support of the return of the child Elián Gonzalez, which took place near the Colón Cemetery. A large group of obviously poor people got into a big pushing and shoving match to make sure they got their free T-shirts distributed by the government.

48. For a recent example of the distinction between "formal" and "substantive" democracy as applied to Cuba, see Ilja A. Luciak, *Gender and Democracy in Cuba* (Gainesville: University Press of Florida, 2007), xvi, xix.

49. Ronald Dworkin, "The 'Devastating' Decision," *New York Review of Books* 57, no. 3 (February 25, 2010): 39; and Ronald Dworkin, "The Decision That Threatens Democracy," *New York Review of Books* 57, no. 8 (May 13, 2010): 63–67.

50. Jill Abramson, "Return of the Secret Donors: In 2010, Corporate Cash, Anonymous Contributions and Other Echoes of Watergate," *New York Times*, October 17, 2010.

51. Eduardo Porter, "The Cost of a Vote Goes Up: How Much Is Spent per Voter? More and More Every Time," *New York Times*, November 7, 2010.

52. For a thorough and critical account of Popular Power in Cuba see Francisco Sobrino, "Reflections on 'Really Imaginary Socialism': Socialism, Democracy and Cuba," *Against the Current* (Detroit) 16, no. 4, n.s. (September/October 2001): 30–34.

53. "Decreto-Ley No. 259 Sobre la Entrega de Tierras Ociosas en Usufructo," *Granma*, 18 julio 2008, 4.

54. "Gobierno quita límites a los salarios," *Cuba a la Mano*, April 12, 2008, http://cubaalamano .net/sitio/client/brief.php?id=5346.

55. Leticia Martínez Hernández, "Trabajo por cuenta propia: Mucho más que una alternativa," *Diario Granma* 14, no. 268 (24 septiembre 2010), www.granma.co.cu/2010/09/24/nacional/ artic10.html.

56. "Pronunciamiento de la Central de Trabajadores de Cuba," *Diario Granma* 214, no. 257 (13 septiembre 2010), www.granma.co.cu/2010/09/13/nacional/artic01.html.

57. Sobrino, "Reflections on 'Really Imaginary Socialism,'" 30.

58. The municipal assemblies can select from the lists proposed by these "commissions of candidacies" the exact number of candidates required to fill each and every position at the higher levels, with half of these candidates to be chosen from among delegates elected to the municipal assemblies. Debra Evenson, *Law and Society in Contemporary Cuba*, 2nd ed. (The Hague: Kluwer Law International, 2003), 25.

59. Sobrino, "Reflections on 'Really Imaginary Socialism,'" 32.

60. Ibid., 31.

61. The anthropologist Amelia Rosenberg Weinreb has described a virtually identical behavior at the official labor union meetings held to elect officers. Weinreb, *Cuba in the Shadow of Change*, 25.

62. Miguel Arencibia Daupés, "Cuba: Entretelones de otras elecciones," *kaosenlared.net*, April 12, 2010, www.kaosenlared.net/noticias/cuba-entretelones-otras-elecciones.

63. "Con unidad monolítica Cuba seguirá adelante, dijo Raúl Castro," *Diario Granma* 13, no. 208 (26 julio 2009), www.granma.co.cu/2009//07/26/nacional/artic27.html.

64. Jean-Paul Sartre, *Sartre on Cuba* (Westport, CT: Greenwood Press, 1974), 86.

65. Luis Conte Aguero, *26 cartas del Presidio* (Havana: Editorial Cuba, 1960), 73. This book was published before Conte Aguero's break with Castro.

66. Fidel Castro, *Un grano de maíz* (Havana: Oficina de Publicaciones del Consejo de Estado, 1992), 76.

67. José Martí, "Resoluciones tomadas por la emigración cubana de Tampa y Cayo Hueso en noviembre de 1891," in *Obras escogidas*, 3: 23, as cited in Dimas Castellanos, *Qué tiene que ver Martí con el partido único*, 27 agosto 2010, www.desdecuba.com/dimas/.

68. Manuel Pedro González and Iván E. Schulman, *José Martí: Esquema ideológico* (Mexico City: Publicaciones de la Editorial Cubana, 1961); and Joan Casanovas, "La nación, la independencia y las clases," *Encuentro de la Cultura Cubana* (Madrid) 15 (invierno 1999–2000): 177–86.

69. Leon Trotsky, *The Revolution Betrayed* (New York: Merit, 1965), 267.

70. For a powerful presentation of the argument of "which side are you on" in the present context, see the concluding section of Hal Draper, "The Two Souls of Socialism," in *Socialism from Below*, ed. E. Haberkern (Atlantic Highlands, NJ: Humanities Press, 1992), 33. See also Peter Sedgwick, "Ghana, Guinea, Guiana: Three Strikes," in *A Socialist Review* (London: International Socialism, 1965), 327–29.

71. Quoted in Alan Riding, "For García Márquez, Revolution Is a Major Theme," *New York Times*, May 22, 1980.

72. Quoted in Allen Young, *Gays under the Cuban Revolution* (San Francisco: Grey Fox Press, 1981), 99.

73. Antoni Kapcia, *Cuba in Revolution: A History since the Fifties* (London: Reaktion Books, 2008), 141.

74. Hugh Thomas, *Cuba: The Pursuit of Freedom* (New York: Harper and Row, 1971), 1202–3.

75. Amnesty International, *Restrictions on Freedom of Expression in Cuba* (London: Amnesty International, June 30, 2010), 9–10.

76. Human Rights Watch, *Cuba's Repressive Machinery: Human Rights Forty Years after the Revolution* (New York: Human Rights Watch, June 1999), 23. According to Human Rights Watch, Díaz Sotolongo twice referred to Castro with the term "king" during an interview that took place in New York on June 11, 1988.

77. Ibid., 42; Amnesty International, *Restrictions on Freedom of Expression in Cuba*, 10–11; and Evenson, *Law and Society in Contemporary Cuba*, 84–85. See also Human Rights Watch, *Cuba: New Castro, Same Cuba; Political Prisoners in the Post-Fidel Era* (New York, November 2009), 4, 28–31.

78. Amnesty International, *Cuba: The Human Rights Situation*, December 1990, 2; and *Human Rights in Cuba: The Need to Sustain the Pressure, an Americas Watch Report* (New York: Americas Watch Committee, 1989), 86–88.

79. Ian Daniels, "Interview with Ana María Simó," *The Torch*, December 15, 1984–January 14, 1985, 8.

80. Human Rights Watch, *Cuba's Repressive Machinery*, 66–68.

81. Evenson, *Law and Society in Contemporary Cuba*, 78.

82. See, for example, Lumsden, *Machos, Maricones and Gays*, xix–xx.

83. Ignacio Ramonet, *Fidel Castro: Biografía a dos voces* (Barcelona: Random House Mondadori, 2006), 486.

84. Fidel Castro interview by Lee Lockwood, *Playboy*, January 1967, 74.

85. "En Cuba hay actualmente 167 presos políticos, según comisión opositora DDHH," Efe dispatch, *El Nuevo Herald*, 5 julio 2010, www.elnuevoherald.com/2010/07/05/759778/en-cuba-hay-actualmente-167-presos.html; "Represión: Elizardo Sánchez; Hubo más de dos mil detenciones de corta duración en 2010," Agencias/La Habana, *Diario de Cuba*, 11 enero 2011, diariodecuba.com; and Patricia Grogg, "DDHH-Cuba: Oposición crítica situación de presos," Reportaje de IPS, *Cuba a la Mano*, 27 enero 2011, http://cubaalamano.net/sitio/client/report.php?id=1242.

86. Those released dissidents who refused to be exiled were placed under a form of probation.

"Disidentes estiman que aún quedan unos cincuenta presos politicos," *cubaencuentro*, 9 abril 2011, www.cubanencuentro.com.

87. Roy Walmsley, *World Prison Population List*, 8th ed. (London: International Centre for Prison Studies, King's College, 2009), www.kcl.ac.uk/depsta/law/research/icps/downloads/wppl_8th_4l.pdf.

88. Evenson, *Law and Society in Contemporary Cuba*, 130.

89. Patricia Grogg, "Pena de muerte: Cuba reafirma moratoria de hecho," Reportaje de IPS, *Cuba a la mano*, 9 diciembre 2010, http://cubaalamano.net/sitio/client/report.php?id=1223.

90. See for example the report by Agence-France Press about Ricardo Alarcón, president of the National Assembly of People's Power, denying that there are political prisoners in Cuba. "Alarcón niega la existencia de presos políticos en la isla," *El Nuevo Herald*, 11 febrero 2009.

91. Mario Mencía wrote an informative book about this experience under the title *The Fertile Prison: Fidel Castro in Batista's Jails* (Melbourne, Australia: Ocean Press, 1993).

92. Armando Valladares, *Against All Hope: The Prison Memoirs of Armando Valladares*, trans. Andrew Hurley (New York: Knopf, distributed by Random House, 1986).

93. Jorge Valls, *Twenty Years and Forty Days: Life in a Cuban Prison* (New York: Americas Watch Committee, 1986).

94. General Arnaldo Ochoa was one of the few people to be given the title "Hero of the Revolution" and was a veteran of the struggle against Batista who also fought in Angola and Nicaragua. He and three other high-ranking Cuban military officers were accused of narcotics trafficking and tried and executed in 1989. To this day, many doubts remain as to whether those were the real reasons for the executions and whether the Castro brothers were not fully aware of what was going on and had not themselves acquiesced to the trafficking, most of the proceeds of which went to Cuban state coffers.

95. Joseph P. Morray, *The Second Revolution in Cuba* (New York: Monthly Review Press, 1963), 38.

96. It is worth mentioning in this context the great impact in Cuba and Latin America of the long interview that Frei Betto, a Brazilian Catholic priest, conducted with Fidel Castro. See Frei Betto, *Fidel Castro y la religión: Conversaciones con Frei Betto* (Mexico City: Siglo XXI Editores, 1986).

97. For an informative and interesting account of how censorship worked inside a Cuban newspaper in the years 2003–2006, see Yusimi Rodríguez, "Freedom of the Press in Cuba," *HavanaTimes.org*, December 8, 2010, www.havanatimes.org/?p=34228.

98. *Weekly Granma Review*, December 17, 1989, 3, as cited by Marvin Leiner in *Sexual Politics in Cuba: Machismo, Homosexuality and AIDS* (Boulder, CO: Westview Press, 1994), 163, 170.

99. In connection with this incident, the Cuban embassy in Pakistan acknowledged in a press release that since 2007 "grave violations of discipline" have been committed by a small group of students "including disrespect for their professors, disregard to the Cuban authorities, failing to attend class, misbehavior, physical aggressions and verbal offenses among the students and, essentially, teaching strikes along with acts of violence." See "Press Release by Cuban Embassy, Islamabad," n.d., www.hec.gov.pk/.../ScholarshipsforGeneralMedicineStudiesCS2007BII/.../Press%20Release,%20Embassy%20of%20Cuba.pdf. See also Juan O. Tamayo, "Cuba: Video Shows Armed Cuban Police Breaking Up Student Protest," *Miami Herald*, September 10, 2010, www.miamiherald.com/2010/09/10/1816918/students-strike-in-cuba-draws.html.

100. Ray Otero, "The Disturbing Frederich Cepeda Case," *HavanaTimes.org*, November 20, 2010, www.havanatimes.org/?p=33437; Luis López Viera, "Frederich Cepeda jugará con Sancti Spíritus 50 Serie Nacional de béisbol," *Juventud Rebelde*, 23 noviembre 2010, www.juventudrebelde.cu; and Circles Robinson, "Cuba Baseball Star Cepeda to Return," *HavanaTimes.org*, November 23, 2010, www.havanatimes.org/?p=33608.

101. For many more examples of the censorship practiced by the ICRT in Cuba, see Alexis

Castañeda Pérez de Alejo, "Si no creyera en la esperanza," *Rebelión*, 25 enero 2009, www.rebelion.org/noticia.php?id=79626.

102. Martín Medem, *¿Por qué no me enseñaste?*, 169.

103. Ian Urbina, "In Cuba, Change Means More of the Same, with Control at the Top," *New York Times*, April 6, 2009.

104. Juan O. Tamayo, "Periodista cubano critica estricto control sobre la información en la isla," *El Nuevo Herald*, 20 octubre 2009, www.elnuevoherald.com/noticias/america_latina/cuba/story/569675.html.

105. Yoani Sánchez was for the *eighth* time denied permission to travel abroad in September 2010. Yoani Sánchez, "En ninguna parte, pero en todas," *Generación Y*, 26 septiembre 2010.

106. "Cuba no permite viaje de Fariñas a recibir premio Sajarov," Associated Press, 14 diciembre 2010.

107. Human Rights Watch, *Cuba: New Castro, Same Cuba*, 100–101. Fernando Ravsberg, the left-wing BBC correspondent in Havana, has discussed some of the absurdities and corruption involved in obtaining a permit to leave Cuba in "Los desertores," BBC Mundo, *Cartas desde Cuba*, February 18, 2010, www.bbc.co.uk/blogs/mundo/cartas_desde_cuba/2010/02/los_desertores.html. For a thorough account of the Cuban government's rules and limitations on travel, see Haroldo Dilla Alfonso, "¿Y qué hacemos con los cubanos emigrados?," *Periódico 7 Días*, 6 febrero 2009, www.7días.com.do/app/article.aspx?id+43636.

108. Lars Schoultz, *That Infernal Little Republic: The United States and the Cuban Revolution* (Chapel Hill: University of North Carolina Press, 2009), 539 and Martín Medem, *¿Por qué no me enseñaste?*, 81–82.

109. Human Rights Watch, *Cuba: New Castro, Same Cuba*, 9.

110. Martín Medem, *¿Por qué no me enseñaste?*, 87–88. For the role and activities of Cuban government agents among the dissidents arrested and sentenced in 2003, see also Daniel P. Erikson, *The Cuba Wars: Fidel Castro, the United States and the Next Revolution* (New York: Bloomsbury Press, 2008), 65–68.

111. Martín Medem, *¿Por qué no me enseñaste?*, 78–81, 117, 120.

112. Human Rights Watch, *Cuba's Repressive Machinery*, 62–65.

113. "Dictatorship of the Proletariat and Socialist Democracy," in *Resolutions of the Twelfth World Congress of the Fourth International (January 1985)*, International Viewpoint, special issue, n.d., 83.

114. Francis Fukuyama, *The End of History and the Last Man* (New York: Maxwell Macmillan International, 1992).

115. For an in-depth discussion of this problem in the context of the Russian Revolution, see chapters 6 and 7 of Farber, *Before Stalinism*.

116. My discussion and analysis here address the phenomena of successful Communist revolutions and the ideological justifications they have used to maintain what I called systematic surplus repression. Other historical situations such as those confronted by the Spanish Civil War in the thirties or Allende's Chile in the seventies require a different discussion, particularly in regard to the totally justified fear of the consequences of the victory of reaction.

117. Friedrich Engels, *The Peasant War in Germany*, trans. and ed. Vic Schneierson (Moscow: Progress Publishers, 1974), 115.

Chapter Two: Economic Development and the Standard of Living since the 1959 Revolution

1. This includes a perforation platform built in China that was supposed to arrive in Cuba in the summer of 2011, opening the way for large-scale exploration of as-yet untapped

crude oil deposits by a consortium led by the Spanish Repsol YPF. "A la espera de platarforma china para explorar en agues del golfo," Efe, La Habana, 5 abril 2010.

2. In 2010, for the first time in its history, Cuba received more than two million foreign visitors by the end of October, representing a growth of 3.4 percent. However, a greater number of tourists may translate into less income for Cuba (i.e., tourists buying less expensive packages), as has been typically happening under the impact of the world recession that began in 2008. "Turismo llegada de visitantes internacionales," O.N.E. (Organización Nacional de Estadísticas, República de Cuba), www.one.cu/publicaciones/06turismoycomercio/llegadadevisitantes/mensual/4.pdf; and "Nuevo récord en arribo de turistas a Cuba," *Cuba a la Mano*, 20 noviembre 2010, http://cubaalamano.net/sitio/client/brief.php?id=8544.

3. Estimates of the amount of remittances vary widely, but in 2003 the Economic Commission for Latin America estimated them at $915 million. See Carmelo Mesa-Lago and Jorge Pérez-López, *Cuba's Aborted Reform: Socioeconomic Effects, International Comparisons, and Transition Policies* (Gainesville: University Press of Florida, 2005), 35.

4. It is interesting to note that in a major speech at the end of 2010, Raúl Castro mocked the tendency of supporters of the regime to blame all the economic ills of the island on the US economic blockade. "Discurso pronunciado por el General del Ejército Raúl Castro Ruz, Presidente de los Consejos de Estado y de Ministros, en la clausura del Sexto Período Ordinario de Sesiones de la Séptima Legislatura de la Asamblea Nacional del Poder Popular, en el Palacio de Convenciones, el 18 de diciembre de 2010, 'Año 52 de la Revolución,' *Granma* 14, no. 354, www.granma.co.cu/2010/12/19/nacional/artic10.html.

5. Omar Everleny Pérez Villanueva, "The Cuban Economy Today and Its Future Challenges," in *The Cuban Economy at the Start of the Twenty-First Century*, ed. Jorge I. Domínguez, Omar Everleny Pérez Villanueva, and Lorena Barbería (Cambridge, MA: David Rockefeller Center for Latin American Studies, Harvard University Press, 2004), 53.

6. Carmelo Mesa-Lago, *Market, Socialist, and Mixed Economies: Comparative Policy and Performance; Chile, Cuba, and Costa Rica* (Baltimore: Johns Hopkins University Press, 2000), 211–12.

7. "Discurso pronunciado por el General de Ejército Raúl Castro Ruz."

8. Ronald Suárez Rivas, "Los caminos del absurdo," *Diario Granma* 14, no. 44 (13 febrero 2010), www.granma.co.cu/2010/02/13/nacional/artic01.html.

9. Freddy Pérez Cabrera, "Cuesta trabajo pensar," *Granma*, 4 junio 2010, 16.

10. Yailin Orta Rivera et al., "Crisis económica mundial también afecta economía cubana," *Juventud Rebelde*, 14 junio 2009, www.juventudrebelde.cu.

11. Carmelo Mesa-Lago, *Cuba in the 1970s: Pragmatism and Institutionalization*, rev. ed. (Albuquerque: University of New Mexico Press, 1978), 34–35.

12. Yailin Orta Rivera, "Especialistas y funcionarios cubanos analizan cómo la Isla puede enfrentar la crisis mundial," *Juventud Rebelde*, 21 junio 2009, www.juventudrebelde.cu.

13. Yaima Puig Meneses, "¿Doble turno o segundo tropiezo?," *Granma*, 28 octubre 2009, 3.

14. Marianela Martín González, "Los pies en el suelo ¿y el grito en el cielo?" *Juventud Rebelde*, 22 agosto 2009, www.juventudrebelde.cu/cuba/2009–08–22/los-pies-en-el-suelo-y-el-grito-en-el-cielo/.

15. Along these lines, Carmelo Mesa-Lago reported that in Cuba from 1966 to 1970 the "inefficient use of capital" was exacerbated by a number of factors including "the emphasis on fixing output targets in physical terms." Mesa-Lago, *Cuba in the 1970s*, 34.

16. Fernando Ravsberg, "La resistencia pasiva," BBC Mundo, *Cartes desde Cuba*, 24 diciembre 2009, http://www.bbc.co.uk/blogs/mundo/cartas_desde_cuba/2009/12/la_resistencia_pasiva.html.

17. Omar Everleny Pérez Villanueva, as cited in Martín González, "Los pies en el suelo."

18. Roberto Campbell Tross, a professor of political economy in Ciego de Avila, Cuba, as told

to Yalín Orta Rivera et al. in "Crisis económica mundial también afecta economía cubana."

19. Fernando Ravsberg, "Los detalles," BBC Mundo, *Cartas desde Cuba*, 23 septiembre 2010, http://www.bbc.co.uk/blogs/mundo/cartas_desde_cuba/2010/09/los_detalles.html.

20. Silvia Martínez Fuentes, "Productividad del trabajo: Entre el ser y el deber," *Diario Granma* 14, no. 36 (5 febrero 2010), www.granma.co.cu/2010/02/05/nacional/artic06.html.

21. Robert E. Quirk, *Fidel Castro* (New York: Norton, 1993), 623–29.

22. René Dumont, *Is Cuba Socialist?* (New York: Viking Press, 1974), 108.

23. Martín Medem, *¿Por qué no me enseñaste?*, 248.

24. Carmelo Mesa-Lago, "Cincuenta años de servicios sociales en Cuba," *Temas*, no. 64, octubre–diciembre 2010, www.temas.cult.cu.

25. Carmelo Mesa-Lago, "La veleta económica cubana: Huracanes internos, crisis mundial y perspectivas con Obama," *Encuentro de la Cultura Cubana* 51–52 (invierno–primavera 2009): 37.

26. Lourdes Pérez Navarro y Yaima Puig Meneses, "Transporte público: Invertir en la calidad," *Diario Granma* 13, no. 305 (31 octubre 2009), www.granma.co.cu/2009/10/31/nacional/artic02.html. For a discussion of similar problems in national interurban transport see Pastor Batista Valdés, "Omnibus nacionales: Ni un boleto más para la impunidad," *Granma*, 18 septiembre 2009, 16.

27. R. Pérez Vera, "Vale la pena analizar nuevos cambios de gestión," letter to the editor, *Granma*, 5 noviembre 2010, 12.

28. Carmelo Mesa-Lago, "La paradoja económica cubana," *El País* (Madrid), July 12, 2009 as reproduced in *Correspondencia de Prensa*, Agenda Radical-Colectivo Militante, 25 julio 2009.

29. Jacques Sapir, "The Economics of War in the Soviet Union during World War II," in *Stalinism and Nazism: Dictatorships in Comparison*, ed. Ian Kershaw and Moshe Lewin (Cambridge: Cambridge University Press, 1977), 227–28.

30. One of these ad hoc economic interventions was the expensive renovation of the School of Law of the University of Havana, which Castro attended in the late forties.

31. Joseph L. Scarpaci Jr., "Winners and Losers in Restoring Old Havana," in *Cuba in Transition*, vol. 10, Papers and Proceedings of the Tenth Annual Meeting of the Association for the Study of the Cuban Economy (ASCE), Miami, Florida, August 3–5, 2000, 290–93.

32. Charles E. Lindblom, *Politics and Markets: The World's Political-Economic Systems* (New York: Basic Books, 1977), 65–75.

33. However, since they are paid in pesos, pensions have become grossly inadequate since the Special Period that began in the early nineties. Because of demographic changes leading to a growing dependency rate, the government recently increased the age of retirement to sixty-five years for men and sixty for women (from sixty for men and fifty-five for women). Although this is still generous by international standards, the government failed to address the more fundamental issues of why young couples don't want to have children (the cause of worsening dependent-to-employed-citizen rates).

34. Mesa-Lago, "La veleta económica cubana," 36.

35. In the CPAs farmers pool their lands and work them together. In the CCSes farmers own and work their own land but join the cooperative for credit, purchasing, and marketing purposes. Jorge I. Domínguez, "Cuba's Economic Transition: Successes, Deficiencies and Challenges," in *The Cuban Economy*, ed. Domínguez, Pérez, and Barbería, 25–26.

36. Armando Nova González, CEEC (Centro para el Estudio de la Ecónomia Cubana), Universidad de la Habana, Cuba, "Valoración del impacto de las medidas más recientes en los resultados de la agricultura en Cuba," presentation at the conference "Cuba Futures Past and Present," Bildner Center for Western Hemisphere Studies, Graduate Center of the City University of New York, March 31–April 2, 2011.

37. This figure does not include the nonproductive personnel working in the UBPCs. See Juan Varela Pérez, "La agricultura necesita poner en orden sus fuerzas," *Diario Granma*, 10

noviembre 2009, www.granma.co.cu/2009/11/10/nacional/artic01.html. For more details on the characteristics and problems of the UBPCs see Juan Varela Pérez, "Unidades Basicas de Producción Cooperativa: Ni trabas ni tutelaje," *Granma*, 19 enero 2010, 3.

38. Since *perfeccionamiento* implies, in Cuban Spanish, a continuing process of aiming for perfection, I think it is appropriate to translate the term as "improvement" rather than as "perfection," which may suggest a finished process.

39. Varios autores, "¿Machucando en baja?," *Juventud Rebelde*, 30 enero 2010, www.juventudrebelde .cu/cuba/2010–01–30/machucando-en-baja/.

40. The article also described other problems in those enterprises such as the lack of autonomy of the local managers and the irrationalities caused by decisions imposed by the central authorities. Lisván Lescaille Durand, Yailin Orta Rivera, and Haydée León, "Vísteme despacio," *Juventud Rebelde*, 6 julio 2010, www.juventudrebelde.cu/cuba/2010–07–03/visteme-despacio/.

41. Sara Sariol Sosa, "Para que no desaparezcan los cafetales," *Diario Granma* 13, no. 288 (14 octubre 2009), www.granma.co.cu/2009/10/14/nacional/artic01.html.

42. Fernando Ravsberg, "El embudo agrícola," BBC Mundo, *Cartas desde Cuba*, 6 mayo 2010, www.bbc.co.uk/blogs/mundo/cartas_desde_cuba/2010/05/el_mundo_agricola_html.

43. Ibid.

44. Juan Varela Pérez, "Distribución y comercialización de productos agrícolas, No es borrón y cuenta nueva, pero se parece," *Diario Granma* 13, no. 194 (13 julio 2009), www.granma.co.cu/2009/07/13/nacional/artic05.html.

45. Juan Varela Pérez, "Baches en las tarimas, ¿pudieron aminorarse?," *Diario Granma* 14, no. 62 (3 marzo 2010), www.granma.cubaweb.cu/2010/03/03/nacional/artic02.html.

46. Juan Varela Pérez, "Pasos perdidos en los envases agrícolas," *Granma*, 20 agosto 2010, 16.

47. Odalis Riquenes Cutiño, "¡Le zumba el mango!," *Juventud Rebelde*, 31 octubre 2009. www.juventudrebelde.cu/cuba/2009–10–31/le-zumba-el-mango/.

48. Leonardo Padura Fuentes, "Cuba: A Debate," IPS (Inter Press Service), September 28, 2010.

49. Yahily Hernández Porto, "Hay que ir al 'grano' en la cuestión del arroz en Cuba," *Juventud Rebelde*, 15 agosto 2009, www.juventudrebelde.cu. In addition to the issues mentioned above, this article notes other problems affecting rice production, such as the insufficient number of dryers to process the wet rice arriving from the fields and the perennial dangers of drought.

50. Pérez, "Baches en las tarimas ¿pudieron aminorarse?"

51. "Economía y desarrollo: Agricultura: La mesa vacía," IPS, 9 marzo 2010. http://cubaalamano .net/sitio/client/articulo_ips.php?id=87; Pérez, "Baches en las tarimas"; Juan O. Tamayo, "Cuban Farmers Seek Fewer Government Regulations," *Miami Herald*, May 18, 2010, miamiherald.com.

52. Cutiño, "¡Le zumba el mango!"

53. Mesa-Lago, "La veleta económica cubana," 40.

54. Reuters América Latina, "Cuba importaría mínimo de 250,000 toneladas de azúcar en 2007," 19 julio 2007; La Alborada mailing list, 20 julio 2007, www.cubamer.org, Washington, DC: Cuban American Alliance Education Fund.

55. Manuel Moreno Fraginals, *El ingenio: Complejo económico social cubano del azúcar* (Havana: Editorial de Ciencias Sociales, 1978), 3: 40. At least part of the relatively low sugar production figures of the fifties has to be attributed to the Cuban government's reduction of production in order to increase prices. This practice was also encouraged by international sugar agreements pursuing the same end.

56. Archibald R. M. Ritter, "Raúl Castro's New Economic Strategy: Context, Viability and Prospects," presentation to the Bildner Center for Western Hemisphere Studies, The Graduate Center, City University of New York, November 29, 2010, figure 3, chart 5,

"Cuban Sugar Production, 1985–2010."

57. Juan Varela Pérez, "Faltaron control y exigencia en la zafra," *Diario Granma* 14, no. 125 (5 mayo 2010), www.granma.co.cu/2010/05/05/nacional/artic01.html, and Juan Varela Pérez, "Industria azucarera: El síndrome del tiempo perdido," *Granma*, 10 marzo 2010, 2.

58. Jorge I. Domínguez, "Cuba's Economic Transition: Successes, Deficiencies and Challenges," in *The Cuban Economy*, ed. Domínguez, Peréz Villanueva, and Barbería, 31–32.

59. Oscar Espinosa Chepe, "Sin azúcar ni país," *Cuba Nuestra: Sociedad Civil*, 19 abril 2010, http://cubanuestra4eu.wordpress.com/2010/04/19/sin-aucar-ni-pais/. For a more in-depth and sober study of the environmental degradation of Cuban agriculture, particularly in the years since the revolution, see chapter 4, "Agriculture and the Environment," of Sergio Díaz-Briquets and Jorge Pérez-López, *Conquering Nature: The Environmental Legacy of Socialism in Cuba* (Pittsburgh: University of Pittsburgh Press, 2000), 79–110.

60. An article in the official press has claimed that during the seventies there was a significant effort to diversify the sugar industry with investments in more than a hundred sugar mills. The article goes on to blame the disappearance of the USSR in the nineties for the collapse of those efforts but says nothing about what happened in the eighties. However, the author was forced to recognize that the decline of sugar diversification was also due to "organizational violations, little motivation, and lack of rigor and standards in preserving the installed means of production. In that somber panorama, many plants remained paralyzed, a situation that endures until today to a greater or lesser degree." Juan Varela Pérez, "Los derivados al rescate de su corona," *Diario Granma, Ciencia y Tecnología*, 4 diciembre 2010, www.granma.co.cu/secciones/ciencia ytec/investigacion/investigacion59.htm.

61. Domingo Maximino Morales, "Cuba: Mi hora de discrepar," *kaosenlared.net*, 11 febrero 2010, www.kaosenlared.net/noticia/mi-hora-de-discrepar. It should be noted that while the ethanol industry in Brazil has been justly criticized for its replacement of agricultural products consumed by the population at large, that was not an issue in Cuba, where for a long time the sugar fields were abandoned and invaded by weeds (*marabú*).

62. Reuters, "Cuba Sugar Ministry to Be Shut in Reform," La Alborada mailing list, April 8, 2010, Washington, DC: Cuban American Alliance Education Fund, www.cubamer.org.

63. Report by Marino Murillo, minister of economy and planning, to the National Assembly of Peoples' Power on December 15, 2010. "Resultados económicos del año 2010 y propuesta de plan para el 2011: Acualización de la política tributaria," *Diario Granma* 14, no. 351 (16 diciembre 2010), www.granma.co.cu/2010/12/16/nacional/artic06.html.

64. Reuters, "Cuba Sugar Ministry to Be Shut."

65. "Hay que hacer producir la tierra, afirma Castro," *Cuba a la Mano*, 2 julio 2008; Andrea Rodriguez, "Cuba entrega tierras ociosas a campesinos," Associated Press, 18 julio 2008.

66. "El gobierno dice estar preocupado porque sólo el 6% de los trabajadores del campo son jóvenes," AFP dispatch reproduced in *cubaencuentro*, 20 mayo 2009.

67. Economics Press Service, "Agricultura: Cambio discreto en fisonomía de tierras ociosas," 14 julio 2009, *Cuba a la mano*, 11 agosto 2009, http://cubaalamano.net/sitio/client/article.php?id=11404.

68. Agencias, La Habana, *Diario de Cuba*, 18–19 abril 2011, www.diariodecuba.com.

69. Dora Pérez, Marianela Martín, Odalis Riquenes, Luis Raúl Vázquez, and Roberto Díaz, "La necesidad no tiene ciclo corto," *Juventud Rebelde*, 22 marzo 2009, www.juventudrebelde.cu/cuba/2009–03–22/la-necesidad-no-tiene-ciclo-corto/.

70. "Economía y desarrollo: Agricultura: La mesa vacía," and Pérez, "Baches en las tarimas ¿pudieron aminorarse?"

71. Paul Haven, "Cuba Admits Failure to Pay Farmers on Time," La Alborada mailing list, September 28, 2009, Washington, DC: Cuban American Alliance Education Fund, www.cubamer.org.

72. Hernández Porto, "Hay que ir al 'grano' en la cuestión del arroz en Cuba."

73. Varios autores, "¿Machucando en baja?"

74. Ravsberg, "El embudo agrícola."

75. Oficina Nacional de Estadísticas (O.N.E.), República de Cuba, Sector Agropecuario, Indicadores Seleccionados enero-septiembre 2010, www.one.cu/mensualprincipalesindicadoresagropecuario.htm.

76. "Discurso pronunciado por el General de Ejército Raúl Castro."

77. Fernando R. Funes Monzote, "Transgénicos en Cuba, necesidad urgente de una moratoria," *kaosenlared.net*, 12 agosto 2010, www.kaosenlared.net/noticia/transgenicos-cuba-necesidad-urgente-moratoria; Patricia Grogg, entrevista al agroecólogo Fernando Funes-Monzote, "Se abre debate cubano sobre transgénicos," reportaje de IPS, *Cuba a la Mano*, 5 octubre 2010, http://cubaalamano.net/sitio/client/report.php?id=1197.

78. According to *Granma*, thirty-nine municipalities were already involved in the "takeoff" stage of the suburban agriculture program by the summer of 2010. Juan Varela Pérez, "¿Despega la agricultura suburbana?, *Diario Granma* 14, no. 183 (1 julio 2010), www.granma.co.cu/2010/07/01/nacional/artico4.html.

79. Patricia Grogg, "Alimentación-Cuba: Agricultura sostenible desde los suburbios," reportaje de IPS, *Cuba a la Mano*, 29 abril 2010, http://cubaalamano.net/sitio/client/report.php?id=1143.

80. Thus, for example, in an exercise of political fiction, Richard Levins claims that urban agriculture "satisfied the need of the country for immediately available food when the economy collapsed after the loss of trade with the Soviet Union and Europe." He goes on to make similar claims for urban agriculture in terms of employment, simplification of distribution, supporting the aims of nutritionists, preservation of green areas, encouragement of neighborhood social interaction, protecting the health of agricultural workers, and restoring the metabolism between town and countryside. It is unlikely that even spokespeople for the Cuban government, who after all live in Cuba, would make such wild claims. Richard Levins, "How to Visit a Socialist Country," *Monthly Review* 61, no. 11 (April 2010): 8, www.monthlyreview.org/100401levins.php.

81. José Antonio Torres, "En la confianza está el peligro," *Diario Granma* 14, no. 130 (10 mayo 2010), www.granma.co.cu/2010/05/10/nacional/artic04.html.

82. Mario Coyula Cowley, "La ciudad del futuro o el futuro de la ciudad," *Temas*, octubre–diciembre 2006: 48, 51–52. For an informative account (with photographs) of garbage dumps by the side of roads in the Havana metropolitan area, see Erasmo Calzadilla, "On the Outskirts of Town with Bruno," *HavanaTimes.org*, January 18, 2011, www.havanatimes.org/?p=36267. *Granma* has complained about how mountains of garbage have even interfered with railroad traffic in central Cuba, let alone being eyesores. Freddy Pérez Cabrera, "¿Hasta cuándo esta indisciplina?," *Diario Granma* 15, no. 27 (27 enero 2011), www.granma.co.cu/2011/01/27/nacional/artic01.html.

83. "U.S. Remains Top Food Source for Cuba," Associated Press dispatch from Havana, reproduced in La Alborada mailing list, March 24, 2007, Washington, DC: Cuban American Alliance Education Fund, www.cubamer.org.

84. Wilfredo Cancio Isla, "Récord histórico en las ventas de E.U. a Cuba," *El Nuevo Herald* (Miami), 12 febrero 2009.

85. Marc Frank, "US Food Sales to Cuba in Steep Decline," Reuters, July 27, 2010. Reprinted in La Alborada mailing list, July 28, 2010, Washington, DC: Cuban American Alliance Education Fund, www.cubamer.org.

86. According to what the Cuban government calls conservative estimates, the direct damage to Cuba resulting from the US economic blockade up to December 2008 was more than 96 billion dollars. This amount would rise to more than 236 billion dollars if the calculation were made according to the present value of the US dollar. Ministerio de Relaciones Exteriores de Cuba, "Informe Cuba vs. Bloqueo 2008," September 18, 2009, www

.cubavsbloqueo.cu/Informe2009/index.html.

87. Jorge I. Domínguez, *To Make a World Safe for Revolution: Cuba's Foreign Policy* (Cambridge, MA: Harvard University Press, 1989), 191–92.

88. Mesa-Lago, *Market, Socialist, and Mixed Economies*, 609.

89. Ibid.

90. A common example pointing to the paradoxes of the GDP as an economic indicator is that the sicker a population is, the more it will consume medical services, thereby raising the GDP for that economy.

91. See, for example, Jon Gertner, "The Rise and Fall of the G.D.P." *New York Times Magazine*, May 16, 2010, 60–71; and "Economic Focus: Measuring What Matters," *Economist*, September 19, 2009, 86.

92. New Cuban adjustments to the GDP index give greater weight to the social services that were previously valued at cost, since they are freely provided to the public. Since 2004, "artificial fees" have been added for use in GDP calculation. This method has been debated, including within the UN Economic Commission on Latin America (ECLA), in terms of its validity and what it means for comparing the Cuban GDP internationally. Omar Everleny Pérez Villanueva and Pavel Vidal Alejandro, "Cuba's Economy: A Current Evaluation and Several Necessary Proposals," *Socialism and Democracy* 24, no. 1 (March 2010): 72.

93. Frank W. Thompson, "Reconsidering Cuban Economic Performance in Retrospect," paper delivered at the conference "The Measure of a Revolution: Cuba, 1959–2009," May 7–9, 2009, Queen's University, Kingston, Ontario, Canada, 3–4, 6, 7. Another version of this piece appeared under the title "The Economy after a Half-Century," *Against the Current*, July/August 2009, 18–19. These two in turn updated Thompson's original article titled "Cuban Economic Performance in Retrospect," *Review of Radical Political Economics* 37, no. 3 (Summer 2005). Thompson went to great lengths to deal with the serious difficulties posed by the comparisons of real GDP per capita in both their intergenerational and intertemporal dimensions. He relied most heavily on the empirical compilations of A. Maddison in *The World Economy: Historical Statistics* (Paris: Organization for Economic Cooperation and Development, 2003). Maddison in turn relied on the work of a number of other researchers.

94. Mesa-Lago and Pérez-López take a somewhat more conservative approach, suggesting that it would have taken at least until 2010 for the Cuban economy to recover its 1989 GDP per capita level (*Cuba's Aborted Reform*, 28). On the other hand, the dissident economist Oscar Espinosa Chepe thinks that the 1989 GDP level was probably reached after 2005. "Economía cubana: Expectativas y peligros," *Encuentro de la Cultura Cubana* (Madrid) 50 (otoño 2008): 214. Thompson, "Reconsidering Cuban Economic Performance in Retrospect," 7, has an estimate close to Espinosa Chepe's and thinks the 1985 levels were recovered in 2006.

95. Domínguez, "An Introductory Analysis," in *The Cuban Economy*, ed. Domínguez, Peréz Villanueva, and Barbería, 7.

96. Asamblea Nacional del Poder Popular, *Noticias del Parlamento*, 17 julio 2007.

97. Thompson, "Reconsidering Cuban Economic Performance in Retrospect," 4, 3.

98. Patricia Grogg, "Home Internet, Distant Dream in Cuba," *HavanaTimes.org*, November 17, 2010, www.havanatimes.org/?=33070.

99. Amnesty International, *Restrictions on Freedom of Expression in Cuba* (London, 2010), 7.

100. Anaysi Fernández, "Cadena de illegalidades," *Diario Granma* 15, no. 27 (27 enero 2011), www.granma.cubaweb.cu.

101. Internet World Stats, "Usage and Population Statistics," www.internetworldstats.com/stats10.htm.

102. "Limitado acceso privado a Internet en Cuba," *Cuba a la Mano*, 1 octubre 2010, http://cubaalamano.net.

103. Grogg, "Home Internet, Distant Dream in Cuba."

104. World Bank, "ICT at a Glance, Cuba." World Telecommunications Indicators Database, International Telecommunications Union, ONE (Oficina Nacional de Estadísticas), República de Cuba, *Tecnologías de la información y las comunicaciones (TIC) en cifras: Cuba 2009* (International Telecommunications Union [ITU], ICT Statistics, 2009); Gerardo Arreola, "En dos años se triplicaron las líneas de celular en Cuba," *La Jornada* (Mexico City), 3 abril 2010, 30; and Marc Frank, "Cuba Reports Little Internet and Telecom Progress," Reuters, June 18, 2010.

105. Amaury E. del Valle, "Cuba tiene más celulares que teléfonos fijos," *Juventud Rebelde*, 14 julio 2010, www.juventudrebelde.cu.

106. For example, Thomas Pogge has shown how the HDI continues to rely on GDP per capita figures with all their attendant deficiencies in comparing countries with very different income distributions. Thomas Pogge, *Politics as Usual: What Lies behind the Pro-Poor Rhetoric* (Cambridge: Polity Press, 2010), 86–90.

107. The indicators in the UN Millennium Declaration of the year 2000, with the purpose of achieving by the year 2015 such goals as universal primary education, elimination of extreme poverty and hunger, promotion of gender equality, and obtaining environmental sustainability, are of course broader in range than the HDI. However, they still do not address or measure most of the economic problems faced by the great majority of Cubans. See Millennium Development Goals Indicators, http://unstats.un.org/unsd/mdg/Host.aspx?Content=Indicators/OfficialList.htm.

108. Lianet Arias Sosa y Lourdes Pérez Navarro, "Salideros: ¿Con el agua al cuello?" *Granma*, 9 enero 2010, 4; Livia Rodríguez Delis, "Asignar y controlar el agua en el Plan de Economía," *Diario Granma* 14, no. 356 (21 diciembre 2010), http://granma.co.cu/2010/12/21/nacional/artic06.html; and "Déficit de agua afecta a capital cubana," *Cuba a la Mano*, 21 enero 2011, http://cubaalamano.net/sitio/client/brief.php?id=8723.

109. Daisy Valera, "Looking for Food," *HavanaTimes.org*, November 5, 2010, www.havanatimes.org/?=32469.

110. Daisy Valera, "A Bus Station as Metaphor," *HavanaTimes.org*, August 7, 2010, www.havanatimes.org/?p=27498.

111. In fact, in 2010 Cuba was listed under the category "Other Countries and Territories" rather than ranked together with the great majority of countries. Nevertheless, Cuba's performance was rated as doing relatively well in some indices (e.g., education) and badly in others (e.g., access to the Internet): 2010 *UNDP Human Development Report*, http://hdr.undp.org/en/media/HDR_2010_EN_Complete.pdf .

112. Mesa-Lago and Pérez-López, chap. 4, "Cuba and the Human Development Index," in *Cuba's Aborted Reform*, 111–30.

113. United Nations Development Programme, *Human Development Report 2009, Overcoming Barriers: Human Mobility and Development* (New York: United Nations, 2009), 179.

114. Lorena Barbería, Xavier de Souza Briggs, and Miren Uriarte, "Commentary: The End of Egalitarianism? Economic Inequality and the Future of Social Policy in Cuba," in *The Cuban Economy*, ed. Domínguez, Pérez, and Barbería, 302–03.

115. Mesa-Lago and Pérez-López, *Cuba's Aborted Reform*, 83.

116. María Elena Benítez Pérez, *La familia cubana en la segunda mitad del siglo XX* (Havana: Editorial de Ciencias Sociales, 2003), 62.

117. However, the revolutionary government had to contend with the sudden exit of a large number of doctors right after the victory of the revolution in the early sixties.

118. Jorge Ibarra, *Prologue to Revolution: Cuba, 1898–1958*, trans. Marjorie Moore (Boulder, CO: Lynne Rienner, 1998), 173.

119. Sergio Díaz-Briquets, *The Health Revolution in Cuba* (Austin: University of Texas Press, 1983), 20–21.

120. Ibid., 28–33.

121. Marifeli Pérez-Stable, *The Cuban Revolution: Origins, Course, and Legacy*, 2nd ed. (New York: Oxford University Press, 1999), 29.

122. Rafael Muci Mendoza, "Neuropatia óptica epidémica cubana: Parte II, Aspectos neuro-oftalmológicos, neurológicos, nutricionales e históricos," *Gaceta Médica de Caracas* 110, no. 2 (abril–junio 2002): 188–93.

123. Redacción Digital, "Logra Cuba tasa de 4,8 de mortalidad infantil en 2009," *Juventud Rebelde*, 4 enero 2010, www.juventudrebelde.cu; Redacción CE, "Mortalidad infantil menor en Cuba que en Estados Unidos," *cubaencuentro*, 26 abril 2010, www.cubaencuentro.com. It was also reported that by the end of 2010 the infant mortality rate had further declined to 4.5 for every 1,000 infants born alive. IPS, "Cuba reporta menor tasa de mortalidad infantil de su historia," *Cuba a la Mano*, 3 enero 2011, http://cubaalamano.net/sitio/client/brief.php?id=8665.

Some critics have argued that Cuba's low infant mortality rates are artificially boosted by statistical manipulation: premature babies who fail to survive, and those who die shortly after birth as a result of having acquired infectious diseases or such illnesses as diarrhea and meningitis, are reclassified as having died in the womb. Michel Suárez, "Un 'timo' mundial," *Diario de Cuba*, 5 mayo 2010, www.diariodecuba.net/cuba/81-cuba/1474-un-timo-mundial.html .

124. Mesa-Lago, "La veleta económica cubana," 37.

125. Mesa-Lago and Pérez-López, *Cuba's Aborted Reform*, 84.

126. Ibid., 84–85.

127. Jorge I. Domínguez, "Cuba's Economic Transition: Successes, Deficiencies, and Challenges," in *The Cuban Economy*, ed. Donínguez, Pérez, and Babería, 21.

128. Anneris Ivette Leyva, "Controlados en descontrol," *Granma*, 9 junio 2009, 4.

129. Letter from A. S. González León, "El negocio de las almohadillas sanitarias," *Granma*, 9 mayo 2008, 11.

130. F. Alonso Amaya, "¿Por qué permitimos estas cosas que no tienen que ver con recursos?," *Granma*, 16 octubre 2009, 11.

131. Padura also called attention to the teacher who takes what is offered by parents interested in their children receiving good grades. Leonardo Padura, "Inside Cuba: Mystery Island," *In These Times*, December 2, 2009, 3A.

132. See a detailed discussion of this issue in Elizabeth Kath, *Social Relations and the Cuban Health Miracle* (New Brunswick, NJ: Transaction, 2010), 143–53.

133. Roberto Veiga González, "Entrevista a Carmelo Mesa-Lago: Estoy disponible para servir a mi patria," *Espacio Laical* (Havana) 1 (2009): 62.

134. Ministerio de Salud Pública, "Información a la población," *Diario Granma*, 15 enero 2010, www.granma.cubasi.cu/2010/01/15/nacional/artic20.html.

135. It remains to be seen whether the public admission of the many deaths at Havana's psychiatric hospital marks a step forward from the regime's past practice of attempting to hide unfavorable health events such as the outbreak of dengue fever in Oriente Province in 1997. See Katherine Hirschfeld, *Health, Politics and Revolution in Cuba since 1898* (New Brunswick, NJ: Transaction, 2007), 3–4.

136. Fernando Ravsberg, ". . . Las verdades que se callan . . ." BBC Mundo, *Cartas desde Cuba*, enero 2011, www.bbc.co.uk/blogs/mundo/cartas_desde_cuba/2011/01/las_verdades_que_se_callan.html.

137. "Sancionados los responsables de los hechos ocurridos en el Hospital Psiquiátrico de La Habana," *Diario Granma* 15, no. 32 (1 febrero 2011), www.granma.co.cu/2011/02/01/nacional/artic05.html.

138. Fernando Ravsberg, "Los recursos de la salud," BBC Mundo, *Cartas desde Cuba*, 29 abril 2010, www.bbc.co.uk/blogs/mundo/cartas_desde_cuba/2010/04/los_recursos_de_la_salud.html.

139. Ibarra, *Prologue to Revolution*, 173. Note the contrast between Cuban prerevolutionary educational realities and the ignorant clichés spouted by foreign apologists for the Cuban government. For example, the noted critic Susan Sontag even claimed, during her Fidelista political phase in the late sixties, that almost all Cubans were illiterate when the revolution came to power! Sontag, "Some Thoughts on the Right Way (for Us) to Love the Cuban Revolution," 14.

140. Ibarra, *Prologue to Revolution*, 162; Agrupación Católica Universitaria, *Encuesta de trabajadores rurales, 1956–57*, reprinted in *Economía y desarrollo* (Instituto de Economía de la Universidad de la Habana) July–August 1972, 206.

141. For a detailed discussion of imperial and uneven economic development in Cuba and its consequences, see chapter 1 of Farber, *The Origins of the Cuban Revolution Reconsidered*.

142. Ernesto Che Guevara, "Sobre el sistema presupuestario de financiamiento," in *Escritos económicos* (Córdoba, Argentina: Cuadernos del Pasado y Presente, 1969), 41.

143. Carmelo Mesa-Lago, *The Economy of Socialist Cuba: A Two-Decade Appraisal* (Albuquerque: University of New Mexico Press, 1981): 164. Thus, the original claims that the 1961 literacy campaign had almost eliminated illiteracy were probably based on wishful thinking, inaccurate data, or a deliberate distortion of the facts.

144. Ibid., 165–66.

145. Ibid., 165.

146. Mesa-Lago and Pérez-López, *Cuba's Aborted Reform*, 87.

147. Domínguez, "Cuba's Economic Transition: Successes, Deficiencies, and Challenges," 21.

148. Dora Pérez, Margarita Barrio, Yahily Hernández, and Jesús Arencibia, "Repasador por cuenta ¿impropia?," *Juventud Rebelde*, 30 marzo 2008, www.juventudrebelde.cu/cuba/2008–03–30/repasador–por cuenta-impropia/.

149. Julio Franco, "Réquiem por el idioma," *cubaencuentro*, 21 julio 2009, www.cubaencuentro .com/es/cuba/articulos/requiem-por-el-idioma-195369; IPS, "Persiste déficit de docentes en la capital cubana," *Cuba a la Mano*, 18 septiembre 2009; and "Decide el Gobierno Revolucionario un incremento salarial para el sector de la educación," *Granma*, 2 julio 2009, 3.

150. Margarita Barrios, "Un curso escolar marcado por las transformaciones," *Juventud Rebelde*, 20 julio 2010, www.juventudrebelde.cu.

151. Luis Felipe Rojas Rosabal, "Retoques a la educación," *cubaencuentro*, 28 agosto 2010.

152. Dora Pérez Sáez, "Cambios promueven la calidad de la educación en Cuba," *Juventud Rebelde*, 14 diciembre 2010, http://juventudrebelde.cu/.

153. Mesa-Lago and and Pérez-López, *Cuba's Aborted Reform*, 87–88.

154. Ibid., 89.

155. Ibid., 90.

156. For an interesting account by a Swedish anthropologist of how and why Cuban families engage in illegal activity in order to make ends meet, see Mona Rosendahl, "Household Economy and Morality during the Special Period," in *Globalization and Third World Socialism: Cuba and Vietnam*, ed. Claes Brundenius and John Weeks (Houndmills, UK: Palgrave, 2001), 86–101.

157. I should note, however, that while his explanations were identical to those of the "culture of poverty," Castro did not use those exact terms.

158. Ramonet, *Fidel Castro: Biografía*, 211.

159. See, for example, Charles A. Valentine's *Culture and Poverty: Critique and Counter-Proposals* (Chicago: University of Chicago Press, 1968); and Eleanor Burke Leacock, ed., *The Culture of Poverty: A Critique* (New York: Simon and Schuster, 1971).

160. Susan M. Rigdon, *Art, Science, and Politics in the Work of Oscar Lewis: The Culture Façade* (Urbana: University of Illinois Press, 1988), 104.

161. Ramonet, *Fidel Castro: Biografía*, 365.

162. Ibid., 365–67.

163. Raquel Marrero Yanes, "Viernes de la ortografía," *Diario Granma* 13, no. 310 (5 noviembre 2009), www.granma.co.cu/2009/11/05/nacional/artic02.html.

164. Leticia Martínez Hernández, "Universidad cubana para todos, pero con calidad," *Diario Granma* 13, no. 204 (22 julio 2009), www.granma.co.cu/2009/07/22/nacional/artic05.html.

165. Margarita Barrios, "Cómo acceder a la universidad," *Juventud Rebelde*, 21 enero 2011, www.juventudrebelde.cu/cuba/2011-01-21/como-acceder-a-la-unversidad/; and "Cuba eleva requerimientos para educación superior," *Cuba a la Mano*, 22 enero 2011.

166. Martínez Hernández, "Universidad cubana para todos, pero con calidad."

167. Joel Mayor Lorán, "Rigor en la enseñanza universitaria," *Granma*, 11 septiembre 2009, 5.

168. Joel Mayor Lorán, "Habrá que estudiar para entrar a la universidad," *Diario Granma* 13, no. 212 (30 julio 2009), www.granma.co.cu/2009/07/30/nacional/artic06.html.

169. "Ministro pide eficiencia a universidades," *Cuba a la Mano*, 13 enero 2011.

170. Martínez Hernández, "Universidad cubana para todos, pero con calidad."

171. Joel Mayor Lorán, "¿La universidad da la espalda a la tierra?," *Diario Granma* 13, no. 314 (9 noviembre 2009), www.granma.co.cu/2009/11/09/nacional/artic01.html.

172. Mesa-Lago, "Cincuenta años de servicios sociales en Cuba."

173. Joel Mayor Lorán, "Formación laboral: Una ardua misión para la escuela," *Diario Granma* 14, no. 153, 2 junio 2010, www.granma.cubaweb.cu/2010/06/02/nacional/artic03.html.

174. Raúl Castro, "Es preciso caminar hacia el futuro, con paso firme y seguro, porque sencillamente no tenemos derecho a equivocarnos," in "Discurso pronunciado por el General del Ejército Raúl Castro," 3.

175. Margarita Barrios, "Después de la secundaria, ¿qué estudiaremos?," *Juventud Rebelde*, 6 marzo 2010, www.juventudrebelde.cu/cuba/2010–03–06/despues-de-la-secundaria-que-estudiaremos.

176. Alina M. Lotti and María de las Nieves Galá, "¿La última carta de la baraja?," *Trabajadores*, 9 mayo 2010, www.trabajadores.cu/news/5/9/bfla-ultima-carta-de-la-baraja.

177. Claes Brundenius, *Revolutionary Cuba: The Challenge of Economic Growth with Equity* (Boulder, CO: Westview Press, 1984), 13.

178. Mesa-Lago, *The Economy of Socialist Cuba*. 121.

179. José Luis Rodríguez, "La economía neocolonial cubana," *Cuba Socialista* 37 (enero–febrero 1989): 121.

180. Louis A. Pérez Jr., *Cuba: Between Reform and Revolution*, 3rd ed. (New York: Oxford University Press, 2006), 228.

181. Mesa-Lago, *The Economy of Socialist Cuba*, 121–22.

182. Ibid., 122; Mesa-Lago, "Búsqueda: El desempleo en Cuba; De oculto a visible," 59.

183. Mesa-Lago, *The Economy of Socialist Cuba*, 122; and Brundenius, *Revolutionary Cuba*, 127.

184. Mesa-Lago, "Búsqueda: El desempleo en Cuba; De oculto a visible," 59.

185. Mesa-Lago, *The Economy of Socialist Cuba*, 124.

186. Fidel Castro, "Resumén de la concentración de trabajadores por la batalla del sexto grado," *El Mundo*, 22 noviembre 1964, 11; "Clausura de curso del Instituto," 12; and "En el IV aniversario de la creación de los CDRs," *Obra Revolucionaria*, septiembre 1964, 19–20, as cited in Mesa-Lago, *The Economy of Socialist Cuba*, 127, 221.

187. Mesa-Lago, "Búsqueda: El desempleo en Cuba; De oculto a visible," 59.

188. Mesa-Lago and Pérez-López, *Cuba's Aborted Reform*, 49–50.

189. Statement by the Minister of Justice of the Republic of Cuba María Esther Reus to the 4th Session of the Working Group on the Universal Periodic Review, Human Rights Council, Geneva, February 5, 2009, www.cubaminrex.cu.

190. Agence-France Presse, "Unos 280,000 jóvenes no trabajan, según un sondeo," March 27, 2008.

191. Gusel Ortiz Cano, Julieta García Rios, Osviel Castro Medel, and Lisván Lescalle Durand, "Empleo juvenil en Cuba. El Cuento de nunca acabar?," *Juventud Rebelde*, 25 noviembre 2007.

192. José Antonio Torres, "¿Cómo se comporta en Santiago la ubicación laboral de los jóvenes?," *Diario Granma* 13, no. 248 4 septiembre 2009, http://granma.co.cu/2009/09/04/nacional/artic06.html.
193. IPS, "Quinta parte de la población cubana no trabaja," *Cuba a la mano*, March 21, 2008.
194. Mesa-Lago and Pérez-López, *Cuba's Aborted Reform*, 50.
195. Mesa-Lago, "Búsqueda: El desempleo en Cuba: De oculto a visible," 60.
196. Ibid., 61.
197. Lourdes Pérez Navarro, "Cuestión de leyes: Indisciplina laboral o un problema por resolver," *Granma*, 11 febrero 2009, www.granma.cubaweb.cu/2009/02/11/nacional/artic04.html.
198. Mesa-Lago, *Market, Socialist, and Mixed Economies*, 193, 207, 225, 260–61, 286–87, 335–36.
299. Of course when we use the Gini coefficient we are necessarily focusing on monetary income alone, leaving aside the problem of nonmonetary income in Soviet-type societies.
200. Claes Brundenius and John Weeks, chap. 1, "Globalization and Third World Socialism," in *Globalization and Third World Socialism*, ed. Brundenius and Weeks (Houndsmill, UK: Palgrave, 2001), 15.
201. Rikke Fabienke, "Labour Markets and Income Distribution during Crisis and Reform" in *Globalization and Third World Socialism*, ed. Brundenius and Weeks, 103–04. The other estimate by Lía Añé was cited by Mesa-Lago and Pérez-López, *Cuba's Aborted Reform*, 72–73.
202. Ángela Ferriol, "Explorando nuevas estrategias para reducir la pobreza en el actual contexto internacional: Experiencia de Cuba." Paper presented at the Seminario Internacional Estrategias de Reducción de la Pobreza, CLACSO/CROP, Havana, cited by Mayra Espina Prieto, "Social Effects of Economic Adjustment: Equality, Inequality and Trends toward Greater Complexity in Cuban Society," in *The Cuban Economy*, 221.
203. Discurso de Raúl Castro a la VII Legislatura de la Asamblea Nacional del Poder Popular, 11 julio 2008, Cuba, Misión Permanente, http://embacuba.cubaminrex.cu/Default.aspx?tabid=8221.
204. Fabienke, "Labor Markets and Income Distribution during Crisis and Reform," 113–14.
205. Omar Everleny Pérez Villanueva and Pavel Vidal Alejandro, "Cuba's Economy: A Current Evaluation and Several Necessary Proposals," *Socialism and Democracy* 24, no. 1 (March 2010): 88.
206. Mesa-Lago, "La veleta económica cubana," 37.
207. Espina Prieto, "Social Effects of Economic Adjustment," in *The Cuban Economy*, ed. Domínguez, Pérez, and Barbería, 228.
208. The figure was provided by Cuban scholar Mayra P. Espina Prieto citing the work of the Cuban economist Ángela Ferriol, in Mayra P. Espino Prieto, chap. 5, "Structural Changes since the Nineties and New Research Topics on Cuban Society," in *Changes in Cuban Society since the Nineties*, ed. Joseph S. Tulchin, Lilian Bobea, Mayra P. Espina Prieto, and Rafael Hernández, with the collaboration of Elizabeth Bryan, Woodrow Wilson Center Reports on the Americas 15 (Washington, DC: Woodrow Wilson Center International Center for Scholars, Latin American Program, n.d.), 92.
209. Cited in Mesa-Lago and Pérez-López, *Cuba's Aborted Reform*, 106.
210. Yenisel Rodríguez Pérez, "Living in the Street," *HavanaTimes.org*, July 6, 2010, www.havanatimes.org/?p=26024.
211. Espina Prieto, "Social Effects of Economic Adjustment," 230–38.
212. Yailín Orta Rivera and Norge Martínez Montero, "La vieja gran estafa," *Juventud Rebelde*, 1 octubre 2006.
213. María Julia Mayoral, "'Canibaleo' en las torres," *Granma*, 19 febrero 2007, 4–5; Ronald Suárez Rivas, "Angular Theft: A High Voltage Problem," *Diario Granma*, año 14, no. 90 (March 31, 2010) www.granma.co.cu/2010/03/31/nacional/artic01.html; and Yaima Puig Meneses, and Lázaro Barrero Medina, "Coto al desenfreno," *Granma*, 4 junio 2010, 10, 13.

214. Lianet Arias Sosa, "Telefonía pública: ¿A quién perjudica el vandalismo?," *Granma*, 5 febrero 2010, 3.
215. Freddy Pérez Cabrera, "Imperdonable derroche," *Diario Granma* 14, no. 345 (10 diciembre 2010), www.granma.co.cu/2010/12/10/nacional/artic10.html.
216. Pastor Batista Valdés, "Para tener y mantener: Hay que apretar la tuerca," *Diario Granma* 14, no. 36 (5 febrero 2010), www.granma.co.cu/2010/02/05/nacional/artic02.html.
217. Lourdes Pérez Navarro, "Para seguir regando piedras en la vía férrea," *Diario Granma*, 16 abril 2010, www.granma.co.cu/2010/04/16/nacional/artic04.html.
218. "Reform in Cuba: Trying to Make the Sums Add Up," *Economist*, November 13, 2010, 43–44; and "Política: El ex encargado de las compras a EEUU habría escapado de la Isla," *Diario de Cuba*, 6 enero 2011, www.diariodecuba.com.
219. Gerardo Arreola, "Cuba condena en ausencia al chileno Max Marambio a 20 años de prisión," *La Jornada*, 6 mayo 2011, www.jornada.unam.mx.
220. Fernando Ravsberg, "Pescadores de río revuelto," BBC Mundo, *Cartas desde Cuba*, 1 abril 2010, www.bbc.co.uk/blogs/mundo/cartas_desde_cuba/2010/04/pescadores_de_rio_revuelto .html; Fernando Ravsberg, "Cuba: Empresario chileno murió de un paro," BBC Mundo, 16 abril 2010, www.bbc.co.uk/mundo/america_latina/2010/04/100416_1640_cuba _rio_zaza_empresario_muerto_baudrand_alf.shml.
221. Esteban Morales, "Corrupción: ¿La verdadera contrarevolución?," UNEAC (Union Nacional de Escritores y Artistas de Cuba), 4 abril 2010, www.uneac.org.cu/index.php ?module=noticias&act=detalle&id=3123.
222. Pedro Campos, "Cuba: El carnet se fue con los sancionadores, la militancia comunista se quedó con Esteban," *kaosenlared.net*, 27 junio 2010.
223. IPS, "Caen ingresos turísticos," 24 diciembre 2009; and IPS, "Crece número de turistas, pero bajan ingresos," *Cuba a la Mano*, 8 junio 2010.
224. "Cuba Expects 2.7 Million Tourists in 2011," *Latin American Herald Tribune*, December 23, 2010. www.laht.com/article.asp?ArticleId=382061&CategoryID=14510.
225. "Metals," *Economist*, November 28, 2009, 109; "Commodities," *Economist*, January 16, 2010, 93.
226. "Discurso pronunciado por el General de Ejército Raúl Castro Ruz."
227. Associated Press, "Cuba Trade with China Fell 31 pct to $1.5B in '09," *Globe and Mail*, June 1, 2010.
228. Yailin Orta Rivera, "Cuba no puede darse el lujo de costear el sobreconsumo eléctrico," *Juventud Rebelde*, 5 junio 2009, www.juventudrebelde.cu.
229. "El plan y el presupuesto serán instrumentos de fundamental importancia para enfrentar con éxito los desafíos del próximo año," intervención del Diputado Osvaldo Martínez, presidente de la Comisión de Asuntos Economícos de la Asamblea Nacional sobre los temas Plan de la Economía Nacional y Presupuesto del Estado, *Granma*, 21 diciembre 2009, 6–7.
230. Yailin Orta Rivera et al., "Crisis económica mundial también afecta economía cubana," *Juventud Rebelde*, 14 junio 2009, www.juventudrebelde.cu.
231. Gerardo Arreola, "Renuncia el presidente del Banco Central de Cuba, en medio de la crisis de liquidez," Economía, *La Jornada*, 5 junio 2009; Marc Frank, "Cuba Says Foreign Ventures Slightly Up after Long Decline," La Alborada mailing list, Reuters India, March 15, 2010, www.cubamer.org, Washington, DC: Cuban American Alliance Education Fund, March 16, 2010; Mesa-Lago, "La veleta económica cubana," 39.
232. Fernando Ravsberg, "Pilotos, tontos y listillos," BBC Mundo, *Cartes desde Cuba*, febrero 25 2010, http://www.bbc.co.uk/blogs/mundo/cartas_desde_cuba/2010/02/pilotos_tontos _y_listillos.html.
233. "Orientan medidas de ahorro de electricidad en todo el país," *Diario Granma*, 23 mayo 2009, www.granma.co.cu/2009/05/23/nacional/artic11.html.

234. Orta Rivera et al., "Cuba no puede darse el lujo de costear el sobreconsumo eléctrico."
235. Alberto Nuñez Betancourt, "Sobre consumo de 40000 toneladas de combustible," *Granma*, 16 mayo 2009. For a later report on the theft of electricity see Jorge Luis Merencio Cautín, "Trampa para tramposos," *Diario Granma* 14, no. 229 (16 agosto 2010), www.granma.co.cu/2010/08/16/nacional/artic02.htm.
236. "Cuba Brings In Austerity Measures: Flickering Lights," *Economist*, June 6, 2009, 38.
237. Marino Murillo, "En el año 2010 debemos trabajar con intensidad y disciplina para lograr el máximo de eficiencia," *Granma*, 21 diciembre 2009, 5.
238. "Discurso pronunciado por el General de Ejército Raúl Castro Ruz."
239. Oscar Espinosa Chepe, "Economía: La otra descapitalización," *cubaencuentro*, 14 octubre 2010, www.cubaencuentro.com; and Mesa-Lago, "Cincuenta años de servicios sociales en Cuba."
240. Mesa-Lago, "La veleta económica cubana," 39.
241. Elías Amor Bravo, "Economía: Cifras del fracaso; Las previsiones de la CEPAL para Cuba anuncian más penalidades," *cubaencuentro*, 23 julio 2009, www.cubaencuentro.com/es/cuba/artículos/cifras-del-fracaso-195971.
242. "Economía: Mesa-Lago; El gobierno 'carece de un plan' para enfrentar la crisis," *cubaencuentro*, 13 julio 2009, www.cubaencuentro.com.
243. "Cuba Says Its Trade Figures Are Improving," Reuters AlertNet, November 1, 2010, La Alborada mailing list, November 2, 2010, Washington DC: Cuban American Alliance Education Fund, www.cubamer.org.
244. Ibid.; Silvia Martínez Puentes, "Productividad del trabajo. Entre el ser y el deber," *Diario Granma* 14, no. 36 (5 febrero 2010), www.granma.co.cu/2010/02/05/nacional/artic06.html.
245. Raúl Castro, "Los modestos resultados ratifican el optimismo y la confianza en que ¡si se puede!," *Diario Granma* 13, no. 209 (27 julio 2009), www.granma.co.cu/2009/07/27/nacional/artic09.html.
246. Will Weissert, "Cuba Eases Property Laws, Could Open Door to Golf," Associated Press, August 28, 2010.
247. Sariol Sosa, "Para que no desaparezcan los cafetales."
248. Varios autores, "¿Machucando en baja?"
249. Mesa-Lago, "La veleta económica cubana," 43.
250. Jorge Luis Merencio Cautín, "Bueyes e implementos no andan bien," *Granma*, 10 marzo 2010, 8.
251. Juan O. Tamayo, "Cuban Farmers Seek Fewer Government Regulations," *MiamiHerald.com*, May 18, 2010.
252. "Pronunciamiento de la Central de Trabajadores de Cuba," *Diario Granma* 14, no. 257 (13 septiembre 2010), www.granma.co.cu/2010/09/13/nacional/artic01.html; Marc Frank and Jeff Franks, "Analysis: Cuba Jobs Reform Brings Opportunity and Uncertainty," Reuters, September 14, 2010.
253. Interview with Tomás Bilbao, executive director of the Cuba Study Group, *Cuba Standard*, October 22, 2010, www.cubastudygroup.org.
254. "Reaching Out to the Cuban People," White House, Office of the Press Secretary, January 14, 2011.
255. Agencias, La Habana, "Reformas: El régimen prodría permitir la entrega de microcréditos externos," *Diario de Cuba*, 12 octubre 2010, diariodecuba.com.
256. Juan Tamayo, "The Rising Cost of Living in Cuba," *El Nuevo Herald*, October 2, 2010, www.miamiherald.com/2010/10/02/1854117/recent-cuts-in-government-subsidies.html; and Gerardo Arreola, "Cuba: Retiro de subsidios a la población, pieza clave de la actual reforma económica," *La Jornada* (Mexico), 30 octubre 2010.
257. "Eliminan en Cuba subsidios a artículos de aseo," *Trabajadores*, 30 diciembre 2010, www.trabajadores.cu/news/eliminan-en-cuba-subsidios-a-artículos-de-aseo.

258. "Aumentan precios de productos agropecuarios," *Cuba a la Mano*, 2 noviembre 2010.

Chapter Three: Cuba's Foreign Policy

1. E. J. Hobsbawm, *The Age of Revolution 1789–1848* (New York: Mentor Books, 1964), 89–91.
2. Ibid., 88–90.
3. Ibid., 90, 93.
4. C. L. R. James, *The Black Jacobins: Toussaint L'Ouverture and the San Domingo Revolution* (New York: Vintage Books, 1963), 139–40.
5. Hobsbawm, *The Age of Revolution*, 102.
6. Ibid., 102–03. For more details about the French foreign policy during this period see Arno J. Mayer, chapter 14, "Externalization of the French Revolution: The Napoleonic Wars," in *The Furies: Violence and Terror in the French and Russian Revolutions* (Princeton, NJ: Princeton University Press, 2000), 533–606.
7. Karl Marx's activities as a union and political organizer have been almost ignored. For a very interesting study addressing this and related topics, see Henry Collins and Chimen Abramsky, *Karl Marx and the British Labor Movement: Years of the First International* (New York: St. Martin's Press, 1965). See also the more recent work by August H. Nimtz, *Marx and Engels: Their Contribution to the Democratic Breakthrough* (Albany: State University of New York Press, 2000).
8. For a very informative and interesting discussion of the various kinds of Jewish radicalism in the tsarist empire, see Robert J. Brym, *The Jewish Intelligentsia and Russian Marxism: A Sociological Study of Intellectual Radicalism and Ideological Divergence* (London: Macmillan, 1978).
9. Isaac Deutscher, *Stalin: A Political Biography* (New York: Oxford University Press, 1949), 388–89.
10. Isaac Deutscher, *The Prophet Armed: Trotsky: 1879–1921* (New York: Vintage Books, 1965), 1: 346–404.
11. Fernando Claudín, *The Communist Movement: From Comintern to Cominform, Part One*, trans. Brian Pearce (New York: Monthly Review Press, 1975), 250–52; Loren Goldner, "'Socialism in One Country': Before Stalin, and the Origins of Reactionary 'Anti-imperialism'; The Case of Turkey, 1917–1925," *Critique* 38, no. 4 (December 2010): 646–47, 655.
12. Claudín, *The Communist Movement*, 130.
13. Ibid., 252.
14. Ibid., 135, 138–39.
15. While there was a growing tendency to defer to Russian views in the Comintern, there were at the same time outstanding foreign Communist leaders such as the German Paul Levi, who stood up to Moscow in the earliest years of the Comintern. See Paul Levi's *Our Path: Against Putschism* and "What Is the Crime: The March Action or Criticizing It?," and David Fernbach's editorial introduction to those pieces in *Historical Materialism* 17, no. 3 (2009): 101–10, 111–45, 146–74.
16. See the monumental study, originally published in 1971, by the French Marxist historian Pierre Broué titled *The German Revolution: 1917–1923*, trans. John Archer, ed. Ian Birchall and Brian Pearce, with an introduction by Eric D. Weitz and in particular chapter 30, "The Rapallo Turn," 599–606 (Chicago: Haymarket Books, 2006).
17. For a detailed account and analysis of Lenin's conflict with Stalin, see Moshe Lewin, *Lenin's Last Struggle* (New York: Vintage Books, 1970).
18. For an illuminating discussion of what has been one of the most misunderstood political ideas in history, see Hal Draper, *The "Dictatorship of the Proletariat" from Marx to Lenin* (New York: Monthly Review Press, 1987).

19. Claudín, *The Communist Movement*, 283.
20. Robert J. Alexander, *Communism in Latin America* (New Brunswick, NJ: Rutgers University Press, 38), 109–111.
21. Jacques Duclos, "On the Dissolution of the Communist Party of the United States," *Cahiers du Communisme*, April 1945.
22. For details about the role of the Soviet Union and the local pro-Moscow Cuban Communists in the early stages of the Cuban revolution, see Farber, *The Origins of the Cuban Revolution Reconsidered*, 137–66.
23. Ramonet, *Fidel Castro: Biografía*, 295, 280, 529–30. For more details on Cuba's involvement in Algeria and Syria, see Piero Gleijeses, *Conflicting Missions: Havana, Washington, and Africa, 1959–1976* (Chapel Hill: University of North Carolina Press, 2002), 30–56, 226.
24. Domínguez, *To Make a World Safe for Revolution*, 175.
25. Of course, US interests in Cuba preceded the twentieth century. For a comprehensive historical account of nineteenth-century US views on annexing the island, see Oscar Pino Santos, "De la Habana al Mississippi: La isla estratégica y la teoría de la anexión, 1800–1898," *Temas* (Havana) 37–38 (abril–septiembre 2004): 146–58.
26. See Farber, *The Origins of the Cuban Revolution Reconsidered*, 69–111, for a detailed discussion of US policy toward Cuba in the early years of the revolution.
27. See ibid., 34–68, for a discussion of the political and ideological background of Fidel Castro and the Cuban revolutionary leadership.
28. Domínguez, *To Make a World Safe for Revolution*, 125–26.
29. This expedition was organized by two Panamanians, Roberto Arias, the husband of the famous ballet star Margot Fonteyn, and the lawyer Rubén Miró. Manuel de Paz Sánchez, *Franco y Cuba: Estudios sobre España y la Revolución* (Santa Cruz de Tenerife, Canary Islands: Ediciones Idea, 2006), 85–86.
30. Domínguez, *To Make a World Safe for Revolution*, 117–18.
31. "Frustró una expedición a Nicaragua el Ejército Rebelde," *Información*, 8 marzo 1959, as cited in de Paz Sánchez, *Franco y Cuba: Estudios sobre España y la Revolución*, 85.
32. Ibid., 118. See a detailed account of the expedition against Trujillo sponsored by the Cuban government in "14 de junio de 1959: Hermosa página de internacionalismo," *Granma*, 12 junio 2009, 4–5. For the August 13, 1959, Cuban government-sponsored expedition against the Duvalier dictatorship in Haiti, see Gerardo González Nuñez, *El Caribe en la política exterior de Cuba (Balance de 30 años: 1959–1989)* (Santo Domingo: Centro de Investigación y Promoción Social, 1991), 36.
33. Farber, *The Origins of the Cuban Revolution Reconsidered*, 121–22.
34. Ibid., 147–48.
35. Ibid., 165–66.
36. Jon Lee Anderson, *Che Guevara: A Revolutionary Life* (New York: Grove Press, 1997), 167; and Carlos G. Castañeda, *Compañero: The Life and Death of Che Guevara* (New York: Knopf, 1997), 62, 181.
37. Farber, *The Origins of the Cuban Revolution Reconsidered*, 56.
38. Régis Debray, "Revolution in the Revolution? Armed Struggle and Political Struggle in Latin America," *Monthly Review*, July–August 1967 (entire issue). A year later *Monthly Review* published an entire issue dedicated to an assessment and critique of Debray's theory under the title "Regis Debray and the Latin American Revolution," 20, no. 3 (July–August 1968). The essay by the Cubans Simón Torres and Julio Aronde titled "Debray and the Cuban Experience" (44–62) deserves special mention, since they challenged Debray's interpretation of what happened in Cuba. Another sharp critique of Debray was presented by James Petras in "Guerrilla Movements in Latin America—II," *New Politics* 6, no. 2 (Spring 1967): 66–72.

39. Domínguez, *To Make a World Safe for Revolution*, 70–75.

40. For an example of a very serious distortion of history relevant to Cuba's foreign policy, see an article commemorating the twenty-fifth anniversary of the murder of Grenadian leader Maurice Bishop, which opened the way to the subsequent US intervention, in the Cuban Communist Party newspaper *Granma*. The article described Deputy Prime Minister Bernard Coard and General Hudson Austin, who led the coup against Bishop, as having been part of a Washington-inspired plot. In fact, Coard and Austin were hard-line Communists who were far more likely to have had ties with Moscow. Aida Calviac Mora, "Maurice Bishop: Símbolo de honestidad revolucionaria," *Granma*, 17 octubre 2008, 5.

41. Fidel Castro speech of August 23, 1968, as translated in *Granma Weekly Review*, August 25, 1968, 2.

42. Initially, Cuba did not explicitly endorse the Soviet invasion but refused to support and voted against (rather than abstain) a UN resolution condemning it, with Cuban foreign minister Raúl Roa claiming that "we shall not vote against socialism." Fidel Castro endorsed the Soviet military action a year after it occurred, but privately commented that Moscow's invasion was "embarrassing for [a] revolutionary movement." The invasion's diplomatic cost for Cuba was high including the loss of a seat in the UN's Security Council that it would have otherwise obtained because of its official leadership of the "nonaligned" countries. Schoulz, *That Infernal Little Republic*, 351.

43. Piero Gleijeses, *The Cuban Drumbeat: Castro's Worldview; Cuban Foreign Policy in a Hostile World* (London: Seagull Books, 2009), 17–18.

44. Carmelo Mesa-Lago, "Cuban Foreign Policy in Africa: A General Framework," in *Cuba in Africa*, ed. Carmelo Mesa-Lago and June S. Belkin (Pittsburgh: Center for Latin American Studies, University Center for International Studies, University of Pittsburgh, 1982), 6.

45. Gleijeses, *Conflicting Missions: Havana, Washington, and Africa*, 368–69.

46. The blog titled *La última guerra: Testimonios de la intervención de Cuba en Angola* (laultimaguerra.com) sometimes carries informative personal accounts by Cubans who served in Angola.

47. Gleijeses, *The Cuban Drumbeat*, 64–66.

48. William M. LeoGrande, "Cuban-Soviet Relations and Cuban Policy in Africa," in *Cuba in Africa*, ed. Mesa-Lago and Belkin, 29–30. LeoGrande claims that Alves had the implicit support of the USSR, but if so, the Soviets did not move a finger to actually do something on his behalf, while the Cubans provided major material support to Neto. For an informative account of Alves's politics and relationship with the Cubans, see Edward George, *The Cuban Intervention in Angola, 1965–1991: From Che Guevara to Cuito Cuanavale* (London: Frank Cass, 2005), 127–31. This important incident is discussed almost in passing in Piero Gleijeses's *Conflicting Missions* (372). This work, supposedly about Cuba's policy in Africa and containing much useful information from archives, conveniently stops in 1976, apparently to avoid discussing Cuba's involvement in Ethiopia, Eritrea, and the Ogaden war. The Cuban government had the book translated into Spanish and celebrated by the official press. Gleijeses was even given a medal by the Cuban authorities in recognition of his "repeated instances of friendship and solidarity with Cuba and its revolution and for his contribution to the publication of the truth about the Cuban presence in Africa." In response, Gleijeses proclaimed: "I have a dream to continue investigating Cuba's foreign policy and to be the bard of this very beautiful epoch." Miguel Ángel Untoria Pedroso, "Condecoran a Piero Gleijeses," *Granma*, 7 noviembre 2003, 2. In his 2009 work *The Cuban Drumbeat*, Gleijeses does discuss Cuba's involvement in the Horn of Africa but only in terms of the conflict between Ethiopia and Somalia and does not say a word about Eritrea (35–40).

49. George, *The Cuban Intervention in Angola*, 32, 35; Gleijeses, *Conflicting Missions*, 169–72; and Domínguez, "Political and Military Limitations and Consequences of Cuban

Policies in Africa," in *Cuba in Africa*, ed. Mesa-Lago and Belkin, 125–26.

50. Thus, for example, in the case of Mozambique, the Cuban government took the lead in training the Departemento de Seguranca de Responsaveis (DSR), which can be translated as Department of Security for Leaders. Cuba had a training system at home to prepare this type of security personnel for their duties abroad. Gillian Gunn, "Cuba and Mozambique: A History of Cordial Disagreement," in *Cuban Internationalism in Sub-Saharan Africa*, ed. Sergio Díaz-Briquets (Pittsburgh: Duquesne University Press, 1989), 86.

51. Mesa-Lago, "Causes and Effects of Cuban Involvement in Africa," 200; Domínguez, *To Make a World Safe for Revolution*, 181.

52. At the Non-Aligned Conference that took place in Havana in 1978, Vice President Carlos Rafael Rodríguez defended the "territorial integrity" of Ethiopia, and in November 1979, Ramón Sánchez Parodi, head of the Cuban Interest Section in Washington, DC, expressed the same sentiment as Rodríguez. Pamela Falk, *Cuban Foreign Policy: Caribbean Tempest* (Lexington, MA: Lexington Books), 100.

53. Nelson P. Valdés, "Cuba's involvement in the Horn of Africa: The Ethiopian-Somali War and the Eritrean Conflict," in *Cuba in Africa*, ed. Mesa-Lago and Belkin, 80, 84.

54. William M. LeoGrande, "Cuban-Soviet Relations and Cuban Policy in Africa," in *Cuba in Africa*, ed. Mesa-Lago and Belkin, 41.

55. Ibid., 39.

56. Wayne S. Smith, *The Closest of Enemies: A Personal Account of U.S.-Cuban Diplomatic Relations since 1957* (New York: W. W. Norton, 1987), 132.

57. Schoultz, *That Infernal Little Cuban Republic*, 313–14.

58. Smith, *The Closest of Enemies*, 40.

59. Ibid., 39.

60. Mesa-Lago, "Causes and Effects of Cuban Involvement in Africa," 199.

61. One hundred sixty-three Cuban "internationalist combatants" died during the war and in the years that the military mission stayed in Ethiopia according to Lourdes Pérez Navarro, "Conmemoran aniversario 30 de la Misión Militar de Cuba en Etiopía," *Granma*, 14 marzo 2008, 7. According to official figures provided by *Granma* on December 6, 1989, 2,016 Cubans died in Angola, of whom 39 percent died in combat, 26 percent of disease, and 35 percent in accidents. In addition, 61 died during the subsequent eighteen months of withdrawal from that country. These figures do not include the wounded, those incapacitated by disease (especially malaria and tropical fever), or any of the hundreds of MIAs, who usually account for double the number killed. George, *The Cuban Intervention in Angola*, 268.

62. For a thorough account of Cuban civilian assistance in Africa until the late eighties, see Sergio Díaz-Briquets and Jorge Pérez-López, "Internationalist Civilian Assistance: The Cuban Presence in Sub-Saharan Africa," in *Cuban Internationalism in Sub-Saharan Africa*, 48–77.

63. George, *The Cuban Intervention in Angola*, 143.

64. For a useful discussion of this issue see Sergio Roca, "Economic Aspects of Cuban Involvement in Africa," in *Cuba in Africa*, ed. Mesa-Lago and Belkin, 163–85.

65. Domínguez, *To Make a World Safe for Revolution*, 115–26.

66. Julia E. Sweig, *Cuba: What Everyone Needs to Know* (New York: Oxford University Press, 2009), 118.

67. Mesa-Lago, *Cuba in the 1970s*, 130. For other unsavory details of the Cuban government's involvement in Mexican politics, see Carlos Ramírez, "Otras traiciones de Fidel," *Zócalo Saltillo*, 26 mayo 2009, www.zocalo.com.mx/seccion/opinion-articulo/otras-traiciones-de-fidel/.

68. De Paz Sánchez, *Franco y Cuba: Estudios sobre España y la Revolución*, 325–26.

69. Ibid., 324.

70. Ibid., 298–99.

71. For a detailed account of the economic relations between Franco's Spain and Cuba after the 1959 Revolution, see George Lambie, "Franco's Spain and the Cuban Revolution," in *The Fractured Blockade: West European-Cuban Relations during the Revolution*, ed. Alistair Hennessy and George Lambie (London: Macmillan, 1993), 234–75.

72. "La actual política norteamericana empuja a Fidel Castro hacia Moscú," *Arriba*, December 22, 1963, 13, as quoted in Lambie, "Franco's Spain and the Cuban Revolution," 257.

73. De Paz Sánchez, *Franco y Cuba: Estudios sobre España y la Revolución*, 332.

74. Schoultz, *That Infernal Little Cuban Republic*, 233–34.

75. De Paz Sánchez, *Franco y Cuba: Estudios sobre España y la Revolución*, 363–68.

76. Ramonet, *Fidel Castro: Biografía*, 459.

77. This was true of left and liberal publications, although, of course, there were Catholic right-wing newspapers such as *Diario de la Marina* that supported Franco.

78. Joaquín Roy, *The Cuban Revolution (1959–2009): Relations with Spain, the European Union, and the United States* (New York: Palgrave Macmillan, 2009), 26–27; de Paz Sánchez, *Franco y Cuba: Estudios sobre España y la Revolución*, 374.

79. Ramonet, *Fidel Castro: Biografía*, 460.

80. De Paz Sánchez, *Franco y Cuba: Estudios sobre España y la Revolución*, 305.

81. Roy, *The Cuban Revolution*, 92–93, 122. The European Union has also opposed the economic blockade as a whole at the votes taken at the United Nations every year (ibid., 70).

82. "96/697/CFSP: Common Position of 2 December 1996 Defined by the Council on the Basis of Article 3.2 of the Treaty on European Union, on Cuba," EUR-Lex Access to European Union Law, http://eur-lex.europa.eu/LexUriServ/LexUriServ.do?uri=CELEX :31996EO697:EN:NOT.

83. Roy, *The Cuban Revolution*, 64.

84. Ibid.

85. Ibid.; "The Lomé Convention," European Commission, http://ec.europa.eu/development/ geographical/lomegen_en.cfm; "The Conou Agreement," European Commission, http:// ec.europa.eu/development/geographical/cotonouintro_en.cfm.

86. "Cuatro horas de entrevista com Fidel Castro," interview by Fernando Morais, *Veja*, July 13, 1977, 43, cited in Mesa-Lago, *Cuba in the 1970s*, 131.

87. This was one of the very few issues on which many right-wing Cuban exiles in south Florida agreed with Castro. The Malvinas/Falkland War was not about national liberation, since no Argentines lived on the very small and thinly populated islands. This war was the continuation by other means of quite reactionary politics on both the side of the brutal military dictatorship of the Argentine "gorillas" and the right-wing Margaret Thatcher administration in the United Kingdom. Of course, a strong case can be made that Argentina rather than Britain should have ultimate sovereignty over the islands, but that does not mean that that particular war was justified and merited support on either side of the conflict.

88. José Manuel Martín Medem, "Marulanda no puede contestar a Fidel," *kaosenlared.net*, 30 noviembre 2008, www.kaosenlared.net/noticia/marulanda-no-puede-contestar-fidel; and Smith, *The Closest of Enemies*, 242–44, 257, 262–63.

89. Yon Sosa and Luis Turcios Lima were both army lieutenants who rebelled against the Guatemalan government in the sixties. Yon Sosa was influenced by Trotskyism and therefore followed a more independent course regarding Cuba, while Turcios Lima was close to the Guatemalan Communists (Partido Guatemalteco de los Trabajadores— Guatemalan Workers Party).

90. Mesa-Lago, *Cuba in the 1970s*, 125.

91. González Nuñez, *El Caribe en la política exterior de Cuba*, 62.

92. For a moving eyewitness account of the events in Grenada that brought about Bishop's downfall and murder and the subsequent US invasion, see Guyanese left-wing leader

Rupert Roopnaraine's "Resonances of the Grenadian Revolution," presented to the colloquium "Remembering the Future: The Legacies of Radical Politics in the Caribbean," sponsored by the Center for Latin American and Caribbean Studies, University of Pittsburgh, April 3–4, 2009, www.normangirvan.info/category/grenadian-revolution/.

93. González Nuñez, *El Caribe en la política exterior de Cuba*, 75.

94. Falk, *Cuban Foreign Policy*, 70.

95. Hal Klepak, *Cuba's Military, 1990–2005: Revolutionary Soldiers during Revolutionary Times* (New York: Palgrave Macmillan, 2005), 254.

96. See, for example, Robert A. Packenham, "Capitalist vs. Socialist Dependency: The Case of Cuba," *Journal of Interamerican Studies and World Affairs* 28, no.1 (Spring 1986): 59–92.

97. Gleijeses, *Conflicting Missions*, 373; and Gleijeses, *The Cuban Drumbeat*, 71–72.

98. Schoultz, *That Infernal Little Republic*, 239.

99. Ibid., 289; and Sweig, *Cuba: What Everyone Needs to Know*, 83–84.

100. Eventually, Eduardo Arocena, the founder of Omega 7, was caught and sentenced to life plus thirty-five years in prison for the gunning down of the Cuban diplomat and several bombings in the New York area.

101. Schoultz, *That Infernal Little Cuban Republic*, 370.

102. Sweig, *Cuba: What Everyone Needs to Know*, 92.

103. Domínguez, *To Make a World Safe for Revolution*, 227–28.

104. Smith, *The Closest of Enemies*, 100, 122–25.

105. Ibid., 118–19.

106. Ibid., 126.

107. Sweig, *Cuba: What Everyone Needs to Know*, 95.

108. It is worth noting that the Platt Amendment was abolished *after* the defeat of the 1933 Revolution by the joint efforts of the Cuban army led by Batista and representatives of US imperialism.

Chapter Four: Cuban Workers after the 1959 Revolution

1. *Granma Weekly Review* 5, no. 3 (August 1970): 3. This speech was translated and published in the *New York Review of Books* 15, no. 5 (September 24, 1970).

2. Speech by Fidel Castro to the leaders of the Central Organization of Workers (CUT) in Santiago, Chile, November 23, 1971, *Granma*, 15 diciembre 1971, 14.

3. US Department of Commerce, Bureau of Foreign Commerce, *Investment in Cuba: Basic Information for United States Businessmen* (Washington, DC: Government Printing Office, 1956), 183.

4. Jorge Ibarra, *Prologue to Revolution: Cuba, 1898–1958*, trans. Marjorie Moore (Boulder, CO: Lynne Rienner, 1998), 170.

5. Debray, "Revolution in the Revolution?," 76–77.

6. Theodore Draper, *Castroism: Theory and Practice* (New York: Frederick A. Praeger, 1965), 77.

7. Hugh Thomas, *Cuba: The Pursuit of Freedom* (New York: Harper and Row, 1971), 1196.

8. Blas Roca, "Huelgas o 'no huelgas,'" *Hoy*, 10 febrero 1959, 1.

9. Fidel Castro, *Discursos para la historia* (Havana: Imprenta Emilio Gall, 1959), 1:137.

10. "Declaraciones del PSP: El PSP pide a los campesinos que impidan pro si mismo las ocupaciones de tierras; Considera innecessaria y peligrosa la Ley 87," *Hoy*, 22 febrero 1959, 1.

11. If such a claim had been correct, Mujal would have been shown to have far greater support in the union movement than the government's supporters had ever given him credit for! Regrettably, some social scientists studying Cuba have accepted the Cuban government's claims at face value. See, for example, Linda Fuller, *Work and Democracy in Socialist Cuba* (Philadelphia: Temple University Press, 1992), 47–56.

12. Marifeli Pérez-Stable, *The Cuban Revolution: Origins, Course and Legacy*, 2nd ed. (New York: Oxford University Press, 1999), 72–73.

13. Law 962, August 1, 1961, in *Gaceta Oficial* (special edition), August 3, 1961, cited in Roberto E. Hernández and Carmelo Mesa-Lago, "Labor Organization and Wages," in *Revolutionary Change in Cuba*, ed. Carmelo Mesa-Lago, (Pittsburgh: University of Pittsburgh Press, 1971), 212.

14. "Declaración de principios y estatutos de la CTC," *El Mundo*, July 6, 1966, cited in Hernández and Mesa-Lago in "Labor Organization and Wages," 212.

15. A good example of this kind of inability to understand the reality of Cuban labor is to be found again in Fuller, *Work and Democracy in Socialist Cuba*, 43–44.

16. Domínguez, *Cuba: Order and Revolution*, 271–72.

17. Raúl Castro, *Revolución*, January 23, 1963, cited in Hernández and Mesa-Lago, "Labor Organization and Wages," 212–13.

18. Fidel Castro, "Los buenos y los malos dirigentes obreros," speech of June 15, 1960, reproduced in *Diario Granma*, 10 junio 2010, www.granma.co.cu/2010/06/10/nacional/artic03.html; Blas Roca, "El nuevo papel de los sindicatos bajo el socialismo," *Hoy*, 28 febrero 1962, reproduced in *Granma*, 16 junio 2010, 3; and Blas Roca, "La disciplina en el trabajo," published as "Aclaraciones de Blas Roca," *Hoy*, 1 julio 2010, reproduced in *Granma*, 1 julio 2010, 3.

19. Hernández and Mesa-Lago, "Labor Organization and Wages," 218–19.

20. Law 1166, September 23, 1964, in *Gaceta Oficial*, October 3, 1964, cited in Hernández and Mesa-Lago, "Labor Organization and Wages," 219–20.

21. Ernesto "Che" Guevara, *Revolución*, June 27, 1961, cited in Hernández and Mesa-Lago, "Labor Organization and Wages," 220.

22. Bunck, *Fidel Castro and the Quest for a Revolutionary Culture*, 136–37.

23. Hernández and Mesa-Lago, "Labor Organization and Wages," 237–38.

24. Bunck, *Fidel Castro and the Quest for a Revolutionary Culture*, 158–59; Mesa-Lago, *Cuba in the 1970s*, 95.

25. Maxine Valdes and Nelson P. Valdes, "Cuban Workers and the Revolution," *New Politics* 8, no. 4 (Fall 1970): 44. The Valdeses in turn drew from information that appeared in *Granma* on September 10, 1970.

26. Hernández and Mesa-Lago, "Labor Organization and Wages," 226.

27. Jorge Risquet, "Comparecencia sobre problemas de fuerza de trabajo y productividad," *Granma*, August 1, 1970, 5–6, cited in Mesa-Lago, *Cuba in the 1970s*, 83.

28. Jorge Risquet, "Palabras en la Plenaria Provincial de la CTC," *Granma*, September 9, 1970, 4–5, cited in Mesa-Lago, *Cuba in the 1970s*, 88.

29. Jorge Risquet, "Speech at the Closing Session of the 6th National Council of the Central Organization of Trade Unions," *Granma Weekly Review*, October 24, 1971, 4, cited in Mesa-Lago, *Cuba in the 1970s*, 88.

30. Valdes and Valdes, "Cuban Workers and the Revolution," 46–47.

31. Mesa-Lago, *Cuba in the 1970s*, 84–86.

32. Pérez-Stable, *The Cuban Revolution*, 128.

33. Fidel Castro, "Discurso en la concentración para celebrar el décimo aniversario de los CDR," *Granma Resumen Semanal*, 4 octubre 1970, 4–5, cited in Mesa-Lago, *Cuba in the 1970s*, 85.

34. Fidel Castro and Raúl Castro, *Selecciones de discursos acerca del partido* (Havana: Editorial de Ciencias Sociales, 1975), 59, cited in Pérez-Stable, *The Cuban Revolution*, 128–29.

35. Pérez-Stable, *The Cuban Revolution*, 129.

36. Ibid., 129.

37. Ernesto Che Guevara, "Discurso en la Convención Nacional de los Consejos Técnicos Asesores," in *Escritos y discursos* (Havana: Editorial de Ciencias Sociales, 1977), 5:38, cited

in Pérez Stable, *The Cuban Revolution*, 102.

38. Ernesto Che Guevara, "Discusión colectiva: Decisión y responsabilidades únicas," in *Escritos y discursos*, 5:200, cited in Pérez-Stable, *The Cuban Revolution*, 102.

39. Ernesto Che Guevara, "Discurso clausura del Consejo Nacional de la CTC, 15 de abril de 1962," in *Escritos y discursos*, 6:133, cited in Pérez-Stable, *The Cuban Revolution*, 102.

40. Hernández and Mesa-Lago, "Labor Organization and Wages," 220.

41. Che Guevara in *Revolución,* February 2, 1963, cited in Hernández and Mesa-Lago, "Labor Organization and Wages," 220.

42. Hernández and Mesa-Lago, "Labor Organization and Wages," 221.

43. Pérez-Stable, *The Cuban Revolution*, 134.

44. Fidel Castro, "Discurso pronunciado en la clausura del II período de sesiones de 1979 de la Asamblea Nacional del Poder Popular," 6, cited in Pérez-Stable, *The Cuban Revolution*, 134.

45. Pérez-Stable, *The Cuban Revolution*, 134.

46. International Bank for Reconstruction and Development, *Report on Cuba* (Washington, DC: International Bank for Reconstruction and Development, 1951), 71.

47. US Department of Commerce, *Investment in Cuba: Basic Information for United States Businessmen*, 24.

48. Valdes and Valdes, "Cuban Workers and the Revolution," 36.

49. Ibid., 37.

50. *Granma*, 8 septiembre 1970, 5; "La microemulación del deber y el honor," *Bohemia* 65, no. 26 (June 29, 1973): 91–92, cited in Domínguez, *Cuba: Order and Revolution*, 275–76.

51. Bunck, *Fidel Castro and the Quest for a Revolutionary Culture*, 166.

52. Ibid., 176.

53. Samuel Farber, "Material and Non-material Work Incentives as Ideologies and Practices of Order," *Review of Radical Political Economics* 14, no. 4 (Winter 1982): 33.

54. Mesa-Lago, *Market, Socialist and Mixed Economies*, 218.

55. Farber, "Material and Non-material Work Incentives," 33.

56. John Montias, "A Classification of Communist Economic Systems," in *Comparative Socialist Systems: Essays on Politics and Economics*, ed. Carmelo Mesa-Lago and Carl Beck (Pittsburgh: University of Pittsburgh Center for International Studies, 1975), 49.

57. Alexander Eckstein, *China's Economic Development: The Interplay of Scarcity and Ideology* (Ann Arbor: University of Michigan Press, 1975), 333; and Charles Hoffmann, *Work Incentive Practices and Policies in the People's Republic of China, 1953–1965* (Albany: State University of New York Press, 1967), 124.

58. Mesa-Lago, *Market, Socialist, and Mixed Economies*, 211–12.

59. Ibid., 221, 211.

60. Pérez-Stable, *The Cuban Revolution*, 156.

61. Mesa-Lago, *Market, Socialist, and Mixed Economies*, 276.

62. Pérez-Stable, *The Cuban Revolution*, 159.

63. Ibid., 281.

64. Mesa-Lago, *Market, Socialist, and Mixed Economies*, 316–17.

65. Ibid., 318.

66. Oscar Ramos Lorenzo, "Nadie quedará desamparado," *Trabajadores*, 1 febrero 2010, www.trabajadores.cu/news/2010/2/1/nadie-quedara-desamparado.

67. Gerardo Arreola, "Castro se propone reducir el gasto," *Página/12* (Buenos Aires), 7 abril 2010.

68. Oscar Sánchez Serra, "Proceso de disponibilidad y reducción de plantillas infladas: Cuba no dejará a nadie desamparado, reorganiza su economía y sus fuerzas productivas," *Diario Granma* 14, no. 272 (28 septiembre 2010), www.granma.co.cu/2010/09/28/nacional/artic03.html.

69. Ibid. A two-step appeal reaching up to the municipal courts was also established, involv-

ing any perceived violation "of the formal aspects of the norms or the procedures that were applied."

70. Lourdes Pérez-Navarro, "Modificaciones del régimen laboral (II): Contratar a estudiantes y trabajadores de otras provincias," *Diario Granma* 13, no. 223 (10 agosto 2009).

71. "Plan que permite pluriempleo en Cuba arroja resultado 'discreto,'" *Invertia*, December 28, 2009, reproduced in La Alborada mailing list, Washington, DC, Cuban American Alliance Education Fund, December 29, 2009.

72. Leticia Martínez Hernández, "Jóvenes al campo: Entre la productividad y el romanticismo," *Diario Granma* 13, no. 297 (23 octubre 2009).

73. Leticia Martínez Hernández, "Comedores obreros: Dar, más que quitar," *Diario Granma* 13, no. 269 (25 septiembre 2009).

74. Oscar Espinosa Chepe, "Economía: Cierre de comedores; ¿Solución efectiva?," *cubaencuentro*, 16 octubre 2009, www.cubaencuentro.com.

75. Yaima Puig Meneses, "Cada trabajador también decide la batalla económica," *Granma*, 11 junio 2010, 5.

76. José Alejandro Rodríguez, "¿Y la sección sindical?," *Juventud Rebelde*, 11 noviembre 2009, www.juventudrebelde.cu/columnas/acuse-recibo/2009–11–07/y-la-seccion-sindical/.

77. CTC, "Pronunciamiento de la Central de Trabajadores de Cuba."

78. Americas Watch, a Committee of Human Rights Watch, *Cuba: Behind a Sporting Façade, Stepped-Up Repression* (New York: Americas Watch, August 11, 1991), 7.

79. Reported to Carlos Moore by several people, including black dissidents Esteban Cárdenas and Gilberto Aldama. Moore, *Castro, the Blacks and Africa*, 306, 416.

80. Pedro Campos Santos y varios compañeros, "Cuba necesita un socialismo participativo y democrático. Propuestas programáticas," *kaosenlared.net*, 17 agosto 2008.

81. Frederick Engels, *Socialism: Utopian and Scientific*, trans. Edward Aveling (New York: Little Marx Library, International Publishers, 1972), 73–75.

82. Orlando Márquez, "Sobre libertad y liberalizaciones," *Palabra Nueva: Revista de la Arquidiócesis de la Habana*, no. 198 (julio–agosto 2010): 2, www.palabranueva.net/contens/1007/0001014.htm.

83. Orlando Márquez, "Sin miedo a la riqueza [Without fear of wealth]," *Palabra Nueva: Revista de la Arquidiócesis de la Habana*, no. 203 (enero 2011), http://palabranueva.net/contens/1101/0001014.htm. Since then, Márquez has also written about the serious problems of the Cuban health system and proposed a number of solutions, including a "combination of the public [health] service with private service." Orlando Márquez, "Reformas: También en salud pública," *Palabra Nueva: Revista de la Arquidiócesis de la Habana* 19, no. 204 (febrero 2011), http://palabranueva.net/contens/pag_opinion1.html.

Chapter Five: Racism against Black Cubans

1. Throughout this chapter, the term *black* is meant to include mulattos (*mulatos*, those of mixed black and white ancestry) in those instances where this latter racial category is not specified. I would have personally preferred to use the term *Afro-Cuban* because it is favored by many politically conscious blacks on the island. However, the term has so far not been adopted by the overwhelming majority of the Cuban people of color, who continue to refer to themselves as *negro* (black) and *mulato*.

2. Marianne Masferrer and Carmelo Mesa-Lago, "The Gradual Integration of the Black in Cuba: Under the Colony, the Republic and the Revolution," in *Slavery and Race Relations in Latin America*, ed. Robert Brent Toplin (Westport, CT: Greenwood Press, 1974), 352.

3. Laird W. Bergad, *The Comparative Histories of Slavery in Brazil, Cuba and the United States* (Cambridge: Cambridge University Press, 2007), 48–49.

4. Ibid., 176–77.
5. Frank Tannenbaum, *Slave and Citizen: The Negro in the Americas* (New York: Knopf, 1946).
6. Franklin W. Knight, "Slavery, Race and Social Structure in Cuba during the Nineteenth Century," in *Slavery and Race Relations in Latin America*, ed. Toplin, 207, 211. See also Bergad, *The Comparative Histories of Slavery*, for a discussion of runaway slaves (202). For Bergad's analysis of rebellions see chapter 7, "Resistance and Rebellion" (202–50), including his assessment of the relative frequency of rebellions in Cuba, Brazil, and the United States (238).
7. Bergad, *The Comparative Histories of Slavery*, 76.
8. Ibid., 180–81.
9. Ibid., 104–05. See also Marvin Harris, *Patterns of Race in the Americas* (New York: Walker, 1964), 70.
10. Bergad, *The Comparative Histories of Slavery*, 61, 105, 196–99.
11. Ibid., 128–29.
12. Ibid., 113.
13. Knight, "Slavery, Race and Social Structure," 210.
14. Harris, *Patterns of Race in the Americas*, 37, 56.
15. Bergad, *The Comparative Histories of Slavery*, 18; and Aline Helg, *Our Rightful Share: The Afro-Cuban Struggle for Equality, 1886–1912* (Chapel Hill: University of North Carolina Press, 1995), 17ff.
16. Bergad, *The Comparative Histories of Slavery*, 274.
17. Masferrer and Mesa-Lago, "The Gradual Integration," 355.
18. Ibid., 356.
19. For an informative discussion of how the views of Céspedes and other independence leaders of the period evolved on the issue of the abolition of slavery, see Ada Ferrer, *Insurgent Cuba: Race, Nation and Revolution, 1868–1898* (Chapel Hill: University of North Carolina Press, 1999), 26 and ff.
20. Cited in Alejandro de la Fuente, *Race, Inequality and Politics in Twentieth-Century Cuba* (Chapel Hill: University of North Carolina Press, 2001), 28. For a discussion of the predominant view that blacks should be grateful and keep silent about their grievances in order not to hurt the independence effort, see Ferrer, *Insurgent Cuba*, 134–35.
21. Ferrer, *Insurgent Cuba*, 69; and Helg, *Our Rightful Share*, 147–48.
22. A close look at the Morúa law shows that it banned not only political organizations organized along the lines of "race" and "color" but political groupings formed by any "class of individuals based on birth, wealth, or professional credentials." Of course, race and color were clearly the principal issues that the law was concerned with. For the full text of the law, see Victor Fowler Calzada, "Contra el argumento racista," *Encuentro de la Cultura Cubana* 53/54 (verano/otoño 2009): 90.
23. De la Fuente, *Race, Inequality and Politics*, 73–75.
24. Helg, *Our Rightful Share*, 225; and Silvio Castro Fernández, *La masacre de los independientes de color en 1912*, 2nd ed. (Havana: Editorial de Ciencias Sociales, 2008), 3, 130, 134.
25. One of these anti-Machado groups was the ABC political organization. The ABC and other white supremacist organizations, influenced by their US counterparts, tried to prevent blacks from obtaining sought-after state jobs. This antiblack campaign culminated in the murder of a member of a prominent black Cuban family in the town of Trinidad in central Cuba. Frank Andre Guridy, "'War on the Negro': Race and the Revolution of 1933," *Cuban Studies* 40 (2009): 49–73.
26. Barry Carr, "Identity, Class and Nation: Black Immigrant Workers, Cuban Communism, and the Sugar Insurgency, 1925–1934," *Hispanic American Historical Review* 78, no. 1 (February 1998): 98–99; and Castro Fernández, *La masacre de los independientes*, 265–67.

27. De la Fuente, *Race, Inequality and Politics*, 219–20.
28. Ibid., 216.
29. Carlos Moore, *Castro, the Blacks and Africa* (Los Angeles: Center for Afro-American Studies, University of California, Los Angeles, 1988), 16.
30. Ferrer, *Insurgent Cuba*, 96; and Helg, *Our Rightful Share*, 99.
31. Masferrer and Mesa-Lago, "The Gradual Integration," 356, 363, 367.
32. Tomás Fernández Robaina, "Un balance necesario: La lucha contra la discriminación al negro en Cuba de 1959 a 2009," *Encuentro de la Cultura Cubana* 53/54 (verano/otoño 2009): 58.
33. See Roberto González Echevarría, *The Pride of Havana: A History of Cuban Baseball* (New York: Oxford University Press, 1999), particularly the photographs of players and teams of various racial backgrounds on pages 304 and 305.
34. De la Fuente, *Race, Inequality and Politics*, 238–40.
35. Jorge I. Domínguez, "Racial and Ethnic Relations in the Cuban Armed Forces: A Non-topic," *Armed Forces and Society* 2, no. 2 (February 1976): 275.
36. Ibid., 281.
37. Masferrer and Mesa-Lago, "The Gradual Integration," 373.
38. Ibid., 371.
39. See, for example, Richard Gott, *Cuba: A New History* (New Haven, CT: Yale University Press, 2004), 119, 138.
40. For an in-depth discussion of Fidel Castro's background in Cuban populist politics, see chapter 2, "Fidel Castro and the Cuban Populist Tradition," in Farber, *Origins of the Cuban Revolution Reconsidered*, 34–68.
41. I am grateful to the historian Ilán Ehrlich, who is working on a biography of Eduardo "Eddy" Chibás, for bringing these facts to my attention.
42. Moore, *Castro, the Blacks and Africa*, 17.
43. De la Fuente, *Race, Inequality and Politics*, 253.
44. Ibid., 252.
45. Lionel Martin, *The Early Fidel: Roots of Castro's Communism* (Secaucus, NJ: Lyle Stuart, 1978), 70.
46. De la Fuente, *Race, Inequality and Politics*, 251.
47. My calculation of the racial composition of the *Granma* fighters is based on my visual inspection of the photographs that appeared in the official daily *Granma* on the fiftieth anniversary of the expedition. There were eighty-one photographs. The picture of the eighty-second participant, José Morán, was not shown. Instead, there was an inscription claiming that there was no available photo and that he had been executed because he became an agent of the Batista dictatorship. *Granma*, 2 diciembre 2006, 3–5.
48. Hugh Thomas, "Middle Class Politics and the Cuban Revolution," in *The Politics of Conformity in Latin America*, ed. Claudio Véliz, (London: Royal Institute of International Affairs Oxford University Press, 1967), 261.
49. Frank Argote-Freyre, *Fulgencio Batista: From Revolutionary to Strongman* (New Brunswick, NJ: Rutgers University Press, 2006), 124–26.
50. A study of 675 women residents of Havana who had participated in the struggle against the Batista dictatorship showed that 82 percent were white, 15 percent mulatto, and only 3.1 percent black. The authors of the study explicitly contrasted this low participation with the heavy black participation in the war of independence against Spain in the 1890s. Elvira Díaz Vallina, Olga Dotre Romay, and Caridad Dacosta Pérez, "Avance de investigación: La mujer revolucionaria en Cuba durante el período insurreccional, 1952–1958," *Revista de Ciencias Sociales* 3, no. 3 (junio 1997): 26.
51. De la Fuente, *Race, Inequality and Politics*, 252.
52. Ibid., 253.

53. Ibid., 253–54; see a reproduction of the cartoon on page 254.

54. Ibid., 261.

55. Ibid., 263.

56. Moore, *Castro, the Blacks and Africa*, 16–17.

57. De la Fuente, *Race, Inequality and Politics*, 263.

58. A different type of exclusion has come to prevail in many of these former private social clubs as they have been taken over by institutions such as the armed forces and the Ministry of the Interior, with access restricted to the members of those institutions and their families. Krause-Fuchs, *Monika y la Revolución*, 200–01.

59. De la Fuente, *Race, Inequality and Politics*, 269, 271.

60. Cited in Moore, *Castro, the Blacks and Africa*, 21.

61. De la Fuente, *Race, Inequality and Politics*, 265–66.

62. Photograph and text in ibid., 271.

63. Moore, *Castro, the Blacks and Africa*, 115–18.

64. Ibid., 117.

65. Esteban Morales Domínguez, "Desafíos de la problemática racial en Cuba," *Temas*, no. 56 (octubre–diciembre 2008): 96.

66. Lázaro Peña, "Problemas del movimiento obrero: Debemos combatir prácticamente la discriminación racial desde los sindicatos," *Hoy*, 29 marzo 1959, 1.

67. Schoultz, *That Infernal Little Republic*, 135. This was a high-cost operation since Almeida's Cuban plane was predictably seized by the US authorities, eager to have the Cuban government pay for the US properties that had just been nationalized in the island.

68. The Catholic Church was an important exception to the government abolition of independent organizations, but it was nevertheless severely constrained in its activities, at least until the relative liberalization of the nineties.

69. Carlos Moore, *Pichón: A Memoir; Race and Revolution in Castro's Cuba* (Chicago: Lawrence Hill Books, 2008), 45–46.

70. Juan René Betancourt, "Castro and the Cuban Negro," *Crisis* 68, no. 5 (1961): 271, 273; De la Fuente, *Race, Inequality and Politics*, 280–85.

71. Mark Q. Sawyer, *Racial Politics in Post-revolutionary Cuba* (New York: Cambridge University Press, 2006), 65.

72. In October 2005, as part of the Cuban government's policy to legalize certain types of organizations, the Abakuá Society was registered as a religious fraternity in the National Registry of Associations of the Cuban Ministry of Justice. María I. Faguagua Iglesias, "El lado oculto del 27 de noviembre: La nación cubana y la Sociedad Abakuá," *Encuentro de la Cultura Cubana* 53/54 (verano/otoño 2009): 65.

73. Cited in Masferrer and Mesa-Lago, "The Gradual Integration," 379.

74. "Negro cubano," in "Poesía-Rap: Textos de Soandry del Río (Hermanos de Causa)," *Encuentro de la Cultura Cubana* 53/54 (verano/otoño 2009): 103.

75. Samuel Farber, "Visiting Raúl Castro's Cuba," *New Politics* 43, 11, no. 3 (Summer 2007): 90.

76. Irene Esther, "Presencia de la mujer negra en la televisión cubana," *Negra Cubana Tenía que ser*, 28 noviembre 2006, http://negracubana.blogia.com.

77. De la Fuente, *Race, Inequality and Politics*, 325.

78. Pedro Alexander Cubas Hernández, "Entre ademanes de lo posible y ardides de lo permitido: Hablar de racismo en Cuba," *Encuentro de la Cultura Cubana* 53/54 (verano/otoño 2009): 47–48.

79. Alejandro de la Fuente, "Recreating Racism: Race and Discrimination in Cuba's 'Special Period,'" Caribbean Project, Center for Latin American Studies, Georgetown University, no. 18 (July 1998): 5.

80. Ibid.

81. Domínguez, "Racial and Ethnic Relations in the Cuban Armed Forces," 283.

82. Henley C. Adams, "Fighting an Uphill Battle: Race, Politics, Power, and Institutional-ization in Cuba," *Latin American Research Review* 39, no. 1 (February 2004): 171.

83. Ibid., 171–72.

84. Ibid., 173.

85. Ibid., 180.

86. Hal Klepak, *Cuba's Military, 1990–2005: Revolutionary Soldiers during Counter-revolutionary Times* (New York: Palgrave Macmillan, 2005), 219.

87. Adams, "Fighting an Uphill Battle," 168, 181.

88. Masferrer and Mesa-Lago, "The Gradual Integration," 363–64, 383; Oficina Nacional de Estadísticas (ONE), Tabla II.3, "Población por color de la piel y grupos de edades, según zona de residencia y sexo," in Cubacuenta, Censo de Población y Viviendas, Cuba-2002, *Granma Digital Internacional*, November 14, 2005.

89. Morales Domínguez, "Desafíos de la problemática racial en Cuba," 98.

90. There are observers who believe that the nonwhite population of Cuba is as high as 70 percent. For various estimates see Moore, *Castro, the Blacks and Africa*, 359–65.

91. The government has announced that a new census will be carried out in September 2012. Agencias, Madrid, "Anuncian un nuevo censo de población y vivienda: Tendrá lugar en septiembre de 2012," *cubaencuentro*, 7 septiembre 2010, www.cubaencuentro.com.

92. Rodrigo Espina Prieto and Pablo Rodríguez Ruiz, "Raza y desigualdad en la Cuba actual," *Temas*, no. 45 (enero–marzo 2006): 48.

93. De la Fuente, *Race, Inequality and Politics*, 319.

94. Espina Prieto and Rodríguez Ruiz, "Raza y desigualdad en la Cuba actual," 48–49.

95. Rodrigo Espina Prieto and Pablo Rodríguez Ruiz, "Race and Inequality in Cuba Today," *Socialism and Democracy* 24, no. 1 (March 2010): 169.

96. Ibid.

97. Cigarettes were eliminated from the ration book in 2010.

98. Espina Prieto and Rodríguez Ruiz, "Race and Inequality in Cuba Today," 169.

99. Espina Prieto and Rodríguez Ruiz, "Raza y desigualdad," 46–47.

100. For a very informative account of the nature and role of rap music in Cuba, see chapter 3, "Fear of a Black Nation: Local Rappers, Transnational Crossings, and State Power," of Sujatha Fernandes's *Cuba Represent! Cuban Arts, State Power, and the Making of New Revolutionary Cultures* (Durham, NC: Duke University Press, 2006), 85–134.

101. Evenson, *Law and Society in Contemporary Cuba*, 130.

102. De la Fuente, *Race, Inequality and Politics*, 323–24.

103. Thus, for example, the union of workers at the electrical utility, one of the most militant and anti-Batista unions in the country, collaborated with the employers in barring blacks from employment in the industry and from membership in its Cubaneleco social club and baseball teams.

104. My approach and perspective are influenced by and draw heavily on the pioneering work of the UC Berkeley sociologist (my former teacher) Robert Blauner. See his *Racial Oppression in America* (New York: Harper and Row, 1972). His disciples (and my fellow graduate students) Stephen Steinberg and David Wellman have continued to work along the paths originally opened by Blauner. See, for example, Stephen Steinberg, *The Ethnic Myth: Race, Ethnicity, and Class in America* (Boston: Beacon Press, 1989); David T. Wellman, *Portraits of White Racism* (New York: Cambridge University Press, 1977); and Michael K Brown et al., *White-Washing Race: The Myth of a Color-Blind Society* (Berkeley: University of California Press, 2003).

105. Interview by Rafael Duharte and Elsa Santos, cited in De la Fuente, *Race, Inequality and Politics*, 324.

106. I want to thank Stephen Steinberg for his help in developing this formulation. Personal communication of June 10, 2010.

107. For a brief historical background of the Abakuá influence among the stevedores of the port of Havana, see David Booth, "Cuba, Color and the Revolution," *Science and Society* 11, no. 2 (Summer 1976): 153–54.

108. Sawyer, *Racial Politics in Post-revolutionary Cuba*, 66–69. Sawyer's summary account is in turn based on the work of other observers and scholars. See, in particular, the more detailed exposition in Moore, *Castro, the Blacks and Africa*, 304–316.

109. Patricia Grogg, "Cuba: Racism Continues," IPS, September 9, 2009.

110. Odette Casamayor-Cisneros, "Todos los negros finos hemos decidido: Nuevos caminos de la expresión racial," *Encuentro de la Cultura Cubana* 53/54 (verano/otoño 2009): 75, and Victor Fowler Calzada, "Contra el argumento racista," *Encuentro de la Cultura Cubana* 53/54 (verano/otoño 2009): 82, 92.

111. Ramonet, *Fidel Castro: Biografía*, 210.

112. Cubas Hernández, "Entre ademanes de lo posible," 54.

113. Norberto Mesa Carbonell, Primer Cofrade, Tato Quiñones, Cofrade, and Tomás Fernández Robaina, Cofrade, "Cofradía de la Negritud: Carta de presentación," La Lisa, julio 1998.

114. "La Cofradía de la Negritud: Un proyecto de acción ciudadana contra la discriminación racial," *Encuentro de la Cultura Cubana* 53/54 (verano/otoño 2009): 112–15.

115. "Cofradía de la Negritud advierte a la CTC sobre posibles despidos racistas," *Diario de Cuba*, 23 septiembre 2010, www.diariodecuba.net.

116. "Presidente cubano reconoce discriminación," *Cuba a la Mano*, December 21, 2010, http://cubaalamano.net/sitio/client/brief.php?id=7547.

117. Associated Press, "TV cubana se lanza al debate sobre el racismo en la isla," Univisión, January 21, 2010.

118. "Acting on Our Conscience: A Declaration of African-American Support for the Civil Rights Struggle in Cuba," AfroCubaWeb, November 30, 2009, http://afrocubaweb.com/actingonourconscience.htm.

119. See Pedro de la Hoz, "Sobre los derechos humanos en Cuba: Un tiro fallido por el flanco equivocado," and Nancy Morejón et al., "Mensaje desde Cuba a los intelectuales y artistas afronorteamericanos," *Granma*, 9 diciembre 2009, 4–5.

120. Moore, *Castro, the Blacks and Africa*, 331–32.

121. Sawyer, *Racial Politics in Post-revolutionary Cuba*, 61.

122. Ibid., 123–24.

123. De la Fuente, *Race, Inequality and Politics*, 332.

124. For a more detailed discussion of the distinction between the "Havana Shore" and "Havana Inland," see Samuel Farber, "Cuba Today and Prospects for Change," *New Politics* 8, no. 1, n.s. (Summer 2000): 167–68.

Chapter Six: Gender Politics and the Cuban Revolution

1. Lumsden, *Machos, Maricones and Gays*, 37. Lumsden also suggests that the massive Spanish twentieth-century migration to Cuba might have reinforced traditional Hispanic sexism long after the end of Spanish colonial rule (40).

2. Tomás Fernández Robaina, "Cuban Sexual Values and African Religious Beliefs," appendix A of Lumsden, *Machos, Maricones and Gays*, 205–07.

3. K. Lynn Stoner, *From the House to the Streets: The Cuban Woman's Movement for Legal Reform, 1898–1940* (Durham, NC: Duke University Press, 1991), 46.

4. Lois M. Smith and Alfred Padula, *Sex and Revolution: Women in Socialist Cuba* (New York: Oxford University Press, 1996), 156.

5. Stoner, *From the House to the Streets*, 45.

6. Bunck, *Fidel Castro and the Quest for a Revolutionary Culture*, 89.

7. Olga Coffigny Leonard, "Mujeres parlamentarias cubanas (1936–1958)," *Temas*, no. 55 (julio–septiembre 2008): 185–86.

8. Bunck, *Fidel Castro and the Quest for a Revolutionary Culture in Cuba*, 89.

9. Coffigny Leonard, "Mujeres parlamentarias cubanas," 187.

10. Smith and Padula, *Sex and Revolution: Women in Socialist Cuba*, 19.

11. Stoner, *From the House to the Streets*, 158–59; Smith and Padula, *Sex and Revolution: Women in Socialist Cuba*, 156.

12. Stoner, *From the House to the Streets*, 164.

13. Ibid., 161–62.

14. Ibid., 192, and Coffigny Leonard, "Mujeres parlamentarias cubanas," 186.

15. Smith and Padula, *Sex and Revolution: Women in Socialist Cuba*, 73.

16. Bunck, *Fidel Castro and the Quest for a Revolutionary Culture in Cuba*, 89.

17. See the first chapter, "The Prerevolutionary Economy: Progress or Stagnation?," of Farber, *The Origins of the Cuban Revolution Reconsidered*, 7–33.

18. For a thorough and comprehensive account of US cultural influence in Cuba, see Louis A. Perez, *On Becoming Cuban* (Chapel Hill: University of North Carolina Press, 1999).

19. Bunck, *Fidel Castro and the Quest for a Revolutionary Culture in Cuba*, 89. Of course, literacy rates were lower in the Cuban countryside. Again, this issue is explored and length in the first chapter, "The Prerevolutionary Economy," of Farber, *The Origins of the Cuban Revolution Reconsidered*.

20. Smith and Padula, *Sex and Revolution: Women in Socialist Cuba*, 89.

21. Ibid., 89.

22. Isabel Larguía and John Dumoulin, "La mujer en el desarrollo: Estrategia y experiencias de la Revolución Cubana," *Casa de las Americas* 25, no. 149 (marzo–abril 1985): 39.

23. José A. Moreno, "From Traditional to Modern Values," in *Revolutionary Change in Cuba*, ed. Mesa-Lago, 479; and Smith and Padula, *Sex and Revolution: Women in Socialist Cuba*, 96.

24. According to an occupational survey carried out in 1952. See Pérez, *Cuba: Between Reform and Revolution*, 232.

25. Lourdes Arguelles and B. Ruby Rich, "Homosexuality, Homophobia, and Revolution: Notes toward an Understanding of the Cuban Lesbian and Gay Male Experience," part I, *Signs* 9, no. 4 (Summer 1984): 686. Along similar lines, Susan Sontag saw Cuba's role as the most popular playground "for the limited exercise of the white middle-class American id on winter vacation" as being of equal importance to sugar and tobacco in defining prerevolutionary Cuba's place in history. Sontag, "Some Thoughts on the Right Way," 14.

26. Rosalie Schwartz, *Pleasure Island: Tourism and Temptation in Cuba* (Lincoln: University of Nebraska Press, 1997), 168.

27. Paul L. Andry, Jr., collector, Papers of Moa Bay Mining Company, Latin American Library, Tulane University, http://lal.tulane.edu/collections/manuscripts/andry.

28. Schwartz, *Pleasure Island: Tourism and Temptation in Cuba*, 115, 148.

29. Of course, many contemporary foreign tourists do not visit Havana, but the number who do far exceed those who visited the capital in the fifties.

30. Pérez, *Cuba: Between Reform and Revolution*, 231–32.

31. For a recent example of a distorted analysis that places organized vice and crime at the very center of Cuban reality in the fifties, see T. J. English, *Havana Nocturne: How the Mob Owned Cuba—and Then Lost It to the Revolution* (New York: William Morrow/Harper Collins, 2007).

32. One notable exception was the Inquisition's sentencing of eighteen "effeminate" sailors in 1571. Marcelo Morales, Cristina Vives, and Sachie Hernández, "Conducta impropia," unpublished manuscript, n.d., 1.

33. Lumsden, *Machos, Maricones and Gays*, 32.

34. Morales, Vives, and Hernández, "Conducta impropia," 6.

35. Emilio Bejel, *Gay Cuban Nation* (Chicago: University of Chicago Press, 2001), 16–27. Bejel also discusses in more general terms Cuban views of homosexuality in the late nineteenth and early twentieth centuries.

36. Ibid., 6–8.

37. Lumsden, *Machos, Maricones and Gays*, 29.

38. Ibid., 30.

39. Thomas, *Cuba: The Pursuit of Freedom*, 767–68.

40. For a corrective see Michelle Chase, "Women's Organisations and the Politics of Gender in Cuba's Urban Insurrection (1952–1958)," *Bulletin of Latin American Research* 29, no. 4 (September 2010).

41. Díaz Vallina, Dotre Romay, and Dacosta Pérez, "Avance de investigación: La mujer revolucionaria," 24–32.

42. Smith and Padula, *Sex and Revolution: Women in Socialist Cuba*, 22–23.

43. I want to thank Michelle Chase for reminding me of this important fact.

44. Smith and Padula, *Sex and Revolution: Women in Socialist Cuba*, 27, 30; Tiffany A. Thomas-Woodard, "'Towards the Gates of Eternity': Celia Sánchez Manduley and the Creation of Cuba's New Woman," *Cuban Studies* 34 (2003): 154–80.

45. Ilja A. Luciak, *Gender and Democracy in Cuba* (Gainesville: University Press of Florida, 2007), 3.

46. Ramonet, *Fidel Castro: Biografía*, 187.

47. Smith and Padula, *Sex and Revolution: Women in Socialist Cuba*, 22–23; Díaz Vallina, Dotre Romay, and Dacosta Pérez, "Avance de investigación: La mujer revolucionaria," 26–27; chapter 5, "The Cuban Insurrection through a Feminist Lens, 1952–1959," in *The Revolution Question: Feminisms in El Salvador, Chile and Cuba*, ed. Julie D. Shayne (New Brunswick, NJ: Rutgers University Press, 2004).

48. Reynaldo González interview with Marvin Leiner, Havana, 1988, in Marvin Leiner, *Sexual Politics in Cuba: Machismo, Homosexuality and AIDS* (Boulder, CO: Westview Press, 1994), 13, 20.

49. William H. Chafe, *Women and Equality: Changing Patterns in American Culture* (New York: Oxford University Press, 1977), 81.

50. Institutions such as the Catholic Church were left with a minimal degree of autonomy and prevented from exercising many of their functions, at least until the early nineties.

51. Smith and Padula, *Sex and Revolution: Women in Socialist Cuba*, 32; Luciak, *Gender and Democracy in Cuba*, 15.

52. Domínguez, *Cuba: Order and Revolution*, 267.

53. Bunck, *Fidel Castro and the Quest for a Revolutionary Culture in Cuba*, 94–95.

54. Pérez-Stable, *The Cuban Revolution: Origins, Course and Legacy*, 107. Unfortunately, ever since the Special Period that began in the nineties, domestic service has returned as a growing occupation for women, and even some men, on the island.

55. Bunck, *Fidel Castro and the Quest for a Revolutionary Culture*, 96–99.

56. Domínguez, *Cuba: Order and Revolution*, 267.

57. Ibid., 269.

58. Smith and Padula, *Sex and Revolution: Women in Socialist Cuba*, 51.

59. Cited in Domínguez, *Cuba: Order and Revolution*, 268.

60. Smith and Padula, *Sex and Revolution: Women in Socialist Cuba*, 39; Luciak, *Gender and Democracy in Cuba*, 25.

61. Bunck, *Fidel Castro and the Quest for a Revolutionary Culture*, 99.

62. Lillian Guerra, "Gender Policing, Homosexuality and the New Patriarchy of the Cuban Revolution, 1965–1970," *Social History* 35, no. 3 (August 2010): 277–78.

63. Maxine Molyneux, *State, Gender and Institutional Change in Cuba's "Special Period": The Federación de Mujeres Cubanas* (London: Institute of Latin American Studies, 1996), 13.

64. Luciak, *Gender and Democracy in Cuba*, 21–23.
65. Ibid., 21.
66. Ibid., 26.
67. Sujatha Fernandes, "Transnationalism and Feminist Activism in Cuba: The Case of Magín," *Politics and Gender* 1 (2005): 442–43.
68. S. Más, "Anticipos de un congreso femenino," *Granma*, 28 febrero 1998, as cited in Isabel Holgado Fernández, *¡No es fácil! Mujeres cubanas y la crisis revolucionaria* (Barcelona: Icaria Editorial, 2000), xx.
69. Fernandes, "Transnationalism and Feminist Activism in Cuba," 445–47.
70. Luciak, *Gender and Democracy in Cuba*, 28.
71. Maxine Molyneux, "Mobilization without Emancipation? Women's Interests, State and Revolution," in *Transition and Development: Problems of Third World Socialism*, ed. Center for the Study of Americas (New York: Monthly Review Press, 1986), 284.
72. Guerra, "Gender Policing, Homosexuality and the New Patriarchy," 280.
73. Moreno, "From Traditional to Modern Values," 482.
74. Sweig, *Cuba: What Everyone Needs to Know*, 29.
75. Larguía and Dumoulin, "La mujer en el desarrollo: Estrategia y experiencias de la Revolución Cubana," 51.
76. Mayda Álvarez Suárez, "La revolución de las cubanas: 50 años de conquistas y luchas," *Temas*, no. 56 (octubre–diciembre 2008): 73.
77. IPS, "Mujeres serán minoría en gobiernos locales," *Cuba a la Mano*, 11 mayo 2010.
78. Luciak, *Gender and Democracy in Cuba*, 65.
79. Ibid., 64.
80. Ibid., 78, and Álvarez Suárez, "La revolución de las cubanas," 74. For photographs of the members of the Council of State, see *Granma*, 25 febrero 2008, 4–5.
81. Luciak, *Gender and Democracy in Cuba*, 79.
82. Ibid., 79.
83. Ibid., 81.
84. Ibid., 82.
85. Ibid., 102.
86. Thus, for example, the Cuban exile feminist Ileana Fuentes believes that if Cuba were a less sexist society, more women would be in a position of leadership and consequently the country would not be in a constant state of war. Ileana Fuentes, *Cuba sin caudillos: Un enfoque feminista para el siglo XXI* (Princeton, NJ: Linden Lane Press, 1994), xxviii.
87. Smith and Padula, *Sex and Revolution: Women in Socialist Cuba*, 45.
88. See William H. Chafe's illuminating discussion of this issue in the US context, where he points out that while black men and women live together in communities, women do not typically have their own exclusive communities; this is one of the differences between the two oppressed groups. Chafe, *Women and Equality*, 57.
89. Mesa-Lago, *The Economy of Socialist Cuba*, 165; Mesa-Lago and Pérez-López, *Cuba's Aborted Reform*, 87–88.
90. Álvarez Suárez, "La revolución de las cubanas," 71.
91. Smith and Padula, *Sex and Revolution: Women in Socialist Cuba*, 99.
92. Ibid., 101.
93. Buck, *Fidel Castro and the Quest for a Revolutionary Culture in Cuba*, 114.
94. Smith and Padula, *Sex and Revolution: Women in Socialist Cuba*, 109.
95. Álvarez Suárez, "La revolución de las cubanas," 69.
96. Ibid., 69.
97. Ibid., 70.
98. Luciak, *Gender and Democracy in Cuba*, 106.
99. Álvarez Suárez, "La revolución de las cubanas," 71.

100. Ibid., 69.
101. Dayma Echevarría León, "Mujer, empleo y dirección en Cuba: Algo más que estadísticas," unpublished manuscript cited by Luciak, *Gender and Democracy in Cuba*, 33–34.
102. Smith and Padula, *Sex and Revolution: Women in Socialist Cuba*, 128.
103. Pérez-Stable, *The Cuban Revolution*, 142.
104. Molyneux, *State, Gender and Institutional Change in Cuba's "Special Period,"* 39.
105. Larguía and Dumoulin, "La mujer en el desarrollo: estrategia y experiencias de la Revolución Cubana," 45.
106. Pérez-Stable, *The Cuban Revolution*, 139–40.
107. Ibid., 137–38.
108. Ruth Lewis, *Four Women: Living the Revolution* (Urbana: University of Illinois Press, 1977), xv.
109. Moreno, "From Traditional to Modern Values," 481.
110. Domínguez, *Cuba: Order and Revolution*, 270. For the full text of the Family Code see *Granma*, 3 marzo 1975.
111. These were the findings of sociologist Marie Withers Osmond in "Women and Work in Cuba: Objective Conditions and Subjective Perceptions," revised version of paper presented at the annual meeting of the American Sociological Association, August 26–30, 1985, as cited by Smith and Padula, *Sex and Revolution: Women in Socialist Cuba*, 141.
112. Krause-Fuchs, *Monika y la Revolución*, 262. A letter published in the weekly complaints section of *Granma* showed that bureaucratic obstacles to the collection of child support payments continue to be a major and apparently insuperable problem. M. García Sosa, "Dificultades para cobro de pensión alimenticia," *Granma*, 4 diciembre 2009, 10.
113. Oficina Nacional de Estadísticas (ONE), *Encuesta sobre el uso del tiempo* (Havana, 2002), as cited in Álvarez Suárez, "La revolución de las cubanas," 70–71.
114. Krause-Fuchs, *Monika y la Revolución*, 270. Krause-Fuchs did not remember the exact date this congress was held, although she says it was either in 1989 or 1990.
115. Smith and Padula, *Sex and Revolution: Women in Socialist Cuba*, 182.
116. Randall, *To Change the World*, 143.
117. Krause-Fuchs, *Monika y la Revolución*, 236–37.
118. Ibid., 237.
119. Sarah Berger Richardson, "'Beans Are More Important Than Guns': Discourses of Motherhood and the Militarization of Women and Food in Cuba," abstract of paper submitted to the international symposium "Cuba Futures Past and Present," Bildner Center for Western Hemisphere Studies of the Graduate Center of the City University of New York, Spring 2011.
120. Benítez Pérez, *La familia cubana*, 98.
121. Ibid., 138.
122. Holgado Fernández, *¡No es fácil! Mujeres cubanas y la crisis revolucionaria*, 155.
123. Ibid., 327.
124. Rosa Martínez, "My Daddy Hit Her Again," *HavanaTimes.org*, May 13, 2010, www.havanatimes.org/?p=24049.
125. Associated Press, "Amid Crisis, Cuba Falls Short on Home-Building," December 17, 2009.
126. Miguel Coyula, "La Habana *toda* vieja," *Temas*, no. 48 (octubre–diciembre 2006): 73.
127. Miguel Coyula, "Un lugar donde vivir, o un lugar para vivir?," *Temas*, no. 58 (abril–junio 2009): 41.
128. Benítez Pérez, *La familia cubana*, 97.
129. Smith and Padula, *Sex and Revolution: Women in Socialist Cuba*, 37.
130. Domínguez, *Cuba: Order and Revolution*, 268–69.
131. Pérez Stable, *The Cuban Revolution*, 142.
132. Smith and Padula, *Sex and Revolution: Women in Socialist Cuba*, 35.

133. Krause-Fuchs, *Monika y la Revolución*, 155.
134. Rosenberg Weinreb, *Cuba in the Shadow of Change*, 58.
135. Smith and Padula, *Sex and Revolution: Women in Socialist Cuba*, 136.
136. Ibid. 142.
137. A. S. González León, "El negocio de las almohadillas sanitarias," letter, *Granma*, May 9, 2008, 11. See also Holgado Fernández, *¡No es fácil! Mujeres cubanas y la crisis revolucionaria*, 66–67.
138. Martín Medem, *¿Por qué no me enseñastes?*, 76–77.
139. Holgado Fernández, *¡No es fácil! Mujeres cubanas y la crisis revolucionaria*, 187.
140. Smith and Padula, *Sex and Revolution. Women in Socialist Cuba*, 71; World Bank, *World Development Indicators* (n.p.: World Bank, updated January 19, 2010), www.google.com/publicdata?ds=wb-wdi&met=sp_dyn_tfrt_in&idim=country:CUBA.
141. Smith and Padula, *Sex and Revolution: Women in Socialist Cuba*, 74.
142. See table 8 of live births and abortions for selected years in Benítez Pérez, *La familia cubana*, 88.
143. Dalia Acosta, "Health-Cuba: Abortion Competes with Contraceptives," IPS, June 1, 2006, http://ipsnews.net/news.asp?idnews=33458.
144. IPS, "Cuba enfrenta aborto con 'píldora del día después,'" November 3, 2009, http://cubaalamano.net/sitio/client/brief.php?id=7400.
145. Molyneux, *State, Gender and Institutional Change*, 38–39.
146. Lourdes Pérez Navarro, "Los cubanos no llegarán a 12 millones," *Diario Granma*, 16 noviembre 2010, www.granma.co.cu/2010/11/16/nacional/artic05.html.
147. World Bank, *World Development Indicators*; Marta Nuñez Sarmiento, "Cuban Development Strategies and Gender Relations," *Socialism and Democracy* 24, no. 1 (March 2010): 143.
148. Orfilio Peláez, "Creció la población cubana en el 2009," *Granma*, 5 enero 2010, 3.
149. Smith and Padula, *Sex and Revolution: Women in Socialist Cuba*, 72. Ian Lumsden also reports that only a small proportion of gay men use condoms. Lumsden, *Machos, Maricones and Gays*, 166.
150. Smith and Padula, *Sex and Revolution: Women in Socialist Cuba*, 73.
151. Krause-Fuchs, *Monika y la Revolución*, 236–37.
152. Ibid., 261–62; Benítez, *La familia cubana*, 88–89.
153. Krause-Fuchs, *Monika y la Revolución*, 262.
154. Ibid., 229. I should note that Krause-Fuchs, born and raised in East Germany, lived in Cuba from 1962 until 1990 and that her testimony is concerned with events that occurred mostly during the seventies and eighties.
155. Holgado Fernández, *¡No es fácil! Mujeres cubanas y la crisis revolucionaria*, 189.
156. For the legal procedures required for Cuban divorces see Lourdes Pérez Navarro, "Cuestión de leyes: La disolución del vínculo matrimonial," *Diario Granma*, 17 marzo 2010, www.granma.co.cu/2010/03/17/nacional/artic01.html.
157. Smith and Padula, *Sex and Revolution: Women in Socialist Cuba*, 155.
158. Benítez, *La familia cubana*, 91; María Elena Benítez as quoted in Tracey Eaton, "For Many in Cuba, Marriage Is for the Birds," *Dallas Morning News*, July 3, 2004.
159. Krause-Fuchs, *Monika y la Revolución*, 262.
160. Allen Young, *Gays under the Cuban Revolution* (San Francisco: Grey Fox Press, 1981), 31.
161. Carlos Franqui, *Retrato de familia con Fidel* (Barcelona: Editorial Seix Barral, 1981), 280–86; Manuel Zayas, "Mapa de la homofobia," *cubaencuentro*, 15 febrero 2010, http://cubaencuenro.com/es/cuba/articulos/mapa-de-la-homofobia-10736.
162. Departamento de Versiones Taquigráficas del Gobierno Revolucionario, "Discurso pronunciado por el Comandante Fidel Castro Ruz, primer ministro del gobierno revolucionario de Cuba, en la clausura del acto para conmemorar el VI aniversario del asalto al palacio presidencial celebrado en la escalinata de la Universidad de la Habana, 13 de

marzo de 1963," *cuba.cu*, www.cuba.cu/gobierno/discursos/1963/esp/f130363e.html.

163. Lumsden, *Machos, Maricones and Gays*, 65–70.

164. Guerra, "Gender Policing, Homosexuality and the New Patriarchy," 274.

165. Thomas, *Cuba: The Pursuit of Freedom*, 1971, 1435; Guerra, "Gender Policing, Homosexuality and the New Patriarchy," 271.

166. Cited from excerpts from *Granma Weekly Review*, May 9, 1971, 5, in Young, *Gays under the Cuban Revolution*, 32–33.

167. Young, *Gays under the Cuban Revolution*, 53; Guerra, "Gender Policing, Homosexuality and the New Patriarchy, 1965–1970," 282.

168. Young, *Gays under the Cuban Revolution*, 34–35.

169. Leiner, *Sexual Politics in Cuba: Machismo, Homosexuality and AIDS*, 117–18.

170. Ibid., 122, 138.

171. Evenson, *Law and Society in Contemporary Cuba*, 187.

172. Leiner, *Sexual Politics in Cuba: Machismo, Homosexuality and AIDS*, 59.

173. Norge Espinosa Mendoza, "Historial en el vacío: Arte, gays y espacio social en Cuba," *Encuentro de la Cultura Cubana*, verano/otoño 2006, 41–42, 92.

174. Lumsden, *Machos, Maricones and Gays*, 144; Yoelvis L. Moreno Fernández, "Avanza reparación del centro cultural El Mejunje," *Juventud Rebelde*, 2 febrero 2010, www.juventudrebelde.cu/cuba/2010-02-02/avanza-reparacion-de-centro-cultural-el-mejunje-/.

175. However, it is worth noting that in spring 2011 *Granma* published a report favorable to the CENESEX campaign against homophobia. José A. de la Osa, "¿Por qué una jornada cubana contra la homophobia?," *Digital Granma Internacional*, 9 mayo 2011, www.granma.cu/espanol/cuba/9-mayo-jornada.html.

176. Mariela Castro, "Los 'prejuicios' frenan la ley de unión homosexual," *Rebelión*, 14 enero 2010, http://rebelión.org/noticia.php?id=98650; "Mariela Castro felicita a México, D.F. por aprobar el matrimonio gay, pero la ley cubana sigue bloqueada," *Diario de Cuba*, 13 enero 2010, www.ddcuba.com/cuba/noticias/2010/mariela-castro-felicita-mexico-df-por-aprobar-el-matrimonio-gay-pero-la-ley-cuban.

177. Alberto Yoan Arego Pulido, "Celebran jornada cubana contra la homofobia," *Juventud Rebelde*, 17 mayo 2009, www.juventudrebelde.cu/; Dalia Acosta, "Cuba: Diversidad sexual, los derechos no esperan," IPS, 17 mayo 2010, www.cubaalamano.net.

178. Matthew Cullinan Hoffman, "Diocese of Havana Denounces Cuban Government's Promotion of Homosexuality," LifeSiteNews.com, June 24, 2008, www.lifesite.news.com/ldn/2008/june/08062606.html.

179. Lumsden, *Machos, Maricones and Gays*, 84; Evenson, *Law and Society in Contemporary Cuba*, 187.

180. Ibid., 83.

181. Fernando Ravsberg, "Cuba: 'Campaña' contra travestis," BBCMundo.com, July 26, 2004, http://news.bbc.co.uk/hi/spanish/latin_america/newsid_3926000/3926441.stm.

182. "Gay Life in Cuba: Not Much Has Changed since Reinaldo Arenas' Time," *LGBT Cuba News Today*, reprinted in *In These Times*, December 2009.

183. Dalia Acosta, "CUBA: Polémica por voto en la ONU," IPS, *Cuba a la Mano*, 30 noviembre 2010, http://cubaalamano.net/sitio/client/report.php?id=1218; "Declaración de la SOCUMES y el CENESEX sobre voto de Cuba en la Asamblea General de las Naciones Unidas," *cubaencuentro*, 2 diciembre 2010, www.cubaencuentro.com.

184. Dalia Acosta, "Cuba: Cancillería explica voto en la ONU," IPS, *Cuba a la Mano*, 2 diciembre 2010, http://cubaalamano.net/sitio/client/report.php?id=1220.

185. Paquito, el de Cuba, "Un paso adelante o cuando la ausencia no quiere decir olvido," http://paquitoeldecuba.wordpress.com.

186. Emilio Bejel, *Gay Cuban Nation* (Chicago: University of Chicago Press, 2001), 110.

187. Sontag, "Some Thoughts on the Right Way," 14.

188. Young, *Gays under the Cuban Revolution*, 15.
189. Lumsden, *Machos, Maricones and Gays*, 64–65.
190. Thomas Harrison, "Socialism and Homosexuality," 19–21, and Sherry Wolf, "LGBT Political Cul-de-Sac: Make a U-Turn," 34, *New Politics* 12 no. 2 (Winter 2009).
191. Lee Lockwood, *Castro's Cuba, Cuba's Fidel*, rev. ed. (Boulder, CO: Westview Press, 1990), 106–107.
192. Ian Lumsden discusses cowardice and how it has been attributed to Cuban gays. Lumsden also points out that the exaltation of physical bravado, which is such an important feature of Cuban machismo, has been relatively absent in Costa Rica, a country that has been involved in fewer military struggles. Lumsden, *Machos, Maricones and Gays*, 53.
193. According to one eyewitness, the prominent Spanish writer Juan Goytisolo, Guevara contemptuously threw Piñera's book across the room as he exclaimed, "Who the fuck reads this faggot here?" ("¿Quien coño lee aquí a ese maricón?"). Juan Goytisolo, *En los reinos de taifa* (Barcelona: Seix Barral, 1986), 174–75.
194. Guerra, "Gender Policing, Homosexuality and the New Patriarchy," 271.
195. Ibid., 271, 283–84.
196. Samuel Feijóo, "Revolución y vicios," *El Mundo*, April 15, 1965, 4, as cited in Guerra, "Gender Policing, Homosexuality and the New Patriarchy," 281–82.
197. Mariela Castro Espín, "Pedir perdón sería una gran hipocresía," Agencia Suiza para el desarrollo y la cooperación COSUDE, 6 octubre 2010, www.cooperacion-suiza .admin.ch/cuba/es/Pagina_Principal/Noticias/Vista_detallada?itemID=195685.
198. This is the title of chapter 9 of Lumsden's *Machos, Maricones and Gays*, 178.
199. Smith and Padula, *Sex and Revolution: Women in Socialist Cuba*, 147.
200. Ibid., 147.
201. Fidel Castro, *Un grano de maíz: Conversación con Tomás Borge* (Havana: Oficina de Publicaciones del Consejo de Estado, 1992), 237–38.
202. Carmen Lira Saade, "Soy el responsible de la persecución a homosexuales que hubo en Cuba: Fidel Castro," *La Jornada*, 31 agosto 2010, 26.
203. Castro Espín, "Pedir perdón sería una gran hipocresía."

Chapter Seven: Dissidents and Critics

1. For an analysis of this and related matters concerning the Batista dictatorship in the fifties see Farber, *Revolution and Reaction in Cuba*.
2. Estimates of the number of those executed vary quite widely, but the most credible estimate is that of the British historian Hugh Thomas, who estimated that there were two thousand executions by early 1961 and perhaps five thousand by 1970. Thomas, *Cuba: The Pursuit of Freedom*, 1460.
3. For a more detailed discussion of this issue see chapters 8–9 of Farber, *Revolution and Reaction in Cuba*.
4. It is worth noting that this statement did proclaim that the necessary changes in Cuban society had to be brought about by the independent and sovereign Cuban people themselves without foreign interventions. "Unidad por la libertad: Mensaje al pueblo de Cuba y a los pueblos del mundo," 15 abril 2007, www.miscelaneasdecuba.net/web/article .asp?artID=9791.
5. For an example of a Cuban woman who is trying to put into practice the rights approach in her everyday life on the island, see Rosa Martínez, "Defending My Rights in Cuba," *HavanaTimes.org*, November 24, 2010, www.havanatimes.org/?p=33640.
6. Thomas Paine, *The Rights of Man*, in Edmund Burke and Thomas Paine, *Reflections on the Revolution in France and The Rights of Man* (Garden City, NY: Dolphin Books, 1961), 323–24. Capital letters and emphasis in original.

7. "Introducción," *Encuentro de la Cultura Cubana* 25 (verano 2002): 3–4. See also the highly critical account written by Pascual Serrano, a well-known supporter of the Cuban regime, in "Gobierno español, estadounidense y fundaciones privadas se unen para financiar el proyecto anticastrista Encuentro," *kaosenlared.net*, September 9, 2009.

8. "Homenaje a la República," *Encuentro de la Cultura Cubana* 24 (primavera 2002): 5–151.

9. See, for example, the collection "Dossier Europa del Este," with articles by Adam Michnik, Vladimir Tismaneanu, Elzbetia Matynia, Miguel Angel Centeno, Tania Rank, and Marcin Krol, in *Encuentro de la Cultura Cubana* 25 (verano 2002): 181–257; and particularly Michnik, "La lógica del compromiso," *Encuentro de la Cultura Cubana* 32 (primavera 2004), in which he warns Cubans against the "utopia" of the third way.

10. "Un hasta luego," *Encuentro de la Cultura Cubana* 53/54 (verano/otoño 2009): 3–4.

11. "Desde Cuba Primera Convención Arco Progresista: Ponencia política," *Cuba Nuestra Digital*, 20 julio 2008, 3, 6, www.cubanuestra.nu/web/article.asp?artID=12543.

12. Patricia Grogg, "Rights-Cuba: Dissidents Work for Racial Integration," IPS, September 3, 2008, www.ipsnews.net/news.asp?idnews=43775.

13. Partido Arco Progresista, "Cuba después del 13 de Septiembre: La posición socialdemócrata," *Cuba Nuestra: Sociedad Civil*, 21 octubre 2010, http://cubanuesra4eu.wordpress.com.

14. Martín Medem, *¿Por qué no me enseñaste?*, 166. Martín Medem was the correspondent in Cuba of TVE, the Spanish television channel. He is clearly a man of left-wing views and very critical of the Cuban government and system.

15. Ibid., 219.

16. Partido Arco Progresista, "La carta de 'Nuevo País,'" 19 mayo 2010, http://partido-arcoprogresista.org/partidoarco/la-carta-de-nuevo-pais/.

17. *New York Times*, April 22, 1997, cited in Schoultz, *That Infernal Little Republic*, 499, 712.

18. Martín Medem, *¿Por qué no me enseñaste?*, 198.

19. "Roca, Sanchez Rap USINT's Internet-Access Policy, ID: 62090, April 27, 2006, Source: US Interests Section Havana," originally accessed at elpais.com, http://www.cablegate-search.net/cable.php?id=06HAVANA9102.

20. Juan Carlos Linares Balmaseda, "Disidencia, 'Ha sido una represión inútil': Elizardo Sánchez Santa Cruz," Cubanet: Prensa Independiente, 17 marzo 2004, www.cubanet.org/Cnews/y04/mar04/18a1.htm.

21. Enrique Patterson, "La mano escondida de la 'gatica de María Ramos,'" *El Nuevo Herald*, October 1, 2003, accessed via LAC News\LATAMCOM INC mailing list.

22. Will Weissert, "Cuban Dissidents Cheer Bill to End US Travel Ban," *Miami Herald*, June 10, 2010, www.miamiherald.com/2010/06/10/1673319/cuban-dissidents-cheer-bill-to.html.

23. Human Rights Watch, *Cuba: New Castro, Same Cuba; Political Prisoners in the Post-Fidel Era* (New York: Human Rights Watch, 2009), 8–9.

24. Human Rights Watch, *Cuba's Repressive Machinery: Human Rights Forty Years after the Revolution* (New York: Human Rights Watch, 1999), 204–213.

25. President Barack Obama's position has been that the economic embargo will stay until Cuba improves human rights and frees political detainees. Reuters, "Castros Sabotage Ending U.S. Cuba Embargo: Clinton," *Washington Post*, April 10, 2010, www.washingtonpost.com/wp-dyn/content/article/2010/04/09/AR2010040904469.html.

26. Even the design of the Cuban national flag was substantially influenced by Masonic symbols. Eduardo Torres-Cuevas, *Historia de la Masonería cubana: Seis ensayos*, (Havana: Imagen Contemporanea, 2004), 96, 149, 164–66.

27. Wyatt MacGaffey and Clifford R. Barnet, *Twentieth-Century Cuba: The Background of the Castro Revolution* (Garden City, NY: Doubleday Anchor, 1965), 243.

28. Mateo Jover Marimón, "The Church," in *Revolutionary Change in Cuba*, ed. Mesa-Lago, 400–02.

29. The text of the pastoral letter is reproduced in Raúl Gómez Treto, *The Church and So-*

cialism in Cuba, trans. Phillip Berryman (Maryknoll, NY: Orbis, 1988), 30–32.

30. Jover Marimón, "The Church," 404; Treto, *The Church and Socialism in Cuba*, 45.

31. Treto, *The Church and Socialism in Cuba*, 43.

32. Ibid., 84–86; Jover Marimón, "The Church," 405.

33. Treto, *The Church and Socialism in Cuba*, 67.

34. For more historical details about the Catholic Church in Cuba in the eighties and nineties written from a sympathetic perspective, see María Isabel Alfonso, "Los ataques al cardenal: Drama en cuatro actos," *cubaencuentro*, 4 junio 2010, www.cubaencuentro.com.

35. David Einhorn, "Catholic Church in Cuba Strives to Reestablish the Faith," *National Catholic Reporter*, March 31, 2006, http://natcath.org/NCR_Online/archives2/2006a/033106/033106o.php.

36. "Monseñor Carlos Manuel de Céspedes pide un debate 'serio' sobre los 'cambios estructurales,'" *cubaencuentro*, September 11, 2009, www.cubaencuentro.com. See also Monseñor Cespedes's detailed proposals in "Cuba hoy: Compatibilidad entre cambios reales y el panorama constitucional," which was published in the Cuban Catholic publication *Espacio Laical*, Suplemento Digital 77, septiembre 2009.

37. Gustavo Andújar, "Medios católicos en Cuba son distintos pero no ajenos," interview by Patricia Grogg, *Cuba a la Mano*, 14 octubre 2010, http://cubaalamano.net/sitio/client/report.php?id=1201.

38. "Obispo reclama espacios en los medios," *Cuba a la Mano*, 12 mayo 2009, http://cubaalamano.net/sitio/client/brief.php?id+6804.

39. AFP, "Castro autoriza misas y cultos en cárceles de Cuba," *El Nuevo Herald*, 15 septiembre 2009, www.elnuevoherald.com/noticias/america_latina/cuba/story/543529.html.

40. Orlando Márquez Hidalgo, "Arzobispado de la Habana—Nota de Prensa," 20 diciembre 2010, http://palabranueva.net/.

41. Einhorn, "Catholic Church in Cuba Strives to Reestablish the Faith."

42. Patricia Grogg, "Rights: Cuba Launches Anti-homophobia Campaign," IPS, March 30, 2009, www.ipsnews.org/news.asp?idnews=46323.

43. "No hay patria sin virtud": Carta pastoral del eminentísimo señor cardenal Jaime Ortega y Alamino en el 150 aniversario de la muerte del Padre Félix Varela," *Encuentro de la Cultura Cubana* 28/29 (verano/otoño 2003): 101.

44. "El cardenal Ortega lamenta el 'estado decadente' de la sociedad," *cubaencuentro*, 9 septiembre 2009, www.cubaencuentro.com.

45. Isabel Morales, "Ortega informará a EEUU de situación en Cuba," *El Nuevo Herald*, 4 agosto 2010.

46. Jackson Diehl, "Can Raúl Castro Modernize Cuba?," *Washington Post*, August 9, 2010, www.washingtonpost.com/wp-dyn/content/article/2010/08/08/AR2010080802398.html.

47. Yoani Sánchez, "La mesa está coja," *Generación Y*, 20 mayo 2010.

48. "Carta abierta al Papa Benedicto XVI," *El Nuevo Herald*, 21 agosto 2010.

49. "La mediación deberá seguir su curso inalterable," editorial, *Espacio Laical*, Suplemento Digital 110, agosto 2010, espaciolaical.org; and Arzobispado de la Habana, nota de prensa, 20 agosto 2010, http://palabranueva.net/contens/pn_notic.htm#1041.

50. When the archbishop of New York, Timothy M. Dolan, was elected president of the United States Conference of Catholic Bishops in 2010, he suggested that he would not countenance other Catholic leaders and organizations taking public positions contradicting that of the bishops. Archbishop Dolan proclaimed that "we're pastors and teachers, not just one set of teachers in the Catholic community, but *the* teachers." Laurie Goodstein, "Dolan Is Picked as the Leader of U.S. Bishops," *New York Times*, November 17, 2010.

51. Anneris Ivette Leyva, "Asiste Raúl a la inauguración de la nueve sede del Seminario San Carlos y San Ambrosio," *Diario Granma* 14, no. 309 (4 noviembre 2010), www.granma.co.cu/2010/11/04/nacional/artic04.html.

52. Martín Medem, *¿Por qué no me enseñaste?*, 48–49.
53. Ibid., 56, 147.
54. Oswaldo Payá, "Opinion: Transparencia para Cuba," *cubaencuentro*, 22 junio 2010, www.cubaencuentro.com.
55. Daniel P. Erikson, *The Cuba Wars: Fidel Castro, the United States, and the Next Revolution* (New York: Bloomsbury Press, 2008), 60.
56. See section 3.A of Proyecto Varela at Democracia Participativa, http://democraciaparticipativa.net/documentos/pvarela.htm.
57. Joaquín Roy, *The Cuban Revolution (1959–2009): Relations with Spain, the European Union and the United States* (New York: Palgrave Macmillan, 2009), 83.
58. The project is named after José María Heredia, an early nineteenth-century Cuban poet who was banished from the island because of his opposition to Spanish colonialism.
59. Agencias, "Disidencia: Oswaldo Payá relanza el Proyecto Heredia," *Diario de Cuba*, 6 octubre 2010, http://diariodecuba.com/derechos-humanos/oswaldo-paya-relanza-el-proyecto-heredia.
60. Documento de trabajo para el programa de transición (Working document for the Transition Program, or WD), 12 diciembre 2003, www.pdc-cuba.org/DIALOGO-NACIONAL-completo.htm or http://democraciaparticipativa.net/documentos/DialogoNacional.pdf.
61. Ibid., segunda parte, programa, introducción al capítulo VIII.
62. Ibid., primera parte, capítulo III, no. 36.
63. Ibid., segunda parte, programa, capítulo VIII, sección 3, nos. 45–47.
64. Ibid., segunda parte, programa, capítulo V, sección 2, nos. 15–16.
65. Ibid., segunda parte, programa, capítulo II, introducción.
66. Ibid., segunda parte, programa, capítulo I, sección 2, no. 42.
67. Ibid., segunda parte, programa, capítulo I, sección 2, no. 41.
68. Ibid., segunda parte, programa, capítulo III, introducción.
69. Ibid., segunda parte, programa, capítulo II, sección I, no. 5.
70. For the full text of the letter that Payá sent to the international news agencies on the occasion of the attempted Venezuelan coup, see Martín Medem, *¿Por qué no me enseñaste?*, 32.
71. Documento de trabajo para el programa de transición, primera parte, capítulo III, no. 30.
72. Ibid., segunda parte, programa, capítulo I, sección 3, no. 48.
73. Ibid., segunda parte, programa, capítulo IX, sección 4, no. 59.
74. Ibid., segunda parte, programa, capítulo IX, introducción.
75. Ibid., segunda parte, programa, capítulo IV, sección 3, no. 26.
76. Ibid., segunda parte, programa, capítulo 9, introducción. Throughout the prerevolutionary republic the Catholic Church unsuccessfully attempted to introduce religion into public education. Immediately after the 1959 revolutionary victory, Enrique Pérez Serantes, the prestigious archbishop of Santiago de Cuba, continued to press the issue, but again without success. De Paz Sánchez, *Franco y Cuba: Estudios sobre España y la Revolución*, 160.
77. Documento de trabajo para el programa de transición, primera parte, capítulo IV, no. 50.
78. Professor Ted Henken's blog *El Yuma* has dozens of links to pro-regime, critical, and dissident blogs: elyuma.blogspot.com.
79. Yoani Sánchez's blog is at http://desdecuba.com/generaciony (readers can select from Spanish or English to read on the site).
80. Salim Lamrani, "Conversaciones con la bloguera cubana Yoani Sánchez (2/2)," *Rebelión*, 15 abril 2010, http://rebelion.org/noticia.php?id=104117. While Sánchez claimed that the interviewer had distorted her replies to his questions, she did not explicitly disclaim this or any of the other substantive answers cited in the interview. See Yoani Sánchez, "La Otra Entrevista," *Generación Y*, 16 abril 2010.
81. Yoani Sánchez, "Chávez ha sido el Viagra que necesitaba el gobierno cubano," interview by Roberto Giusti, *El Universal* (Caracas), 4 abril 2010, http://politica.eluniversal.com/

2010/04/04pol_art_chavez-ha-sido-el-v_1818183.shtml.

82. Yoani Sánchez, "Piratas del Caribe," *Generación Y,* 1 junio 2010, www.desdecuba.com/generaciony/?p=3495.

83. Yoani Sánchez, "Mi Pedacito," *Generación Y,* 1 noviembre 2010.

84. Reinaldo Escobar and Yoani Sánchez, "Arrogance, Totalitarian and Hegemonic," reproduced on *El Yuma,* 1 marzo 2010, elyuma.blogspot.com.

85. "09HAVANA592: GOC da señales de 'moverse hacia adelante,'" *Las Razones de Cuba,* 23 diciembre 2010, http://razonesdecuba.cubadebate.cu/cablegates-wikileaks/09havana592-goc-da-senales-de-moverse-hacia-adelante/.

86. "¿Que hiciste cuando vinieron buscando al inconforme?," *Generación Y,* 29 diciembre 2009.

87. Haroldo Dilla, "Y sin embargo, Cuba se mueve," *Periódico 7 Días* (Dominican Republic), January 3, 2010, www.7dias.com.do/app/article.aspx?id=66531.

88. A cable from the US Interests Section in Havana revealed by Wikileaks cites its chief, Jonathan Farrar, as describing "one political party and organization" telling him "quite openly and frankly that it needed resources to pay salaries and presented him with a budget in the hope that USINT would be able to cover it." "Wikileaks 2009: U.S. Bets on Dissidence Delivered by Cuban Youth," *Progresso Weekly,* December 16, 2010, http://progreso-weekly.com.

89. Jules R. Benjamin, *The United States and the Origins of the Cuban Revolution: An Empire of Liberty in an Age of National Liberation* (Princeton, NJ: Princeton University Press, 1990), 188.

90. See the informative discussion of Guillermo J. Grenier in "The Cuban-American Labor Movement in Dade County: An Emerging Immigrant Working Class," in *Miami Now: Immigration, Ethnicity and Social Change,* ed. Guillermo J. Grenier and Alex Stepick III (Gainesville: University Press of Florida, 1992), 133–59.

91. On Jorge Mas Canosa see chapter 5, "The Man Who Would Be King," of Ann Louise Bardach's *Cuba Confidential: Love and Vengeance in Miami and Havana* (New York: Random House, 2002), 126–50.

92. Americas Watch and the Fund for Free Expression, Divisions of Human Rights Watch, *Dangerous Dialogue: Attacks on Freedom of Expression in Miami's Cuban Exile Community* 4, no. 7 (August 1992): 3, 15, 27.

93. Guillermo J. Grenier and Lisandro Pérez, *The Legacy of Exile: Cubans in the United States* (Boston: Allyn and Bacon, 2003), 91.

94. Schoultz, *That Infernal Little Cuban Republic,* 521.

95. Grenier and Pérez, *The Legacy of Exile: Cubans in the United States,* 98.

96. Americas Watch and the Fund for Free Expression, *Dangerous Dialogue: Attacks on Freedom of Expression,* 26.

97. Ibid., 9–11.

98. I use the term "terrorist" in its strict sense of those who deliberately attack noncombatant civilians. These groups and individuals rarely distinguished between unarmed civilians and the security and police forces of Castro's government.

99. Americas Watch and the Fund for Free Expression, *Dangerous Dialogue: Attacks on Freedom of Expression,* 26.

100. Ibid., 20, 21, 3.

101. Ibid., 14, 16, 24–25.

102. Ibid., 12.

103. Grenier and Pérez, *The Legacy of Exile,* 79–80. For an informative and insightful discussion of the white Cuban leadership in Miami and racial politics in the city, see chapter 7, "Racial Politics in Miami: Ninety Miles and a World Away," in Sawyer, *Racial Politics in Post-revolutionary Cuba,* 154–74.

104. Grenier and Pérez, *The Legacy of Exile*, 101–15, for an informative and interesting discussion of the Elián González controversy in Miami.

105. For an informative discussion of corruption, extortion, and protection rackets in Cuban American Miami, see Bardach, *Cuba Confidential: Love and Vengeance in Miami and Havana*, 101–25.

106. David Rieff, *The Exile: Cuba in the Heart of Miami* (New York: Simon and Schuster, 1993), 84–103.

107. For a detailed discussion of Posada Carriles and his record see chapter 7, "An Assassin's Tale in Three Acts," in Bardach, *Cuba Confidential: Love and Vengeance in Miami and Havana*, 171–222.

108. Ann Louise Bardach, "The GOP's Bill Ayers?," *Slate*, October 15, 2008.

109. Christopher Marquis, "Bush Proposes a Plan to Aid Opponents of Castro in Cuba," *New York Times*, May 7, 2004.

110. Oscar Corral, "Exiles Offer Post-Castro Cuban Plan: A Proposal Released by Cuban-American Congressional Leaders and Members of Cuban Exile Groups Offer, a Blueprint for a Transition to Democracy," *Miami Herald*, February 21, 2004, 1; Schoultz, *That Infernal Little Republic*, 549.

111. Martín Medem, *¿Por qué no me enseñaste?*, 41, 158.

112. Ibid., 61, 158; and Schoultz, *That Infernal Little Republic*, 549.

113. Martín Medem, *¿Por qué no me enseñaste?*, 203.

114. "U.S. Plan Ineffective by Design. Our Opinion: Revamp Cuba Programs and Lift Travel, Remittance Restrictions," op-ed, *Miami Herald*, November 19, 2006; and Frances Robles, "Cuban Dissidents Ask U.S. to Lift Travel, Aid Limits," *Miami Herald*, November 28, 2006.

115. "Martha Beatriz, off the Reservation?," *Cuban Triangle: Havana-Miami-Washington Events and Arguments and Their Impact on Cuba*, May 7, 2008, http://cubantriangle.blogspot.com/2008/05/martha-beatriz-off-reservation.html.

116. Grupo de Trabajo de la Disidencia Cubana (Cuban Dissidence Task Group), "The Homeland Belongs to All," translated by the Cuban Humanist Evolutionary Movement (MHEC), www.cartadecuba.org/Homeland%20Belongs.htm.

117. Committee on Human Rights, National Academies, Advisers to the Nation on Science, Engineering, and Medicine, "Cuban Economist Vladimiro Roca Released from Prison," www7.nationalacademies.org/humanrights/Vladimiro_Roca_release.html.

118. Andrés Oppenheimer, *Castro's Final Hour: The Secret Story behind the Coming Downfall of Communist Cuba* (New York: Simon and Schuster, 1992).

119. José Luis Méndez Méndez, "Dos batistianos preocupados," *Cubadebate*, reproduced in *Rebelión*, 1 febrero 2010, www.rebelión.org/noticia.php?id=99671.

120. Mirta Díaz Balart, Mario and Lincoln's aunt, married Fidel Castro in the late forties and divorced him several years later. They had a son, Fidel Castro Díaz Balart (who is therefore a cousin of the two congressmen), who was trained as an engineer in the Soviet Union and for many years headed Cuba's nuclear energy agency. The congressmen's father and grandfather were prominent members of Batista's government.

121. Elysa Batista, "Bitter Election for Congress Behind, Republican Rivera Ready to 'Work Tirelessly,'" *Naples Daily News*, November 7, 2010, www.naplesnews.com.

122. Sweig, *Cuba: What Everyone Needs to Know*, 240.

123. Ginger Thompson, "Restrictions on Travel to Cuba Are Eased," *New York Times*, January 15, 2011.

124. For the views and perspectives of Cuban Christian Democrats (Partido Demócrata Cristiano) on current events, see *Cuba 2.0: Publicación Digital del PDC-Cuba* 9 e-newsletter (pdc.cuba@gmail.com).

125. Consenso Cubano, www.consensocubano.org/eng/pillarscc.htm, n.d. More recently, Consenso Cubano issued a declaration affirming support for, among other things, private enterprise in

the context of the changes taking place on the island. "Consenso Cubano emite declaración sobre situación económica en la Isla," *cubaencuentro*, 11 febrero 2011, cubaencuentro.com.

126. Daivid [*sic*] Adams, "Bringing Hope to Cuba: Youth Group Finds Role in Parents' Cause," *St. Petersburg Times*, October 11, 2009, reproduced on Cuba Study Group, October 12, 2009, www.cubastudygroup.org.

127. Bendixen & Associates, "National Poll of Cuban Americans on Changes to Cuba Policy," www.bendixenandassociates.com/Cuba_Flash_Poll_Executive_Summary.html.

128. "Cuban Americans Split over U.S. Embargo on Cuba: Poll," Reuters, September 1, 2009, www.bendixenandassociates.com/press/reuters-september12009.html.

129. Michael Miller, "Miami Cubans Now Overwhelmingly Favor Lifting Travel Ban," *Miami New Times* (blog), July 27, 2010, as reproduced in La Alborada, mailing list of the Cuban American Alliance Education Fund, July 28, 2010, www.cubamer.org.

130. Guillermo J. Grenier and Hugh Gladwin, "Comparisons among Eight FIU/Cuba Polls: 2007," Institute for Public Opinion Research, Florida International University, Miami, www2.fiu.edu/~ipor/cuba8/CubaComp.htm. I want to thank Professors Jorge Domínguez and Guillermo Grenier for alerting me to this problem of ambiguity and helping me to interpret it.

131. These issues are explored at length in Farber, *Revolution and Reaction in Cuba*.

132. For an interesting and informative discussion of *Pensamiento Crítico* see Kepa Artaraz, *Cuba and Western Intellectuals since 1959* (New York: Palgrave Macmillan, 2009), 40–44, 78–81, 129–32.

133. Velia Cecilia Bobes León, *Los laberintos de la imaginación: Repertorio simbólico, identidades y actores del cambio social en Cuba* (Mexico City: Colegio de México, Centro de Estudios Sociológicos, 2000), 204–06.

134. See Julio Carranza Valdés, Luis Gutierrez Urdaneta, and Pedro Monreal González, *Cuba: La restructuración de la economía; Una propuesta para el debate* (Havana: Editorial de Ciencias Sociales, 1995). For useful accounts of the events surrounding the repression of the CEA critics, see Mauricio Giuliano, *El caso CEA: Intelectuales e inquisidores en Cuba; Perestroika en la Isla?* (Miami: Ediciones Universal, 1998); and Alberto F. Álvarez García and Gerardo González Nuñez, *Intelectuales vs. revolución? El caso del centro de Estudios sobre América, CEA* (Montréal: Ediciones Arte D.T., 2001).

135. Personal communication from Haroldo Dilla, September 30, 2010.

136. Espina Prieto and Rodríguez Ruiz, "Raza y desigualdad," 44–54.

137. "El 26 de julio de 1953 en la cultura política cubana," *Temas*, no. 46 (abril–junio 2006): 77–96.

138. "Quo vadis, universidad? Un simposio cubano," *Temas*, no. 57 (enero–marzo 2009): 76–88.

139. Arturo Arango, "Tribuna: Arturo Arango; Cuba: Los responsables del futuro," UNEAC (Unión de Escritores y Artistas de Cuba), 15 mayo 2010, www.uneac.org.cu/index.php?module=noticias&act=detalle&id=3219.

140. Esteban Morales Domínguez, "Corrupción: ¿La verdadera contrarevolución?," 9 abril 2010, www.uneac.org.cu/index.php?module=noticias&act=detalle&tipo=noticias&id=3123.

141. Esteban Morales Domínguez, "Algunos retos de la enseñanza de la economía política," diciembre 2010, www.uneac.org. (Note: article is no longer on the website.)

142. "Expulsado de la UNEAC el escritor Manuel García Verdercia por 'uso indebido' de internet," *Diario de Cuba*, 22 enero 2010, ddcuba.com/cuba.

143. Silvio Rodríguez, interview by Fernando García, *La Vanguardia* (Spain), November 2008.

144. "Cuba: El cantautor Silvio Rodríguez dijo que Cuba 'pide a gritos una revision,'" *Agencias y Público*, Havana, 27 marzo 2010.

145. Pablo Milanés, "El socialismo cubano se ha estancado," interview by Carlos Fuentes, *Público.es*, December 29, 2008, www.publico.es/culturas/186756/el-socialismo-cubano-se-ha-estancado.

146. "Cuba: Entrevista a Pablo Milanés, 'Quiero un cambio en Cuba cuanto antes,'" interview by Rafael J. Alvarez, *El Mundo* (Madrid), March 13, 2010.

147. Juan Carlos Chavez, "Carlos Varela condena actos de repudio contra las Damas de Blanco," *El Nuevo Herald*, 5 mayo 2010, www.elnuevoherald.com/2010/05/04/711870/carlos-varela-condena-actos-de.html.

148. Rafael Hernández, "Diálogo imaginario sobre política cubana," *La Jornada*, 14 abril 2010, www.jornada.unam.mx/2010/04/14/index.php?section=mundo&article=029a1mun.

149. Ironically, Juan Marinello (1898–1977) was the most prominent intellectual and presidential candidate of the old Stalinist, pro-Moscow Cuban Communist Party.

150. See Julio César Guanche, "Por un consenso para la democracia (en diálogo con Roberto Veiga)," *Espacio Laical*, Suplemento Digital 111, octubre 2010; and Roberto Veiga González, "Compartir la búsqueda de nuestro destino," *Espacio Laical*, Suplemento Digital 113, octubre 2010.

151. Ariel Dacal Díaz, "Por qué fracasó el socialismo soviético," *Temas*, no. 50/51 (abril–septiembre 2007): 4–15. Dacal also participated in a symposium titled "Por qué cayó el socialismo en Europa oriental?," *Temas*, no. 39–40 (octubre–diciembre 2004), 91–111.

152. See for example the article by Pedro Campos Santos, "Cuba: Qué confusión!," *kaosenlared.net*, June 2, 2009.

153. Pedro Campos Santos y varios compañeros, "Cuba necesita un socialismo participativo y democratico: Propuestas programáticas; Presentación para su discusión pública al pueblo, a los trabajadores y a los revolucionarios cubanos, con miras al VI Congreso del Partido Comunista de Cuba," *kaosenlared.net*, 17 agosto 2008.

154. Pedro Campos Santos, "Hay que cerrar el paso a la provocación imperialista," *Boletín del Socialismo Participativo y Democrático* (Havana) 2, no. 12, (March 23, 2010), SPD-36.

155. Pedro Campos, "Cuba Needs Dialogue, Not Violence," *HavanaTimes.org*, April 14, 2011, www.havanatimes.org/?p=41550.

156. Pedro Campos Santos, "Expulsan de su trabajo a colaborador cubano de Kaosenlared," *kaosenlared.net*, May 13, 2009, www.kaosenlared,net/noticia/expulsan-trabajo-colaborador-cubano-kaosenlared.

157. Armando Chaguaceda y Dmitri Prieto, "La esperanza asumida: Bitácora—criolla y crítica—de otro exorcismo colectivo," *Espacio Laical Digital*, abril 2010, 116.

158. Ibid., 117.

159. "Observatorio Crítico hacia el 2011," comunicado de prensa de la Red Protagónica Observatorio Crítico, Havana, 19 diciembre 2010.

160. Chaguaceda y Prieto, "La esperanza asumida: Bitácora—criolla y crítica—de otro exorcismo colectivo," 118; and Pedro Campos, "Dump the Bureaucracy," *HavanaTimes.org*, May 20, 2010, www.havanatimes.org/?p=24318.

161. Chaguaceda y Prieto, "La esperanza asumida: Bitácora—criolla y crítica—de otro exorcismo colectivo," 118; Patricia Grogg, "Sociedad-Cuba: Memoria inconclusa," IPS, *Cuba a la Mano*, 4 diciembre 2010, http://cubalamano.net/sitio/client/report.php?id=1221; and Isbel Díaz Torres, "The Abakuas in the Streets of Havana," December 4, 2010, *Havana-Times.org*, www.havanatimes.org/?p=34106.

162. In an interview, Circles Robinson, a founder of *HavanaTimes.org*, related that initial pressure had been placed on two *HavanaTimes.org* writers, but since then the contributors have been able to continue without further problems. State security has questioned some of them for matters more related to their community and environmental activism, although the topic of *HavanaTimes.org* did come up. "More Glasnost, Less Perestroika," *Weekly Worker* 848 (January 13, 2011).

163. "Carta en rechazo a las actuales obstrucciones y prohibiciones de iniciativas sociales y culturales," Red Protagónica Observatorio Crítico, 18 diciembre 2009, reproduced and translated in *El Yuma*, elyuma.blogspot.com.

164. Erasmo Calzadilla, "Supreme Court Upholds My Firing," *HavanaTimes.org*, September 11, 2010, www.havanatimes.org/?p=29194.

165. Campos Santos y varios compañeros, "Cuba necesita un socialismo participativo y democrático."

166. Chaguaceda y Prieto, "La esperanza asumida: Bitácora—criolla y crítica—de otro exorcismo colectivo," 119.

167. Armando Chaguaceda, "Revolution & Regime in Cuba," *HavanaTimes.org*, March 26, 2010, www.havanatimes.org/?p=21990.

168. Ibid.

169. Theodore Draper, *Castro's Revolution: Myths and Realities* (New York: Frederick A. Praeger, 1962).

170. For the principal documents of the "war of the emails," see "Ciclo 'La política cultural del periodo revolucionario: Memoria y reflexión,'" Centro Teórico Cultural Criterios, www.criterios.es/cicloquinqueniogris.htm.

171. Michelle Chase, "Cuba's Generation Gap," *NACLA Report on the Americas*, November/December 2008, 9–13.

172. For an informative account of the hip-hop movement in Cuba, see chapter 3, "Fear of a Black Nation: Local Rappers, Transnational Crossings, and State Power," in Fernandes's *Cuba Represent!*, 85–134; Eugene Robinson, *Last Dance in Havana: The Final Days of Fidel and the Start of the New Cuban Revolution* (New York: Free Press, 2004).

173. This ban has since been removed by Raúl Castro's government. Cubans who have access to hard currency and can afford the places previously reserved exclusively for tourists are now able to use them.

174. For the role played in this incident by Eliecer Dávila, the articulate student who confronted Alarcón, see Erikson, *The Cuba Wars: Fidel Castro, the United States and the Next Revolution*, 277–79.

175. Wikileaks (subject: The U.S. and the Role of the Opposition in Cuba), "Traducción íntegra del cable en el que funcionarios de EEUU expresan sus opiniones sobre la disidencia en Cuba," http://www.rebelion.org/noticia.php?id=118854.

176. On November 1, 1962, the US military submitted an estimate to the White House on the number of US casualties there would be in an invasion of Cuba. There would have been 18,484 casualties (killed, missing, and wounded), 4,462 of which would have come the first day. See Alexandr Fursenko and Timothy Naftali, *One Hell of a Gamble: Khrushchev, Castro, and Kennedy, 1958–1964* (New York: W. W. Norton, 1997), 298. Of course, changed conditions—especially new military technology and diminished internal support for the Cuban government—would affect any such estimate today.

Conclusion: Cuba Might Not Be a Socialist Democracy, But . . .

1. Ian Kershaw and Moshe Lewin, "Afterthoughts," in *Stalinism and Nazism: Dictatorships in Comparison*, ed. Ian Kershaw and Moshe Lewin (Cambridge: Cambridge University Press, 1997), 344–45.

2. For a more detailed discussion of uneven modernity and uneven development in prerevolutionary Cuba, see the first chapter of my book *The Origins of the Cuban Revolution Reconsidered*.

3. This was a serious problem since the very beginning of the revolution. For example, the handbook *Alfabeticemos*, issued in 1960 to the campaign against illiteracy, was also a political education manual with a glossary of frequently used words and phrases. For instance, the word "ambition" was defined as "unbridled passion to gain wealth, power . . ."

and the Soviet Union was described as a "nation formed by the union of several republics that have a socialist regime and where the exploitation of man by man does not exist and where the means of production belong to the people."

4. Karl Marx, *Critique of the Gotha Program*, in *The Marx-Engels Reader*, ed. Robert C. Tucker, 2nd ed. (New York: W. W. Norton, 1978), 531.

5. James Petras, "The Responsibility of the Intellectuals: Cuba, the U.S. and Human Rights," *Canadian Network on Cuba*, May 1, 2003, www.canadiannetworkoncuba.ca/Documents/Petras-1may03.shtml.

6. Karl Marx and Frederick Engels, *The Communist Manifesto: Road Map to History's Most Important Political Document*, ed. Phil Gasper (Chicago: Haymarket Books, 2005), 40; and Frederick Engels, *Anti-Dühring: Herr Eugen Dühring's Revolution in Science* (New York: International Publishers, 1976), 183.

7. This type of sentiment has been expressed by businessmen regarding the viciously anti-Muslim Narendra Modi, chief minister of the Indian state of Gujarat. Heather Timmons, "Inspiring Growth and Doubts: Polarizing Politician Is Loved by Businesses," *New York Times*, February 9, 2011.

8. Marx and Engels, *The Communist Manifesto*, 55.

9. Hal Draper, *Karl Marx's Theory of Revolution* vol. 2, *The Politics of Social Classes* (New York: Monthly Review Press, 1978), 284–86.

10. Cited in ibid., 278–87.

11. Cited in ibid., 281–82.

12. Ibid., 283.

13. Ibid.

14. Hal Draper, *Karl Marx's Theory of Revolution* vol. 1, *State and Bureaucracy* (New York: Monthly Review Press, 1977), 437.

15. Ibid., 438.

16. Ibid., 436.

Epilogue

1. VI Congreso del Partido Comunista de Cuba, *Lineamientos de la política económica y social del partido y la revolución*, aprobado el 18 abril 2011, "Año 53 de la Revolución," Lineamiento 265, página 34, www.cubadebate.cu.

2. Ibid., Lineamiento 297, página 37.

3. Ibid., Lineamiento 286, página 35.

4. Leticia Martínez Hernández and Yaima Puig Meneses, "Sesionó reunión ampliada del Consejo de Ministros," *Diario Granma* 15, no. 60 (1 marzo 2011), www.granma.co.cu/2011/03/01/nacional/artic06.html.

5. As of May 2011, 309,728 Cubans were legally self-employed in nonrural occupations. Of these, 22 percent were involved in the preparation and sale of food and 4.5 percent in private transportation. It is worth noting that 68 percent of the self-employed did not previously have a job, while only 16 percent had been state workers and another 16 percent were retired. Ivette Fernández Sosa, "Trabajadores por cuenta propia sobrepasan las 300,000 personas," *Diario Granma* 15, no. 141 (21 mayo 2011), www.granma.co.cu/2011/05/21/nacional/artic05.html.

6. "Eliminan en Cuba subsidios a artículos de aseo," *Trabajadores*, 12 diciembre 2010, www.trabajadores.cu/news/eliminan-en-cuba-subsidios-a-artículos-de-aseo.

7. Anneris Ivette Leyva, "Sobre los recientes acuerdos del consejo de ministros. Continuar facilitando el trabajo por cuenta propia," *Diario Granma* 15, no. 147 (27 mayo 2011), www.granma.co.cu/2011/05/27/nacional/artic01.html.

8. *Proyecto de Lineamientos de la política económica y social del Partido Comunista de Cuba* (Draft guidelines for economic and social policy of the Communist Party of Cuba), 4, www.cubadebate.cu/wp-content/uploads/2010/11/proyecto-lineamientos-pcc.pdf.

9. The final guidelines approved at the congress provide an even less adequate list of the economic problems confronting the country, *Lineamientos del Partido Comunista de Cuba*, introducción, página 7.

10. Carmelo Mesa-Lago, "La veleta económica cubana, huracanes internos, crisis mundial y perspectivas con Obama," *Encuentro de la Cultura Cubana* 51–52 (invierno–primavera 2009): 39; and Elías Amor Bravo, "Economía: Cifras del fracaso; Las previsiones de la CEPAL para Cuba anuncian más penalidades," *cubaencuentro*, 23 julio 2009, www.cubaencuentro.com/es/cuba/artículos/cifras-del-fracaso-195971.

11. Marc Frank, "Cuba Bows to Pressure to Reform Its Economy," *Financial Times*, December 3, 2010, www.ft.com/cms/s/0/e6fc6374-06d9-11e0-8c29-00144feabdc0.html#axzz-187qw6wgg.

12. "El Sexto será un congreso de toda la militancia y de todo el pueblo," *Diario Granma* 14, no. 314 (9 noviembre 2010), www.granma.co.cu/2010/11/09/nacional/artic03.html.

13. "Discurso pronunciado por el General de Ejercito Raúl Castro Ruz, Presidente de los Consejos de Estado y de Ministros, en la clausura del Sexto Período Ordinario de Sesiones de la Séptima Legislatura de la Asamblea Nacional del Poder Popular, en el Palacio de Convenciones, el 18 de diciembre de 2010: 'Año 52 de la Revolución,' *Diario Granma* 14, no. 354 (19 diciembre 2010), www.granma.co.cu/2010/12/19/nacional/artic10.html.

14. *Lineamientos de la política económica y social del partido y la revolución*, Lineamiento 96, página 18.

15. Ibid., páginas 5, 9.

16. Ibid., Lineamientos 01, 02 and 03, páginas 10–11.

17. Ibid., Lineamiento 53, página 24.

18. Ibid., Lineamiento 176, página 26.

19. Ibid., Lineamiento 174, página 26.

20. Ibid., Lineamiento 111, página 19.

21. José Alejandro Rodríguez, "¿Economía cubana de mandatos o de utilidades?," interview by Joaquín Infante, *Juventud Rebelde*, 12 diciembre 2010, www.juventudrebelde.cu.

22. *Lineamientos de la política económica y social del partido y la revolución*, Lineamiento 55, página 15.

23. Ibid., Lineamiento 170, página 25. The phrase "asegurar que los salarios garanticen que cada cual reciba según su trabajo" is somewhat vague and ambiguous. However, I believe I am justified in translating it as "work performance" in light of Lineamiento 20 discussed below and, more generally, because of the government's repeated insistence on this method of compensation during the last several years.

24. Ibid., Lineamiento 169, página 25.

25. Ibid., Lineamiento 41, página 14.

26. From a report by Marino Murillo, minister of economy and planning, to the national assembly of Peoples' Power, December 15, 2010. Marino Murillo, "Resultados económicos del año 2010 y propuesta de plan para el 2011. Actualización de la política tributaria," *Diario Granma* 14, no. 351 (16 diciembre 2010), www.granma.co.cu/2010/12/16/nacional/artic06.html.

27. Raúl Castro, "Informe central al VI Congreso del Partido Comunista de Cuba," *Juventud Rebelde*, 16 abril 2011, www.juventudrebelde.cu.

28. Anneris Ivette Leyva, "A la empresa lo que es de ella, y a la función estatal lo suyo," *Diario Granma* 15, no. 103 (13 abril 2011), www.granma.cubaweb.cu/2011/04/13/nacional/artic01.html.

29. *Lineamientos de la política económica y social del partido y la revolución*, Lineamiento 14, página 12.

30. Ibid., Lineamiento 16, página 12.
31. Ibid., Lineamiento 11, página 11.
32. Ibid., Lineamiento 17, página 12.
33. Ibid., Lineamiento 18, página 12.
34. Ibid., Lineamiento 20, página 12.
35. Ibid., Lineamiento 23, página 12.
36. Ibid., Lineamiento 68, página 16.
37. Ibid., Lineamiento 35, página 13.
38. Ibid., Lineamiento 121, página 20.
39. "Conclusiones del 6to. Congreso del Partido Comunista de Cuba: Discurso de clausura del 6to Congreso del Partido Comunista de Cuba, pronunciado por el General de Ejército Raúl Castro Ruz," *Diario Granma* 15, no. 109 (19 abril 2011), www.granma.co.cu?2011/04/19/nacional/artic04.html.
40. Gerardo Arreola, "Sexto Congreso del Partido Comunista de Cuba: Ascenso jerárquico a dos de los mayores operadores de la economía cubana," *La Jornada*, 20 abril 2011, 3, www.jornada.unam.mx/2011/04/20/index.php?section=politica&article=003n1pol.
41. Haroldo Dilla Alfonso, "Al combate corred, generales," *cubaencuentro*, 25 abril 2011, www.cubaencuentro.com.
42. "El Sexto será un congreso de toda la militancia y de todo el pueblo," 4.
43. See the original version in *Proyecto de Lineamientos de la política económica y social del Partido Comunista de Cuba*, Lineamiento 142, p. 21.
44. Ibid., Lineamiento 162, página 23.
45. Ibid., Lineamiento 19, página 8.
46. Ibid., Lineamiento 14, página 8.
47. Ibid., Lineamiento 16, página 8.
48. VI Congreso del Partido Comunista de Cuba, *Información sobre el resultado del debate de los lineamientos de la política económica y social del partido y la revolución*, mayo 2011, 3; "Año 53 de la Revolución," Fundación de Investigaciones Sociales y Políticas, www.fisyp.org.ar/modules/news/article.php?storyid=804/.
49. Raúl Castro, "Informe central al VI Congreso del Partido Comunista de Cuba," 3.
50. VI Congreso del Partido Comunista de Cuba, *Lineamientos de la política económica y social del partido y la revolución*, 11. Author's emphasis.
51. "Actividades autorizadas para el ejercicio del trabajo por cuenta propia," *Granma*, 24 septiembre 2010, 5; and Archibald Ritter, "Raúl Castro's New Economic Strategy: Context, Viability and Prospects," presentation to the Bildner Center for Western Hemisphere Studies, Graduate Center of the City University of New York, November 29, 2010.
52. Gerardo Arreola, "Atenuará Cuba impuestos a los microempresarios," *La Jornada*, 21 abril 2011, 15, www.jornada.unam.mx/2011/04/21/index.php?section=mundo&article=015n1mun; and Leyva, "Sobre los recientes acuerdos del consejo de ministros."
53. Carmelo Mesa-Lago, "Búsqueda: El desempleo en Cuba, de oculto a visible," *Espacio Laical*, abril 2010, 62–63; and Leticia Martínez Hernández and Yaima Puig Meneses, "En materia de tributos, más valen las cuentas claras," *Granma*, 22 octubre 2010, 4–5.
54. Archibald Ritter, "Partido Comunista de Cuba, Projecto de Lineamientos de la Política Económica y Social, Viable Strategic Economic Re-orientation and/or Wish List?," *The Cuban Economy–La Economía Cubana*, November 10, 2010, thecubaneconomy.com.
55. Marc Frank, "Cuba autoriza créditos para impulsar sector privado," Reuters, 30 marzo 2011, http://lta.reuters.com/article/domesticNews/idLTASIE72T1BT20110330?sp=true.
56. Mesa-Lago, "Búsqueda: El desempleo en Cuba, de oculto a visible," 62; and Samuel Farber, "Where Is Cuba Headed?," *SocialistWorker.org*, September 20, 2010.
57. "Más ventas minoristas para trabajo por cuenta propia," *Cuba a la Mano*, 26 noviembre 2010.
58. I want to thank Charles Post for helping me to formulate this paragraph. Many of the

arguments defending the Cuban government can be found in articles written for *Links: International Journal of Socialist Renewal*, links.org.au. The website Rebelión at rebelion.org is very supportive of the Cuban government and also contains many articles putting forward these sorts of views. Among the most prominent defenders of the Cuban regime is Argentinian social scientist Atilio Boron. Boron was invited to visit the island in March 2009 and was even granted an interview with Fidel Castro. See his "Una reunión en primera persona con Fidel," *Página/12*, 14 marzo 2009, www.pagina12.com.ar/diario/elmundo/4-121514-2009-03-14.html. Not surprisingly, Boron has praised, without any significant criticism, the recent economic turn by the Cuban government. See Atilio Boron, "Cuba: Tiempo de cambio," *kaosenlared.net*, 26 noviembre 2010, www.kaosenlared.net/noticias/cuba-tiempos-de-cambio.

59. Guillermo Almeyra, "Cuba: Un documento peligroso y contradictorio (III)," *La Jornada* (Mexico City), 28 noviembre 2010.

60. Ibid.; parts 1 and 2 of the same article published in *La Jornada* on November 14 and November 21, 2010. The entire article was translated into English and appeared under the title "Cuba: A Dangerous and Contradictory Document," in *IV Online Magazine: IVP 430*, November 2010, www.internationalviewpoint.org. Almeyra has continued to regularly cover events in Cuba leading to, and after, the Sixth Party Congress. See, for example, "Después del congreso del Partido Comunista de Cuba," *La Jornada*, 1 mayo 2011, www.jornada.unam.mx/2011/05/01/index.php?section=opinion&article=018a1pol. For another perspective supporting workers' self-management but that does not raise, as Almeyra does, the need for democracy in the Cuban political system and society as a whole, see Camila Piñeiro Harnecker, "Risks in Expanding Non-state Enterprises in the Cuban Economy," *The Bullet*, Socialist Project E-Bulletin 437. December 6, 2010, www.socialistproject.ca/bullet/437.php. In all fairness, I must point out that most proponents of a capitalist "market economy" also support a democratization of Cuban society, although along the lines of liberal rather than socialist democracy. See, for example, Ritter, "Partido Comunista de Cuba: Proyecto de Lineamientos de la Política Económica y Social, Viable Strategic Economic Re-orientation and/or Wish List?," 3.

61. Haroldo Dilla Alfonso, "Congreso del partido: La insoportable levedad de los lineamientos," *cubaencuentro*, 17 noviembre 2010, 2, www.cubaencuentro.com.

62. "Raúl en Shanghai," *Granma*, 21 abril 2005, 8.

63. "Cuba se guía por reformas chinas, dice Alarcón," *Cuba a la Mano*, 26 noviembre 2010, http://cubaalamano.net/sitio/client/brief.php?id=8565.

64. Frank, "Cuba Bows to Pressure to Reform Its Economy."

65. Esteban Morales was readmitted to the party in July 2011. At the time of this writing, it is unknown whether he will resume his appearances in the mass media or what, if any, promises he may have made to the party authorities.

66. It is revealing that the lay Catholic website Espacio Laical organized in 2010 a panel discussion including a wide range of views on the topic of hope in Cuba today. See "La esperanza en Cuba hoy," *Espacio Laical* 6, no. 22 (abril–junio 2010), http://espaciolaical.org/contens/22/ind_main22.htm.

67. Rosenberg Weinreb, *Cuba in the Shadow of Change*, 27.

68. See the interview with Carlos Saladrigas, a wealthy Cuban American capitalist and head of the Cuban Study Group, in which, during a visit to Cuba, he expressed an interest in investing on the island provided certain legal guarantees were met by the Cuban government. "No es fácil cambiar, pero lo hice," *Palabra Nueva: Revista de la Arquidiócesis de la Habana* 20, no. 207 (mayo 2011), http://palabranueva.net/contens/pag_sociedad3.html.

69. Javier Corrales, "The Gatekeeper State: Limited Economic Reforms and Regime Survival in Cuba, 1989–2002," *Latin American Research Review* 39, no. 2: 50–51.

Selected Bibliography

Books and Pamphlets

Agrupación Católica Universitaria. *Encuesta de trabajadores rurales. 1956–57*. Reprinted in *Economía y desarrollo* (Instituto de Economía de la Universidad de la Habana), (julio–agosto 1972), 188–212.

Álvarez García, Alberto F., and Gerardo González Nuñez. *Intelectuales vs. revolución? El caso del Centro de Estudios sobre América, CEA*. Montréal: Ediciones Arte D.T., 2001.

Americas Watch. *Human Rights in Cuba: The Need to Sustain the Pressure, an Americas Watch Report*. New York: Americas Watch Committee, 1989.

Americas Watch and the Fund for Free Expression. *Dangerous Dialogue: Attacks on Freedom of Expression in Miami's Exile Community*. Washington, DC: August 1992.

Amnesty International. *Cuba: The Human Rights Situation*. London: Amnesty International, December 1990.

———. *Restrictions on Freedom of Expression in Cuba*. London: Amnesty International, June 30, 2010.

Artaraz, Kepa. *Cuba and Western Intellectuals since 1959*. New York: Palgrave Macmillan, 2009.

Bardach, Ann Louise. *Cuba Confidential: Love and Vengeance in Miami and Havana*. New York: Random House, 2002.

Bejel, Emilio. *Gay Cuban Nation*. Chicago: University of Chicago Press, 2001.

Benítez Pérez, María Elena. *La familia cubana en la segunda mitad del siglo XX. Cambios sociodemográficos*. Havana: Editorial de Ciencias Sociales, 2003.

Benjamin, Jules R. *The United States and the Origins of the Cuban Revolution: An Empire of Liberty in an Age of National Liberation*. Princeton, NJ: Princeton University Press, 1990.

Bergad, Laird. *The Comparative Histories of Slavery in Brazil, Cuba and the United States*. Cambridge: Cambridge University Press, 2007.

Betto, Frei. *Fidel Castro y la religión: Conversaciones con Frei Betto*. Mexico City: Siglo XXI Editores, 1986.

Bobes León, Velia Cecilia. *Los laberintos de la imaginación: Repertorio simbólico, identidades y actores del cambio social en Cuba*. Mexico City: Colegio de México, Centro de Estudios Sociológicos, 2000.

Brundenius, Claes. *Revolutionary Cuba: The Challenge of Economic Growth with Equity*. Boulder, CO: Westview Press, 1984.

Bunck, Julie Marie. *Fidel Castro and the Quest for a Revolutionary Culture in Cuba.* University Park: Pennsylvania State University Press, 1994.

Carranza Valdés, Julio, Luis Gutierrez Urdaneta, and Pedro Monreal González. *Cuba: La restructuración de la economía; Una propuesta para el debate.* Havana: Editorial de Ciencias Sociales, 1995.

Castro, Fidel. *Un grano de maíz.* Havana: Oficina de Publicaciones del Consejo de Estado, 1992.

Castro Fernández, Silvio. *La masacre de los independientes de color en 1912.* 2nd ed. Havana: Editorial de Ciencias Sociales, 2008.

Chafe, William. *Women and Equality: Changing Patterns in American Culture.* New York: Oxford University Press, 1977.

Claudín, Fernando. *The Communist Movement: From Comintern to Cominform, Part One.* Translated by Brian Pearce. New York: Monthly Review Press, 1975.

Conte Aguero, Luis. *26 cartas del presidio.* Havana: Editorial Cuba, 1960.

De Paz Sánchez, Manuel. *Franco y Cuba: Esudios sobre España y la revolución.* Santa Cruz de Tenerife, Canary Islands: Ediciones Idea, 2006.

Díaz-Briquets, Sergio. *The Health Revolution in Cuba.* Austin: University of Texas Press, 1983.

Díaz-Briquets, Sergio, and Jorge Pérez-López. *Conquering Nature: The Environmental Legacy of Socialism in Cuba.* Pittsburgh: University of Pittsburgh Press, 2000.

Domínguez, Jorge I. *Cuba: Order and Revolution.* Cambridge, MA: Belknap Press of Harvard University Press, 1978.

———. *To Make a World Safe for Revolution: Cuba's Foreign Policy.* Cambridge, MA: Harvard University Press, 1989.

Draper, Hal. *Karl Marx's Theory of Revolution,* vol. 1, *State and Bureaucracy.* New York: Monthly Review Press, 1977.

———. *Karl Marx's Theory of Revolution,* vol. 2, *The Politics of Social Classes.* New York: Monthly Review Press, 1978.

———. *The "Dictatorship of the Proletariat" from Marx to Lenin.* New York: Monthly Review Press, 1987.

Dumont, René. *Is Cuba Socialist?* New York: Viking Press, 1974.

Engels, Frederick. *Socialism: Utopian and Scientific.* Translated by Edward Aveling. New York: International Publishers, 1972.

Enzesberger, Hans Magnus. *The Consciousness Industry: On Literature, Politics and the Media.* New York: Seabury Press, 1974.

Erikson, Daniel P. *The Cuba Wars: Fidel Castro, the United States and the Next Revolution.* New York: Bloomsbury Press, 2008.

Evenson, Debra. *Law and Society in Contemporary Cuba.* 2nd ed. The Hague: Kluwer Law International, 2003.

Farber, Samuel. *Before Stalinism. The Rise and Fall of Soviet Democracy.* Cambridge: Polity Press, 1990.

———. *The Origins of the Cuban Revolution Reconsidered.* Chapel Hill: University of North Carolina Press, 2006.

———. *Revolution and Reaction in Cuba, 1933–1960: A Political Sociology from Machado to Castro.* Middletown, CT: Wesleyan University Press, 1976.

Fernandes, Sujatha. *Cuba Represent! Cuban Arts, State Power and the Making of New Revolutionary Cultures.* Durham, NC: Duke University Press, 2006.

Ferrer, Ada. *Insurgent Cuba: Race, Nation and Revolution, 1868–1898.* Chapel Hill: University of North Carolina Press, 1999.

Franqui, Carlos. *Retrato de familia con Fidel.* Barcelona: Editorial Seix Barral, 1981.

Fuente, Alejandro de la. *Race, Inequality and Politics in Twentieth-Century Cuba.* Chapel Hill: University of North Carolina Press, 2001.

George, Edward. *The Cuban Intervention in Angola, 1965–1991: From Che Guevara to Cuito Cuanavale.* London: Frank Cass, 2005.

Gleijeses, Piero. *Conflicting Missions: Havana, Washington, and Africa, 1959–1976.* Chapel Hill: University of North Carolina Press, 2002.

Gómez Treto, Raúl. *The Church and Socialism in Cuba.* Translated by Phillip Berryman. Maryknoll, NY: Orbis, 1988.

González Nuñez, Gerardo. *El Caribe en la política exterior de Cuba (Balance de 30 años, 1959–1989).* Santo Domingo, Dominican Republic: Centro de Investigación y Promoción Social, 1991.

Grenier, Guillermo J., and Lisandro Pérez. *The Legacy of Exile: Cubans in the United States.* Boston: Allyn and Bacon, 2003.

Giuliano, Mauricio. *El caso CEA: Intelectuales e inquisidores en Cuba; Perestroika en la Isla?* Miami: Ediciones Universal, 1998.

Helg, Aline. *Our Rightful Share. The Afro-Cuban Struggle for Equality, 1886–1912.* Chapel Hill: University of North Carolina Press, 1995.

Hobsbawm, E. J. *The Age of Revolution, 1789–1848.* New York: Mentor Books, 1964.

Holgado Fernández, Isabel. *¡No es fácil! Mujeres cubanas y la crisis revolucionaria.* Barcelona: Icaria Editorial, 2000.

Human Rights Watch. *Cuba: New Castro, Same Cuba; Political Prisoners in the Post-Fidel Era.* New York: Human Rights Watch, November 2009.

———. *Cuba's Repressive Machinery: Human Rights Forty Years after the Revolution.* New York: Human Rights Watch, June 1999.

Ibarra, Jorge. *Prologue to Revolution: Cuba, 1898–1958.* Translated by Marjorie Moore. Boulder, CO: Lynne Rienner, 1998.

Klepak, Hal. *Cuba's Military, 1990–2005: Revolutionary Soldiers during Counter-revolutionary Times.* New York: Palgrave Macmillan, 2005.

Krause-Fuchs, Monika. *Monika y la Revolución: Una mirada singular sobre la historia reciente de Cuba.* Tenerife, Canary Islands: Centro de la Cultura Popular Canaria, 2002.

Leiner, Marvin. *Sexual Politics in Cuba.* Boulder, CO: Westview Press, 1994.

Lewis, Oscar, Ruth M. Lewis, and Susan M. Rigdon. *Four Men: Living the Revolution; An Oral History of Contemporary Cuba.* Urbana: University of Illinois Press, 1977.

Lewis, Ruth. *Four Women: Living the Revolution.* Urbana: University of Illinois Press, 1977.

Lindblom, Charles E. *Politics and Markets: The World's Political-Economic Systems.* New York: Basic Books, 1977.

Lockwood, Lee. *Castro's Cuba, Cuba's Fidel.* Rev. ed. Boulder, CO: Westview Press, 1990.

Luciak, Ilja A. *Gender and Democracy in Cuba.* Gainesville: University Press of Florida, 2007.

Lumsden, Ian. *Machos, Maricones and Gays: Cuba and Homosexuality.* Philadelphia: Temple University Press, 1996.

MacGaffey, Wyatt, and Clifford R. Barnet. *Twentieth-Century Cuba: The Background of the Castro Revolution.* Garden City, NY: Doubleday Anchor, 1965.

Martín Medem, José Manuel. *¿Por qué no me enseñaste cómo se vive sin ti?* Mataró, Spain: El Viejo Topo, 2005.

Mencía, Mario. *The Fertile Prison: Fidel Castro in Batista's Jails.* Melbourne: Ocean Press, 1993.

Mesa-Lago, Carmelo. *Cuba in the 1970s: Pragmatism and Institutionalization.* Rev. ed. Albuquerque: University of New Mexico Press, 1978.

———. *The Economy of Socialist Cuba: A Two-Decade Appraisal.* Albuquerque: University of New Mexico Press, 1981.

———. *Market, Socialist, and Mixed Economies: Comparative Policy and Performance; Chile, Cuba, and Costa Rica.* Baltimore: Johns Hopkins University Press, 2000.

Mesa-Lago, Carmelo, and Jorge Pérez-López. *Cuba's Aborted Reform: Socioeconomic Effects, International Comparisons, and Transition Policies.* Gainesville: University Press of Florida, 2005.

Molyneux, Maxine. *State, Gender and Institutional Change in Cuba's "Special Period": The Federación de Mujeres Cubanas.* London: Institute of Latin American Studies, 1996.

Moore, Carlos. *Castro, the Blacks and Africa.* Los Angeles: Center for Afro-American Studies, University of California, Los Angeles, 1988.

———. *Pichón: A Memoir; Race and Revolution in Castro's Cuba.* Chicago: Lawrence Hill Books, 2008.

O'Connor, James. *The Origins of Socialism in Cuba.* Ithaca, NY: Cornell University Press, 1970.

Padura Fuentes, Leonardo. *El hombre que amaba a los perros.* Mexico City: Tusquets Editores México, 2009.

Partido Comunista de Cuba. *Lineamientos de la política económica y social del partido comunista de Cuba.* 18 abril 2010. www.granma.co.cu./secciones/6to_congresso_pcc/folleto%20lineamientos%20vi%20cong.pdf.

Payá, Oswaldo. *Documento de trabajo para el Programa de Transición* 12 diciembre 2003. www.pdc-cuba.org/DIALOGO-NACIONAL-completo.htm or http://democraciaparticipativa.net/documentos/DialogoNacional.pdf.

Pérez, Louis A., Jr. *Cuba: Between Reform and Revolution.* 3rd ed. New York: Oxford University Press, 2006.

———. *On Becoming Cuban.* Chapel Hill: University of North Carolina Press, 1999.

Pérez-Stable, Marifeli. *The Cuban Revolution: Origins, Course and Legacy.* 2nd ed. New York: Oxford University Press, 1999.

Quirk, Robert E. *Fidel Castro.* New York: W. W. Norton, 1993.

Ramonet, Ignacio. *Fidel Castro: Biografía a dos voces.* Barcelona: Random House Mondadori, 2006.

Randall, Margaret. *To Change the World: My Years in Cuba.* New Brunswick, NJ: Rutgers University Press, 2009.

Rieff, David. *The Exile: Cuba in the Heart of Miami.* New York: Simon and Schuster, 1993.

Rosenberg Weinreb, Amelia. *Cuba in the Shadow of Change: Daily Life in the Twilight of the Revolution.* Gainesville: University Press of Florida, 2009.

Roy, Joaquín. *The Cuban Revolution (1959–2000): Relations with Spain, the European Union, and the United States.* New York: Palgrave Macmillan, 2009.

Sartre, Jean-Paul. *Sartre on Cuba.* Westport, CT: Greenwood Press, 1974.

Sawyer, Mark Q. *Racial Politics in Post-revolutionary Cuba.* New York: Cambridge University Press, 2006.

Schoultz, Lars. *That Infernal Little Republic: The United States and the Cuban Revolution.* Chapel Hill: University of North Carolina Press, 2009.

Schwartz, Rosalie. *Pleasure Island: Tourism and Temptation in Cuba.* Lincoln: University of Nebraska Press, 1997.

Shayne, Julie D. *The Revolution Question: Feminisms in El Salvador, Chile and Cuba.* New Brunswick, NJ: Rutgers University Press, 2004.

Smith, Lois M., and Alfred Padula. *Sex and Revolution: Women in Socialist Cuba.* New York: Oxford University Press, 1996.

Smith, Wayne S. *The Closest of Enemies: A Personal Account of U.S.-Cuban Diplomatic Relations since 1957.* New York: W. W. Norton, 1987.

Stoner, K. Lynn. *From the House to the Streets: The Cuban Women's Movement for Legal Reform, 1898–1940.* Durham, NC: Duke University Press, 1991.

Sweig, Julia E. *Cuba: What Everyone Needs to Know.* New York: Oxford University Press, 2009.

Thomas, Hugh. *Cuba: The Pursuit of Freedom.* New York: Harper and Row, 1971.

Trotsky, Leon. *The Revolution Betrayed.* New York: Merit, 1965.

Young, Allen. *Gays under the Cuban Revolution.* San Francisco: Grey Fox Press, 1981.

Articles, Chapters, and Essays

Adams, Henley C. "Fighting an Uphill Battle: Race, Politics, Power, and Institutionalization in Cuba." *Latin American Research Review* 39, no. 1 (February 2004): 168–82.

Álvarez Suárez, Mayda. "La revolución de las cubanas: 50 años de conquistas y luchas." *Temas* no. 56 (octubre–diciembre 2008): 67–77.

Arguelles, Lourdes, and B. Ruby Rich. "Homosexuality, Homophobia, and Revolution: Notes toward an Understanding of the Cuban Lesbian and Gay Male Experience, Part I." *Signs* 9, no. 4 (Summer 1984): 683–99.

Betancourt, Juan René. "Castro and the Cuban Negro." *Crisis* 68, no. 5 (1961): 270–74.

Booth, David. "Cuba, Color and the Revolution." *Science and Society* 11, no. 2 (Summer 1976): 129–72.

Bravo, Elías Amor. "Economía: Cifras del fracaso; Las previsiones de la CEPAL para Cuba anuncian más penalidades." *cubaencuentro,* 23 julio 2009. www.cubaencuentro.com/es/cuba/artículos/cifras-del-fracaso-195971.

Campos Santos, Pedro, y varios compañeros. "Cuba necesita un socialismo participativo y democrático: Propuestas programáticas; Presentación para su discusión pública al pueblo, a los trabajadores y a los revolucionarios cubanos, con miras al VI Congreso del Partido Comunista de Cuba." *kaosenlared.net,* 17 agosto 2008.

Carr, Barry. "Identity, Class, and Nation: Black Immigrant Workers, Cuban Communism, and the Sugar Insurgency, 1925–1934." *Hispanic American Historical Review* 78, no. 1 (February 1998): 83–116.

Casamayor-Cisneros, Odette. "Todos los negros finos hemos decidido. Nuevos caminos de la expresión racial." *Encuentro de la Cultura Cubano* 53/54 (verano–otoño 2009): 74–81.

Chaguaceda, Armando. "'Revolution' and Regime in Cuba." *HavanaTimes.org,* March 26, 2010. www.havanatimes.org/?p=21990.

Chaguaceda, Armando, and Dmitri Prieto. "La esperanza asumida: Bitácora—criolla y crítica—de otro exorcismo colectivo." Suplemento Digital, *Espacio Laical,* abril 2010.

Chase, Michelle. "Cuba's Generation Gap." *NACLA Report on the Americas,* November–December 2008, 9–13.

———. "Women's Organisations and the Politics of Gender in Cuba's Urban Insurrection (1952–1958)." *Bulletin of Latin American Research* 29, no. 4 (September 2010): 440–58.

Coffigny Leonard, Olga. "Mujeres parlamanterias cubanas (1936–1958)." *Temas* no. 55 (julio–septiembre 2008): 185–97.

Corrales, Javier. "The Gatekeeper State: Limited Economic Reforms and Regime Survival in Cuba, 1989–2002." *Latin American Research Review* 39, no. 2 (2004): 35–65.

Coyula, Mario. "El trinquenio amargo y la ciudad distópica: Autopsia de una utopía." *Centro Teórico-Cultural Criterios*, 19 mayo 2007. www.criterios.es/cicloquinqueniogris.htm.

———. "La ciudad del futuro o el futuro de la ciudad." *Temas* no. 48 (octubre–diciembre 2006): 49–55.

Coyula, Miguel. "La Habana *toda* vieja." *Temas* no. 48 (octubre–diciembre 2006): 72–76.

———. "Un lugar donde vivir, o un lugar para vivir." *Temas* 58 (abril–junio 2009): 40–49.

Dacal Díaz, Ariel. "Por qué fracasó el socialismo soviético." *Temas* no. 50/51 (abril–septiembre 2007): 4–15.

Díaz-Vallina, Elvira, Olga Dotre Romay, and Caridad Dacosta Pérez. "Avance de investigación: La mujer revolucionaria en Cuba durante el período insurreccional, 1952–1958." *Revista de Ciencias Sociales* 3, no. 3 (June 1997): 24–32.

Domínguez, Jorge I. "The Cuban Economy at the Start of the Twenty-First Century: An Introductory Analysis." Chapter 1 of *The Cuban Economy at the Start of the Twenty-First Century*, edited by Jorge I. Domínguez, Omar Everleny Pérez Villanueva, and Lorena Barbería. Cambridge, MA: David Rockefeller Center for Latin American Studies, Harvard University Press, 2004, 1–16.

———. "Cuba's Economic Transition: Successes, Deficiencies, and Challenges." Chapter 2 of *The Cuban Economy at the Start of the Twenty-First Century*, edited by Jorge I. Domínguez, Omar Everleny Pérez Villanueva, and Lorena Barbería. Cambridge, MA: David Rockefeller Center for Latin American Studies, Harvard University Press, 2004, 17–48.

———. "Racial and Ethnic Relations in the Cuban Armed Forces: A Non-topic." *Armed Forces and Society* 2, no. 2 (February 1976): 273–90.

Draper, Hal. "The Two Souls of Socialism." In Hal Draper, *Socialism from Below*, edited by E. Haberkern. Atlantic Highlands, NJ: Humanities Press, 1992.

Espina Prieto, Mayra. "Social Effects of Economic Adjustment: Equality, Inequality and Trends toward Greater Complexity in Cuban Society." Chapter 7 of *The Cuban Economy at the Start of the Twenty-First Century*, edited by Jorge I. Domínguez, Omar Everleny Pérez Villanueva, and Lorena Barbería. Cambridge, MA: David Rockefeller Center for Latin American Studies, Harvard University Press, 2004, 209–44.

Espina Prieto, Rodrigo, and Pablo Rodríguez Ruiz. "Raza y desigualdad en la Cuba actual." *Temas* no. 45 (enero–marzo 2006): 44–54.

Espinosa Mendoza, Norge. "Historial en el vacío: Arte, gays y espacio social en Cuba." *Encuentro de la Cultura Cubana* 41/42 (verano–otoño 2006): 83–92.

Fabienke, Rikki. "Labour Markets and Income Distribution during Crisis and Reform." In *Globalization and Third World Socialism*, edited by Claes Brundenius and John Weeks. Houndmills, UK: Palgrave, 2001, 102–28.

Farber, Samuel. "The Cuban Communists in the Early Stages of the Cuban Revolution: Revolutionaries or Reformists?" *Latin American Research Review* 18 (March 1983): 59–83.

Fernandes, Sujatha. "Transnationalism and Feminist Activism in Cuba: The Case of Magín." *Politics and Gender* 1 (2005): 431–52.

Fernández Robaina, Tomás. "Un balance necesario: La lucha contra la discriminación al negro en Cuba de 1959 a 2009." *Encuentro de la Cultura Cubana* 53/54 (verano/otoño 2009): 57–62.

———. "Cuban Sexual Values and African Religious Beliefs." Appendix A of *Machos, Maricones and Gays: Cuba and Homosexuality* by Ian Lumsden. Philadelphia: Temple University Press, 1996.

Fornet, Ambrosio. "El quinquenio gris: Revisitando el término." *Centro Teórico-Cultural Criterios*, 30 enero 2007. www.criterios.es/cicloquinqueniogris.htm.

Fowler Calzada, Victor. "Contra el argumento racista." *cubaencuentro* 53/54 (verano–otoño 2009): 74–81.

Grenier, Guillermo J. "The Cuban-American Labor Movement in Dade County: An Emergent Immigrant Working Class." In *Miami Now: Immigration, Ethnicity and Social Change*, edited by Guillermo J. Grenier and Alex Stepick III. Gainesville: University Press of Florida, 1992.

Guanche, Julio César. "The Crisis of the Scissors." *Revista: The Harvard Review of Latin America* 8, no. 12 (Winter 2009). www.drclas.harvard.edu/revistaweb/1960s/cuba/guanche.

———. "Por un consenso para la democracia (en diálogo con Roberto Veiga.)" Suplemento Digital *Espacio Laical*, 111 (octubre 2010).

Guerra, Lillian. "Gender Policing, Homosexuality and the New Patriarchy of the Cuban Revolution, 1965–1970." *Social History* 35, no. 3 (August 2010): 268–89.

González Marrero, Claudia. "La novela policial en Cuba durante la década del 70: Una literatura comprometida." *kaosenlared.net*, 25 octubre 2008.

Gunn, Gillian. "Cuba and Mozambique: A History of Cordial Disagreement." In *Cuban Internationalism in Sub-Saharan Africa*, edited by Sergio Díaz-Briquets. Pittsburgh: Duquesne University Press, 1989.

Guridy, Frank Andre. "'War on the Negro': Race and the Revolution of 1933." *Cuban Studies* 40 (2009): 49–73.

Harrison, Thomas. "Socialism and Homosexuality." *New Politics* 12, no. 2 (Winter 2009): 16–26.

Kershaw, Ian, and Moshe Lewin. "Afterthoughts." In *Stalinism and Nazism: Dictatorships in Comparison*, edited by Ian Kershaw and Moshe Lewin. Cambridge: Cambridge University Press, 1997.

Knight, Franklin W. "Slavery, Race and Social Structure in Cuba during the Nineteenth Century." In *Slavery and Race Relations in Latin America*, edited by Robert Brent Toplin, 204–27. Westport, CT: Greenwood Press, 1974.

Lambie, George. "Franco's Spain and the Cuban Revolution." In *The Fractured Blockade: West European-Cuban Relations during the Revolution*, edited by Alistair Hennessy and George Lambie. London: Macmillan, 1993.

Larguía, Isabel, and John Dumoulin. "La mujer en el desarrollo: Estrategia y experiencia de la Revolución Cubana." *Casa de las Americas* 25, no. 149 (marzo–abril 1985): 37–53.

Marimón, Mateo Jover. "The Church." In *Revolutionary Change in Cuba*, edited by Carmelo Mesa-Lago. Pittsburgh: University of Pittsburgh Press, 1971.

Masferrer, Marianne and Carmelo Mesa-Lago. "The Gradual Integration of the Black in Cuba: Under the Colony, the Republic and the Revolution." In *Slavery and*

Race Relations in Latin America, edited by Robert Brent Toplin. Westport, CT: Greenwood Press, 1974.

Mesa-Lago, Carmelo. "Búsqueda: El desempleo en Cuba, de oculto a visible." *Espacio Laical*, abril 2010. http://espaciolaical.org.

———. "Cincuenta años de servicios sociales en Cuba." *Temas*, no. 64 (octubre–diciembre 2010). www.temas.cult.cu.

———. "Cuban Foreign Policy in Africa: A General Framework." In *Cuba in Africa*, edited by Carmelo Mesa-Lago and June Belkin. Pittsburgh: Center for Latin American Studies, University Center for International Studies, University of Pittsburgh, 1982.

———. "Economía: Mesa-Lago: El gobierno 'carece de un plan' para enfrentar la crisis." *cubaencuentro*, 13 julio 2009. www.cubaencuentro.com.

———. "La veleta económica cubana: Huracanes internos, crisis mundial y perspectivas con Obama." *Encuentro de la Cultura Cubana* 51–52 (invierno–primavera 2009): 35–47.

Molyneux, Maxine. "Mobilization without Emancipation? Women's Interests, State and Revolution." In *Transition and Development: Problems of Third World Socialism*, edited by Center for the Study of America. New York: Monthly Review Press, 1986.

Morales Domínguez, Esteban. "Algunos retos de la enseñanza de la economía política." Diciembre 2010. www.uneac.org.cu/index.php?module=noticias&act=detalle&id=3219.

———. "Desafíos de la problemática racial en Cuba." *Temas* 56 (octubre–diciembre 2008): 95–99.

———. "Corrupción: ¿La verdadera contrarevolución?" UNEAC (Unión Nacional de Escritores y Artistas de Cuba), 4 abril 2010. www.uneac.org.cu/index.php?module =noticias&act=detalle&id=3123.

Moreno, José A. "From Traditional to Modern Values." In *Revolutionary Change in Cuba*, edited by Carmelo Mesa-Lago. Pittsburgh: University of Pittsburgh Press, 1971.

Pérez Villanueva, Omar Everleny. "The Cuban Economy Today and Its Future Challenges." Chapter 3 of *The Cuban Economy at the Start of the Twenty-First Century*, edited by Jorge I. Domínguez, Omar Everleny Pérez Villanueva, and Lorena Barbería. Cambridge, MA: David Rockefeller Center for Latin American Studies, Harvard University Press, 2004.

Pérez Villanueva, Omar Everleny, and Pavel Vidal Alejandro. "Cuba's Economy: A Current Evaluation and Several Necessary Proposals." *Socialism and Democracy* 24, no. 1 (March 2010): 71–93.

Pino Santos, Oscar. "De la Habana al Mississippi: La isla estratégica y la teoría de la anexión, 1800–1898." *Temas* 37–38 (abril–septiembre 2004): 146–58.

Rosendahl, Mona. "Household Economy and Morality during the Special Period." In *Globalization and Third World Socialism*, edited by Claes Brundenius and John Weeks. Houndmills, UK: Palgrave, 2001.

Sobrino, Francisco. "Reflections on 'Really Imaginary Socialism': Socialism and Democracy in Cuba." *Against the Current* 16, no. 94, n.s. (September/October 2001): 30–34.

Sontag, Susan. "Some Thoughts on the Right Way (for Us) to Love the Cuban Revolution." *Ramparts*, April 1969, 6–19.

Thomas, Hugh. "Middle Class Politics and the Cuban Revolution." In *The Politics of Conformity in Latin America*, edited by Claudio Véliz. London: Oxford University Press, 1967.

Thomas-Woodard, Tiffany A. "'Towards the Gates of Eternity': Celia Sánchez Manduley and the Creation of Cuba's New Woman." *Cuban Studies* 34 (2003): 154–80.

Thompson, Frank W. "The Economy after a Half-Century." *Against the Current*, July–August 2009, 18–19.

Varios autores. "La esperanza en Cuba hoy." *Espacio Laical* Suplemento Digital, 6, no. 22 (abril–junio 2010).

Varios autores. "Por qué cayó el socialismo en Europa oriental?" *Temas* 39–40 (octubre–diciembre de 2004): 91–111.

Varios autores. "Quo vadis, universidad? Un simposio cubano." *Temas* 57 (enero–marzo 2009): 76–88.

Varios autores. "El 26 de julio de 1953 en la cultura política cubana." *Temas* 46 (abril–junio 2006): 77–96.

Veiga González, Roberto. "Compartir la búsqueda de nuestro destino." *Espacio Laical* Suplemento Digital, 113 (octubre 2010).

Wolf, Sherry. "LGBT Political Cul-de-Sac: Make a U-Turn." *New Politics* 12, no. 2 (Winter 2009): 32–37.

Zayas, Manuel. "Mapa de la homofobia." *cubaencuentro*, 15 febrero 2010. http://cubaencuentro.com/es/cuba/artículos/mapa-de-la-homofobia-10736.

Index

Gleijeses, Piero, 125, 316n48
Godínez, Elisa, 167
Gómez Manzano, René, 250
González, Elián, 247, 248, 250, 297n47
González Poey, Alfredo, 153
González, Reynaldo, 191
Gorbachev, Mikhail, 123
Gore, Al, 120
Goytisolo, Juan, 334n193
Grammy Awards, 247
Granma (newspaper), 26, 42, 88, 93,
    207, 234, 278
    described with three adjectives, 256
Granma (province), 202
Granma (ship), viii, 167
Grau San Martín, Ramón, vii
Great Britain. *See* United Kingdom
Greece, 101
Grenada, 105, 316n40
Grenier, Guillermo J., 245
Grievance Commissions, 142–43
Grupo de Acción por la Libertad de
    Expresión de la Elección Sexual
    (GALEES), 215
Grupo de Administración Empresarial
    S.A. *See* GAESA
Grupo de Apoyo, 266
Guanche, Julio César, 22, 258
Guantánamo, 60
Guantánamo (province), 84, 205
Guantánamo Naval Base, 130, 160
Guatemala, 110, 120, 121, 223
Guerra, Félix, 262
Guerra, Lillian, 218
Guevara, Alfredo, 211
Guevara, Ernesto "Che," 5, 8, 19, 76,
    108, 109, 142, 153
    economic policies and, 148, 149
    birthday commemoration, 234
    homophobia of, 217
    on strikes, 138
Guillén Landrian, Nicolás, 36
Guillén, Nicolás, 36, 180
Guinea, 105
Guisa, 60
Guiteras, Antonio, 108

Gutiérrez, Rafael, 153
Gutiérrez Urdaneta, Luis, 256
Guyana, 122

Habana Libre Hotel, 182
Habanguanex, 58
Habanos, 89
Haile Selassie I, 114, 115
Haiti, 68, 75, 96, 97, 107, 108
    emigration, 162, 164, 244
Haitian Revolution, 159
Harlem, New York City, 172
Hart, Armando, 40
Havana, 37, 53, 230, 260
    agriculture and, 61
    blacks, 163, 172, 183
    bombings, 126
    buses, 58
    canteen closures, 152
    concerts, 253–54
    day care centers, 206
    education, 77
    gays, 189, 210, 211
    health care, 73, 75–76
    prostitution, 188, 190
    remittances and, 86
    shantytowns, 87, 205
    "social dangerousness," 174
    supermarkets, 55
    unemployment, 84
    unionism, 153
    water supply, 71
    See also East Havana; Old Havana
HavanaTimes.org, 242, 259, 262,
    341n162
Havel, Vaclav, 228
Helms-Burton Act, ix, 120, 128, 245
Heredia Project, 238–39, 337n58
Hermanos al Rescate. *See* Brothers to
    the Rescue
Hermanos de Causa, 173–74
Hermanos Saíz. *See* Asociación
    Hermanos Saíz
Hernández Castro, Hiram, 259
Hernández Cata, Alfonso, 189
Hernández, Rafael, 258

About Haymarket Books

Haymarket Books is a nonprofit, progressive book distributor and publisher, a project of the Center for Economic Research and Social Change. We believe that activists need to take ideas, history, and politics into the many struggles for social justice today. Learning the lessons of past victories, as well as defeats, can arm a new generation of fighters for a better world. As Karl Marx said, "The philosophers have merely interpreted the world; the point, however, is to change it."

We take inspiration and courage from our namesakes, the Haymarket Martyrs, who gave their lives fighting for a better world. Their 1886 struggle for the eight-hour day, which gave us May Day, the international workers' holiday, reminds workers around the world that ordinary people can organize and struggle for their own liberation. These struggles continue today across the globe—struggles against oppression, exploitation, hunger, and poverty.

It was August Spies, one of the Martyrs targeted for being an immigrant and an anarchist, who predicted the battles being fought to this day. "If you think that by hanging us you can stamp out the labor movement," Spies told the judge, "then hang us. Here you will tread upon a spark, but here, and there, and behind you, and in front of you, and everywhere, the flames will blaze up. It is a subterranean fire. You cannot put it out. The ground is on fire upon which you stand."

We could not succeed in our publishing efforts without the generous financial support of our readers. Many people contribute to our project through the Haymarket Sustainers program, where donors receive free books in return for their monetary support. If you would like to be a part of this program, please contact us at info@haymarketbooks.org.

Shop our full catalog at www.haymarketbooks.org or call 773-583-7884.

Also from Haymarket Books

Class Struggle and Resistance in Africa
Edited by Leo Zeilig • Employing Marxist theory to address the postcolonial problems of several different countries, experts analyze such issues as the renewal of Islamic fundamentalism in Egypt, debt relief, trade union movements, and strike action. Includes interviews with leading African socialists and activists. ISBN 9781931859684

Exile: Conversations with Pramoedya Ananta Toer
Pramoedya Ananta Toer, Andre Vltchek, Rosie Indira, edited by Nagesh Rao • This is the first ever book-length interview with Pramoedya, a novelist and writer widely regarded as the artist who gave expression to a revolutionary vision of Indonesian cultural identity. ISBN 9781931859288

Field Notes on Democracy: Listening to Grasshoppers
Combining fierce conviction, deft political analysis, and beautiful writing, this essential new book from Arundhati Roy examines the dark side of democracy in contemporary India. Roy looks closely at how religious majoritarianism, cultural nationalism, and neo-fascism simmer just under the surface of a country that projects itself as the world's largest democracy. ISBN 9781608460243

Fields of Resistance: The Struggle of Florida's Farmworkers for Justice
Silvia Giagnoni • In Immokalee, Florida, the tomato capital of the world—which has earned the dubious distinction of being "ground zero for modern slavery"—farm workers organized themselves into the Coalition of Immokalee Workers and launched a nationwide boycott campaign that forced McDonald's, Burger King, and Taco Bell to recognize their demands for workers' rights. ISBN 9781608460939

From Rebellion to Reform in Bolivia: Class Struggle, Indigenous Liberation, and the Politics of Evo Morales
Jeffery R. Webber • Evo Morales rode to power on a wave of popular mobilizations against the neoliberal policies enforced by his predecessors. Yet many of his economic policies bear striking resemblance to the status quo he was meant to displace. Drawing on dozens of interviews with leading Bolivian activists, Jeffery R. Webber examines the contradictions of Morales's first term in office. ISBN 9781608461066

History of the Russian Revolution
Leon Trotsky • Regarded by many as among the most powerful works of history ever written, Trotsky's account of the events of 1917 reveals the October revolution's profoundly democratic, emancipatory character. Collected in a single, portable volume, with a thorough new index. ISBN 9781931859455

The Palestine Communist Party, 1919-1948:
Arab and Jew in the Struggle for Internationalism
Musa Budeiri • This history of the Palestinian Communist Party upends the caricature of the Israeli-Palestinian conflict as an ancient religious blood feud. Musa Budeiri shows how the complex history of the Palestinian Left before the Zionist destruction of historic Palestine was defined by secularism and solidarity between Arab and Jewish workers. With a new introduction and afterword by the author. • ISBN 9781608460724

The Pen and the Sword: Conversations with Edward Said
Edwar Said and David Barsamian, introductions by Eqbal Ahmad and Nubar Hovsepian • Gathered here are five wide-ranging interviews with the internationally renowned Palestinian scholar and critic Edward Said (1935–2003). In conversation with David Barsamian, director of Alternative Radio, these interviews cover a broad range of topics: the Israeli-Palestinian conflict; Professor Said's groundbreaking work of literary scholarship, *Orientalism*; music; and much more. With an introduction by Eqbal Ahmad and a new introduction from Nubar Hovsepian, this is an indispensable introduction to one of the twentieth century's foremost critical intellectuals. • ISBN 9781931859950

The Politics of Combined and Uneven Development:
The Theory of Permanent Revolution
Michael Löwy • Drawing on the prescient insights of Leon Trotsky, Michael Löwy shows how modern economic development across continents can only be understood as a process of ferocious change, in which social formations fuse, come into tension, and collide—and how the resulting ruptures make it possible for the oppressed and exploited to change the world. ISBN 9781608460687

Sin Patrón: Inside Stories from Argentina's Worker-Run Factories
Edited by the lavaca collective, foreword by Naomi Klein and Avi Lewis • In 2001, the economy of Argentina collapsed. Unemployment reached a quarter of the workforce. Out of these terrible conditions was born a new movement of workers who decided to take matters into their own hands. *Sin Patrón* lets the workers themselves tell the story of how they took over control of their workplaces, restarted production, and democratically decided how they would organize their work. ISBN 9781931859431

Vietnam: The (Last) War the U.S. Lost
Joe Allen, foreword by John Pilger • In addition to debunking the popular mythology surrounding the U.S.'s longest war to date, Allen analyzes three elements that played central roles in the U.S. defeat in Vietnam: the resistance of the Vietnamese, the antiwar movement in the United States, and the courageous rebellion of soldiers against U.S. military command. ISBN 9781931859493

About the Author

Samuel Farber was born and raised in Marianao, Cuba, and came to the United States in February 1958. He obtained a PhD in sociology from the University of California at Berkeley in 1969 and taught at a number of colleges and universities, including UCLA and, most recently, Brooklyn College of the City University of New York, where he is a professor emeritus of political science. His scholarship on Cuba is extensive and includes many articles and two previous books: *Revolution and Reaction in Cuba, 1933–1960* (Wesleyan University Press, 1976) and *The Origins of the Cuban Revolution Reconsidered* (University of North Carolina Press, 2006). He is also the author of *Before Stalinism: The Rise and Fall of Soviet Democracy* (Polity/Verso, 1990) and *Social Decay and Transformation: A View from the Left* (Lexington Books, 2000). Farber was active in the Cuban high school student movement against Fulgencio Batista in the 1950s and has been involved in socialist politics for more than fifty years.